Sport in Canada

Sport in Canada

A HISTORY

Don Morrow AND Kevin B. Wamsley

OXFORD
UNIVERSITY PRESS

OXFORD
UNIVERSITY PRESS

8 Sampson Mews, Suite 204, Don Mills, Ontario M3C 0H5
www.oupcanada.com

Oxford University Press is a department of the University of Oxford.
It furthers the University's objective of excellence in research, scholarship,
and education by publishing worldwide in

Oxford   New York

Auckland   Cape Town   Dar es Salaam   Hong Kong   Karachi   Kuala Lumpur   Madrid
Melbourne   Mexico City   Nairobi   New Delhi   Shanghai   Taipei   Toronto

With offices in

Argentina   Austria   Brazil   Chile   Czech Republic   France   Greece   Guatemala   Hungary   Italy   Japan
Poland   Portugal   Singapore   South Korea   Switzerland   Thailand   Turkey   Ukraine   Vietnam

Oxford is a trade mark of Oxford University Press in the UK and in certain other countries

Published in Canada by Oxford University Press

Library and Archives Canada Cataloguing in Publication

Morrow, Don
Sport in Canada : a history / Don Morrow and Kevin B. Wamsley.

Includes bibliographical references and index.
ISBN 978-0-19-543115-5

1. Sports—Canada—History—Textbooks. 2. Games—Canada—
History—Textbooks. I. Wamsley, Kevin B. II. Title.

GV585.M65 2009   796'.0971   C2009-903595-2

Oxford University Press is committed to our environment.
This book is printed on paper that contains a minimum of 50% post-consumer waste.

Printed in the United States of America.

2 3 4 5 – 14 13 12 11

Contents

Contents

Preface

Sport in Canada: A History is the second, updated edition of a textbook designed for use in undergraduate university and college courses that focus on the place of sports and games in Canadian life, both historically and, to a lesser extent, in contemporary society. Its content and organization are based primarily on how we have selected content and delivered it in our Canadian Sport History classes over the past few decades. In this respect, it is not a definitive study of Canadian sport that exhausts all topics, facts, dates, and significant events and people in the country's long history. Rather, it is *a* history: a selection of issue-based chapters discussing how people related to one another through sports, games, and pastimes throughout Canada's history. In this framework, we have attempted to provide narratives where feasible and important, and to assess the broader social context within which pastimes, games, and sports emerged or disappeared, the forces that have shaped them, and some of the individuals who have figured prominently.

As the reader will surmise, some of the activities discussed in the book do not have the characteristics of current sports, or the patterns of behaviour were not consistent with how Canadians understand sport today. What early Canadians considered 'sporting' sometimes bore little resemblance to modern sport. Yet, there are similarities in how people a century ago related to one another through physical activity and through common notions about the body that remain significant, even in today's society.

Many social activities in early Canada were instructive, explaining how Aboriginals related to Europeans, and how men related to men, women to men, and women to women through various gendered and social class-influenced notions and values about their bodies. Understanding the social restrictions placed upon people's bodies and social lives and the value structures that persuaded them not to participate in certain physical activities helps to explain the sporting behaviour and the social meanings associated with it for those who did play games and sports. Therefore, Victorian ideologies that rendered some middle-class women as passive but supportive spectators of men's sport, for example, explain some of the social meanings related to male participation, while underscoring the place of middle-class women in Canadian society. In any society, ideas about 'femaleness' draw meanings from ideas about 'maleness', and vice versa. To discern the brands of masculinity or femininity reinforced or celebrated through sporting relations is to know symbiotic connections and forms of opposition between them. An understanding of these relationships provides some of the tools necessary to understand society more broadly. Further, people of distinct social classes did not share all values. Social classes and gender orders were fragmented. Not all middle-class men were involved in organized sport, for example. But, in some cases, men adhered to particular codes of masculinity that differed according to social class, specifically and intentionally distinguishing gentleman from labourer, a relationship played out through physical activity that was meaningful for them and instructive for us as historians.

We have organized some of the early chapters in the book in a chronological fashion, exploring the games and pastimes of Aboriginal Canadians, the fur traders and garrison soldiers, and early colonists. We arranged the remaining chapters of the book according to the issues at hand, for example, the relationship between amateurism and professionalism, gender, government, organized sport in Montreal, sport and journalism, the Olympic Games, and, finally, a brief examination of some of the current issues in Canadian sport. These chapters explore issues that we think were and are significant in the organization of sport and that help to inform the popular understandings of what sport was at the time and what it means today.

The main analytical framework for the book considers the forces of class, gender, and race as primary in any discussion of sporting relations in Canadian history, and we have attempted to weave this analytical context throughout the book. We have used a broad array of secondary source materials from the growing body of literature produced by Canadian sport historians. To provide some of the best evidence and most interesting examples available, we cite the specific research findings of these authors whenever possible so as not to gloss over the outstanding primary source research that they have performed over the past 30 years. In addition, we draw on secondary sources from the broader Canadian social history literature. And finally, we cite and summarize our own research on various topics in Canadian sport history. Since our examination of sport here is not exhaustive, and we do not claim to have factored in all contributions to the sport history literature, we have included an extensive and revised 'Bibliography of Canadian Sport History' listing books, articles, theses, and dissertations that have been written about Canadian sport in a historical context. This should be an excellent secondary source guide for undergraduate students who are required to write research papers specifically grounded in Canadian sport history. We hope that our colleagues will inform us if we have inadvertently omitted any publications or theses so that they might be included in later editions. For the specific use of instructors and students in undergraduate classes, we have included 'Issues Boxes' in each chapter (intended to be snapshots of historical issues in Canadian sport) and lists of study questions at the end of each chapter. These questions focus on what we consider to be some of the main points of interest or importance for each issue or era in Canadian sport history. We have also included some websites that might be useful for students interested in electronic sources or just beginning to survey their topics for further research. Noticeable also is the fact that within each chapter we have bolded key terms and created a Glossary to help clarify and standardize the use of historical concepts and/or unusual terminology.

During the past year that we have spent revising the book, we have been fortunate to have the support of a number of individuals, most of whom we know, and some anonymous. First, we wish to thank Peter Chambers, Developmental Editor, Higher Education Division; Jacqueline Mason, Sponsoring Editor at Oxford University Press; Jessie Coffey, copy editor; and the anonymous reviewers of the original project proposal who provided insightful criticism of and commentary on our plans for the book. We also thank the anonymous reviewers of the manuscript, who gave outstanding constructive criticisms and suggested important changes to make the book more useful for readers and students of Canadian sport history. Special thanks go to Professors Mike Heine and Jim McKay, who read draft versions of chapters and recommended editorial and content changes, and to Gordon MacDonald and Toby Rider for their editorial work on the Canadian Sport Bibliography. In the latter regard, we extend our appreciation to Dr Alan Metcalfe for his contributions toward gathering and compiling various iterations of the bibliographic entries. And it is with gratitude and respect that we acknowledge each other for finding the gifts in each other's style of doing and writing history.

Finally and most importantly we thank our partners and families for their encouragement and patience during the compacted process of revising 'the book'.

Don Morrow and Kevin B. Wamsley
University of Western Ontario
London, Ontario
January 2009

Reviewers

We gratefully acknowledge the contributions of the following reviewers, whose thoughtful comments and suggestions have helped to shape this new edition.

Patrick Harrigan, University of Waterloo
Charlene Weaving, St. Francis Xavier University
Nancy B. Bouchier, McMaster University
Stephen Wenn, Wilfrid Laurier University
Robin Anderson, University of the Fraser Valley

Cover Photo Credits

Gymnastic group, Montreal, QC, 1891. Wm Notman & Son. © McCord Museum, II-95016.

Hurdle race on snowshoes, Montreal, QC, 1892. Wm Notman & Son. © McCord Museum, VIEW-3147.0.

Audrey Cook and sister Sarah, St Moritz, Switzerland, 1927. Anonymous. © McCord Museum, MP-1993.59.11.

Ross-Hodgson Curling Match, Woodlands, Dorval, QC, 1916. Thm. C. Finley. © McCord Museum, MP-1980.126.2.11.

Champion Ladies Curling Team, 1925. © South Peace Regional Archives, 2002.57.32.

Boxers, McGill Boxing, Wrestling, and Fencing Club, Montreal, QC, 1925. Wm Notman & Son. © McCord Museum, II-263756.

Rowing scull and team, near Montreal, QC, 1924. Wm Notman & Son. © McCord Museum, VIEW-22027.

Lawn bowling group, copied for Mr H.L. McDougall in 1908. Anonymous. © McCord Museum, II-169624.0.

Dedication

This revised edition is dedicated to the wonderful group of graduate students who we each have supervised over the course of our careers. They have challenged and inspired us to strive to be better historians. We are very proud of their success and wish to recognize that the future of Canadian sport history is in capable hands.

CHAPTER 1

Introduction

Sport is a form of culture recognized by all Canadians. Reporting on sports is ubiquitous in communications media—television, newspapers, Internet, radio; it is practised, watched, and facilitated by people of all genders and ages and of many social, economic, and ethnic backgrounds. Even those who dislike participating in or watching sport, or who are otherwise disinterested, find it difficult to avoid because sport extends into many other aspects of our lives. Some Canadians are fanatical in their consumption and participation. Indeed, some people structure their lives around it with the ebb and flow of sporting seasons, cyclical championships, and festivals—at international levels, at Canadian national competitions, at provincial levels, at community levels, and by individuals in their daily and weekly routines. Some study sport in university and college academic programs. Sport is an aspect of government policy and it has been used as an instrument of international policy and political leverage and to promote cultural and national unity—even to define what is Canadian to the country and to the world. Billions of dollars are exchanged annually for sports equipment, clothing, club memberships, registration fees, the building and maintenance of sport facilities, professional athletes' salaries, event tickets, memorabilia, 'official' and game-worn jerseys, air travel and accommodations for athletes and spectators, elite sport training programs, coaching development, sport administration, and bidding for and hosting national and international events. Sport is pervasive in Canadian society.

Many Canadians have emotional attachments to particular sporting events, and they can recall moments in sport that measure and define their values. Such events elicit nostalgic recollections and excitement about where they were and what they were doing at those moments. For example, many Canadians can remember where they were when Paul Henderson scored the goal to secure victory over the Soviet Union for Team Canada in 1972, or when Donovan Bailey won gold in the men's 100-metre dash at the 1996 Olympics in Atlanta. Canadians are interested in debating who are, or were, the greatest hockey players, the best teams, the best boxers, or sprinters, or ice skaters. Even non-participants express their interest in some events, as when non-golfers talked about Mike Weir's victory at the 2003 Masters tournament in Augusta, Georgia. Canadians love sport.

However, only some Canadians participate in sport at highly competitive levels; only select sports are supported by government funding or have professional leagues; only particular sport facilities (e.g., skating rink arenas for hockey, figure skating, and leisure skating) are available in most Canadian communities. The common understanding remains that sport is a predominantly male domain of interest and expertise, even though more women and girls than ever before are participating in sport at all levels. Why do some sports, such as hockey, remain popular while others fade from interest? Why are Canadians so interested in the success of national teams and in hosting the Olympic Games? Why are professional athletes paid multi-million dollar salaries? Why do some Olympic athletes become cultural icons? Why are the nation's hopes and dreams said to rise and fall with sporting victories and defeats? The answers to some of these questions are to be found in the study of the history of Canadian sport.

Sport history is a relatively recent addition to academic sub-disciplinary studies in social history. Indeed, sport and physical activity were long considered rather insignificant areas of study. In addition to the sport history disciplinary experts, who emerged from physical education programs during the late 1960s, some traditional historians dabbled in the social history of sport. More than three generations of Canadian sport historians have been plying their craft in Canadian universities (see Bibliography). Today, sport history is studied in university popular culture or social history courses and in physical education (kinesiology) faculties, as it has been for decades. The visibility of sport in contemporary society suggests the social significance of sport in Canadian history.

People have been playing sports and games in these territories for hundreds, likely thousands, of years. Yet, in the past 100 years, the engagement of sport at one or another level of personal consumption has significantly increased for Canadians. Where does one begin to interpret this rather complex social phenomenon? We have selected some individuals over others for elaboration and have analyzed particular places in Canada at the expense of others. Some chapters contain more specific details and information about individual Canadians, while others focus on social analysis and factors that seem at first glance unrelated to sport. Our intent throughout this second edition of *Sport in Canada* has been to examine Canadian sport history thematically, to provide an intermittent narrative for analysis in interpreting Canadian sporting evolution. Rather than a linear approach, this record assembles a spiralling of events for contextual analysis; certain themes and issues are amplified or explained, often within different contexts.

The first chapters deal specifically with eras of pre-contact between Aboriginals and Europeans; the arrival of the French and life in New France; conquest by the English, the establishment of British rule in the colonies, and the development of British institutions and rural social life; the post-rebellion, pre-Confederation era and the emergence of the middle classes; and the post-Confederation era of national development and international political interest. Specific topical attention is given to the organization of sport in Montreal; to case studies on the emergence of the sports of lacrosse and baseball; to significant sporting personalities; to the idea of amateurism as an organizing principle in early Canadian sport; and to the symbiotic relationship of the print media with the evolution of early- to mid-twentieth century Canadian sport.

Other chapters approach specific issues for the significant influence they had on mobilizing social meanings and people's understandings of, and experiences in, sport within broader socially defined concepts, such as 'gender' and 'the nation'. The cultural significance of the Olympic Games and physical education as a disciplined study are explored in later chapters, which address longer periods of time in Canadian history. And, finally, a chapter on current issues briefly examines the present environment of sport in Canada, including professional sport and high performance Olympic competition. The changing economic structure of sport, the cracks and fissures evident in such high-level environments, including pain, violence, and discrimination, are discussed here.

Where possible, we bring our analysis close to the modern period, although such topics as sport and industrialization are bound to earlier periods. Although current attitudes and opinions influence our beliefs about sport, it is problematic to superimpose these ideas upon the past. We must attempt to see the past without expectations, to appreciate the forces at play and the individuals involved within their specific historic contexts. It makes no sense to argue that the Scottish immigrants who curled on frozen rivers in the late 1700s were not participating in 'real' sport. It is more instructive to understand who was there, who was not there, and why they were curling—what this activity meant to them. It is practical, moreover, to understand contests in nineteenth-century tavern arm-wrestling within the context of competition during this period, through masculine codes of behaviour in particular social settings including the subculture of the tavern, than to compare the activity to later forms of club and professional sport that appeared to be more organized and regulated. More specifically, studying how people in the past related to one another through the physicality of competition for fun, for symbolic or economic gain, or for whatever other reasons, expands Canadian social history along many dimensions, providing a more complete picture of society that intimately connects to the more traditionally invoked political, religious, and economic interpretations of the forces affecting the daily lives of Canadians.

Long before the arrival of Europeans, Aboriginal peoples played games, competed, and tested one another physically. Attitudes towards the body were spiritually as well as physically significant. Survival, skill, fun, and a sense of dedication to community life and responsibility characterized such activities as Aboriginal people participated in a variety of games in particular regions of the continent. Contact with Europeans changed Aboriginal life, including the games they played and how they related to other Native groups through traditional cultural practices. However, cultural change did not occur unidirectionally. The Europeans had different views about their bodies, different skills and practices, and, consequently, learned new survival skills and competitive practices from Native groups wherever they met. They also altered the sports and games from their homelands according to the new environments and social relationships. French and English Canadians learned from one another, from the Loyalists who came north after the American Revolution, and from Native people, with each at times clinging to tradition or modifying physical practices when moved to do so by force, expediency, necessity, or choice. Sports and games were mutable and were subject to interest; negotiation; forms of control; and the influences of religion, politics, economy, the military, gender, race, ethnicity, and social class.

Fur traders, soldiers, trappers, and labourers carried and learned notions of masculine honour, which became enshrined in the practices of their professions and celebrated through competitions with Aboriginal people and their working peers. For the bachelor subcultures of the bush and the garrison, social life meshed closely with work and a sense of vigorous physicality struck similar chords in both aspects of their lives. Seasonal celebrations, games playing, and competitions in horse racing, and even fencing, marked a part of social life in New France, as settlers entertained themselves during the long Canadian winters and elites sought to augment their social status through informal competitions. The English brought different cultural influences, establishing legislation and laws that ensured revenues from the alcohol consumption of settlers to support government expenditures and public works and to make certain there was recourse to punish the public 'nuisances' of drunkenness, revelry, and the various conflicts emanating from the growing population of the colonies. British elites socialized in clubs and a limited number of social organizations, while the average citizen frequented the tavern and revelled in post-workday gatherings and work bees. Cricket matches and hunting, fishing, and riding events brought like-minded sporting gentlemen together, reaffirming privilege and responsibility to British institutions.

During the pre-Confederation era, middle-class men increasingly asserted themselves in public life and some chose sport as a meeting ground for the celebration of a new sporting masculinity, combining the social aspects of club membership and the public display of physical capabilities, while in part creating and sustaining a symbiotic relationship with the passive and domestic femininities of the Victorian middle-class family. Middle-class sporting clubs provided exclusivity in the form of a social outlet that distanced professionals from the working-class culture while emulating the senses of privilege and entitlement of urban gentlemen. The doctrine of amateurism ensured a class separation through sport for the remainder of the nineteenth century as amateur organizations, such as the Montreal Amateur Athletic Association, assumed control over competitive amateur sport in central Canada.

In 1867 the Confederation of former British colonies created opportunities for new meanings through sport. National championships, national teams, and international competitions where athletes represented the Dominion of Canada held a new cultural cachet for supporters, patriots, sportsmen, and even government leaders. Women were excluded, for the most part, from joining men's sport clubs and some formed women-only sport organizations of their own. Moral entrepreneurs, who sought to inculcate Christian values in Canada's young men, competed against the economic entrepreneurs, the new sports promoters who traded on civic boosterism and the spectator appeal of sport to make money. The late nineteenth- and early twentieth-century civic boosterism and town rivalries waged through sports such as hockey and baseball challenged the ideological propriety exercised by the gentlemen amateurs. The gambling and excitement afforded by horse racing and boxing continued to hold sway over spectator appeal.

By the turn of the century, some Canadian athletes competed for American colleges, some women played sports at university, and Canada looked outward to test itself more frequently in international competition. The Olympic Games offered the primary outlet for athletes, just as the world fairs and expositions of the day measured Canada's success in manufacturing, mineral excavation, and agricultural production. Participation and loss in the First World War reminded Canadians that the military drill exercises of the nineteenth century were still relevant in schools and that organized sports prepared men and boys for the defence of the nation. A post-war sense of Canadian pride (reaffirming that trained men's bodies were indices of a nation's progress), economic prosperity in general, and a relaxation of some of the Victorian codes of appropriate femininity brought more attention and interest to men's and women's sports in the 1920s. The print media both reflected and contributed to the widespread interest in sport as male and female journalists were hired full time by major Canadian newspapers to comment and capitalize on escalating interests in sport. While Canadian readers followed American professional baseball in the press through the summer, Canadian professional hockey thrived during the winter. Lopsided victories in international hockey, particularly at the Winter Olympic Games, and the popularity of the sport at all levels across the country convinced Canadians that hockey was our game and that the best male hockey players were icons of Canadian popular culture. The Second World War brought some men's and women's sports to a grinding halt, but professional hockey, represented by the monopoly National Hockey League (NHL), prevailed, even though some star players left for war.

The post-World War II era, leading into the Cold War period, accelerated the symbolic significance of victory in competitive, elite-level sports to unprecedented heights of political and personal emphasis. Following the entry of the Soviet Union in the 1952 Olympic Games and through to the 1980s, technology, training, sport science, professional coaching, and massive funding fuelled an us-versus-them rivalry between East and West nations. Sport became a fundamental tenet of international policy for the wealthiest nations of the world. Part of the success and popularity of the Games was attributable to the ostensibly amateur Olympic ethos—the so-called purity of sport—lorded over by the International Olympic Committee (IOC). With the enhanced competitive levels of international hockey, particularly emphasized in the Soviet Union, the international hockey supremacy at world championships and the Olympics could no longer be assured by the Canadian amateurs. Consequently, the Canadian players, fans, and government leaders faced what were perceived to be dismal international results on a backdrop of hockey's deeply felt cultural significance and the knowledge that NHL players were not eligible to compete in the Olympic Games.

The professional sports of hockey, American baseball, and Canadian football thrived as spectator and media broadcast events. The Canadian Broadcasting Corporation (CBC) helped to sustain the NHL's monopoly over professional hockey, while its weekly show, *Hockey Night in Canada*, maintained the highest television ratings in the country. For NHL owners, who constantly appealed to the players' love of the game through their management structures and contract negotiations, hockey was profitable. Given the profit margins enjoyed by owners, the players remained underpaid. The advent of players' unions in all of the major professional sports ushered in a new era for rates of player pay. In a matter of decades, between the 1960s and the 1980s, salaries ballooned from thousands of dollars for star players to millions. Players had always been commodified—bought and sold by owners—but with such huge sums of money at stake, television contracts, sport clothing, and paraphernalia, player health and commitment became more expedient issues within the realm of professional sport. The so-called amateur athlete was not immune to the process of sport commodification.

In a sense, the athlete had long been an object of national interest, with performance and value measured by medals. However, with the increased symbolic significance of the Olympic Games, the stakes became significantly higher for competing nations. Even in the days of the amateur athlete, national teams and individuals accepted sponsorships, money, and products from governments, universities, and shoe and ski manufacturing companies. The Games themselves became objects of commercial interest as extensive advertising opportunities permitted multi-million dollar television contracts and corporate sponsorship arrangements. Large companies sought to align themselves with the Olympic image to increase their visibility worldwide, to gain consumer confidence through value association, and to sell more products. The Olympic Games became a primary outlet to sell products and styles of consumer behaviour; the multi-billion dollar agreements from television and global corporations permitted the Olympics to be sold at ideological, even educational, levels throughout the world. In much the same way science had been the 'new religion' of the previous era, performance and profit prevailed by the end of the twentieth century.

For the early civic leaders and government promoters of immigration and economic development in the late nineteenth century, sport provided valuable opportunities to market Canada and Canadian communities, while simultaneously arousing patriotic sentiments and a sense of Canadian identity in individuals. Sport was entertaining and fun, something that inspired or touched people deeply, making it vulnerable to political, social, and economic movements and initiatives. The community boosterism of earlier eras ultimately gave way to the political jockeying of the Cold War period. This freshly nationalized significance was translated into profit and profiteering both in professional sports and in the sports formerly considered amateur—even if profit translated into symbolic forms of gain and revelling in personal achievement was predicated on the defeat of others. Sport had not necessarily become more complicated, but it had changed. Canadians find a great deal of joy in sport, even if it is exclusionary and inequitable at a number of different levels. They still have their heroes, icons, and favourite teams. They lace up their blades, shoot hoops, throw the pigskin, and go to the gym. *Sport in Canada* is our version of how that came to be.

CHAPTER 2

Games and Contests
in Early Canada

. . . they are constantly playing ball, the favourite game, laughing and singing, and the ball they play with is the skull of a walrus. The object is to kick the skull in such a manner that it always falls with the tusks downwards, and thus sticks fast in the ground. It is this ball game of the departed souls that appears as the aurora borealis [northern lights], and is heard as a whistling, rustling, crackling sound. The noise is made by the souls as they run across the frost-hardened snow of the heavens. If one happens to be out alone at night when the aurora borealis is visible, and hears this whistling sound, one has only to whistle in return and the lights will come nearer, out of curiosity.[1]

Knud Rasmussen's poetic retelling of an old Inuit mythological story about football in the Arctic conveys the deep spiritual and cultural connections between people, the environment, and the pleasures of physical play. He speaks to a timeless significance and to a long history of games and sports within the modern geographical boundary of Canada. Historians and archaeologists argue that humans have inhabited these territories for more than 10,000 years.[2] From the earliest years to the present day, through ceremonies and rituals, informal and formal gatherings, institutionalized and legislated activities, generations of people—Aboriginal, French, English—competed with one another, danced, played, watched, gambled, and actively engaged in cultural forms that came to be known and celebrated as sport.

Traditional Games and Pastimes

The **First Nations** of Canada were the earliest players in the regions of North America later to be called Canada. Like European government officials, church representatives, and colonists before them, modern historians tend to universalize these Native cultures into a collective—North American Indians—in spite of striking diversities in language, customs, and social, religious, subsistence, and trading practices that beg for a contemporary, regionalized, and localized understanding of the many peoples and their cultural practices. Reports from priests and missionaries, fur traders, travellers, and explorers provide the initial but limited basis of historical understanding to date. The distinctly European or outsider interpretation that emerges from these accounts illustrates Aboriginal culture in part, but more accurately demonstrates the various political, social, economic, or religious interests that outsiders invoked in their relationships with Native Canadians. Consequently, Aboriginal Canadians had their histories written for them. We attempt to recognize the plurality of Native cultures, the uniqueness of relations between individuals and groups, and to trace the differences and similarities in how meanings about the physical body manifested themselves in Aboriginal cultures through the practice of games and sports, from the earliest contact between Europeans and Aboriginals, through the period of European domination. This material can refer to but a small sample of the hundreds of unique games and contests practised for hundreds of years across the continent.[3]

Recent histories and research on Native sport have incorporated the memories and stories of Aboriginal elders whose recollections in some cases offer more detail and completely different social meanings—less romanticized and less judgmental accounts of **traditional games** in their contexts without the interpretive biases of colonizers.[4] Thus, with respect to traditional games and practices, specific historical studies of early Aboriginal cultures have provided a unique lens for viewing the complexities of social life in early Canada. These studies help us to understand aspects of the past and even some of our current interpretive biases, created by our contemporary perceptions of sport. From a wide range of sources, it is evident that physical and gambling games, skill development, subsistence techniques, confrontational competitions organized principally around survival within a nomadic or semi-nomadic lifestyle, and fun were fundamental and significant aspects of kinship, gendered, and interpersonal relations.[5]

One methodological approach to categorizing Native cultures in Canada has involved a division by language and tribal or band affiliation, in addition to geographical location. Francis et al., for example, identify the North Pacific, Plateau, Plains, Subarctic, Arctic, and Eastern Woodlands in their schemata.[6] The western part of one of these regions, the Subarctic, is the homeland of the Athapaskan or Dene peoples. The Athapaskans are divided into at least 18 regional groups,[7] and these regional groups, in turn, are subdivided into a great number of smaller, more localized groups, often with their own distinct cultural traditions and customs. These numerous local groups constitute the foundation of Athapaskan social organization. This circumstance demonstrates the erroneousness of assigning abstract characteristics to all 'Indians' in North America or Canada. In their respective home territories, the regional and local Athapaskan groups followed a traditional subsistence lifestyle based on constant, regular travels on the land. The groups travelled to reach the areas where they could harvest the resources on which they depended for their survival: caribou herds, fishing spots, and berry-gathering grounds. The conceptual constraints European explorers and settlers brought with them—constraints based on a differing understanding of time, space, and private property—influenced their understanding and the later histories of Aboriginal cultures. For example, the idea that the Athapaskans, like their northern Inuit neighbours, travelled not to get home but to 'be home',[8] ran counter to **Eurocentric** assumptions (some of which we sustain even now), underlying the necessity for travel. By contrast, for the Athapaskans the nomadic life expressed a deep connection to the land, a connection that was also expressed through the physical characteristics of the group members—men,

Blackfoot migration. (Professor Buell, Library and Archives Canada, C-00178)

women, and children—who had to be strong and fit to sustain such a lifestyle. Fur traders and travellers marvelled at the strength of Athapaskan women, who pulled sleds burdened with supplies and other gear or carried heavy packs from camp to camp. In one instance, a traveller was astounded to see that a 12-year-old girl was able to carry a 60-pound pack for 16 miles in one day.[9] The men, too, demonstrated extreme fitness as they pursued game for miles, ahead of the mobile camps.

The games of the Dene and Inuit, such as wrestling matches and the running of races, celebrated and enhanced strength, endurance, and resistance to pain and served as a forum where groups shared their culture, ceremoniously, when they met. Among the Inuit, for example, before missionaries and fur traders introduced the handshake as a greeting between travellers, men wrestled. Visitors showed respect for their hosts by accepting challenges in boxing, wrestling, or other painful contests like the arm pull or finger pull. Songs, dances, and contests such as the high kick or blanket toss also marked the gatherings among Inuit groups.[10]

Such contests and games were also the basis of education for children to prepare them for their lives on the land. Inuit of the Arctic, Athapaskans of the western Subarctic, and the Algonquian peoples in the East all embraced similar traditions that fostered analogous social relationships based on the groups' close connections to the land. As mentioned above, what mattered then and what matters today, from the Aboriginal perspective within this context, are how these social relationships and traditions were and are shaped at regional and local levels.[11] Boys learned bow and spear skills, in addition to tracking techniques, and developed the rigorous levels of endurance necessary for the hunt. The hopes Athapas-

Fishing in the rapids near Sault Ste-Marie, Ontario. (Detroit Photographic Co., Library and Archives Canada, PA-164372)

kan parents held for their children's physical development were identifiable by particular objects they attached to clothing by way of a symbolic symbiosis, such as hawk's feet which denoted speed and power. Chief Miska Deaphon explains the connection between symbolic object and skill: 'for boys to hit targets—chicken hawk eyes; for boys to fight well—porcupine tails; for boys to climb fast up a hill—spruce hen head or ptarmigan foot; for boys and girls to work hard—arm sinews of a bear'.[12] An analogous symbolic and spiritual awareness was evident in the more southerly regions of the Iroquois Five Nations, where longhouses unifying extended families were adorned with crests of animals, birds, or reptiles, in part to signify the physical strengths embodied in the life cycles of those animals.[13]

Running games and races were practical training for hunting but they also symbolically celebrated the abilities of noted runners in the communities. Indoor races in winter shelters and relays for speed and endurance, sometimes with backpacks filled with rocks, represented extensions not only of the functional requirements of daily living and survival but also more personal meanings of identity and exchange. **Gendered** notions of physical achievement in Aboriginal cultures were reaffirmed, in some cases directly linked to male hunting prowess and in other cases to female strength. In the caribou chase games played by Dogrib, Sahtu Dene, Slavey, Tanana, and Gwich'in Athapaskan boys, for example, the 'hunters' chased and attempted to tag a runner who dragged a piece of animal skin representing a caribou, bear, or moose.[14] For Athapaskan women and girls, on the other hand, it was often their physical strength that was tested in such games as moose-skin ball, a custom corresponding to the fact that the women were usually responsible for most of the physical labour involved in moving camp and in many tasks of daily life.[15] In this game, two compet-ing teams passed the ball from player to player, while not permitting it to touch the ground. But games and physical prowess were not only important in terms of their functional sig-nificance for preparing the people for the physical and technical skills necessary for survival in the traditional way of life. In relationships and systems of exchange within and between genders, between young people and elders, and between groups and communities, physical skills and prowess also provided symbolic meanings and the celebration of spiritual values when the people gathered and shared their songs, their stories, and their games. Gender, therefore, is socially constructed and should not be extracted and isolated from broader meanings about community, spirituality, and the connection of physical practices to every-day life; rather, it must always be viewed in relation to other aspects of individuality, family life, and community.

The ability to endure pain and hardship was a necessity in everyday life and celebrated in the traditional games. Among the Inuit, the ability to show indifference to pain held symbolic and practical value for people of all ages. The participants' abilities to endure the pain caused by the game explicitly determined the outcomes of the mouth pull and ear pull. Competitors tested strength through the stick pull, pole push, stone-lifting, finger pull, and wrestling, among other activities, in both Dene and Inuit cultures.[16] Specialized ball games, such as moose-skin ball and football, snow snake, bow and arrow, and tug of war were similar to other traditional games in that little equipment was required, an important consideration for people who travelled year-round and who could rely only on their own—and, that is to say, most often the women's—physical strength when camp and equipment had to be moved.

One of the most popular games common in most regions outside of the Arctic was the hand game, a complex group activity where teams of players worked together using hand signals and body actions to hide small objects or tokens in their fists, or sometimes under a blanket, as drums were played and gambling songs sung by the drummers.[17] Such fun and exciting gambling games also served important practical purposes including the redistribu-tion of tools, goods, and food shared among families and between visiting groups.

Similar traditions of very physical, competitive, and co-operative games, gambling, and strategic training for daily life and survival formed the basis of cultural life for families and regional groups in the southern regions of Canada. Of these games, travellers and observers recounted some more frequently than others, in part because of their idiosyncratic interests and in part because of the commonality observed between groups and the sheer energy and excitement that such events invoked among participants and observers. For example, historians often refer to shinny, probably because of its identification as a precursor to Canadian ice hockey. Aboriginals of the Northwest Plains played **shinny**, as did the Han, Deg Hit'an, and Gwich'in of the western Subarctic, in winter.[18] In both versions, players used a shinny stick to contact a hide-covered ball or a puck either on open plains or ice, with a considerably large playing surface and with goal lines or poles for scoring. In this context, the types of games enjoyed by Aboriginals tended to relate directly to the forms of subsistence adopted in response to the varieties of landscape in traditionally travelled areas.[19] Natives played shinny in the flat Great Plains region and in the coastal Far West, where people relied on hunting and fishing as opposed to agriculture. It is reasonable to assert that such running games were excellent training for subsistence while positioning the skill and strength of young men in visible demonstrations to be admired by all. Rough play and endurance games, such as shinny, prepared men for war and combat,[20] particularly when population patterns changed and when the later consequences of the fur trade and the exchange of European goods extended hostilities between groups.

Lacrosse

Although not played in all regions of Canada in the early days, historians have identified lacrosse as the most important Aboriginal game.[21] Some histories of lacrosse situate the early game in the context of other ball games in the Americas by analyzing a number of important purposes the activity served in Native life, including the redistribution of resources, the establishment of respect among neighbouring groups, the production of religious meanings about life and death, its utility in healing the sick, and its importance in honouring the Creator. Natives played lacrosse (called *tewaarathon* by the Mohawks) in three regions—the Northeast in the Iroquoian Confederacy or Five Nations, the Great Lakes region, and the Southeast of the present United States. The Iroquoian, Algonquian, and Sioux used similar sticks; in the Southeast the Chickasaw, Choctaw, and Cherokee used two sticks with netted pockets to play. All groups played on varied ground surfaces, sometimes extending for miles between two goals and involving entire communities of male players.[22] Mott cites fur trader Peter Grant in a particularly detailed account of lacrosse played by the Ojibwa:

> The 'hurdle' is their favourite game; not only their young men, but men advanced in life sometimes engage in it. On this occasion they strip naked, save their breech clouts, head dress, a few silver ornaments on their arms and a belt around their waist; their faces and bodies are painted in the highest style. Each man is provided with a hurdle, an instrument made of a small stick of wood about three feet long, bended at the end to a small circle, in which a loose piece of net work is fixed, forming a cavity big enough to receive a leather ball, about the size of a man's fist. Everything being prepared, a level plain about half a mile long is chosen, with proper barriers or goals at each end. Having previously formed into two equal parties, they assemble in the very middle of the field, and the game begins by throwing up the ball perpendicularly in the air, when, instantly, both parties form a singular group of naked men . . . [trying] to catch the ball. . . . Whoever is so fortunate as to catch the ball in his hurdle, runs with it towards the barrier with all his might, supported by his party, while his opponents pursue him and endeavour to strike it out. He who succeeds in doing so, runs in the same manner towards the opposite barrier and is, of course, pursued in his turn. If in danger of being overtaken, he may throw it with his hurdle towards any of his associates who may happen to be nearer the barrier than himself. . . . The best of three heats win[s] the game, and, besides the honor acquired on such occasions, a considerable prize is adjudged to the victors.[23]

This is only one account of a game played in different regions of the continent for centuries. The technical aspects and the equipment may have been similar over the years but, certainly, the context within which the game was played between different communities, in different eras, varied tremendously.

Montagnais making a bark canoe. (Alexander Henderson, Library and Archives Canada, PA-149709) >

All accounts of lacrosse come from Jesuit missionaries, fur traders, and travellers at a time when relations between Aboriginal groups were changing. Before European contact, the ball games involved sets of relations and meanings between Aboriginal groups only, without any influences of the Christian missionaries whose presence compromised the community positions of traditional medicine men and shamans, and before the trading of European goods that made the outcomes of games more significant. Pre-contact warfare was less destructive and less pervasive; the ball games emphasized traditional religious meanings, dedications, and social relationships. The exchange of goods was facilitated in part by the outcomes of games, which were a 'binding force' between regional groups and allies.[24] All relations between Aboriginal groups changed following European contact and, consequently, so did the traditional games.

Relationships with the French and English altered the balance of power among Native groups, a result of favoured trade pacts and alliances and, therefore, access to manufactured tools and weapons.[25] This had a direct influence on trade and social relations between Natives. In addition to such sweeping economic shifts, the military disasters resulting from the American Revolution forced the relocation of the surviving Native families. Further, the European invasions generally left surviving Aboriginals—those who did not succumb to disease—confined to limited areas of land, and Christian influences altered the religious meanings of the time-honoured ball games. Some Aboriginal groups, such as the Mohawks, still played lacrosse out of respect for the past but the game's web of inherent meanings linked to the traditional ways of life had been severely dislocated, as Fisher cogently summarizes:

Now defeated and divided, Iroquois nations could not hope to achieve military victory. When they adopted farming, the ball game no longer served as a mechanism for reinforcement of their military might. When they became economically dependent on whites, militarily and politically weakened, and partially assimilated into European culture through Christianity and sedentary agriculture, ball play ceased to function as a means of maintaining traditional notions of tribal integrity, autonomy, and survival.[26]

Native written accounts about traditional societies do not exist; however, the memories of elders and stories of the **oral traditions** are important for identifying some of the social and symbolic meanings about physicality in early Aboriginal societies. The observations of non-Native travellers also are useful sources. In concert, these accounts permit us to consider the significance of games in earlier eras; to recognize that pre-contact Aboriginal societies had long economic, political, and religious histories; and to see how the contact between Europeans and Aboriginal peoples forever changed both.

Contact with Europeans

After centuries of continental isolation, excepting a brief visit from the Norse in about AD 1000 and minimal Norse contact to the fourteenth century, the Portuguese, Spanish, French, Dutch, and English sent ships to North America in the fifteenth and sixteenth centuries. By the early 1600s, an annual trade had developed between the French and the Algonquians of the St Lawrence region. The consequences of the relations between Natives and Europeans over the next few hundred years are summarized by Nichols:

> In 1513, when Europeans first reached North America, between five and ten million native people lived in what are now the United States and Canada. During the next several centuries American Indian populations fell drastically because several million Europeans invaded, overrunning and often destroying the tribal societies. This long-running multi-racial encounter brought violence and warfare that alternated with periods of peace. . . . Often trade, cooperation, and goodwill coexisted with greed, brutality, and violence. In these circumstances ethnocentrism, misunderstanding, miscalculation, incompetence, and criminality all played central roles as they poisoned relations between tribal peoples and the intruding Europeans.[27]

The trade of the late 1500s and the expansion of inland trade routes through the 1600s brought about alliances between particular Aboriginal groups and the French in New France or parts of eastern Canada and the United States.[28] An expanding network of exchange relationships between Natives and newcomers in the economic domain or the cultural sphere also included shared experiences in contests of physicality, tests of strength, races, and games. Samuel de Champlain, who eventually stabilized the fur trade and struck alliances with the Algonquians, Montagnais, and Hurons, ordered hunting and fishing, cultural celebrations, drinking, and feasting to combat the ravages of life in the 'new world', declaring in 1606 *L'ordre de bon temps*—the order of good times, of mirth or good cheer. Of the first social order in New France, Champlain wrote:

We spent this winter very pleasantly, and had good fare by means of the Order of Good Cheer which I established, and which everyone found beneficial to his health, and more profitable than all sorts of medicine we might have used. This Order consisted of a chain which we used to place with certain little ceremonies about the neck of one of our people, commissioning him for that day to go hunting. The next day it was conferred upon another, and so on in order. All vied with each other to see who could do the best, and bring back the finest game. We did not come off badly, nor did the Indians who were with us.[29]

A member of Champlain's party, playwright Marc Lescarbot, who presented *Theatre de Neptune*, wrote: 'At night after grace was said, he resigned the Colar of the order, with a cup of wine, to his successor in that charge, and they dranke one to another.'[30] In 1608, Champlain established a protected enclave of buildings at Stadacona or what the Algonquians called *Kebec*. Champlain solidified trade relations with his new allies by joining war parties against the Iroquois and by wintering among the Hurons, who began to trade furs with the French during the 1620s.

When the Hurons were vanquished, by the Iroquois and by the diseases carried by European traders and missionaries, their position in the fur trade was assumed by men who travelled to New France and worked independently. Known as the *coureurs de bois* or the runners of the woods, these men lived inland among the Algonquians and delivered furs to New France.[31] Similar to the Jesuit missionaries, who travelled widely to convert Aboriginals to Christianity, the fur traders adopted a lifestyle that demanded physical strength, skill with the canoe and with snowshoes, and endurance. Many accounts written by missionaries and travellers depict Aboriginals as uncivilized savages, who required baptism and assimilation to French culture to advance as a people. Ironically, the Natives civilized the French, teaching the survival skills of the canoe and snowshoe, enlarging agricultural knowledge, and guiding the intricacies of travel, including sometimes the provision of fresh meat, in an environment that was harsh for the unprepared. Even the Jesuits, whose religion contained elements of Christian asceticism and focused on the afterlife while forgoing the pleasures of the flesh, were required to exhibit high degrees of fitness and endurance to attend to distant settlements such as Huronia. This involved arduous long-distance travel during all seasons of the year. A Jesuit recalls a journey from 1651:

We set out again at three in the morning by terrible tracks through scrub so thick that at each step we had to search for a place to put down our feet or our snowshoes. Several times I took the wrong turning because it was impossible in the dark to follow the tracks of those who went ahead. Then we came upon lakes covered in slippery ice where it was extremely dangerous to proceed in snowshoes, because of uneven ice and melted snow.[32]

Life in the bush was extremely difficult for the uninitiated French traders until they successfully adopted the techniques of Aboriginal travellers. As the new middlemen of the fur trade, the *coureurs de bois* assumed a unique place in Canadian lore. The trade required these men to establish cordial relations with Aboriginal hunters and trappers, to travel extensively year-round, and to obtain furs; therefore, they spent more time inland than in

Trading parties meet at Fort Pitt. (O.B. Buell, Library and Archives Canada, PA-118768)

New France and, consequently, gained a reputation for being unruly, wild, and uncivilized men of the bush when they returned to post and settlement. They wrestled, fought, ran races, paddled, and drank with one another and with Native men, in symbolic exchanges of physical prestige, thereby establishing hierarchies of physical empowerment that delineated both economic and social standing. Yet, administrators and colonists respected their physical skills and their abilities to survive in what they considered to be extremely dangerous and volatile circumstances. Governor Frontenac's[33] early impressions of the legendary physical prowess of the *coureurs de bois* attested to this:

> unless one had witnessed it one could not believe the exhaustion of those men, dragging the boats, most of them had been in the water a great deal of the time up to their armpits and bouncing on rock so sharp that some of them had legs and feet running with blood, yet their gaiety was undiminished and as soon as they got back to camp, some of them began to jump around, to perform gymnastics, and all manner of games.[34]

The runners of the woods came to be both revered and feared. They relied on their endurance and physical skills for subsistence and survival and, hence, developed masculine identities closely linked to the physical demands of their labour: strong, swift, and enduring, combined with a fierce independence and a lack of deference to the authority of French administrators. Governor Denonville's report to France is revealing:

. . . you are aware Mon Siegneur, that the coureurs de bois are a great evil, but you are not aware how great this evil is. It deprives the country of its effective men, makes them debauched and incapable of discipline.[35]

The priests and administrators of New France had little control over unruly behaviour, since the traders represented the main link to the increasingly distant supply of furs and, through their intimate relations with Aboriginal suppliers, they could barter with the English or pay representatives to trade for them when opportunity arose. Eventually, the fur traders became icons of a rough but only half-respected manhood or **bush masculinity**.

The fur trade also directly influenced gender hierarchies within Native communities; through marriage to French traders, Aboriginal women gained more influence over trading relations and access to goods, enhancing their own status in the community. Multi-levelled interests of such partnerships ranged from companionship and sexual contact, to handicraft skill in making snowshoes and moccasins, to the broader politics of community access to European manufactured goods and the sustaining of good relationships with the French.[36] The boundaries between Aboriginals and the French were 'at best ill-defined'.[37] Joseph La France was a second-generation *coureur de bois* and the child of a fur trade partnership, his father a fur trader from Quebec, his mother from the Ojibwa people near Sault Ste Marie. Achieving some notoriety during his life as a fur trader, La France travelled more than 17,000 miles by canoe and another 500 miles overland, once having paddled 40 days upstream, including 36 portages from Montreal to Lake Nipissing, after running afoul of the Governor.[38] La France traded fur with various Native groups along his routes to ensure safe passage and to avoid capture by the French, who sought to regulate the fur trade by establishing trading posts and restricting the unlicensed traders.

European Settlement

In New France in 1627, the Company of One Hundred Associates assumed seigneurial title to all lands in order to promote colonization and to support the work of the missionaries. The Company in 1633–34 granted 50 tracts of land—*seigneuries*—to seigneurs, or landholders, who in turn arranged for their distribution to rent-paying settlers, or **habitants**. Seigneuries divided the land along the St Lawrence River into long, narrow portions leading back from the riverfront. Seigneurs built flour mills and churches for the habitants, who cleared portions of the land, helped to build roads and bridges, and provided some military service to the Crown.[39] Habitant life was physically challenging for those who survived the voyage from France and the first winter. Building shelter was the first concern in addition to hunting game to be stored for winter. Felling trees, sawing lumber, raising even small buildings, stumping, and removing rocks with minimal tools were extremely strenuous tasks. It followed, then, that strength became one of the most significant aspects of habitant physicality in New France. As in Aboriginal cultures and in the bachelor subculture of the fur trade, masculinity or aspects of exemplary manhood among the habitants connected intimately to the strengths and skills valued in the labour process. In order to promote colonization and to increase the population during the 1660s, 800 French women, known as the *filles du rois* (daughters of the King), travelled to New France to claim husbands (or to be claimed as wives) and start families.

A trapper and the tools of his trade. (Library and Archives Canada, C-003280)

These women of France—some provided with money or supplies and clothing by the Crown, others who were educated[40] and carried money of their own—were bound by their marriages to hard field labour and harsh winter conditions with sparse provisions and under threat of attack or military invasion. They were confronted with remarkable challenges in their lives.[41] With the family constituting the most important unit in New France, public and private life was essentially undifferentiated; women and men worked together and fought enemies together.[42]

The organization of the seigneurial system directly influenced social gatherings of families in New France and forms of entertainment during the cold winter months. Due to the layout of the long, narrow plots, houses were built in close proximity. Neighbouring families bonded through extended seasonal celebrations, wedding feasts, singing, drinking, and card-playing. The physically demanding agricultural work, of course, depended on the seasons. During the summer months, habitants worked from dawn to dusk; during the winter months men applied to work in the fur trade to supplement supplies and income while women managed family businesses and farms at home. Such a lifestyle concerned the administrators of New France, who preferred the establishment of trades that would service the growing population and lessen its dependency on the diminishing returns of the fur trade. The Roman Catholic Church, too, attempted to dissuade parishioners from pursuing the rougher forms of entertainment such as drinking, gambling, and fighting, and from mingling with the opposite sex before marriage.

Although the historical literature highlights the leadership of the clergy in New France, there is evidence to suggest that the habitants remained somewhat independent from Church authority and were reluctant to renounce their predilection for less respected entertainments.[43] The Jesuits equated dancing among unmarried couples with sin and debauchery. A cleric criticized social entertainments of this sort: 'Assemblies, balls, and country parties were infamous . . . mothers who brought their daughters to them were adulteresses, that they only availed themselves of these nocturnal pleasures to put a veil over their shamelessness and over fornication.'[44] A local Bishop unequivocally expressed his comments towards mixed dancing in Montreal in a letter of complaint to the Governor:

> Although balls and dances are not sinful in their nature, nevertheless they are so dangerous by reason of the circumstances that attend them and the evil results that almost inevitably follow . . . nevertheless, since the youth and vivacity of mademoiselle, their daughter, requires some diversion, it is permitted to relent somewhat, and indulge her in a little moderate and proper dancing, provided that it be solely with persons of her own sex, and in the presence of madam, her mother; but by no means in the presence of men or youths, since it is this mingling of sexes which causes the disorders that spring from balls and dances.[45]

Conquest

At the formal end of the Seven Years War in 1763, the British assumed control of the districts of Montreal, Quebec, and Trois-Rivières, but in contrast to the expulsion of the Acadians from what would become Nova Scotia, the 70,000 habitants, merchants, and colonial elites remained in the former New France.[46] For the French Canadians, the Catholic Church remained prominent in cultural life, as did the language, customs, and values passed down from previous eras. For Aboriginals in the Canadas, the Iroquois in particular, the conquest by the English meant that all connections to traditional lands and territories would be called into question. Following the capitulation of New France to the British, Aboriginal territories became even more compressed. Disease continued to ravage Native populations and, empowered by legislation, immigrants and waves of **Loyalists** from the United States began to assume ownership of lands for settlement and development.

The ceding of the Hudson's Bay region to the English through the Treaty of Utrecht in 1713 had opened up new land to the fur trade. The Hudson's Bay Company had hoped to capitalize on these northerly resources in the 1780s, after the fall of New France, but met competition from the North West Company organized by Scottish and American traders in Montreal. Commercial rivalries between the two companies, sustained until their merger in 1821, expanded northern and western trade routes far beyond the travels of the *coureurs de bois* of the previous era. A new group of hearty, competitive employees of the North West Company, the *voyageurs*, displaced the remaining Aboriginal travellers in the fur trade. As had been the case with European men before them, legends of their skill, strength, and stamina emerged from the bush. A paternalistic relationship of master and servant existed between *bourgeois* and *voyageur*, varying according to circumstances and those involved and sometimes bordering on the cruel and discriminatory. Masters even threatened servants through starvation and dismissal; yet, it remained workable, since the voyageurs were often reasonably accepting of subordinate relations but could resist, revolt, or challenge their masters.[47]

In the beginning, social and economic hierarchies among *voyageurs* related to the differing occupations within the trade; later, as more British assumed the role of *bourgeois* while French Canadians, Métis, and Iroquois from Kahnawake[48] took on the role of workers or engagés, divisions in the hierarchy became more ethnically based. A canoeman's notoriety and the territories he covered conferred social distinctions based upon the physical capacity of the task. The wintering *voyageurs* worked the interior and considered

Issues in Canadian Sport History

The Voyageur: Estimated Facts and Feats

Average weight	155 pounds
Average height	5'4" to 5'6" (restricted by canoe leg room)
Paddle rate	40 per minute
Distance travelled per day (without portages)	75 to 100 miles
Distance travelled per day (with portages, varying)	50 miles
Load responsibility per paddler	Six packs or 'pieces' plus personal pack
Pack weight	60 to 90 pounds
Personal pack weight	40 pounds, held in place by the portage collar placed around the head and straps around each pack
Portaging	Stops or 'poses' were spaced at distances of ¼ to ½ mile over the length of the portage; some portages were up to 9 miles in length
	Each voyageur jogged with 2 packs or sometimes 3 (as many as 4–7 have been recorded) and jogged back for the next load
Estimated caloric intake per day	7,200; primarily salmon, whitefish, and pemmican
Estimated caloric burn	6,990 over a 15-hour day
	Records show working days of up to 18 hours; for example work day began at 2:30 AM; breakfast at 7:30 AM; lunch at 1:30 PM; camp at 9:30 PM; start again at 4:30 AM.

themselves more physically hearty. They were the *hommes du nord*, or north men, and had little respect for the summer-employed *mangeur du lard*, the 'porkeater', also referred to as 'greenhorn' or 'tenderfoot'. The north men prided themselves on travelling and living hard, and scorned the Montreal-based porkeaters for their 'easy' lifestyles in the fur trade.[49] However, strength and paddling abilities did not readily translate into authority and higher pay. Paddlers earned less than steersmen, interpreters, and guides, who wielded specific technical authority.[50] Among *voyageurs*, masculine identity linked intimately to the labour process, and intense, competitive rivalries came to define relations between crews and among individual crewmen.

For the canoemen, paddling rhythm, endurance, and the strength to haul packs and supplies over long and difficult portages defined ability, efficiency, and the success of the trade. The physical abilities of the *voyageur*, then, translated to both economic reputation as a good worker and to social reputation as a respectable man. Immense strength and physical endurance became markers of masculine identity for every *voyageur* and highly valued characteristics of exemplary manhood for the profession and for outsiders who marvelled at the legends of their physical feats. Significant rituals such as the baptism of novices,[51] departure celebrations, and physical competitions underscored a deep

The fur trade at Fort Chippewa. (Library and Archives Canada, C-001229)

awareness of the dangers of the profession, the risk-taking and bravado of the men, and the importance of physicality in defining both identity and a marked distinction from their masters, the *bourgeois*.

All trips varied in length and crews differed in habits and strategies, but a typical day for a voyageur consisted of rising during the middle of the night, paddling until breakfast at dawn, a midday lunch of pemmican, paddling 40 to 60 strokes per minute or the equivalent of five to six miles per hour, and then night camp, struck between eight and ten in the evening. *Voyageurs* measured time and distance by the number of 'pipes'—stops for smoking tobacco—they enjoyed. It may be true that British travellers' literature and Canadian authors of the nineteenth century romanticized and stereotyped the life and feats of the voyageur,[52] but it is evident that 12–15 hours of paddling per day was common among crews. When in the canoe, the *voyageurs* kept paddling rhythm by singing, which ensured consistent pace and, therefore, extended distance each day throughout the trip. The number of songs in one's repertoire was also a marker of identity and reputation. However, the portage—carrying packs and canoes around rapids—placed all emphasis on individual performance, sometimes to a dangerous extent. If rapids could not be poled or the empty canoe dragged, then the traders carried their packs to stations or poses, approximately one-quarter mile apart. The *voyageurs* divided the Grand Portage, at nine miles in length, into 16 poses. Packs of furs ranged from 80–100 pounds each, and every voyageur was responsible for three packs and 40 pounds of personal belongings. The average load was two packs, although some records indicate that the strongest men carried as many as five or even seven packs beyond the usual quarter mile without stopping. *Voyageurs* shuffled or jogged between poses and then returned for the next load. It is possible that some accounts exaggerated such feats; but others record that the condition of strangulated hernia commonly afflicted the men, leading at times to death.[53] Such intense competition marking crew strength and individual stamina juxtaposed economic and social aspects of the profession, creating a fusion of identity and physical prowess in a dynamic that was symbiotic, if not pathological. Some observers, such as the Jesuit missionary Jean de Brébeuf, deplored the social value placed upon physical prowess in the fur trade:

> All the fine qualities which might make you loved and respected in France are like pearls trampled under the feet of swine, or rather mules, which utterly despise you when they see that you are not as good pack animals as they are. If you could go naked and carry the load of a horse upon your back, as they do, then you would be wise according to their doctrine, and would be recognized as a great man, otherwise not.[54]

In addition to the competitions readily organized on the trail and on the water, contests of strength, fist fights, brawling, drinking, and racing lent symbolic weight to, and enhanced, their positions within the social hierarchy of the profession. Crews challenged one another to contests of endurance in long-distance canoe races. In one contest, crews raced from the north to the south end of Lake Winnipeg, for 48 hours without stopping, before they eased off and camped.[55] More violent and aggressive contests, during fun and revelry, served to desensitize the *voyageurs* to the inherent risks of their lifestyles and helped to prepare them for the challenges they constantly faced in the bush.[56] However, in many respects, the *voyageurs* actively created the hardships and challenges of the profession, the codes of competition on portages that they adhered to and respected, and participated in the construction of their own identities and reputations as exemplars of a violent, but competent, bush masculinity. Further, these men structured their reputations in opposition to other men, including their masters, underscoring the value of material possessions; domestic qualities, including romance and sexual exploits; and the '*voyageur*' capacities for strength and song. The recollections in 1825 of retired voyageur Alexander Ross capture the complexities and subtleties of these social relations:

> I have now been forty-two years in this country. For twenty-four I was a light canoeman. . . . No portage was too long for me; all portages were alike. My end of the canoe never touched the ground till I saw the end of . . . [the portage]. Fifty songs a day were nothing to me, I could carry, paddle, walk and sing with any man I ever saw. . . . No water, no weather, ever stopped the paddle or the song. I have had twelve wives in the country; and was once possessed of fifty horses, and six running dogs, trimmed in the first style. I was then like a Bourgeois, rich and happy: no Bourgeois had better dressed wives than I; no Indian chief finer horses; no white man better harnessed or swifter dogs . . . I wanted for nothing; and I spent all my earnings in the enjoyment of pleasure. Five hundred pounds, twice told, have passed through my hands; although now I have not a spare shirt to my back, nor a penny to buy one. Yet, were I young again, I should glory in commencing the same career again. I would spend another half-century in the same fields of enjoyment. . . . There is no

life so happy as a voyageur's life; none so independent; no place where a man enjoys so much variety and freedom as in the Indian country.[57]

The exaggerations of Ross's account are less important, historically, than the values he identifies with the fur-trading life. Seeking to trade on the historic images and reputations of the *voyageurs*, in a more refined social setting, fur trade merchants who had spent time in the interior formed an exclusive social organization in Montreal in 1785 called the Beaver Club. The 'real' *voyageurs*, paddlers and labourers, were not welcome to this club where men of mercantile distinction ate, sang, and often drank themselves to sleep. Lavish dinners and enormous quantities of wine provided a backdrop to the sharing of stories about their adventures in the wilderness, even though they had no part in heavy paddling or portaging in the fur trade business. However, the more physical forms of masculine prowess, appropriated in self-aggrandizing stories, made for better impressions, particularly when members of Montreal's elite male citizenry visited the club. Social organizations, such as the Beaver Club and others, served to socially distance the men from labourers and from women, and permitted them to make connections to aristocratic elites or maintain ideological solidarity in distinction to the gentry if it suited them.[58] The club permitted middle-class men to invoke their connections to the romance of the wilderness, as successful and manly businessmen, while forging new business ties within the emergent commercial sector of Montreal. Self-appointed, respectable men selectively borrowed and romanticized the values inherent in rougher versions of bush masculinity in respectable settings, without the discomfiting presence of unruly labourers.

Similarly, authors in the nineteenth century romanticized the lifestyles of those whom they considered nation builders and the forebears of early Canadian manhood. Authors such as Robert Ballyntine and the Canadian patriot and lacrosse enthusiast, George Beers (see Chapter 5), lionized the *voyageurs* in their respective representations of the exotic and the wild, and both engaged in literary mythmaking at a time when the long tradition of the fur trade was declining. Ballyntine's depiction of the *voyageurs* in *The Young Fur Traders* combines 'the light gay-spirited and full muscular frame of the Canadian with the fierce passions and active habits of the Indian. And this wildness of disposition was not a little fostered by the nature of their unusual occupation.'[59] Beers's interpretations were similarly romantic: 'Nature in all her freedom, unrestrained by the customs of civilization, has made the voyageurs a peculiarly intrepid, romantic race—with rather a tendency to be savage.'[60]

Conclusions

As the viability of the fur trade as a commercial enterprise declined in the Canadas, stories, songs, and literary musings sustained a residue of cultural representations of this earlier era in history. Nineteenth-century interpretations of the battles between French and English, the development of the colonies, and the civilization of the savages belied the unfettered destruction of centuries-old traditions, ways of life, and the outright slaughter of countless peoples. However, the cultural significance of strength, skill, and the physicality of the habitants was not forgotten; rather, it was recast by the French Canadians themselves within the network of social contexts and ideas attributed to the 'progressive' society of the Victorians, Loyalists, and immigrants who sought to build state, economy, and social order during the 1800s. They, too, played games and sports, danced, drank, and established social institutions to celebrate particular social values imbued with relations of class, gender, and race, and passed laws to diminish others. Under the dim lights of the aurora borealis, the social landscape of the continent had changed irrevocably.

Related Websites

General History
http://www.canadiana.org/citm/index_e.html

North American Indigenous Games
http://www.virtualmuseum.ca/Exhibitions/Traditions/index.html

New France
http://www.tfo.org/television/emissions/rendezvousvoyageur/en/world/context/fromcoureur.html

Early Maps
http://www.kstrom.net/isk/maps/royalproc.html

Montreal
http://www2.ville.montreal.qc.ca/archives/500ans/portail_archives_en/accueil.html

Study Questions

1. Why is it difficult to understand the history of traditional games in North American Aboriginal societies?
2. What purposes did games and physical competitions serve in Native communities?
3. In comparison to the evidence available for early Aboriginal Canadians, what ideas did the French have about their bodies relating to religion, work, and play?
4. What was the role of competition in the life of a fur trader?
5. How did religion, patterns of settlement, and the economy influence physical activity in New France?
6. What qualities of manliness were revered in early Canada? Do these values persist today?

CHAPTER 3

Games, Pastimes, and Sporting Life in British North America

——————◆——————

The taverns then lined each side of the way,
As thick as the milestones in Ireland today;
And then the farmers all thought it was fine,
If they got as far as the London Proof Line.

—Biddulph Township poet, W.W.
Revington, inspired by the 12 popular
taverns lining the few short miles between
London and Elginfield[1]

In addition to the relatively unregulated public spaces, rivers, lakes, fields, and common grounds, the tavern, club, and **garrison** were the most important social institutions in the post-Conquest/pre-Confederation era (1763–1866) where games and sports occurred with some frequency. Never innocent amusements, these physical activities demonstrated how the English, French, Aboriginals, Irish, Scots, Loyalists, and others related to one another; the values they shared or resisted; their political, economic, and religious interests; their aspirations, irritations, loves and fears, manhood and womanhood, freedoms, and restraints. Evidence of how these people played and competed can be found in nineteenth-century newspapers, travellers' literature, diaries, government and judicial records, and in the legislation invoked to regulate the affairs of British North Americans.

Although there is ample evidence that throughout the nineteenth century people played, competed, drank, or fought for money, fun, and pride, the reasons others did not play are equally significant. Settlement, conquest, and the removal of Aboriginal peoples to reserves altered indigenous games and dances, fragmenting the traditional cultures that Aboriginals attempted to preserve and that nineteenth-century

Pioneer Saloon, Dawson City, Yukon Territory [1898–1910]. (National Museum of Canada, Library and Archives Canada, PA-013511)

Euro-Canadian officials sought to suppress or to put on public display. Immigrants brought games and social traditions with them but not in a unidirectional process of diffusion or transplantation from the Old World to the New. Rather, in addition to policies of British imperialism and processes of state formation in the Canadas, the symbolic meanings attached to pastimes related directly to newly emerging relations between established settlers, new arrivals, and within the social institutions they sought to create. Further, the attachment to the landscape and geography unique to the colonies and the patterns of population growth were both factors in the emergence of sport and other forms of culture.

The English established governing institutions in British North America to organize behaviour and to regulate property ownership and access, possessions, trade, religion, government, economy, and values about life and living. The inextricably linked class, gender, ethnicity, and race are particularly useful analytical categories for historians to describe how and why people played, the interests that they pursued, the unseen forces that influenced their lives, and how these factors related to their social positions or daily existence on the social and cultural landscape. It is important to examine some of the broader social institutions and the political and economic contexts in which colonial life was situated to understand the social place the various pastimes, games, and sports enjoyed by citizens of different classes in the urban and rural areas of British North America during the early nineteenth century.

Settlers' log home built along the Tartigou River in Quebec. (Alexander Henderson, Library and Archives Canada, PA-149763)

The British Elite

Although the political settings in each region of the British North American colonies were unique, similarities in governance and access to economic and social influence prior to the 1840s served to shape many parameters of social life in Upper and Lower Canada (Ontario and Quebec) and the Maritimes (Nova Scotia, New Brunswick, Prince Edward Island, and Cape Breton), including sports, games, and pastimes. The appointment of British elites—who tended to be Anglican, Tory military officers—to public office led to the establishment of self-perpetuating networks of administrative interest in which officials were bonded together by a political and social 'like-mindedness'. At local levels, wealthy families favoured by land-granting policies formed alliances with governing elites, giving rise to vast networks of political and economic patronage. In Upper Canada, family continuity and local prominence were intimately connected. Similar political oligarchies ruled in Halifax, Fredericton, and St John's, in addition to the network of elites known as the **Family Compact** in Upper Canada and the **Château Clique** in Lower Canada.[2] In Upper Canada, the Macdonnell, Jones, Robinson, Sherwood, Boulton, Buell, Howard, Burritt, and Jessup family names frequented the role of the House of Assembly and senior administrative positions.[3] Patronage appointments, such as those of the business savvy Ingersoll brothers to offices of postmaster and land registrar in the old Brock District, were the norm.[4] For elites, such like-mindedness in religious and social values provided context for certain class- and gender-based social behaviours expressed through forms of culture, including sport, that emerged during this period. A common deference to hierarchical order, juxtaposing church and state, by elites and their allies served to legitimize the laws and legislation passed to govern town and country life in the colonies. The Family Compact buttressed its political power with significant revenues from the Crown reserve lands established in support of the Church of England or Anglican Church.[5]

The Reverend Easton preached to Montreal citizens in 1810:

> this duty of being submissive and obedient to the constituted civil authorities should come with peculiar energy to the hearts of British subjects. If we respect Christianity we must for that very reason respect our civil rules, and unite them in promoting the peace and happiness of society. These two kinds of regard are inseparably connected . . . [and] . . . it may be observed the Christian duty of al- legiance is not founded on the personal characters of our rulers, but entirely on the offices which they hold.[6]

These two kinds of regard—Christianity and civil rules—were invoked through legislation and bylaws to regulate and shape citizen behaviour in towns and rural districts. However, ruling was not just a matter of legislation and law: 'rule must appear practically in the behaviour, activity, understandings, etc. of those who are ruled.'[7] Colonial governments endowed local justices of the peace with various powers to regulate and punish criminal activities and public nuisances. However, before 1840 an absence of connections between central authority and rural areas limited the efficiency of inspectors and officials.[8]

Public Nuisance and Public Purse

One of the principal targets of such legislation was the public house, inn, 'grog shop', or drinking establishment. In the early period of post-Conquest settlement by Loyalists and European immigrants, taverns and inns provided food, drink, and shelter for travellers. Decades later, local taverns were primarily houses of entertainment where men and women drank, socialized, gambled, played, sang, laughed, argued, and fought. Bearing in mind the sheer numbers of establishments, the numbers and varieties of patrons, the volumes of government ordinances and church and temperance sermons against them, and the significant revenues for the public purse, the tavern was the most important social institution in nineteenth-century Canada.[9]

The earliest legislation regulated the drink trade, primarily to collect revenues for public expenditures. 'Sin taxes' were one of the foundations of colonial society, from a social, regulatory standpoint extending to one of government economic viability. The government administrative purse depended on the 'sins' of the people and on the subsequent taxes on certain pastimes. The first liquor-related law in Upper Canada, passed in 1793, established a fund for the payment of the salaries for the officers of the Legislative Council and House of Assembly.[10] Justices of the peace were empowered to limit the number of licences distributed and to make inquiries into the 'life, character, and behaviour' of licence applicants, providing ample opportunities for local politicking in the licensing process.[11]

In addition to providing a mechanism to impose a regulative authority over public drunkenness, legislation criminalized public gambling games as activities dangerous

The Colonial Hotel at Soda Creek, British Columbia. (Frederick Dally, Library and Archives Canada, C-008076)

to the moral fibre of the colonies. Gambling, as an alternative form of material gain, challenged the commonly held notions about class entitlement which were informed, in part, by the emerging Protestant work ethic.[12] With respect to private and public space, class values and a distinct gender order pervaded all behavioural legislation. The elite men of the Beaver Club in Montreal, for example, could gamble and often drank until they passed out, without fear of legal or social repercussions. However, average citizens, women in particular, drinking in taverns (public spaces) were subject to increasing scrutiny, as were the owners of these establishments. Respectable citizens of Montreal, self-appointed crusaders against the tavern game of billiards, were concerned that the game, when unchecked, created moral degradation; the implication was that when played among gentlemen in private quarters it could be respectable.[13] An Act to regulate public tables stated:

> Whereas much inconvenience has arisen from the increased number of billiard tables throughout this province; And whereas it is essential to the happiness and welfare of all of his Majesty's subjects therein, that the licensing of billiard tables, in future, for the more effectual prevention of the evils and inconveniences arising therefrom, be considered an object of legislative interference.[14]

Between 1792 and 1840 in Lower Canada, the liquor and tobacco trade, in addition to billiard licences, provided 6–34 per cent of total annual revenues.[15] As the temperance movement gathered support, legislators had to wrestle with the temperance lobby on the one hand and the lucrative revenues from licences and tariffs on the other. Governments had direct regulatory, educational, and financial interests in the pastimes of the people.

In addition to the sermons of ministers and priests about leisure behaviour, the governing elites supported the establishment of institutions dedicated to education and the improvement of agriculture and manufacturing. William Botsford Jarvis, John Elmsley, William Henry Boulton, John Beverly Robinson, and Henry John Boulton, for example, were instrumental in promoting agricultural education and the establishment of **agricultural societies** in Upper Canada.[16] In Lower Canada, the government provided funds for societies in Quebec, Montreal, and Trois-Rivières during the 1820s and decreed that all counties[17] should have agricultural societies for the 'production of superior agricultural products' to be displayed at local **fairs**.[18] Elites considered funds for agricultural societies and mechanics' institutes as money well spent toward the improvement of citizens and economic development.[19] Legislation stipulating that Catholic rectors, Protestant clergy, and legislative or executive councillors could be honorary and voting members of these societies was another assurance that elites would sustain control over economic and political interests in British North America.

Town ordinances and legislation offer a glimpse into social life, an indication of what activities were regulated or prevented. In addition to billiards, the legislation positioned cards, dice, tables, tennis, bowls, shooting off fireworks, or just standing on street corners as 'idle' behaviour—social events to be monitored by local justices or even prohibited.[20] The inherent moralizing evident in behavioural legislation underscored the class distinctions of early Canadian society. The clubs and private dwellings of elites shielded them from the sort of public scrutiny that they sought to enforce on others. Yet, excessive drinking was not limited to farmers and labourers, or the poor and indigent, as the language of the law and the sermonizing in local newspapers would have one believe; all segments of society—magistrates, clergymen, government officials, rich and poor, men and women, and some children—drank alcohol on a daily basis at home, at work, and as a social ritual at gatherings or public houses.[21] Early in the nineteenth century, business owners commonly provided rum rations for their labourers, a practice borrowed from the military and the British Navy that was sometimes revoked as a manner of punishment.[22] Furthermore, one could not attract sufficient numbers of workers to logging, barn-raising, or harvest bees without appropriate quantities of liquor.[23]

The church–state link also extended through laws prohibiting certain activities on Sundays. Priests and ministers expected colonists of Protestant and Roman Catholic faiths to observe religious services and rituals on Sundays; the Protestant Sunday was restrictive in British North America and eighteenth-century legislation in Nova Scotia, New Brunswick, and Prince Edward Island prohibited Sunday sports, games, play, **fowling**, and fishing, under threat of fine.[24] However, such laws were difficult to enforce, particularly in Lower Canada, where the French continued to enjoy a **continental Sunday**—church leaders permitted a few drinks, games, and social activities after Mass.[25] Some turn-of-the-century opposition to the continental Sunday and the enjoyment of games existed in Montreal, particularly to bowling and billiards[26] on the Sabbath, and local magistrates voiced similar concerns in 1810 about the distractions that these amusements created:

young and idle persons assemble together in numbers on Sundays and holydays, for the purpose of play and amusement, in the streets, squares, and other places of the town and suburbs, instead of attending Divine worship.[27]

Officials attempted to curtail activities such as horse racing that had long been popular among elites, merchants, and habitants in New France,[28] and fighting, cursing, or public drunkenness near the churches during services.[29] Local laws defined and then targeted other public nuisances, including bathing or swimming naked within town limits, as in Montreal in order to prevent 'indecent' bathing,[30] and in Charlottetown where people sometimes swam nude near the wharfs, which for some was 'repugnant to the rules of morality and decorum'.[31]

Good Hunting

Early hunting and fishing legislation initiated control over lands, forests, streams, and lakes away from the towns, defining appropriate seasons for particular species of birds, mammals, and fish.[32] Where Aboriginal peoples had travelled and hunted for centuries, Canada became known as a hunters' paradise for tourists, travellers, and wealthy men who owned large parcels of land.[33] The physical experiences of hunting helped to create social hierarchies for all men—Aboriginal, fur trader, and British gentleman. Hunting laws reinforced the class-based assumption that gentleman hunters were more rational, fairer to wild game, and more responsible than subsistence hunters, farmers, and Aboriginals.[34] For the British and colonial recreational hunters, class values blended with masculine identities to frame these experiences, in part securing a place for these men in the literature for their readership as conquering proprietors of the Canadian wilderness, at the expense of the more physically skilled Aboriginal guides who were positioned as savage, but noble, lesser men. In matters of physical ability such as hunting, where comparisons could be drawn between men of different classes or when the British compared themselves to Aboriginal men through racial distinctions, there was always tension in masculine identities.[35] Class- and race-based excuses could always usurp the shortcomings evident in physical ability to preserve the social distinctions that gave meaning to middle-class and gentry masculinities. Relations between same sexes were as significant historically as relations between opposite sexes in reproducing class and gender orders.

However, the process of British imperialism and land appropriation ran far deeper than organizing property and managing wildlife; imperialists organized the ways that people understood the land and its aesthetic qualities. British sportsmen, travellers, and authors appropriated the landscape of nineteenth-century Canada by imposing scientific and aesthetic interpretations or 'gazes' by mapping, by applying the Linnaean system of classifying plants and animals, and by constructing landscape in terms that were familiar to the British readership.[36] Through such systematizing and aesthetic construction of the landscape, the imperialist sportsmen gave the land cultural meaning to bring it under the auspices of British control.[37] For inhabitants, game laws asserted the primacy of the gentleman hunter and fisher in 'managing' wildlife and, more broadly, a certain control over public lands. In short, nature was organized into consumable forms.[38] On their own lands, elites could do as they pleased. Early legislation permitted subsistence hunting by Aboriginals and 'poor' settlers at all times of the year, but the process of scientizing wildlife, imbued with the moral codes of 'proper' seasons, hunting techniques, and stock management for hunters and fishers, created a permanent foundation for the socially meaningful organization of nature in Canada.[39]

Bachelors and Clubs

In confines that were predominantly male such as the fur-trading posts and the garrisons throughout the colonies, sports, games, and contests alleviated boredom and provided fun, excitement, and entertainment during traditional holidays such as Christmas. For example, football and fist-fighting were the most popular pastimes at the York Factory trading post from the late 1700s to the mid 1800s. Men gathered frequently to play football and to gamble on the outcomes of their matches. Football was sometimes a reward provided by the Chief Factor if the men consumed less alcohol than usual during Christmas. This strategy was not always successful, as is evident in the records for 25 December 1823: 'stormy weather as has been the usual custom at this place . . . part of the Men and some of the Gentlemen turned out to a game of football which was not kept up with much spirit probably from the Severity of the Weather combined with a previous too free use of the Bottle.'[40] In addition to the often violent football matches, the fur traders employed fisticuffs to solve their disputes and to test one another, particularly after bouts of heavy drinking.[41]

Military officers in all of the garrison towns of British North America patronized the sport of horse racing during this era.[42] The British garrisons, staffed by regular troops and officers, provided military protection and a sense of domestic stability for colonists in Halifax, Saint John, Quebec, Montreal, Kingston, Niagara, and London. The public display of parading soldiers—orderly, trained, and in uniform—announced a permanency to the growing towns, a reminder of Crown and homeland, and a symbolic, exemplary manhood. Conversely, when mustered by local administrators to quell public disturbances, the garrisons served as a violent threat to would-be strikers, rioters, or disturbers of the peace. For the townspeople, their presence was, on the one hand, comforting, and lucrative for the shops when soldiers spent military pay on supplies and entertainment. On the other hand, the bachelor subculture of the garrison soldiers who lived in relative social isolation tended towards drinking, brawling, and sexual conquest when they were on leave in town.[43]

Against the backdrop of local military regimes that secured British territories, and in addition to the establishment of patriarchal property laws, the constructions of ideas about maleness and femaleness served to consolidate further gender identities in British North America. In the late eighteenth and early nineteenth centuries, middle- and upper-class men increasingly organized activities or distinct forms of culture to create and sustain **gender polarities** that reinforced relations between men and women and positioned them into different social domains.

Loyalist women from the United States who resettled in eastern Ontario found themselves dependent on a more paternalist and patriarchal British regime. The post-Conquest society increasingly marginalized women from matters of public commerce. Bourgeois men, merchants, and business owners interested in social and economic distinction sought the insulation of urban-based private clubs to pursue economic and political interests. The men of the Beaver Club in Montreal celebrated their attachments to masculine bravado in the wilderness and drank themselves unconscious, not to distinguish themselves to female admirers and spouses but rather to impress other men, their peers.[44] Thus, they isolated

Hunting camp set up near Cobourg, Ontario. (C. Lawes, Library and Archives Canada, PA-125812)

themselves by excluding lower orders of men and all women, yet often invited members of the local aristocracy to patronize or visit. The social effect was part of a broader process of creating separate spheres for middle-class men and women, emergent through the nineteenth century.[45] Similarly, fur-trading Scottish merchants formed Canada's first sporting club at Gillis's Tavern in 1807, the Montreal Curling Club, as a fraternal organization conceived under the auspices of sport. As for the men of the Beaver Club, food, drink, and revelry were the order of the evening. The club met every two weeks 'to dine on salt beef and greens' with the losers of the curling match paying for a bowl of 'whisky toddy, to be placed in the middle of the table for those who may chuse [sic] it.'[46] Wherever the Scots settled, there was curling (see Chapter 4). Several sources describe the Scottish soldiers curling on the St Charles and St Lawrence rivers as early as the period of the Seven Years War, between 1756–63.[47] A well-known story is of a French-Canadian farmer who reacted to the Scots playing on the ice: 'Today I saw a band of Scotchmen, who were throwing large balls of iron like tea-kettles on the ice, after which they cried "Soop! Soop!" and then laughed like fools. I really believe they ARE fools.'[48] The Scots established curling clubs in Halifax, Kingston, Quebec, Fergus, West Flamborough, Toronto, Milton, Galt, Guelph, Hamilton, and Scarborough before 1840.[49] Other men's sport clubs organized in Montreal, with a population of 22,500 by 1825[50] and the 'cradle'[51] or 'birthplace'[52] of Canadian sport, included a hunt club and cricket club, formed in response to the challenges of officers in the garrison.[53] Sports such as cricket permitted refined, competitive rivalries to be acted out between men without the dangers of a brawl or the influence of common worker associations of wrestling or challenges of strength. For all classes of men, participation and outcome signified masculine honour in any sort of physical contest. However, when acts by elite peers slighted manly honour, gentlemen took recourse more dangerous than cricket matches.

The Honour of Public Men and Domestic Women

For elites, their immediate followers, and the backwoods aristocracies of the Canadas rank, status, and family name embodied distinction and honour, the symbolic characteristics of social standing. Middle-class men, too, aspired to aristocratic ideals of manliness. The *voyageurs* found class honour in carrying heavy packs with speed, the tavern brawler in fights with fists and implements; however, when confronted with insults or denigration or harm, whether professional or personal, gentlemen invoked the ritual ceremonies of attack known as the duel. Honour was a prerogative of manhood bound to preserving family name, wealth, and influence in the social, political, and economic spheres. Consequently, honour was a paradox for the gentry, a tricky balance between the coveting of distinction and constant apprehension over reputation.[54] Like-mindedness, the linking of political appointment and social position, provided solidarity for governing elites; yet sustaining personal honour was a matter of great anxiety for these men, since any question of integrity threatened their status among peers. Gentry masculinities were unique in British North America because hereditary title and family longevity in the regions did not exist. Therefore, men had greater concern for preserving codes of status and appropriate conduct, particularly in small, socially elite enclaves such as York (Toronto).[55] Men responded to personal insults directed at times towards spouses and their sexual virtues, or other family members, with a challenge to a duel: a violent ritual between the two parties using pistols. At least 24 known challenges occurred in Upper Canada from 1793 to the 1840s before legislation outlawed duelling. Violence and intimidation were more prevalent, historically, in unstable hierarchies.[56]

Following the insult and the subsequent issue of a public challenge, seconds or observers joined the two men, often early in the morning, on the outskirts of town, to ensure that the duel was carried out fairly. Unlike the tavern brawl, where the outcome was most significant, the duel was a matter of due social process to satisfy the party who had been affronted. It did not matter if the offending party was killed or maimed, provided that the appropriate challenge was issued and the duel conducted in the prescribed manner. Although duellists were tried in court, they were often acquitted if they had followed the agreed-upon rules of killing.[57] The duel served to validate gentrified notions of chivalry, a public symbol of the anxieties and insecurities of aristocratic manhood.

The defence of women's sexual virtue demonstrated the paternalist focus of masculine honour and distinguished chastity as a fundamental feature of femininity for the gentlewoman.[58] Women were not permitted the option of physical confrontation to defend their own honour; however, men could defend against slights, insults, and dishonour by placing their bodies in harm's way in recognized acts of courage. Middle- and upper-class women's passivity came to define a genteel femininity, while fuelling an aggressive paternalism in masculine ideals wielded in defence of women or in opposition to the feminine ideal to impress or challenge other men. In spite of such notions about femininity, womanhood in this era was far from passive and genteel. Rural and urban women defended

Issues in Canadian Sport History

The Duel, Upper Canada 1833
Excerpts from the *Perth Courier*, 30 June 1905

A quarrel between the two friends and fellow law-students arose out of some words in reference to a young lady, who afterwards became the wife of Wilson. One was accused by the other of having spoken slightlingly of the lady in question; the lie was given and a blow given by Lyon to the other separated the two friends forever. Lyon was much the stronger and larger man, and Wilson was unable to retaliate effectually, and for the time the fracas ended between them, only to be retailed, with the flourishes added to it, so consistent with our erring human nature, by five hundred tongues within an hour or two after. The young lady who was the innocent inspiration of the altercation and assault, was a Miss Elizabeth Hughes.

Henry La Lievre was a man of powerful frame and herculean strength, full of courage, handsome, reckless and not troubled with scruples where self-interest or feelings of revenge came into play. Judge Hughes says he harbored feelings of resentment against Wilson because he desired an intimacy with Miss Hughes, but unsuccessfully, and he imagined Wilson was the cause of his failure, and was desirous of 'getting back' at Wilson by engaging him in a duel with Lyon, who was known to be a sure shot under ordinary conditions. Be this as it may, La Lievre, who was well acquainted with both parties in the quarrel, undertook, true to his disposition, to obtrude his advice upon them as to the right mode of settling their difference, urging, with his strong, persuasive powers, blended with ridicule and appeals to their courage and pride, the youths to wipe out the score by mortal combat. He was successful.

Wilson sent a challenge to Lyon: the latter accepted, both very unwillingly it is said, to resort to this dreadful alternative; and a meeting with pistols was arranged for the early morning of June 13th. The weapons were regular duelling pistols, surreptitiously taken, it is said, from a store in town, and returned after the deadly issue. The summer wind blew softly among the trees, the sun shone brightly and the birds sang joyously as the young men, with beating hearts, appeared on the ground, crossing the bit of wood from the Scotch Line to the river bank. Along with Lyon came La Lievre, his fire-eating second. Wilson's second was a young Scotchman named Simon Fraser Robertson, son of Captain Robertson, and brother of Mrs. (Hon.) Roderick Matheson, whose position of supporter of his principal was evidently opposed to his desires, as he strove at a critical time to effect a reconciliation between the belligerents. A surgeon, as was usual, was in attendance. The duel went on.

The first fire proved harmless to either. It has been said that the pistols for this shot were loaded only with blank cartridge, but Judge Hughes claims that Wilson's temple was grazed and his hair brushed by a flying bullet from Lyon's pistol. Reade and Robertson, now did their best to have the affair end there, and Lyon was willing to apologize to Wilson, but La Lievre would not hear of it. 'Load up again,' said he, and his ferocious counsel prevailed. His vindictive nature could not bear to allow the 'affair of honor' to end in this bloodless way, and the pride of the young men came to his aid.

The pistols were again charged, and there was no doubt this time that they were loaded with ball. When the word fire was given both weapons went off together. Lyon's bullet went harmlessly by, but the shot of Wilson carried death with it. Simultaneously with the report, Lyon was seen to throw up his hands, and then fall to the ground motionless. When taken up he was dead. The bullet from Wilson's pistol passed under his extended arm, passed through his body, piercing the heart. Wilson and Robertson were horrified at this ending and at once gave themselves up to the authorities.

Wilson was kept in Perth jail some three months, until the next Johnstown district assizes were held at Brockville, where he was tried before Chief-Justice Robinson, and acquitted. It is said that young Wilson's impassioned appeal to the jury was a masterpiece, and at this critical period of his career he showed himself worthy of the high standing he was to attain afterwards in law and in the judiciary.

One can view these pistols in the Perth Museum and visit Last Duel Park in Perth.

themselves violently, and worked with strength and endurance in the fields and in early industry; however, social institutions including government, church, school, and private organizations such as men's clubs increasingly promoted idealized femininities tied to notions of dependency, domesticity, chastity, and relative weakness—in contradistinction to the daily experiences of most women.

The early social and sporting clubs provided urban middle-class and elite men relatively insular sites for entertainment, under the guise of business and gentlemanly interests. Such segregation reinforced the notion of separate spheres for men and women and, further legitimized a more exclusive social life for men. Within the context of these social values about appropriate womanhood and manhood, publicly contested acts of courage or honour, such as the duel or street fight, or symbolic contests, such as hunting, arm wrestling, cricket, and horse racing, encouraged specific notions about the public display of people's bodies. In proper contexts, men were socially empowered by displays of physicality. For women, pressure for appropriate dress and decorum reinforced the idealized values of ornamental womanhood, that is to say, a disempowered public physicality.

The often-cited passage from the *Kingston Gazette*, in 1812, about women enjoying a simple swing in public underscores some of the pressures that gentlewomen faced from critics of both sexes: 'an exercise which, allowably beneficial to the health when practiced in the proper place, loses that merit when a delicate girl mounts a lofty and dangerous swing just after leaving a warm tea room, and at that hour of all others when the chilly dew is most prejudicial to even a strong constitution.' The women of Kingston responded to their critics: 'we shall without the least hesitation recommence the favourite amusement, with the season that permits it.'[59] The dislocation between experience and social expectations must, at times, have seemed ridiculous to women.[60] But not only women who had the temerity to engage in physical activity in a public space were the targets of the male observer's censure. As travellers, women, like men, were dependent on taverns for overnight lodging, food, and whisky. And their presence in the tavern, as a public venue, brought with it the same strictures faced by those women who chose to engage in physical activities. Traveller Joseph Pickering, in 1826, notes his disgust at the behaviour of young ladies in a local tavern:

some smart lasses came in during the evening, who live just by, most of whom took a smoke with the landlord and the landlady, passing the short black pipe from one to another. Disgusting as this practise is, it is not so much so as one in common use in the eastern part of Maryland, of girls taking a 'rubber' of snuff— that is, taking as much snuff as will lie on the end of the forefinger out of a box, and rubbing it round the inside of the mouth![61]

Later, as settlers and as citizens, women visited taverns for entertainment and many worked at inns or sold liquor out of their back kitchens.[62]

Work Bees and Physical Prowess

In spite of extensive evidence of women's involvement in drinking and tavern brawling during the nineteenth century and in working the farm fields of the Canadas, there are few records, with the exception of dancing, of female participation in the physical activities and contests of rural **bees** and celebrations. Quilting bees were an important social activity for women in rural Upper Canada and, in all likelihood, women were involved in the harassment rituals of the **chivaree**.[63] The informal competitions of the work bee evening drew attention to some of the physical abilities that distinguished the more powerful men.

The promise of work and liquor attracted labourers, both local and transient, to rural gatherings including logging, stumping, harvest, and building-raising bees. After the day's work was completed and food and drink served, music, dancing, and inevitable physical challenges entertained the workers. Physical competence, of course, was an important signifier to working men of all ages. Wrestling, boxing, lifting contests, and arm-wrestling contests celebrated the role of physical strength in the labour process.[64] The reputation of transient labourers, who relied on work parties and seasonal employment for their livelihoods, depended specifically on physical ability. As had been the case with the voyageurs, physical skill for farm workers was a matter of personal pride and identity. However, bodily strength served as an economic asset for labouring men, and so the sporting contests at the end of the day reinforced important hierarchies as both practical and symbolic.

Habitants passed on the legends from New France about feats of heavy lifting, village giants, and strongmen, such as the grandfather of Louis Cyr (see Chapter 6), as did settlers during the following era in all parts of British North America, underscoring the importance of strength as a signifier of both cultural value and masculine identity. The strain of pioneer life and the physical demands of everyday tasks were unavoidable realities for both men and women, and went hand in hand with the processes of land and rock clearing, stumping, shelter and home building, and even carrying grain to the mill. From the Hercules of the North, Grenon, in New France to the trapper and lumberman Joseph Montferrand, the stories grew by the decade. By the early nineteenth century, the value of strength as a signifier of male identity moved beyond local demonstrations and gatherings to professional tours. Claude Grenache, once a farmer and blacksmith, toured the United States and entertained crowds with his exhibitions of strength as the 'Canadian Samson'.[65] Tales of such men as Modeste Mailhout, the 'Canadian Giant', and Angus McAskill, the 'Cape Breton Giant', celebrated size and strength and local pride in their astounding accomplishments related to and deriving meaning from everyday life and work.[66] Some of these meanings about strength and honour were sustained for some time, but others about social life, sports, and

A barn-raising bee organized near Brampton, Ontario. (John Fletcher Cole, Library and Archives Canada, PA-164911)

games changed significantly in direct relation to the political and economic shifts marking the pre-Confederation era.

The British Elite

Following reformer Robert Gourlay's initial early criticism in 1818 of the Family Compact and its strict control over politics, others agitated for political change against the Tory elite in the Canadas. Lieutenant-Governor Sir John Colborne responded to the problem by encouraging loyal supporters of Tory elites to settle in the 'politically troubled' areas of the province.[67] In Woodstock, a group of retired military and naval officers received large land grants to settle the area. In addition to the economic stimulus injected into the community, the elites brought the aristocratic values of English country life and the social activities as well.[68] The officers established and asserted their social presence in the community through activities such as riding to the hunt, steeple chasing, and cricket.

The sport of cricket became popular as early as 1830 in the garrison towns and other locations where the ex-officers settled and in private schools such as Upper Canada College. An often-cited example of the cricket match between men of the college and 'the gentlemen of Toronto' represented a roll call of provincial elites.[69] Elites initiated British sporting traditions such as cricket to provide stability in the colonies. Hence, Lieutenant-Governor Colborne, at Upper Canada College, attempted to:

foster in the new institution a love of the old manly British Field Sports, a love which has always been a characteristic of English Public School men and is, indeed to the present day. And so in obtaining the services of English graduates for the College, Sir John not only obtained men who had the highest educational qualifications, but also those who would encourage and stimulate among the boys a love of healthy and manly games, which the astute governor rightly judged to be a powerful factor in developing among the lads a healthy self-reliant spirit that would fit them to cope in after years with the many arduous and difficult problems incidental to the development of a new country.[70]

The celebration of sports and social traditions staked out an aristocratic territory for the elite, affirming values for British Loyalists yet undoubtedly causing irritation among others who resented the former's favoured position in the community and the power they wielded. Political agitation by reformers, Methodists, and other non-Anglicans excluded from power and influence culminated in the failed rebellions of the late 1830s in Upper and Lower Canada. Forced to deal with the precarious state of political affairs, the British government, through the Durham Report, came to recognize the problems of the extensive networks of patronage in the Canadas and the conflicts between legislative and executive authority in New Brunswick and Nova Scotia.[71] During the resolution of these conflicts, prominent Methodist educator Egerton Ryerson (see Chapter 9) steered the reform-minded Methodists somewhere between radicals such as William Lyon Mackenzie and the old Tories, including John Strachan, bringing moderate Tories and some reformers into positions of political influence.[72]

The judiciary executed some rebels in widely attended public hangings, a violent and visible form of punishment that served to secure order and power for a shaken government.[73] In the aftermath of these conflicts, the pre-rebellion patronage networks persisted, through the continued collaboration of church leaders, until they were replaced by political policies that favoured entrepreneurs and a new commercial elite. During the 1840s, businessmen and professionals increasingly assumed political positions. They relied on local electoral support and duly rewarded it with favourable investment legislation that enabled local patrons to realize financial gains in subsidized public works projects such as railroads, harbours, and canals.[74] Lord Durham envisioned an assimilation of the French and recommended the union of the Canadas to absorb the debts of Upper Canada, a precursor to the union of all British North American colonies. The two Canadas became Canada East and Canada West, the Province of Canada, a process overseen by Charles Poulett Thompson, Lord Sydenham. New alliances formed and, thus, changing economic and social imperatives shaped and influenced cultural values in the pre-Confederation period.

Pre-Confederation and the Emergence of the Middle Classes

The **temperance** lobby gained considerable ground, supported by many groups, including the Methodists. Its advocates argued that alcohol was a cause of poverty and crime and lobbied for restrictive legislation in all regions.[75] In a commissioned report on temperance, Dr Sewell testified that moral suasion against liquor consumption would 'advance the interests of the

Travelling by stage coach to the Clinton Hotel in British Columbia. (Charles Gentile, Library and Archives Canada, C-088907)

working classes—to elevate them in moral scale".[76] Legislators provided the means to deal more effectively with public nuisances, such as brawling and drunkenness, implemented in the form of restricted hours, liabilities of tavern owners, and limiting the numbers of licences available. Such measures, in concert with the business strategies of the emerging commercial elites, served a broader movement to create a rational workforce and rational business practices.[77]

Given the economic implications of enforcing temperance legislation for governments and administrators, the liquor acts were neither effective nor enforced.[78] Through the pre-Confederation era, the tavern remained immensely popular for public entertainment. In 1846, officials issued 2,096 tavern licences in Canada West, and one can only speculate about the number of unlicensed establishments that served liquor. Licence fees and alcohol taxes comprised more than one-half of the total inland revenues for the province that year.[79] It has been estimated that one tavern existed for every mile of road;[80] citizens of Kingston complained that 65 taverns served a town of only 4,000;[81] 100 taverns and 45 stores were selling liquor in the London district by 1843; 30 taverns operated on 70 miles of roads between Brantford and London;[82] the High Constable of Montreal reported 883 licensed and unlicensed establishments in the city;[83] and 3,655 citizens were charged with drunkenness in Halifax between 1862 and 1866, a testament to the ineffectiveness of the liquor laws in curbing the consumption of alcohol.[84]

In addition to socializing and treating,[85] people gambled, fought, and sometimes enjoyed the various entertainments organized by tavern owners, including staged

Playing cards to pass the time on a steamer voyage on British Columbia waters. (Charles Gentile, Library and Archives Canada, C-088876)

boxing matches, cock-fighting, dog fights, bear-baiting, bull-baiting, billiards, and cards.[86] Customers frequented a pit for cock and dog fights at Black Daniel's shanty in Halifax and were entertained by a character known as 'Jack the Rat', who bit the heads off mice and decapitated rats for quarters at the New York City Tavern.[87] Charles McKiernan's beer-guzzling bear at Joe Beef's Tavern was legendary in post-Confederation Montreal.[88] Many rural taverns continued to offer lodging and food for travellers, as, later, did Joe Beef's in Montreal for transient and homeless clientele, which also served as a place to locate manual labour jobs, but urban taverns in general during the pre-Confederation period became facilities to sell alcohol for the purpose of entertainment. This sort of public drinking was a break from the monotony of everyday work and home life.[89] Within the context of gender and the social positioning of idealized femininities, temperance literature and sermons increasingly chastised women for visiting the disreputable tavern, reinforcing further the social privileges of all classes of men.[90] Women depended explicitly on character references for employment and, when they lived without husbands or outside of their fathers' houses, accusations of lewd behaviour or imputed associations with public houses tarnished their reputations and limited job opportunities. Middle-class social reformers accused women who worked in taverns or as prostitutes of leading men astray or damaging their morals.[91] Reformers viewed women as the arbiters of morality in Victorian British North America.

It became increasingly evident that the middle classes preferred to drink in hotels and establishments that were more elegant and respectable, such as the Tecumseh Hotel in London or the British American House in Kingston, creating social distance between those and 'underclass' taverns. Middle-class men sought to distance themselves socially from labourers through various institutions and invoked a new, rationalized morality to justify their inability to reach the status of the older landed elites. Unlike gentrified masculinities, where family name in part determined class honour, middle-class men equated honour with respect earned through hard work, appropriate behaviour, and upstanding business practices. In short, they sought to personify the Protestant work ethic. These men placed social emphasis on education, temperance, and a rational responsibility to the workplace. Social reformers rejected drinking in the workplace by labourers and they rejected the ritual of the duel—a residual expression of gentry manly honour—as barbaric and uncivilized, and banned it through legislation in 1847.[92] The potential outcome of the duel ran contrary to the emerging Victorian notion of the stable family, with father and husband as its loyal and dedicated head.[93] Public leadership in the economy, politics, and social life were the prerogative of middle-class men, whereas idealized femininity embodied domestic, charitable, and moral distinctions. In this sense, middle-class gender identities consisted of a series of binary opposites within the masculine and feminine, in part based on appropriate social activities. Guidebooks, sermons, and newspapers represented idealized notions of the stable family.[94] Yet, the emergence of middle-class men's clubs, which provided social leadership and participation opportunities in benevolent societies, sport clubs, and educational and political organizations, removed men from their homes regularly, contradicting the notion of the idealized family. As in the previous era of governance by the landed elite, legislation targeted the activities of the lower orders and protected the rights of property owners and club members.

Temperance advocates and Protestant church leaders lobbied for Sabbath laws preventing the profanation of the Lord's Day by sports, games, drinking, and the operation of public mail and trains on Sundays.[95] After Colonel Prince introduced a bill in 1845, he withdrew it for Canada East following lengthy discussion in the House of Assembly because it was determined to be 'directly in opposition to the established customs and habits of Lower Canadians', a reference to the custom of the habitants who had gone hunting after Mass for many years.[96] In Canada West, however, it became illegal in 1845 to play at 'skittles, ball, foot-ball, rackets, or any other noisy game, or to gamble with dice or otherwise, or to run races on foot, or on horseback, or in carriages, or in vehicles of any sort . . . or fishing or hunting or shooting', in addition to engaging in other work and business enterprises. The Act also stipulated that people should not 'bathe in any exposed situation in any water within the limits of any incorporated City or Town, nor within view of any place of Public Worship, or private residence, on the Lord's Day'.[97] The laws forbidding activities are useful indicators of the sorts of activities in which people commonly participated.

As an alternative to regulatory legislation, elites continued to promote agricultural associations, plowing matches, local fairs, mechanics' institutes, and literary associations,[98] thus demonstrating a shift towards publicly funded programs of social and economic betterment driven by the emergent middle classes of businessmen, professionals, and the new commercial elite. Citizens also lobbied for civic holidays and cultural celebrations, including sport, organized around such events as the Queen's birthday.[99] Hunting and fishing legislation continued to legitimize the scientific rationalization of nature, the preservation of wildlife stocks for sport hunters and fishermen, while setting bounties in the regions for the destruction of animals such as wolves and foxes that threatened livestock production.[100]

Conclusions

The post-rebellion, pre-Confederation era marked significant shifts in the organization of sport in British North America. From the turn of the century, the garrison officers had organized almost every aspect of horse racing in British North America, providing horses, prizes, bets, and officials. These officers were also responsible for the organization of sporting clubs in many parts of the colonies, including cricket, horse racing, track and field, curling, sleighing, snowshoeing, and aquatics.[101] At the garrisons, officers organized cricket matches,[102] rowing regattas, tandem exercises, and foot races among themselves for the soldiers and eventually for townspeople. In Halifax, officers lent organizational expertise and social status to sporting events, contributing to the development of sport in the community. Military officers served as patrons, officials, and judges, building positive relationships in the community and filling their leisure time with sport.[103] Sport and the organization of social events such as theatrical presentations connected military officers to local elites and enabled a smoothing of relations necessary when rowdy soldiers attracted unwanted attention in town.[104] As soldiers and officers of the garrisons arrived and departed according to their postings, so too did the organization of sporting events and patronage by garrison personnel.

Undoubtedly, the social connections between officers and business leaders directly influenced local interests in sport and the organization of sporting clubs. The garrison men, who brought expertise and a specific physical presence to social life in the towns, ensured long-term popular followings for some sports.[105] Indeed, one cannot overestimate the influence of these sporting events on the middle-class men who sought to organize sports and sporting clubs in the towns of the new Dominion. Sporting clubs emerged as important sites for middle-class men to celebrate and demonstrate public forms of rationalized manliness and a connection to what they perceived to be British culture and to new, Canadian versions of sport. Middle-class men were the primary organizers of sporting clubs in Montreal, where, by the 1860s, organized sports were a significant part of the cultural landscape.[106]

Related Websites

General History
http://www.canadiana.org/citm/index_e.html

Taverns
http://ist.uwaterloo.ca/~marj/genealogy/tavern.html

Pioneer Life
http://www.uppercanadahistory.ca/finna/finna2.html
http://www.linksnorth.com/canada-history/upper.html

Duels in Ontario
http://www.lanarkcountytourism.ca/SevenWondersVoting/LastDuelPark.pdf

Wrestling History
http://ejmas.com/jmanly/articles/2001/jmanlyart_leyshon1_0701.htm

Confederation Maps
http://www.collectionscanada.gc.ca/confederation/023001-2101-e.html

The Beaver Club
http://www.rootsweb.com/~qcmtl-w/BeaverClub.html

Curling
http://icing.org/game/history/historya.htm

Cricket
http://www.canadacricket.com/history.htm

Study Questions

1. What were the influences of social class on sports and pastimes in British North America?
2. How does the notion of honour factor into our historical understanding of competition and physical contests?
3. What influence did a changing economy have on sport from the early to mid nineteenth century?
4. What gender polarities were created in middle-class social life?
5. What was the role of government in the pastimes of early Canadians?
6. How was 'manliness' defined and celebrated by different groups prior to Confederation?

CHAPTER 4

Transitions to and Control of Organized Sport in the Nineteenth Century

At a meeting which was held in the Railway Y.M.C.A. last evening a basket ball league was organized and composed of the following shops:—Machine, blacksmith, car and erecting shops. The first of a series of games was played between machine and blacksmith shops after the meeting and resulted in an easy victory for the former. . . .

—Toronto Globe, 20 December 1898

The nineteenth-century transition from pastimes, impromptu games, and sports to highly organized competitive sport was related to a complex set of changes that altered society and sport. Where taverns, individuals' and churches' bees, garrisons, and garrison officers carried the initiative for early games and sports, it was a variety of other social, technological, and organizational changes that transformed the physical activities, recreations, games, and pastimes into what we recognize as more modern forms of organized sport. Coalitions of particular interests, such as those of the Scots and of the Montreal middle class, developed strong sporting organizations as the process of industrialization altered society in general. Technological changes rested behind some new features that emerged in organizing sport. The *Toronto Globe* quotation above mentions the railway, the YMCA, competitors from new and different social classes, and a new sport—basketball. All were products of the **Industrial Revolution**. This chapter explores the impact of technological change, the Montreal middle class, and the infusion of the amateur ideal on the development of organized sport in nineteenth-century Canada.

Technology: A Catalyst in Sport Conversion

Technological changes did not happen in a vacuum;[1] human agency and initiative went hand in hand with the changes wrought through technological evolution. The competitiveness encouraged through the emerging economy turned interests in forms of culture to rival towns. One of the great accelerators towards organized sport was directly related to advancements in transportation. In the early years of the nineteenth century, British North Americans had some options for travel: if by road, they could walk, take a stagecoach, or, in the winter, use snowshoes or ride in a sleigh or calèche (in Lower Canada); if water was the mode of transport, travellers could take a skiff of some type, a flat-bottomed bateau, a canoe, a sailing schooner if larger waterway travel was desired, or, after 1809, they could pay a fare for a **steamboat**. All of these modes were relatively time-consuming. In 1800, it took two to three days to travel by stagecoach between Montreal and Quebec City; even at mid-century, the stagecoach took four days between Montreal and Toronto. Only mail carts and wagons could make the overland journey to the Maritimes. Furthermore, the stagecoach was expensive—$5.00 to travel from York (Toronto) to Niagara in the early 1800s. Obviously, long and rigorous journeys were not conducive to inter-town sporting competitions. Only wealthy gentlemen could afford the time and expense since inter-club games in, say, cricket or curling during the 1830s and 1840s placed those competitions within the context of a half-week's holiday: a day to travel to the competition, a day to play, and a day to return home.[2]

The development and dispersion of sport were influenced by the steamer in many ways. Early horse-racing events were enhanced by enterprising steamboat proprietors donating prizes. And, as early as 1833, steamers created special trips to shuttle spectators to horse-racing venues. Track and field, or 'athletic games', as they were called, such as those in Cornwall on the Queen's birthday in 1865, attracted thousands of spectators brought to the games by steamship companies. Steamboat franchises gave special rates for rifle tournaments in the 1860s, and for bicycle races and baseball matches in the 1880s; often these special rates were made possible by hotel proprietors' donations to the steamship companies. Perhaps more than any other sport, rowing enjoyed tremendous interest, directly because of the steamers. Spectators who could afford the special fare and race judges/officials could follow the race literally and at a proximity that permitted an intimate view of the participants and the intricacies of rowing technique. A number of excellent press sketches show rowing competitors surrounded by flotillas of watercraft.[3] With bands on board, rowing spectatorship became an attractive feature to the sport even though zealous captains often created serious problems for the competitors by swamping them, albeit inadvertently.[4]

As much as the steamer did for sport, its major drawback was still the time it took to get to events. The advent and rapid spread of railways prompted a spectacular rise in the amount of competitive sporting activity in Canada. From modest amounts of track at mid-century, government grant inducements led to the rail links between communities. For example, in southwestern Ontario during the 1850s, monetary incentives for rail lines longer than 112 kilometres meant that cities like Toronto, London, Hamilton, and Guelph were joined by rail. This accounts in large measure for the success of early professional baseball teams and leagues in those cities. By Confederation, some 3,200 kilometres of rail lines connected towns and cities in Ontario, Quebec, and the Maritimes, and by 1885 the '**last spike**' had been driven in the Rocky Mountains; by 1900, there were almost 30,000 kilometres of rail lines 'from sea to sea' in Canada.[5] By 1866, the half-week trip from Montreal to Toronto had shrunk to a mere 16 hours. Where 60 years earlier it had taken days just to get from Montreal to Quebec City, by 1885 it was only a five-day trip from Montreal to

Port Moody, British Columbia. By the 1890s, baseball on the Prairies was invigorated by railway expansion as teams in geographical proximity—such as those from Medicine Hat, Lethbridge, and Calgary—were quickly linked.[6]

Railways fascinated the public just as the steamers did; simply riding on a train was a special occasion. For sport, the railway had three primary influences: reduction in time, regularity of competitions, and the promotion of multi-club and multi-sport events. Thirty-two teams from Canada and the United States competed at the Burlington Bay curling bonspiel in 1858 as a direct result of rail transport. Individual sports like snowshoeing were promoted for participants and spectators alike via the faster travel and by creative uses of 'rolling stock', with rail cars providing grandstands at snowshoe competitions. Similarly, extra cars could be added when events such as horse racing drew larger crowds than anticipated. There is evidence that a railway company paid Canada's premier oarsman, Ned Hanlan (see Chapter 6), some $3,900 in 1878 to compete in an event close to rail lines.[7] Because railway companies prided themselves on the accuracy of their schedules, the repercussions for organizing sport were quite profound. Instead of suggesting 'sometime' during 'some day' for a competition, sporting events could be pinned down to an exact time of day. And, if one game time could be predicted and scheduled accurately, then several games in a series of competitions could be prearranged. For team sports, this permitted league play, a whole new concept and new level of organization for sport. Thus, for lacrosse, baseball, and hockey, season schedules could be established at the start of any given season. For everyone involved—players, teams, spectators, and promoters—this regulative principle provided an unheard of level of efficiency in sport. Within cities, street railway systems in Montreal, Halifax, Toronto, Saint John, Ottawa, Winnipeg, Victoria, and other cities facilitated intra-city sport with readily available transportation, special rates, and even spur lines constructed for special sporting events.[8]

Communication changes affected the rate, magnitude, and direction of sporting developments. That is, communication changes had a catalytic impact on changes in the production and dispersion of sport. During the early years of the nineteenth century, the modes of communication were word of mouth, letters, and the press, all of which were linked to methods of transport and therefore slow to transmit current or up-to-date 'news'. From less than 20 newspapers at the time of the War of 1812 to 10 times that number by 1850 (owing to the development of the steam presses and advertising revenue), the number of newspapers grew to 1,200 by the end of the century. Early sporting reports prior to mid-century were less focused on the sporting events and more devoted to social descriptions, such as in this Novascotian report of an 1833 Halifax horse-racing event:

> The Races were continued with great spirit on Thursday and Friday. The weather was delightful and the concourse of spectators on both days, and particularly on the former, was very great. The western side of the citadel was covered with gay groups . . . while some seventy tents ranged alongside the base of Camp Hill, dispersed the elements of mirth and hilarity. . . . The winning post was, however, the great rallying point for lovers of the turf, of both sexes. The elite of rank and fashion occupied a large booth, and a range of carriages extending north from it.[9]

Press reports mirrored the privileged class interests in sports such as horse racing and cricket and to some extent rowing, especially in the Maritimes. Newspapers helped to foster a climate of interest in sport by communicating about games and events. There is some evidence that '**challenge matches**' for such events as track and field competitions were arranged through advertisements in the press. With the invention of the telegraph, press reporting grew rapidly. And, because the results of events in, say, Fredericton could be read about in the Toronto press by the next day, this particular improvement in communication meant greater following and attention to more sports via newspapers, not just locally but also in the contraction of geographical distance via the telegraph's impact. Even into the early years of the twentieth century, crowds gathered around telegraph stations to 'listen' to live reports of matches in hockey, as they did for the Stanley Cup events of 1902.[10]

All of these technological changes were expanded by the economic boom and prosperity of the country in the 1850s and 1860s. Demand for Canada's wheat and timber was high during the **Crimean War** years and British capital was bestowed to build more railway lines. Responsible government, achieved in the Canadas in 1848, brought a level of stability that combined with economic affluence and international promotion campaigns to attract immigrants to the country; during the 10 years after 1851, Canada's population increased by 37 per cent. As more people came to Canada under such prosperous circumstances, interest in forms of culture, including sport, increased significantly. Press coverage given to sports increased dramatically, to the point of headline space devoted to rowing, cricket, and lacrosse. Even more recreational activities were given coverage. For example, an ice-skating mania enveloped central Canada—'from Gaspé to Sarnia'[11]—during the 1860s; the press reflected the widespread interest to the extent that when masquerade skating events were held, the local papers provided a list of the names of the guests and their costume personalities in the next day's paper.[12] When the Atlantic telegraph cable was completed in 1866, it meant that the transmission of information from sporting matches between Canada and Great Britain was more rapid and allowed for greater immediacy of results. Having the latest sporting results through changing technologies became a matter of great social interest.

Just as transportation and communication changes directly affected the evolution, dispersion, and organization of sport, so, too, did changes of various articles of sporting equipment provide a significant impact on the design and systematization of sport. Some equipment changes were subtle and others were more substantial; in the latter case, inventors often took out letters of patent in anticipation of widespread adoption of new designs. In all cases, the extent to which equipment could be mass-produced meant greater accessibility to sport, cost reductions in equipment for everyone concerned, and greater uniformity of play. With specific reference to the organization of sport, equipment uniformity was critical regarding the standardization of play, rules, codes, and other regulations—the hallmarks of middle-class social organization. During the nineteenth century, sporting goods stores did not exist; therefore, sport enthusiasts relied on clothing companies or other outlets for equipment. Consider a few examples of the manner in which equipment availability and changes affected particular sports.

In Aboriginal lacrosse, as in most forms of the nineteenth-century game, the stick strings comprised a very small area; the traditional game was more of a running game. When Montreal players adopted and adapted the game the expanse of string increased dramatically in order to support an increased passing style of play. Interestingly, Aboriginals crafted and mass-produced the adapted stick at St Regis and a Canadian family, the Lallys, in the early twentieth century almost exclusively manufactured the wooden sticks until

A Notman composite of the Montreal Amateur Athletic Association Bicycle Club, 1885. (Notman Photographic Archives, 26.273 view, courtesy of the McCord Museum of Canadian History, Montreal)

they were 'plasticized' in the 1970s.[13] Different-coloured uniform jerseys and knickers were in vogue by the 1880s, making the teams literally colourful and certainly much more distinctive than the whites of all cricket players. Primarily, it was the cheap stick—50 cents in Confederation year, 25 cents by 1900—that contributed to the standardization and great expansion of lacrosse across Canada at all levels of play. Baseball equipment manufacture, especially bat production, was largely American but the resulting price of 10–35 cents per bat had the same growth effect in baseball as it did in lacrosse.[14] And a parallel situation existed in hockey, with sticks ranging in price from 25 cents to one dollar by the 1890s, while almost any object—including frozen horse dung in northern Ontario cities—could be used as a 'puck' in that sport.

One invention that seemed to captivate all Canadians was the bicycle. Originally, it was in the form of a 'high-wheeler' with a front wheel some 1.2 metres in diameter and a rear wheel of only 25 centimetres. It is believed that the first one in Canada was just such a 'boneshaker' (so named because of their solid steel frames and solid rubber tires) brought to Glace Bay in 1865.[15] These early bicycles were used primarily for recreation, not for transportation, due to poor roads and the expense—about $150—of owning one. And yet, it was not long before bicycle clubs were formed for recreational riding and for racing. By the 1880s, racing on the high-wheelers was common in most large cities. When the 'safety' bicycle—with wheels of equal size and diameter—was invented near the end of that decade, the bicycle became even more popular, though still expensive (about $50 for children's bicycles); they were widely advertised in the press and catalogues during the 1890s.[16] Historians also have noted the impact of the safety bicycle, in its drop-frame format for females, on the physical emancipation of women by relieving the conventions of cumbersome dress to allow women to become more involved in leisure, sport, and recreation pursuits.[17]

Montreal—The Cradle of Organized Sport

In addition to technological changes in recreational and sporting equipment, the phenomenon of urbanization and urban growth, with the clustering of the population in cities, had profound effects on the organization of sport. Most sporting activities in British North America before the middle of the nineteenth century were prompted by impulse. Pioneer sports associated with such social occasions as work bees and with taverns were spontaneous and loosely organized. Very few of the structures and necessities of organized sport that we take for granted today—clubs, teams, budgets, commercial support, leagues, playing schedules, facilities, and so forth—were present or established in Canadian sport before 1850. The first and most significant changes took place in Montreal in a distinct incubation of organized Canadian sport.

That Montreal became a kind of mecca for Canadian sport in the nineteenth century was logical in view of its geographical, economic, cultural, and commercial advantages.[18] The city was the metropolitan nexus of a vast Canadian hinterland that had once made Montreal the great outlet for the fur trade and for which the city was now a railway terminal, maritime port, and manufacturing and financial centre. The population of 58,000 in 1851 increased to over a quarter of a million 50 years later. Though English-speaking Montrealers outnumbered French-speaking citizens for only the 40 years before Confederation, the development and organization of sport, and its spread beyond the Montreal region, were due mostly to the efforts of Anglophones.

The first event in Canada that signified organization in any sport was the formation of the Montreal Curling Club (MCC) in 1807 by 20 elite citizens of Montreal, all of them Scottish (see Chapter 3). This is the oldest sport club in continuous existence in Canada,[19] a record that is a tribute to the energetic efforts of the Scots as well as to Canada's many successes in international curling events for well over 150 years. There has been considerable debate about the origins of the 'roarin' game'. Pieter Bruegel's 1565 painting, 'Hunters in the Snow', clearly depicts curling in the foreground, an indication that the game was commonplace in Bruegel's native Holland. Nevertheless, Scotland has argued vehemently for recognition as the birthplace of curling, and the game was well enough established in that country by the end of the eighteenth century that a small group of its emigrants in Montreal—civic leaders, most of them wealthy merchants who were members of the North West Company of fur traders—met at Gillis's Tavern to establish officers and draw up the club 'rules'. In the early nineteenth century, several societies and clubs had been formed by Montreal's elite. The St Andrew's Society, the Natural History Society, the Horticultural Society, the Theatre Society, and the Beaver Club, for men connected with the fur trade, each had been formed around a common interest. In the first half of the nineteenth century, sporting clubs in Canada were primarily social. The earliest (1807) rules of the Montreal Curling Club reflected social concerns and exclusivity more than playing procedures. These stipulations, preceded by a four-line club motto, were followed by 21 signatures, but nowhere were there any playing rules for the game of curling. Fraternizing and dining were uppermost; in fact,

Curling on the St Lawrence River, Montreal, 1878—a Notman composite showing the Governor General, the marquis of Lorne, and his wife in the middle foreground, and seated across the ice, wearing a top hat, Sir John A. MacDonald. (Notman Photographic Archives 48.781–11, courtesy of the McCord Museum of Canadian History, Montreal)

evidence suggests that only two or three of the original members even knew how to curl, or had curled, prior to 1807.[20]

In spite of the severity of Montreal winters and of outdoor playing conditions on the St Lawrence River—'sheds' were occasionally made and rented out for shelter—great strides were later made in the development of the sport in Montreal. Equipment was minimal and, at first, crude in that stones, literally, were curled. Even cannonballs were tried, but the iron was such a strong heat conductor that they stuck to the ice. Most players and clubs fashioned their own curling stones and even named them (Tinto or Black Meg, for example). Many of these stones had been recovered from riverbeds, outdoor ice facilities being the most common venues in the first half of the nineteenth century.[21] Rules and playing regulations were codified by the MCC in 1820, complete with restrictions concerning the use of the club's stock of stones—very likely natural boulders or 'irons' (granites cracked in the intense cold) of various shapes and sizes fitted with makeshift handles or crude finger holes. One can envision the club secretary and a hired hand, or even 'ice managers', carting the stones and brooms ('besoms') by sled to the river on a frosty Wednesday afternoon in February. Laboriously they cleared a 30- or 40-metre strip of ice, etched the necessary 'house' markings, and prepared the stones for the six or eight curlers. Often MCC members had to compete with the ice harvesters, whose job it was to cut blocks of ice to supply to the

Montreal Curling Group, circa 1905. (Canada Patent and Copyright Office, Library and Archives Canada, PA-029045)

hotels and taverns of Montreal. Conflicting encounters between the two groups—curlers and cutters—must have been frequent and perhaps sometimes comical. Dressed warmly, the curlers arrived at the appointed place of meeting on the ice, formed two teams of, say, bachelors versus benedicks (married men), and proceeded to curl. Three hours later, they retreated to their favourite tavern to engage in whisky toasts ('bumpers'). While it appears that actual games were not all that frequent, the MCC's existence was continuous and its members met regularly, if only to socialize and to conduct the affairs of the club.[22]

Maintaining its social and ethnic exclusivity, the MCC played a leadership role in the formation of other curling clubs, especially new ones created during the 1830s in such southern Ontario towns as Guelph, Fergus, and Galt, where Scottish immigrants had settled. Rules and regulations, such as codes of conduct deemed appropriate to the game's adherents and club members' moral and financial obligations, as well as refined aspects of the method of play developed by the MCC during the 1820s and early 1830s, were passed along to the new 'brothers of the stone' in Ontario. By the end of the 1840s, the MCC had lent some of its stones to rinks outside Montreal, had affiliated with the Grand Caledonian Curling Club in Scotland to maintain cultural ties and to participate in the standardization of curling rules, had stimulated two new curling clubs in the city—the Thistle (1843) and the Caledonia (1850)—and had come to be recognized generally as Canada's senior curling society. Although exclusive and restrictive, the MCC represented a major first step towards, and a strong precedent for, the creation of other sport clubs in Montreal.

The MCC exemplified the fact that before sport became organized, it was the exclusive preserve of a small, select segment of Montreal society.[23] Officers of the garrisoned regiments brought organization and growth to sport in Montreal and other cities in British North America prior to 1850. After 1814, Montreal became the headquarters of the British imperial forces in Canada. The officers were well educated and imbued with the sporting experiences and traditions of Rugby, Eton, Chester, and Harrow. Modern sport—cricket, rugby football, soccer, track and field, and so forth—was organized, codified, and disseminated to the Empire via these British public school graduates. Equally important was their code of conduct of gentlemanly behaviour and 'manliness', and the vaunted character development that was assumed to flow automatically from participation in the great public-school games. This cult of athleticism, as it was labelled near the end of the nineteenth century, was glorified in the famous epigram, 'The battle of Waterloo was won on the playing fields of Eton', and in the ringing verse from Sir Henry Newbolt's **Vitai Lampada:**

> There's a breathless hush in the Close tonight Ten to make and the match to win A bumping pitch and a blinding light, An hour to play and the last man in. And it's not for the sake of a ribboned coat, Or the selfless hope of season's fame But his captain's hand on his shoulder smote—Play up! Play up! and play the game.[24]

A belief in the supremacy of 'games' in the building of men's characters emanated from one of the nineteenth century's fundamental belief systems regarding the link between athletic skill and the construction of moral fibre—muscular Christianity (see Chapter 8). This tradition was zealously carried to British North America by military personnel (see Chapter 3).[25]

Garrison officers possessed the leisure time, money, and administrative skills to impose some organization on the sporting activity of their choice.[26] The Hunt (1829), Cricket (1829), Tandem (1837), and Racquet (1839) clubs all were formed by the officers of the Montreal garrison, along with like-minded members of the social elite in the city. The Montreal Hunt Club kept and trained a kennel of hounds and engaged in fox hunting by 'riding to hounds' on horseback. Equally exclusive was the Racquet Club at the corner of Craig and St Peter Streets, which was used for early forms of handball, tennis, and squash and which is regarded as the first club of its kind in North America. But cricket, the sport of the British gentleman, and horse racing, the revered 'sport of kings', seemed to be the most favoured activities. Tandem clubs were merely ostentatious winter displays of military colour, horses, and sleighs. Meetings and contests were sporadic, entirely dependent on the whim of the officers, who of course also decided on venue, equipment, rules, prizes, and so forth. When troops were withdrawn from Canada for the Crimean War during the 1850s, there was a dramatic decline in Montreal sporting events—strong evidence of the garrison officers' importance in Montreal sports.

Snowshoers' Ethic

A series of events that provided a significant incentive to organized sport stemmed from the earliest known gatherings of about a dozen prominent Englishmen, from the highest strata of Montreal society,[27] to engage in long-distance outings or 'tramps' on snowshoes.[28] Aboriginals, *coureurs de bois*, Nor'Westers, military units, and European men living in the

A snowshoe outing, c. 1878. (Alexander Henderson, Library and Archives Canada, C-022233)

bush used the snowshoe to facilitate winter transport. But it was not adopted for recreational and sporting use until these 12 Montreal men engaged in regular tramps and then, in 1843, formalized their interest in snowshoeing by creating the Montreal Snow Shoe Club (MSSC). It is not generally known that snowshoeing was the pivotal and transitional activity through which Montreal sport was ushered into the modern era of commercial organized sport. Proximity to the reserve at Caughnawaga provided a distinct influence in the development of snowshoeing in Montreal because the Iroquois living there were a constant source of both quality snowshoes and competition.

In the early years of the MSSC, tramping was the most common activity of members. During the winter months, the snowshoers mustered twice weekly at an appointed rendezvous and time. The snowshoeing tramps were disciplined and orderly. At the rendezvous, the ranking club officer was appointed leader and follow-the-leader was the protocol. An experienced snowshoer was appointed by the leader to be 'whipper-in', that is, to bring up the rear of the file and keep the group together. Compass in hand, the leader took his charges on various cross-country excursions in the vicinity of Montreal. By the 1860s and 1870s, new snowshoe clubs in the city—among them the Beaver, the Alexandria, and St George's—followed the example of the MSSC and adopted blanket coats, pants, sashes, and distinctive toques to signify club affiliation. Members of the MSSC were known as the Tuques Bleus and their activities were romanticized frequently in the press, as on the occasion of an 1873 torchlight procession of snowshoers:

Softly, silently, like the snow flakes upon which they trod, with the peculiar roll of the shoulders and jogging of the hips went the band of athletes, the livid torches illuminating their picturesque costumes, their bright turbans, their fleecy bashiliks [i.e., hoods] and their cerulean tuques. Tramp tramp like the stroke of fate went their webbed foot-falls.[29]

Sumptuous dinners and tavern stops were hallmarks of the growing snowshoeing fraternity in Montreal by 1867. At the taverns, many toasts were drunk, there was dancing among the men, and self-laudatory ballads were sung to celebrate the 'manliness' of snowshoeing. Women were not allowed into snowshoe club membership. The last verse of the 'Song of the Montreal Snow Shoe Club' exemplifies the snowshoers' prevailing perspective on women:

All pretty girls take my advice, On some vain fop don't waste your 'lub,'
But if you wish to hug something nice, Why marry a boy of the Snow Shoe Club.
Then each night, with wild delight, You'll sing success to the Snow Shoe Club.[30]

By the mid-1870s, the MSSC frequently was requested to put on musicals and concerts in Montreal and surrounding towns. These shows, featuring singing and tableaus of the tramping, racing, and dining activities of club members, propelled the MSSC into the public spotlight, especially since all concert proceeds went to charity.

Racing was the competitive branch of snowshoeing, a complement to its more recreational tramping aspect. Once again, it was owing to the MSSC's initiative that racing formats were standardized. By the mid-1860s, a typical racing card listed eight events: a race for Indians of two to four miles; an open one-mile race; a hurdle race; a half-mile boys' race; a 100-yard dash; a half-mile garrison race; a club race of two miles; and an open half-mile dash. The greatest test of stamina and training was the two-mile race, an event open only to members of the host club. The hurdle race also required considerable skill since only the tail of the snowshoe was allowed to touch the large wooden equestrian hurdles. Winter racing venues were horse-racing tracks and lacrosse and cricket grounds. Carefully ploughed and packed quarter- and half-mile tracks provided the best racing conditions. Whenever grounds with a grandstand could be used, entrance fees were levied; ladies were always admitted free of charge. Bands were hired and vendors sold food and beverages. By the late 1870s, winter weekends in Montreal were crowded with snowshoe-racing events hosted by different clubs. Gambling popularized the races: newspapers published betting odds and the *Montreal Gazette* actually printed race cards on which past performance and betting information was listed.[31]

The calibre of performance was admirable. Five-minute, fifty-second miles were common by 1870. Top racers achieved 13.5 seconds in the 100-yard dash, a time that was only 3.5 seconds slower than a competitive footrace at that distance in the same period. Some racers drove nails through their snowshoe frames for better traction under icy conditions. In general, the performance times of non-Natives were surpassed by those of Natives, who were nonetheless victims of social and racial discrimination—they were never assimilated into competitive snowshoeing and were never considered for membership in any snowshoe club in nineteenth-century Montreal. However, because of their perceived innate skill and demonstrated excellence in the sport, and because they were a crowd-drawing feature, the

A drawing of a mile-long snowshoe race for the Worthington Cup, Montreal, c. 1879. (From the *Scrapbook of the Montreal Amateur Athletic Association, volume 14.* Courtesy of Don Morrow)

'Indian race' was the first event on every race card. All other events were understood to be closed to Natives.

There was an unfortunate side to these distance races. Incentives were offered to Native competitors to perform at near-maximum speed for, say, the first mile of a three-mile race, so that spectators could sadistically witness their agony in the last stages of the race while betting on individual runners. Often clubs offered novelty events for Natives that had as their objective ridicule and entertainment for the spectators. For example, at a winter sports day in 1875, hosted by the Volunteers at Decker Park, four Natives were entered in a 100-yard snowshoe 'potato race' in which each competitor had to pick up the potatoes placed every yard along the stretch and return them, one at a time, to a basket at the starting line. Such degrading practices were prevalent in track and field and lacrosse. Excluded from Euro-Canadian competitions and held up to ridicule or induced to perform to exhaustion, Natives were treated as lower-class athletes by the middle-class organizers of sport even though—or perhaps because—they were perceived to have superior skill.

These snowshoeing events set the example for the organization of Montreal sport. By the later 1870s there were 20 thriving snowshoe clubs in the city. Of those, the MSSC was the 'senior' club, and also the largest, boasting 400 members. But it was its administrative efficiency and panache that played a leading role in Montreal sport. The adoption of club colours and uniforms; the discipline and ritual attached to tramping; well-organized racing events complete with Natives, bands, caterers, manicured tracks for the racers, and comfortable seating for spectators; the lure of gambling on racers and races; snowshoeing's association with commendable values such as manliness; and attention to charity, as demonstrated by the donation of concert proceeds—all these traditions of the MSSC influenced and shaped the conduct of sport generally in Montreal, and later were spread to other parts of the country via Montreal-established national sport governing bodies such as the Amateur Athletic Association of Canada.

Ice-skating was a complementary, and at times rival, sport to snowshoeing. During the 1860s, an ice-skating mania enveloped eastern Canada at all levels of society. Like snowshoeing, ice-skating could be practised for its own sake as a pastime or it could be organized into competitions for speed or skill. Most public skating was relegated to natural ice on rivers and ponds, but the sport's popularity, the indoor sheds of Montreal's three curling clubs, and the increasing tendency towards 'clubbing' in Montreal sport combined to prompt well-to-do citizens in the west end of the city to proffer shares for the building of the magnificent Victoria Skating Rink on Drummond Street. Completed in 1863, the red-brick rink was spanned by a semicircular framed roof that rose to a height of 16 metres and was supported on the inside by huge wooden arches anchored in the ground. Around the perimeter of the 1,350 square metres of ice was a three-metre-wide raised platform for promenading. Above this, in a horseshoe shape on three sides of the rink, was a gallery with enough space to seat 700 people. At the west end over the entrance was a bandstand and a private gallery for the rink's directors. Fifty large windows lighted the interior by day; by night 'six pendant stars, each having about 50 gas burners', or about 300 jets of gas, illuminated the rink. Its elaborate design was paralleled by its exclusiveness: membership was restricted to, and carefully controlled by, Montreal's social elite in a 'blackball' voting system.[32]

Nevertheless, the Victoria Rink became the fashionable winter meeting place in Montreal during the 1860s and 1870s. It was not unusual for spectators and skaters to be served five o'clock tea. Moreover, the fancy dress carnivals and masquerade skating events staged frequently each winter were popular and colourful pageants of winter recreation in the city.[33] Hundreds of skaters came to the rink dressed as such historic figures as Marie Antoinette, Henry VIII, or as pirates or princesses. The next day, the Montreal papers published a complete list of those in attendance and the characters they represented or the costumes they wore:

> But what a dazzling sight it is; no wonder the aisles and galleries are packed with spectators to such an extent that the marvellous elasticity of the human body is demonstrated to a nicety. All eyes are attracted to the shifting, changing scene upon the sparkling ice . . . . Here is the tall sunflower bending her graceful form to elude the half naked savage, who, with swarthy visage and glittering nose ring, lifts his cruel spear to smite his prey.[34]

So renowned were these skating masquerades that the world-famous **Notman photographic firm** completed a composite picture of one such occasion entitled 'The Skating Carnival, 1870', which conveys both the spectacular aspect and the social cachet of skating in nineteenth-century Montreal. Notman's composites used huge painted backgrounds on canvas—in this case the interior of the rink—on which individual hand-painted photographs of hundreds of characters taken in the studio in pre-planned poses were superimposed. The entire process for such a composite took about a year and a half to complete.[35] The final

A Notman composite of a skating carnival in the Victoria Rink, Montreal, 1870. (Library and Archives Canada, C-15302)

product was a coloured, framed photograph/painting that measured approximately 1.5 by 2 metres. The sale of smaller black-and-white photographs of both the composite and the individual staged portraits provided the funding for the composite production.

Until the 1890s, ice-skating in its recreational figure-skating and speed-skating forms was overshadowed by snowshoeing in Montreal. In fact, as other indoor and outdoor rinks were gradually constructed during the 1870s and 1880s, their proprietors often advertised a snowshoe race on the ice surfaces to attract paying crowds to skating and racing events. But eventually the various kinds of ice-skating were developed into popular competitive sport forms, and the Victoria Rink was at the forefront of this development. For example, Montreal's Louis Rubenstein trained at the Victoria Rink and went on to capture the Canadian, American, and world figure-skating championships by 1890 (see Chapter 6). Similarly, the first Stanley Cup hockey game in 1893 at the Victoria Rink was contested between two Montreal teams; the dimensions of the rink, 56 by 24 metres, provided the standard for North American ice-hockey rinks for decades. The impact of this facility in Montreal, then, was widely felt in the development of organized winter sports.

Summer Sports Changes

Summer sports were also fuelled by Montreal's prominence and its sportsmen. The summer counterpart to snowshoeing was lacrosse, and the overlap between these two sports accounts for the growth and development of lacrosse in its early years. Impromptu games among Natives and between Native and non-Native teams led in 1856 to the formation of Canada's first lacrosse organization, the Montreal Lacrosse Club (MLC), by several of the members of the Montreal Snow Shoe Club. Lacrosse grew slowly in Montreal and until the 1860s only a few other clubs were formed. But during that decade zealous promotion by MLC member Dr George W. Beers, a dentist, accelerated the development of the sport (see Chapter 5). By the end of Confederation year there were 80 clubs in Quebec and Ontario and lacrosse went on to flourish as one of the most widespread and popular sports in Canada.

Other summer sports existed in Montreal by the 1870s, but not with the popularity, prominence, or frequency of participation of lacrosse. Although the Montreal Cricket Club was formed in 1843, cricket remained a closed sport, devoid of any concerted, overt attempts to popularize it in Montreal. Even when the 'Gentlemen of England' played the Montreal Cricket Club in 1872, their appeal seemed to be confined to upper-class cricket aficionados—even though in London, Ontario, they attracted some 3,000 spectators. Baseball, by contrast, seemed to draw its adherents from among the lower classes of society and was not very well developed in Montreal until the end of the nineteenth century. In the Maritimes, baseball's development fell to an emerging middle class.[36] However, baseball was an industrial sport played by factory workers, or rude 'mechanicals', as they were sometimes called. It gained its first foothold in southern Ontario through a reliance on industrial communities linked by railways. Toronto, in fact, was the site for the initial efforts towards the organization of baseball when the Canadian Base Ball Association was formed in 1876 in that city[37] (see Chapter 5).

Unquestionably the greatest change in the organization of competitive sport was ushered in by the bicycle. On 1 July 1874, a Montreal resident, A.T. Lane, rode through the streets of Montreal on one of the first bicycles ever seen in North America. It was a 'plain-bearing, socket steering high wheeler', or a penny-farthing bicycle. As the penny-farthing became mass-produced in Britain and France, other Montreal citizens acquired this new amusement, and under Lane's initiative the Montreal Bicycle Club (MBC) was formed in 1878. It was only the third bicycle club in North America; the other two were in Boston and Bangor, Maine.

Although roads in the nineteenth century were never clear of broken glass, wire, garbage, horse dung, and potholes, by 1881 MBC cyclists organized 'outings' or rides into the country after the fashion of the Montreal Snow Shoe Club tramps. They wore dark-blue braided patrol jackets and knee breeches, fore-and-aft peaked caps with a tiny gold winged wheel at the front, blue-ribbed stockings, and blue canvas shoes. In this costume, 20 to 50 men rode in paramilitary formation through the Montreal countryside. Club rides were mustered by the MBC bugler and occasionally 12 men were picked to perform maneuvers—marching drills on high-wheel bicycles—at public gatherings, exhibitions, track and field meets, and lacrosse contests. Cycle races on dirt, cinder, or board tracks as well as on open roads were quickly popularized. The MBC was instrumental in the formation and development in 1882 of a national body—the Canadian Wheelmen's Association—to govern, regulate, and promote competitive cycling. With the invention and mass production of the 'safety' bicycle in the late 1880s, the MBC 'rode' the crest of public popularity in cycling and promoted racing and cyclists' rights within the city and throughout the province.[38]

Starting a bicycle race, 1895. (H.J. Woodside, Library and Archives Canada, PA-016114)

The Formation and Domination of the Montreal Amateur Athletic Association

The Montreal Bicycle Club was the third club in the triumvirate that in 1881 formed Canada's first multi-sport club, the Montreal Amateur Athletic Association (MAAA). In essence, the MAAA brought order to the random development of sport in Montreal when the prestigious Montreal Snow Shoe Club amalgamated with the Montreal Lacrosse and Montreal Bicycle Clubs in order to acquire grounds and a club facility. It was incorporated by an Act of the Quebec legislature, but this was merely a legal necessity for property acquisition. There was no grand design for the development that would give the MAAA such a dominant sports leadership position in Montreal and across Canada.[39]

Yet the timing and the foresight of the members of the three founding clubs were fortunate. In 1881, the MAAA acquired the former Montreal Gymnasium, located at what is now the northwest corner of Mansfield and Maisonneuve. Early gymnastics enthusiasts in the city—perhaps inspired by the interest in physical fitness engendered by the American Civil War—had formed a joint stock company in 1867 with members subscribing as shareholders. Within one year, the Montreal Gymnasium was built and equipped for $13,800. Complete with all forms of gymnastics apparatus, a billiard room, and two bowling alleys, the Gymnasium was run as a non-profit business and was initially financially successful. But within two years it was in difficulty, owing to its inability to collect the shareholders' promised subscriptions and to attract new members from a public more interested in lacrosse, ice-skating, and snowshoeing than in physical culture alone. In a last attempt at solvency, the Montreal Gymnasium merged with the Mercantile Library Association in 1874. Given suitable accommodation for its books, periodicals, and reading facilities, and a few other concessions of usage, the library in return assumed the company's $4,000 debt; the union provided only temporary relief. Use of the facility dwindled and the debt continued to increase.

In terms of success, renown, and growth, the Snow Shoeing and Lacrosse Clubs overshadowed the Gymnasium Company during the 1870s. The two sporting clubs required permanent club quarters and Angus Grant, a notable snowshoer, was the guiding force in the eventual amalgamation of these two clubs and the Montreal Bicycle Club. In 1877 Grant was a director of the Gymnasium Company and president of both the MSSC and the MLC. The two clubs made arrangements to rent space from the Gymnasium Company in order to conduct business affairs and, when the MSSC and the MLC united from 1878 to 1881, they were referred to only as 'the associated clubs' in the Montreal press; the meaning of the term was clear to all. Members of the associated clubs enjoyed their preferred activities as well as gymnastics, boxing, fencing, single sticks, billiards, shooting, and bowling, which were also available within the Gymnasium building. Grant was instrumental in inviting the members of the Montreal Bicycle Club to join the other clubs in buying the Gymnasium by assuming all liabilities and the mortgage on the building at a total cost of $13,000. Thus the Montreal Amateur Athletic Association was formed in 1881. The bicycle wheel became the basis of the MAAA's emblem—a winged wheel, the Canadian counterpart to the New York Athletic Club's winged foot. The wheel symbolized the MAAA as the hub or central organization, with the various recreational and sporting branches represented in the spokes. In the rim of the wheel was cast the Association's motto, *jungor ut implear*: 'I am joined that I may be complete.'[40]

With an initial base of approximately 600 people, the MAAA membership increased threefold within three years. By the end of the century, total membership was 2,600. In 1888, outdoor grounds were acquired in Westmount at the junction of St Catherine Street and Hallowell Avenue, where, for $70,000, the MAAA built a pavilion, grandstands, and a cinder track surrounding a large outdoor playing field, and acquired a second clubhouse. All outdoor team events and most recreational activities were conducted at the Westmount grounds. The Association was successful financially. Owing to its tax-exempt status as a non-profit organization, it was able to rely on only two sources of income: membership fees, set at $10 annually and $100 for life membership, and gate receipts from events held in its outdoor grounds. The Association's board of directors, elected from the major sporting clubs, administered all activities, and this was the key to the MAAA's quickly acquired position of power in Montreal and in Canadian sport. The officers of the Association were middle-class businessmen, and they were well able to conduct the affairs of the MAAA. Indeed, they became highly qualified 'professional' administrators of sport.

The directors skillfully built a pyramidal sport structure. At the base was mass recreation for its members (bowling, billiards, tobogganing, ice-skating, etc.). An ascending hierarchy of team sport through junior, intermediate, and senior levels was maintained, to be conducted intramurally, municipally, provincially, nationally, and internationally. Meticulous attention to every detail, including the early adoption of new equipment and devices to enhance sport, attracted members and events to the Association. A revolutionary electric timer was purchased for the track, along with brass distance markers installed on the inner rim; the latest pulley-weight apparatus was placed in the gym; a 'home trainer' or stationary bicycle was purchased for offseason cycle practice as early as 1883; gym cleats for tug-of-war practice were installed in the late 1880s; and a rowing machine was set up near the bowling alleys for training purposes. In addition to hosting popular spring track and field championships locally, the MAAA's annual Fall Games attracted the best athletes from the Manhattan and New York athletic clubs, and prior to 1909, the Canadian track and field championships were repeatedly held on the MAAA grounds.

In the late 1870s there was an increasing emphasis on sport outcome and on the winning of championships and trophies. This led to dishonest practices among teams, athletes, and clubs in Montreal and elsewhere. For example, teams were strengthened by the tacit importation of paid players to supplement club players, so that the amateur ideology of the clubs was corrupted by what came to be called, pejoratively, professionalism. Fixed outcomes, widespread and unregulated gambling, and lack of standardized, codified rules created unfair conditions in sport. To correct them, the MAAA actively sought involvement and control in competitive sports. From its inception it advocated the ideal of nineteenth-century amateurism. This British-based value system in sport emphasized the virtues of character-building through sport, fair play, adherence to rules, and, most important of all, the notion of playing solely for the joy of contest. To remedy the increasing trend towards an unofficial, corrupt 'professionalism', the MAAA followed the lead of British and American sport systems and organized the Amateur Athletic Association of Canada in 1884 (renamed the Canadian Amateur Athletic Union in 1898). MAAA executives dominated the affairs of this national amateur sport governing body into the first decade of the twentieth century.

The MAAA's winged-wheel emblem became synonymous with efficiency in the organization of, and success in, sport on national and international levels. Appropriately, the MAAA held the Canadian Wheelmen's Association's national cycling championships in 1886 and again in 1894. Five years later the Association hosted the World Bicycle Meet. Cycling fever in Montreal, fanned by MAAA initiative, was celebrated when an entire issue of the *Montreal Daily Star* (2 May 1896) was devoted to the bicycle.

Members of the MAAA conceived and became the principal organizers of the world-famous Montreal **Winter Carnivals** that were staged annually between 1883 and 1889.[41] Propelled and financed by civic **boosterism**, the carnivals were effective lures to the tourist industry—even more so than festivals of winter sport. Notwithstanding any underlying motives, the carnivals featured week-long activities in ice-skating, masquerade balls on skates, tobogganing, snowshoeing, and ice-hockey contests. The crowning event each year was a fireworks display at the ice palace constructed in Dominion Square. For the 1883 Winter Carnival:

The palace will consist of nearly 10,000 blocks of ice, each about 40 x 20 inches in size, and will cost about $3,200. It will face on Dorchester Street, the facade being 160 feet and the greatest depth 65 feet. The walls will be castellated and of different elevations, and three thick partitions of ice will trisect the building. Doors, however, will be cut in these walls so that the public can roam about the interior at will. The main tower standing about 76 feet in height will be a marvel of frozen architecture. . . . Numerous windows will be left at intervals in the walls of the structure which will be filled in with thin ice afterwards.[42]

Ice Palace for the 1884 Montreal Winter Carnival. (George Arless, Library and Archives Canada, PA-028746)

City clubs and businesses decorated horse-drawn floats to be paraded around Montreal during Carnival week and driven to the ice palace for the big evening. When the crowd of 50,000 had gathered, 1,500 snowshoers representing every club in Montreal, each carrying a lighted torch, marched eight abreast down Peel Street to surround the castle and initiate a mock battle with a spectacular 'pyrotechnic display'. This winter festival always ended with hundreds of musical instruments and thousands of voices mingling in the strains of 'God Save the Queen'. But the great Montreal Winter Carnivals of the 1880s became too complex, too commodified, and lost their special winter Mardi Gras appeal as a result of commercial interests and increasing attention to the 'bottom line'. The carnivals were halted in 1889.

The Winter Carnivals represented only one facet of the MAAA's influence. Its members were instrumental in the formation and administration of many national governing bodies, including rugby football, hockey, cycling, baseball, figure skating, bowling, and water polo between 1882 and 1906. During the 1890s, the MAAA hosted the Amateur Skating Association of Canada championships, and in 1897 this 'powerhouse' of Canadian sport staged the world speed-skating championships. Numerous Canadian titles were won by MAAA athletes in lacrosse, snowshoe races, cycling, steeplechases, track and field, figure skating, ice hockey (including the championships of seven consecutive Amateur Hockey Association of Canada victories and four Stanley Cup victories between 1886 and 1902),[43] bowling, billiards, football, fencing, speed skating, and boxing between 1881 and 1909. Even Canada's first Olympic gold medallist, Étienne Desmarteau (the champion 56-pound hammer-thrower in the 1904 St Louis Olympic Games), was a product of MAAA training.

Through meticulous administration and the prestige achieved through success and reputation, the MAAA gained power and influence in the organization of Canadian sport. The Notman firm took hundreds of photographs of MAAA events and preserved them in composite photographs that were displayed at exhibitions around the world. Sporting clubs from all over the continent wrote to the MAAA for copies of its constitution and modelled their own organizations accordingly. The Hamilton Amateur Athletic Association, the St Paul Amateur Athletic Association, and the Abegweit Amateur Athletic Association were only a few of the MAAA clones.

By 1900, there were almost 250 sport clubs in Montreal, with 24 leagues operating in seven different sports. For the most part, potential chaos was averted by the MAAA, which brought sound administration and organization to this flowering of amateur sport. Most of the growth was in team sports—notably lacrosse, rugby football, ice hockey, soccer, and baseball—and was the result of the entrance into sport of members of the working class. French Canadians were involved in lacrosse and snowshoeing, but participants in organized sport were mainly English-speaking Montrealers, whose middle-class ideology of amateurism was paramount in the structure and governance of sport. A trend towards commercialism, without adherence to any amateur ideals, was accelerating in spectator team sports. In addition to and complementing this direction in team sports, recreations of the working class—cycle races, prizefighting, cockfighting, skating, and billiards—were engaged in and enjoyed (in direct contravention, incidentally, of Sabbath laws against such activities). Gambling, swearing, and drinking were adjuncts of these commercially-based activities, in contrast to the uplifting moral ideology associated with the amateur ethos.[44] Indeed, even in the midst of Montreal's middle-class values, individuals from the city's Irish and Catholic working class founded the Shamrock Lacrosse Club (SLC), whose matches with the Montreal Lacrosse Club were perennial favourites that 'pitted English against Irish, Protestant against Catholic, and mechanic against clerk'.[45]

Control in Sport: The Amateur Ideal

[An amateur is] one who has never competed in any open competition or for public money, or for admission money, or with professionals for a prize, public money
or admission money, nor has ever, at any period of his life taught or assisted in the
pursuit of Athletic exercises as a means of livelihood or is a laborer or an Indian.
—*Constitution and By-laws of the Montreal Pedestrian Club, 1873*

The ebb and flow of the development of Canadian sport was not as open-ended or democratic as might be expected. On the contrary, concomitant with the organization and expansion of sport, governing authorities brought quite rigid control measures that were contrived partly to maintain fairness in competitions but, even more, to control who competed with whom. For most of the nineteenth century, sport was the prerogative of upper- and middle-class men; there was no need to control sport because these gentlemen of the early hunt clubs, tandem clubs, snowshoe clubs, and curling clubs founded their organizations to play sport and to socialize among themselves. Rules—for example, those of the first known sport club in Canada, the Montreal Curling Club of 1807 discussed earlier in this chapter—were first social and second athletic in nature. The regulation of sport in those early years was not an issue. With the dispersion of sport among different social classes around Confederation, codes of behaviour and social class exclusion that had been assumed in sport were contested. The Montreal Pedestrian [walking] Club's definition of an amateur, cited above, was the first clearly articulated effort by sporting officials in Canada to bring measures of control to sport. As a value system, amateurism dominated the Canadian sporting landscape beginning in the last two decades of the nineteenth century and continuing until well into the twentieth century, buttressed by the like-minded amateur values of the Olympic Games. As Kidd notes in *The Struggle for Canadian Sport*:

> The earliest 'amateur codes' restricted participation on the basis of class and race, reflecting the upper classes' desire to reproduce the social hierarchies of Victorian England and the British Empire and to maintain the primacy of sports as an expression of manly honour and elegant display.[46]

How, then, did the amateur ideal become the prevailing code of Canadian sport during the late nineteenth and early twentieth centuries?

Amateur Derivations

Some background information is necessary to understand how such a value system as amateurism—so obviously discriminatory—could become the ruling force in Canadian sport. Essentially, the ideal of amateurism had its modern roots in Great Britain. The British Henley Rowing Club stewards promulgated their definition of an amateur in the late 1870s. That definition and restriction stated that an amateur was 'one who is not, among other things, by trade or employment a mechanic, artisan or laborer'.[47] It is clear that this definition was constructed to exclude the lower classes from competing in rowing and that the definition only characterized what an amateur is not rather than what an amateur is. The latter fact is characteristic of every definition of an amateur or amateurism that ever existed. In the case of the Henley definition, the intent of the prestigious club's rowing stewards was to maintain social distinctions in sport so that manual labourers would not compete alongside the more privileged classes. And there was some sense that manual labourers held some physical advantage over middle- and upper-class competitors; not only was this perceived to be an unfair advantage, but the whole notion of members of the lower classes beating their higher-class countrymen was just not conceivable in that era; indeed, such an idea was repugnant to the elite. Within 10 years of the articulation of the famed Henley amateur regulation, payments to athletes became an issue in rowing and rugby football; therefore, the restriction was added that amateur athletes in England could not receive remuneration for their athletic prowess.[48] The whole issue of paid athletes erupted in soccer to such a degree that the very existence of that sport was threatened[49] and led to even tighter amateur restrictions. Several historians interpret the amateur rule in late nineteenth-century Britain as an 'instrument of class warfare' that had its roots and meaning in a concept of 'pure' sport among British sportsmen, who were imbued with the persistent sporting traditions of the upper- and middle-class public schools[50] (called private schools in Canada).

Canadian Amateur Ideals and Definitions

In the United States in the late 1870s early definitions of 'amateur' emanated from the National Association of Amateur Oarsmen, which stated that:

> An amateur is any person who has never competed in an open contest, or for a stake, or for public money, or for gate money, or under a false name, or with a professional for a prize, or where gate money is charged; nor has ever at any period of his life taught or pursued athletic exercise as a means of livelihood.[51]

Devoid of the social class tinges of the Henley definition, this regulation emphasizes the escalating 'problem' of paying athletes. Any such athlete was axiomatically labelled a 'professional', more as a term denoting paid-to-play than any inherent notion of quality of player. By implication, amateurism was the absence of professionalism. So, too, in Canada, rowing brought attention to the concept of amateurism with the Canadian Association of Amateur Oarsmen's 1880 definition:

> An amateur is one who has never assisted in the pursuit of athletic exercises as a means of livelihood, who rows for pleasure and recreation only during his leisure hours, and does not abandon or neglect his usual business or occupation for the purpose of training for more than two weeks during the season.[52]

In Canada, as we have seen, the reach of a landed gentry did not extend as far as it did in Great Britain, but there was definitely an affluent upper class able to afford the time and expense of sporting competitions in the first half of the nineteenth century. As industrialization progressed, more and more members of all classes were able to enjoy sport, either as spectators or as participants. In horse racing, for example, traditionally an upper-class pastime, when the lower classes became able to 'intrude' into the racing venues, participate in the attendant gambling, and behave in a manner not in keeping with upper-class ideals (let alone the economic implications when towns and farms were abandoned for days), organizers tried all manner of strategies—such as moving the events further from towns and, in some cases, cancelling the races altogether—to control the 'rowdy' elements.[53] Similarly, in competitive sports like lacrosse, baseball, and rowing, paid players began to infiltrate the contests. Canadian rowing organizers, then, comparable to and following the lead of their British and American counterparts, took the initiative to frame an amateur definition of exclusion in an effort to ensure the influence of certain middle- and upper-class values in sport. Inherent in that 1880 definition were the notions that amateurs competed for 'pleasure' and that they were not employed as athletes since they were to have their 'usual business or occupation'.

And yet Canada was in no way free from the taint of ethnic discrimination in sport. Consider the revealing last seven words of the Montreal Pedestrian Club's 1873 amateur definition quoted at the start of this chapter: '. . . or is a laborer or an Indian'. The origins of such discrimination precede this definition by decades. During the early part of the nineteenth century, blacks settled in clusters around Dresden and Chatham in Ontario as well as in Nova Scotia, and constituted a very small minority group in Canada. In 1835 there was a thriving 'turf' or horse-racing club in Newark in Upper Canada. The written rules of that club were typically social in nature until that year, when it was stipulated that 'no black man will be allowed to compete under any pretext whatsoever.'[54] There was never any reason given for this ban on black competitors but we can speculate that horse racing, the 'sport of kings', was a socially exclusive affair at Newark. Did a black man forget his 'place' and attempt to enter a race? Did white people not want him to compete as their equal? Was

St John, New Brunswick's 'Paris Crew', 1871. (G.P. Roberts, Library and Archives Canada, C-014065)

the intruder a stable 'boy' who knew more about and was more adept at the sport than the white club members? Was he both black and a common manual labourer who should not be allowed to compete with gentlemen? We don't know the answers to these questions; possibly both racial and class biases prevailed. Almost 30 years later, in 1863, one William Berry submitted his application to enter the Toronto Bay Championship Rowing Regatta. On race day, the competitors lined up for the start and, lo, Berry was black. The other competitors, all Euro-Canadians, refused to row the race.[55] Once again, it would seem, a perceived social 'inferior' had intruded into sport's exclusive preserve. Since there were no published rules of exclusion, race officials set out over the next few years to warn other competitors about the racial background of their opponents. So, for example, William Berry was designated on the race card as 'William Berry (coloured)', or 'Black Bob Berry', or, 'Western Canadian of African descent'. For the Toronto regatta, Berry kept submitting his name but received the curt response that 'coloureds are barred' from the races. Finally, in 1868, race organizers felt Berry would be defeated easily and allowed his entry to stand. Berry won the event and aroused so much consternation in doing so that one white competitor, Tom Loudon, challenged Berry to two more races, both of which Berry won. Berry went on to win many more races; however, his case and the experience of the Newark turf club demonstrate how power and control were wielded in the early years of organized sport.

Snowshoeing and lacrosse exemplified exactly the same social exclusivity and pattern of control when event organizers decided Indians were eligible only for certain contests and not others. At the time of Confederation, Aboriginals were not allowed to compete in 'Canadian' lacrosse championship matches. In this instance they were deemed, by implication, not to be Canadian. The reason behind their exclusion was directly related to their outstanding skill levels and the desire of white officials to control competition.

The Founding of a National Organization to Manage Amateur Sport

As more and more members of all social classes and races became able to compete in sports that had been socially exclusive, the whole issue of control became paramount. What Canadian sport moguls perceived was the trend in the United States and Great Britain towards written rules about eligibility under the banner of amateur restrictions. Clearly, the trend in sport, especially in sports clubs, was away from 'social first, athletic second' to clubs and sports whose members and participants placed more of a premium on competition, not social conviviality. Rowing had taken an amateur regulation leadership role in all three countries—Great Britain, the United States, and Canada. However, track and field, or 'athletics', as it was known, was becoming more and more popular. That sport, as we have previously discussed, was highly promoted by the Scots in their Caledonian Games. By the late 1870s, talented track and field competitors could make a tidy sum of money by travelling a circuit of the Games in southwestern Ontario, winning events, and selling their material prizes.[56] Thus, in modern terms, track and field events—at least the ones organized by the Scots—became 'professional' events in that they fostered a direct and sanctioned commercial aspect. This trend, combined with the use of paid players in lacrosse and baseball, led to the formation in 1884 of Canada's first parent body or custodian of the amateur ideal, the Amateur Athletic Association of Canada (AAAC), at the instigation of the powerful Montreal Amateur Athletic Association.[57] With the founding of the AAAC, the control of virtually almost all sports, certainly the propagation of the amateur ideal, was firmly attached to one organization.

The AAAC's first amateur definition formulated to control sport was patterned exactly after the US National Association of Amateur Oarsmen's 1879 definition (cited earlier), with the addition of this second sentence: 'This rule does not interfere with the right of any club to refuse an entry to its own sports.'[58] This definition followed the international pattern in that it said what an amateur was not. It did not speak of fostering or promoting track and field but of restrictions; in fact, the stated aim of the AAAC was to '*regulate*' competition on the 'cinder path' (tracks were often made of cinder)—and it was noteworthy for the sentence granting the AAAC and its affiliate clubs/organizations absolute right of exclusion. Executive members of the AAAC promoted a model of sporting regulations based on what many historians refer to as meritocratic principles.[59] That is, amateurism was designed to be highly exclusive and required participants to conform to upper middle-class values of the way to play sport.[60]

To understand how amateur moguls became so stringent, it is important to comprehend how quickly sport proliferated and how quickly the shift had been made towards high-quality competition. Simply put, sport achieved higher and higher quality of performance owing to its growth, more highly skilled athletes, better organization by interest groups, and the technological and social changes discussed in earlier chapters. At the same time, we must also remember that the prevailing notion of a professional athlete in Canada during the late nineteenth century was equated with a form of prostitution.[61] The term 'professional' was used to characterize any athlete who sold his—women were not yet competing at this level—athletic talent to the highest bidder or for the most gain, or who might be persuaded to fix outcomes of contests and generally dupe the public for profit. There were exceptions to this professional perception. For example, in Chapter 5 we will explore how the commercial basis for baseball was established and respected by paying customers who wanted to see good sport played well, and by promoters willing to pay to bring American players to Canadian towns. Similarly, we will see in Chapter 6 how Canada's first individual world champion in any sport, Ned Hanlan, was an openly declared professional in his quest to become the very best in his sport. However, lacrosse, rugby football, track and field, and ice hockey were 'semi-professional' or covertly professional[62] in that some athletes accepted money while pretending to be amateur. Other popular individual sports—such as bicycle racing and speed skating—contained distinct categories for professionals and amateurs, but no mixed events of the two categories were approved by the AAAC.

As senior leagues in team sports became more competitive, with greater emphasis on winning championships, the more concentrated and numerous were the efforts to build quality teams while pretending to adhere to the amateur strictures of the national amateur governing body. Thus, in many ways, creating and enforcing amateur codes or regulations was akin to the proverbial throwing a blanket over a postage-stamp-sized problem. And yet, at the time it was as though the middle-class amateur enforcers could not see any other way to control the outbreak of cheating amateurs—'shamateurs', as some called them—and professional practices and maintain their control over the 'right' way to participate in sport. Moreover, the feeling was that two of the fundamental principles of sport would be destroyed by professionalism, those of fair play, in the British tradition, and its corollary, uncertainty of outcome. Fairness, of course, was fairness to a middle-class perception of reality.

Actual charges of professionalism were rampant during the 1890s, especially in team sports; even paid referees were banned from playing amateur sport of any kind and were fixed instead with the professional label.[63] Jobs or placements, sponsorships, end-of-season performance bonuses, and outright payments to athletes were made under the disguise of amateurism. The staunch AAAC instigated two-year residence rules in an effort to prevent players during a single season from constantly hopping teams to the next highest bidder. And the same group spent most of its time with the arduous and complex tasks of investigating charges of professionalism, suspending proven violators of the amateur code (or, in perverted jurisprudence, suspending athletes whose only guilt was that they could not 'prove' their amateur innocence), and reinstating athletes who had transgressed the code, been suspended, and were ready to repent and willing to follow the strictures of simon-pure amateurism.[64] The AAAC was extremely successful in its quest to uphold the values of amateurism and control competitive sport because of the unified concern over sport corruption and because this national body set up annual national track and field championships and required all member clubs to host at least one track and field competition per year, thereby boosting track and field's popularity and the attendant code of amateur regulation.

The prime concern of this organization during the 1890s was to 'abolish everything in the shape of professionalism from athletic sports.'[65] That is, the national body was not content merely to govern amateur sport; instead, it pointed itself with a vengeance at the abolition of professionalism. Control of sport was its avowed goal, and its prestige was rising. At first, the AAAC was centred in Ontario and Quebec; Nova Scotia joined the national body in the late 1880s and British Columbia did the same in 1893. As well, international athletes applied to compete in the Association's national championships as early as 1887. With the founding of the modern Olympic Games in 1896, the amateur code so embedded in Canada was given global support that increased as the Games became more popular. In the same vein, the AAAC formed an alliance with the powerful Amateur Athletic Union of the United States to become the Canadian Amateur Athletic Union (CAAU) in 1898.[66] Coincident with its name change, the governing body's focus shifted from mere regulation of athletes mainly in track and field; instead, the Union vowed to 'advance' and 'improve' all sports among amateurs and stated an even loftier objective, i.e., 'to encourage systematic physical exercise and [physical] education in Canada'.[67] Clearly, the CAAU was puffing its athletic chest. However, the prevailing trend in the evolution of sports—at least in team sports—seemed to be towards an even higher-quality, commercial brand of sport at the top levels. The amateur code appeared to be swimming upstream.

While the CAAU preached ironclad opposition to professionalism and sought to foster amateur sport, prestigious trophies like the Stanley Cup in hockey and the Minto Cup in lacrosse were governed by trustees outside the realm of the CAAU. Despite all manner of suspensions and regulations in the name of amateurism, professional or non-amateur lacrosse, hockey, and, to a lesser extent, rugby football[68] were flourishing by 1905. The situation became chaotic; professionals claimed to be amateurs; players were literally selling themselves to the highest bidder. Policing the amateur ideal was almost impossible. So convinced were amateur guardians that the evil in sport was professionalism, that if an amateur athlete was found to have played a game with or against a professional athlete, doubts were cast on that athlete's amateur standing. Trends and pressures towards more commercially-based sport escalated and created an athletic-behaviour bubble waiting to burst. Between 1901 and 1905, the Executive Committee of the CAAU dealt almost exclusively with allegations, suspensions, and questions concerning the issue of amateur athletes playing with or against professionals—should the mere association of amateurs in competition with or against professionals, knowingly or unknowingly, result in loss of amateur status?[69] In lacrosse, for example, team members accused of professionalism were forced to file affidavits of innocence testifying to their bona fide amateur status before a judge[70] or else faced suspension. However, the evolution of lacrosse was such that paying players was almost required at the top or senior levels of competition. The National Amateur Lacrosse Union petitioned the CAAU in 1903 for a special concession to allow declared professionals to compete with and against amateurs in lacrosse. At first the CAAU was unequivocal in its negative response. One year later, the amateur governing body tried a compromise by telling its member clubs and organizations, inclusive of lacrosse, that all teams and players formerly suspended as professionals would be reinstated as amateurs if they agreed to abide by the strict amateur guidelines after a six-month transition.[71] It was a band-aid measure in the turmoil surrounding the regulation, control, and development of sport in Canada. Pressure was such that in 1905 the CAAU granted, only to lacrosse, the right to allow professionals to compete with and against amateurs.[72]

The Athletic War

The exemption for the good of the 'national sport' was radical and quite unconstitutional, short-lived as it was. Within a year, the CAAU rescinded its decision. In Montreal, the founding organization of the AAAC in 1884, the Montreal Amateur Athletic Association (MAAA), was struggling with its lacrosse supremacy in the face of rising team travelling costs, accident insurance rates, and facility maintenance expenses.[73] Lacrosse, among other sports, became at its senior levels a business, no longer a pleasant pastime. Amid heated internal debate, the MAAA Board of Directors and its members voted in 1906 overwhelmingly to allow its amateurs to play with or against professionals without jeopardizing their amateur status.[74] The Montreal press gushed its admiration for the move with headlines such as, 'The M.A.A.A. to Cut the Gordian Knot'. Within the month, the National Amateur Lacrosse Union followed suit, adopted the same resolution, and became the National Lacrosse Union.[75] With the combined powers of the MAAA and the NLU directed towards the new practice that was openly touted as commonplace in cricket and soccer in the mother country, royal sanction and divine blessing seemed imminent. By the fall of 1906, sentiment in the Montreal public press favoured following the same course in rugby football and ice hockey.[76] The CAAU spoke volumes in its silence. Finally, the Union declared itself in a bold stand against the traditionally powerful MAAA and stood adamant in its strict policy of amateurism. It became a power struggle between the seat of Canadian organizational sporting development in the nineteenth century—Montreal—and the emerging centre of sport governance—Toronto. When the CAAU made its position clear, the MAAA withdrew from the organization it had been instrumental in founding. An athletic 'war' was declared.[77]

For about two and a half years this war dragged on with an almost perfect 'Montreal versus the rest of Canadian amateur sport' split in belief systems. The MAAA created a new governing body, the Amateur Athletic Federation of Canada (AAFC), claiming 'jurisdiction over all athletes and all athletic sports in Canada'.[78] Members and executives of both the CAAU and the AAFC were caught in the sweeping social changes of the times. As Canada was experiencing economic prosperity with the settlement of the western provinces via the energetic immigration policies of Clifford Sifton, so too was sport—team sports in particular—accelerating towards commercial interests, sponsors, spectators, gate receipts, and general administrative costs, including the desire of athletes to be fairly remunerated for the 'product' they delivered to the public. So, while the newly formed AAFC represented a bold effort to try to deal with such changes, their tactic of circling their wagons around Montreal in the hopes that the rest of Canadian sport would join them was outdated. Although seemingly strengthened by the powerful American AAU pledging affiliation with the AAFC and concomitant non-recognition of CAAU member athletes, it was not enough. The CAAU, on the other hand, went on a concerted campaign to recruit more clubs and athletes to affiliate with its organization and attendant amateur belief system. The regulatory body divided the country up into provincial self-governing regions, all allied to the central Union. From some 16 sporting clubs in 1906, the CAAU boasted 900 sporting clubs with some 60,000 athletic members by 1908.[79]

The pivotal event in drawing the athletic war to a close was a set of events connected to the 1908 London Olympic Games. Colonel Hanbury-Williams, representing the British Olympic Committee in Canada, called a meeting of CAAU and AAFC representatives to be held in the Governor General's offices in Ottawa late in the fall of 1907. The intent was to declare a temporary truce to the war for the unified good of the country and its athletes regarding participation in the Olympic Games.[80] It is evident from the venue chosen for the meeting that sport itself had acquired considerable prestige. A truce was reached and, as if to underscore their goodwill, both organizations published Christmas greetings to all

Tom Longboat, 1907 (Charles Aylett, Library and Archives Canada, C-014095)

Issues in Canadian Sport History

The Tom Longboat Controversy

The Tom Longboat controversy began when one official of the AAFC, Leslie Boyd, then president of the MAAA, colluded with the American Athletic Union's president, James E. Sullivan, to try to get Olympic marathon favourite, Tom Longboat, declared a professional to disqualify him from running the Olympic marathon.[82] Longboat's fame was international in scope and his running prowess was unquestioned. And as a Toronto-based runner he therefore was affiliated with the CAAU. When the letter of protest against Longboat was published by the AAFC in a variety of Canadian newspapers, Canadians were incensed. The *Ottawa Journal,* for example, labelled Boyd's actions as 'nationally disloyal and dishonourable.'[83] It was the major failing point of the AAFC. In effect, the collusion with the United States governing body in the Longboat incident fractured the Montreal-based group. Ironically, Longboat not only did not win the 1908 Olympic marathon event, he collapsed somewhere around the 30-kilometre mark, the apparent victim of an overdose of strychnine. Strychnine, in lower dosages was once used in medications as a central nervous system stimulant. During this time period, it was common to gamble on the outcome of famous athletic events. Speculation in some analyses is that someone in Longboat's training retinue gave him the overdose in order to capitalize on the betting odds by preventing Longboat from achieving a highly expected victory.[84]

amateur athletes in both the Montreal and Toronto presses.[81] The truce lasted only until the next summer when controversy erupted over the amateur status of Canadian and world marathon running champion, Tom Longboat.

In September 1908, the Canadian Olympic Committee publicly denounced Boyd's actions and the AAFC's support for Boyd based on the 1907 truce agreement. After one last but failed effort by the AAFC to get Longboat to accept money for winning a race in Williamstown, Pennsylvania, delegates of the Federation came to Toronto in the spring of 1909 to appeal for athletic peace.[85] By Labour Day that year, the 'peace' was negotiated in Ottawa and hailed in the daily press:

> **The Barriers Are Now Raised—Athletic Peace Comes at Last**
> The A.A.U. of Canada was formed here yesterday by the amalgamation of the A.A.F. of C. and the C.A.A.U. The hatchet was buried forever and neither side claims a victory, both declaring that they have acted for the betterment of Canadian athletics only.[86]

Renewed Amateurism

The new CAAU remounted the pedestal of nineteenth-century amateur values. All athletic members were pledged to the strict enforcement of the amateur ideal with a general sense of having rescued sport from professionalism.[87] 'New' amateur definitions merely reinvented the amateur wheel of control in sport. At the same time, this renewed advocacy for amateur ideals reflected the prevailing 'Gospel of Order'.[88] The amateur ideal was one of moral belief about 'right' values, just as it was a method for exclusion of unwanted behaviour and competitive formats. As for hockey and lacrosse, the CAAU regarded them as 'money-making mediums for groups of mercenary promoters'[89] (note the implicit negative value attached to professionalism in these two sports). New trophies were created to honour and promote amateur values in hockey with the Allan Cup and, in lacrosse, with the Mann Cup. The theory was that these new trophies would be CAAU-controlled and would provide incentives to wean the wayward sports back to the fold. Hockey entrepreneurs countered with the 1910 creation of the National Hockey Association, a declared professional hockey body and forerunner of the National Hockey League. The athletic war in Canada was a significant conflict in the history of Canadian sport because its results so firmly entrenched the amateur ideal in Canadian sport. Significant change did not happen; instead, the resolution of the 'war', in real terms, only served to embalm and enshrine an outmoded or, at best, unstable amateur ideal.

With specific respect to the development of avowed professionalism in Canadian sports, hockey and lacrosse were indeed the trend-setters in the establishment of a commercial basis for sport. Both were popular team sports by the late nineteenth century; both lent themselves to spectator appeal owing to their fast-paced and often violent nature; and both had prestigious trophies donated and named after governor generals.[90] In addition, public sentiment was shifting, if judged by the public press. For example, just prior to the athletic war, in reference to an exciting lacrosse game in Toronto, the *Star* gushed: 'Talk about your professionals spoiling the game! Not much. Those fellows were just as anxious to win and worked just as hard as if they were simon pure amateurs and in the final, their joy was just as great.'[91]

Professional Hockey

The lacrosse example led hockey promoters to recognize that spectators were attracted to high-quality competition that, in turn, was related to enforced practice sessions. The connection of professional sport to higher-quality sport began to be forged. Early professional leagues in both lacrosse and hockey published lists naming which athletes were professionals in order to instill confidence in the paying public. In fact, as early as 1908, if a professional athlete performed poorly in a game, the press quipped that he should soon apply for amateur reinstatement.[92] What really launched professional hockey was the mining boom, in copper and steel, in northern Michigan and northern Ontario. Small towns and cities like Houghton,[93] Calumet, and Sault Ste Marie (both the American and the Canadian cities of the same name) were able to support professional hockey financially as early as 1904. Mining money was used to promote and fund the league. Artificial ice was not needed because of the northern locations of the teams. The International Hockey League prospered and the prestige attached to winning the Stanley Cup—a challenge-based trophy at the time—grew to the extent that a team from Dawson City, Yukon, travelled by dogsled, boat, and train all the way to Ottawa to contest for the Cup in 1905.[94] Virtually unknown towns in northern Ontario—Haileybury, Cobalt, Kenora, and New Liskeard, for example—'prospected' for hockey talent in zealous efforts to win the coveted trophy, and in 1907 Kenora did win it.[95]

It was not long before the more populous central and southwestern areas of Ontario developed professional hockey leagues. Business entrepreneurs formed the National Hockey Association (the NHA, the earliest name of what would become the National Hockey League) in 1909. What cemented the notion of being professional was the adoption of the first professional contract in Canada, the NHA contract of 1910. This two-page agreement was signed by each player and each club's representative. The contract included a 'reservation clause' to bind each player to a team and it revealed an intense concern for proper behaviour of each player in its stipulation that:

> should the [player] at any time or times be intemperate, immoral, careless, indifferent or conduct himself in such a manner, whether on or off the ice, as to endanger or prejudice the interests of the [hockey club] . . . the [latter] shall have the right to discipline, suspend, fine or discharge the [player] . . . . .[96]

The NHA was perceptive in its awareness of the need to develop the image of its professional athletes as good citizens, no different in that respect from amateurs. This contract is significant in Canadian sport in that it symbolized and cemented a businesslike basis for hockey. Moreover, as quality of play was quickly perceived to be higher in professional hockey, the distinctions of both higher performance and signing a business contract became attached to the concept of the professional athlete. No longer perceived to be a 'prostitute', a 'pro' was someone who was professional in his skill, in moral deportment, and in the legitimacy of his business—sport. As a result, such early professional hockey players as Edward 'Newsy' Lalonde and 'Cyclone' Taylor became respected household names and hockey heroes.[97]

Within a very short period of time, the NHA implemented rule changes to enhance hockey games as a product. For example, in 1911 the Association reduced the number of players on the ice from seven (the seventh player had been a 'rover') to six in order to open up the game's offence and thereby enhance its entertainment value.[98] At the same time, the NHA imposed a salary limit of $5,000 per team for the 16-game schedule, thereby making it less expensive to ice a team and controlling the possibility of escalating salaries. It is intriguing that 'control' in professional hockey was fuelled by monetary restrictions while in amateur sport control was related to restricting playing privileges. The NHA executives quite understandably perceived their goal as maximizing profits. Players had little say in rule changes or running of the league, whereas in amateur sport players often had been on managerial committees.[99] Two brothers, Frank and Lester Patrick, were players on one of the NHA's early teams, the Renfrew Millionaires.[100] Disenchanted with playing in the NHA, the brothers returned home to Victoria, British Columbia, and approached their father, who had made his fortune in the lumber industry, to fund the construction of some artificial ice rinks in the Lower Mainland in an effort to start a west coast professional hockey league. Within a few years, the Pacific Coast Hockey League (PCHL) was created with franchises and rinks in Vancouver, Victoria, Portland, and New Westminster.[101]

The Patricks lured players from the NHA to join the rival league. With the end of the mining boom in Ontario and Michigan, the NHA's fortunes were not as strong as they had been. The resourceful brothers acted as players, coaches, managers, and alternated as league presidents during the PCHL's growing years. They implemented a variety of innovations, such as the blue line and forward passing, in order to enhance the game. By 1914, the status of the PCHL was such that the Stanley Cup was contested by the season-winning team from each rival league in a best-of-five series (the Stanley Cup competition had been a two-game, total-goals system). Seven years later, the success of professional hockey in the two leagues led to the formation of a four-team Western Canadian Hockey League—Edmonton, Calgary, Regina, Saskatoon. However, the NHA had expanded into major American cities such as New York, Chicago, and Boston and had changed its name to the National Hockey League (NHL) in 1917. Weakened by escalating salary demands and an unstable basis for funding in the western provinces, the PCHL and the Western Canadian Hockey League amalgamated in 1923. Finally, in 1926, Lester Patrick sold the franchise to the NHL. Some 22 major rule changes to hockey are attributable to the Patricks. That two men could have so much influence, changing the shape and direction of one sport, was unheard of in amateur sport. Clearly, money was their power in controlling the evolution of hockey; they approached the sport as a business enterprise first and foremost and cleverly marketed hockey for its retail value.

The changes to hockey inspired other sports, like baseball and football, to venture more openly into the realm of commercialized sport, either by setting up professional leagues across Canada, as baseball did around 1912, and/or by conducting sport in a more professional manner, as football did, with training camps and the employment of skilled coaches.[102] This is not to imply that professionalism was readily or universally accepted. The phrase 'turn pro' held a very negative connotation well into the 1920s. However, circumstances and events connected with the First World War broke down some of the pejorative connotations attached to being a 'pro'. The very fact that professional athletes fought for their country brought to public view their credibility. Even the Canadian AAU relaxed its strictures of playing with and/or against professionals, during the war.[103] Rising prestige came to the CAAU and its amateur principle with the growing prestige attached to the Olympic Games. Canada was well recognized for its gold and other medal achievements in the 1908 London and 1912 Stockholm Olympic Games.[104] One of the strongest committees of the CAAU became the Canadian Olympic Committee, whose mandate was tied to the guardianship of the Olympic amateur ideal and whose connection to the CAAU solidified the control of amateur sport in the country.

Thus, there were competing trends for the control of Canadian sport by the 1920s. While the CAAU was building power, Canadian professional hockey interests and developments were such that by 1926 the NHL became a two-division league with a five-team American division and a five-team Canadian division. That structure lasted until the Depression, when the NHL became a six-team league with only two Canadian teams, Montreal and Toronto. Part of the life and 'death' of hockey[105] was its professionalization and its selling out to American interests. Canadians were enticed and enchanted with the professional hockey product brought live into their living rooms by Foster Hewitt's radio broadcasts of NHL games, beginning in 1931 from Maple Leaf Gardens in Toronto.[106] At the same time, the nation revelled in its Winter Olympic amateur hockey supremacy of the 1920s and 1930s. By the 1930s, open professional sport such as that promoted by the NHL, was a fixture in the Canadian sporting landscape; yet, amateurism was still the prevailing ideal in most competitive sports. Thus, in the latter regard, the CAAU sought to retain its control and jurisdiction and to police 'shamateurs' or semi-professionalism (paid players pretending to be amateurs) in sport.

Conclusions

In the quarter-century since it had been formed from the crystallization of Montreal sport, the MAAA was outstripped by the diffusion of sport throughout Canada. At the same time, the leaders of the MAAA were instrumental in shaping the development of organized sport out of the technological and social changes that occurred over the course of the nineteenth century. In flexing its muscle during the athletic war, the Association erred in assuming that its reputation alone would magnetically draw sport organizations to its perspective. While Montreal had been the cradle—albeit gilt-edged—of organized sport in Canada, and it had been nurtured by the MAAA, a single association in one large city was no longer able to control sport across the country. Toronto-based sport administrators of the Canadian Amateur Athletic Union engineered the formation of a national governing body with tiers of provincial, regional, municipal, and club representation. The Federation of the MAAA was forced to amalgamate with the Union in 1909, thereby reaffirming traditional amateur ideals.

'Amateur' and 'professional' were not just labels for athletes in the construction of Canada's sporting landscape. Instead, they represented ideals and values about how sport should be played, who should play, and under what set of circumstances. Canada's amateur sports governing bodies defined, codified, and directed a wide spectrum of sports through to the 1970s when the Canadian Amateur Athletic Association finally disbanded in deference to government control of sport. Though severely weakened when the Canadian Olympic Committee established itself as a free-standing organization outside the CAAU umbrella in the early 1950s, the conservatism of sport as an institution is such that it seems a wonder that amateurism prevailed as a value system for more than 100 years. And it seems that the evolution of elite sport was towards a professional standard, not just in terms of monetary inducements and salaries, but in the sense of the excellence of performance and high-quality sport.

————— ◆ —————

Related Websites

Canada Science and Technology Museum
http://imagescn.technomuses.ca

Multi-links for Snowshoeing in Canada
http://www.out-there.com/htl_ssh.htm

Montreal History and Images
http://www.virtualmuseum.ca/PM.cgi?LM=Gallery&scope=Gallery&LANG=
English&mark=&AP=M_E_display&Page=MCCDI.html

Montreal History Links (including professional sport history)
http://www.geocities.com/ericsquire/montreal.htm

McCord Museum of Canadian History
http://www.mccord-museum.qc.ca/

Significant Dates in Canadian Railway History
http://www.railways.incanada.net/candate/candate.htm

Penny Farthing Bicycles
http://www.thewheelmen.org/sections/links/links.asp

Who Rides Penny Farthings?
http://www.wuk.at/hochrad/wer/wer_eng.php

Curling History Overview
http://icing.org/game/history/historya.htm

Women's Amateur Athletic Federation of Canada and Women's Sport History
http://www.caaws.ca/e/milestones/women_history/index.cfm

History of Amateur Hockey in Canada
http://www.hockeycanada.ca/6/8/3/0/index1.shtml

Study Questions

1. How was competitive sport altered by technological changes? That is, how was the form and conduct of sport transformed by these changes?
2. In what ways does technology impact sport today?
3. What cultural, social, and economic factors enabled Montreal to exert such impact on the organization of Canadian sport? What city or cities exert control over Canadian sport today?
4. How was amateurism both a value and a discriminatory control measure in Canadian sport? What other control measures are built into organized sport and how are they maintained?
5. What were some of the other issues surrounding marathon runner Tom Longboat's career? Are these issues still prevalent today in other cases and circumstances?
6. What is the current meaning of 'professional' as it applies to athletes? Are there any amateur athletes today?

Case Studies in the Growth and Institutionalization of Sport: Lacrosse and Baseball

Lacrosse and baseball provide an excellent window for viewing the specific ways that sport became patterned and established in the period following Confederation and up to almost the end of the twentieth century. In many ways, the development of these two sports represents the efforts of a new nation to achieve distinction. Whereas cricket was distinctively rooted in Great Britain, lacrosse and baseball were more **colonial**. While there is some overlap in the periods of popularity of baseball and lacrosse, the latter sport first reached a crescendo of Canadian interest in the decades following Confederation and subsequently dwindled in its allure and allegiances right around the First World War. Baseball gathered sporadic momentum just prior to the turn of the twentieth century and all but replaced lacrosse in cross-Canada enthusiasm by the 1920s and 1930s. For both sports, the emphasis in this chapter is on their rise to popularity within the context of their sporting times. Similarly, both sports illustrate how a way of playing a sport was shaped into the way of playing—in short, these sports became institutionalized in Canada.

The Native Game[1]

The depiction by the American artist George Catlin (1796–1872) of lacrosse in the early nineteenth century conveys a distinct and profound image of the Aboriginal origins of the game. Catlin's painting shows hundreds of athletic-looking Natives engaging in a ball-and-stick game; more significantly, it evokes the motion and struggle of these early contestants. There were some 40 variations of lacrosse—also known as baggataway or tewaarathon—engaged in by Ojibwa, Choctaw, Mohawk, Seneca, Cherokee, Huron, Iroquois, and other tribes at least as early as the first North American explorers observed them. The best evidence indicates that inter-tribal contests were rare, perhaps because of the subtle differences in playing forms, but more likely because of the purpose of Aboriginal lacrosse:

the games were ritual affairs.[2] Ceremoniously dressed in plumed headdresses, decorated with iridescent paint, and wearing elaborate beadwork belts, Native players contested to honour a fallen warrior,[3] paralleling in purpose the funeral games for Patroclus in Homer's **The Iliad**, or for medicinal purposes, to bring a sick person back to health. The games often lasted for days and required tremendous skill and endurance.

Although lacrosse was perceived by early missionaries and travellers to be crude and dangerous, and despite the seemingly chaotic appearance of the game, modern research has emphasized the ritualistic nature of the contests, the skills required, and the emphasis on values such as discipline, leadership, physical skill, physical conditioning, and tribal unity.[4] Most often a single racket about one metre long was used, but in a few tribes the contestants carried one stick in each hand. In either case the top end of these hickory sticks was bent over to form a small hoop or crook that was netted with leather thongs. The hoop of the stick was only large enough to hold the ball, which was made of wood or buckskin and stuffed with hair. The Indian name of the game alluded to the ball, but the Europeans in Canada named it for the stick, calling it 'la crosse' because the stick resembled a bishop's crosier.[5]

The form of the early stick suggests that lacrosse as played by the Natives must have been more of a running than a passing game. The object was to drive the ball through two sets of poles or posts erected at each end of the field, affording prime occasions for wagering on the outcome[6]—a significant aspect of the sport that was inherited by European settlers in the nineteenth century. By far the most notorious and most repeated account of early lacrosse concerns a contest witnessed by Alexander Henry during the **Pontiac rebellion** of the 1760s and described in his *Travels and Adventures in Canada* (1809). The game in question was played between the Chippewa and the Sauk at Fort Michilimackinac on the occasion of the birthday of George III, 4 June 1763. The two teams conspired to use the contest to mask an intended attack on the British fort. Having drawn the officers out of the fort to view the game, at a prearranged signal Ojibwa charged the fort, killed over 70 soldiers, and took many others—including **Alexander Henry**—prisoner. The massacre and capture of the fort are a major feature of the folklore and history of lacrosse, and very likely perpetuated the idea that Indian lacrosse was brutal.

The *Montreal Gazette*, on 1 August 1833, carried the earliest newspaper reference to lacrosse in a report on an all-Indian game that represented merely one element of an initiation ceremony for five new chiefs.[7] The best-known and most visible Native centres of lacrosse in British North America were the Caughnawaga (Iroquois) reserve near Montreal and the St Regis (Iroquois) reserve near Cornwall. Although there were some attempts to package the Indian sport for white spectatorship in the mid-1830s, there are no records of non-Natives playing lacrosse until the Montreal 'Olympic' Games match in 1844.[8] The major thrust to competitive lacrosse came with the formation of the Montreal Lacrosse Club (MLC) in 1856.

The Montreal Lacrosse Club and the 'National' Game

In the early years of the MLC, members met in the field behind St James the Apostle Church, piled their surplus clothes in a heap, and played a lacrosse match among themselves before breakfast. The bond linking the men was their joint membership in and enthusiasm for the activities of both the Montreal Snow Shoe Club (MSSC) and the MLC.[9] Although there are no formal records of matches, it seems likely that the formation of the MLC was prompted by sporadic games during the 1840s and 1850s between MSSC members and the Caughnawagas. The MLC's leadership in the game is evident in an 1858 photograph, the first one taken of a non-Aboriginal lacrosse team.[10] The stick is seen to be of floor-to-shoulder length, but the major change from the Aboriginal style of racket was a much larger hoop or crook at the top and a greatly increased expanse of interwoven thongs (made from rawhide, gut, or clock strings) to form a flat surface of stringing some 20 centimetres wide at the top and tapering down to the shaft about one-third of the length of the stick. Clearly this transformed lacrosse stick signalled major changes, such as an increased emphasis on passing the ball.

Before 1860 there were no established playing rules. Instead, rules were understood among devotees; playing conditions and standards of acceptable conduct were mutually agreed upon by participants before a match. With only three non-Native clubs in Montreal—the MLC, the Hochelaga (1858), and the Beaver (1859)[11]—rule formalization was not deemed necessary. In fact, the social aspect of getting together and playing the early games seemed to be stronger than the interest in winning.[12] A noticeable injection of enthusiasm for the game and its standardization resulted from the visit to Canada of the Prince of Wales and his entourage in August 1860. Newspapers followed his every move. Upon his arrival in Montreal he was ushered into the grounds shared by the Montreal Cricket and Lacrosse Clubs to witness a 'Grand Display of Indian Games'.[13] The 'games' were actually two lacrosse contests sandwiched between an introductory Indian war dance and a concluding Indian foot race. Featured in the first lacrosse match were an Iroquois team and an Algonkian team, with 30 players a side. But the special event of the day—for which the Prince asked that the first contest be halted!—was a game between 25 selected Natives and 25 'gentlemen players of Montreal'. The **Prince of Wales** medal was eventually awarded to the Native team.[14]

More important than the event itself was the subsequent publication of the first lacrosse rules in a brochure entitled 'The Game of Lacrosse'.[15] Advertised in Montreal newspapers beginning on 15 September 1860,[16] it contained notes on the construction of a stick, sketches on methods of throwing and catching the ball, tactical points on checking, dodging, and goalkeeping, and a set of eight playing rules:

1. No swiping is allowed.
2. No tripping, holding, or any such unfair play is allowed.
3. Throwing the ball with the hand is prohibited, though if in a struggle, and opponents around, it may sometimes be kicked with the foot.
4. Picking up the ball with the hand is not allowed, except in extreme cases, where the Crosse cannot get it, such as in a hole, etc.
5. After every game the players change sides, unless the players who tossed up agree otherwise.
6. If a ball flung at the goal is caught by the 'goal-keeper' but breaks through his Crosse and enters the goal, it is in. Or, if a player of either side puts the ball in by accident, it is game for the party who were attacking that goal.
7. In facing, neither of the 'facers' shall attempt to gain the ball till 'three' is counted.
8. When a player is posted in a certain position, he must remain there, unless a favourable chance presents itself for him to leave it, and then he should return to his former position.[17]

These 'rules', which obviously left a great deal to the imagination, reflect not only an initial attempt to formalize the sport but an embryonic stage of lacrosse development.

Before 1867, lacrosse was played on fields of varying dimensions (some were almost a kilometre in length) with teams that fluctuated between 10 and 60 players. Goalposts with no cross bar or net, often surmounted with a single pennant or 'flag', were planted in the ground at either end. With the transformation of the stick in the 1850s, lacrosse moved away from the mass attacks of the Native running game and became more of a passing game that emphasized teamwork and positional play. Goals were likely infrequent since a match was won when the first goal was scored (a goal in the terminology of the time was a 'game'). From all accounts, spectator interest was minimal and the sport was confined to a triangular region bounded by Montreal, Cornwall, and Ottawa.

Expansion of the sport was inspired almost single-handedly by a Montreal dentist, Dr George William Beers. In 1861, lacrosse boasted nine clubs in Montreal, but the American Civil War dampened the spread and development of the game until Beers undertook the task himself. Born in Montreal in 1843, he attended Phillips School and **Lower Canada College** and was then apprenticed to a Dr Dickenson to complete his formal education in dentistry.[18] A product of Montreal's burgeoning sport environment during the 1840s and 1850s, Beers was picked as one of the goalkeepers for the match played before the Prince of Wales, and under the pseudonym 'Goalkeeper' he wrote the 1860 brochure. An ardent patriot, he was one of the founders of the Victoria Rifles Volunteers militia unit, formed during the Fenian raids of the early 1860s, and recruited members of the Montreal and Beaver lacrosse clubs. He retired from military service in 1881 with the rank of Captain.[19]

George Beers's propagandizing of things Canadian was clearly in evidence during the decade of Confederation. By 1865 he had published three articles in popular magazines— 'A Rival to Cricket', 'The Voyageurs of Canada', and 'Canada in Winter'—all with distinct national themes.[20] Within the dental profession he founded and published the *Canadian Journal of Dental Science*, the first attempt at dental journalism in Canada. Unquestionably, George Beers adopted a leadership posture in his vocation and avocation, and in the latter respect he was nothing short of a 'flaming lacrosse evangelist'. Capitalizing on the nationalistic fervour of the Confederation year, Beers provided several stimuli towards the expansion of lacrosse. In Montreal newspapers, for example, he wrote several articles under the banner 'The National Game', in which he argued the merits of lacrosse over the imported, revered sport of cricket.[22] Beers was responding to an article published one day earlier under the pseudonym 'Stumps', who had argued that cricket alone, an established sport of the British upper classes in Canada, deserved to be heralded as the new Dominion's national game. Beers's lengthy response was uncharacteristically mild, very likely because he was in the throes of attempting to nationalize lacrosse by riding the crest of pro-Confederation enthusiasm.

In the spring of 1867 there were about 10 lacrosse clubs in Canada; by the end of October there were 80, with some 2,000 members, and Beers was the catalyst for this expansion. On 1 July 1867, the MLC adopted 17 rules as the official 'Laws of Lacrosse'; drawn up by Beers and published in the *Montreal Gazette* on 17 July 1867, they were made available for sale through that newspaper's offices. The publication and dissemination of these rules had a crucial impact on the evolution of the sport. Uniformity of playing regulations is a hallmark of modern competitive sport, and common rules are the very foundation on which the spread of any sport depends. Beers's new 'Laws of Lacrosse' standardized the number of players at 12, the nature of the ball (India rubber), playing positions, the use of umpires (quasi-referees), and the method for determining the outcome of a match (best 3 out of 5 'games' or goals, instead of the previously unpredictable system of 'first goal wins'). Beers's rules provided an instant recipe for competition; all that was lacking was a competitive structure.

In 1867, Beers and the members of the MLC prompted lacrossists in the Montreal, Cornwall, Ottawa, and Toronto areas to attend a lacrosse convention in Kingston, Ontario,[23] to adopt formally a common code of playing rules, and to organize a national association to promote and perpetuate lacrosse as the national sport of Canada. Kingston, a central location, was strategic in Beers's conscious effort to expand the sport outside Montreal; it was also the site of the Provincial Exhibition. The Kingston Lacrosse Club issued an official invitation and 52 delegates representing 27 clubs assembled in Kingston's Temperance Hall on 26–27 September 1867. One of the major outcomes of this convention was the formation of Canada's first sport governing body, the National Lacrosse Association (NLA), with a mandate to administer the sport by codifying and enforcing rules, and to encourage all clubs to join the Association.[24] A detailed constitution was drafted and published verbatim in several newspapers, including the *Montreal Gazette* on 15 October 1867.

Without question, the formation of the NLA was a brilliant stroke of promotional strategy that resulted almost immediately in the proliferation of lacrosse clubs in Quebec and Ontario. In Toronto alone, 13 new clubs—the Maple Leaf, the Osgoode, the Toronto, the Ontario, and several military teams—were formed and playing within one month of the convention.[25] Thus the two major urban centres in Canada embraced lacrosse and effectively secured its future. Montrealers figured prominently in the executive of the NLA; the inveterate snowshoer, Nicholas 'Evergreen' Hughes (a founding member of the MSSC in 1843), was elected president and Beers was elected to the central administrative position of secretary-treasurer. Another testament to Beers's recognized organizational efficiency was the virtual adoption of his 'Laws of Lacrosse' with only minor modifications, such as the appointment of a referee in matches and the standardization of field length to a minimum of 150 yards (approximately 137 metres).

In effect, the establishment of the NLA constituted an overt attempt to popularize a particular sport at a time when sport in general was the preserve of the upper classes. Moreover, the NLA was part of Beers's drive to enshrine lacrosse as Canada's national game. He claimed repeatedly that lacrosse had been sanctified as Canada's national game by an Act of Parliament, and this came to be believed. For example, Henry Roxborough, in *The Story of Nineteenth-Century Canadian Sport* (1966), declared: 'Lacrosse is especially linked with Confederation Year, for the Dominion's first parliament had proclaimed it to be Canada's national game.'[26] However, nowhere in the Dominion's first parliamentary session is lacrosse even mentioned. And no Montreal or Toronto newspaper in 1867 reports such a proclamation or enactment. The 1894 edition of the *Dictionnaire Canadien-Francais* stated that lacrosse became the national game of Canada on 1 January 1859.[27] Beers wrote a book on the sport, entitled *Lacrosse: The National Game of Canada* (1869),[28] in which he made the following claim:

> I believe that I was the first to propose the game of lacrosse as the national game of Canada in 1859; and a few months preceding the proclamation of Her Majesty, uniting the Provinces of Canada, Nova Scotia and New Brunswick, into one

A lacrosse match on the Shamrock Grounds, Montreal, 1867. (Library and Archives Canada, C-87235)

> Dominion, a letter headed 'Lacrosse—Our National Field Game' published by me in
> the *Montreal Daily News*, in April 1867, was printed off and distributed throughout
> the whole Dominion, and was copied into many of the public papers.[29]

Beers was only 16 years old in 1859. Furthermore, in a year when only three lacrosse clubs—
all in Montreal—were known to exist, it seems unlikely that such an Act would have been
considered. *The Canadian Parliamentary Proceedings and Sessional Papers* and the *Journals
of the Legislative Council of the Province of Canada* reveal that Parliament was not even
in session in either January or July 1859 and that no mention of lacrosse was made in
those publications during the entire year. As for the 1867 letter, only selected issues of the
April 1867 editions of the *Daily News* could be located; but every April and May issue of
the *Montreal Gazette*, the *Montreal Herald*, the *Ottawa Citizen*, and the *Toronto Globe* were
combed, to no avail, to ferret out Beers's letter. No sporting contests at all were mentioned
by the *Globe* and the *Gazette* in April 1867. Considering that the British Parliament passed
the Act to create the Dominion of Canada on 29 March 1867, April would have been a good
month to begin such a publicity campaign. All research[30] suggests that any such campaign
must have been by word-of-mouth only, or was a figment of Beers's fervent imagination.

Beers, it would seem, invented the whole national-game concept, which nevertheless
managed to gain acceptance by a kind of consensual validity: if something is claimed to
be true enough times, it is often accepted as truth—then and now. By late 1867, the sport

was indeed surrounded by a 'national' aura; for example, the formation and acceptance of the name National Lacrosse Association had its own connotation; and the Association's provision of a banner for 'championship' play bore the slogan 'Our Country and Our Game'.[31]

Public Popularity and Winning

Lacrosse was a featured event in many **Dominion Day** celebrations. Five thousand Montreal spectators watched the Caughnawagas defeat the Montreal Lacrosse Club, whose members wore white caps, white jackets with red cuffs, grey knickerbockers with a red sash, and black stockings.[32] These costumes promoted the public popularity of lacrosse over cricket; lacrosse was all colour and rapid motion whereas—to all but devout cricketers—cricket was cream in colour and almost slow motion. In late October the *Gazette* stated:

> Every Saturday afternoon particularly, the Parks and Commons are crowded with Lacrosse players, from the Professor who doffs the gown for the occasion, to the little urchin who can barely scrape together 50 cents to purchase a Crosse.[33]

In November 1867, T. James Claxton, the millionaire head of a Montreal wholesale dry goods company,[34] donated four championship 'flags' (poles topped with banners in goal-flag style and valued at over $250) for challenge competition in the city.[35] Together with the NLA's banner—'Our Country and Our Game'—and the City of Toronto championship medal, the emphasis in lacrosse had shifted from social conviviality to more intense levels of competition.

The years between 1868 and 1885 were pivotal in the development and growth of lacrosse in Canada. With an established set of rules, a governing agency, 'championship' incentives such as the Claxton flags and the NLA banner, and the promotion of the national-game concept, lacrosse moved towards a greater emphasis on winning. Moreover, as skills were refined, the game increasingly became a drawing card. In 1876, for example, 8,000 spectators attended a game in Toronto between the Montreal Shamrocks and the Toronto Lacrosse Club.[36] The Shamrocks embodied the spiralling emphasis on winning lacrosse games.[37] Formed in **Griffintown** along the Lachine Canal in 1867, the Shamrock Lacrosse Club was composed of Irish Roman Catholic working-class members in an era when the playing fields were dominated by middle-class Protestants. In 1876 when the Shamrocks met the Toronto club, which had an Irish Protestant membership, there was a built-in rivalry that could only enhance the emphasis on winning from a spectator point of view. Although lacrosse and other team sports were slowly evolving towards more intensive competition and its attendant behaviours, the Shamrocks were ahead of their time in their total dedication to winning first and foremost. They were constantly accused of dirty play and ungentlemanly conduct, and subjected to media attributions such as the 'unwashed' and 'denizens of Griffintown' (insulting allusions to the Shamrocks' working-class origins and to the district of Montreal in which they and their supporters lived); they won three times as many championship matches as the Toronto club, their closest rival, between Confederation and 1885.[38]

The Shamrocks represented only the tip of the iceberg of the lacrosse phenomenon that was crystallizing. It was not merely a matter of behaviour fitting only the 'denizens of

Griffintown'. Protests and disputes over game outcomes among 'crack' or first-class teams were common during the 1870s. As early as 1867, Natives were barred from playing for white clubs in 'championship' matches, which operated on a challenge basis before 1885 rather than through the league structure that is common in modern sport. The ban against Natives in such competitions was due both to social exclusivity and to a perception that they naturally possessed superior skills in lacrosse. At the same time, commercialism first crept, then galloped, into lacrosse as it became a gate-taking sport in the 1870s. For example, $100 was offered as top prize for the winning team at a Paris, Ontario, lacrosse tournament in 1868,[39] and in 1875 the Shamrocks played the Caughnawagas for the 'championship of the world' and a $500 cash prize.[40]

The expense of maintaining high-calibre lacrosse clubs escalated in the 1870s. Teams and their organizers had to contend with rising costs in transportation, facility lease or purchase, facility maintenance, and spectator attractions—hiring bands to play at the matches, printing programs, installing telegraph connections to cater to fan interest and media demands, and hiring groups or vendors to sell refreshments. Clubs became heavily dependent on admission revenues—about 25 cents plus 10 cents more for a grandstand seat at most matches before 1885, despite initial newspaper criticism that this practice smacked of professionalism. But the emphasis on winning and the commercialization necessitated professional practices. Skilled lacrosse players were offered inducements— cash bonuses and job placements—by teams recruiting non-local talent. Lacrosse clubs and the NLA were actually run by professional administrators, middle-class businessmen who had an interest in sport but seemingly possessed a rigorous loyalty to pristine amateurism. The only way the NLA could control player inducements was to institute, in 1877, a residence rule to prevent 'tourist' lacrosse players from jumping from team to team.[41] It was a band-aid measure that did not stop the flow of commercialism in lacrosse. As had been the case with the Indian brand of lacrosse, gambling was entrenched in the sport by the 1870s. At various venues of the clubs in Ontario and Quebec as early as 1870, the NLA put up posters prohibiting gambling on site and threatened to expel violators. Yet both the *Toronto Globe* and the *Montreal Gazette* frequently reported betting information throughout the 1870s. Moreover, the Shamrocks actually promoted betting. One of the club's officers, the owner of the Tansey House, sold pools at his tavern. After one victory over Toronto in 1881 the *Star* estimated that Shamrock supporters collected over $15,000 in bets.[42] The *Montreal Gazette*, in 1869 and 1876, also reported pool-selling at Tansey's.[43]

Lacrosse was being propelled, via human agency, against the grain of an idealistic value system—amateurism (see Chapter 4)—that was used as a policy and a means of regulating the sport. Although commercialism and gambling were by-products of the 1870s, an emphasis on winning and rumours of scandals in other sports, such as 'pedestrianism' (any foot race) and rowing, made organizations like the NLA wary of the 'intrusion' of professionalism; it was a canker to be eradicated. At first, the link between money and professionalism was subjected to minor control. In 1876, Article IX of the revised NLA constitution stated:

> No Club in the Association shall play for a money challenge except with Indians. Any club playing for money (except as aforesaid) shall be suspended from membership in the Association.[44]

But playing for a stake or wager apparently continued to be a problem. Natives were almost axiomatically labelled professional by virtue of their skill. By 1880, Aboriginal teams were excluded from NLA championship games on the basis of race and perceived skill advantage and were assigned professional status by the NLA. In the same year, the NLA changed its name to the National Amateur Lacrosse Association (NALA) and adopted a formal policy of strict amateur membership (i.e., non-Native players and no monetary connections to players except travel and accommodation expenses) and enforcement.[45] This was a futile effort to stem the tide of commercialism. Frustrated by their inability to control semi-professional and professional practices—such as direct payments to players by clubs—the Montreal Lacrosse Club actually withdrew from the NALA between 1880 and 1882.

By the late 1870s and early 1880s, the popularity and dispersion of lacrosse had outstripped the most optimistic dreams of that eccentric lacrosse salesman, George W. Beers. Competitive levels of organized lacrosse were categorized on the basis of proficiency into junior, intermediate, and senior divisions. Although Ontario was the 'hotbed' of the sport, by 1881 Manitoba—whose first lacrosse club, the Prince Rupert, was established in 1871—had two clubs affiliated with the NALA: the Garry and the Winnipeg.

A major contributor to the widespread and rapid rise to popularity of lacrosse was its spectator appeal. Not only was it fast-paced, colourful, and easy to understand, but it was a rugged body-contact sport that led to disputes and rough or violent play. Since the goals were only two sticks placed about two metres apart, the players, umpires, and spectators were often in disagreement about whether the ball had passed inside, outside, or over the top of the goals. By the mid-1870s, lacrosse reports in the newspapers were filled with descriptions of game delays over the alleged incompetence of officials and of excessively rough and even violent behaviour (slashing, fouling, and fighting). Between 1867 and 1885, the incidence of disputes and rough play during championship matches was more than double that of exhibition or regular games.[46] Rules against foul play, cross-checking, deliberate charging, interfering, and threatening to strike appeared as early as 1878 and reflected the spread of such behaviours. But they were very likely crowd-drawing features; rough sport was irresistible to many and part of the 'manliness' of the game (see Chapter 8).

There were more positive aspects to lacrosse. Skill levels accelerated from 1867 to 1885. As the game evolved and players became more experienced; they refined positional play and offensive and defensive tactics. Basic skills of throwing and catching evolved from early underarm patterns to sidearm and overhand techniques. Beers's *Lacrosse: The National Game of Canada*, which was filled with lacrosse mechanics, was widely sold in 1869 and again in 1879 when it was reprinted. Two publications that were virtual plagiarisms— 'Hints to Players by a Native' printed in an 1871 issue of *Canadian Magazine*[47] and W.K. McNaught's *Lacrosse and How to Play It*[48]—served to disseminate and enhance playing skills and thereby advanced the sport.

Showcasing the Game

Perhaps one of the strongest unifying factors in the spread and acceptance of lacrosse was its export as a showcase activity and as a symbol of Canada to Great Britain in 1867, in 1876, and again in 1883. Nineteenth-century Canadian sport thrived on cordial sporting ties with England, and British North America had imported most of its sport, as well as its traditions and values, from English and Scottish immigrants. A precedent for international tours was established in the late 1850s when an English cricket eleven toured British North America. Canada, in turn, sent teams of marksmen to the world-famous annual rifle championships at Wimbledon. Acting on an offhand suggestion, Captain W.B. Johnson of the Montreal Lacrosse Club engaged 16 Caughnawagas to leave Canada on 12 July 1867 and tour England to demonstrate lacrosse. But Johnson was mainly interested in the financial prospects of the venture; the visit was not publicized and was short-lived and of little consequence.[49]

In the mid-1870s another MLC member, Dr Thomas Archer, moved to London, England, and persuaded the Thames Hare and Hounds Club to form a lacrosse club. Subsequently Archer corresponded with Beers to explore the possibilities of a tour. Beers persuaded Mr Charles Rose to visit Britain in 1875 to solicit support for a lacrosse trip. With the verbal and financial encouragement of the celebrated Hurlingham Polo Club, it was decided that lacrosse teams would be sent to Britain. Public subscriptions were sought in Montreal, a Committee of Management of the MLC was struck, and discussions about ensuring success were predicated on sending one team of Natives along with a white team.[50] The trip was at least partially envisaged as a Canadian image-builder: 'Thousands will go to see Canada's game to one who would go to hear Canada's immigration agents.'[51]

Beers, of course, primarily desired to sell lacrosse to Great Britain not only as a game but also as a symbol of Canada. Before the teams' departure, the Montreal press gave details of the trip under the banner 'Young Canada'. In Britain, the press used material from Beers's book to educate its readers on the nature of the game, but the real media emphasis was laid on its Aboriginal origins, including the 1763 Fort Michilimackinac incident (although the press was careful to point out that Iroquois were not involved in that massacre). The fact that this historical buildup in all the British papers ran parallel to the games suggests that it was pre-packaged and pre-released by Beers. The tour was drenched in Aboriginal imagery; the Natives themselves were Beers's advertising gimmick and his drawing-card for the British.

The teams played 16 games during their month-and-a-half foray through Ireland, Scotland, and England. The order of ceremonies was repeated for each match. The Natives were escorted to centre field in their playing costumes, which consisted of red-and-white striped 'guernseys' (jerseys, or tunics) and knickers, with white hose (or red-and-yellow striped knickers); blue velvet caps overlaid with much ornamental bead work and topped by two or three scarlet feathers; and tight-fitting sashes and waist belts of blue velvet with a large letter C (for Caughnawaga) on the front. In addition, all the Natives wore earrings and many silver-coloured finger rings. Against the stark green backdrop of the cricket grounds on which they played, and the creams of the cricket players, they were vivid to say the least. Next, the 13-member MLC team came onto the grounds wearing white **guernseys**, grey tweed knickers, and dark brown hose. After brief introductions to the chief dignitary present, the match commenced.

The British reaction was most favourable and 3,000–5,000 spectators attended each of the games. Enthusiastic descriptions of the Natives and the equipment used in lacrosse were plentiful in the British press. The most eloquent characterization of a lacrosse stick was rendered in the *London Daily Telegraph*: 'a spoon of Brobdingnagian size and Filigree pattern'.[52] Both teams had been carefully coached to be above reproach; the players were commended repeatedly for their exemplary behaviour in the intervals between matches, whether touring cairns, castles, or collieries. Always on such occasions, away from the playing fields, the Natives were asked to wear their lacrosse outfits. Between games they

The Canadian lacrosse team that toured England and Ireland in 1883; Dr Beers is in the centre. This is the first known use of the maple leaf emblem to denote a 'national' team in Canadian sport. (Courtesy of Don Morrow)

were urged to hold snowshoe races on the grass, to dance 'war dances' or the 'green corn dance', or to hold mock 'powwows'. During the contests Keraronwe, who spoke English very well, made 'wild verbal ejaculations' and frantic gestures to his teammates. **James Fenimore Cooper** could not have contrived a more colourful image of stereotypical 'Indian-ness' for these early 'Harlem Globetrotters' of lacrosse.

Near-sanctification came to the tour when Queen Victoria requested that a private game be played before her at Windsor Castle on 25 June 1876. This audience was interpreted even in Toronto as indicative of 'the estimation in which this country is held by the highest person in the Empire'.[53] Before the game, Keraronwe read the Queen a speech—inscribed on a colourfully decorated piece of birch-bark—in his native tongue. The irony was that both the speech and the artwork on the birch-bark were fashioned by Mrs H.W. Becket, the wife of one of the MLC players.[54] After the match and the usual snowshoeing displays, the monarch presented each player with an autographed picture of herself.

Back in Montreal the teams were extolled as 'representatives of the young manhood of Canada' at a civic reception in the Victoria Rink (heavily decorated with lacrosse sticks and snowshoes).[55] Financially, the trip, which cost nearly $12,000, broke even; however, its success must be measured in terms of the lacrosse-Canada-Aboriginal symbolism promoted to the British. Seven years later, in 1883, a more upscale tour was organized, specifically to use the lacrosse-'Indian' image to sell Canada to potential British immigrants. George Beers was, once again, the tour organizer. Two teams of Caughnawagas and MLC players combined with six Toronto Lacrosse Club players for the 1883 tour. Glowing tributes to and expansive coverage of oarsman Ned Hanlan's triumphs in Great Britain gave firm evidence that the link between sporting prowess and Canadian nationhood had developed greatly since the 1876 tour. This was Beers's chance to exert the lacrosse muscle of Canada. Furthermore, there had been only two British lacrosse clubs in existence before the 1876 tour, but in 1883 it was estimated that there were around 150.[56] In some ways this meant that the teams faced a stronger challenge than they had encountered in 1876.

The tour was frantic; 62 matches were played in 41 different cities in just over two months—a heavier schedule than that of most modern professional baseball teams. It is notable that no member of the Shamrocks was invited to go on the tour, even though the team was the most successful in Canada by 1883. Were the working-class Shamrocks not the 'proper' group to build a Canadian image? (Several references in the Montreal press during the tour forecasted an 1884 Shamrocks tour of the British Isles.) The players docked in Liverpool and the tour started in Scotland. The teams went on to London for games in its vicinity, then to the southwest coast of England, followed by games in the southeast. They then ventured into the Midlands and the manufacturing towns before touring northern cities and, finally, municipalities in Ireland. In all, they travelled over 9,000 kilometres by train in Britain, mostly at night. Extracts from British press accounts that were republished in the *Toronto Globe* and the *Montreal Gazette* indicate that the dominant image was exactly the same as that of the 1876 tour; the Natives—dressed in scarlet this time—dominated. The 'Canadian Gentlemen' (were Natives not Canadian gentlemen?) were dressed in bright blue with a white maple-leaf crest—perhaps the first used in association with Canadian sport—encasing the letter 'C' emblazoned on their jerseys.

The 1883 tour went well beyond the subtle advertising of its 1876 counterpart. The distinct role of both teams was to act as a collective immigration agent. With the unprecedented co-operation and financial support of the federal Department of Agriculture, team members distributed 150,000 immigration flyers certified by the Governor-General, and a total of 120 cases, each weighing 660 kilograms, containing copies of a special supplement of the *Canadian Illustrated News* that described Canada's resources in words and pictures.[57] Beginning in the 1870s, Canada had stepped up its immigration methods— in fierce competition with those used by the United States, Australia, and Africa[58]—and the 1883 tour was a state-driven propaganda campaign that used lacrosse as the delivery system. As if the written barrage was not enough to saturate British lacrosse audiences, Beers arranged to have lectures or speeches about Canada's resources given in every city. An MP and two ordained ministers accompanied the teams for this purpose, and their messages were often reprinted in the British press.[59] The valuable work of the lacrosse players in bringing the country into greater prominence was applauded by the federal government,[60] and Beers was acclaimed for writing some 300 letters in answer to immigration queries while in Britain.[61] The dominant image portrayed to the British public during the 1883 tour was that of a young, resourceful nation that had carried on the sporting tradition of Great Britain through its national Aboriginal game of lacrosse. The entire tour must have been an endurance contest for the players. The fact that they did not rebel, and that public reaction to the games was excellent (if judged by glowing letters written home by the players and by crowds that numbered up to 8,000 per game), is a tribute to the organizational prowess of Beers and the players' devotion to him, and to the immigration device.

League Play and Commercialization

By the mid-1880s, lacrosse was a major, perhaps *the* major, popular team sport in Canada. Undoubtedly the fame of the lacrosse tours enhanced the attraction to the sport for both players and spectators. The British blessing on lacrosse combined with the forces of commercialization, professionalism (in the true sense of the word), and organizational changes to develop the game. For example, at the 1885 NALA convention, a league or series system of matches was adopted for senior lacrosse competition.[62] That is, instead of a challenge system of games a league schedule for the season was created and a playoff format was established. The initiation of the league system launched lacrosse into the format of modern sport and provided an organizational framework that triggered considerable change and growth in the sport. Next to Beers's contributions to the image of lacrosse as the national game, this development was the most important change in the game's history. In the 30-year period preceding the First World War, lacrosse activity intensified in Quebec and especially in Ontario. Although the game was launched in the major cities of the Maritimes during the 1880s and 1890s,[63] it never gained a firm, established acceptance. Saint John, Halifax, Pictou, Windsor, Springhill, and other centres formed clubs, played sporadically, and disbanded. It seems that in the Maritimes the British sports of cricket and rugby football, as well as the American pastime of baseball, were of more interest than lacrosse.[64] By contrast, rivalries among cities in Ontario and Quebec were so intense and the emphasis on winning so strong that disputes over the league system plagued the NALA constantly for three years after its implementation. Toronto clubs rebelled in 1887 and formed a rival second league, the Canadian Lacrosse Association (CLA). Most Ontario clubs became affiliated with the CLA while Quebec and eastern Ontario clubs remained loyal to the NALA. By 1889, the CLA had established 11 geographical districts to provide manageable leagues for the various levels of play. The two associations actually had to agree to draw a boundary line at Peterborough for recruitment of top players for the senior championship series. Fractionalization occurred in 1889 when the Shamrocks, the MLC, and the Toronto, Cornwall, and Ottawa clubs broke off all affiliation and created a Senior League with home-and-home matches (one home and one away game for each pair of teams).[65]

All of these organizational changes in the late 1880s resulted in a dilution of lacrosse management and inconsistent administrative direction in the development of the sport. When the Senior League became an elite league in its own right, the governing bodies were severely weakened and were left to organize junior and intermediate levels of lacrosse during the 1890s. The CLA became the largest association, governing rural lacrosse strongholds within a 160-kilometre radius of Toronto (southern Ontario was a baseball Mecca).[66] Recognition of the Toronto heartland of lacrosse—although the Athletics of St Catharines was the most successful club between 1885 and 1914[67]—was demonstrated in 1901 when the Globe Publishing Company donated the Globe Shield for senior CLA supremacy (thereby replacing the CLA banner).[68] Presumably Globe spokespersons felt that lacrosse promotion was a significant campaign tool to increase newspaper sales, but the existence of a major trophy also enhanced championship prestige.

In the two decades surrounding 1900, lacrosse developed rapidly in the western provinces. Manitoba and British Columbia in particular became major centres of the sport. With a precedent for the structural system established in Ontario and Quebec, lacrosse was able to develop very quickly from intra-club matches to challenges to championship play to league structures in Winnipeg, Brandon, Portage La Prairie, Vancouver, Victoria, and New Westminster. The change in 1887 from the best two of three or three of five goal systems in the East[69] to a 2–2.5-hour time limit was easily adopted in the West. The New Westminster Salmonbellies emerged from their late 1880s triangle of competitions with Vancouver and Victoria and travelled east in 1890 to play the best teams in Toronto and Montreal. With a 5–1 win–loss record, the Salmonbellies returned to a tumultuous reception in their home town: 'The Royal City stood on its head to welcome home the conquering heroes, and they hung a gold locket around the scarred neck of each player.'[70]

By the mid-1890s, the CLA and the NALA were geographic misnomers because they were regional sport governing bodies. The British Columbia Amateur Lacrosse Association (BCLA) governed the sport in that province, while most major prairie city lacrosse clubs were under the umbrella of the Western Canadian Lacrosse Association (WCLA). In fact, by 1900, the WCLA boasted club memberships from Fort William and Port Arthur (now Thunder Bay), through Minneapolis and St Paul, to cities in southern Alberta. All sport governing bodies relied on and adopted the rules and constitution of the established NALA. Although leadership in lacrosse generally flowed from east to west, major innovations, such as the use of goal nets in the BCLA in 1897, did affect the game across the country.[71] Lacrosse became a truly national championship sport in 1901 when the Governor-General, the Earl of Minto, donated a cup for challenge competition among the champions of the senior lacrosse leagues in Canada. As the emblem of national supremacy the Minto Cup engendered intense competition over the next 13 years. Significantly, British Columbia teams held the Minto Cup without a loss between 1908 and 1914. In fact, they dominated early twentieth-century lacrosse at the elite level, stimulated by the Salmonbellies' new style of lacrosse tactics—they turned from methodical positional play using long passes towards free-flowing, shorter passes, hitting the open man, and a run-run-run offence.[73]

Rough play increased during the 1890s and the early years of the twentieth century. Violent play was repeatedly blamed on incompetent referees, whose powers were extended beyond ejecting players from contests to imposing heavy fines. But the referees were merely scapegoats for the competitive emphasis in lacrosse, especially elite lacrosse, which prospered despite the pretense of amateurism. Native 'ringers', or skilled players, were imported for teams in the East and West and the recruitment of outstanding white players for financial inducements was prevalent in amateur circles. Hypocritical and inconsistent enforcement of amateur regulations was at the root of the strife that existed among the NALA, the CLA, and the Senior League during the 1890s.[74] Although commercialism was basic to elite lacrosse, it was discountenanced at least publicly—as if an admission that money was a critical factor in the health of the sport would somehow destroy it. Suspensions of entire lacrosse teams from competitions were frequent, as when a court trial in 1898 disclosed that each member of the Capital Lacrosse Club of Ottawa had accepted a $100 bonus.[75] The whole conflict between amateurism and professionalism/commercialism reached a chaotic crescendo in 1904. In an effort to deal openly with the situation, the founding lacrosse club of Canada, the MLC, petitioned its governing body to allow known professionals to play with and/or against amateurs.[76] Although this was a significant, viable request that offered a workable solution, it was directly antithetical to strict amateur regulations. Within two years this initiative resulted in a protracted athletic war over the concession to professionals implemented by the MLC (see Chapter 4). Its resolution—a return to strict amateur regulations—was a giant step backward. Meanwhile, gambling and pool-selling on lacrosse matches continued unabated. In spite of the 1910 donation of the Mann Cup by railway magnate Sir Donald Mann to stimulate amateur lacrosse competition at the elite levels, and despite the formation in 1912 of a truly national governing body—the Canadian Amateur Lacrosse Association—commercially supported teams remained fundamental to elite lacrosse. In fact, two of the professional associations, the National Lacrosse Union and the Dominion Lacrosse Association, had become joint stock companies, with capital stock of $14,000 and $20,000 respectively.[77]

By 1914, the glorious years of the heyday of lacrosse were drawing to a close. The tug-of-war between amateur ideology and commercial forces was apparent in the promotion and development of the sport and yet both were viable—two ways of playing lacrosse, not merely the way of playing by vaunted amateur principles. The raiding of players was widespread at the professional level; amateur leagues were weakened because the best players were siphoned off from them. Salary wars were common among elite teams, and clauses were implemented in player–owner agreements to bind players to specific teams. Lacrosse moguls placed their emphasis on elite lacrosse and did not take sufficient measures to stimulate the sport in school or church leagues.[78] Lacking strong grassroots player development, and with amateur–professional fragmentation at the top levels, lacrosse fell into decline. On the commercial side, the sport faced the geographical dilemma that still plagues Canadian professional sports: a huge country with a relatively small population. Spectators were the only source of revenue, and there just were not enough of them. Although the game could not sustain itself commercially, amateur lacrosse was mired in commercial trends. Newspapers had great difficulty keeping track of the various leagues, divisions, clubs, and levels and gradually reduced their coverage of the sport. Meanwhile, media and public attention turned to the emerging and increasingly popular team sports of baseball, football, and ice hockey.[79]

The halcyon days of lacrosse were the years between 1867 and 1885 when George Beers and the great tours brought the game into prominence as a national symbol of Canada. That symbol was tarnished, since lacrosse originated with Canada's Natives, who were shamefully used in the transformation of the sport from its Aboriginal to its modern form. Although lacrosse re-emerged during the Depression as box lacrosse (boxla) and has been promoted in that form at various times over the past 50 years, interest in this sport has been confined to pockets of southern Ontario, parts of Quebec, and southern British Columbia (and much more prominently in American colleges and universities on the eastern seaboard). Of considerable intrigue, in 1994 both hockey and lacrosse were declared Canada's national sports—for winter and summer respectively—by the federal Parliament in the National Sports Act. For lacrosse—now played by men's and women's teams in localized areas and among a variety of educational institution-supported teams—the government sanction is fitting tribute to its heritage as a significant form of Canadian culture.

Baseball Roots

Unlike the team sports of lacrosse, football, and hockey, which originated and developed in Montreal, the Canadian origins of baseball were in southwestern Ontario. Its development is far more community-rooted and commercially-based than the more controlled, early evolution of lacrosse. Ultimately, baseball was infused into almost every city and community in Canada, a distinct difference from lacrosse. Though profoundly American in its later development, with its star players, rules, leagues, and large financial backing, baseball was not 'invented', as legend has it, by Abner Doubleday in Cooperstown, New York, in 1839.[80] A game occurred one year earlier in Beachville, Ontario, halfway between Woodstock and Ingersoll. It was played in a form remarkably similar to the so-called 'New York' rules later established by the New York Knickerbrocker Club in 1845.[81]

Baseball must have had its origin in children's ball games—throwing and catching the ball, then batting it with a stick to a catcher. The loose development of a team composed of pitcher, catcher, batters running to bases, and fielders had obvious connections with the English games of rounders and even cricket. The Beachville game of 4 June 1838 was described by Adam E. Ford (1831–1906) in a letter published in part in the *Ingersoll Chronicle* on 20 May 1886 and later appeared in full in *Sporting Life*. The game, between the Beachville club and the Zorras, players from two neighbouring townships, was held on a holiday, **Militia Muster Day** (this was only six months after the Mackenzie Rebellion in Toronto), and took place in a field behind Enoch Burdick's shops. Four bases, called 'byes', marked the infield area, and there were foul areas—corroborating the early departure from cricket's 360-degree 'fair territory' (the 'oval') surrounding the batsman. Hits and runs were numerous, since the real fun was in getting runners out by 'plugging', that is, the runner, when caught between bases, could be tagged or hit (plugged) by a ball thrown at him. No one wore gloves; the score was kept by notches on a stick; and games lasted from six to nine innings. Games played earlier than 1838 (so Ford suggested) were declared finished when one team reached 18 or 21 runs. Finally, the players—Ford noted that the number per team varied between 7 and 12—ranged in age from 15 to 24. Ford named them all.[82] His letter and contemporary support for its veracity establish baseball as one of the earliest team sports in Canada. Moreover, it underscores the village roots of the game. Vestiges of the 1838 rules—namely, the use of 11 players and four bases and a common striker's box/home bye—remained in the Woodstock–Ingersoll area until at least 1860. The more popular New York game—which used 9 players and 3 bases—was in vogue in the United States and in other Ontario communities.

Generally speaking, cricket and rowing were the emerging summer sports in the 1850s and 1860s. For one thing, they benefited from the organizational skills and support of the local elite. Baseball was very much a working-man's sport and caught on quickly in Woodstock, Ingersoll, and even in the larger centre of Hamilton. In 1854, the year the Great Western Railway completed its main line (Niagara Falls–Hamilton–London–Windsor), the Hamilton Young Canadians became the first known organized team, with an executive, a membership fee, and a regular place to play.[83] They played the New York game, where every player had to be put out before the side was retired. The founders of the club were William and James Shuttleworth, a clerk and a shoemaker, and the members represented a wonderful array of working-class occupations: five clerks, three shoemakers, two turners, two labourers, and a coach manufacturer, a saloon-keeper, a painter, a marble-cutter, a brakeman, a tinsmith, one maker each of brooms, horse-collars, cigars, watches, carriages, and many others.[84] This overwhelming representation of the working class at both the playing and organizational levels also characterized other clubs in nearby communities, like the Dundas Mechanics, and eventually across the country, and (at least among the players) puts a stamp on baseball today.[85] It has had the salutary effect of exempting early southwestern Ontario baseball, relatively speaking, from the class manipulation so prevalent in other sports (such as lacrosse). As Bouchier points out, contrary to the organizational strictures of lacrosse:

throughout the nineteenth century Canadian baseball possessed no single sport governing institution to regulate various levels of competition. Without such a superstructure defining the range of 'legitimate' practices and meaning associated with the sport, baseball could never be totally controlled by middle class reformers.[86]

Brewing Professional Baseball

The most prominent team of the 1860s was the Woodstock Young Canadians, who played their first match in 1861 and were undefeated by a Canadian team until 1867, when they were beaten by the Dundas Independent Club.[87] Coopers, shoemakers, a carriage-maker, a blacksmith, a painter, and a grocer made up the Woodstock club in 1862, and three-quarters of these players were Ontario-born.[88] This club was instrumental in introducing the concept of baseball 'championship' play when, in 1863, they solicited subscriptions to purchase a silver ball, the winner of which would be designated the champion baseball club in Canada. It must not be assumed or implied that middle-class and professional men did not relish participating in, and watching, informal baseball games. The merchants and clerks from the 'Detroit and Windsor' sides of Ingersoll's King Street, for example, frequently challenged their business competitors from across the street.[89] Similarly, players from various districts of Woodstock's commercial area divided themselves up geographically to form teams; on one occasion employees working between 'Farrell's Hotel to Watson's Corner' played against those from 'White's to Woodroofe's blocks'.[90] Rarely, if ever, did men from dissimilar occupational backgrounds compete against each other. A further indication of the organization being brought into the sport was the formation of the Canadian Association of Baseball Players at Canada's first baseball convention held in Hamilton at the time of the Provincial Exhibition, on 30 September 1864.[91] Of course, this national designation was a misnomer; only southwestern Ontario teams were involved, although there were a few clubs in Victoria, BC, in 1863. The only evidence of clubs outside Ontario and British Columbia is in Montreal, where there was a baseball subsidiary of the Montreal Foot Ball Club in 1865, and in Halifax, where there were two clubs in 1867.[92]

By the end of the 1860s, community-rooted baseball teams were playing more and more inter- rather than intra-community games. For example, several Canadian teams placed quite well in the three categories (classes) of competition in an 1867 Detroit tournament.[93] One of the most extensive reports of early Canadian baseball appeared in the *Brampton Times* on 3 July 1868 and described a contest between Streetsville and Brampton. The account—in a self-satisfied tone typical of newspapers at the time—reveals a number of things about early baseball. The ludicrously uneven score in the five-inning game, 70–9, was quite common in an era when strikers (batters) could wait for their choice of pitches, when no player wore a glove (as the game increased in speed and the ball became more resilient, most players dusted rosin on their hands), and when fielders and infielders were usually quite inept at catching and throwing. 'Fly catches', or catching a fly ball, were not much practised, since a ball caught after the first bounce registered the same out. Streetsville used at least two American players in the contest and they were very likely 'crack ballists'. The players were praised for their 'gentlemanly bearing'—a moral expectation of the upper strata of athlete in most sports at the time—and this suggests either the desire to impose a measure of elite respectability on the working-class game, or that there were no fights among the players. The one umpire was an American, who probably stood behind the pitcher to make all calls in the game, a custom retained by baseball until well into the twentieth century, although some umpires gravitated to a place behind the catcher during the 1880s. Moral reformers were concerned about drinking and gambling and '**rowdyism**' at baseball games in these early years, even in small towns like Ingersoll and Woodstock, Ontario.[95]

In 1864, Woodstock played Guelph, beginning a rivalry in which Guelph came out on top, becoming the leading baseball town of the 1870s. The Guelph Maple Leafs wore only their work clothes and a red maple leaf sewn onto their shirts, but within two years they had adopted a formal set of bylaws.[96] Heated games between the two teams, with fights in the bleachers, were not uncommon. For example, on 4 August 1868 in Woodstock, 'toughs' from that town roamed the stands to provoke Guelph spectators and players. The lure of competitive baseball in southwestern Ontario seemed to outweigh its more sordid characteristics. Over the Dominion Day weekend in 1869, Woodstock hosted a three-day tournament, complete with substantial cash prizes derived from a $10 entrance fee to competing clubs and from subscriptions solicited from local businessmen. Some 5,000 people—at least a thousand in excess of Woodstock's entire population—watched Ingersoll defeat the Woodstock and Guelph clubs in the first-class competition.[97] Not to be outdone by Woodstock, London, the metropolis of southwestern Ontario, one month later held a much larger three-day tournament, involving 11 teams from eight Ontario towns alongside the Provincial Exhibition. The Guelph team won and received $150 in gold.[98] Nevertheless, disagreements over the rights to the prestigious Silver Ball trophy,[99] emblematic of the so-called Canadian championship, reached the point of threatened legal action. These games began in earnest the fierce community rivalry/loyalty that has been so much a part of baseball to this day.

At the helm of Guelph's rise to baseball dominance was entrepreneur George S. Sleeman (1841–1926). A prominent brewer during the 1860s and 1870s, he was civic-minded and absolutely committed to promoting and developing Guelph in any way possible. He was instrumental in the construction of the Guelph Opera House, brought the Provincial Fair to Guelph, was the owner of the first street railway in the city, and eventually became mayor of Guelph for a six-year term.[100] He was astute in recognizing the potential in baseball not only to enhance community spirit but to promote the city.

Sleeman's first contact with baseball was tied to the mid-1860s formation of his own factory team, the Silver Creeks. Games were held in the empty lot beside his brewery and Sleeman himself paid all expenses for equipment and road trips. His players were quite literally 'home brews'. The Maple Leafs, of course, were by far the better team. When Sleeman, along with 3,000 others, accompanied the Leafs to Woodstock for the 1869 Canadian championship game, the expertly played and exciting contest (which the Leafs won) must have been a revelation to the businessman.[101] He began to put money into the team and in the early 1870s, when baseball clubs existed throughout Ontario,[102] the Guelph Maple Leafs were acknowledged as the best team. The Leafs, with which the Silver Creeks had merged by 1873, employed the tactic of hiring two American players. In an era when money in almost any other sport (except in professional rowing and the Scots' Caledonian Games) was anathema to the conception of 'true' sport, Sleeman invested in the Leafs, realizing that money was essential, indeed critical, to the maintenance of the game.

In 1874, Sleeman was elected president of the Maple Leafs. One of the first things he did was to devise a set of club rules governing player behaviour in public.[103] Fines that ranged from $5 to $25 were deterrents. The strategy was sound. Players were often praised

Guelph's Maple Leaf Baseball Club, 1874. (From the *Montreal Amateur Athletic Association Scrapbook, volume 14.* Courtesy of Don Morrow)

for their 'gentlemanly' playing and bearing, both on and off the field. In June of 1874, Sleeman took the team at his own expense to Watertown, New York for the 'World' semi-pro championship. The Leafs won and took the $450 first prize. They won the Silver Ball both that year and the next. Correctly anticipating that the reputation of the Leafs would attract other teams, players, and fans to come to Guelph, Sleeman built the Wellington Hotel near the baseball grounds.

Sleeman worked hard to maintain Guelph's baseball pre-eminence. The Sleeman Papers at the University of Guelph are files, five centimetres thick, of correspondence to and from Sleeman for 1876 and 1877, containing letters regarding match dates, travel rates, equipment purchases, and (most abundant) player recruitment. Clearly, Sleeman must have known that the continuing quality of his baseball product depended on the calibre of players. In that regard alone, Sleeman's talent hunt was extraordinary. The Leafs' prowess in 1874 and 1875 was well known and candidates for his team wrote him from all over North America. For example, one such letter from the Sleeman collection reads, in part:

> The St. Louis Red Sox manr [manager] want me to play with them next season but
> I don [sic] like to stay there so I thought I would write to you and let you know that
> I will play with your team next season of (6) months commencing the 15th of April
> until the 15th of October to be paid in equal payments the first of every month. If

those figures suits [sic] you let me know immediately as I would like to have my contract signed as soon as possible for if I cannot make any terms I want to answer my other letters.

This was written on 16 November 1876 by T. Dolan of St Louis, Missouri. Similar letters came from Chicago, Brooklyn, Philadelphia, Ottawa, and many other places. Most correspondents were careful to praise their own talents. For example, on 25 August 1876 Mr Salisbury declared: 'I pitch both the in curve and out, also rising and falling balls.' Sleeman, who usually offered $100 per month plus board and transportation to and from Guelph, almost single-handedly set in motion the commercial chain of events that compelled other communities and clubs to follow suit.

On 7 April 1876, at the Walker House Hotel in Toronto, the Canadian Base Ball Association (CBBA) was formed at a convention held for that purpose.[104] Sleeman was elected president of the five-team league. The London Tecumsehs, the Guelph Maple Leafs, the Toronto Clippers, the Hamilton Standards, and the Kingston St Lawrence each paid the required $10 fee to enter 'championship' play, to be composed of four games against every other team (each team would play 16 'championship' games). The team achieving the greatest number of victories would be declared the winner. The CBBA copied the constitution and bylaws verbatim from the National Base Ball Association of the United States.[105] A 'Judiciary Committee' of five members—the real power or functional executive of the CBBA—decided on all matters of dispute, awarded the 'championship stream' (pennant), and set the 25-cent admission to all championship games, with the visiting clubs to receive 40 per cent of the game's cash receipts after expenses were deducted. Clearly, the injection of commercialism into the CBBA was inspired by Sleeman's success with his semi-professional Guelph team.

As for Sleeman himself, he remained heavily involved with the Leafs until the end of the 1877 season. His final baseball hurrah was his direction and promotion of a barnstorming tour by the Maple Leafs in 1886, a 54-game journey through Canada and the United States (as far away as Wheeling, West Virginia). For Sleeman and for baseball, the tour was highly successful. The Leafs won 47 games. On game nights, Guelph citizens swarmed around the telegraph offices to catch game reports. When the Leafs returned, 3,000 people gathered at the train station to greet them. This was the final tribute to Sleeman who, in a few years, had not only masterminded the rise to international success of the Leafs but made an imprint on baseball in general by helping to found the CBBA.

Between the mid-1850s and 1876, baseball's thread of development stretched from Hamilton to Woodstock to Guelph and then to London, which had a team as early as 1856. The London and Forest City clubs amalgamated in 1868 to form the Tecumseh Club (named after the Tecumseh Hotel in London where the 1868 club was formed); by 1876 it was one of the best-known teams in North America, playing serious professional baseball by American rules and with American players.[106] The real force behind the Tecumsehs was Jacob Lewis 'Angel' Englehart. Only 29 years of age in 1876, Englehart ran his own petroleum producing and refining company. By 1880, he was vice-president of the Imperial Oil Company, and his personal net worth was estimated at around $100,000.[107] With the formation of the CBBA in April 1876, London's oil baron set out to run the Tecumseh club in a business-like manner. Its executive body was a grade up the social hierarchy from the early organizers of Canadian baseball and bespoke an advancement in managerial sophistication beyond the one-man-rules and style of earlier times. Forty per cent of the 129 officers of the CBBA itself were white-collar workers and another 27 per cent were of the mercantile class (shopkeepers and hotel owners). Interestingly, 12 of the 129 CBBA personnel were existing or future mayors.[108] Englehart, then, represented the movement towards baseball organizers who were small manufacturers and/or local businessmen—an entrepreneurial orientation comprising a more broadly based group than the established businessmen and professionals who controlled major amateur sport organizations during the last third of the nineteenth century.[109]

Londoners were showered with top-notch baseball games in 1876. In addition to the series games, the Tecumsehs played 36 exhibition games against a variety of American teams, winning 31 of these games, strong evidence of their high quality. Londoners attended games held locally in crowds ranging from 2,000 to 6,000, proof positive to Englehart and others of the potential market for professional baseball. When Ed Moore, treasurer of the Tecumseh organization, umpired the third game of the London–Guelph 1876 series, he apparently bet on the Tecumsehs with a friend, the winner of the bet to receive a box of cigars. The Tecumsehs were indeed victorious, but Sleeman protested the result to the CBBA judiciary committee, which upheld the protest and declared the contest null and void.[110] The *Toronto Globe* was quick to forecast doom for baseball:

> There seems to be a good deal of feeling manifested on both sides, each club accusing the other of having professional players engaged, and neither of them giving the charge a direct denial. That there should be any foundation for such charges is having a disastrous effect upon the popularity of Base Ball; for when it begins to lose the character of a genuine amateur amusement . . . and partakes of the nature of a speculation in the engagement of mercenaries, and as a game for gamblers, its sordid side is sure to extinguish whatever favour it may have possessed, at least in the eyes of the Canadian public.[111]

The journalist was obviously influenced by the conservative British ideals of amateurism and proper moral behaviour so well entrenched in most Canadian sports emerging during the 1870s. However, baseball was heavily influenced by American forces, Canadian local entrepreneurs, and rural communities, not by British tradition or by large urban sporting configurations (such as the MAAA).

In February 1877, the Tecumseh and Guelph organizations decided to join the International Base Ball Association (IBBA), comprised of the two 'Canadian' entries and five strong American teams: the Alleghenys, Live Oaks, Ohio Buckeyes, Manchester, and Rochester. The Tecumseh executive raised subscriptions to build Tecumseh Park (now Labatt Park) on the outskirts of London and brought in five new American players, retaining five from the 1876 team. At the start of each Tecumseh season (from 1876 to 1878), the London papers printed the name, playing position, height, and weight of each of the players. Since home runs were rare in an era of a dead or heavy ball (made with less India rubber than in the 1850s or 1860s), the intent was probably to introduce the hired 'meat-on-the-hoof' and, by extension, to imply athletic prowess by height and weight information. Numerous pictures of baseball teams of the 1870s reveal sturdy players, almost all of whom wore full moustaches. The most important ingredient of a successful baseball team was not the players' size but the 'battery', that is, the pitcher and the catcher. In 1877, crowds were drawn in great numbers and were rewarded by high drama and high-quality

Tecumseh Park in 1871, London Tecumsehs versus Syracuse Stars. (Edy Brothers, Library and Archives Canada, PA-031482)

baseball. The Tecumsehs, after 47 wins, 26 losses, and 7 ties, played in the final game of the IBBA championship, a crowd-thrilling one, against the Alleghenys in London on 3 October 1877. Englehart's team emerged victorious, giving rise to the notion that a 'Canadian' team had beaten the Americans at their own game.

Correspondence in the Sleeman Papers reveals that the Tecumseh executive, who remained virtually unchanged over the three-year period, administered the club meticulously as a business whose product was high-quality baseball. Their avowed aim was not to make a profit; rather, they sought to promote the sport, along with the London community. Their sophistication was reflected in their stationery, which carried the name Tecumseh Base Ball Club in script; flanking it in the top left corner was a finely sketched naked torso of a North American Indian (their idea of Tecumseh?) in hunting pose and surrounded by trees. Nevertheless, London's inflated baseball bubble had burst by mid-July 1878. The Tecumsehs were not as dominant and the crowd size diminished. Moreover, there was widespread belief that the Tecumsehs threw a game against the Syracuse Stars in early July.[112] Even the suspicion of fraud is unacceptable in both sport and business. Tecumseh game attendance waned and when in mid-August it was clear the Tecumsehs could not win the series, a fickle executive, led by Englehart, 'resolved that the nine be paid off on Saturday and released from their engagement'.[113] This was done and the team folded. Professional baseball in a small town or city, without the protection of an umbrella organization, was a fragile thing and remained so whenever high-calibre baseball was embarked upon.

National Diffusion

From the late 1870s onward, baseball's diffusion throughout Canada at all levels—from spontaneous games and informal play to elite professionalism—was phenomenal. Top athletes in the sport, normally American imports, were called 'ballists'. Although Canadian newspapers focused on American major league baseball between 1880 and 1884, baseball matches were prevalent in Victoria and New Westminster, often against clubs from the state of Washington, and inter-town matches were being played among Halifax, Saint John, Moncton, Truro, and Pictou. Unlike most Canadian team sports and forms of competition, Canadian baseball was structured on a north–south basis. That is, it continued to look to the United States for all levels of competition and for players in semi-professional and professional leagues until well into the twentieth century.[114] The American influence that pervaded the sport in Canada was therefore its most stabilizing influence. Although teams and leagues in the 1880s and 1890s may have appeared, disappeared, and in some cases reappeared, this pattern was not baseball's 'malady', as one sport historian implies.[115] Rather, it was how baseball survived. Its tide never ceased in Canada.[116]

In the mid-1870s, there were six teams in the Saint John Baseball Association in New Brunswick for which most players practised at 5:30 AM in order to be at work by 7:00 AM.[117] When the great fire of Saint John occurred in 1877, baseball died out for two years owing to both the destruction of the city and the fact that many of the ballplayers moved west to look for jobs. In the early 1880s, the Saint John Cricket Club was active, and baseball bounced back in 1884. In that era, children made their own baseballs, 'centred on the nose of a sturgeon and covered with yarn'.[118] A tremendous rivalry developed between the team of the Protestant Saint John Athletic Association and the Shamrocks, and high-calibre baseball resulted. Up to 2,000 fans attended games between the two teams, a demonstration of support that led to the formation and two-year existence of the professional New Brunswick Base Ball League, beginning in 1888. Moncton and Fredericton completed the four-team league.

Both Saint John clubs recruited heavily in Maine and Massachusetts for American players. American college students, especially good 'batteries', were financially induced to spend the summer in New Brunswick and play 'Canadian' baseball under aliases in order to protect their amateur status south of the border.[119] In 1890, Moncton had only three Canadians on its team.[120] With the professional treadmill set in motion, baseball became a fact of civic and spectator interest. Housewives, doctors, clerks, lumbermen, merchants, and fishermen could be seen sitting in the grandstand or standing along the sidelines.[121] Moreover, the CPR Telegraph Company erected a scoreboard at the corner of King and Germain streets in Saint John for the benefit of those who could not get into the game. During games, the corner was a veritable hive of betting activity. Inevitably the question arose: which was the best baseball team in the Maritimes? To decide the issue the Saint Johns met the Halifax Atlantas in a three-game series that lasted only one game because it was determined that the umpire had been 'bought off' by the Atlantas. This scandal created ill feeling between the two municipalities for some time; but for baseball it was just part of the perpetually repeated evolutionary process. When the Shamrock fans got out of control in an 1890s contest against the Saint Johns, the latter team withdrew from the league and Moncton followed suit, owing to the same financial difficulties that plagued the weaker teams in Ontario's CBBA 1876 series.

Between 1890 and 1905 Saint John retreated to 'amateur' baseball—amateur in the sense that the inclusion of paid players was not declared, just known. The best intercity teams were the Roses, Starlights, Gashouse, YMCA, Strawberries, and Alerts. The Alerts and the Roses were notorious throughout the 1890s for bringing in paid American batteries, but since there was no amateur affiliation or governance, the practice was regarded as part of baseball. A good local pitcher like Jim Whelly of the Alerts in the 1890s often came home with his hat full of silver dollars. The contests between teams were usually played for $100 a side as well as 75 per cent of the gate receipts. As elsewhere, money was a necessity in the Maritimes for the survival of good teams and leagues.[122] The Halifax Orients even travelled with a theatrical group, using performance receipts to cover expenses. Several leagues folded in Halifax over lack of financing. Although baseball on Prince Edward Island was insulated from intercity competition with other Maritime locales, it took root mainly in the rural communities of Pisquid, Tracadie, Peakes Station, Roseneath, Stanhope, and Baldwin's Road during the 1890s. In the same decade there was a strong network of intracity contests in Charlottetown.[123]

In the western provinces and territories, baseball teams had a fledgling existence in the 1870s. By the early 1880s lacrosse was the favoured summer sport in Manitoba, and soccer and rugby had a greater following than baseball.[124] In 1885, the three best baseball clubs in Winnipeg—the CPR, the Metropolitans, and the Hotelkeepers (financed by hotel proprietors)—actively recruited the best players in the province and gave them good jobs in return for baseball service. But each team inevitably began to import salaried players, usually batteries, from the United States to remain competitive and financially viable in the Winnipeg Base Ball League.[125]

Fuelled by the Winnipeg newspapers' extensive coverage of all North American professional leagues—one hotel even offered daily telegraphed reports of games on the continent—Winnipeggers were said to be suffering from baseball mania in 1886. All kinds of groups in the city, such as printers, civil servants, and lawyers, formed baseball teams for sheer enjoyment. The three-team Manitoba Baseball League of 1886 was at the top of the baseball echelon and enjoyed the status of being the first professional sport league on the Prairies. Games typically drew 10 per cent of the city's population of 20,000. However, by the late summer of 1886, baseball began to fall into disrepute over betting. Open gambling on the final score, margin of victory, hits by various players, and total game score—of which the umpire might have pre-game knowledge—raised public concern, which increased when collusion by players to fix outcomes was suspected. Attendance declined, teams disbanded, and the league collapsed. A tournament style of baseball prevailed for the next 16 years. In 1902, Winnipeg obtained a franchise in a North Dakota and Minnesota professional league and the city's baseball fans absorbed the quality games along with the misfortunes of financial difficulties, corruption, and occasional rough play until 1914.[126]

From the late 1880s until the First World War, many prairie cities and towns had baseball teams at all levels up to the tournament format (on weekends and holidays). Lethbridge, Wiste, Medicine Hat, Sturgeon, and Edmonton all generated the same civic pride in baseball prowess.[127] Consider the recollections of one prairie pioneer, circa 1910:

Everything in them days you could say was baseball. Every town would have a pasture with a chicken wire backstop, and when you was gonna have a game you'd chase the town cows off it and scrape up the cow plops and that was about it. Town teams always played town teams. Like there would be a town down the line and they'd wire us they'd be up on a Saturday afternoon. It was baseball in them days too, good ball. There was none of this spares business and four or five pitchers. Not then. If your pitcher had a sore arm, well maybe he'd trade off with the shortstop and the shortstop would pitch that game and so it went.[128]

In Quebec's Eastern Townships, baseball flourished after the turn of the century and French-Canadian rural communities promoted the game through schools, churches, and challenge tournaments.[129] Though Montreal was an early centre of amateur sport, notably lacrosse and rugby football, baseball was for a time resisted there. This was perhaps logical, given the game's informal structure linked to commercial adventures in gambling and player imports, and its professional tendencies. Nevertheless, the Montreal Base Ball Club (affiliated with the prestigious MAAA) competed in an 1886 and 1887 league made up of the Beavers, the Gordons, and the Clippers until the Gordons resigned to try professional baseball (unsuccessfully).[130]

In Ontario, baseball blossomed in the 1880s and 1890s. At the grassroots level, village networks were thriving: Burnamthorpe, Caledon, Cheltenham, Churchville, Ebenezer, Forks of the Credit, Malton, Palgrave, Stanley Mills, Terra Cotta,[131] and many other communities carried on the rural traditions of baseball with games on civic holidays and with challenge and tournament formats. At the same time, 'ringers' playing under aliases (top-flight players brought in from outside) and loaded baseball bats were common at the elite levels of the sport, but so was tremendous fan support. For example, the Alton Aetnas were one of the best teams in the province from 1893 to 1907. Formed in 1875 by Samuel Barber, a carriage-maker and blacksmith, and J.F. Holden, a druggist and station master, the Aetnas attracted rural fans within a 30-kilometre radius:

> Wherever the team travelled, there, too, went its supporters. Farmers of the surrounding district forsook their ploughs, mechanics in the village laid down their tools, Alton men and women alike donned their Sunday best, and went out to cheer their Aetnas, at home or abroad.[132]

'Abroad' implied an invitation from Owen Sound to play at that centre's Railroad Conductors' Picnic in 1893. Public subscriptions from Alton residents were used to make up the $100 wagers on games, such as one with Orangeville for which local carriage-maker Sam Boggs in 1897 used his traction threshing engine to pull three farm wagons, covered with tarpaulins and decorated with humorous signs, to Erin. It was a community-driven promotional stunt and typified the popularity and festive atmosphere of late nineteenth-century baseball.

The attractions of the game at holiday gatherings organized by churches, schools, local business entrepreneurs, and small civic-based institutions were just not strong enough to ensure the development of professional baseball throughout Canada. While most towns flirted with commercial or professional practices, only the largest urban centres—Toronto, Montreal, Winnipeg, Victoria, and Vancouver—had large enough populations to sustain clubs during both winning and losing seasons.[133] In Toronto, and later in Montreal, pro baseball became viable and tremendously popular, beginning in 1885.

In that year, five prominent Toronto citizens—Deputy Police Chief Stark, Peter Ryan, E. Strachan Cox, William Macpherson, and Thomas Hunter—met at the Rossin House to form the executive of the Toronto Base Ball Club.[134] They formed a joint stock company, paid out $4,200 in salaries, grossed $8,500 in receipts, and at the end of the season placed third behind Hamilton and London in the Canadian Baseball League, of which Guelph was a fourth member. (The league's name was a misnomer typical of central Canadian sport organizers.) The following season (1886), the Torontos moved baseball into the realm of commercial entertainment by joining with the powerful International League of the United States. With this it remained, in spite of some name changes and one five-year absence in the 1890s, until 1967. Sunlight Park, Toronto's first baseball-specific facility, was completed in 1886 for $7,000 on eight acres of land south of Queen Street East, adjacent to the Don River. All 2,000 seats were cushioned, armed, and backed, and the grandstand was covered.[135] Over the next few years the Toronto press gilded the pro-team athletes with nicknames. W.W. 'Peekaboo' Veach, 'Daisy' Davis, Bob 'The Wig' Emslie, and Ned 'Cannonball' Crane (arguably one of the fastest pitchers in baseball at the time) became household names in the late 1880s, strengthening the popularity of baseball in the process. Toronto won the 1887 International League championships.

When teams in the International League began jumping from one league to another, the Torontos retreated to quasi-amateur baseball from 1890 to 1895. (Meanwhile, strictly amateur baseball in Ontario at the senior, intermediate, and junior levels prospered.)[136] In 1896, Toronto joined seven American teams in the Eastern League. The next year the team moved into the new Hanlan's Point Stadium on Toronto Island. Lol Soloman owned a restaurant on the island, as well as the Toronto Ferry Company, which purchased the Toronto franchise to lure the people over to the island. In the same year, Montreal was able to buy the Rochester franchise in the Eastern League. A Canadian baseball great, 'Tip' (James Edward) O'Neill (1858–1915), who played with Woodstock before beginning a memorable 10-year career in St Louis that included nearly 1,400 hits and 52 home-runs, was president of the league. In 1898, the popular Montreal Royals were organized. Playing in the newly built stadium in Atwater Park, they won the pennant the first year. (They lasted, in this incarnation, until the First World War.) Thus, by the turn of the century, viable professional baseball had arrived in Canada's two principal metropolitan centres, in spite of conservative amateur ideas such as those expressed in *Saturday Night* in 1895:

> The true nature of professional baseball is well shown in the present relation held
> by Toronto to the Eastern League. There is not a Toronto man, or even a Canadian,
> in the whole aggregation of game-losers wearing the Toronto colours; the manager
> of the club is Mr. Chapman of Rochester, and the money that floats the venture is
> Buffalo money.[137]

This observation, deriding the by now accepted high American component of Canadian teams, was rooted both in outdated amateur ideals and in the reality of the advent of commercial baseball. Professional baseball became permanently established in Toronto. The Canadian delirium for the game in general and for professional baseball in particular loomed.

The Boom Years of Baseball, 1900–1920

Between 1900 and 1920 baseball was easily Canada's most popular sport.[138] Even in Quebec the game spread via the league system of competition among anglophones in urban areas. French Canadians, who were playing in small colleges in Montreal and Trois-Rivières in the 1870s and 1880s, adopted the challenge and tournament format of the game. Newfoundlanders took up the game some time around 1913 when the St John's Amateur Base Ball League was formed at the instigation of the employees of the Imperial Tobacco Company, the Bank of Montreal, and the Reid-Newfoundland Railway. When Imperial Tobacco's vice-president, G.G. Allen, donated a silver cup for championship play that year, baseball games were a natural activity for the Wednesday afternoon commercial half-holidays.[139] Such leagues featuring industrial sponsorship were a major component of baseball across Canada during its golden years, but in Newfoundland the war stymied it and it never really took root there again.

In the Maritimes and the West, semi-professional leagues continued to flourish and abate. On Prince Edward Island strong junior, intermediate, and senior city leagues were in full swing in Charlottetown and Summerside. These tiers eventually enabled the organization of an Island Championship Series and Maritime play-downs between 1925 and 1935, although PEI teams seldom performed well in the regional championship.[140] The New Brunswick–Maine League of pro ball enjoyed two years of financial success, beginning in 1911, but fan support, the league, and the sport itself dwindled during the war years. Revived in the 1920s, New Brunswick baseball went through the intercity, semi-professional, professional, amateur cycle repeatedly in the twenties and thirties.[141] Nova Scotia teams, by contrast—at least those from Halifax, Yarmouth, and Springhill (the renowned 'Fencebusters')—were very strong and attracted 5,000 fans at Halifax for games against New England teams in the hope that the Bluenosers could 'lay a whuppin' on American teams.'[142] In Cape Breton, where baseball had been avidly played in the coal-mining towns of Sydney, Sydney Mines, Glace Bay, and New Waterford, among other places, since the early years of the century, the all-Canadian Colliery League had a short but remarkable existence in the 1930s. When the league turned professional in 1937 the games, players, and feats of the Glace Bay Miners, the Steel City team of Sydney, and the New Waterford Dodgers became famous throughout the Maritimes and in New England. However, the First World War brought it to an end.[143]

The Western Canada League was formed in Alberta in 1906, and in Saskatchewan high-calibre teams with intriguing names like the Saskatoon Quakers and the Regina Bonepilers were popular.[144] Between 1910 and 1915, railway travel expenses in the western provinces—even in the north–south direction of competitions—plagued commercial baseball development. Curtailed even further by war, western baseball was promoted by countless tournaments at the grassroots level and by barnstorming tours of good American and Canadian teams. Westerners even tried to formalize gambling pools, but they were closed down in 1923 by the Manitoba Court of Appeal. During the 1920s, tournaments in the West were sponsored by rummage sales and merchants in order to offer $1,000 prizes.[145]

From Manitoba to British Columbia—where baseball was at a feverish pitch with 60 teams in Vancouver's Sunday school baseball league—strictly amateur baseball was very popular in the first 20 years of the century. Twilight leagues were formed in several centres as early as 1908, while the Sunday school leagues were strongly supported and well organized in Edmonton, Calgary, and New Westminster, as well as in Vancouver.[146] YMCAS

An early baseball game on the Prairies between Lethbridge and Calgary at Lethbridge, Alberta, 21 January 1905. (Courtesy of the Glenbow Archives)

also provided baseball leadership and facilities across the West (and across Canada). At senior and other levels the sport was greatly curtailed by the war, although many exhibition matches raised money for the Red Cross. Military baseball leagues kept the sport alive at the grassroots level, while professional leagues like the International League carried on with business as usual.[147] Professional franchises like the Toronto Maple Leafs (formerly the Toronto Baseball Club), were shrewd in portraying the patriotism revered during the war years. The *Toronto Globe* carried a large photograph of the Maple Leafs taking rifle practice in their baseball uniforms.[148]

Such propaganda was only the tip of the media iceberg during baseball's 'golden era' in Canada. The country was literally saturated with game coverage. With nationwide baseball activities stimulated by more and more American college imports, barnstorming teams, and international leagues, Canada's other summer sport, lacrosse, was deprived of player and spectator interest as baseball skyrocketed. The massive expansion of baseball at all levels and the involvement of so many teams, leagues, and American interests can only be understood against the backdrop of press influence. The major newspapers in Canada, from Halifax to Vancouver, show that baseball in 1915 ranked first in percentage coverage of all other sports. Furthermore, 50 per cent of the baseball coverage in the same papers between 1885 and 1915 was concerned specifically with American leagues, especially major leagues.[149] The frequency and prominence of newspaper coverage of predominantly American league baseball in the Canadian press outranked even that of hockey in Halifax, Montreal, Toronto, Winnipeg, and Vancouver between 1927 and 1935. Even though the National Hockey League was booming in these years, and in 1928 and 1932 Canadian teams won Olympic gold medals, press coverage still favoured American professional baseball.[150]

And it was during the years of the First World War and the decades immediately following the war that women's softball became so popular. Factory-sponsored teams and church and youth organizations, among others, provided rational recreation in a variety of sports, like softball, for working-class women.[151] Early softball leagues for women were founded in Toronto by such leaders as Mabel Ray and Alexandrine Gibb. Companies like Eaton's in Toronto and the Hudson's Bay Company in the West sponsored a variety of sports for female employees, including softball.[152] During the 1920s and 1930s, women's industrial leagues in softball flourished, as did many other levels of the game, all part of major changes in sport and society (see Chapter 8 and Chapter 9) that served to support women playing sport at all levels. As with men's sport promotion and organization, Toronto seemed to be a hub for women's softball development fuelled by zealous sportswriters, such as Phyllis Griffiths, Alexandrine Gibb, and Bobby Rosenfeld, who campaigned for women's involvement in sport through major Canadian newspaper sports columns (see Chapter 7).

Toronto and Montreal: Major League Baseball

At the hub of Canadian sport in general, and Canadian baseball in particular, was Toronto and its vaunted professional baseball team. Between 1900 and 1910 it played in three different parks and changed ownership twice. In 1900, 52 Toronto businessmen spearheaded by Ed Mack, a tailor, Jes Applegath, a hatter, and Thomas Soole, a printer, paid $8,000 to the Toronto Ferry Company to buy the Toronto franchise and move from the Hanlan's Point park to another park, given the name Diamond Park, on Fraser Avenue, east of Dufferin and south of King Street West.[153] As well as continuing the importation of American players, the executive brought Edward Grant Barrow from the US as manager for a salary of $1,500, plus $300 if the team finished second or first.[154] Barrow was the creative genius behind the building of the New York Yankee dynasty of the twenties, thirties, and forties.

Torontonians flocked to games motivated by publicity extravaganzas and lured by the aura of baseball culture. On the opening day of the 1901 season, 13 tallyhos (horse-drawn carriages) formed a parade to transport players in uniform, sportswriters, and equipment led by the Queen's Own Rifles along Simcoe, King, Yonge, and Queen streets before thousands of spectators, until the entourage stopped in front of the then new City Hall for speeches and introductions.

By 1906, the Toronto franchise was worth $25,000. The team returned to Toronto Island in 1908, but a fire destroyed the stadium in 1909 and it was back to Diamond Park until a new 18,000-seat stadium, Maple Leaf Park, was built at Hanlan's Point. (This is where 19-year-old Babe Ruth, a pitcher for the minor-league Providence Grays, on Labour Day, 5 September 1914, struck his first professional home run, against the Torontos.) Bags of peanuts by the thousands were sold at the games in pre-hot dog days. This was a time when players were not above physically attacking umpires (for which appropriate fines were levied), incidents that could not help but excite spectators. A rowdy atmosphere infested the games, which on 4 August 1906 was deplored in *Saturday Night*:

> In the first instance the visiting Rochester players made their exit from the grounds in the most approved theatrical style, that is, amid a shower of mud, stones and other more malodorous missiles [rotten cabbages], hurled by the riff raff of hood-lums who, somehow or other, form the entourage of baseball and baseball players.

Maple Leaf Stadium, Toronto, 1922. (Courtesy of the City of Toronto Archives)

Nevertheless, *Saturday Night* reported in its issue of 16 May 1908 that the 'true fan' goes to the game every afternoon during the season, 'his mind quite controlled by sheer adoration of baseball' and the 'mere finance and travail of toil may go hang for all of him while the season lasts.'[155]

Fans in Toronto (and Canada) became riveted on the game when the first news of major league baseball was leaked in one small corner of the sports page in the dead of winter, and reports gradually included rumours of trades, player injuries, and pennant hopes, grew into larger articles on training camps in the southern United States, and then full pages were devoted to major league coverage. Press reports were not banal items but were written in a lingo that satisfyingly cocooned baseball fans in their own cotton-wool world of the sport: 'So the Cincy [Cincinnati] push dodged the hook and went away from that place with two notches in their tally stick.'[156] In Toronto, a simple 'Out at first!' in 1909 could engender more discussion, it was said, than the election of an Anglican bishop or a dispute over the earlier chapters of Genesis.[157] Even W.A. Hewitt, of the Ontario Hockey Association and a guardian of the amateur principle, travelled with the Torontos. He once purchased with Tommy Ryan (the Canadian inventor of five-pin bowling and founder of the Miss Toronto Beauty Contest) the 'Paragon Score Board', which was operated at Shea's Theatre, the Star Theatre, and Massey Music Hall during the World Series games. A telegraph agent and announcer received the reports and dramatized the games on an electric board whose lights indicated balls and strikes, runners on base, and when balls were hit and where they landed. Capacity crowds filled these theatres until rental costs became prohibitive.[158]

The combination of commercialism, pastoral afternoons at the park, and rabid fans enhanced the excitement of the game itself. Torontonians left work early on Wednesday afternoons or ventured out early on Saturday mornings, eventually to fight their way out of the streetcars and across the railway tracks to the docks to board the ferries to Toronto Island. Waves of spectators, laden with hampers of food, were unloaded at Hanlan's Point to line up for tickets, tour the sideshows, ride the merry-go-round or roller coaster, go through the 'Tunnel of Love', or maybe even take in the vaudeville acts at the outdoor theatre before going to see the game. Once inside the stadium, the hypnotized fan yielded to the environment of baseball in a way that people not interested in the sport find difficult to understand:

> Once you are there you are caught in the maelstrom of baseball emotion. You enter into the mob-spirit of yourself. You act like one of your antediluvian ancestors. It is all you can do to keep from climbing up into the rafters, hanging by one foot, and spitting at the umpire. Your manner of eating peanuts isn't entirely human. And the things you shriek at the respectable middle-aged official who prevails over the plate. And all because of what a number of American gentlemen do to a horsehide American ball with bats made in Chicago or Philadelphia.[159]

This was *Saturday Night*, again, venting its sarcasm against the Americanization of Canadian baseball in 1912. But of course no one cared. Baseball was public theatre in Toronto, as elsewhere, and the involvement was total.

The Montreal Royals were revived in 1928 when the Syracuse franchise in the International League was acquired by Althanase David and Ernest Savard. They played in the new 22,000-seat Delormier Downs stadium. A few years later, in 1931, the Royals, and the stadium, ran into financial trouble. They were saved by three investors (one of them was Pierre Elliott Trudeau's father, Charles-Émile Trudeau) and went on to many successes. Until they were dissolved in 1961, the Royals won seven International League pennants, and in 1946 and 1948 they won both the pennant and the Little World Series. In 1945 an event occurred that put the Royals into the historical limelight: the hiring of Jackie Robinson.[160] The Royals club had been bought by the Brooklyn Dodgers in 1944 and was Brooklyn's top farm team when its general manager, Branch Rickey, assigned Robinson to the Royals in 1945 as part of a scheme to launch him as the first black player in the major leagues.[161]

For many years black players were seen in Canada only on all-black teams playing against all-white teams. A breakthrough in integration occurred in Montreal with the Quebec Provincial League, which began in 1935, with Alfred Wilson, who played for one season as pitcher and outfielder. For two years, 1936 and 1937, an all-black team, the Black Panthers, made up mostly of American southerners played in Montreal. The atmosphere of semi-tolerance in Montreal—players could live wherever they liked—probably influenced Robinson's placement with the Royals. When he arrived in Montreal he felt he was accepted. But when the Royals played in Louisville in the Little World Series, spectators shouted, 'Go back to Canada, black boy!' On his return to Montreal:

> We discovered that the Canadians were up in arms over the way I had been treated. Greeting us warmly, they let us know how they felt. . . . All through that first game, they booed every time a Louisville player came out of the dugout. I didn't approve

Issues in Canadian Sport History

Black Players in Canadian Baseball

Many black players of exceptional skill played baseball in Canada in the last decades of the nineteenth century, but sadly they met with immediate hostility.[162] (In the United States, where the hostility was greater, all-black teams were formed.) Bud Fowler (b. 1854), an American, played briefly for Guelph in 1881, but in spite of his obvious ability he was soon released. The *Guelph Herald* reported:

> We regret that some members of the Maple Leafs are ill-natured enough to object to the colored pitcher Fowler. He is one of the best pitchers on the continent of America and it would be greatly to the interest of the Maple Leaf team if he were re-instated. . . . He has forgotten more about baseball than the present team ever knew and he could teach them many points in the game. We are glad, however, to find that it is only a few in the team who have done so.[163]

Canadian-born Jimmy Claxton (b. 1892) left Canada as a child and achieved prominence with the Oakland Oaks, of the Pacific Coast League, and never returned. Ollie Johnson, born in Oakville, Ontario, played with the Cuban Giants, a black team based in Buffalo; though he returned to Oakville and died there in 1977, he never played baseball there. Hamilton-born Bill 'Hippo' Galloway joined the Woodstock team in 1899 but prejudice eventually led him to leave the country and join the Cuban Giants.

Jimmy Claxton, born in 1892 on Vancouver Island, was the first black player in organized baseball (San Francisco Oaks, 1916) in the twentieth century. (Marc H. Blau Collection)

of this kind of retaliation, but I felt a jubilant sense of gratitude for the way the Canadians expressed their feelings.[164]

When the Royals won the Little World Series, Robinson was mobbed as a hero. The adulation prompted an American reporter to make the following often-quoted observation: 'It was probably the only day in history that a black man ran from a white mob with love, instead of lynching, on its mind.' Robinson played his first game for the Dodgers, as first baseman, on 15 April 1947. (Roy Campanella followed Robinson with the Royals in 1947 before he, too, joined the Dodgers.) Some 20 years later, a Canadian-born black player, Ferguson ('Fergie') Jenkins (b. 1943) began his spectacular climb to the top. From the 1960s to 1983 he was a pitcher for the Texas Rangers, the Boston Red Sox, and the Chicago Cubs, pitching 284 wins, 3,192 strikeouts, and attaining a major league record by a pitcher of 363 putouts. He won the Lou Marsh Trophy in 1974, was Canadian male athlete of the year four times, and was elected to the Canadian Baseball Hall of Fame in 1987.

In the early 1920s, the Toronto Baseball Club wanted a new stadium on the main land for the Maple Leafs, who were playing in the International League. Plans for a War Memorial Stadium on Fleet Street were drawn up in March 1922.[165] It was to be paid for by the city and the cost was estimated at $400,000, which was later cut back to $150,000. It was an issue in the civic elections of 1 January 1923 and was voted down as being too expensive (the estimated cost had by then risen to $263,000). In 1924, the Toronto Harbour Commission, an agency of the federal government formed to develop harbour lands, asked for a grant of land on the same site. The Commission responded to renewed pressure from the club for a stadium and realized that it would be a money-making proposition. Plans for a poured-concrete building were drawn up by Chapman, Oxley, and Bishop—the architects of several major Toronto buildings (including that of the Harbour Commission)—and Maple Leaf Stadium opened on Fleet Street in 1926. Costing $300,000 and seating 17,500, it was the most up-to-date stadium in the minor leagues. In that first year 220,000 fans watched the Leafs play.

In the 1930s, baseball had a rocky history in Toronto.[166] Maple Leaf Stadium was not near public transport, and while the opening games were well attended, spectator interest declined in the summer. In 1931, the club, which was responsible for taxes and rent, fell behind in payments and lost control of the stadium to the Harbour Commission. The first night game, against Rochester, was on 28 June 1934, and did not begin until it was dark, which meant 10 o'clock, and because the floodlights seemed to slow the play down, it did not end until 1 AM. The crowd was not pleased, although there was jubilation over Ike Boon's hitting a homer for the Leafs. The dismal record of the Leafs in the 1930s ended with their taking last place. (Seven of the team's players and managers over the years were elected to the International League Hall of Fame.) But games continued during the war, in spite of the fact that most of the younger players were in the services.

The Leafs won their eighth league pennant in 1943 and there were many notable players in the forties: pitchers Luke 'Hot Potato' Hamlin, who retired at the end of the 1948 season with a 91–58 won–lost record, Burleigh Grimes, Nick 'Jumbo' Strincevich, Dick Conger, and Tom Ananicz; hitters Ed Sanicki and Bill Glynn; catchers Gene Desautels and Stan Lopata, and a great many more, some of whom graduated to the majors. During the war, over a quarter of a million troops were allowed into the stadium free as guests of the Maple Leaf Baseball Club.

The next decade has been called the Leafs' Fabulous Fifties because Jack Kent Cooke assumed ownership, and not only bought top-flight players but introduced innovations that grabbed the attention of post-war Torontonians who wanted to be entertained. Sunday baseball was introduced. Fireworks, music, stunts, and entertainers drew huge crowds and the Leafs soared. For example, in 1954 they won 97 games. The most valuable player that year was Elston Howard, whom Cooke had borrowed from the New York Yankees; he hit a homer in his first game. Among the large array of star players Cooke acquired were hitters Mike Goliat, Lew Morton, Rocky Nelson; pitchers Lynn Lovenguth, Don Johnson, and Eddie Blake; and catcher Andy Anderson. The Leafs won the pennant again in 1956 (8–7 against Rochester) when Ed Stevens scored the winning run on a hit by Hector Rodriguez.

The Leafs entered their final decade in the 1960s. Cooke left Canada in 1961 and oversaw the team's activities, and the club's losses, from California. No player captured public interest—players seemed to come and go without making names for themselves—and attendance at games decreased. In 1964, Cooke sold his interest in the Leafs to a group headed by Robert Lawson Hunter and Sam Starr, and a new organization—Toronto (Community) Baseball Ltd—evolved. This lasted only until 1967. On 4 September, when the Leafs played their final game, only 802 spectators watched them lose, 7–2, to Rochester. The end came at a meeting of the International League in Cleveland on 17 October 1967. The club was sold and the stadium was demolished the next February. Cooke had longed to enter the major leagues but was discouraged by the high cost of doing so. A Canadian team did not accomplish this until 1969, and it happened not in Toronto but in Montreal, when a new team, the Montreal Expos, partly owned by Charles Bronfman, was admitted to the National League. The Expos played their first game on 9 April 1969 at New York's Shea Stadium, beating the Mets 11–10. On 14 April, they played their first Montreal game in Parc Jarry, where Mack Jones hit the first homer and they beat the St Louis Cardinals 8–7. They remained in Parc Jarry until 1977, the year they moved to the new 60,000-seat Olympic Stadium and achieved their first winning season. (The unpopular stadium—the Big Owe—made headlines because its cost reached the financial 'stratosphere': $1.2 billion.) The Expos quickly earned a huge following and sparked a revival of national interest in baseball. Between 1979 and 1983, they had the best overall winning percentage in the National League (.548) and in 1987 they finished only four games out of first place. Sadly for the continuance of professional baseball in Canada, the Montreal franchise was moved to Washington to start in the 2005 season. The major reason was the ever-present problem in most Canadian professional sport enterprises—too small a population base to support big league sporting franchises consistently.

It took a while for Toronto to catch up with Montreal by acquiring a major league team of its own. The Toronto Blue Jays—formed by Imperial Trust Ltd, Labatt's Breweries, and the Canadian Imperial Bank of Commerce—were admitted to the American League and began to play in Toronto's CNE Stadium, which was renovated for them, on a snowy day in April 1977. After a very slow start they had their first winning season in 1983, for a fourth-place finish. The Blue Jays have had many top players, including Dave Stieb, Alfredo Griffin, Lloyd Moseby, Willie Upshaw, George Bell—who was named the league's most valuable player in 1987, Carlos Delgado, Roger Clemens, Jack Morris, and Roberto Alomar.

They played their first game in Toronto's new SkyDome on 5 June 1989 against Milwaukee, two days after the official opening of the stadium. Financed by private investors, the province of Ontario, and Metropolitan Toronto and costing more than $560 million ($319 million over the estimate of 1986), including $30.6 million for the giant video-screen scoreboard, SkyDome has catapulted Toronto, and Canada—which had entered the major leagues of baseball so recently—into worldwide prominence as a provider of space-age facilities for the mass enjoyment of sport. The stadium, seating 52,000 for baseball, 54,000 for football, and up to 65,000 for concerts, is part of a huge complex that includes restaurants, a health club, a hotel, and a broadcast network. But above all its innovations—

and, visibly, above the stadium itself—is its retractable roof, which almost miraculously realizes the sports lover's dream of being able to enjoy baseball and football out of doors while still receiving fairly speedy protection from inclement weather. (The plan for the retractable roof began to germinate on a cold fall day in 1982 at the CNE Stadium when Ontario Premier Bill Davis and Metro Toronto Chairman Paul Godfrey, who had wanted a domed stadium in Toronto since 1969, were among the fans whose enthusiasm for the Grey Cup game was almost snuffed out by the freezing, drizzling weather.) Bought by Rogers Communications on 2 February 2005 and renamed The Rogers Centre, the SkyDome is considered, in the context of Canadian sport history, a monumental symbol of the end of one era and the beginning of another.

More than any other sport, baseball—which has been called America's national pastime—is firmly entrenched in the popular culture of both the United States and Canada. Examples are endless. The phrases 'striking out', 'dig in', 'home run', 'touching base', 'out in left field', 'two strikes against you', 'lead-off man', 'take a rain check', and 'throwing a curve' are among our everyday expressions. The song 'Take Me Out to the Ball Game', the mock-heroic poem 'Casey at the Bat' (written in 1888 by Ernest Lawrence Thayer), and Abbott and Costello's skit 'Who's on First?' are known to almost everyone, at least by their titles. In theatre, *The Umpire of 1905* enjoyed a long run in Chicago, and *Damn Yankees* (1955), based on the Douglass Wallop novel *The Year the Yankees Stole the Pennant*, is a classic American stage and film musical. Hollywood has apotheosized Lou Gehrig and Babe Ruth, and produced *The Bingo Long Traveling All-Stars and Motor Kings*, about the Negro leagues of the 1930s, *Eight Men Out*, and *Bull Durham*. In literature, the distinguished American novelist Bernard Malamud wrote *The Natural* (1952), which treats comically the mythic view of the American hero in terms of baseball. And a Canadian, William Kinsella, has celebrated baseball in his 1982 novel *Shoeless Joe* (on which the film *Field of Dreams* was based) and in collections of memorable short stories. In *The Thrill of the Grass*, he describes a community effort to replace artificial turf with sods of real grass during a baseball strike. 'What do you think about artificial turf?' the narrator asks a new acquaintance. 'Hmmmmf', he snorts, 'that's what the strike should be about. Baseball is meant to be played on summer evenings and Sunday afternoons, on grass just cut by a horse-drawn mower.'

Conclusions

Nostalgia for the past seems to be part of baseball's mythology. Yesterday it was two teams with a ball and a bat playing on a wide stretch of grass in a village, on the sand-lot of a town, or in a city park, half surrounded by spectators standing or sitting in bleachers. (Max Braithewaite's 'Why Girls Should Not Play Baseball' in *The Night We Stole the Mountie's Car* is a classic tribute to country baseball.) Today, we have Montreal's Olympic Stadium and Toronto's gigantic outdoor/indoor Rogers Centre—or our own living rooms, where we see virtually nothing but an electronic image of the plays themselves, as far removed as possible from the game played on grass, passionately observed by townsfolk on a summer evening.

In the long history of baseball in Canada, teams have formed and folded; leagues have been created and disbanded; American 'imports' (known at various times as 'baseball's foreign legions') have been lured to teams from Halifax to Victoria; local entrepreneurs have sponsored high-calibre teams; competitions have been played out in tournaments, challenges, and barnstorming tours; one intra-city competition has led to another and then another; the cycle of amateur teams leading to semi-professional teams leading to professional teams leading to the demise of professional teams and the resurgence of amateur teams. This unceasing ebb and flow has been at the core of the Canadian baseball experience and has simply proved that the game has an invincible hold on the public's affection. When the games of the Expos and the Blue Jays reached millions on television, the popular interest in Canadian baseball attained a height that could not have been imagined 100 years ago. This might raise the question: Will baseball maintain its strength and popularity, or will interest decline through overexposure? Thinking of the unbroken, though checkered, nationwide history of Canada's two major league teams, and of what has been called 'the perfect game' with its potential for excitement and suspense, for the glorification of teams and of individual players in their demonstrations of power, precision, and speed and even of the game's unlimited generation of statistics, which a true fan delights in memorizing, one cannot foresee any decline in interest. The setting may have changed in scale, but the game is the same; the skill simply increases.

But there is another ingredient that should not be overlooked. Baseball feats, and memories of games, lend themselves to fantasizing, as in Hugh Hood's story 'Ghosts at Jarry' and in many stories by Kinsella. In the introduction to his collection *The Thrill of the Grass*, Kinsella writes: 'I am often asked about the relationship of baseball and magic. I feel it is the timelessness of baseball which makes it more conducive to magical happenings than any other sport.' Baseball is unique among sports in its capacity to seize the imagination. Finally, it is important to underscore the different processes of evolution of baseball and lacrosse and how the way of playing each was dramatically different. Baseball in Canada began, almost, in an experimental process driven by two entrepreneurs, Sleeman and Englehardt. During the period when lacrosse was at its zenith of popularity, about 1880 to 1910, baseball was played and actively promoted and seemed to take root in civic and/ or community boosterism, inspired, in part, by its widespread promotion in the United States. Lacrosse began as a middle-class sport with indigenous roots and an omnipresent value system shrouded in amateur ideals. Montreal middle-class clubs controlled its development, as did the prevailing code of the amateur idealists—professional lacrosse was almost an underground activity. Field lacrosse thrived in the industrial era while baseball seems adaptable and somehow more timeless in its popularity.

Related Websites

Lacrosse History on Wikipedia
http://en.wikipedia.org/wiki/Lacrosse

CBC Radio Audio Excerpts about Lacrosse History
http://archives.cbc.ca/search?q=lacrosse&RTy=0&RC=1&RP=1&RD=1&RA=0&th=1&x=0&y=0

Canadian Lacrosse Association
http://www.lacrosse.ca/

Baseball's Beginnings in Canada
http://www.craigmarlatt.com/canada/symbols_facts&lists/baseball.html

Historian William Humber's View on Canadian Baseball History
http://www.humbersport.org/essays/Bakers.html

Dr Barney and Dr Bouchier's Account about Adam Ford
http://www.la84foundation.org/SportsLibrary/JSH/JSH1988/JSH1501/jsh1501e.pdf

Western Canada Baseball History
http://www.attheplate.com/wcbl/

Study Questions

1. What factors were different in the evolution of lacrosse and baseball?
2. How was discrimination a part of both baseball and lacrosse?
3. How important are international sporting tours in spreading a nation's reputation? Give examples of other Canadian tours in other sports (hockey, for example).
4. What does the designation 'national sport' mean to society? Why do governments designate a sport as being 'national'?
5. Given baseball's widespread playing and spectator appeal, why is it not our 'national sport' instead of hockey and lacrosse?
6. What are the strengths and weaknesses in Barney's and Bouchier's argument that baseball was 'invented' in Canada?

CHAPTER 6

Stars and Heroes: Hanlan, Rubenstein, Cyr, Scott, and Johnson

One of the intriguing ways to look at sport within a particular era is to examine the sport 'stars' or heroes to determine their impact on sport and society and, in turn, the meanings society attaches to each star. Sports heroes provide windows or texts through which we can see how communities eulogize and celebrate their stars.[1] Sports stories, similar to myths, often focus on particular individuals and provide basic images and metaphors that inform the perceptions, memories, and even aspirations of society. Our selection of the five heroes discussed in this chapter is not particularly profound. We sought to examine different sports, different ethnic backgrounds, different societal impacts, and different historical time periods. In the latter respect, we move from the 1870s to the late 1980s, in an effort to explicate the heroic and the heroes in the context of their sporting and cultural times. Ned Hanlan, Louis Rubenstein, Louis Cyr, Barbara Ann Scott, and Ben Johnson achieved not only national but world championship status in rowing, men's figure skating, weightlifting, women's figure skating, and sprinting. Rubenstein was a Montreal Jew, Hanlan a Torontonian of Irish extraction, Cyr the eldest of 17 children of rural French-Canadian parents, Scott an Ottawa debutante, and Johnson a black athlete of Jamaican descent. Our examination of their careers reveals, among other things, the magnetic attraction to sport heroes, and to sport itself, felt by Canadians from all walks of life.

Edward (Ned) Hanlan (1855–1908)

Ned Hanlan was Canada's first individual world champion in sport. Hanlan's sport—**single-sculls** rowing—was one of the most popular spectator sports in Canada during the last half of the nineteenth century. In fact, if public interest, press coverage, international success, and numbers of clubs are criteria, rowing may well have been the major sport at the time.[2] The earliest known regatta took place in 1820 at Quidi Vidi Lake, Newfoundland. Fishing skiffs were the boats used at early regattas in the Maritimes. Garrison officers in the eastern provinces provided the competitive impetus in the sport by importing racing shells from England and Scotland and by organizing clubs and regattas in major cities. There were at least six rowing clubs in Saint John, New Brunswick, during the 1840s.[3] By the mid-nineteenth century a boatbuilding rivalry developed between Saint John and Halifax that led quickly to standardization in the sport as well as to rivalries among various eastern cities. In Ontario, Barrie and Toronto supported a large number of rowing clubs and numerous regattas by the late 1850s. Four-oared crews were the popular form of racing prior to 1860 and no crew was more famed than that of Saint John, which won many events in the United States and Canada during the 1850s and 1860s.[4] In the **Confederation** year a four-oared crew from that city won the world amateur rowing championships held on the Seine in Paris, thereby earning the title 'Paris Crew', which stuck with them in competitions over the ensuing four years.

The popularity of rowing had more than a little to do with gambling and lucrative prizes. Without stringent amateur distinctions (see Chapter 4), the Saint John crews commonly won $2,000 per race, plus undisclosed amounts in side bets.[5] In any sport there is always an urge to find the best or the fastest person, and in rowing this led naturally to the evolution of a popular trend towards single sculling. George Brown of Herring Cove, Nova Scotia was one of Canada's most prominent early scullers. Five times between 1864 and 1875, Brown won the Cogswell Belt, one of the most coveted prizes in North American rowing. In Toronto, Thomas Tinning, hailed as the 'father' of modern rowing because of his mastery of the sleek shell, 'The Cigarette', won the prestigious Toronto Bay Rowing Regatta many times during the late 1850s and early 1860s. Eventually, Tinning sold his 13-kilogram craft to Ned Hanlan, who was world single-sculls champion from 1880 to 1884.

Hanlan's Irish lower-class family background did not endear him to Toronto's snobbish upper- and middle-class British sportsmen, who were dominant in the organization of rowing. Ned's father was a fisherman who also ran a hotel on Toronto Island, and Ned gained his early rowing practice in a fishing skiff, either in the pursuit of angling or in the business of illegally smuggling rum across Lake Ontario to his father's hotel.[6] He won several four-oared and singles sculling races as a teenager in the early 1870s and won the Ontario singles championship in 1875. Shortly thereafter, he came close to being caught by the police for illegally supplying liquor to his father's hotel; Hanlan left Toronto in late May 1876 and carried out his plans to race at the Centennial Regatta in Philadelphia on the Schuylkill River. After he won the regatta, the City of Toronto, overlooking his indiscretion, received him with a tumultuous welcome. No doubt the adulation directed at Hanlan was fuelled by major media attention that focused on the events of the American centenary celebrations.[7] At this moment, Hanlan was an athlete who had broken the law, won a sporting competition, and was fêted as a hero—a combination that would be repeated again and again and would lend a rather shadowy character to the triumphant rowing career that followed. It is intriguing how sport and its heroes and their actions have so often been perceived as somehow outside 'real' life just because of sporting prowess.

Hanlan's external advantages in his sport were two: his backers, and his mastery of the technological innovation of the sliding seat. Five Toronto businessmen—Dave Ward, Col. Albert Shaw, J. Rogers, Jack Davis, and H.P. Good—recognized the lucrative potential of 'handling' Hanlan as a promising rower if he were backed by a small consortium. Sometime between 1875 and 1876, these men formed the Hanlan Club, which managed all negotiations and arrangements, leaving Ned free to train and row.[8] At a time when the professional athlete was regarded as something of an athletic prostitute because of fixed contests in several sports (see Chapters 4 and 5), Hanlan competed only for money, usually $500 to $1,000 a side, before 1878. His club set up all contests and even had Hanlan and his opponents advertise an upcoming race by making whistle-stop tours between Toronto and Barrie. Hanlan reportedly accepted $3,900 from various railroad companies after an 1878 train tour to promote a race with Wallace Ross, the champion oarsman from Saint John.[9]

Hanlan was apparently the first sculler to master the use of the sliding seat, which his backers had imported for him from England. It was a form-fitting wooden seat fixed to wheels that rolled back and forth in parallel tracks with the oarsman's stroke and recovery motions. Hanlan was diminutive compared to most scullers, weighing only 70 kilograms, and standing 75 centimetres high. Perhaps that was part of his appeal; his small size made him appear to be the underdog. He needed the added leverage the sliding seat gave him and he trained and worked hard to perfect his technique because it made possible a longer stroke, a longer lever arm, and a much more efficient

Edward Hanlan, 1878. (Notman and Sandham, Library and Archives Canada, C-025318)

sculling motion. Other oarsmen, wearing slippery, chamois-padded shorts and committed to catching the blade in the water and then prying against a fixed foothold with tremendous upper-arm strength, could not see the logic behind Hanlan's up-and-back motion in the boat—nor, it seems, could they manage his technique. Some newspaper reports suggested that Hanlan must have had some kind of **blacksmith's bellows** propelling his craft underneath the **keel**. It is to Hanlan's credit that he was able to surmount the intricacies of the sliding seat; already blessed with natural talent, it made him a formidable opponent.

In 1878, Hanlan engaged in a series of races with Charles Courtney, the American amateur champion from the Philadelphia races (Hanlan had won the professional championship in the same set of races), at Lachine, Quebec. The three races were well publicized and extremely popular, but they were marked by controversy.

There is a strong possibility that the backers of the two athletes 'arranged' to have Hanlan win the first, lose the second, and win the third race in order to profit by a dramatic series of contests.[10] Given ensuing events and Hanlan's frequently questionable behaviour throughout his career, a fixed set of races seems highly probable.

The twelve **articles of agreement** signed by Hanlan and Courtney for their race on 3 October 1878 stated that they were to row 'a 5 mile race with turn'; the race was to be for $2,500 a side; 'the referee, after preliminary warning, shall start the race by the word "go"'; the race was to be rowed in smooth water, otherwise there would be a postponement; and it was to be governed by the laws of boat racing as adopted by the National Association of Amateur Oarsmen. The last two articles read:

> 11th. This race is not to be rowed for, and is not to involve or affect, the championship of either the United States or the Dominion of Canada, now held by the said Edward Hanlan.

> 12th. It is hereby further mutually agreed that the said Edward Hanlan or his representatives do hereby guarantee the sum of $5,000 in the form of a purse, and as much more as may be raised for the purposes of the said match.

The main concerns were, as far as possible, to ensure equality in the racing conditions and payment procedures for the stakes. Before 20,000 spectators, Hanlan won the first match by a small margin of one-and-a-quarter boat lengths, thereby leaving some doubt about the superiority of one oarsman over the other.

Hanlan's backers did an admirable public relations job, producing the 37-page *Sketches of the Champion Oarsmen: Hanlan and Courtney*,[11] financed by advertising revenue from Montreal businesses. It included an account of Canadian rowing successes, early life stories of each athlete, their records to date, the articles of agreement, and preliminary comments on race conditions. The publication was not merely good advertising; it also gave the conduct of the races an aura of legitimacy and business acumen. Further dignity was added to the event with the distribution of an official program of the 'Championship Boat Race', which featured handsome sketches of the competitors, a full list of the officials, and advertised prices for spectators that ranged from 50 cents for a grandstand seat to $10 for a place on the press steamer that would follow the boats with the referee. Preceding the main event were an Indian war-canoe race of three miles, with a $30 first prize and a 'squaw race' with 'not less than 12 squaws in each canoe' for a $15 first prize. The latter event was an echo of the racism prevalent in at least two other sports of the period, lacrosse (see Chapter 5) and snowshoeing (see Chapter 4). Over the five-mile course of the main event, flags were hoisted on the judges' **barge** to give information to the public on the progress of the race at every half-mile. And, of course, the flags provided good information for betting during the race. If Hanlan was ahead, a red flag was raised; if Courtney was in the lead, a white flag was raised; a blue flag indicated the race was in suspense. Overall it was a masterfully orchestrated piece of entertainment.

Hanlan's narrow margin of victory at Lachine was characteristic of his entire career. Some have thought that Hanlan 'refused to row away from his victims and allow them to suffer an ignominious defeat'.[12] But it is more likely that Hanlan, for whom rowing provided his livelihood, won his races by narrow margins to maintain uncertainty about the outcome, which is the very foundation of all professional sport and its attendant gambling. His technical advantage and talent made him so much better than his opponents that it would have been career suicide always to pull ahead of them at the outset of a race and to stay far ahead, as he could have done. Hanlan and his backers were much too clever to have him go all out in any single event for fear of losing the element of gambling speculation.[13]

Betting on horse-racing events, snowshoeing contests, and matched rowing events was the addiction of the era. Odds were published in the newspapers before every one of Hanlan's races, and gambling outlets and pool-selling ventures were widely available at the contest sites. In selling pools, the operator ran an auction on the athletes. The highest bidder selected his favourite athlete, established odds on him, and the operator then auctioned the odds on the second athlete. Bids on the second athlete had to be close to the odds established by the original highest bidder. Pool-selling worked best when the outcome was uncertain. Front-page headlines were blatant in providing gambling information—for example: 'Toronto Men Putting Their All on Hanlan' (*Toronto Mail*, 2 Oct. 1878). For the Lachine race, 'pools were sold . . . in the Windsor Hotel which presented the appearance of an exchange in one of the Metropolitan Cities of the world.'[14]

Preparations were elaborate for the second Hanlan–Courtney match at Chatauqua, New York, in 1879. In the months following the Lachine race, a great deal of newspaper controversy over Hanlan's and his backers' tactics was aired in the American *Spirit of the Times* and the *Toronto Globe*.[15] In the midst of the disputes Hanlan was shipped to England, where he defeated John Hawdon and William Elliott and added the English championship to his Canadian and American titles.[16] Uncharacteristically, Hanlan won the English contest by 10 lengths. Very likely he performed to capacity solely to annex a title; he was now rowing to establish gambling opportunities in his own country. Again, Hanlan was the toast of the town when he returned to Toronto. A three-mile flotilla followed Hanlan's steamer into the Toronto harbour. One editorial in the *Ottawa Citizen* proclaimed that Hanlan should be knighted for his British victory,[17] a clear indication of the lionization that accompanies superlative sporting feats. The *Toronto Globe* heavily advertised a 'Hanlan Gala Day', during which Hanlan would be presented in full racing costume to the audience attending the performance of *HMS Pinafore* at the Horticulture Gardens.[18] Meanwhile, at Chatauqua a grandstand for 50,000 spectators was erected and a stomach-tonic manufacturer, Hop Bitters of Rochester, provided a $6,000 purse in exchange for five per cent of the gate. A special railway spur-line was constructed into the rowing venue to carry a half-mile-long observation train; steamers sold tickets for $5 per person and hotel rates skyrocketed from $1 to $12 per day.[19] But the race never took place. The night before the contest, 15 October 1879, Courtney's boat was sawed in half. Hanlan rowed the course alone, but the incident was regarded as scandalous in sporting circles. All manner of accusations were made against Hanlan, Courtney, their sponsor, and backers, but no resolution of the 'greatest sports crime ever committed' was found.[20]

Controversy and intrigue seemed inextricably united to Hanlan's athletic career. For one encounter in 1879, against the American Jimmy Riley on Kempenfelt Bay (near Barrie, Ontario), Hanlan was described as 'fat as a bullock' and 'unfit' when the two finished the four-mile race tied for first:

> . . . of course it is just possible that his miserable condition may have something to do with this . . . it is more than possible that he threw away what ought to have

A composite of photographs and painting (the painting by Frederic Marlett Bell-Smith) of Ned Hanlan racing Fred Plaistad, Toronto Bay, 15 May 1878. (Courtesy of the Metropolitan Toronto Library, T-13375)

been a very easy victory by trifling with Riley for the sake of making it a close finish. But if, as some appear to think, the Champion of Canada, the United States and England has descended to the practices of crooked sprint runners [fixed foot races], it will be some time before the people of Canada will go wild over another aquatic hero.[21]

On the contrary, the Hanlan 'mania' never seemed to abate. There was an inevitable backlash, however. In letters to the editor of the *Globe*, disgruntled critics of the 'betting fraternity' associated with Hanlan's races and those who favoured more 'noble' and 'manly' sports such as cricket, shooting contests, and yacht races, were vituperative in their summation of Hanlan's impact. For example:

The fever that has fairly seized the feeble-minded portion of the masses has now been raging for several months past. Column after column has been and is still being devoted to it, until great numbers of people have become so surfeited with what are termed 'aquatics' that they begin to loathe them as Jews do swine. It is said that enough is as good as a feast, but it is very evident that some of the journals labour under the impression that the reading public can never have too much of this simple boat race, where one professional proved himself faster than the other, a fact that is weighing upon some minds so much that they are actually led to make the ludicrous declaration that the honour of nations hung upon this sculling contest.[22]

Perhaps Hanlan's fans were mainly drawn from the working class and gambling elements, whose values were different from those of the upper and middle classes who espoused sport for sport's sake.

Some 100,000 spectators were drawn to the third Hanlan–Courtney race in 1880 on the Potomac River in Washington. Both Houses of Congress adjourned; businesses closed; hats, shoes, and cigars named after the oarsmen were on sale everywhere; pickpockets disguised as clergymen roamed the crowds; partisan spectators wore the colours of their favoured oarsman; a system of coloured balloons and rockets was set up to provide spectators with information on the progress of the scullers; and gambling was as rampant as ever: 'the city swarmed with strangers. In pool rooms, at hotels, and even on the streets, rolls of money were waved by persons who sought wagers.'[23] During the race, **hawkers** and speculators alike ran along the shores shouting, 'Five hundred to three hundred on Hanlan!' or 'Two to one or any amount on the Torontonian!'[24] Courtney folded early in the race and Hanlan won easily, thereby satisfying his Canadian public and quieting detractors of his racing prowess. Only one title remained to be won.

In November 1880 Hanlan defeated the 198-centimetres-tall Edward A. Trickett for the championship of the world in the Oxford–Cambridge boat race on the Thames. The race drew as many spectators along the course as had attended the Hanlan–Courtney encounter on the Potomac. Never in doubt, Hanlan's victory is less revealing of his prowess in this particular case than of his grandstanding conduct. Adorned with a broad moustache, he was always regarded as a handsome man and a crowd favourite, and in this race with Trickett he was the consummate showman. His behaviour—described on other occasions as 'clowning', 'harlequinading', and 'games-manship'—amounted to nothing short of sideshow entertainment and the complete humiliation of his opponent. At various points over the course Hanlan blew kisses to the crowd, stopped to chat or wipe his brow or fan himself. Once he feigned fatigue and slumped over in his boat. As Trickett pulled alongside, Hanlan smiled to the crowd, who went wild with appreciation, and he rowed away from his opponent using alternate strokes of each oar.[25] Unsportsmanlike and technically unethical, such behaviour was nevertheless part and parcel of Hanlan's cockiness and irresistible fan appeal. It is more than noteworthy that the prestigious MAAA, the main instrument of implementation of amateur regulations in Canada (see Chapter 4), invited Hanlan, the consummate professional and world rowing champion, to its gymnasium stage to present a 'tableau' of his rowing technique. All Hanlan did was sit on a stationary rowing machine, mounted on stage, and pretend to row amidst audience applause and adulation. It is intriguing, then, that Hanlan's impact knew few boundaries in an era when professional athletes were not normally held in high regard.

Ned Hanlan defended his world title six times before relinquishing it in 1884 to Australia's William Beach, a physically powerful blacksmith who had learned the sliding-seat technique.[26] Because of his renown, Hanlan was unable to profit financially by matched races during his reign as world champion. For income-producing events, he was relegated for the most part to staging rowing exhibitions and performing 'trickster' feats, such as rowing in a straight line using only a single oar.[27] On his tours of Australia he was honoured, wined, and dined, and his commercial interests were not readily obvious to many Australian sportsmen and reporters. Hanlan also hypnotized much of the rowing public in that country. Diamond rings, pins, buttons, and bracelets were presented to him as gifts in Australia even after his loss to Beach.[28] Hanlan stayed in Australia for over half a year, hoping to regain his title in 1885, but in that he did not succeed. He even returned to Australia in 1887. In the interim, and while on this second tour, he frequently failed to show up for arranged races, made excuses for losing, and fouled his opponents during races.[29] True to form, he turned his trips to Australia into commercial exhibitions, putting on aquatic displays and rowing in exhibitions anywhere he could command spectators and a significant gate.[30]

Hanlan eventually coached oarsmen at two universities, Columbia and Toronto; operated his father's hotel on Toronto Island for a while; and, like Rubenstein in Montreal (see below), was a city alderman for Ward 4 in the late 1880s. In addition to dazzling the world with his talent and showmanship in rowing in the decade prior to 1884, he was regarded personally as a friendly, attractive, humorous man. The *Toronto Globe* claimed that he was single-handedly the greatest immigration agent for Canada in the last third of the nineteenth century.[31] In spite of the shadow cast on his reputation by manipulative tactics and unethical practices he was a classic sports hero whose character flaws were overlooked in deference to the perceived significance of his athletic prowess. At his death he was given a civic funeral in St Andrews Presbyterian Church and 10,000 people filed past his **bier**.[32] In 1926, the City of Toronto spent $17,000 to erect a commissioned bronze statue of Hanlan near the Princes' Gates of the Canadian National Exhibition Grounds in Toronto (the statue still stands there), and he was enshrined in a six-verse poem published in the *Toronto Telegram*.[33] Hanlan's achievements and clear adulation are fascinating facts in the history of Canadian sport. His case is indicative of how society projects its values—like competition and winning—onto a sporting champion.

Louis Rubenstein (1861–1931)

A fascinating contrast to Ned Hanlan in impact and athletic distinction was the more altruistic Louis Rubenstein, who grew up in Montreal at a time when snowshoeing, curling, and ice-skating became increasingly popular.[34] Exactly who or what it was that attracted him to skating is unknown, but the Victoria Rink, with its colourful skating pageants and masquerades, must have played an important role. Perhaps the publication in 1869 and the subsequent popularity of Mary Elizabeth Mapes Dodge's *Hans Brinker or the Silver Skates* fuelled the youngster's interest in skating, but an article in the *Montreal Herald* (18 April 1891) speculates simply, and probably accurately, that Rubenstein 'loved skating' as a boy, and that with 'practice and ambition' he developed his skills. Whatever his early motivation, Rubenstein directed his attention to the sport of 'fancy' skating and in 1878, at the age of 17, he won the Montreal championship.[35]

The development of Rubenstein's career in skating paralleled the growth in popularity of winter sports in Montreal during the late 1870s and 1880s (see Chapter 4). He was the right person in the right place at the right time. After moderate success in sporadic competitions, he won the Canadian figure-skating championship at the Victoria Rink in 1883 and retained it for the next seven years. In this period, the Montreal Winter Carnival—of which ice-skating was one of the sporting competitions—was staged annually and became immensely popular as a tourist attraction. Rubenstein's talent was honed during the 1880s by competing with skaters from Toronto, Montreal, Brooklyn, New York, and Somerville, Massachusetts, and with his two brothers, Abraham and Moses. He outclassed all those skaters.

The single factor in Rubenstein's rise to premier 'fancy skater' was his unprecedented ability to trace and retrace figures on the ice with tremendous accuracy and precision. One hundred years ago, precision skating was the only form known to North Americans. Figure skating was—as the name implies—the tracing and retracing of figures on ice, and Rubenstein's skill was appreciated and applauded. As early as 1884, and again in 1885, he was invited 'at the request of some prominent residents' to give skating exhibitions and take part in competitions in eastern Canada—in Saint John, St Stephen, Newcastle, Bathurst, Chatham, Moncton, and Halifax.[36] In 1884, one poster advertising Rubenstein's expected exhibition in St Stephen, New Brunswick, described his coming as 'The event of the season.'[37] By 1889, the Montreal press fairly burst with praise for Rubenstein:

> Most Montrealers are acquainted with the champion's style and he went through the list yesterday with all his wonted grace and precision, some of the figures executed being marvels of skill and patient practice while the apparent ease with which he surmounted the difficulties of the cross cut and other intricate movements was a sight worth going to see.[38]

It is difficult to appreciate Rubenstein's skill without understanding some basic elements of his sport as it was conducted during his time. Because of the lack of standardization among host clubs for skating competitions, the skaters signed 'articles of agreement' (as did Ned Hanlan in his rowing races), or minor contracts, that delineated the details of the events. Originating in track and field, articles of agreement were a common means of ensuring uniformity for events in a variety of sports. The articles for figure skating stipulated the list of figures (the 'lists', as they were known) to be skated, their specific order, and the point value for each figure. The point values for judging the figures in each category varied from two for basic locomotive-type steps to 15 for double-eight figures skated entirely on one foot. Often the lists differed markedly from competition to competition and disputes were common. For example, in the seasons of 1883 and 1885, arguments between Rubenstein and H. Robinson, a Toronto speed skater, over the lists were aired in the *Montreal Gazette*, a further testimony to the public's strong interest in this sport.[39]

As a member of the Victoria Skating Club, Rubenstein was naturally partial to its list of figures, not only because he was accustomed to them, but because the club was 'the most important one in the Dominion, if not on the continent'.[40] Further, he noted, the club's list had governed all the 'important competitions', such as those for the Dufferin and Bantin medals. In short, Rubenstein contended that he was advocating 'correct' lists, that is, those originating with the Victoria Skating Club. Because of its prestige, the success of the skating competitions in the Montreal winter carnivals, and the press description of Rubenstein as 'the finest figure skater in Canada',[41] Montreal took the leading role in standardizing and organizing the sport. How they did so, to Rubenstein's advantage, provides an interesting case history of nineteenth-century Canadian sporting politics.

On 1 November 1887, a circular was sent to all rinks in Canada giving 15 days' notice of a meeting to form a national governing body to administer both speed and figure skating.[42] Thanks to so little warning, the resulting Amateur Skating Association of Canada was

Louis Rubenstein, 1890. (Courtesy of Don Morrow)

Montreal-dominated. One of its first duties was to codify the list of figures and, of course, the list adopted was the one favoured by Rubenstein and the directors of the Victoria Rink. Regulations to govern competitions were formulated and 21 categories of figures for the championship list were established. Included were the use of inside and outside edges, forward and backward rolls, changes, figure eights, figure threes, rocking turns, grapevines, toe- and flat-foot spins. The club published its 'List of Figures to be Skated at Tournament',[43] in all of which Rubenstein had become extremely skilled.

In addition to his advantage of location, Rubenstein enjoyed the distinct benefit of time—time to train, to compete, and to give exhibitions—that accounts in large measure for his success in a sport demanding precision from constant repetition and practice. He was a partner in the family business of Rubenstein Brothers, a silver-, gold-, and nickel-plating and manufacturing firm in Montreal. Among nine children, Louis and his four brothers shared sporting interests and the firm donated medals for skating competitions as early as 1884.[44] A bachelor, Louis was free from the constraints of family responsibilities. In 1886 alone, he spent five consecutive weeks travelling to and from Picton (Ontario), Detroit, New York, and various places in Vermont, giving skating exhibitions and engaging in competitions.[45]

By virtue of acquiring the United States championship in both 1888 and 1889,[46] Rubenstein was considered the best figure skater in North America by the end of the decade. Recognition of his athletic excellence was widespread and he won many tributes. The *Montreal Gazette* reported that the Ottawa press referred to Louis as 'King of the Ice'.[47] After a visit to Quebec City, Rubenstein was presented with a gold pin 'set with emeralds and diamonds as a souvenir of his visit to the Ancient Capital'.[48] The ice skate manufacturers Barney and Barry of Springfield, Massachusetts, gave Rubenstein 'a pair of the finest skates their celebrated firm can turn out . . . as a mark of appreciation and esteem of the world's fancy skater'.[49] When news of the St Petersburg (Russia) 'world' championship—staged to commemorate the twenty-fifth anniversary of the St Petersburg Skating Club—reached Montreal in mid-December 1889, the choice of the most appropriate and deserving representative to be sent by the Amateur Skating Association of Canada was a foregone conclusion.

Four hundred dollars was raised through private donations to defray Rubenstein's expenses. In early January 1890, he boarded the Cunard Royal Mail steamer *Etruria* in New York carrying letters of introduction from Canada's Governor-General, Lord Stanley, to the Foreign Office and the British ambassador in St Petersburg. Rubenstein knowingly embarked on an adventure, and he entered czarist Russia at the height of the **pogroms** and other organized anti-Semitic practices taken against Jews in that country. Prophetically (and insensitively), the Montreal press stated that 'our skaters can now wait confidently for the cablegram that shall inform us that the redoubtable Louis has either carried off the championship in triumph or is snugly incarcerated in the Trubetskoi Bastion.'[50] Indeed, Rubenstein received extensive newspaper coverage during his two-and-a-half month absence from Montreal, often in the form of his published letters home. When it was all over and Rubenstein was interviewed in Montreal's **Bonaventure Station**, a reporter asked him for his perception of Russia. In jocular fashion, and with characteristic wit—surprising in view of the obstacles he faced and the discrimination he suffered in St Petersburg—he responded:

> Well, before I went there I had an idea that Russia was a country somewhere in Europe but I did not know exactly where its boundaries began or left off; that one end of it was somewhere near India and the other near Constantinople; and the principal productions of the country were Nihilists and nitroglycerine, and that it was governed by a man whose family name was Romanoff and whose business it was to get up every morning and light the sun.[51]

Upon his arrival in St Petersburg, Rubenstein registered at the Grand Hotel d'Europe. He used the four weeks available before the contest to familiarize himself with the outdoor conditions under which he would have to compete. There were no indoor rinks in the city, and wind, the glare of the sun, and extreme cold were the most common problems confronting skaters at the competition. To Louis, the ice felt 'like stone' and made figure-tracing very difficult. Above all, the skating standards were much different in St Petersburg than those under which he had gained such an advantage in Montreal:

> Instead of what we call our list in Canada there are three separate competitions in Russia. The real figure skating or what we call list skating goes under the name diagram skating in Russia. Then there are two other departments—special figures and specialties—and in these there is a tendency to acrobatic work, which would not be recognized as fine skating in Canada.[52]

In short, the evolution of figure skating in Europe was closer to the modern, twentieth-century form of figure skating that had, until relatively recently, included both compulsory and freestyle components. Rubenstein expressed his distaste for 'acrobatics' succinctly when he commented on skaters doing a spread-eagle: 'it was a physical impossibility for some men to look directly north and compel the toes of the right foot to point exactly east, and the toes of the left foot exactly west.'[53] At the time of the St Petersburg event there was no international organization to standardize competitions. The International Skating Union was not established until 1894.[54]

As if the pressures of different conditions and styles were not enough to challenge Rubenstein, he was not spared the effects of Russian **anti-Semitism**. Within a few days of his arrival he was required to go to the municipal police office. Asked if he was a Jew, he responded affirmatively. His passport was seized and a few days later he was taken from skating practice to another police station, only to be told to leave the country within 24 hours. When he asked the reason, he was told: 'You are a Jew, and there is no necessity to further discuss the matter. We cannot permit Jews to remain in St Petersburg.'[55] Rubenstein made his plight known to the British ambassador, Sir Robert Morier, who intervened on Louis's behalf. Ultimately the prefect of police had Rubenstein roused from sleep to meet with him. The skater was told he would be allowed to compete but that he must leave Russia immediately after the contest. Rubenstein's passport was returned with the words 'British subject' crossed out and replaced by 'L. Rubenstein, Jew'.[56]

Apparently Rubenstein's skating talents quickly attracted other competitors and coaches, who came to watch him practice. Finally, on Valentine's Day 1890, the North American press announced his victory in the unofficial world championship event. Within two days the title was rescinded—but it was finally re-awarded. In spite of disadvantages, including the alleged bias of the nine judges, Rubenstein defeated all the other skaters from Vienna, Stockholm, Norway, Finland, Moscow, and St Petersburg by securing first place in two of the three 'departments' in the competition.[57]

Rubenstein returned from St Petersburg in triumph. He was besieged by reporters in both New York and Montreal, but a death in his family subdued his homecoming welcome. He retired from competition in the sport in 1892, after finishing in a first-place tie in the 1891 United States championships.[58] His triumph in, and devotion to, skating led him to write Lessons in Skating (1900).[59]

It is tempting to think of Rubenstein as nothing more than a pioneer and brilliant practitioner of figure skating. But his contribution to sport encompassed many activities as an athlete and/or administrator in other sports and sporting organizations. He also exhibited a tireless devotion to the promotion and conduct of cycling. Attracted to the prestigious Montreal Amateur Athletic Association by the lure of membership and participation in the Montreal Bicycle Club in 1882, Rubenstein showed an active interest in long-distance cycling. Between 1883 and 1886 he placed consistently among the club's top seven cyclists, accumulating the most mileage in a given season. For example, his total in 1885 was 452 miles, and that distance was achieved at a time of high-wheelers, or penny farthings, and poor roads.[60] In competitive cycle racing, he worked on committees concerned with issues of 'Cyclists' Rights' in the city, campaigned for various events, and officiated as a scorer, starter, timekeeper, handicapper, course charter, and judge. Between 1893 and 1900 he served as Montreal's delegate to the Canadian Wheelmen's Association (CWA, the national sport governing body in bicycle racing) and became its president in 1899,[61] which title, or that of honorary president, he retained for the next 18 years. During the late 1890s, he travelled all over eastern Canada to promote the formation of bicycle clubs and their affiliation with the CWA. When Montreal was awarded the World Bicycle Meet in 1899, all confidence was placed in Rubenstein for its efficient functioning. To advertise the meet, his own bicycle club formed a group called 'Rubenstein's Greatest Canadian Bicycle Band', which travelled with him to play selections from Wagner and Beethoven at bicycle races leading up to the world championship.[62] The races of the World Bicycle Meet were conducted on a special third-of-a-mile board track constructed at Queen's Park. Together with its masquerade bicycle parades, moonlight tours, and banquets, the meet was a tremendous success and Rubenstein was involved in every phase of it.

Rubenstein was most interested in sports that required precision, patience, and practice. During the winter in the 1890s he played billiards and bowled (ten-pin) at the

Montreal Amateur Athletic Association and curled at the St Andrew's Curling Club. He was elected president of the Canadian Bowling Association in 1895, the same year he was made honorary secretary of the Amateur Skating Association of Canada.[63] In the latter capacity he 'pulled the labouring oar' for the World Speedskating Championships held at the MAAA grounds in 1897 and was presented with a handsome diamond pin for his efforts.[64] In 1907, he was instrumental in forming the International Skating Union of America, in opposition to the strictures imposed on amateur skaters in both the United States and Canada. Two years later he became its president.[65] It is clear that his administrative abilities were much in demand. In 1911 he was elected president of the Montreal branch of the Royal Life Saving Society,[66] and two years later he became president of the MAAA.[67] Throughout his life he maintained some kind of involvement in sport. During the First World War he campaigned for and worked hard to complete an indoor swimming pool in Montreal. In tribute to his efforts, the $50,000 'Rubenstein Baths' was officially opened in 1916.[68] At the end of the war he was elected president of the Young Men's Hebrew Association and retained the post until his death in 1931. For a similar period Rubenstein represented the St Louis ward in Montreal as alderman.[69]

People who knew Rubenstein in his later years remarked on his selfless devotion to serving others and on his affable personality.[70] At social gatherings, or 'smokers', he was noted for his recitations and his renditions of favourite comic songs, such as 'McCracken's Dancing School', 'Only a Cat', and 'Pay No Rent'.[71] He was inducted posthumously into both the Canadian Sports Hall of Fame and the Jewish Sports Hall of Fame in Israel. His penny-farthing bicycle is preserved in the Chateau de Ramezay in Montreal, where in 1939 a drinking fountain was erected in his honour at the corner of Mount Royal and Park Avenue. And a 1960 publication, Frank Andrews's *Rejoice We Conquer*, contains a poetic tribute to and an account of his 1890 world championship.[72] Thousands of mourners witnessed his funeral cortege in January 1931.[73]

Louis Cyr (1863–1912)

Montreal and Toronto were the recognized centres of Canadian sport in the nineteenth century, and Rubenstein and Hanlan were their much vaunted English-speaking world champion heroes. But Montreal could also boast of a French-speaking hero, Noe-Cyprien Cyr, or Louis Cyr. Born in Saint Cyprien de Napierville, Quebec, Cyr is often remembered, or billed in contemporary accounts of weightlifting, as the 'strongest man who ever lived'. (His biographer, Ben Weider, entitled his book *The Strongest Man in History: Louis Cyr*.)[74] Unlike the accomplishments of Rubenstein and Hanlan, Cyr's were not well publicized during his lifetime, partly because weightlifting was in its infancy. It was not standardized into formal competitions, with uniform weights or weight classes. As a result, some of the information about Cyr's life and athletic career is shrouded in myth or has become legendary. At the same time, his achievements, renown, and impact on his sport, and on French Canadians, and his early leadership in weightlifting, have ensured his place in the pantheon of great Canadian athletes.

Eight kilograms at birth, Cyr inherited his adult size from his mother. She was reputed to be 183 centimetres tall and weighed over 114 kilograms, while his father, a farmer-butcher, was of normal size. In his prime, Louis's vital statistics were:

Weight:	144 kg
Height:	179 cm
Biceps:	61 cm
Neck:	56 cm
Forearms:	48 cm
Chest:	152 cm
Waist:	114 cm
Thighs:	84 cm
Calves:	71 cm

Cyr was only five centimetres taller than Ned Hanlan but his weight was more than double Hanlan's. Apparently his paternal grandfather, himself a village strongman, was a primary influence, encouraging Cyr as a growing boy to develop his strength;[75] strength was a coveted virtue in French-Canadian culture, especially since the economy of much of rural Quebec was based on hard physical work in the lumber-woods and associated forestry industries.[76] Cyr's inherited physique and his environment combined to shape his physical development and interest in weightlifting.

Undocumented stories abound concerning the adolescent Cyr's feats of strength in arm wrestling and lifting heavy loads. At 15, having quit school three years before, Cyr moved with his family to Lowell, Massachusetts, where he lived for four years and worked at odd jobs in the area. During that time he became proficient in English, an advantage and facility that would work in his favour as a public performer. Married to Melina Comtois when he was 19, he moved back to Quebec and worked as a lumberman in the backwoods. Accounts of his strength spread by word of mouth. Finally, in 1885, the reigning strongman, David Michaud, challenged Louis to a boulder-lifting competition. Cyr won the contest by successfully raising one end of a boulder, thought to weigh some 226 kg, and became the unofficial champion strongman of Canada.[77] Following his victory he made a brief tour of the province, giving demonstrations of his prowess.

Near the end of 1885, having saved some money from his tour and after putting in a short stint as a policeman in Montreal, Cyr purchased a tavern called Carré Chaboillex and used it as both a stable economic base and a stage from which to demonstrate his strength and attract paying customers.[78] From there he toured parts of Canada and the United States as a weightlifter for the remainder of the 1880s. During this time he learned to do something that Hanlan had honed to an art; he realized that it was wise to out-lift an opponent by only the smallest margin necessary to win; to dominate lifting events would mean little doubt about the outcome and therefore interest would decline. Cyr's tactic, in the absence of organized competitions, was to issue newspaper or word-of-mouth challenges to strongmen, wherever he was visiting, to test their strength against his. For example, Cyr published a declaration in the *Montreal Gazette* on 24 June 1885:

> I hereby challenge any man in the world, bar none, to a heavy weightlifting contest, without harness, for any sum from one hundred dollars to five hundred dollars a side. Yours truly, Louis Cyr.

By 1889, he had achieved enough distinction and fame to be invited to perform before the Prince of Wales in London's Royal Aquarium Theatre. Cyr reportedly astounded a crowd of 5,000 by raising a 250-kilogram weight off the floor with a one-finger hold on a hook attached to the top of the weight. At the same event he pressed a 124-kilogram barbell from his shoulder with one arm, and, after backing under a platform loaded with weights totaling 1,864 kilograms, raised the platform on his back by straightening at the knees.[79] Such uncommon lifts became trademarks of Cyr's skill and talent.

Throughout his career, Cyr controlled and entertained his audiences both by his impressive demonstrations and by allowing anyone to verify any of the weights he used. For a while, he fancied himself a modern **Sampson**, wore a tight-fitting costume, and grew his hair long after the fashion of the Biblical character; he even used his hair to twirl people around while they held onto his locks.[80] One of his more dramatic exhibitions was to have harnesses strapped to his arms, bent at the elbow in a muscleman pose. The other ends of the harnesses were attached to two pairs of horses that, on a given signal,

Louis Cyr, c. 1890. (Library and Archives Canada, C-086343)

pulled away from either side. In reality, the pairs were actually pulling against each other through Cyr's shoulders: the signal to the horses was precisely timed or Cyr would have been injured for life. Still, from his first performance of this act in 1891 at Sohmer Park, Montreal, it became a favourite.[81] It was reenacted on television in the late 1980s in an American Express commercial.

During the 1890s, Louis Cyr toured Europe and the United States, putting on exhibitions and meeting challenges wherever and whenever he could. Without standardization in his sport, and with no organized ruling body, his weightlifting bordered on a circus performance. In fact, he occasionally travelled with the Ringling Brothers and Barnum and Bailey. Yet his weightlifting records were documented. Probably the most impressive of these were established in 1896 in Chicago's St Louis Arena:

1. right and left arm, 85 kg.
2. left shoulder lift with arm 70 kg.
3. iron cross with 44 kg. in right hand, 40 kg. in left
4. 35 consecutive right arm presses with 74 kg.
5. 251 kg. one finger lift

6. lifted 86 kg. with 2 arms straight in front of his body
7. lifted 448 kg. with one hand
8. lifted 197 kg. from right shoulder without use of knees
9. restrained 4 horses for 55 seconds
10. in one motion, raised or snatched 158 kg. over his head.[82]

Since many of these feats are unorthodox by modern standards and technique, it is difficult to make contemporary comparisons. More significant is the fact that during his lifetime no one could equal Cyr's feats or best him in his self-proclaimed billing as the world's strongest man. He was in a class by himself, as exceptional in his skill, in his way, as were Hanlan and Rubenstein in theirs.

Cyr's appeal was not merely confined to, or defined by, his absolute strength. To complement his talent he nurtured a flair for theatrics, making spectacular and unforgettable entrances.[83] Often when he appeared on stage, the curtain was drawn to reveal Louis, wearing a tight-fitting costume that accentuated his physique, spotlighted in erect stance, arms akimbo. He learned to manipulate the collective emotions of his audiences by building tension before a stunt or by delaying a difficult lift to the very edge of audience patience. In addition, he frequently used members of the crowd in his feats: twirling people from his hair; loading a platform with all the 'fat men' in the audience for his famous back lift; or lifting up a woman seated in the palm of his hand. Once he balanced on his chin a ladder, at the top of which his wife was seated.[84] Such show business tactics had a magnetic appeal to audiences. So popular was Cyr during his 23-week tour of Europe in 1889 that his originally scheduled two-week booking in the South London Music Hall was extended to a full month.[85]

In declining health by 1906, and aged 43, Cyr performed his last competition in Montreal against Hector Decarie, 12 years his junior. Although victorious, Cyr announced that he was relinquishing his title to Decarie and retired from weightlifting.[86] Overindulgence in food and liquor had left him with heart ailments. An asthmatic, Cyr died of Bright's disease on 10 November 1912; his funeral in Montreal was attended by thousands.[87]

In their abundance of talent and in their approaches to sport as entertainment, Cyr and Hanlan were similar. However, Cyr's career had the added dimension of becoming part of Quebec folklore in his lifetime. One researcher found, in sampling 84 Canadian newspapers on dates coincident with significant performances by Cyr, that he was not at all known across Canada; his Canadian renown was apparently confined to Montreal and vicinity.[88] He was not the celebrated hero Hanlan was, but his historical reputation approaches legendary proportions, especially among French Canadians. In that respect, he is a stark contrast to the dominant and prevailing middle-class Anglophone values so firmly attached to organized sport in Montreal during his lifetime.

Barbara Ann Scott (1928–)

In apparent sharp contrast to the colossal strength of Louis Cyr are the perfection and grace embodied by Barbara Ann Scott in her career as an outstanding figure skater in the mid-twentieth century. Different in sex than the three heroes discussed above, Scott had no less an impact in her athletic feats and in her role as a Canadian sport hero; in fact, in the latter regard, in many ways she may have had greater impact owing to the media attention lavished on her. Although Scott's era seems removed from the late nineteenth- and early twentieth-century period of Hanlan, Rubenstein, and Cyr, her influence as an athlete and as a person derived from what she was made to be by the contemporary press.

Barbara Ann's major skating titles can be summarized quite succinctly: national junior champion in 1939; Canadian senior and North American ladies champion for four years beginning in 1944 and ending in 1948; European and world champion in 1947 and 1948; Olympic gold medalist in 1948. From 1949 to 1954 she skated professionally in a variety of ice shows and revues.[89] Between 1947 and 1973, ostensibly the 'golden age' of Canadian figure skating, Canada won 44 world and Olympic figure skating medals, 13 of them gold medals.[90] And yet skating analysts placed her at the end of an era of skating style owing to her skill and perfection in skating school figures. As one writer expressed it, 'she produced her skillful and artistic expression of skating art as if from

Barbara Ann Scott, Olympic Women's Figure-Skating Champion, St Moritz, 1948. (Courtesy of Library and Archives Canada)

out of a box in which everything was perfectly packed and orderly.'[91] Her training towards that discipline began early, at the age of six when she began skating at the prestigious Minto Skating Club in her home city of Ottawa. Hailed by the *Ottawa Journal* that year, she was dubbed the 'darling of the show' for her performance in the club ice follies. Her father, a retired military colonel, and her mother, who always seemed to sit at 'the side of the rink wielding the symbols of skating mother-dom, a pair of number nine knitting needles',[92] made the decision to support their youngest of three children by taking her out of formal schooling and hiring a tutor,[93] thereby allowing her the time to train during the day. For four months each year Barbara Ann practiced school figures and free-skating techniques for eight hours each day; in the summer months, she attended skating schools in Kitchener, Ontario, Lake Placid, New York, and in Schumacher, near Timmins in northern Ontario. Clearly, she worked extremely hard and was a dedicated and disciplined athlete, facts not readily reflected in the press of the day.

During her international competitions in 1947 and 1948, judges perched on their hands and knees to scrutinize her figure tracings and re-tracings and all were consistently awed with her precision in these etchings. Her free-skating routines were marked by careful conservatism with **axel spins**, **double Salchows**, and **stag leaps** (her trademark) that were equally and consistently flawless on the indoor rinks of North America or on the highly unpredictable ice conditions of outdoor rinks throughout Europe. Her coaches— Melville Rogers, Otto Gould, and Sheldon Galbraith[94]—were integral components in her extraordinarily successful career. And yet this excellence was produced within a particular social context that often masked her tremendous athleticism; in stark contrast to the darkness and horrors of war, Barbara Ann was sweet and petite. In that regard, she was a classic example of the eventful hero, the right person in the right place at the right time.[95] *Time* magazine on 2 February 1948 featured her in full colour on its cover as 'Ice Queen'; one week earlier, in the same magazine, she had been the focal point of its feature article, 'Babes in Iceland', coincident with her performance at the European championships. For that competition, it was quipped that 'Prague's newspapers burned up a month's supply of flashbulbs photographing her on ice.'[96] More ebullient was the descriptive portrait held up to Canadians at that time:

> Barbara Ann, with peaches-and-cream complexion, saucer-sized blue eyes and rosebud mouth is certainly pretty enough. Her light brown hair (golden now she bleaches it) falls page-boy style on her shoulders. She weighs a trim, girlish 107 pounds [49 kg], neither as full-bosomed as a Hollywood starlet nor as wide-hipped as most skaters. She looks in fact like a doll that is be looked at but not touched.[97]

Indeed the little doll image was paramount, far outstripping any tributes to her athleticism. Her daisy-like eyes[98] drew viewers into her photographic 'doll-eyed'[99] visage. Her fans were reminded constantly about her own affection for dolls. She practiced ventriloquism with her **Charlie McCarthy** doll as a young competitor and carried her good luck charm, Junior, a stuffed koala bear, everywhere, including at the 1948 Olympic Games. Even Scott was aware of the image she portrayed, as evidenced by her 1968 reference to professional skating rigours, 'they wind you up and put the smile on and out you go.'[100] Engineered by the media, the doll image was literally manufactured and marketed during the 1950s. For $5.95, Canadians could purchase a Barbara Ann Scott doll, wearing either a pink or blue skating costume.[101]

The doll-like image flowed almost naturally from Scott's appearance, the media attention to her appearance, and the sport of figure skating itself, which combines the precision and beauty of dance with the athletic skills of the gymnast. Yet, more than anyone else, Barbara Ann Scott was the media's vehicle for a re-entrenchment (or new wave) of traditionalism that encouraged female domesticity at the expense of competitive involvement. The ideal female athlete, in the prevailing social view, was one who engaged in 'feminine' sports such as diving, synchronized swimming, golf, tennis, and figure skating. In Scott's case, she did not merely symbolize this ideal of a young woman, she was the ideal that became the symbol, or so she was made to be. Her publicity agent during her professional career, George B. Evans, the same man who orchestrated Frank Sinatra's appeal to **bobby soxers** a decade earlier, used to state, 'She's the widest-eyed, blue-eyed gal I ever met. And I fear she's real.'[102] Real she was, but the image was unreal and superficial.[103]

Scott's fame and the attendant media image spread from Ottawa to London to Europe 'like a wind-whipped prairie fire'.[104] In 1948, Scott's photographs in Czechoslovakian newspapers were double (17) in number to those of the red-headed, Hollywood 'bombshell'

Rita Hayworth, who had visited Prague one year earlier.[105] Scott was repeatedly described in the Canadian press as neat, precise, ladylike, calm, tiny, dainty, unpretentious, charismatic, sweet, and above all, feminine. She was literally a national beauty queen on skates. Consider these assorted but consistent 'athletic' descriptors of Scott during her 1947 and 1948 seasons: 'fairy princess of Ottawa', 'charming figure in emerald green', 'darling of Davos', 'cover-girl of Canadian skating', 'Ottawa's own pin-up girl', and 'young lady of the flashing toes'.[106] Clearly, she was a pretty female first and foremost, an athlete a distant second. She was extracted from sport and put on a different pedestal from that of her male counterparts—out of literally hundreds and hundreds of stories and pictures of Scott in the Canadian media during the late 1940s, rarely were these articles and pictures contained in the sports section. Instead, they appeared on the front page or the cover page of the second section, and often there were three to four pages of coverage about her.[107] She was sensationalized for her femininity, not her prowess as an athlete: 'On the centre section of the ice, under gleaming floodlights, a tiny figure in turquoise lamé dress stood poised to begin her performance. . . . The tiny figure whirled in great effortless leaps. . . . Figure flowed into figure with the easy grace of a mountain stream.'[108] And: 'Miss Scott, in a striking pure white costume and white gloves with a skull-cracker cap of red and white, made the figures 'take' with her flashing skates.'[109]

What is revealing in these typical press descriptions are the emphases upon the 'tiny figure', 'effortlessness', legs being 'pushed', making the figures 'take', her 'striking' costumes, and 'flashing' skates. In the media and consequently in the public image, Scott could not merely skate hard or skate with finesse to success. Instead, she 'pirouetted to victory'.[110] Her plane could not just land in Sydney, Nova Scotia, for re-fuelling en route from her post-Olympic performance in Europe; instead, the *Halifax Herald* dramatized the event in storybook fashion: 'Canada's fairy princess of figure skating came home in a shiny air chariot today.'[111] It was the stuff of dreams and romance and youth and the rhetoric of heroism, albeit rather different from male heroism. Even the music Scott chose for her free-skating competitions fit the feminine image like an angora muff: 'Babes in Toyland', the 'Copelia Ballet', 'Ave Maria', 'Les Patineurs', and 'the Gazelle'. At municipal receptions for Canada's darling skater, the standard welcome to her by the local bands was so apropos— 'Let Me Call You Sweetheart' (for Hanlan, it had been 'Hail the Conquering Hero Comes'). Newspaper descriptions of these receptions and attendant banquets had the unmistakable air and terminology more characteristic of a bridal shower than a civic tribute to a world champion athlete.[112]

Barbara Ann's achievements were not unheralded, just couched differently. She was the first female athlete ever to be accorded an official reception by the Ontario legislature[113] and members of the federal House of Commons applauded her Olympic victory, in session, on 6 February 1948.[114] The irony of this level of political recognition is that no level of government could be persuaded to fund her European and world championship campaigns one year earlier. And yet she became the 'girl whose twirling skates spun a web of romance to entrance the hearts of millions',[115] even to the point of inspiring Reverend Mother Mary Thomas Aquinas (her pen name was Maria Sylvia) of the Joan of Arc Institute to compose and publish a 30-line poem, 'Homage to Barbara Ann', in French.[116] Scott was an avid campaigner for the Canadian Red Cross, and the press wasted no time in printing publicity photographs of her wearing the familiar white armband, surmounted by a red cross to add to her repertoire of 'right' values and femininity that was held up to Canadians. And how stunning was the contrast to the values applauded in Ned Hanlan. On Valentine's Day 1948,

Saturday Night scooped all others by publishing a stunning portrait-photograph, by the internationally renowned Montreal photographer Yousuf Karsh, surrounded by tiny hearts and figure sketches of a skater, the whole of which was captioned with a poem, 'Canada's Valentine', written in her honour by Mary Lowrey Ross:

> Dear Barbara Ann: Your Public would
> Prefer to show its gratitude
> With tributes rare and wonderful,
> And, preferably, tangible.
> A rope of pearls, a wrap of mink
> A private, indoor skating rink,
> A larger Buick[117] still and creamier
> With testimonials from the Premier
> But since such gifts are out of line
> We send you this simple Valentine
> A license issued to your art,
> To skate school figures in our heart.[118]

All of the feminine imagery was carefully contrived, but superficial. It kept her an athlete in disguise. Barely mentioned were her qualities of sacrifice, tenacity, determination, her lonely quest for athletic excellence through thousands of practice hours, a real person working towards an admirable human achievement. As she once stated: 'In a slightly scary way I sometimes feel as though I, Barbara Ann, didn't exist at all. I often seem to be something people have conjured up in their minds, something they want to believe I am, something a little bit better than perfect, which no one can be.'[119]

When she 'turned' professional, some of the pristine quality of her amateur image was diminished in the press. Yet throughout her career, her shopping sprees in Paris gleaned more coverage than any of the three times (1945, 1947, and 1948) she won Canada's highest athletic award, the Lou Marsh Trophy (see Chapter 7). She was awarded France's sport medal of honour; yet that fact was buried in one sentence at the end of one press article in 1947.[120] She was an accomplished equestrienne and pilot, yet the press marvelled at her ability to understand the 'complex controls and mechanisms' in the cockpit of an airplane en route to Montreal and Toronto.[121] The press measured Scott in exterior fashion just as she was measured for the gallery of champions in Tussaud's Wax Museum in London, England.[122] The full measure of Barbara Ann was never taken. The author of *Skate With Me* (1950) and *Skating for Beginners* (1953), Scott was better known by the highly romanticized book by Cay Moore, *She Skated into Our Hearts* (1948).[123]

Voted more newsworthy than the Prime Minister of Canada in 1947, the significance of Scott as either a world-class athlete or as the epicentre of the propagation of an image as the female ideal has never really been analyzed. In a brief but more perceptive analysis of Scott in 1975, Susan Swan remarked that 'For women who grew up while she was a skating star ... she was almost [as] important an influence as a mother. She was a female role model that not only said all there was to say about femaleness at that time but a model that implied being female meant being perfect.'[124]

One has only to glance through the advertisements in magazines in the late 1940s and early 1950s to realize just how pervasive was the image of the trim, blonde, neat,

Issues in Canadian Sport History

The Richard Riot of 1955

Maurice 'Rocket' Richard (1921–2000) played for the Montreal Canadiens from 1942 to 1960; arguably, he was the star of the National Hockey League (NHL) in his era and dominated the game in the same way Wayne Gretzky dominated professional hockey during his career. Richard was the first player to score 50 goals in 50 games (in the 1944–45 season) and the first to score 500 goals in a career. He played on eight Stanley Cup teams and served as captain for five of those in consecutive victories from 1955–60.[125]

Very similar to Louis Cyr's impact on French Canadians, Richard was absolutely idolized throughout his playing career; to his fans, he was the very symbol of French Canadian sporting excellence in a sport dominated by English Canadians as players, coaches, and administrators. Part of the

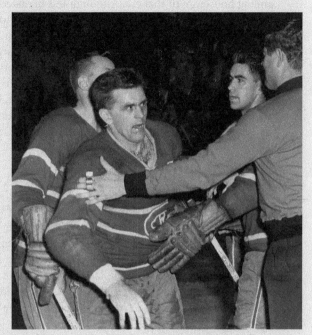

Maurice Richard, left, was suspended by NHL President Clarence Campbell for the final three regular season games and the entire 1955 Stanley Cup playoffs. (The Canadian Press)

mystique of Richard's heroism is attached to the Richard Riot of 1955. On 13 March of that year, Richard attacked Hal Laycoe of the Boston Bruins; while accounts vary, Richard later claimed he retaliated against a high-stick from Laycoe. Nevertheless, Richard did attack both Laycoe and one of the game's officials. Three days later, NHL President Clarence Campbell presided over an official hearing into the incident; the decision Campbell made was to suspend Richard for the remainder of the season inclusive of the playoffs. The suspension was the longest ever given for an NHL on-ice incident. Local media were deluged with outrage from fans.

On 17 March 1955, Campbell and his fiancée attended the Canadiens game against the Detroit Red Wings at the Montreal Forum. Amidst shouting protestors, the crowd frenzy reached its pitch when an exploded tear gas bomb led to the evacuation of the arena. Outside, in St Catherine street, shops were looted and a half-million dollars in damage was done in an area up to 15 blocks from the Forum. Injuries abounded and arrests were made as the riot progressed until it abated at three o'clock in the morning.[126] Richard ended up making a radio plea to his fans to abide by the decision and stop the unruly behaviour. The incident remains one of the most memorable and malicious events in the history of Canadian sport. Some critics perceive the event to have been a precursor to Quebec's **Quiet Revolution** of the 1960s.

smiling housewife of that era. Although less heralded than her peak amateur years, Scott's professional career—the shows, the cross-country tours, the skating demonstrations, the public appearances—served to perpetuate and ingrain the female image created during her peak amateur years. Armed with their Barbara Ann Scott dolls, young Canadian girls dreamed of being Barbara Ann. In reality, Scott achieved far more acclaim than her achievements warranted. Without question, she is one of Canada's most accomplished and decorated athletes. However, the primary focus of public and press attention was never on her athletic achievements; rather, her fame was couched in a carefully constructed set of images, all tied to prevailing cultural perceptions of femininity.

Ben Johnson (1961–)

Somewhat akin to Maurice Richard, what distinguishes Ben Johnson's career and heroic status is controversy on the world stage of sport. If the sawing of Courtney's boat before the second (1879) Hanlan–Courtney rowing race was 'the greatest sports crime ever committed'[127] in that era, the stripping of Ben Johnson's 1988 (Seoul) Olympic gold medal for the 100-metre sprint event is one of the most scandalous affairs in the history of modern sport. Although this distinction places Johnson more toward anti-hero than hero, he is still perceived as a star of considerable magnitude. Consider this perspective on sports 'outcasts and villains' from an article written 10 years after the Seoul Olympic Games:

> In sports outcasts and villains are durable, more than even many of the heroes who shared their eras. They remain on display in memory, jogging recall of thin righteousness or steaming prejudice or crude injustice. The great Indian decathlete Jim Thorpe, stripped of his medals, was destroyed culturally. Jack Johnson, who became the first black heavyweight champ in 1908, was the victim of his times and white sexual fear; Jack was as personal as the lock pick scratching at the bedroom door. Later, Sonny Liston was also taken personally; Sonny, it was imagined, wanted into your bedroom, not for your wife but for her jewels and the wall safe. Now there is Ben Johnson, the aging sprinter who will not retire to his spidered attic of history.[128]

Villain or victim or both, Johnson remains a significant star in the Canadian cultural consciousness.

Comparable to Hanlan, Cyr, and Rubenstein, Johnson came from a minority background. Born in Falmouth, Jamaica, Johnson was the fifth of six children born to Gloria and Ben Johnson Sr, a telephone repair worker.[129] Young Ben's childhood activities included swimming and running—his mother remembers him running everywhere—but nothing formal in the way of organized sport. In the mid-1970s, when Johnson was 15, his family emigrated to Scarborough, Ontario. Quiet, shy, and possessing a slight stammer in his speech, Johnson attended, and finished, high school. In 1977, his older brother Edward, who was a sprinter of considerable talent, introduced Ben to Charlie Francis, coach of the Optimist Track Club at Lawrence Park Collegiate Institute. Francis was a former Canadian sprint champion in the early 1970s and was a member of the Canadian Olympic team for the 1972 Games in Munich. Not only was he Johnson's long-standing coach through to the Olympic Games in 1988, he was the national sprint coach for nine years leading up to those Games.

Under Francis's tutelage, Johnson won the 100-metre Canadian junior championship in 10.66 seconds in 1979. After that, his rise to national caliber status was relatively meteoric. He was named to the Canadian Olympic team for the Moscow Games in 1980; however, Canada boycotted the Games as a national protest against the Soviet invasion of Afghanistan.[130] In 1982, he won two silver medals at the Commonwealth Games in Brisbane, Australia, one medal in the 100-metres, the other in the 4 x 100-metre relay team. At the 1984 Los Angeles Olympic Games, he won bronze in the same two events as in Brisbane; later in the same year, at a meet in Zurich, Switzerland, he established a new Canadian 100-metre record of 10.12. In 1985, after seven consecutive losses to American sprinting sensation Carl Lewis (winner of four gold medals in Los Angeles), Johnson finally beat him and then added the World Cup championship in Canberra with a time of 10 seconds flat.

Ben Johnson races as a junior in the relay event at a meet in Sudbury, Ontario in 1980. (Photograph by Claus Anderson)

In terms of world level sprinting achievements 1986 and 1987 were Johnson's watershed years. In the former year, he beat Lewis three times, including a decisive, widely televised event at the Goodwill Games in Moscow, thereby establishing his reputation and contributing to the national level hype over 'Canada's own' Ben Johnson. For the 1986 Commonwealth Games in Edinburgh, Johnson was elected flag-bearer and he won gold in the 100-metres at these Games. By the end of that year,

> Johnson was finally acknowledged as the Number One ranked 100-meter man in the world. He had recorded ten finishes under 10.10 seconds, his average 100-meter time in 1986 was a stunning 10.025 seconds....Every time he came out to the track, Johnson looked bigger and stronger and more determined.[131]

His athletic achievements escalated from the previous year. Between 15 January and 7 March 1987 Johnson set and/or re-set world indoor sprint records in the 50 metres

Ben Johnson winning the Olympic 100-metre gold medal ahead of American Carl Lewis. (ROMEO GACAD/AFP/Getty Images)

(5.55 seconds) and 60 metres (6.41 seconds) in four major national and international races. Significant recognition of his banner years came in a variety of forms. In both 1986 and 1987, Johnson won the Lionel Conacher Award for best Canadian male athlete of each year, and he won the Lou Marsh Award (see Chapter 7) given annually by a panel of journalists in recognition of being Canada's top athlete.[132] On 29 April 1987, a little more than a month after setting his 60-metre indoor world record, Ben Johnson was invested as a Member of the **Order of Canada**, a most significant and fitting acknowledgement from the federal government for his world-class sprinting achievements.[133] For Johnson, his crowning achievement—one that came 10 years after meeting his coach Charlie Francis—was his stunning 100-metre world record performance of 9.83 seconds, set on 30 August 1987 in Rome, Italy at the World Track and Field Championships.[134]

For the next year, Johnson held onto the title of fastest man on earth. He became a lucrative marketing commodity with some reports claiming he earned as much as $480,000 per month in endorsements.[135] Johnson's arch-rival, Carl Lewis, became outspoken in his insinuation about 'some' track and field athletes relying on banned substances after Johnson's world record achievement in Rome. The very clear implication was that Johnson was among that group. For Canadians, if judged by the national media, Lewis's accusations served to dump fuel on the fire of expectations leading up to the Seoul Olympic Games in September 1988. Lewis, to the Canadian media, was the brash, outspoken American vocalizing sour grapes over his loss of number-one-world-sprinter status to 'Big Ben'.[136] As if to add more to the conflagrations of hype,[137] Johnson seemed to be enjoying his lucrative lifestyle while retreating from a number of races with proclaimed hamstring injuries. When Lewis defeated Johnson in Zurich in August 1988, the first meeting of the two sprinters since the Rome event, doubt crept into the national consciousness about Johnson's Olympic chances for a gold medal.

The Games of the 24th Olympiad opened on 17 September 1988 in Seoul, Korea, a torn and battle-weary city. The war atmosphere raised the spectre of the 'Olympic massacre' in Munich 16 years earlier. By contrast, the very symbol of peace and charity, Mother Theresa was visiting Canada and the country's United Church had just voted to permit the ordination of gay ministers. In sport, not only were Canadians anxious about Johnson's chances of victory, but the nation had been rocked by the Edmonton Oilers' August decision to trade Wayne Gretzky to the Los Angeles Kings in the NHL.[138] As Brantford, Ontario poet laureate John B. Lee expressed it,

When Gretzky went to L.A.
my whole nation trembled
like hot water in a tea cup when a train goes by.[139]

'King Carl', as the media dubbed Lewis, had publically declared in Zurich that he would never again lose to Ben Johnson. Lewis was Johnson's nemesis of **brobdignagian** proportions and the national foreshadowing for the Olympic 100-metre event was not optimistic. Even the Canadian press acquiesced and opined all hopes rest on 'three women and a horse'.[140] Somewhat ironically, Big Ben the sprinter was replaced in the media aspirations by Ian Miller's show jumping horse, Big Ben.

Akin to the 'where-were-you' memories of major events such as the assassination of President John F. Kennedy or men landing on the moon, most Canadians who were alive in 1988 have some recollection of Ben Johnson speeding to Olympic gold in a world record time of 9.79 seconds on 24 September 1988. Embedded in the collective memory is the image of Johnson, dressed in bright red track shorts and top, muscles rippling, leading the whole pack of runners from the start, then, almost at the finish line, raising his right arm, index finger extended to proclaim his number one status, while simultaneously looking over his left shoulder to see Lewis well behind him.[141] Newspaper headlines were declarative and succinct:

Benfastic
Ben Triumphs
Our Ben's Best
Big Ben Grabs Gold, Record

Against the backdrop of Canadian Olympic performances and athletes described as 'faltering', 'drowning', and 'choking', Johnson's world record and gold medal were not just an event triumph but an overwhelming injection of hubristic euphoria among the Canadian population.

Sixty-two hours later, the world learned that Johnson's urine samples had shown significant amounts of the anabolic steroid **stanozolol** and he was disqualified for using a banned substance. The front page of the *Toronto Sun*, in bold headlines, asked, 'Why, Ben?' and carried the caption, 'Canada's shame'.[142] The *Toronto Star* was more graphic in its expression of the impact of the scandal; the star carried an editorial cartoon of a Johnson-caricature, head down, body pinned to a wall by a gigantic 'steroids'-needle that pierced the Canadian flag over Johnson's heart; on the floor, beneath his feet, lay his gold medal.[143] Reminiscent of the child's query 'Say it ain't so, Joe', to baseball player Joe Jackson who was declared guilty of conspiring to fix the 1919 World Series, another paper asked, 'Say It Ain't So, Ben', while others were less kind and more spiteful with labels of Johnson as, 'Fastest Junkie on Earth' and 'Bennies Johnson'.[144] Canadian euphoria evaporated as quickly as it had grown.

Athletic justice in the Ben Johnson scandal was swift. At first, Johnson and Charlie Francis unequivocally denied using steroids. On 3 October 1988, *Sports Illustrated* ran its weekly issue with the front cover featuring a picture of Ben Johnson in full sprint stride, overlaid with one word, 'Busted!' Inside the issue was a stunning piece of investigative journalism with just too much evidence about how, where, for how long, and from whom Johnson had received steroids.[145] During the week after the announcement, the Canadian media were feverish in their addiction to and quest for information and stories on the scandal; on a daily basis most major papers devoted from five to eight pages on the story. Simply put, Ben Johnson got caught but not just in any sporting event; he was caught on the world stage, in the Olympic cauldron of sport, in the 100-metre event that defines the modern Games and leaves its victor with the revered title of 'world's fastest human'.

Not long after the Games the federal government established the 'Commission of Inquiry Into the Use of Drugs and Banned Practices Intended to Increase Athletic Performance'. The commission was headed by Ontario Appeal Court Chief Justice Charles Dubin and the process and resultant report became known as The Dubin Inquiry.[146] Released in 1990, the *Dubin Report* resulted in the establishment of an independent, non-profit Canadian anti-doping agency that became responsible for drug-testing, policy, practice, and implementation in Canada. In their testimony to the Commission, both Johnson and Francis admitted to the use of steroids. Following the release of the *Dubin Report*, Charlie Francis wrote and published his book, *Speed Trap: Inside the Biggest Scandal in Olympic History*.[147] Obviously, the book presents Francis's perspective on the events; however, one of the major admissions in the text is that Johnson participated in a sophisticated steroids program beginning in 1981. As a result of the Dubin findings, Francis's book, and other incriminating evidence, Ben Johnson was stripped of his world records. *Track and Field News*, the guru organ of the sport, annually awards its prestigious title, 'athlete of the year'. For 1987, the award citation reads,

> 1987 — Said Aouita (Morocco) 1500/Mile, 5000
> (Ben Johnson [Canada] led voting at time, but retroactively stripped of honor)[148]

Sadly, Johnson's decision-making and actions have resulted in a very clearly defined national embarrassment. Steven Jackson has argued that 'media discourses [showed] overwhelming resentment toward Ben Johnson, revealing both racist and ethnocentric attitudes and practices within Canada.'[149] For example, Jackson's research demonstrates that before Johnson's rise to fame, the media labeled him as 'Jamaican immigrant'; once his track prowess became established, they referred to him as 'Jamaican-Canadian'; by 1987, coincident with his World title attainment, he was 'Canadian'. After his disqualification, Johnson re-gained his hyphenated label, 'Jamaican-Canadian'.[150] In Jackson's final analysis Ben Johnson's legacy was such that 'he brought the end of innocence to Canada's highly self-idealized reputation as the "fair play" nation. Canada's response was strategic damage control initiated through the Dubin Inquiry.'[151] In short, Ben Johnson became somewhat of a pariah in his adopted country.

Since the Johnson scandal, there have been many other athletes found guilty of using banned substances to enhance athletic performance, Carl Lewis among them.[152] Regardless of his guilt, Ben Johnson was a world-class athlete, perhaps iconic in representing the pressures of high performance sport in his era. He was briefly reinstated and competed in the 1992 Barcelona Olympic Games, but inauspiciously finished last in his semi-final heat after stumbling out of the blocks. A year later, he was found guilty of doping at a race in

Montreal and was banned for life by the International Amateur Athletic Federation. He subsequently coached several athletes, developed a clothing line (whose motto was 'Catch Me'), and ran stunt events such as one in Prince Edward Island where he ran against a horse and a stock car. With a touch of poignant and sardonic humour, Johnson appeared in a series of television advertisements for Cheetah Power Surge 'energy-drink' beverages. In the ads, Johnson was asked, 'Ben, when you run, do you Cheetah?' and he responds, 'Absolutely, I Cheetah all the time.'[153] Interestingly, owing to Johnson's decision to sue his former lawyer for 37 million dollars,[154] the 'shamed sprinter' was named the *Toronto Star*'s 'newsmaker of the year' in 2008,[155] 20 years after the Olympic scandal. Such is the power of the media and the elevated status society accords to its sporting heroes.

Conclusions

The careers of these five famous sports figures—Hanlan, Rubenstein, Cyr, Scott, and Johnson— not only represent exceptional athletic achievement but also illuminate the enthusiasm for, and the significance of, sport in nineteenth- and twentieth-century Canada. And they provide evidence in Canadian sports history of the impact athletic heroes have on their society in any era. Their stories have been, and continue to be, important in our culture.

Related Websites

Louis Cyr: Wikipedia
http://en.wikipedia.org/wiki/Louis_Cyr

Louis Cyr
http://www.municipalitestjeandematha.qc.ca/louiscyr.html (click on the photo of the statue to read his memorial)

Ned Hanlan: Canada's Sports Hall of Fame
http://www.cshof.ca/accessible/hm_profile.php?i=163

Children's Literature on Hanlan
http://www.umanitoba.ca/outreach/cm/vol14/no4/fireonthewater.html

Hanlan—Early Tobacco Card
http://www.rowinghistory-aus.info/world-pro-sculling/1884.php

Rubenstein Brothers Company
http://www.rubenstein.ca/html/eng/history.html

Barbara Ann Scott Photo Gallery
http://www.canoe.ca/2002GamesBarbaraAnnScott/home.html

The Skating Gallery—Scott's Pro Career with Ice Revues
http://theskatinggallery.com/php/programs.php3?sub=Barbara%20Ann%20Scott& page1

Barbara Ann Scott Doll
http://www.antique67.com/articles/BarbaraAnnScott_dolls/BarbaraAnnScott_ dolls.php

YouTube's Video of the Seoul Olympic Games 100-metre Final
http://www.youtube.com/watch?v=cCh5QswxQ6k

CBC **Archives of Video Clips on Ben Johnson**
http://archives.cbc.ca/sports/drugs_sports/topics/1392/

Audio Collage of the Dubin Inquiry Hearings
http://archives.cbc.ca/sports/drugs_sports/clips/8964/

National Film Board of Canada: *The Hockey Sweater*
http://www3.nfb.ca/collection/films/fiche/?id=13316

Study Questions

1. What distinguishes a hero from a legend?
2. Is a heroine different from a hero?
3. Was Cyr, a French Canadian, treated any differently by the press or public from other heroes?
4. Is there historical evidence that racial discrimination in sports was prevalent in Canada?
5. What are the prominent issues in the controversy over the use of drugs in elite sport?
6. What were the impacts of these five stars on society?
7. To what kinds of societal privileges or exemptions should stars/heroes be entitled?
8. Are heroes obliged to uphold and reflect social values?

CHAPTER 7

Sports Journalism
and the Media

———◆◆◆———

Mediated transmissions of sport and about sport are a fact of everyday life in contemporary Canadian culture. To mediate means, in one nuance, to transfer something from one place to another. Media are the various means of mass communication—newspapers, magazines, radio, and television—distributed from the people involved in their production to the mass markets of media consumers. Journalism is one facet of media production wherein reporters cover, research, and write stories and produce images/photographs for the press, periodicals, e-zines, and/or photo-journal formats. In the gathering and production of mediated events, consumers are presented with factual information, opinion pieces, editorial perspectives, investigative journalism, and on-the-spot images of events.

Canadian media expert Marshall McLuhan coined a phrase about the media that has become one of the most widely quoted axioms about interpreting mediated sources: 'the medium is the message', meaning that the way by which a message is sent is as important, if not more important, as the message itself.[1] For example, for one of the largest spectacles in modern society—the Olympic Games—consumers rely on media transmissions for viewing *the* Games; however, in point of fact, for millions of patrons, the media are *the* Olympic Games because we can only know the Games from the 'feed' we receive from various broadcasting networks and their producers. Thus, we are subjected to the biases and perspectives of particular broadcasters, just as we are from news events sent to us from anywhere in the world by whatever source they are transmitted. In Canada, we have a very large media distribution agency, **the Canadian Press** (CP). In today's terminology:

The Canadian Press along with its French-language counterpart, La Presse Canadienne, is Canada's not-for-profit, multimedia news agency. We have been keeping Canadians informed and telling people the story of their country for almost 90 years.... Many Canadians are familiar with THE CANADIAN PRESS credit on countless newspaper stories and photos capturing memorable events, as well as the radio news reports from our broadcast journalists. However, most may be surprised to learn that much of the Canadian content online comes from The

Canadian Press as well. We are also the exclusive distributor of The Associated Press in Canada. The Canadian Press World Desk editors sift through a massive file of international news stories from AP, the world's largest news agency, looking for stories of particular interest to Canadians.[2]

Almost 100 years ago, the Canadian Press Limited re-distributed news from the **Associated Press**—currently the oldest and largest news organization in the world with 243 bureaus in 97 countries—until the CP established itself as its own agency in 1917. Although having a central news agency can mean that we receive a lot of 'homogenized' news, in sports reporting Canada has an extensive number of sports journalists who have mediated their often colourful and unique views on sporting events locally, nationally, and internationally.

This chapter explores some of Canada's earliest and most well known sports journalists—newspaper journalists—in order to show the nature of sports reporting and the symbiotic relationship of the media with the evolution of Canadian sport within the context of the sporting times. We have selected both male and female sport journalists whose writing and careers evolved during the first half of the twentieth century. The relationship of these newspaper journalists and the press in general with other media formats such as magazines and radio, where appropriate, is discussed, albeit very briefly.[3] Our intention in focusing on newspaper journalists is to provide significant insight into the inextricable interconnectedness between one primary media form with the development of sport and the meanings attached to sport.

Lou Marsh and the Rise of Canadian Sport Journalism

As noted in Chapter 4, most nineteenth-century newspaper reports about sport were very factual and, in the first part of the century, more focused on the social aspects of the events in respect of the privileged classes who were able to afford to play sport. Printing newspapers at the time was a cumbersome process; steam-powered cylinders were the norm, typesetting often was done by hand, and typewriters were not in common usage until the 1880s. The boon for sports coverage came when telegraph services paralleled the railway line development within provinces and across Canada. By the late nineteenth century, factual sports reporting—who did what, and where, and when—became more common. For major sporting events in larger urban areas, such as Stanley Cup games, crowds gathered outside telegraph stations to get 'first-hand' accounts of the games.[4] With regard to newspapers in Canada, the evolution of a separate section and the transition to a sports page(s) was a gradual shift that took place around 1892 to 1914, depending upon the size of the newspaper and its revenues. One of the earliest sports editors was William Abraham Hewitt, father of the famous Canadian hockey broadcaster, Foster Hewitt. William served at *Toronto Star* as sports editor from 1900 until 1931. Of intrigue and technological interest is that in his autobiography, *Down the Stretch: Recollections of a Pioneer Sportsman and Journalist*, William Hewitt proclaimed that over his 36 year career, he wrote all his stories by hand and never used a typewriter.[5]

The same year that Hewitt became sports editor of the *Star* (1900), he hired a junior reporter, Lou Marsh, who had been with the paper since 1893, to serve as his assistant.[6] For the next 36 years, Marsh 'lived his life on the inner rim of the sports wheel', as one writer quipped.[7] During his career, Marsh earned himself a national reputation for his colourful journalism:

Just before Canadiens and Leafs played at Maple Leaf Gardenns Saturday night [7 March 1936], the teams lined up at the centre ice opposite each other and the audience rose with bared heads and stood in silence while the big clock ticked off one minute. It was another testimonial to the memory of the late Lou Marsh.[8]

One year and one month later, 8 January 1937, the Canadian Press announced that Dr Phil Edwards, 'the dusky flash of three Canadian Olympic teams', had been selected as the first recipient of the Lou Marsh trophy.[9] Every year since then, the name of Lewis Edwin (Lou) Marsh has been resurrected annually, when a select panel of sport journalists vote to name Canada's best athlete, male or female, amateur or professional; it is the highest national sport honour a Canadian athlete can achieve.[10] At the top of the octagonal, black marble Lou Marsh Memorial Trophy is an etched plaque carrying Marsh's image and his column masthead:

> With Pick and Shovel
> Knocks and Boosts
> Slams and Salve
> By Lou Marsh
> Sports Editor of the Star

And so it is that a sportswriter is equated with Canada's highest athletic honour. What did a sportswriter do to merit the honour of being equated with the pinnacle of athletic excellence? A great deal can be learned about Canadian sport from examining the 'Pick and Shovel' columns in terms of the sporting ideals espoused by Marsh, as well as by studying the style and techniques he employed in his journalism.

One of Marsh's advantages in sports reporting was his own athletic background. He played football from a young age, an interest which culminated in playing for the Toronto Argonauts as quarterback. He joined the Irish Canadian Track Club as a reputable sprinter. He both raced against and coached one of Canada's best sprinters, Hamiltonian Bobby Kerr who eventually won the 1908 London Olympic Games 200-metre event.[11] Perhaps the most famous athlete coached or trained by Marsh was long distance runner, Tom Longboat. While Longboat was managed by Tom Flanagan within the Irish Canadian Club, it was Marsh who served as Longboat's coach and aid during his two most famous marathons, the 1907 Boston marathon (won by Longboat) and the controversial 1908 London Olympic Games marathon during which Longboat collapsed, ostensibly from an overdose of strychnine, a central nervous system stimulant[12] (see the Issues box on Tom Longboat in Chapter 4). More distinguished than his athletic career was Marsh's success and renown as a referee in both boxing and ice hockey. In the latter regard, he was recognized as a referee of the highest calibre up to and including Olympic and professional levels (the NHL). For example, Marsh refereed the first professional hockey game ever played in New York's Madison Square Gardens in December 1925. At the time, referees commonly wore white shirts, black ties, and blue pants, blatant targets for the expectorant from tobacco-chewing fans. In the physically aggressive Northern Ontario Hockey League, Marsh was known to use a cow bell instead of a whistle in order to keep games under control.

An angler, hunter, and golfer of average frequency, Lou Marsh was devoted to sailing, on water and ice, and to motor boat racing. When the small outboard crafts were invented and first displayed skittering over Toronto Bay, Marsh coined the term 'sea-flea' to characterize

The original Lou Marsh Trophy. (Courtesy of Canada's Sports Hall of Fame)

them. Over the years, Marsh owned seven racing sea-fleas, each named 'Pick and Shovel' (I, II, III etc.). Apparently, he was as well known for the sea-flea term as he was for his characteristic, patented jerk of the thumb over his shoulder that motioned many a delinquent player to the penalty box when he was refereeing hockey. In his later years, Marsh was a respected steward for at least four different horserace courses (Long Branch, Dufferin, Kenilworth, and Metropolitan) in Ontario. He attended and reported on every Olympic Games between 1908 and 1932 and refereed Olympic ice hockey games in 1924 and 1932. Baz O'Meara, sometimes touted as the dean of Canadian sportswriters, wrote that Marsh 'loved controversy, the heat of athletic conflict, the smoke and fire of the sports pit'.[13] Frederick Wilson, former sports editor of the *Globe* adjudged that 'Lou Marsh knew more about a greater variety of sports than any other man in the sporting world.'[14] All of Marsh's athletic involvement was done in concert with his full-time job with the *Toronto Star*, often covering events in which he coached or refereed.

Married with two daughters, he served in France during the First World War, in which he attained the rank of major before he was injured and forced to return home. Thereafter, he insisted that no one address him by his official rank since the war was over. Many people described his character as gruff and forceful, traits which carried over from perceptions of his role as hockey and boxing referee. His writings and his actions reveal a generous man, full of humour, whose single aggravation was hypocrisy, in whatever form, in sport. He was a sport crusader but one who campaigned with the insight and empathy gained from his many years as a competitor and knowledgeable observer of competitive sport.

And what of his journalism? Simply stated, it was unique. He wrote as he talked; a literary critic very likely would say that he floundered with dots and dashes and exclamation marks. His paragraphs were brief—frequently just one sentence in length—and punchy. Marsh's colleagues pinpointed his writing style with the following adjectives: terse, pungent, sparkling, snappy, crisp, breezy, racy, graphic, vigorous, colourful, slangy, and unvarnished.[15] No matter how they might be framed, Marsh's columns were always readable, not pedantic. For example, he contrived his own lexicon, and even made up words such as those that he often used to start sentences:

> Ferinstance
> Whoinel
> Buleeve muh
> Safunnything
> Lottsa
> Howja
> Diddin I tellyuh

Such lingo served to endear him to his readers and to invite a loyal following. In the same vein, he made up original terms, likely intended to have the same seductive impact as his sentence-starters:

Horn-rimmed cheaters = reading glasses
Wooer of My Lady Nicotine = cigarette smoker
Show the saffron = to be yellow or a coward
Wibble wobblers = race walkers
Corrugated pill = golf ball
Bell ringers = hockey referees
Mitfest = boxing match
Cauliflower culture = boxers
Scow with an Evinrude wasp on her tail = motorboat
Mastodonic acrobats = professional wrestlers
Pavement pounders = long distance runners

By using such terminology, Marsh created a distinctive style of sport writing and, more importantly, he was able to present his point of view graphically, concisely, and with varying degrees of humour. He had a special gift of being able to say in one sentence what it might take others three or four sentences to explain. For example, Marsh once characterized the irascible Toronto Maple Leaf player King Clancy as '170 pounds [77 kg] of barbed wire and nitro[glycerine]'.[16] All of these devices, and many more, made his 'Pick and Shovel' column one of the most widely read single pieces of sports journalism in Canada, and, to a certain extent, in the United States.[17]

The 'pick and shovel' epithet on his column masthead became his trademark and represented Marsh's consistent attempts to dig into sport in all of its ramifications. Where he saw fit, he could be caustic about anyone or any practice he felt deserved stinging criticism; at the same time, he often awarded 'bouquets', as he called them, to any person, athlete, or administrator in the sporting realm who he believed warranted praise. More characteristically, Marsh enveloped his comments in humour. Typically, the last paragraph of his columns contained a joke about stereotypically impecunious Scotsmen, or, ethnic and racist quips (characteristic of that period) about Chinese, Black, or Jewish groups. Most of his comic comments were intended to tickle his readers' interest, yet with a specific point. For example, when he wished to emphasize a hockey team's poor marksmanship, he played upon the team name suggesting that the Niagara Falls Cataracts be re-named the Niagara Falls Astigmatisms. Or, he would use a definition such as 'A hick town is where they play seven-man, half-hour period hockey, lift the puck from end to end, time the game by the town hall clock, and pay the referee off in eggs.'[18] Similarly, he was not content merely to report the result of an event such as a small bonspiel held in Lindsay, Ontario. Instead, he integrated the results with the fact that the winning team—all members of a small, rural community—was awarded floor lamps as the first prize. The implicit humour, not lost to his readers, was the assumed fact that none of the team members lived in a house with electricity.[19]

From a historical perspective, Marsh's use of wit provides insight in to the nature of sport during the first third of the twentieth century; the hick town definition is a prime example. By contemporary standards, his Jewish jokes might be seen as made in bad taste. Very likely, he intended them as harmless humour. For example, when Fanny Rosenfeld, voted Canada's female athlete of the first half-century, departed for Amsterdam for the 1928 Olympic Games, Marsh warned her well-wishers to 'be careful who you say, "bring home the bacon" to' when her train departed from Toronto.[20] After Rosenfeld's photo finish in the 100-metre final, Marsh quipped:

> Fanny Rosenfeld's first remark after the 100-meter final, 'Was I first or second?'
>
> ★　★　★
>
> Her second remark when informed that the official decision was 'second,' was, 'If I had won, they would have presented me with a synagogue—now all I'll get will be a pew.'[21]

Racist or not, Marsh's intention and effect, as always, was to attract readers. People wanted to read what 'Old Pick and Shovel' had to say about sport each day in his column.

Marsh wrote in an easy, straightforward manner, apparently always striving to reach a wider readership. The only classic literary device he employed was the simile. Several examples follow:

- On attending a six-day bicycle race in 1933, Marsh stated that he felt '…as comfortable as a Bedouin suddenly set down of the shores of Baffin Bay'.[22]
- When miniature or Tom Thumb (the diminutive folklore character) golf became popular in the 1930s, Marsh employed a comparison close to the heart of all Depression era farmers. He said the game was 'spreading like an epidemic of grasshoppers'.[23]
- After a Montreal Canadiens' hockey contest in 1931, Marsh stated that the team's two stars, Aurel Joliat and Howie Morenz, 'went through the Leafs' defense like a Kansas cyclone through a chicken coop'.[24]
- In 1925, he noted that Canadian National Exhibition sports director, Elwood A. Hughes was 'as busy as a yellow dog with exzema'.[25]
- While campaigning for greater forward passing allowances in ice hockey at a time when the game was very static and forward passing was greatly restricted, Marsh opined: 'For thrills a 6–5 hockey game lays over a 1–0 hockey game like an ostrich would over a hummingbird's egg'.[26]

Humour and similes were hallmarks of Marsh's columns; they were the techniques that made his journalism so appealing to readers interested in points of view, or colourful, encapsulated descriptions and commentary that went beyond the level of more standard, factual reporting of sports. The latter was readily available in the sports pages of Canadian newspapers; however, columnists like Marsh provided a kind of punctuation to the events, all in obvious efforts to sell newspapers to sport-hungry populace.

Comparable to all writers, Marsh needed and skillfully used a 'hook', that is, an interest-grabbing device designed to draw readers into his column. These leads included poems written by 'Wilfred', the poet laureate of the 'Pick and Shovel' column, such as this verse of universal appeal to golf enthusiasts:

> Doesn't it get
> Your dander

Up
When the
Ball
Stops dead
On the lip
Of the cup?[27]

And in Marshian effervescent enthusiasm over an exciting game, he wrote:

Hot Hannah!
And likewise Torrid Tilly!!
And also Jingery Juila!!!
Wotta battle! Wotta battle![28]

Similarly, he would close his column with a mild joke or, more commonly, with a personal sign-off; for example, 'So long folks, the muskies and the bass are calling. See you Monday night.'[29] Even his self-mocking closings must have been endearing for readers: 'Wanted—a golf caddy. Steady employment, April to November. Must not be able to count over 100. Apply to Pick and Shovel editor.'[30]

In between the lead and the closing comment was sporting coverage and comment that burst with plum-pudding richness. Marsh's informality in writing could be noted in his apologies for ever having to use the 'cap I' and in his consistent reminders to 'Mr Compositor' to be sure to include a certain form of punctuation or spelling. Marsh believed in amateur sport, professional sport, and, unlike his contemporary amateur sport governing officials (see Chapter 4), allowing amateurs to compete with and against professionals, particularly in individual sports like the very popular bicycle races of the 1920s and 1930s. Consistently throughout his career, Marsh railed against the hypocrisies in amateur sport. He blasted everyone from Ontario's Premier Hepburn to amateur hockey officials and owners who condoned and encouraged shamateursism (the practice of paying athletes while claiming they were amateur) to the athletes who duped the public with amateur pretensions.[31]

Marsh's national and international appeal was also engendered and revealed in some poignant descriptions of such sporting events as an August 1928 eight-oared rowing race between Canada and the United States, a tremendous piece of sporting journalism.[32] Similarly, his annual descriptions and analyses of the America's Cup yacht races and the Harmsworth Cup motor boat races over the pretzel-shaped Detroit River course were always well written and dramatic in style. Two other columns were highlighted by his peers and contemporaries. One was his description of opening night at Madison Square Gardens on the occasion of the first NHL game played in New York.[33] The second was a non-sporting eulogy penned in tribute to his Boston bull terrier, Bubs, Lou Marsh's shadow. He lamented, 'I know you will pardon me if this column isn't very cheery this morning—'Bubs' is dead. He wasn't any bigger than a minute, but he was all dog—all grit—and tougher than gutta percha.'[34] Indeed, it is difficult to read the entire column today and not to feel a deep sense of loss at Bub's death.

Marsh was comfortable and competent in discussing politics in sport, proposed rule changes in hockey, athletic personalities, and personalized stories of past or contemporary sports figures. In the latter regard, his athletic obituaries were especially well known.[35] He could even make the trivial task of cleaning out his own desk drawers into an enjoyable read. Occasionally, Marsh overstepped the boundaries of his readers' tolerance for his opinions. For example, he once made a very detailed case for Australian Bobby Pearce being a far superior oarsman to Toronto's beloved Ned Hanlan[36] (see Chapter 6). It was heresy to his readers and Marsh let his readers express their views by printing their opinions in his column. Just as quickly, he could recover their loyalty through his appeals for charity in the form of the *Star*'s Fresh Air Fund, the Santa Claus Fund,[37] the Stew Car Ticket Fund, or just an appeal for relief for those how were forced into the soup lines during the Depression.

With a knack for clarity of expression, Marsh could explain the mania for whippet dog-racing in New Orleans, or the meaning and significance of the Diamond Sculls victory on the famed London, England Henley course.[38] Equally well he could explain the intricacies of less well known sports, like sailboat racing, while at the same time educating his readers about sporting legends like the famous Maritimes' racing vessel, the ***Bluenose***:

> Captain Angus Walters of the schooner Bluenose demands a real outside course for a race with the Columbia, the U.S. fighting schooner champion. He wants some place where there is wind and water. Anything under 20 knots is a zephyr to these hardy toilers of the sea. Up here, anything over six knots is a wind and over 20 knots a gale.[39]

Lou Marsh wrote many, many sporting articles during his 43-year career that were not part of his 'Pick and Shovel' column. For example, when William A. Hewitt retired in 1931 and Marsh was appointed to the office of sports editor on 16 October 1931, he began writing another column entitled:

> Stop! Look! Listen!
> In One Ear—Out Next Edition

Yet it was clearly his 'Pick and Shovel' column that was equated with Marsh's prowess and impact as a sporting journalist. Over the door of his office at the *Star* was a beautifully crafted wooden pick and shovel; at his funeral, one of the largest ever witnessed in Toronto, was a huge floral pick and shovel sent by his admiring co-workers. Obviously, Marsh wrote during a period when sport flourished in Toronto and throughout Canada and, therefore, he wrote to a very receptive audience. At the same time, his journalism fulfilled a purpose that good television sports commentary has taken over in the past 40 to 50 years—colourful, knowledgeable, and insightful commentary on sport. And, his impact was not at all confined to central Canada; even in Winnipeg and Vancouver Marsh was hailed as the 'dean of Canadian sportswriters'.[40] Unique were his insights into sport; while his columns did not quantify sport, they most certainly qualified it.

Sporting Extras: Ted Reeve and Versifying Sport

Just after the Second World War, George McCullagh, owner of the *Toronto Globe and Mail*, bought the *Toronto Telegram* for three and half million dollars. McCullagh commented on the purchase, 'That was a hell of a lot of money, but it was worth it—just to get Ted Reeve.'[41] There is no question but that Edward 'Ted' Reeve was hired by the *Toronto Telegram*

Ted Reeve, enlisting for Sportsmen Battery with Conn Smythe at Maple Leaf Gardens, 1939. (Courtesy of the Archives of Ontario, F 223-1-1-12)

in the late 1920s in an effort to rival the growing public interest in the *Star*'s daily sports columnist, the 'caustic' Lou Marsh. Clearly, sports journalism was a symbiotic part of the sporting landscape in Canada.

Implicit in Reeve's column title, 'Sporting Extras', was the assumption of some element of 'more-than' mere sports reporting. When Reeve began his column in 1928, the newspaper sales rivalry in Toronto was at its peak. At the time, the sport pages in both the *Star* and the *Telegram* varied from two to four full pages in length with Marsh's and Reeve's columns each representing less than five per cent of the total sports page space in their respective papers. The public appetite for 'more-than' sports reporting was echoed in the parallel tactics of the same newspapers to hire women's sport columnists. In 1928, the *Star* hired Alexandrine Gibb, women's amateur sport organizer extraordinaire,[42] to write a column entitled, 'No Man's Land of Sport'. Gibb retained this position for almost 20 years. The *Telegram* countered the *Star*'s initiative in 1928 with the appointment of Phyllis Griffiths to write 'The Girl and the Game' column. In Toronto, then, there was a strong impetus to attract readers with specialized sport columnists. Ted Reeve was a prominent part of that enterprise.

Reeve was born in the Beaches district of Toronto in 1902. Like Marsh, Reeve had considerable athletic experience. He played at high level amateur and professional level lacrosse and football. In the former sport, he was a member of two different teams, in 1929 and 1930, which won the Mann Cup, emblematic of the Canadian championship. Similarly, in football, as a member of the Toronto Balmy Beach club, he was instrumental in winning the Grey Cup in 1927 and again in 1930. During the 1930s, he coached the Queen's University football team, winning three provincial titles (the Yates Cup).[43] During the Second World War, Reeve 'in his late-thirties at the time, served as a gunner in the Sportsman's Battery, the 30th Light Anti-Aircraft, organized by Toronto Maple Leafs' owner Conn Smythe'.[44] Not only did his sporting background serve him as a journalist, but while growing up in the Beaches District of Toronto, the young Reeve worked in his mother's bookstore and apparently used every opportunity to read, even to the point of consuming an entire set of the *Encyclopedia Britannica*. He avowed that his favourite author was Charles Dickens, an influence that is borne out in examining the style and nature of his columns throughout his writing career, from roughly 1928 to the mid-1970s.

Before examining Reeve's journalism (we will consider the writing done during the same era as Marsh, for the sake of comparisons in a time context), it is important to realize how important sport was to Canadians during the 1920s and especially during the 1930s. Whereas one might expect a Depression economy to have devastated sport as a potentially perceived activity of less importance within the social and economic milieu, such was not the case. Instead, there were many changes to sport, most notably the trend toward an increasing interest in professional team sports such as hockey, football, and lacrosse (notably its indoor derivative, box lacrosse). With respect to professional sport, one factor in its escalation in popularity was the fact that it was an avenue of employment; logically then, during the Depression, professional sport interests depleted athletic talent from senior amateur leagues. The appeal of that brand of sport as entertainment led to seemingly highly incongruous events such as the completion of Maple Leaf Gardens in 1931.[45] A study of a cross-section of Canadian daily newspapers found that the sports news ranked second, just behind human interest stories during this era.[46] With the unemployment rate so high, leisure time increased and sport became a pastime of choice for both participants and spectators alike.[47] The entertainment value and the very likely morale-boosting aspects of sport contributed symbiotically to the significance of the sports page and specialized journalists such as Ted Reeve.

Toronto was a sports thirsty city during the 1920s and 1930s. In all probability, the prosperity brought by mining in northern Ontario and by agricultural and dairy farming in southwestern Ontario meant that Toronto was less vulnerable to the economic changes of the period. Baseball leagues abounded in the city, from the Maple Leafs professional team playing in the International League to the myriad amateur softball leagues; baseball sport coverage in the papers reflected not only local participant and spectator interest in the game, but also the very popular interest in the American major league game.[48] A tremendous amount of press coverage was consistently given to the Toronto Maple Leafs, the Ontario hockey association teams, and the Metro hockey leagues. In addition, the gambling attraction to sport resulted in a high frequency of reporting of boxing, wrestling, and horseracing.[49] Noting these trends in sporting interests and the consistent coverage given to popular male sports in the Toronto press, Reeve was probably hired not only to balance Marsh's popularity but even more to enhance the sporting zeal of *Telegram* readers and attract new ones. Ultimately, the reason newspapers exist is to make a profit from sales and subscriptions; the goal of any newspaper business is to sell newspapers. Reeve did not disappoint. Whereas Marsh was an established writer near the end of his career during this period, Reeve was new. His strategy was to cater to the prevailing rabid interests already established in baseball, hockey, boxing, football, and so forth; his columns mirror the dominant trends in Toronto sporting interests and press coverage.

Reeve gave Toronto readers exactly what they wanted to read. In general, October's columns were almost exclusively devoted to football. In his columns, game recounts were frequent; however, he also provided considerable insight into the technicalities of the game, as one might expect from his professional playing expertise. He pinpointed 'shoelace snatching tackles'[50] and the 'unknown soldiers' of the wing line who were unheralded relative to the flash of the offensive 'starry halfs'.[51] Reeve's bias for the 'manly art of smashing lines'[52] giving way to a developing preference for more kicking and passing is testament to the masculine values attached to football that were reinforced during this period. When the forward pass was being introduced, in contrast to the exclusive and traditional ball-carrying style of Reeve's playing era, the sportswriter did his best to make its adoption look like a foolish prospect. He wrote, 'the greatest open-field and close formation ball-carrying of the coming autumn will be done by the referees.'[53] However, once spectator interest in the more exciting passing game reverberated in greater fan appeal, Reeve quickly aligned his views to coincide with popular acceptance of the innovation. As straightforward as this type of insider expertise might seem, Reeve was quite skilful in creating images with messages, even related to his beloved sport of football. For example, with a touch of humour and a twist of irony, almost Dickensian in style, Reeve proclaimed that each Fall the 'music of swiftly turning turnstiles can be heard quite clearly on the autumn air.'[54]

In keeping with the prevailing masculine trends and values of the sports page—and perhaps in deference to the newly-hired female sports columnists—Reeve devoted very little attention to women in sport. A short poem was all he could devote to the first Canadian women's team to be sent to the 1928 Olympic Games:

> Myrtle and Smitty
> And Fanny and Flo
> And Ethel and Jean
> Are the girls that will go.[55]

When he did mention women's sport, it was more derisive or semi-mocking than it was to underscore the quality of the sport or to pay tribute to its devotees. He once remarked:

> Girls' basketball is quite a game
> When played with proper zest
> It puts roses on the cheeks
> And Lilies on the chest.[56]

And, 'we have never seen females moving matters with such speed since the day slickers sold for $1.98 in the basement.'[57] There were some, albeit very few, indications that he appreciated the talent of certain female athletes (such as track athlete Jean Thompson, the 'Penetang Pansy'[58]) but he embodied the stereotypical male, conservative, and sexist viewpoint on female athletes and he propounded that perspective to his readers.

By contrast, Reeve was skilled at promoting, embellishing, and making a case for select male athletes for their prowess or for some inequity in their situations. For example, when sprinter Percy Williams was excluded from the 1927 Canadian championships on the basis of a coin toss and then went on to win double gold medals in the 100-metre and 200-metre events at the 1928 Amsterdam Olympic Games, Reeve lashed out, with mild rebuke, at track and field officials by branding them as 'those whose conversations are filled with split seconds.'[59] Irked by fathers who had been successful elite athletes and then pushed their sons toward greatness, Reeve once quipped about Joe Wright Jr, who won the Diamond Sculls at the British Henley in 1928:

> I always knew the boy would row,
>   Said Joseph Wright, the pater
> The way he rode in his baby cart
>   Assure me of the matter.[60]

Reeve's columns often exhibited cases or issues highlighting human traits in sport, yet he always seemed to be conscious of the limits of his universe and the maximum stretching point of his readership. Whereas Marsh blasted the phoniness of professional wrestling, Reeve treated it consistently as serious sport, as though it were sacrosanct territory; this was in keeping with his perceived readers' interests in the sport. When he really wanted to make a point or be direct, he used a persona to speak, an indirect, self-deflecting technique. This too was part of his literary devotion to Dickens; his personae were carefully chosen, often with flamboyant names: Moaner McGuffrey, or The Moaner was one of his favourites, and so were Alice Snippersnapper and Nutsy Fagan. The latter two were very Dickensian-derived characters. He also used the editorial 'we' or more phonetically-named characters like Hassen Ben Sober (his game-predicting fortune teller) or his Indian poet, Young Chief Hiawalkamatter. These guises allowed Reeve to come out of his shell. On his own, he could pronounce, in subtle fashion, 'Dicky [a baseball player] was fined one thousand dollars for punching an opponent whereas Schmeling and Sharkey [in professional boxing] split one hundred fifty thousand for refraining to hit each other. Blessed are the meek.'[61] Moaner, on the other hand, could be much more blunt:

> The amateur official proud
> Sighed deeply as he saw the crowd
>   That watched the Dukes and Fleas.
> He said, 'From this we may assume
> The amateurs will have a boom
>   Which leaves me ill at ease,
> For games are only amatoor
> As long as all the gates are poor.'
>   —Moaner McGuffrey[62]

In the final analysis, all of his character derivations were but clever journalistic devices designed to create a loyal readership.

Similar to Marsh and for exactly the same reasons, Reeve developed and used his own vernacular. For example, university athletes were 'hands from the fact foundry', the boxing ring was the 'Coliseum Clout Court', hockey players were 'rubber rushers', and goalies were 'twine minders'. Furthermore, his voracious reading and literary skills allowed him to compress meaning into a very few words. He once expressively defined a baseball knuckle ball as 'made off the back of the fingers by remote control'.[63] This analysis of Reeve's journalism provides another window of insight into early sport journalism in Canada, at least with respect to the dominant gender in sport.

In the Women's Sportlight: Myrtle Cook and the Promotion of Women's Sport

Within the Toronto newspaper system, the hiring of two female sport columnists was significant. Phyllis Griffiths wrote her column, 'The Girl and the Game' in the *Telegram* from 1928 to 1942; Alexandrine Gibb's 'No Man's Land of Sport' ran in the *Star* from 1928 to 1940. Two other sports-writing pioneers who advocated strongly for greater involvement and greater recognition of women in sport were Bobbie Rosenfeld and Myrtle Cook. Rosenfeld's column published in the *Globe and Mail* from 1939 to 1958 was entitled 'Feminine Sports Reel.' Myrtle Cook wrote 'In the Women's Sportlight' for the *Montreal Daily Star* from 1929 to 1971.

We will focus on an analysis of Cook's journalism because it parallels, in time, the two male columnists discussed above and because it was written in Montreal and, therefore, provides a different background environment than the Toronto-based journalists. It should be noted that all of the columnists discussed in this chapter were nationally and often internationally known for their journalism and that they were leaders in the development of quality sport journalism in Canada. Our assumption, often verified by tributes and accolades given to these journalists, is that the fact that their writing careers spanned at least two decades, in all cases, and almost five decades in two cases (Reeve and Cook), is that their tenure meant the newspapers realized the value-added component of having specialized sport journalists in selling newspapers in major urban centres.

The sporting landscape for women in the 1920s was in no way comparable to that for men. Although some women at the elite levels of competitive sport were active in skating, cycling, tennis, and basketball,[64] their participation lacked both the organizational structure and hierarchy of leagues that were common for boys and men in sport. Even with the formation of the Women's Amateur Athletic Federation in 1926, there was no institution or means to promote competitive sport at most levels, let alone at the national, elite level of sport. Lack of facilities and coaches were major obstacles to women's sporting development as were societal attitudes toward women competing in sport. If there was one sport that did exhibit considerable organization and widespread play across the nation during the pre-Second World War years, it was women's softball. By the 1920s, within larger cities there were industrial league baseball leagues with teams sponsored by various companies and institutions such as Bell Telephone and the Canadian National Railway in Toronto.[65] However, national championships, other than in basketball, were almost non-existent for women. Major championships in the 1920s were Toronto-centric in that promoters, like CNE sports director Elwood Hughes, picked Toronto area athletes for track and field events; 'Canadian' championships tended to involve representatives from the Toronto area to the exclusion of Quebec, the Maritimes, and the Western provinces. Five of the six women selected to represent Canada at the 1928 Amsterdam Olympic Games were either from Toronto or living in the city in order to train. One of the members of that famous group, the 'Matchless Six', was Myrtle Cook. Her much-deserved recognition as the 'matriarch'[66] of

Canadian women at Stamfordbridge, England in 1925. (© Bettmann/CORBIS)

modern athletics for Canadian women has to do with the examples she set as an athlete and even more with her role in promoting women's sport as a Montreal sports journalist; in the latter regard, she quite literally advanced women's role in sport beyond the Toronto area.

Born in 1902 and raised in Toronto, Cook won her first track competitions while attending Riverdale High School. Following graduation, she joined the local YM–YWCA and also the Toronto Ladies Athletic Club in 1924. Her earliest major competitions were as a member of 440-yard (approximately 400 metres) relay teams. In 1925 she was a member of the Canadian team that travelled to Stamfordbridge, England, to compete against the English and French relay teams. At this prestigious event, Cook and the women's team placed second on a 660-yard course, a commendable achievement for the very first international track competition involving Canadian women.

In 1926 Cook joined the newly-formed Canadian Ladies Athletic Club as both athlete and coach. Two years later, she travelled to New York to run the 100-metre dash; she won the world indoor sprint title.[67] Within two months, at the Canadian Championships (which were also designated as the Olympic trials) in Halifax, Cook ran the 100 metres in 12 seconds flat—a new world record. Cook was appointed captain of the women's team who travelled to compete in the 1928 Amsterdam Olympic Games. Unfortunately, after two false starts, Cook was disqualified in the 100-metre final.

However, on the final day of the Games, Cook anchored the women's relay team and was instrumental in winning a gold medal and setting a world record for the event.[70] Although barely noticed when the team left for the Games, Cook and her five track and field teammates were well celebrated when they came home:

The magnitude of the accomplishment and the popularity of the team were reflected in the heroes' welcome they received upon their return to Canada. 'The Matchless Six' returned to ticker tape parades in Toronto and Montreal. The press estimated that 200,000 people jammed Toronto's Union Station and adjacent Front Street and another 100,000 lined the parade route.[71]

Cook continued competing and maintained her Canadian championship status in the 100-metre and 60-yard events until 1931.[72] When she

Myrtle Cook, world record holder in sprinting, shown in 1926. (Courtesy of the City of Toronto Archives, James Collection 8172)

retired from competitive sport in 1931, it was after seven consecutive years of being an international calibre athlete; in the context of the very nascent development of Canadian women in elite track and field events, this longevity is exemplary, just as the whole Canadian women's track and field success in 1928 is noteworthy. In 1976, 48 years after the Matchless Six achieved their fame, Christie Blatchford, currently one of the most well respected journalists in Canada,[73] proclaimed:

When Jane Bell and Ethel Smith ran—with Bobbie Rosenfeld and Myrtle Cook—in Amsterdam in 1928, they wore bloomers. They trained before and after work. Athletes did work then. They ran whenever they could run and before the 1928 Games, they had not run together before…. They were champions, and they deserve to be treated now as champions. As rare and special Canadians, they deserve treatment at least equal to that which will be given to our elected representatives who are a cent a dozen.[74]

The 1928 Olympic Games Women's 100-Metre Final Controversy

The 1928 Olympic Games' women's 100-metre final was fraught with controversy and disappointment for the Canadian team and, ultimately, for Canadians. Though the nation eventually basked in the medals obtained by the team, Cook's disqualification was a shock. In an interview with Myrtle Cook in 1981, she claimed that she did false start once, but not the second time (two false starts warranted disqualification at the time). She felt that her reputation and world record status resulted in intimidation from the German starter. Apparently, the starter stood directly behind Cook; convention then was for the starting pistol to be pointed downward in the lower hand, with the other arm raised for timers to see. When the gun was fired, the starter's raised arm was lowered. Cook stated that the starter kept the pistol very close to her backside and that it made her nervous. Alexandrine Gibb's account of the alleged false starts, while biased, corroborated the unfairness accorded Cook.[69]

Cook's experience as a sprinter and coach would suggest at least the possibility of a contentious ruling of false starts. Moreover, when the race was completed, there was a very close finish between Canadian team member Bobbie Rosenfeld and American Betty Robinson. Canadians at the Games were convinced Rosenfeld had won.[70] Athletes and officials, including Madame Alice Milliat of France, then-president of the International Women's Federation, urged Dr A.S. Lamb, president of the Amateur Athletic Union of Canada, and the only person who could act officially, to protest the decision. He refused in spite of the fact that the chief placing judge was an American.

In 1929, Cook moved from Toronto to Montreal in order to establish a branch of the Canadian Ladies Athletic Club (CLAC) in that city. Acquiring the use of the YMCA facilities, she coached and directed the track and field division of the CLAC branch. In April of that year, she was hired by the *Montreal Daily Star* to write a column she entitled, 'In the Women's Sportlight'.[75] Montreal did not have nearly the women's sport infrastructure that Toronto's female athletes enjoyed. High schools were the major institutions supporting sporting activities for young women. Softball and some basketball teams existed, but they were basically in the category of unstructured recreation. Thus, one of the first functions of Cook's column was to serve as a channel of communication for aspiring athletes in the large urban metropolis. In one of her earliest columns, she entreated her readers in this fashion:

> Girls in sport, this is your column...use it to tell what you are doing, and what you can do. The results of inter-city and provincial games are generally regarded as a sort of mirror of civic and provincial prowess. From now on the girls in Montreal will have their own domain in this column. Let's make the mirror show results![76]

Thus, Myrtle Cook's column and the focus of her journalism were very different than the columns of Lou Marsh and Ted Reeve. The latter wrote to attract and feed the athletic appetite of male athletes and spectators who enjoyed a well developed system and network of sport in Toronto, in Canada, and internationally. While those columns might seem more 'advanced' in terms of quality of writing and insight than those written by Cook, Griffiths, or Gibb, it is not a fair comparison given the early development of women's

The Matchless Six greeted at Union Station, August 1928. Left to right: Myrtle Cook, Jean Thompson, Ethel Smith, Florence Bell, Ethel Catherwood, Fannie Rosenfeld, Miss A.E.M. Parkes (Chaperone), and Dorothy Prior. (Courtesy of the City of Toronto Archives, Fonds 1266, Item 14109)

competitive sport in Canada. In Cook's case, it is interesting that she became the nexus for the development of women's sport in Montreal, the very city that served as the cradle for organized, male sport in the nineteenth century (see Chapter 4). Cook's column was instrumental in developing a cohesive community of female, competitive athletes via such basic functions as recruiting sportswomen, informing them about events, championing their performances, and encouraging more widespread development of women's clubs and women's involvement in competitive sport endeavours.

In bulletin board fashion, Cook's early columns published times and locations of club practices and encouraged girls graduating high school to join or form clubs in order to continue their sporting activities. To bolster those efforts, she attended many high school athletic meets and competitions both to support young women and to recruit them via printing their names and photographs in the *Star*. When good athletes were identified by their prowess, Cook made it her business to remind them that in order to compete in sanctioned amateur sporting events, they had to be members in good standing with the

Women's Amateur Athletic Federation of Canada (WAAF) and be in possession of amateur qualification cards issued by the Amateur Athletic Union of Canada. Thus, in her column, she constantly reminded athletes of the standards they needed to meet as well as the means by which the amateur cards could be obtained.[77] This amateur advocacy role was very important in that it made Quebec women eligible for competitions for which they previously would have been denied entry. In the same vein, Cook commended the formation of new clubs—such as the St Lambert's Club and the St Columbia Athletic Club—and gave them lots of publicity for their events, thereby enhancing public exposure of the club network and its athletes to her readers.

The impact of Cook's endorsements to organizations was felt almost immediately in Montreal. By late 1929, some 23 new basketball teams were formed outside of the high schools; doubtless, the inter-city rivalry and growing popularity of basketball catalyzed this growth in the number of teams together with the column promotions provided by Cook. Significantly, organizations like the Caledonian Society and the prestigious Montreal Amateur Athletic Association (MAAA, see Chapter 4), which had been bastions of organized sport for men, began to sponsor events for women. For example, the MAAA sponsored the Canadian track and field championships in 1929, very likely inspired both by Cook's prowess as an athlete and the rapidly rising popularity of her column.[78] Other clubs, namely the Montreal Police Amateur Athletic Club, the Lachine Rowing Club, the Order of the Blue Goose, and local lacrosse, cricket, and shooting clubs followed suit to the extent that tennis leagues and other competitions within their respective spheres were offered for developing female athletes. The merging of women's sporting events within male-dominated clubs and organizations was a very important integrative accomplishment for women's sport in Canada.

Cook used her journalistic role to counter the ever-present, stereotypical frail image of women athletes. Lead by the powerful president of the AAU of Canada, Montreal's Dr Arthur Lamb, who had voted to abolish women's athletics at the Olympic Games,[79] the prevailing male perspective was that most forms of athletic activity were too strenuous for women (see Chapter 8). Cook constantly received negative comments about the 'propriety' of female athleticism. Her reaction was to use her column as a mouthpiece to deflate the myths espoused by those opposed to women in sport. The following is one strongly worded example of how she interceded on women athletes' behalf:

> Those who were in the stands on Saturday and saw the girls compete in their track events at the M.A.A.A. meet, realized that a new type of girlhood is growing up on this Island; the woman athlete. She is a significant phenomenon. Watch her. And do not think for a moment that this new athleticism will entail a loss of femininity. None of the female athletes…picked up any hints of masculinity along with their new capacity for sprinting.… Prejudice against women taking part in athletics still exists…and can be removed by attendance at the Dominion track and field championships at the M.A.A.A. grounds on Monday.[80]

When the 800-metre competition was taken off the list of Olympic track events for women—after the 1928 Olympic Games, ostensibly because of its male-perceived taxing impact on female physiology—Cook countered the hypocritical decision by highlighting the new world record established by Corine Rossburg for swimming 61 hours continuously.[81] She also pointed out the inequity of the fact that the 800-metre event would be run at the 1932 British Empire Games.[82] For the same reasons, and in the same vein, Cook detailed Japanese world record long jump holder, Kinuye Hitomi's career in her column and gave significant publicity to Amy Johnson when she made her solo plane flight from England to Australia in 1930.[83] Prejudice on the basis of gender was not something with which male journalists ever had to contend.

Without question, Cook envisioned an important part of her role as one that highlighted Canadian achievements. In the early 1930s, the American media boasted about their new athletic wonder, Mildred 'Babe' Didrickson. Cook pointed out that Didrickson's much-heralded 100-metre time had been equalled by Canada's own Bobbie Rosenfeld long before the American gained recognition for the achievement. Myrtle opposed the hyperbole of American reports concerning Didrickson:

'Babe' Didrickson is deserving of much credit, but until she accomplishes something extraordinary, calling her a new athletic marvel is a bit thick. Her jump [long jump] distance was a mark easily within reach of numerous Canadian girls.[84]

Her intent herein was probably not to discredit the American's performance; rather, her efforts were to convince Canadian women and men that the country's female athletic accomplishments were exemplary and important to recognize. Another manner in which Cook worked to achieve the same thing was to print picture of female athletes within her column, as she did throughout the 1930s, in order to showcase prominent athletes as models for all Canadian women. Very likely, the effect of these images and their corresponding stories demonstrated Canadian women's sporting excellence from local to national levels.

As the proliferation of women's sport continued, assisted by energetic and committed columnists like Cook, Griffiths, and Gibb, it became increasingly apparent that one of the barriers to women's elite competition in some sports was the lack of rule standardization at the national levels. For example, in the western provinces and Ontario, women played basketball using 'men's' rules, which permitted full court play of all players on the floor; women in Quebec and the Maritimes played under the more restrictive, static-position 'women's' rules. In order for the WAAF to sanction standardized, national championships, there had to be consistent rules. Therefore, Cook used her column to promote the more exciting and dynamic game opportunities provided for in men's rules. By 1931, Cook's efforts resulted in both the Montreal Ladies Basketball League and the Quebec Women's Basketball Association adopting the new rules thereby making teams eligible for Dominion championships.[85] In similar fashion, Cook constantly used her column to bridge communication gaps between provincial sport organizations and national level governing bodies for women's sport.

It is clear from examining Myrtle Cook's journalistic endeavours that the nature of women's sporting journalism was much different than their male counterparts. Cook's writing career and concomitant promotion of women's competitive sport at all levels was paralleled by her work as a sport manager. For example, she was on almost every British Empire/Commonwealth Games committee and Olympic Committee from 1932 to 1972. During both of those sets of Games in the 1950s, she served as press liaison officer.[86] In 1955, Cook became the first woman inducted into the Canadian Sports Hall of Fame and each year, she is commemorated when the Myrtle Cook Trophy is presented to the most outstanding

MAMIE MOLONEY, the Vancouver Sun's social editor, writing a guest column for Hal Straight, takes sport scribblers to task like this:

"Sports writers, for years past, have been practically alone in the field of turning the English language inside-out for their own fiendish uses.

To the uninitiated, like us, it has been an utter impossibility to interpret the average sports writer without a glossary, or even to guess what game he was writing about.

Proof of our contention is offered in the following paragraphs:

A typical sentence in a sport's story about baseball:

"Harry is a fancy Dan and when he steps up to the dish his best bingles are bloopers. He's a sucker for a sinker and he usually goes to war on a change of pace."

Which, being interpreted means:

"Harry is the kind of ball player, who, by his antics, makes everything look much harder than it really is, and when he takes his place at home plate, his best batting efforts are softly hit balls which are fortu-

An example of Rosenfeld's column, "Feminine Sports Reel", extracted from the *Globe and Mail*, 26 October 1940. (Courtesy of http://jwa.org/exhibits/wov/rosenfeld/ and Don Morrow)

young Canadian athlete in any sport.[87] The Trophy's targeted group seems entirely apropos to the role Cook played in promoting sport for new and aspiring athletes.

One of Myrtle's teammates from the 1928 Games, Bobbie Rosenfeld, pursued a career in sports journalism through her column, 'Feminine Sports Reel' in the Toronto *Globe and Mail* from 1937–58. Rosenfeld was an incredible athlete who eventually was voted (in 1950 by a Canadian Press poll) as Canada's 'Female Athlete of the Half Century'.[88]

Crippled by arthritis in 1929, Bobbie—or her more familiar, Fannie—returned to competitive sport in 1933 to play softball and hockey; she retired from sport at the end of that year. Rosenfeld held a particular philosophy about the purpose of her column. At the outset, she stated that her column would reflect what she believed about sport for girls and women; she believed that 'sports competition, when properly organized and directed, has a contribution to make to the education of women.'[89] The Jewish Women's Archive has assembled a full website in tribute to Rosenfeld; their summary of her writing style merits reprinting:

For eighteen [sic] years, Rosenfeld covered women's sports with wit and 'refreshing candor.' She celebrated female pioneers in everything from bowling to rodeo riding, and wrote with authority on softball, basketball, hockey, track-all the fields she had once dominated. Along the way she mocked herself and most everyone else, recommended taffy and orange juice to cure hangovers, and occasionally reminisced about the golden age of girls sports, 'when the Cook and the Rosenfeld held sway. . . (kind of snooty, eh!)'.

But perhaps more importantly, Rosenfeld used her column to advocate for women athletes. She debunked the sexist attacks that insisted women looked, 'better with a frying pan than a tennis racquet.' She encouraged girl's sports in the schools, asserting that, 'competition when properly organized and directed has a contribution to make to the education of women.' Throughout the years, Rosenfeld continued to remind a too-often forgetful public that girls were 'in sports for good'.[90]

Because sport columnist styles vary considerably over time, it is worth printing scanned images of one of Rosenfeld's columns from 1940[91] to capture the nature of writing about women's sport in this era. Her semi-mocking tone, her spunk and sarcasm, and her use of colourful language and expressions is readily apparent in the excerpt reprinted on the previous page.

Conclusions

The symbiotic relationship between the media and sports is complex, varied, variable, and fascinating. This chapter has explored the form and function of a selection of prominent male and female sport journalists who made major contributions to writing about sport in the first half of the twentieth century. Marsh, Reeve, Cook, Gibb, Griffiths, and Rosenfeld were all pioneering sport journalists in Canada. In different ways, they each sought both to promote sport for Canadian men and women and to provide insights about issues—social, athletic, and political—in sport. Journalists, in many ways, punctuate sport; that is, they provide contemporary meaning to sport and sporting issues. There were, and are, many other journalists aside from the ones highlighted in this chapter—William A. Hewitt, Bas O'Meara, Henry Roxborough, and Elmer Ferguson, to name but a few of the more prominent writers in large cities—and countless 'scribes' in smaller newspapers across the country. Both the Canadian Press, where syndicated, and the American Press reprinted stories from the more well known Canadian journalists.

National magazines such as *MacLean's*, *Saturday Night*, *The Canadian Magazine*, *Chatelaine*, and *The Star Weekly* often, though not regularly, provided in-depth articles about Canadian sport and/or Canadian athletes. Scott Young, father of currently famous Canadian rock-singer, Neil Young, was a sports columnist with two or three different Toronto newspapers from the 1940s to the 1970s; in addition, Scott Young was nationally known for his children's books, particularly those about hockey heroes in his juvenile fiction series, *Scrubs on Skates* (1952), *Boy on Defence* (1953), and *A Boy at the Leafs Camp* (1963).

Radio coverage of sport was a phenomenon that began in the early 1920s. Many baseball fans in North America still prefer to listen to professional American baseball broadcast on the radio. For most Canadians, the 'voice of hockey' was William Hewitt's son, Foster who began broadcasting hockey games in 1923. Perched in his gondola high above the ice of the Maple Leaf Gardens, Foster's game coverage was a household feature to the broadest spectrum of Canadians. His game sign-on was legendary, 'Hello, Canada, and hockey fans in the United States and Newfoundland' (before Newfoundland joined Confederation in 1949) as was his trademark, 'He shoots…he scores!' Hewitt broadcast *Hockey Night in Canada* for 40 years, and then came out of retirement in 1972 to cover the Summit Series between Canada and the former Soviet Union. From the eighth game of that series emanated Hewitt's second most remembered phrase embedded in the consciousness of Canadians, 'Henderson has scored for Canada.'

In modern sport, media coverage now extends to e-zines, blogs, specialized websites on particular sports, single-sport television stations, fantasy sports' websites, international coverage of almost every sport played at elite levels, and sport commentary television stations—all are readily available to the sport consumer of every age. Messages, to paraphrase McLuhan who was quoted at the beginning of this chapter, can be selected from a broad menu of media and broadcasters inclusive of the ribald reporting of Canada's own Don Cherry.

Related Websites

The Canadian Press
http://www.thecanadianpress.com/home.aspx?ID=58

The Associated Press
http://www.ap.org/

The Canadian Association for the Advancement of Women in Sport (CAAWS)
http://www.caaws.ca

Canada's Sports Hall of Fame
http://www.cshof.ca/

Lou Marsh on Wikipedia
http://en.wikipedia.org/wiki/Lou_Marsh

Ted Reeve's Honoured Member, Canadian Sports Hall of Fame Biography
http://www.cshof.ca/hm_profile.php?i=366

Myrtle Cook Tribute
http://www.collectionscanada.gc.ca/women/002026-225-e.html

Jewish Women's Archive of Bobbie Rosenfeld
http://jwa.org/exhibits/wov/rosenfeld/

Study Questions

1. What factors would you consider important in choosing Canada's best athlete each year? Why?
2. What qualities make up good sports writing? Which ones make up good sports broadcasting?
3. Describe the differences in the nature of sport coverage by Canada's earliest sport journalists.
4. Write an obituary for two of the sport journalists mentioned in this chapter. How would you research information about each one? How would you decide what to include?
5. How would you describe the gender differences in sport in the first half of the twentieth century? Consider such variables as opportunity, equality, sexism, levels of success, and any other comparative measures you might discern.

CHAPTER 8

Gender, Body, and Sport

———⬥◆⬥———

Considering the obvious biological differences between men and women, it might appear 'natural' that they should act and feel in different ways. However, throughout history, sport, leisure, and physical activity have been cultural arenas[1] where people *learn* how to act, feel, and interpret the world like men or women. People have always organized sports and other competitive physical activities to celebrate certain aspects of manhood or womanhood, defined by shared roles of participation or spectatorship and by cultural norms. At the individual level, people traded on the social, political, and economic rewards embedded in physical activities. In Canada's history, therefore, sports, games, and pastimes could be interpreted as cultural markers demonstrating how people related to one another, struggled for authority and power, included some and excluded others, celebrated lifestyle and community values, and had fun. Women and men in historically specific eras experienced social life differently—through their bodies, in public and private spaces, in access to rewards—and this is evident in how they played and competed. Social class, race and ethnicity, economics, nationalism, medicine and science, and religion have been factors influencing how men and women understand and assume their places in society, the kinds of behaviour considered appropriate at any given time, and how they experience their bodies in relation to others. Some used sport to solidify class-based relations but others to resist and to change these dominant social meanings. In this sense, sport could be empowering, disempowering, or sometimes both.

Often, people participated in patterns of physical activity as a strategy for separating themselves by class or race, or they invoked social meanings to distinguish themselves through ethnic or religious solidarity. People experienced hierarchies of social difference first-hand, for example, through their exclusion from private clubs or at structural levels, where the reasons for daily experiences of unequal access to rewards remained hidden and could not be understood easily. However, not all of the experiences and feelings embedded in social life were bifurcated completely by distinctions such as social class. People of different social classes or ethnicities sometimes experienced their bodies through physical activity in similar kinds of ways. To distinguish themselves socially from common citizens, the middle

For more than 100 years, boys and girls have learned and continue to learn about their bodies through sport. (Courtesy of Kevin Wamsley)

classes and elites of mid-nineteenth-century British North America identified violence and drinking (called intemperance) as working-class and underclass problems; yet, they, too, drank alcohol and engaged in violent confrontations and rough forms of culture, but they rationalized their behaviour through institutions, clubs, and codes of honour legitimated by peers and privileged by law. People had their feet planted in many worlds. In spite of the imposition of exclusionary rules, hierarchies of difference, and ideologies strategically invoked to promote social distinction, people's experiences of sports and pastimes cut across lines of class, gender, and ethnicity.

Sports, Games, and Gender in Early Canada

As noted in Chapter 2, the social divisions of labour in Aboriginal cultures in part determined the sorts of values celebrated through games and competitions. The skills embedded in traditional games for men and women related to their engagement with the land and their abilities to survive, endure hardship, and contribute to the life of the community.[2] Contact with Europeans directly influenced the gender orders of Aboriginal communities. In some communities, marital relationships with fur traders, who provided greater access to manufactured goods and weapons, enhanced the social and political status of women.[3] Jesuit priests disrupted the spiritual influences of medicine men in Aboriginal communities and chastised Native men for the control that women had in determining partnerships, and for what the priests considered extramarital relations.[4] Ultimately, war, disease, forced reserve settlements, and the imposition of European law on the colonies displaced the communal arrangements of labour, travel, and social life in Native communities. The tyranny of the **residential schools** stripped Native Canadians of their social traditions and language; the reserve system rendered tenuous the connections to the land embedded in traditional sports and games; therefore, only weakened and disjointed fragments of the older Aboriginal ways of life, appropriated by Europeans, remained in the nineteenth century.

In the colonial, bachelor subcultures of the fur trader, soldier, and missionary, masculinity or the commonly understood ways of being a man related to labour, travel, survival, and, for the missionaries particularly, religion. For both fur trader and soldier, their physical labour was the primary means to survival and limited economic sustenance. Skilled traders successfully navigated lands and waters, relied on strength and endurance to complete their voyages, and depended on such qualities to form a basis for personal reputation, which ensured more work. Soldiers relied specifically on the technical, physical skills of battle for survival, the fundamental basis of their pay. The Jesuit missionaries— whose religion included a form of Christian asceticism that denied the pleasures of the body in earthly service and in anticipation of the more important afterlife—relied on strength, endurance, and the skills of seasonal travel to further their work. Priesthood and celibate manhood were infused with a religious commitment to a mind–body duality that ultimately subsumed the physical, accepting the rigours of a harsh environment foremost in creating the bodily sensations of hunger, cold, exhaustion, and pain.[5]

Sports and games, competitions between men, served as entertainment and fun for traders and soldiers, while reinforcing and sustaining the connections between bodily skill and masculine identity. These men lived in unstable circumstances, confronting death as a matter of course and employing or enduring violence when necessary. Consequently, they fought to solve disputes, to test one another and compete for symbolic social rewards, for personal pride, or just to defend themselves. Fur traders ran foot races, paddled, and snowshoed against other traders and Aboriginal men.[6] Physical competence was fundamental to masculine identity and contributed to extant social and economic hierarchies.

During the colonial period, most families were engaged in subsistence economies, surviving from season to season, year to year, on what could be produced on the family farm in addition to those provisions that had to be bartered or bought. Men and women worked together to clear land, build shelter, plant and harvest crops, carry grain to the mill, and to defend the property.[7] The differences between men and women were a matter of degree, not kind, even though men still tended to dominate the relationship.[8] Women's identities, in general, related to household production, as opposed to the later social emphasis on sexual reproduction during the Victorian period. With the arrival of Loyalist settlers and the appointment of elites to political power in the Canadas and the Maritimes, attitudes about deference, honour, and masculine entitlement in the public sphere became entrenched in British North America.[9] As their husbands made legislative decisions and developed colonial policies, elite women exercised informal power in the private sphere. However, publicly exercised power was more visible and continued producing further social, political, and economic opportunities for men.[10]

Militarism and Manhood

As had the soldiers of New France, British North American soldiers assumed the role of colonial protectors. At a time of uncertainty with respect to attack, the civilians and ex-soldiers in these settlements assumed military roles. The War of 1812 presented new opportunities for people to embrace notions of loyalty and patriotism to the Crown and to their new home in commonly understood terms. Men were bound to protect the imperial colonies, homes, and families from the American threat. Thus, the military charged manhood with meanings about loyalty to the new country—underscored somewhat by the idea of protecting one's family. This linking of public and private spheres of manhood in British North America influenced many levels of society: it provided for a practical defence of territories; it served in the ideological construction of a British imperialism supposed to be favoured by God, which was fundamental to colonial administration; and it reaffirmed the positions of men as heads of households, protectors of British property, and defenders of home and family, and, therefore, the 'rightful' leaders in politics, government, and economy. Conversations, speeches, and sermons spoke to the heroism of men and by default promoted the cultural dependency of women. Morgan argues that:

> although the soldier could not symbolize Upper Canadian womanhood, he could reassure women and children that their persons and homes were protected by a beneficent patriarchal force. Wives, daughters, and sisters did not need to fear that their own troops would fall prey to the kind of vicious masculinity inherent in the American invaders.[11]

Militarism cut across class lines, beyond elites, linking patriotism and loyalty to working-class masculine identities with respect to family order, protection, and the civic responsibility of defending British property. Fighting for God, empire, family, and self provided the inspiration necessary to mobilize men to war—and personal sacrifice, if required. Such values were just as significant in times after and between wars. The symbolic value of sacrificing one's body or just accepting the threat of death for empire and family fostered senses of entitlement and control in other areas of life, connecting intimately with other patriarchal institutions such as religion and law to create opportunities in public life for men, while legitimizing a more domestic and private place for women.

The Social Elite

Elites had a sense of social and political entitlement secured by patronage appointments. They were dependent somewhat on family name or gentlemanly status, one's reputation in many aspects of life, and connected to a broader network of like-minded colonial elites. As argued in Chapter 3, fear and honour went hand in hand. All elites wished to preserve their social status and coveted approval. All elites feared or remained anxious about preserving manly honour and this, in part, determined how they related to one another socially. The violence of the duel among men who considered themselves highly civilized relative to their lesser-classed contemporaries signified the boundaries of responsibility for these social privileges; yet, acquittals and favourable treatment from the judiciary following death or wounding in a duel legitimized this colonial social structure of patronage and privilege.

The cricket match and the hunt presented safer opportunities for the display of a civilized, British masculinity that required physical competence, yet remained cultured, at times when a call to arms was not imminent. A sense of preserving a refined physical masculinity, among peers, through cultural activities remained more significant to men and women of the same station than it did for citizens of lower classes, for whom physical exertion was an integral part of daily life.[12] Through these formal social occasions, men, women, and children learned the proper, gendered codes of conduct:

> Propriety, and convention, particularly regarding appropriate behaviour, circumscribed club affairs. Ladies and gentlemen partook of the festivities and watched the game while sipping tea and resting comfortably in tent-covered stands. Cricket provided opportunities for children to learn the social niceties considered appropriate to their social station, with young boys wearing their finest clothes as they helped with the game and practiced their throwing, batting, and fielding skills at the sidelines.[13]

Yet, it was the same men of cultured refinement who meted out violent punishments to criminals convicted of murder, assault, or even treason. Violent, public punishments countered threats to other citizens and enforced property laws, while stabilizing the presence of an emerging governing process or state in the colonies.[14] The public hangings that followed the 1837–8 rebellions sent a powerful political message about social order and discipline in the empire to the massive crowds that gathered to watch and to readers who followed the events in local newspapers.[15]

Gender Identities and the Working Class

The children of workers and farmers internalized codes of conduct for appropriate masculine and feminine behaviours at social events, outside the church, and in the fields. In the early 1800s, the interactions between men and women at social events and competitions, and at work bees, provided opportunities for learning about gender. Men competed with one another in contests of strength and tested one another in impromptu wrestling matches and fist fights.[16] Evidently the symbolic value of strength and physical competence was more significant for men even though labouring women demonstrated strength, endurance, and a range of physical skills on a daily basis. In spite of the daily practicalities of life for labouring women and men in early Canada, people considered strength to be a masculine virtue. The legend of the strong man, such as the early fur trader, voyageur, or habitant, or the actual 'strongman'—the entertainer who organized demonstrations and travelling shows—remained popular through the nineteenth century (see Chapter 6). Men and women celebrated these social values when they gathered after workdays; and, later in the century, the residual symbolic significance of strength and physical skill persisted in public events such as local fairs and exhibitions.[17]

Violence

Frequently attached to commentaries on masculine strength and physical competence in diaries and newspapers of the nineteenth century was the idea of violence or of violent confrontation. Some women defended themselves and killed attackers in New France,[18] committed violent political acts in the Maritimes,[19] committed assault with some frequency, and fought alongside male partners in the taverns of the Canadas.[20] Yet, violence was not considered appropriately feminine in any context for women of any social class or ethnicity. Some men murdered, raped, and assaulted women they knew, and complete strangers; men also committed the same, severe violent acts against other men. Women murdered and assaulted men and other women much less often.[21] Colonial society positioned women, categorically, as victims, a distinction that spoke to common values about the abilities and expectations of men to defend not only themselves, but women also, and about the 'inherent' physical weakness of women. Ideologies of protection and provision lent considerable weight to the construction of separate spheres for men and women, strategically reinforced by the distinction of public from family life. Thus, the social understanding of violence as a masculine domain, one in which violence was expected and endorsed in response to physical challenges and confrontations, could only serve to perpetuate men's violence in both domestic and public contexts. Both rural and urban communities revered strong men and good fighters, but only under fair or justified circumstances. The fact remained: women did not ordinarily engage in impromptu physical challenges or fight for fun or honour.[22]

For the bachelor fur trader, garrison soldier, logger, and the tavern-goer, arm wrestling, wrestling, and fist-fighting created hierarchies of reputation and character. Physical skill also gave economic value to men's bodies. Men fought with one another over social, economic, political, ethnic, and personal matters. Serious fighting frequently occurred in taverns in conjunction with the consumption of alcohol but also in the workplace, field, or at the work bee. Physical competence in fighting provided a sense of stability for men in uncertain economic conditions, or solidarity among work crews, such as the loggers in Ottawa, who picked fights along their travel routes. Skilled or violent fighters such as the Donnellys of Lucan, Ontario, used the threat of violence to ward off business competition,[23] even attacking rival business owners; their fighting skill gave them reputations in local taverns as the toughest, most fearsome men in the London area.[24] Gangs of men from Goderich, Seaforth, and Clinton, Ontario, roamed the countryside taverns, drinking and picking fights for fun. Protestants fought Catholics, local men picked fights with British soldiers, and white men attacked black and Aboriginal men. Observing that fights drew crowds regularly, tavern owners capitalized by organizing boxing matches and charging admission.[25]

The sense of masculine honour embodied in violent physical challenges crossed class boundaries and found expression in a range of contests from the duel to the fist fight. Professionals, businessmen, and elites fought over gambling issues, horse races, and women. Middle-class reformers opposed such violent means of resolving disputes and increasingly sought redress in the courts as a more civilized solution.[26] Creating opportunities for a wider participation in public life, middle-class men organized social activities in which they could participate with men of their own social standing, demonstrate manly physical abilities in controlled circumstances, and celebrate a vigorous and virile manhood for the admiration of women and other men—sport. Organized sport provided a venue to regulate participation and celebrate the emergent social and economic values of competition without the uncertainty and risk of the tavern altercation. Sport was a public forum for physical manhood, tempered by Christian values yet sometimes rationalizing the pleasures of perceived violence and aggression.[27]

Organized Sport

Social and sporting clubs expanded the sphere of public activities for men in the economic domain, positioning as market-related skills the controlled aggression and competition of middle-class masculinities. Simultaneously, the exclusivity of men's sport reinforced domesticity for middle-class women, where nurturing and child-rearing demonstrated the qualities of appropriate femininity or womanhood.[28] Shifts in rural and urban economies from sustenance to small profit eventually devalued women's work in the home and, coupled with the lack of economic options for unmarried women, served to contract opportunities for women in the public sphere.[29] For men, however, the sporting clubs of the pre- and immediate post-Confederation eras, such as the Montreal Snowshoe Club and the Beaver Club of the early 1800s, created male-only space for the celebration of a physical manhood, augmented by drink, food, manly exercise, and songs of ability, virility, and conquest.[30] These men preserved their class- and race-based masculine enclaves by invoking the doctrine of amateurism, a nineteenth-century ideological invention that reserved sport for men who had the time and money for leisure (see Chapter 4). Sporting clubs remained exclusive by rule and regulation, the administrative control markers of mid-nineteenth-century middle-class men, and they secured the notions of empowered, male physicality that provided the hierarchical distinctions that shielded the membership, events, and competitions from stronger working-class or Aboriginal men, who were deemed inferior in all respects and hence could not be afforded an opportunity to display their physical superiority. Male-only space also cut across class- and race-based boundaries. Fraternal organizations for traditionally marginalized groups, including men of colour and disabled war veterans, provided a sense of social legitimacy and patriotism, even though such all-male groups remained segmented by class.[31] Sporting clubs, fraternal organizations, and other forms of public life drew men out of the home and away from the family, directly undermining the family role of the middle-class man promoted by the ideal of domesticity.

Like the aristocratic notion of honour of the previous era, sport provided a sense of physical empowerment, one that was coveted, but at the same time created conditions invoking the anxiety of losing in competition. The doctrine of amateurism ensured that 'lesser' forms of masculinity would not taint respectable manhood, but also made certain that men risked the shame of physical incompetence only among their class peers. Although wielded as an instrument of men's power, organized sport was fraught with social contradictions like all other competitive activities and it exposed the weaknesses of manhood as much as it celebrated manly victory.

The invention of race as a biological distinction helped white men deal with their fears of physical incompetence. The snowshoe clubs of Montreal did not permit Aboriginal members and even organized separate races for Indians and 'squaws' to enhance their gate receipts.[32] Consequently, club members rationalized the physical and technical abilities of skilled Aboriginal men and women by suggesting they had unfair natural abilities; the same classes of people rationalized the repression of nonwhites through the doctrine of race, categorizing others as uncivilized, lesser peoples. Inversely, but to the same effect, the British imperialist sport hunters, aristocrats and gentlemen, romanticized the Aboriginal male as noble savage. Their skilled guides, all with superior knowledge of hunting and travelling, some with muscular physiques, became less threatening to the often unskilled gentlemen hunter when positioned as socially and racially inferior. Thus, the social empowerment embedded in the manly exercise of sport hunting was preserved.[33]

Middle-class men's sporting clubs rejected outright the participation of women, even though they sometimes participated in skating, tobogganing, croquet, swimming, and tennis; women formed their own sporting clubs, such as the Montreal Ladies Archery Club, organized in 1858, and the Prince of Wales Club for women's snowshoeing in Montreal in 1861.[34] For men, the admiration of well-dressed ladies who applauded their physical exploits in club activities and competitions provided them a sense of identity, a pride in their bodies, and made them 'feel like men'.[35] Moreover, men's sporting events provided opportunities for young women to meet marriage partners,[36] 'to attract and wed "promising" young men who would provide them with support'.[37] Of fancy-dressed women who skated for fun at the rinks in Hamilton, Quebec, and Montreal, sport enthusiast and railway clerk Forbes Geddes recalled in 1862, 'many a match has resulted from attentions first received there.'[38] However, competitive sports such as rackets, Geddes concluded, were no place for Hamilton ladies. He wrote: 'The Misses Thomas and Mrs Rose were at the Racket Court. It is proposed to have a Lady's Day at the Court, so that the Gentlemen may not be caught "dishabillé" to use a mild term. But many think it is not a proper place for the soft sex. I agree.'[39] Until the last decade of the nineteenth century, competitive sport for women in Canada was unusual and, in popular consciousness, bordered on the burlesque.[40]

The increasing influence of **muscular Christianity**, in part celebrated in middle-class sporting clubs, was a direct reaction to emerging female leadership in the Protestant church.[41] Further, the values of toughness and strength celebrated by working-class men were incompatible with an increasingly feminized Christian faith.[42] These tensions, part of the gender order of community-based religion, were dispelled somewhat by physical activities supposedly 'favoured by God'.[43]

Education and the Gender Order

While some learned how to be men in the taverns and fields of British North America, and in the sporting clubs of Montreal, others were educated in the public schools of England. It was here that gentlemen and imperial leaders absorbed their academic and physical training, couched in the rhetoric of **social Darwinism**, which linked strength and manhood, Christian morals, and fair play to the success of empire and to the 'survival of the fittest'. Popular Victorian authors such as Charles Kingsley and Thomas Hughes 'adapted this emerging sense of individual possibility, moral and political, to their own profoundly religious confidence in personal and social salvation through service and strenuousness.'[44] Such chivalric ideals embedded in the notion of muscular Christianity gained favour in the schools of England and private schools of Canada, so that by mid-century a ruling elite was inspired by the images, language, and values of medieval chivalry.[45] Expanding earlier school strategies to control the behaviour of boys through sport, headmasters, teachers, authors, and sportsmen leveraged sport for its potential for turning boys into men, the leaders of nations. To be masculine or manly through sport meant being the opposite of being feminine or womanly. Early snowshoers,[46] schoolboys, and cricketers alike, through songs and revelry, made it clear that their exercises were not womanly:

What in the world is the use of a creature
All flabbily bent on avoiding the pitch,
Who wanders about, with a sob in each feature
Devising a headache, inventing a stitch?
There surely would be a quick end to my joy
If possessed of that monster—a feminine boy.[47]

Rough sports, violent and pain-inflicting rituals to build toughness, and hierarchies of power sustained through fighting between boys presented a model, adopted in part by private schools in British North America and the Dominion of Canada, such as Upper Canada College, Lower Canada College, Ridley College, Lakefield College, and St John's College. In addition to describing the rituals of cold baths, floggings by teachers, and beatings by prefects, in the recollections of Thomas Aldwell from Trinity College School: 'Games were important: football, foot-races, and cricket. But again there was no coddling. A boy had to fight for survival, had to learn to run and dodge and put everything he had into the contest or he was marked a failure.'[48]

As discussed in Chapter 9, physical activity remained absent from school training for boys and girls who did not have access to private schools. Children worked regularly in the fields with their parents, an important contribution to household production; as such, at that time, educators did not raise the issue of fitness in relation to health as a social concern.[49]

Following the Crimean War, the American Civil War, and the withdrawal of British troops from the garrisons during the 1860s, the British encouraged the establishment of local militias, rifle companies, and a volunteer force as an inexpensive alternative to permanent military troops.[50] In addition, educators, often ex-military officers, emphasized military drill in the schools for boys as an integral aspect of training. School and social activities linking masculinity with military patriotism were powerful tools of nation-building in the Confederation era. Teachers organized calisthenics as the primary physical education exercises for schoolgirls from Confederation to the end of the nineteenth century.[51] In private schools, middle- and upper-class girls and young women had the most wide-ranging opportunities to explore their bodies through physical activity.[52] Elite women also exercised and participated in sports such as hockey, basketball, tennis, and fencing at universities including McGill, Toronto, Dalhousie, and the Halifax Ladies College.[53]

Science, Morality, and the Politics of Appearance

In addition to religious values, political and economic limitations, the overarching cultural constructions of the domestic sphere for middle-class women, namely fashion, gender, and health concerns, served to restrict the range of expressions of physicality available to these Victorian women. For middle- and upper-class women, clothing and appearance were indices of social station and devices used to attract men. A social obsession with style and appearance, driven in part by public norms and in part by concern for domestic security, carried considerably more weight than day-to-day practicality. Consequently, fashion usually compromised and limited physical movement, comfort, even health. The corset, for example, bound women's bodies into an appealing shape, even though it was painful, restrictive, and its long-term use in some cases constricted organs and caused death. In addition to such physical abuses, the corset contributed to creating submissive women.[54] Women's fashion reinforced the polarities of gender construction, with hoop skirts, corsets, and layers of clothing literally restricting physical movement, thereby adding to the public empowerment of men, their supposed social opposites, while constricting their own social options.

As urban centres increased in population and deadly diseases such as cholera and smallpox devastated families and entire city blocks, everyone—but the middle classes and public officials in particular—turned to physicians in matters of public health.[55] The idea of science as an important foundation of human knowledge and the role of medicine, based on these scientific principles, influenced public attitudes about the body. The scientific and medical communities entrenched the gendering of professional knowledge, even as women's bodies became subservient to broader social pressures. The control exerted by the medical profession over health concerns and exercise needs pressured women to comply with the oppression.[56] The sentiments of the profession are captured by the *British Medical Journal* in 1867, one of the premier periodicals that provided information to practising physicians:

> As a body who practise among women, we have constituted ourselves, as it were the guardians of their interests, and—in many cases—the custodians of their honour. We are, in fact, the stronger and they the weaker. They are obliged to believe all that we tell them and we, therefore, may be said to have them at our mercy.[57]

One of the ways that popular culture absorbed scientific knowledge was through exercise and sport.[58] Indeed, the medical profession played a significant, even dominant, role in determining which physical activities were safe or appropriate for women.[59]

As evident in the above quotation, doctors conflated medical advice with the social and moral concerns of motherhood and sexuality. Strenuous exercise, doctors argued, could cause uterine displacement and other serious reproductive problems, incapacitating women for the responsibilities of womanhood. Dr Edward Clarke's theory of menstrual disability, widely accepted in medical circles, claimed that mentally and physically taxing exercises were dangerous to the female bodily constitution.[60] This contributed to public concerns over women's participation in sport. The theory that women were naturally and chronically weak, with only a certain amount of mental and physical energy, had strong influences on the medical profession and, as a result, on public attitudes towards women's participation in exercise.[61] Thus, the medical discourse of the late nineteenth century naturalized the posited biological differences between men and women in social and moral terms, contributing widely to the reproduction of separate spheres. Exercise for women, the medical literature purported, ran counter to the rules of nature; doctors fearful of the ravages of exercise debated whether sport depleted energy, causing serious harm.[62] Some doctors went so far as to argue that higher education could be taxing on women's health. Such thinking suggested that biology prevented women from developing their intellect, a convenient assumption to sustain the absence of women from politics, law, and other forms of public life.

The idea that humans possessed limited amounts of energy was related to theories of vitalism or vital energy, suggesting that certain activities depleted the stores of said energy and decreased the natural lifespan. These arguments linked exercise to notions about sex and masturbation, two activities theorized to deplete one's vital energy. Doctors suggested that women lost vital energy through menstruation, pregnancy, lactation, and masturbation. The emphasis for men, according to this theory, was the loss of seminal fluid from excessive sex and masturbation.[63]

Biological theories blended with social, moral, and religious values to influence attitudes about appropriate behaviour. Protestants legitimized the religious economic imperative (the work ethic) through legislation that criminalized loitering.[64] The social theory that non-working, idle hands caused trouble in society blended with medical notions that idle hands led to masturbation, which was damaging to human health.[65] Women having been cast in the role as moral arbiters of Victorian society, the responsibility for sexual control or restraint rested on their shoulders. Men, it followed, had natural but barely controllable sexual urges that had to be kept in check by women. Conservative fashion styles of middle- and upper-class women, designed to cover legs, arms, ankles, and wrists, hid women's bodies from the eyes of supposedly oversexed men. While presenting certain class distinctions for women, designers ensured that fashion styles referenced feminine attractiveness without intimating overtones of sexual desire. Further, since strenuous exercise, movement, and perspiration were considered socially vulgar for women, clothing, by design, restricted movement.[66] Consequently, clothing, from social wear to bathing costumes, was layered, voluminous, and impractical; exercise of any sort for women who were dressed 'appropriately' was difficult.[67] In the case

Bathing suit on the shores of Lake Winnipeg. (Library and Archives Canada, PA-181073)

of swimming, the bathing costume, when wet, could weigh in excess of nine kilograms, rendering the exercise quite dangerous for women who strayed into waters that were too deep.[68] Religion, medicine, domestic relations, and the 'maleness' and 'femaleness' created and sustained through competitive sport, politics, and economy all combined to influence commonly held ideas about how women's and men's bodies were to be displayed in public.

The Bathing Machine

The bathing machine was essentially a change room on wheels, in use from the late 1750s in England to the early twentieth century. The device was also used in North America. It was approximately six feet in length and eight feet high, with wooden or canvas walls, and a roof and a bench inside for sitting. Horses or attendants drew the cart to lake or sea-side and the bathing machine provided privacy for women while they changed into their bathing costumes. Some carts were outfitted with a flag to indicate that the bather had changed her clothing and was ready to swim. Once near the water, attendants assisted the bathers down the steps and into the water.

From Tobias Smollett's *The Expedition of Humphrey Clinker*:

Image to yourself a small, snug, wooden chamber, fixed upon a wheel-carriage, having a door at each end, and on each side a little window above, a bench below—The bather, ascending into this apartment by wooden steps, shuts himself in, and begins to undress, while the attendant yokes a horse to the end next the sea, and draws the carriage forwards, till the surface of the water is on a level with the floor of the dressing-room, then he moves and fixes the horse to the other end—The person within being stripped, opens the door to the sea-ward, where he finds the guide ready, and plunges headlong into the water—After having bathed, he re-ascends into the apartment, by the steps which had been shifted for that purpose, and puts on his clothes at his leisure, while the carriage is drawn back again upon the dry land; so that he has nothing further to do, but to open the door, and come down as he went up—Should he be so weak or ill as to require a servant to put off and on his clothes, there is room enough in the apartment for half a dozen people.[69]

Fighting Re-'cycled' Arguments

During this era some men and women rejected the restrictions placed on women's participation in exercise. Female physicians, such as Mary Putnam Jacobi and Elizabeth Blackwell, defended higher education for women and challenged the social determinism of science and medicine.[70] Physical educators such as Frederic Barnjum preached about the benefits of exercise for men and satirized common notions labelling women the weaker sex. His public address delivered 11 January 1867 lampoons Victorian attitudes towards the body:

What shall we say of girls, who, by the conventional rules of society, are debarred from taking more than the semblance of exercise. They have not the same opportunity for romping as boys. Poor little missie must walk home in the most genteel manner possible, perhaps indulging in a softened laugh with some companion[,] her arms carefully hugged to her sides, motion of the lower extremities only being permitted, added to which her poor little body is in all probability forced in by one of those instruments of death called corsets, binding up the naughty muscles that are begging and praying to be let loose and have an opportunity of strengthening themselves, and the young lady is considered to be in a highly satisfactory condition

if she is pale and weak; but no matter, it is the natural thing for girls to be weak . . .
(I) do not hesitate to say that any young lady placed under the care of an intelligent,
well-educated teacher, cannot fail to attain a degree of health which otherwise she
never would have dreamed of.[71]

Canon R.W. Norman, writing to *The Educational Record* 14 years later agreed, suggesting
that both boys and girls should be engaged in supervised gymnastics, tennis, snowshoeing,
skating, rowing, and swimming exercises.[72]

The introduction of the safety bicycle during the 1890s created opportunities for some
middle-class women to exercise in public. Initially for men only, the first popular models
were the ordinary or the penny farthing, a high-wheeled, expensive vehicle restricted to
young men of the middle classes.[73] The sheer size of the penny farthing prevented the young
and old from riding, in addition to women concerned with wearing the appropriate hoop
skirts and long dresses in public. The bicycle, like the horse in previous eras, conferred social
power to its rider. The higher the rider on his bicycle, the higher a man's self esteem.[74] For the
middle-class men who organized cycling clubs, it was an exciting enterprise that appeared
daring and risky to onlookers, a marker of manhood to be respected for its technical aspects
by other men and for its demonstrations of sheer bravado by admiring women.[75] Men
pedalled the ordinary to speeds of 20 miles per hour, a fearsome sight for both horse-
drawn carriages and pedestrians. Men formed clubs to legitimize the activity, a reaction in
part to the growing public criticism that cyclists were a menace to safety on town streets.
Cyclists frequently wrote to local newspapers to educate the public about respectability and
the control demonstrated by physically competent riders, to allay public fears, to enhance
their status as cycle owners, and to generate excitement for events and competitions. The
daring high-wheelers brought the gentleman athlete's body to public prominence, creating
a carnivalesque atmosphere at simple rides and gatherings. The most talented riders and
racers gained reputations in the press, and fellow cyclists positioned the unmarried men
as dashing young icons of exemplary manhood, available for the admiration of the young
women of the community. The price of bicycles restricted the activity by class; and the
rhetoric of risk made it a men's activity. However, bicycle advocates countered arguments
about the danger of riding by describing spills and accidents as humorous 'headers'. A fine
line of social commentary in the newspapers made cycling risky enough to be exciting and
appealing but safe enough to be respectable in the public eye.

The arrival of the smaller-wheeled safety bicycle helped vault curious women into the
saddle, often incurring the disdain of both men and other women. Critics raised concerns
over safety and reproductive health, and the ill effects of perspiration, all of them reacting
negatively to the appearance of physically active women in the streets. Some doctors
brandished cycling as a public exercise of female masturbation, perpetrated by immoral
women who derived orgasmic pleasures from the bicycle seat.[76] Others dismissed this
criticism as pure mythology and even praised the bicycle for its contribution to dress reform
and the introduction of split skirts and bloomers for female cyclists.[77] Opponents viewed
the split skirt as men's trousers or 'bifurcated bags' that created 'unholy desires' among
boys and men;[78] but the Rational Dress Society, an organization that protested against
the physically debilitating effects of women's fashion, adopted it as an official emblem.[79]
The physically emancipating effects of the bicycle were restricted to only some women of
the middle class. However, by the 1890s, the presence of female cyclists on public streets[80]

Cyclist Mabel Williams, Ottawa, 1898. (Library and Archives Canada, PA-132274)

energized other changes in social values and practices, shifting some of the public attitudes in favour of women's limited participation in exercise and some sports. In addition, educational thought changed somewhat, with the introduction of more physical activity for girls and women; newly patriotic ideals of motherhood emerged, supported by a limited sector of the medical community— it was now thought that light exercise could contribute to the physical requirements of motherhood; and sports and games such as lawn tennis and competitive activities for women at private schools and universities[81] demonstrated that rigid Victorian attitudes were beginning to lose their stranglehold on parts of society.[82] However, many doctors continued to use exercise prevention and prescription as a means of professional control over women's bodies and women's health; exercise prescription, albeit limited, operated on the principle that muscularity was damaging to mother-hood.[83] For the majority of citizens—men and women— competitive sport and rigorous exercise remained distinctly male enterprises well into the twentieth century.

Sport and the Legitimation of Male Violence

No other institutionalized cultural activity in Canadian history has contributed more to naturalizing violence in society than sport. Early organized sports such as cricket, rowing, track and field, snowshoeing, and for some time baseball served as venues for gentrified or genteel masculinities, where Christian men celebrated social distinction and attempted to distance themselves from working-class men, since violence was associated with labourers and the 'rough' elements of society. However, in the middle-class sports of lacrosse, hockey, rugby, and later baseball,[84] violence was common on the fields, pitches, and ice surfaces, as well as in the stands. Class divisions and fragmentations split opinions on appropriate social behaviours for men. Many professionals and parliamentarians did not approve of sport at all. For some middle-class men in the sporting clubs, muscular Christians all, bourgeois notions of the gentleman, domestic provider, and father gave way to the celebration of toughness and empowered physical masculinity on the pitch. These men did not play lacrosse, hockey, and rugby gently, even though the idea of fair play remained a distinct component of sporting honour. Lacrosse matches of the 1860s, 1870s, and 1880s were rife with slashing, punching, tripping, body-checking, and bloody, violent melees.[85] To preserve a class distinction, men rationalized the aggression practised through sport as a rite of passage, a character-building enterprise that built stronger, better men and, therefore, a stronger nation.[86] Rough play, when tempered by the Christianized notion of fair play, masked the contradictions of respectable violence.

A significant problem for men who considered themselves respectable was their enjoyment of violence as a form of entertainment. Tavern owners had long understood their patrons' fascination with fighting and had organized matches for paying customers. Promoters took this idea beyond the tavern and began organizing boxing matches as spectator events. In order to evade local police, the matches were organized in remote areas, some only accessible by boat or train. Since the promoters paid the boxers from the gate receipts, the sport was known as prizefighting. Two Ontario matches in

The football snap, Edmonton Eskimos, c. 1919. (Courtesy of Frank Cosentino)

particular, one at Long Point and one at Point Dover, led to a federal ban on prizefighting. Anticipating a riot and the usual drunkenness and gambling associated with boxing, the sheriff of Norfolk County and 71 members of the 39th Battalion boarded the steamship *Annie Craig* on 18 January 1880 to prevent the fight at Long Point from occurring. On 12 May 1880, members of the 39th and 44th Battalions prevented the fight at Port Dover. Parliamentarians debated the issue of boxing within the social contexts of intemperance, gambling, morality, amateurism, and appropriate manhood. One of the main issues was the cost of calling out the militia. Federal legislation banned prizefighting in Canada in 1881.[87] Moral entrepreneurs and commercial entrepreneurs, each wishing to capture sport for their own purposes, waged similar kinds of debates in Canadian communities. Moral entrepreneurs promoted sport to build character in boys and men in an effort to battle loitering on city streets, to fight intemperance, to reform the rough tavern behaviour of the unemployed underclass and working-class men, and formal attempts were pursued to use sport to bring men back to the church and religion through the social gospel.[88] In addition to other sports, Young Men's Christian Associations offered amateur boxing programs to men and boys.

The commercial entrepreneurs sought to make money through sport by selling tickets to events, using the once-popular ideologies of amateurism only to secure a decent reputation for their entertainment product. They capitalized on town boosterism—the interest that people had in supporting the reputations of their towns through various competitions, including sport. In most towns of Canada, civic boosterism, being competitive with other towns, created difficulties for defenders of the amateur ideal. In sports such as baseball and hockey,[89] owners and promoters relied on gate receipts and thus turned to the recruitment of star players from other cities for pay. Spectators tended to be more interested in victories than in the preservation of the gentleman amateur. This had a direct impact on how games

The principles, Luther McCarty versus Arthur Pelkey, promoted by Tommy Burns, Calgary, 1913. (William J. Oliver, Library and Archives Canada, C-014060)

were played and watched. Rivalries between players and spectators often resulted in violent play on the ice, spectator violence directed towards players, and brawls between spectators of different towns.[90] Violent play sometimes led to the deaths of players, including Alcide Laurin in 1905 and Bud McCourt in 1907, both killed during hockey games after being struck over the head with sticks. Luther McCarty died in Calgary in 1913 during a boxing match, informally billed as the 'White Heavyweight Championship'.[91] But in these cases and others that followed, a culturally accepted level of violence in sport, tied to the development of manly character as a patriotic exercise, rendered the courts reluctant to prosecute sports violence. Generally, Canadian courts left sport leagues to police themselves through the first half of the twentieth century.[92] The sporting community and the judiciary viewed sporting deaths as unfortunate accidents. Moreover, many justices hearing such cases voiced their approval of the kind of training that sport provided for boys and men, and members of the court often attended the major sporting events in the community.[93]

Promoters and supporters successfully redefined boxing as a demonstration of what they referred to as scientific skill and technique to distance it from the previously unregulated prizefights and street brawls. Couched in the new 'religion' of modern society—science—they attempted to neutralize the negative perceptions of the violence integral to boxing matches.[94] They hoped that urban boxing matches would attract all classes of society. By the early twentieth century, petitions to host or to prevent boxing matches forced lively debates among many town councils.[95] Following the exploits of John L. Sullivan, Jim Corbett, Jim Jeffries, and Canada's first heavyweight boxing champion of the world, Tommy Burns, early fans came to identify the heavyweight champion title as the pinnacle of sporting manhood. Produced blow by blow for newspapers, then by telegraph tickertape, then by fight films, fans could follow every round of heavyweight matches. The seriousness of this manly enterprise became evident when Tommy Burns lost the title in 1908 to Jack Johnson, the first black fighter acclaimed heavyweight champion. Johnson's victory sent ripples of racist discontent around the world, as white supremacist sentiment boiled over and a crisis in white masculinity emerged, one that continues to the present day. The voluminous rhetoric that had crowned white men as the natural leaders in all social affairs, including sport, was rendered meaningless overnight. The initial response of critics was to label boxing as a savage and corrupt enterprise and black fighters as savages who lacked intelligence, while promoters, ex-fighters, and the white public scoured the earth for a 'Great White Hope' to dethrone Johnson, the new symbol of black physical supremacy.[96] Previously, all heavyweight champions and fighters in other weight classes had refused to fight black boxers. Consequently, the boxing world denied talented boxers such as Canada's Sam Langford and George Dixon opportunities for boxing glory.[97]

All classes of men and some women attended boxing matches, including doctors, lawyers, police, and firemen. Tommy Burns, a boxing promoter in Calgary following his defeat, used 'ladies' days' for women to watch sparring, essentially to bring respectability to his events.[98] Baseball promoters used this strategy as well.[99] In addition to later swimming and diving competitions, boxing was one of the first sports to present male athletes with bared bodies in public. At a time when residual Victorian attitudes about the body prevailed, sport provided new public venues for the voyeur and presented the athlete as an object, now uncovered, of erotic desire.

The most accolades reserved for a trained, uniformed, masculine appearance were accorded to community firemen. During civic celebrations, the visits of distinguished state guests, and parades, newspaper commentaries identified firemen as the best-looking, muscular exemplars of Canadian manhood.[100] Similar to the soldier, militiaman, rifle shooter, and police officer, the fireman was a symbol of male protection over weaker men, women, and children, and significant more practically—if ineffectively—for his work in fighting the fires that ravaged the wooden buildings of the period. Volunteer firefighting companies in small towns provided venues for working-class men to obtain honour and pride in the public sphere and to share in town boosterism through their skills at firefighters' competitions and public demonstrations of fire extinguishing.[101]

Social reformers thought that the industrialization of the workplace was softening the bodies of men. Anthropologists demonstrated a new fascination with bodies, using standardized measurements of limbs, heads, and even penises as indicators of an imputed inferior or superior intelligence or propensity for criminal activity, or even simple poverty. Such measurements culminated in pictures and sculptures of what the anthropologists termed the 'perfect' bodies of males and females, adding to the rather arbitrary cultural distinctions drawn between men and women.[102] Sport, they argued, should counter the adverse effects of sedentary forms of desk labour in offices. The popularity of the strong man, Canadian Louis Cyr the most famous among them (see Chapter 6), gave way to the scientized demonstrations of strength and the body beautiful, popularized by bodybuilder, showman, and publicist Eugen Sandow. Sandow made a considerable fortune posing nearly nude in scenes of heroic muscularity with animal skins and weapons, showing his body as a symbol of masculine beauty.[103] Sandow's *Physical Culture* magazine and his contemporary

Bernarr Macfadden's *Physical Development* magazine portrayed the body 'builder' as a romantic, virile man. Macfadden offered $1,000 for a contest held at Madison Square Garden to determine the 'Most Perfectly Developed Man in America'. Similar contests were held for women, and within this subculture, female bodybuilders, such as Minerva, were photographed and admired. Macfadden, one of the first influential supporters of women's bodybuilding, argued that women, too, could achieve strength and beauty through exercise.[104] Early male physique photography of near nudes and, later, full nudes added the genre of male muscular development to the more casual depictions of male nudes in paintings and photographs by Thomas Eakins.[105]

The First World War to the 1930s

The cult of competitiveness—celebrated in part through working-class sports and made possible through a shorter workweek, town boosterism, the sports promoter and entrepreneur, and the emergence of the sports page—carried organized sport beyond the middle- and upper-class enclaves of the nineteenth century to Canadian popular consciousness in the twentieth century. Men returning from the violence and brutality of the First World War brought their deep emotional scars into family and public life. One of the consequences of the war was an increased interest in the violent sports of boxing and hockey, and a heightened sense of awareness of opportunities to celebrate nationalism and patriotism through sport. For women, the war had opened up work opportunities in factories, manufacturing, and professions such as teaching and nursing. Culminating in the right to vote in Canada, women secured a more public place within work, society, and culture in the 1920s.

Young Women's Christian Associations, with 14 branches in Canada by 1900, provided 'respectable' exercise facilities for women, while private schools such as the Somers School of Physical Training and the Margaret Eaton School[106] offered opportunities for women to exercise and study physical culture.[107] Ethel Mary Cartwright instructed a program for playground supervisors at McGill, following the work of the National Council of Women to develop urban playgrounds in Canadian municipalities. By the First World War, organized women's basketball and hockey teams existed across the country, in addition to some softball teams. By far the most famous Canadian sport team of this era was a group of women known as the Edmonton Commercial Graduates basketball team.[108]

Coached by J. Percy Page, the Grads played competitive basketball from 1915 to 1940 across Canada and Europe, defeating the majority of women's and men's teams that they faced.[109] The fact that a well-respected man served as manager and coach of the team, and his wife acted as chaperone on trips, stemmed criticism against these single women, who travelled around the world playing a competitive sport. Businesses in Edmonton provided jobs for the Grads and Page raised local funds for their travels from sponsors and gate receipts. Like their male sporting peers, whose participation in sport secured their masculine identities and reputations, the Grads willingly adhered to codes of feminine conduct, such as dressing and acting like 'ladies' and refraining from behaviours that the coach considered unladylike, including smoking, drinking, and chewing gum. Page forced them to leave the team once they married. The Grads served as role models to young sporting women, and their itinerary included a visit to the Berlin Olympics in 1936 for exhibition matches, while Percy Page used his coaching success and celebrity to build a career in politics.[110]

The Edmonton Commercial Graduates Basketball Team, 1922. (Courtesy of Don Morrow)

Throughout the 1920s and early 1930s, the Grads and other female athletes faced criticism, moral judgment, and a public eye bent on assessing their looks and womanhood rather than their skills. In this era, the press judged male athletes according to competitive performance and good character. At times, as in the case of swimmer Johnny Weismuller, who played Tarzan in Hollywood movies, the masculine physique received attention by virtue of physical form and facial features. Newspaper accounts of sport competitions judged women first by beauty, then by character and deportment, and last by performance.[111] Some argued that sport made women 'mannish', giving women undesirable physical characteristics.[112] Consequently, when members of the press considered a female athlete beautiful and feminine, they focused almost exclusively on these qualities in their reporting. Ethel Catherwood, the gold-medal-winning high jumper from Saskatoon, became an icon of Canadian feminine sporting beauty, referred to as 'The Saskatoon Lily' during and after the 1928 Olympics. Successful female athletes gained public praise for traits of femininity, one of the costs of women's acceptance on the public stage of Olympic and international sport, a venue that most people still considered appropriate for men only. If female athletes could be beautiful and graceful, heterosexual, participate in gender-appropriate sports, and eventually be good wives and mothers, then their participation in sport did not compromise traditional social values. A feminized athlete could not challenge the celebration of manhood through sport and thus did not displace men as the 'real' athletes of the era. The new leaders of Coubertin's Olympic Games, Count Henri Baillet-Latour and

Ethel Catherwood, 1928 Olympic High Jump Champion, shown in 1930. (Courtesy of the City of Toronto Archives, James Collection 8174)

Avery Brundage, eventually accepted the premise of women's participation, provided, they argued, that it was in events such as swimming, fencing, and tennis but not in the strenuous masculine sports such as shot-putting.[113] Sporting women, like Hollywood stars, became the cultural icons of femininity.

Dress code regulations at the Olympics notwithstanding, female athletes, as interested as men in winning and performance, altered their competitive outfits to suit their sports.[114] Changes in fashion made the Olympic swimming and diving pools, and indeed any venues where women and men displayed their partially or lightly clad bodies, a new and exciting locale for the sport sexual voyeur. Yet, the press and the organizers of sport continued to treat men and women differently, sustaining a gender order through sport that was residually Victorian. Maxwell Stiles of the *Los Angeles Examiner* described the march-in of Canadian athletes in 1932 at the Los Angeles Olympics:

> The Canadian girls are undoubtedly the prettiest and most wholesome looking group of girls who have arrived for the competition. They constitute a denial of the general idea that a woman athlete must be built like a baby grand piano and have a face like a hatchet. Their ages range from 16 to 21, and they are here to show the world that Canada has some splendid young women who are good-looking and who know how to conduct themselves.[115]

Internationally, by the 1930s, male sport leaders had assumed control over women's athletics and Olympic sports, generally. The feminization process and its long-term consequences were the costs of women's participation. In Canada, the AAU did little to promote women's sport in the 1920s, in spite of the success of the Women's Olympics and a growing number of women participating in athletics and team sports. In response to an invitation for a Canadian team to attend an all-expenses-paid competition in England, the AAU asked Alexandrine Gibb to organize trials for athlete selection for the team. Gibb learned from this international experience, particularly from the British Women's Amateur Athletic Association, and she sought to form a similar organization in Canada when she returned home.[116] She became the first president of the Canadian Ladies Athletic Club, later sanctioned in 1926 by the AAU as the Women's Amateur Athletic Federation of Canada. Coast-to-coast paid membership totalled 3,300 by 1935, with sports such as hockey, basketball, softball, skiing, and swimming recognizing its authority.[117] Women's sport leaders acknowledged the dominant influence of men but were willing to negotiate a path for women to assume positions of executive authority in various sports.[118] There were still many influential men in the sporting world, such as Arthur Lamb, head of the Canadian Olympic contingent in Amsterdam, who voted against women's participation in future Olympics. Female journalists such as Alexandrine Gibb, Phyllis Griffiths, and sport stars Fanny Rosenfeld and Myrtle Cook all wrote columns about women's sport in Canada (see Chapter 7), bringing women's experiences and triumphs to the sport pages. Both men and women debated over whether women should use men's rules in such sports as basketball or girl's rules. Proponents of different rules for women argued that men's sports were becoming too competitive, too violent, and too commercialized and that women should be given a more healthy and educational alternative to the male model.[119] Gibb's columns assured the public that sporting women maintained femininity in the face of continuing social and medical arguments against women's participation in exercise and sport throughout the 1930s.

The Second World War and the Cold War

The Second World War brought a halt to the Olympic Games of 1940 and 1944, while owners of the National Hockey League teams and Major League Baseball in the United States attempted to operate their leagues in spite of the loss of many players to the war effort. Baseball owners in the United States organized the All-American Girls Professional Baseball League in 1943 to help bring spectators back to ballparks during the war years when Major League rosters were depleted. Scouts recruited talented Canadian women, such as Marion Watson (Stanton) of Chatham, Ontario, and Saskatchewan's Bonnie Baker, to American teams, where they were required to attend charm schools before playing. Under threat of fines, league founder P.K. Wrigley insisted that they wear makeup and long hair to look like ladies. Watson recalled: 'They kept a pretty good check on you, just for your own reputation. They wanted ladies and didn't want any bad reputations around the league. You had to be an athlete, but a lady also.'[120] Players had to sneak out of their rooms to avoid curfew and chaperones if they wanted to socialize in local bars.[121] This women's league lasted until 1954.

The feminization process in sport encouraged by leaders of the International Olympic Committee (IOC) and International Sport Federation leaders served to channel women into artistic and aesthetic sports in the post-war era, while others strove to maintain the image of beauty and domesticity in the press. Women made significant contributions to the war effort overseas and in the workforce at home. But upon the return of men to Canada, government and the press encouraged women to return to their homes as wives and mothers, their 'rightful' place. Such attitudes, popularized and propagated in schools, magazines, books, and social commentary of the post-war era, reinforced the norm of the nuclear family in Canada, with husband as provider and wife as domestic worker and mother to the country's next generation. In spite of the new Cold War emphasis on cultural competition and the Soviet expansion of women's sport, the Canadian public insisted that its female athletes maintain their wholesome image.[122] One social reaction caused by the feminization of the artistic sports was a feminization of men who participated in them. Within the gendered ideological framework constructed for sport in this era, how could men who participated in sports such as figure skating, which was identified as appropriately feminine, possibly be masculine?

In the post-war era, men's hockey supremacy, as indeed a great portion of the Canadian sporting imagination, was sustained by the NHL monopoly, brought live to households by radio during the 1930s, 1940s, and 1950s, and by television in the 1950s and 1960s. The Canadian Football League (CFL) was established in 1958, and likewise reinforced the popularity of violent spectator sports for men. The commercialization of these sports, the wide celebration of sport superstars, and the profit objectives of professional sport teams created unique labour relations, where the dreams of boys and the responsibilities of men strategically intertwined to create a mythical fraternal community.[123] Athletes depended on their bodies for pay and stardom and, as such, were willing to play through pain and injury to keep a spot on the roster. A masculine subculture normalizing bravado, when it came to issues of health, or perpetrating violence to protect a teammate or as a strategy to win became widely accepted and actively endorsed as seemingly immutable traditions by players, managers, doctors, and owners in the confrontational sports.[124] Men retreated further, it has been argued, into the fraternal comfort of combat sports such as football, hockey, and boxing during the 1970s and 1980s, on the heels of the feminist movement and social gains by women in other areas of society.[125]

The 'good versus evil' ideological battle of the Cold War period, played out significantly through the Olympic Games, was mimicked as well in professional wrestling and roller derbies that existed on the margins of sport culture as popular entertainment. In the post-war context, these narratives connected to the emergence of Hollywood heroes in film and those appearing later on television such as the Lone Ranger, Maverick, Davy Crockett, Matt Dillon, and the new superhero comic figures such as Superman. Such cultural narratives offered up a passage from boyhood to manhood, a construction of masculine identity that seemed uncomplicated when framed in terms of the binary opposition represented by 'good' and 'evil'. Hollywood women were beautiful, glamorous, and dependent on male heroes, while the comic book hero, Wonder Woman, was athletic and yet assuredly female.

Also on the margins of post-war popular culture, in the United States the AAU's 'Mr America' contest replaced Macfadden's 'perfect' man pageants. The Charles Atlas ad campaign alerted men to the ostensible perils of being 'wimps' on the beach; Bob Hoffman[126] and the Weider brothers brought public consumers to the bodybuilding industry in North America. Professional bodybuilding promoters joined with British and European organizers, forming the International Federation of Bodybuilders, inaugurating the 'Mr Olympia' and 'Mr Universe' competitions.[127] In this context of competition, more muscle meant more man, an ironic interpretation since many bodybuilding followers were homosexual and the well-muscled body ran counter to popular notions of the effeminate or homosexual man.[128] Steve Reeves, the best-known bodybuilder of the 1950s and 1960s, who played the role of adventuresome warrior in Hollywood movies, worked and trained in an era when male bodybuilders remained on the margins of popular culture.

The arrival of Arnold Schwarzenegger, the most celebrated bodybuilder to date, announced a new era for the popular acceptance and admiration of muscular development, embraced by television and movie audiences worldwide, and over the following decades the weight training and diet supplement industries became multibillion dollar enterprises.[129] Women, too, have competed internationally for bodybuilding titles since gaining official

Start of the women's marathon swim, Canadian National Exhibition, Toronto, 1935. (Courtesy of Don Morrow)

status internationally in 1978. Women's bodybuilding has gained a considerable following but remains relatively unaccepted within social norms, even though competitors have attempted to maintain a feminine image and organizers prevent them from performing specific 'masculine' poses.[130] Extreme muscle development remains a marginalized aspect of physical culture for women; generally, people still consider muscularity a masculine attribute. The women's fitness movement legitimized body 'shaping' for women, in the context of standardized beauty and body-type norms, through aerobics, dance fitness, and an assortment of toning products and devices. Female self-improvement, the driving ideology of the fitness industry, is gendered with respect to the body type promoted, one that requires just enough exercise to make one firm, athletic, and thin, presumably to attract the attention of men.[131]

Just as the issue of what rules to adopt was difficult for activists promoting women's sports in previous eras, the issue of opportunity for girls to play organized sport at competitive levels remained complicated for decades. Future track star Abby Hoffman had no opportunities to play competitive hockey growing up in St Catharines, Ontario, during the 1950s. Hoffman created a media stir when officials discovered that she was a girl playing in the boys' league.[132] Some 30 years later, in 1985, Justine Blainey earned a spot on a boys' hockey team in the Metro Toronto League, but was then barred from playing by the Ontario Hockey Association.

As demonstrated in many sports that women now play, including football, the physical limitations of women that were long perpetrated through specific cultural understandings about sport were pure myth. (Courtesy of Kevin Wamsley)

Blainey's case, taken to the Ontario Court of Appeal and an Ontario Board of Inquiry, raised issues of inequality in the Canadian sport system. The Board ruled that the Ontario Hockey Association could not bar girls from competing for positions in the league.[133] On the one hand, feminists argued that the Blainey case was a victory for human rights; on the other, advocates for women's sport argued that it would lead to the demise of girls' hockey.[134] Rules in women's hockey prevent heavy body-checking and prescribe considerably less violence than in the men's game. Women's hockey is currently more popular than ever, having gained considerable press since the gold medal win of the women's national team at the 2002 and 2006 Winter Olympics. However, recent studies suggest that elite women's sport is plagued with problems similar to men's; women report similar responses, a willingness and cultural imperative towards playing through pain and injury.[135] Further, in order to market their sports or to raise money for competition and travel, some female athletes have posed naked. The women's national cross-country ski team posed naked for a calendar to raise funds for the team. Athletes like Waneek Horn-Miller of the Canadian national women's water polo team, who posed nude for the cover of *Time* magazine, celebrated a certain empowerment of the athletic body. Critics suggest that such acts add to the trivialization and sexualization that female athletes have been fighting against for almost a century.

The feminization processes or channelling of women into the appropriate 'feminine' sports, endorsed and encouraged by Olympic leaders and through the Olympic Games from the 1930s to the present, contributed to the sexualization of female athletes, generally, to the creation of the child athlete in such sports as gymnastics, and to body image crises among young athletes in the artistic sports in particular. The qualitative sport emphasis on increasing risk ostensibly to demonstrate progress and to heighten spectator appeal has resulted in diminished body proportions for athletes in gymnastics and figure skating. The complicity of judges, coaches, and international officials in promoting a 'biomechanical' model as the aesthetic body ideal has led some athletes to chronic eating disorders and compulsive training, sometimes ending in death.[136]

Serious health issues related to body image developed for boys as well. The post-bodybuilding movie career of Arnold Schwarzenegger in the 1980s and a long list of well-muscled contemporaries, including Sylvester Stallone, or more recently Dwayne 'the Rock' Johnson, John Cena, Hugh Jackman's portrayal of the comic book character Wolverine, and the latest James Bond, Daniel Craig, helped to naturalize hyper-muscularity as a form of manliness or masculinity in the popular media. Further, the successful marriage of age-old professional wrestling with contemporary bodybuilding by sport entertainment entrepreneur Vince McMahon has placed a cast of wrestling heroes and villains in contemporary sport channel spotlights. Boys have learned from Olympic athletes, professional wrestlers, and bodybuilders that anabolic steroids will improve performance and build muscle. A consequence of the prevalence of hyper muscularity in the entertainment industry has been an increased use of steroids by boys who are intent on becoming muscular as a marker of exemplary manhood.

Conclusions

Sport has always been a cultural location where men and women have built and learned identities about how to be masculine or feminine. For more than 100 years, sport has been organized to celebrate the attributes of competitive, strong, and sometimes violent men, usually at the expense of weaker men and most women. However, in spite of this gender ordering, people have resisted the popular attitudes of the day to carve out a unique place for their own brands of participation and understanding. Nevertheless, sport remains one of the foremost institutions where economic and symbolic rewards are distributed unequally to its participants, a process that separates the men from the boys and the girls.

Related Websites

Gender Education and Advocacy
http://www.gender.org/

Laboratory for Leisure, Tourism and Sport: Readings in Violence and Sport
http://www.sp.uconn.edu/~yian/frl/19viol.htm

Sport and Masculinity
http://www.aafla.org/9arr/ResearchReports/boystomen.pdf

Fashion History
http://www.fashion-era.com

Edmonton Commercial Graduates Basketball Team
http://www.collectionscanada.gc.ca/women/002026-229-e.html

Bodybuilding History
http://www.sandowplus.co.uk/

Sport and Eating Disorders
http://www.caringonline.com/eatdis/topics/athletics.htm

Study Questions

1. What do we learn about traditional masculinities and femininities when we study sport in Canada before the Second World War? How do they influence our ideas about behaving appropriately today?
2. What historical conditions help to explain why modern sport is violent?
3. What compromises did women make to be involved in competitive sport?
4. How is our understanding of human musculature gendered?
5. How can our understandings of sport in the past help to explain the gender order of the present?
6. What social factors shape our perceptions about the athletic body, the nude body, and the athletic nude body?

CHAPTER 9

Physical Education, School Sport, and Physical Fitness

———◆◆◆———

The windows in the sides of the building should be placed as high as possible; they should be about three feet high and about six feet wide; there should be as many of them on both sides as can be put in; there should be a large window or several windows in one end of the building, the other end being a dead wall. The windows should all work on pivots. The doors should be placed at the end of the building containing the window or windows. A large door for bringing in sawdust, etc., may be placed at one side. The end of the building having the dead wall should have a plank floor for about twenty feet from the wall, so that it can be used, if necessary, for the purpose of school entertainments, gymnasium choral society, hand ball, etc., and it should be entirely free from apparatus. The trapeze and flying rings should be in the central portion of the building, the point from which they are suspended being sixteen feet from the ground; the point of suspension for the row of side rings can be any height from thirteen to sixteen feet from the ground. The building must be properly heated and ventilated; if heated with stove, it and the stationary gymnastic apparatus should be properly placed at the end of the building containing the doors and windows. The flooring, except at the dead wall end of the building, should consist of sawdust or sand, about one foot and a half deep; this should be sprinkled with water every morning, about an hour before the first class commences to exercise, and again at noon if necessary. A locker should be provided, where the movable appliances can be securely kept when not used by the class.[1]
    —*Description of an ideal, late nineteenth-century high school gymnasium,*
from E.B. Houghton's Physical Culture (1886)

On 29 September 1961, a federal government bill (C-131) entitled 'An Act to Encourage Fitness and Amateur Sport' received royal assent.[2] This act symbolized a new—and renewed—commitment on the part of Canada's government to involve itself in the administration of sport and, to a lesser extent, fitness. How extensively governments have been able to be involved in sport, recreation, fitness, and leisure is a checkered history. We have seen in previous chapters how the government used legislation to control sport, as it did in Upper Canada with the 1845 Act to Prevent Profanation of the Sabbath (see Chapter 3). Royal visits, such as the one in 1860, were occasions when sport was used to showcase the colony. Federal donations to the Dominion Rifle Association and its regional associations between 1868 and 1908 totalled $1.5 million. And we have seen how the government used sport as propaganda, as it did with the 1883 lacrosse tour to the United Kingdom under the sponsorship of the federal Department of Agriculture (see Chapter 6), and the federal government over the years has involved itself in supporting and promoting and basking in the reflected glory of Olympic sports. Finally, examples are legion of politicians associating with sporting events (former Prime Minister Pierre Trudeau kicking off the Grey Cup game), or being photographed with famous athletes (Mayor King of Ottawa seemed always to be at civic receptions and tributes to Barbara Ann Scott), or just being around athletes (Ontario Premier Mitch Hepburn was a family friend of Lionel Conacher).

However, prior to the Fitness and Amateur Sport Act, there was no formulated policy or official position on the government's perceived role in, contribution to, or sponsorship of sport; indeed, the word 'sport' did not appear in the **British North America Act** when the provinces entered into a Confederation in 1867. And there is no reason to assume there should have been any mention of it since the development of public sport was in its infancy. Where governments, provincial and federal, did become involved with promoting or legislating physical activity was within the school systems of our provinces. It is instructive and important to understand how curricular physical education was streamed towards physical fitness, a kind of education *of* the body. Sport, for a long period of time, was perceived as extracurricular. Implicit in this bifurcation of physical activity modes in Canada, then, was the notion that physical fitness was more 'educational' than sport and/or that sport was not properly aligned with educational objectives. This chapter explores the process by which the physical education system was developed within schools and universities and the role those institutions played in the development of sporting opportunities for Canadian youth.

Egerton Ryerson: Teaching Teachers to Teach Physical Education

Historians cite the 1909 Strathcona Trust[3] as the first major, federal financial incentive towards physical education/fitness in Canada.[4] And some of those historians perceive the impact of the Trust to be one of the most important developments in curricular physical education.[5] During its time, the most vocal opponent of the Trust was the man generally hailed as the 'father' of physical education in Canada, Dr Arthur Stanley Lamb. At the 1933 Canadian Physical Education Association's annual meeting, Lamb spoke about the 'imbecilic notions' of the federal **Militia Department**, the government body charged with implementing the terms of the Trust, and the 'irreparable harm' done by the department's instructors by promulgating the 'automatic tin soldiers' concept of physical education in the schools.[6] Lamb, a Montreal-based medical doctor and director of physical education at McGill, based his objections to the Trust on his firm belief in the value of play, games, and sports in education.[7] Both views of the Trust, the one emphasizing its harmful nature and the other proclaiming its important contributions to Canadian physical education, have considerable merit. The apparent split between sports and games versus curricular physical education in schools is a fact. Before examining the context and full implementation of the terms of the Trust, it is important to examine events within Canadian education that led to its enactment. In doing so, we can better understand the significance, positive and negative, of this important governmental initiative, especially against the backdrop of sporting evolution in Canada.

Norman O. Brown, in his classic psychoanalytic study of history, *Life against Death*, stated that Western civilization has come through '2000 years of higher education based on the notion that [the human being] is essentially a soul for mysterious accidental reasons imprisoned in a body'.[8] Sport has only recently become a significant part of the curriculum in Canadian schools and universities. Whereas educational institutions in the United States have long regarded sports and games in physical education classes as legitimate components of the curriculum, schools in Canada have relegated sport instruction to extracurricular status. In fact, physical education as a branch of instruction in Canadian schools, considered historically, is rooted in activities such as military drill, rifle shooting, calisthenics, and gymnastics. Because the British North America Act placed education under provincial jurisdiction, and because Ontario's system of education was one of the first to become organized, the focus here will be mainly on Ontario schools and universities. Since education in Canada conformed to a religion that placed primary emphasis on the mind and the spirit, it was little concerned with development of the body, or indeed with the integration of body and spirit. Moreover, as educational systems developed first at the apex of the institutional pyramid—in universities and private colleges—public education in Ontario before the mid-nineteenth century was abysmal by any standard. The first educational Act, passed in 1807, concerned itself solely with secondary or 'grammar' schools. Nine years later elementary or 'common' schools were recognized officially, although responsibility for them was entrusted to individual communities that could erect a schoolhouse and pay for the teacher.[9]

Prior to 1850, pioneer settlement conditions, prevailing social mores that favoured the elite (sons of the elite, especially), and public apathy were major deterrents to a strong educational system in Ontario. Teaching was not regarded as a noble profession; the typical teacher was male and British-born, often an ex-soldier.[10] Rural schools were crude and curriculum quality varied widely. Few teachers or administrators in a rural-agrarian society were concerned with the nature of the physical activity of their pupils (unless they were inconvenienced by it). As one historian of Canadian education said, 'There were no playgrounds nor [*sic*] **Closets**—the Highway was occupied for the Former and the adjoining woods for the latter.'[11] Play was equated with idleness and was therefore not viewed by educators as an agent of the child's physical or moral development:

> Schools were the right arm of the churches in the moral and ethical training of
> the young. Children were regarded as basically evil and depraved creatures whose
> salvation depended on their being disciplined severely.[12]

If a 'common' school had any facility for play or games it was purely at the whim of a particular teacher or community. In 1826, opposite a schoolhouse in Bertie Township, 'fastened to the boughs of lofty beech and maple trees are placed two swings, made of the bark of the elm and basswood . . . one for the boys and one for the girls.'[13] Similarly, grammar (secondary) schools, which emphasized the classics, seldom offered pupils physical education. An exception was Upper Canada's earliest school, the 'Old Blue School' in York (Toronto). It was opened in 1807 as the Home District Grammar School, and 18 years later acquired the Reverend Dr Thomas Philips as headmaster:

> The ground surrounding the School, which in primitive times was slightly undulating, had been cleared of the stumps, and a space of a few hundred square feet was selected for the good old English sport of Cricket, which was cultivated from 1825 under the enthusiastic direction of Mr. George Anthony Barber who accompanied Dr. Phillips to York as his principal Assistant in the School.[14]

Barber is the acknowledged 'father' of cricket in Ontario, owing to his involvement with Upper Canada College in later years.[15] The provision he made for cricket at the Home District School was decidedly unusual. In most schools, marbles and peg-tops were the common amusements for pupils, and fighting was probably the only kind of vigorous physical activity in which pupils indulged. Physical education, either as systematized physical training or as sports and games, was non-existent. The only official nod to the importance of physical fitness before 1840 appeared in the *Report on Education* prepared by Dr Charles Duncombe and submitted to the **House of Assembly** in 1836:

> An education should be such as to give energy and enterprise to the mind, and activity to the whole man. This depends, in part, upon the physical constitution. Hence the necessity of preserving a sound state of bodily health. To secure this, temperance and proper exercise are requisite. But what exercise is best, as part of a student's education, is still unsettled. Without stopping to discuss that point at large here, in my opinion, the best kind of gymnastics are the exercises of the field and of the shop, in some kind of useful labour.[16]

That Duncombe should associate 'gymnastics' with manual labour, the better to enhance the productivity of society, was quite in keeping with the prevailing view that education was properly an instrument of social policy.[17] Reform needed to happen.

Into this educational wasteland came Dr Egerton Ryerson, who is generally recognized as the founder of the provincial and national systems of education. A **Methodist** itinerant or 'saddle-bag' preacher until he was 41 years old, he was appointed Ontario's first superintendent of education in 1844.[18] He remained throughout his career, and his life, a living embodiment of the Protestant work ethic. While a practising minister, he had been extremely self-disciplined and ascetic—an unlikely candidate to champion the cause of physical education, as he did many years later. Ryerson's first known exposure to a sporting event was when he attended a horse race, a sport that was least likely to appeal to him because of the atmosphere it created. All social classes were lured to the races by prospects of gambling. Tents were set up on the hills surrounding the open racetrack, where roulette wheels and other betting contrivances and quantities of drink were the main attractions. While the elite wagered money, the lower classes made their bets in goods such as salt pork, cedar shingles, pork sausage, tanned leather, blacksmiths' bellows, and so forth. Pickpockets and swindling were rampant, a general rowdyism took over, and smaller communities suffered the loss of workers for two or three days. Because of the 'demoralizing activities surrounding the events', Halifax abolished horse racing by municipal enactment for over a decade before mid-century.[19] Little wonder, then, that in his diary entry for 4 May 1824 Ryerson recorded his aversion:

> I watched today a large concourse of people assembled to witness horseracing. I stood at a distance that I might observe an illustration of human nature. Curiosity and excitement were depicted in every countenance. What is to become of this thoughtless multitude? Is there no mercy for them. Surely there is. Why *will* they not be saved? Because they *will* not come to Him.[20]

However, 35 years later, Ryerson boasted of his new-found pleasure in rowing a skiff to Toronto Island and back, in walking long distances, in riding, hunting, and swimming.[21] By the 1860s, he was converted to seeing the value of physical exercise for its own sake: 'I feel better than at any time during my tour. All who have known me and seen me in former years say how well and healthy I look. I owe this in a great degree to my boating and riding.'[22] In fairness, sport was more ingrained in the social landscape by the 1860s, and at the 1824 horse race, Ryerson may have been repelled not by the sport itself but by the gambling, drinking, and rowdiness that accompanied it.

Dr Egerton Ryerson. (Courtesy of Don Morrow)

Ryerson was impressed by the work of the great English educator, Dr Thomas Arnold, headmaster of Rugby (1828–42).[23] In the light of this interest, he probably read *Tom Brown's Schooldays* (1857), a novel about rugby by one of Arnold's pupils, Thomas Hughes, who advocated what later became known as '**muscular Christianity**'—a combination of Christian principles and physical courage, self-reliance, love of sport, and school loyalty. This book had a great impact on English public schools and helped to create the 'cult of athleticism'—an overemphasis on sport and games in schools and universities throughout the British Empire.[24] Ryerson's efforts to reform the school system in Ontario, however, focused on mass rather than elite education, and he garnered his information and ideals for education in general, and physical education it particular, from a European tour to study systems of instruction on the Continent. His *Report on a System of Public Elementary Instruction for Upper Canada*, published in 1846, was based on observations he had made in Holland, Belgium, Germany, Switzerland, and Britain in 1844–5, and in the United States, where various systems of physical education already existed. In it he included physical training among the many subjects he recommended to supplement the study of the three Rs:

> On the development of the physical powers I need but say a few words. A system of instruction making no provision for those exercises which contribute to health and vigour of body, and to agreeableness of manners, must necessarily be imperfect. The active pursuits of most of those pupils who attend the public Schools, require the exercise necessary to bodily health; but the gymnastics, regularly taught as a recreation, and with a view to the future pursuits of the pupil, and to which so much importance is attached in the best British Schools and in the Schools of Germany and France, are advantageous in various respects,—promote not only physical health and vigour, but social cheerfulness, active, easy and graceful movements. They strengthen and give the pupil a perfect command over all the members of his body. Like the art of writing, they proceed from the simplest movement, to the most complex and difficult exercises—imparting a bodily activity and skill scarcely credible to those who have not witnessed them.
>
> To the culture and command of all the faculties of the mind, a corresponding exercise and control of all the members of the body is next in importance. It was young men thus trained that composed the vanguard of **Blutcher's army**; and much of the activity, enthusiasm and energy, which distinguished them, was attributed to their gymnastic training at school. A training which gives superiority in one department of active life, must be beneficial in another . . . .
>
> The youth of Canada are designed for active, and most of them for laborious occupations; exercises which strengthen not one class of muscles, or the muscles of certain members only, but which develop the whole physical system, cannot fail to be beneficial.
>
> The application of these remarks to Common Day Schools must be very limited. They are designed to apply chiefly to boarding and training, to Industrial and Grammar Schools—to those Schools to the Masters of which the prolonged and thorough educational instruction of youth is entrusted.[25]

He advocated physical training for its health benefits, although under prevailing conditions—lack of facilities and a general lack of interest—few teachers or pupils at the time were actually affected by his plea.

Recognizing that the key ingredient in quality education was teacher training and the establishment of a profession, Ryerson brought to fruition in 1853 the construction of the first teacher training institution in the province: the Toronto Normal and Model School. Significantly, the original buildings included two 'Play Sheds', similar in appearance to two roofed railway platforms set back to back, and two acres of 'Grounds for Gymnastic Exercises of Students and Pupils'.[26] Ryerson also appointed Mr Henry Goodwin as 'gymnastic master' of the Normal and Model School, at a salary of £50 per annum.[27] Goodwin was an Irish-born soldier who had fought at the Battle of Waterloo. When he received his discharge in 1818 he enlisted in the King's Light Infantry and was made head drill instructor. Recognized and honoured in five European countries for his proficiency in gymnastics and fencing, he emigrated to Canada at the age of 55 and opened a school to teach calisthenics and riding. Two years later, Lord Elgin recommended Goodwin

Toronto Normal Play Sheds, c. 1855. (Courtesy of Don Morrow)

to Ryerson. Canada's first instructor of physical education was 57 when he was hired; surprisingly, at age 77 Goodwin was still the gymnastics master at the Normal School, and at Upper Canada College, Bishop Strachan's Ladies School, and Mrs Nixon's Ladies School as well. He also tutored privately! (Goodwin's widespread employment may have resulted from necessity—he fathered 16 children by two wives.)[28] Goodwin was respected for his skills, if judged by the number of Toronto families who hired him for private instruction.

Ryerson made provision for teachers to receive instruction in physical training—likely in military drill, light apparatus gymnastics (vaulting benches, parallel bars), calisthenics, and fencing. Ryerson's reports in the 1850s and 1860s included references to the Normal School timetable, which incorporated drill for men and calisthenics for women for at least two hours per week.[29] But Goodwin's impact on physical education in Ontario seems to have been slight; as late as 1877, only 17 per cent of the province's teachers had any professional teacher training whatsoever.[30]

The only two authorized texts for physical training within Ryerson's Department of Education were Charles Spencer's *Field Exercises and Evolutions of Infantry Drill* and *The Modern Gymnast*.[31] Both were published in Britain and both were geared to adult readership and use—with no provisions for the instruction of children. The training of teachers in military drill suggests that physical training in the schools during Ryerson's tenure (1844–76) was mainly valued as a means of instilling discipline in pupils.

Through his monthly *Journal of Education for Upper Canada* (first issued in 1848), an official publication, Ryerson did his utmost to have apparatus gymnastics inaugurated in Ontario schools. There is considerable doubt that his *Journal*—intended as a disseminator of information to all levels, from education administrators to the teachers—was even picked up by school trustees, let alone passed on from them to teachers. Nevertheless, it reflects Ryerson's early enthusiasm for physical training and a sincere desire to promote the subject in his quest for ways to improve practical education. Between January and September 1852, Ryerson published in the *Journal* a series of articles entitled 'Physical Training in Schools'.[32] Intriguing as the engravings of gymnasts performing elaborate exercises on novel pieces of apparatus may have been to readers, they provided little benefit to teacher or pupil. Still, Ryerson made an important start in educating the new teaching profession about physical exercise.

A few articles during the 1850s continued to advocate apparatus gymnastics for males and light calisthenics for female students. In the latter regard, an article in 1857 strongly advocated the use of a 'backboard', literally a board strapped to the back, as a postural exercise device for girls.[33] During the 1860s, the articles became decidedly militaristic in nature,[34] possibly owing to the influence and proximity of the **Civil War** to the south. The actual introduction of drill into schools led to considerable controversy, especially over its inclusion in elementary schools; as a result Ryerson devoted 10 pages in 1866 to various articles that stressed the necessity and importance of military drill in the schools.[35] His efforts to vindicate drill were predictable, since he was a social conservative. By the end of his term he was advocating this favoured form of physical training for public schools:

> The Boys to be arranged in companies, sized from both flanks, numbered and told off in half-companies and sections. To be put through the formations, Right, Left and Right and Left About as a Company. To increase and diminish the Front. To form a company Square, Fours, Right, Left, Deep. Calisthenics for Girls.[36]

Military drill was convenient; instructors—often discharged military personnel—were abundant; equipment was inexpensive and minimal; it could be conducted outside; and it fostered, or exemplified, prompt obedience by 'miniature adults', who were of course males. Military drill, which Ryerson called military gymnastics, was taught throughout the 1860s in many elementary and secondary schools, especially in cities and the larger towns of Ontario. It reinforced the pedagogical emphasis on educating boys, with a resulting neglect of curriculum development for girls. The subject was optional in the elementary schools and was at the discretion of the trustees. In 1876, Toronto became the first city to introduce a regular system of military training into public schools.[37] In the rest of the province, the fledgling educational system and its slow rate of development prevented many of Ryerson's ideas on physical training from being realized until late in the century.

Despite Ryerson's efforts, actual physical training programs in the schools during his tenure were minimal. Although playground development around schoolhouses increased, play and games were relegated to recess. But even then: 'When admonition, remonstrance and reproof fail in securing proper attention, the offender is required to stand on the floor during a part or the whole of the playtime.'[38] Before 1876, the only evidence of curricular physical training at the secondary school level was at the Galt Grammar School and the Hamilton Central School.[39] As for facilities, public opinion would not permit school boards to spend taxpayers' money on 'frills' such as gymnasiums or playgrounds.

The Extracurricular and the Curricular

Any sports that occurred in the schools up to the 1870s were organized under the teachers' own initiatives—as in the case of George Barber's promotion of cricket at the Old Blue School. By the late 1860s, sporadic contests in track and field, cricket,[40] lacrosse, and rugby football took place at some secondary and private schools, but always as extracurricular activities outside regular classroom instruction. Prior to Confederation, the private schools—in keeping with the precedents and traditions of the vaunted British public schools—were at the forefront of any sporting developments in educational institutions. Between 1868 and 1900, schools and universities 'were often the nurseries in which new games were practised and then spread into the community'.[41] In 1887, when the first Canadian cricket 'eleven' visited England, five of the team members were Upper Canada College 'old boys'. Contemporary newspaper accounts reveal a pattern of carrying sport into society at large via former student athletes who continued to play rugby football and association football (soccer) in the 1870s and 1880s, and ice hockey in the 1890s. Sport dispersion occurred to a certain extent within Ontario's secondary schools, with soccer becoming the most widespread secondary-school sport before 1900.

Emerging sports, such as baseball and lacrosse, and even cricket, were not prominent among institutes of higher education—perhaps owing to their being played mainly in the summer when universities were not in session and schools were closed. By contrast, universities nurtured track and field and the Canadian Amateur Athletic Association, as well as by the numerous Scottish Caledonian societies, strongly promoted it[42] (see Chapters 4 and 5). Thus, universities and private schools were significant contributors to the emergence of organized competitive sport in the late nineteenth century. However, their contribution was elitist—in the sense that a university education was a privilege available to a very small minority—and it was unsystematic, because sport activities were energized in a haphazard fashion by interested people outside the formal framework of education.

Sports and games were never included in the nineteenth-century physical education curriculum, in spite of the emergence of two general trends in educational philosophy: a new recognition of the importance of childhood and of child-centred activities, and the recommended inclusion of practical subjects into the school curriculum, such as bookkeeping, drawing, music, health, temperance—and physical education.[43] Still, before 1908 the only exercise facility that any elementary school could boast of was the great outdoors. The use of gymnasiums began at the secondary level. In order to become a collegiate institute in 1882, any one of Ontario's 104 high schools was required to have 'suitable buildings, outbuildings, grounds and appliances for physical training'.[44] Thereafter, Department of Education 'circulars' were distributed widely and frequently to induce and to police curricular change in physical training. Although they are more indicative of intent than actual practice, such circulars provide clues to prevailing ideals about physical training. For example, an 1885 circular recommended the following equipment for a high school gymnasium (with the usual dismissal of the needs of girls):

Dumb Bells	Fixed Parallel Bars
Bar Bells	Trapezium
Leaping Rope	Pair of Rings
Leaping Pole	Row of Rings

Horizontal Beam	Elastic Ladder
Vaulting Bar L	adder Plank
Vaulting Horse	Inclined Ladder
Vertical Rope	Rosary or Knotted Rope
Vertical Pole	Mast

For girls a suitable supply of **Indian Clubs** should be provided.[45]

Drafted directly from the British book, *The Modern Gymnast*, the list was premature: it was a long time before schools wanted, could afford to buy, or in some cases could accommodate such elaborate equipment.

More significant incentives to curricular physical training in secondary schools occurred in 1886 and 1887, when regulations for upgrading existing facilities and equipment were tied to increased government grants. Though drill, gymnastics, and calisthenics were made 'obligatory' subjects the teaching of physical training continued to have a subsidiary role in the curriculum:

> Now that the Collegiate Institutes have gymnasia, and Regulation 50 is explicit as to the requirements, there will probably be an improvement; but so long as the July examinations are so vitally important to both teacher and pupil, physical education will, in many cases, be subordinated to even the least important of the examination subjects.[46]

In fact, where gymnasiums were constructed—in Guelph, Hamilton, Lindsay, and elsewhere—they were more often used as auditoriums, assembly halls, or even as extra classroom space.[47] When they *were* used for physical education classes—it never occurred to anyone to permit games to be played in them—the prevailing viewpoint was a holdover from Ryerson's era. Sports and games in public education were 'rational amusements', best left to informal organization by students themselves, and drill, gymnastics, and calisthenics were tolerated as adjuncts to more academic pursuits. Furthermore, teachers could not teach what they did not know: without lesson plans, nineteenth-century teachers could not instruct in any subject, let alone a new one.

James L. Hughes and E.B. Houghton

The first important and useful guide for physical instruction was a small book published in 1879 by the foremost educator of the period, James L. Hughes: *Manual of Drill and Calisthenics: Containing Squad Drill, Calisthenics, Free Gymnastics, Vocal Exercise, German Calisthenics, Movement Songs, The Pocket Gymnasium, and Kindergarten Games and Songs.*[48] Hughes (1846–1935) was appointed inspector of public schools in Toronto in 1874. He was 'an **Orangeman**, a **Mason**, an athlete, and unquestionably an administrative success'.[49] An ardent patriot, he focused mainly on military drill in his manual—which caused it to be reviewed harshly in an 1880 issue of the *Canadian Education Monthly*. Nevertheless, the drill content was in keeping with the precedent Ryerson had set and it conformed to the equipment, facilities, and teacher competence of the era. If any educator had enough sporting background and expertise to develop sports and games in the curriculum, it was

Hughes. Yet his training for 'proper' education was steeped in discipline and obedience. Furthermore, his three brothers were all high-ranking military officers,[50] a fact that must have reinforced his tendency to stress military drill in the schools. Ratified by the Ontario Teachers Association, Hughes's manual advocated teaching proper form in saluting, marking time and marching, squad formations, and so forth. Though there was some public opposition to treating children in elementary schools as 'little soldiers', drill was entrenched as the proper 'system' of physical instruction in secondary schools and even at the University of Toronto. Hughes's manual, which excluded any concept of curricular instruction in sports and games, simply consolidated its presence.

In 1886, E.B. Houghton, a retired physical training instructor from Chatham, wrote a book that advocated important changes in physical education. Authorized by the Minister of Education and available to teachers for 50 cents, *Physical Culture*[51] became the recommended textbook on physical training in the Toronto and Ottawa Normal schools.[52] It was useful, popular, and a harbinger of landmark transitions in the concept of physical training for students. First and foremost, it was suited to actual school conditions and teacher preparation. Drill was included (but only occupied 20 per cent of the book) to uphold prevailing practice: 'That the drill may assimilate with that in use by the volunteers and regulars, so that if at any future time the pupil should join the volunteers or Military School, he will have nothing to learn or unlearn as far as Squad Drill is concerned.'[53]

The second section of Houghton's book, 'Calisthenics', which advocated the use of straight lines and squads after the military fashion—every schoolchild from then until now has been subjected to squads, straight lines, and precision in physical education classes—was organized from simple to complex exercises. Free exercises, the use of climbing and skipping ropes, and stretching and flexibility exercises were all illustrated with sketches of the movements for teachers, and the section on gymnastics described different exercise series for dumbbells and stationary ropes—far more practical than the apparatus gymnastics advocated earlier by Ryerson and others.

As Ontario education in general was male-oriented—the government grant for educating girls in high school was exactly half that for boys—the most progressive aspect of Houghton's book was that nearly half of it was devoted to physical training for girls. *Physical Culture* offered girls basic exercises containing elementary movements that resembled dance or postural positions; dumbbell exercises, which were almost the same as those for men; and 50 pages devoted to Indian-club exercises. The origin of the name 'Indian club' is obscure, but it resembled a wooden bowling pin and weighed one to one-and-a-half pounds. (The largest mass producer of Indian clubs was the American sporting goods manufacturer A.G. Spalding.) Houghton was full of admiration for them as exercise tools for women:

> The illimitable number of combinations that may be effected in Artistic Indian Club swinging, the exceeding grace and beauty of the movements, the poetry and rhythm of motion, especially when accompanied by music, the operation of the mental faculties in conjunction with the physical, the splendid exercise which it gives to the body, especially the upper portion, the fact of both sides being equally employed, the great ease and freedom of carriage acquired through its practice, mark it as being pre-eminently adapted as an exercise for ladies.[54]

 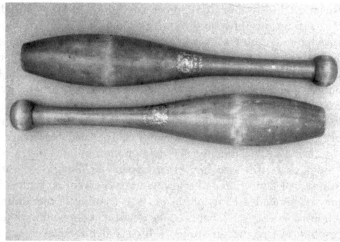

Left: Female Indian Club Exercise, from Physical Culture, 1888 edition. *Right*: Indian Clubs made by Spalding. (Courtesy of Don Morrow)

Indian-club movements were made in patterns—circles and 'ellipses' of various combinations—and mainly involved the arms, with some trunk-twisting. Still, girls were finally involved in physical training, and Houghton's text was a reservoir of practical information for teachers (including the ideal gymnasium configurations described in the opening quotation for this chapter).

Concurrent with the publication of Houghton's work were major curricular changes directed at education in health ('hygiene') and at the kindergarten movement. Increasing social sensitivity to sanitary living conditions resulted in the creation in 1882 of the Provincial Board of Health and the subsequent release into the schools of a spate of books on health, physiology, temperance, and hygiene. These books, such as *Public School Physiology and Temperance* (1893), dealt with the treatment and prevention of illnesses, the dangers of alcohol abuse, and bodily functions. They went through multiple editions, evidence that they were widely distributed and used in the schools. Some of the books even contained small chapters proclaiming, briefly, the benefits of physical exercise. By 1893, hygiene was a compulsory subject on the high school entrance examination,[55] and throughout the 1890s, the Ontario Education Association's annual meetings were flooded with speeches on the topic of health practices.[56]

Both health teaching and kindergartens in the 1880s created a favourable environment for the development of physical training courses. Kindergartens, and the international kindergarten movement, were predicated on the concept of the importance of play to childhood learning. Previously, play had been considered antithetical to 'real' intellectual education; but kindergartens literally brought it inside the school walls from the playground outside. James L. Hughes was most responsible for implementing the kindergarten movement in Ontario.[57] Opposition, based on objections to expensive fads in education, was strong and rural schools in particular had difficulty in developing kindergartens; but by 1900 there were well over 100 kindergarten classes in the province. It was the kindergarten movement of the 1880s and 1890s that laid the foundation for the acceptance of child-centred physical activity—play. And yet, the concept was not extended so that play could be valued and taught at all levels of the school system. Drill and calisthenics were ingrained in teachers at normal schools and they were highly resistant to change.

Both Hughes's and Houghton's books had a direct impact on schools through extensive use. *The Annual Reports of the Minister of Education for Ontario* actually listed the numbers of elementary pupils taking each subject. If the number taking physical training is expressed as a percentage of those taking the most common school subject—spelling—the early 1870s statistics revealed that only 3.5 per cent received any physical training. By 1880, there was a fivefold increase to 18 per cent. Ten years later, immediately following the publication of *Physical Culture*, almost half of all Ontario elementary pupils received some instruction in curricular physical education and the trend gradually increased to 70 per cent by 1905. These figures reveal nothing about the nature or quality of instruction. Since Houghton's manual was the one used in all normal schools, it seems reasonable to assume that it was not only responsible for the increase

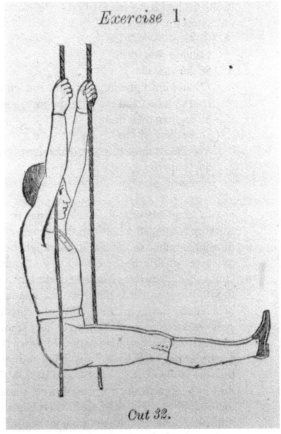

Male rope exercises, *Physical Culture*, 1888 edition. (Courtesy of Don Morrow)

in curricular instruction but provided the basis for teaching. At the same time there can be no doubt that drill prevailed as the main thrust of physical education for boys. Compulsory physical training was on the horizon, but at the close of the century the Dominion Education Association revealed the prevailing attitude to curricular sports and games, calling them a 'sporadic exercise' that:

> cannot be called training in a proper sense—to which young men in college subject themselves in the form of boating, baseball, football, lacrosse etc., with the belief that they are doing great things for themselves, yet instead often planting in their bodies the seeds of irremediable troubles . . . .[58]

Such activities were considered much inferior to calisthenics, 'the exercise that in kind and quantity is directed by the most enlightened science'. Objectives for physical training in the schools were shifting from an emphasis on discipline and obedience to more health-related concerns for bodily development. Even in primary grades, growing health awareness was evident:

> Children who drill
> Seldom are ill
> For sinking, tiptoeing, and right and left going,
> And shouting and clapping and measured out tapping,
> Strengthen their limbs,
> Drive away whims,
> Make faces shine brightly, make spines grow uprightly;
> So, I suppose,
> Illness all goes.[59]

In secondary schools, drill remained the basis of all physical training, thanks to a close working relationship between the Department of Education and the federal Department of Militia. Public opinion and the enlightenment of some educators softened the military overtones of drill in the elementary schools, but in secondary schools military drill for young men seemed to be accepted without question. Moreover, small monetary grants ($50 to $100) were available after 1890 to secondary schools that employed a drill instructor and held regular classes in drill.[60] This inducement was apparently effective; the mid-1890s were peak years for the numbers of secondary school students taking drill and calisthenics.[61] But a letter written by the young Arthur Meighen (Conservative Prime Minister of Canada twice, briefly, in the 1920s), who was living and attending school in St Mary's in 1892, suggests that the students were opposed to drill. Meighen and his fellow students, who believed drill to be 'practically a waste of time', pleaded with the Minister of Education to write them a note excusing them from 'this obligation so unnecessary and so embarrassing'.[62] The minister declined to give permission. Beginning in 1898, grants had entrenched cadet corps in Canadian high schools.

By 1907, the Education Department in Ontario had passed five 'regulations' concerning obligatory physical training in high schools and collegiate institutes developed around Houghton's drill and calisthenics exercises. The fourth regulation provided a glimmer of hope for the future of physical education classes and sport development within the schools: 'During the months of May, June, September, October, and November, the Principal may substitute for drill etc. such sports and games as he may approve.'[63] Although it was some years before this regulation was sanctioned and practised, it suggests that the Education Department could no longer ignore the interests of students and the popularity of sport in society at large.

Team Sports and the Universities

Early in the twentieth century, sport was promoted outside educational institutions by various regional, provincial, and national sport governing bodies. Team sports—such as lacrosse, football, baseball, and ice hockey—were especially popular; and the modern Olympic revival began in 1896 in Athens (see Chapter 11). It was well established that sport was energized, administered, and controlled by its own devotees—no level of government and no educational or entrepreneurial agency assumed any responsibility for its development. School or university officials who wished to become involved in sport at any level did so under their own volition. Sport remained at the periphery rather than at the core of educational environments.

Even though sport in the university remained outside the curriculum, it developed much more rapidly there than at the pre-university level. This was undoubtedly because it was entirely in the hands of students who formed teams, challenged other university teams, created team (university) spirit, and inaugurated leagues in the 1890s. Leadership in sport development was provided by McGill University, the University of Toronto, and Queen's University. Canadian football's enduring tradition as the major sport in most contemporary Canadian universities grew out of early matches among these three institutions. Moreover, a series of games in 1874 between McGill and Harvard is thought to be the source both of Canadian-style football and of the American hybrid.[64] Canadian intercollegiate football was inaugurated in 1881 with the first annual McGill–Toronto game; Queen's established its football foundation in matches against the Royal Military College during the 1880s, and in the 1890s ventured into intercollegiate competitions with Toronto and McGill.[65] Ontario university teams dominated both provincial and national football competitions during the last decade of the nineteenth century.

Although there is considerable debate about where the first game of ice hockey originated, it is reasonably well established that three McGill students devised the first modern rules for the game in the late 1870s.[66] By merging and adapting the rules from field hockey, lacrosse, and rugby football, these students were able to bring uniformity to the game and establish it firmly within the structures of late nineteenth-century Canadian sport. Montreal teams dominated the Stanley Cup during the 1890s and Queen's University teams were frequent challengers for the prestigious trophy throughout the decade; University of Toronto teams were competitive in provincial leagues.[67]

Universities assumed the dominant role in competitive sport development, especially in football, ice hockey, and track and field. In 1906, the Canadian Intercollegiate Athletic Union was formed as an umbrella governing body for affiliated universities and colleges.[68] Whereas students had originally been responsible for the organization of university sport, the creation of the CIAU signalled a bureaucratic structure that increasingly wrestled control of university sport from informal student organizations and transferred it to university officials and administrators. Although for many years the management of university athletics was monopolized by the University of Toronto, Queen's, and McGill,[69] and the contribution of universities to general sporting development is beyond question, the issue arising from the creation of the CIAU was the function of sport within an educational framework.

There seemed to be a 'natural adherence to the English tradition of games and sports'[70] that served to keep sport in rational perspective. But after 1910, commercial trends affected the function of sport, or some sports, at Canadian universities, particularly the increasingly popular sport of Canadian football, which was 'the university game' of this period. Between 1909 and 1924, universities in central Canada dominated major football competitions, including those for the Grey Cup.[71] Football players were 'shoe-horned' into post-secondary institutions; American players were recruited; athletes were subsidized;[72] professional coaches, such as Frank Shaughnessy at McGill, were hired. Spectators flocked to the university game while 'the music of swiftly turning turnstiles [could] be heard quite clearly on the autumn air.'[73] Alma mater became enveloped in pigskin[74] until municipal and commercial interests wrenched football away from university dominance, leaving post-secondary institutions after 1925 with a rich legacy of football traditions and the prospect of playing the game at a lower level among themselves.

The third leading sport at Canadian universities prior to 1920—track and field—was popularized throughout the school system, from grade schools to tertiary levels of education, in 'field days', 'sports days', and 'annual games'. Intra-school competitions led to interscholastic competition and, in turn, to continued participation at the intercollegiate level. The spread of track and field across all levels of ability and education ought to have triggered comparable models in a variety of sports,[75] but this did not happen. There was always a hierarchy of sporting importance, intercollegiate sport being at the apex of a weakly developed system of school sports. Even in established universities, intramural sports of every conceivable variety were implemented by the 1920s, but their budgets were only a fraction of those devoted to the 'major' intercollegiate sports of football and hockey. Universities seemed more interested in raising the level of their intercollegiate competition from 'intermediate' designation to 'senior' than in developing curricular and extracurricular sports' opportunities for all students at all ability levels.[76] Significantly, the Women's Intercollegiate Athletic Union (WIAU) was formed in 1923, thereby recognizing, sanctioning, and promoting women's competitive sport in post secondary institutions, albeit mostly in Ontario and Quebec universities.

The organization of Canadian university sport remained relatively stable until just after the Second World War. In the mid 1950s, the CIAU collapsed over jurisdictional issues among member organizations. Regional organizations governed intercollegiate sport in Ontario, Quebec, the Maritimes, and the western provinces until the modern CIAU was revised in 1961. Critical to the CIAU's reinvigoration was the influx of significant funding from the federal government; this money was of great support in financing technical assistance/leadership, travel costs throughout the provinces, and the development of sport policies consistent with high performance sport initiatives across the country. The formation of the Canadian Women's Intercollegiate Athletic Union (CWIAU) in 1969 was a hallmark in the independent organization of women's intercollegiate sports. Gender issues such as equitable funding, student support, and facility allocation have been constant issues within universities during the twentieth century, ameliorated initially with complementary policies to the American-based Title IX. The latter legislation was enacted in 1972 as a strong measure of law to prohibit discrimination under any education program or activity receiving federal financial assistance.[77] After mergers between the CIAU and the CWIAU in the late 1970s, and significant funding changes within university systems, the CIAU voted in 2001 to change its name to Canadian Interuniversity Sport (CIS).[78] In contemporary Canada, universities play a major role in promoting sport and recreation for student fitness and in the development of high-level competitions and skilled athletes in a wide variety of sports.

Drill and the Strathcona Trust

In elementary and secondary schools, sports remained decidedly extracurricular until well into the 1930s. Strong competitive leagues existed in sports such as lacrosse, baseball, football, and track and field, and the Toronto Public Schools Amateur Athletic Association was the dominant model of interscholastic organization. With the installation of wooden-floor gymnasiums in secondary schools and universities—mostly during the 1920s—competitive sport participation in basketball, volleyball, boxing, fencing, wrestling, and apparatus gymnastics was promoted.[79] But the persistent dominance of physical education by militaristic interests continued to retard the progressive development of sport within the educational framework. Public displays of drill work and the strutting of prestige and patriotism by cadet corps were common early in this century. The principal of Prescott High School stated in 1907:

> When cadet corps boys at target practice score bull's-eyes at 200 yards with a Lee Enfield rifle that kicks like a broncho, they've got guts. When the same boys, marching past a red-tabbed Inspecting Officer from Ottawa, give him such a snappy eyes-right that he says they are the smartest corps in the country, they've got esprit de corps. When the corps took part in such celebrations [May 24th festivities] they marched from the old High School, down Main Street, past bevies of fair damsels who waved frilly handkerchiefs, to the green expanse of the Fort Field, where a big Union Jack floated proudly under the blue Canadian sky.[80]

Mass pageants of marching, ceremonial drill, and physical exercises—conducted with and without rifles—were held frequently and publicly on the grounds of Toronto's Canadian National Exhibition.[81] The time was ripe for advancing military instruction in the schools and the Department of Militia was quick to take advantage. The success of Sir Frederick Borden, the federal Minister of Militia, in persuading **Lord Strathcona** to provide funds to equip a 500-man contingent for the Boer War (the Strathcona Horse) led Borden to approach Strathcona for money again in 1909. He agreed to donate half a million dollars to 'encourage physical *and* military training in the schools'. Prime Minister Sir Wilfrid Laurier made a stirring acceptance speech before members of the House of Commons, lauding Strathcona's generosity.[82] The following day, 25 March 1909, the *Toronto Globe*, 'Canada's national newspaper', reacted with front-page headlines and feature articles, such as the one headed:

> Physical and Military Training in the Schools
> Ten Thousand Dollars Yearly
> Offer Stirs the House to a Burst of Patriotism

The basic concept of the scheme, later known as the Strathcona Trust, was to invest the principal sum at four per cent, to yield $20,000 annually for use by elementary and secondary schools across the Dominion. Reaction was mixed. Some school boards embraced the concept, but opposition was mounted by the executive of the Trades and Labour Congress, the Peace and Arbitration Society, a committee of the Toronto Methodist Conference, and the trustees of the Ontario Education Association.[83] A member of the last group proclaimed:

> I see designing enthusiasts aiming at a huge organization which will furnish a fresh crop of emoluments and tinsel honours at the expense of the great mass of the people, creating in time a small army of inspectors, drillmasters and officials of all kinds, added to our already costly and overgrown military establishment.[84]

The vision was prophetic.

Sir Donald Smith, Lord Strathcona, 1908. (Wm. Notman and Son, Library and Archives Canada, C-017767)

The Strathcona Trust was actually two-pronged: it was meant to encourage both military *and* physical training, not merely to propagate cadet corps at all educational levels; and it was intended by both Strathcona and its architect, Borden, to be only a 'stimulus or inspiration'[85] to school boards to foster the growth of curricular physical education. In spite of initial opposition, by 1911 the Trust was fully in place in all provinces except Quebec, which never did enter agreement. As might be expected, it was administered with precision and efficiency and dominated by the Department of Militia on local, provincial, and national committees. Since the funds were available by province, on a per capita school-aged-child basis, some schools obtained only a few dollars in any given year. But instructors—drill sergeants—were donated to school boards and creative plans were implemented to pool resources so that drill and exercise competitions could be held among schools and school boards. Uniform *syllabuses*, first published in 1911, then updated in 1919 and 1933, were used to train teachers in the Strathcona system at all teachers' colleges. The First World War likely reinforced the perceived need for drill-based programs in the schools.[86]

The Strathcona Trust may have suited the educational climate in Ontario, where mere lip service was being paid to the importance of physical education, but it represented a giant step backward for child-centred education and for the incorporation of sports and games into the curriculum. Instead of trying to educate the whole child, body and mind, the schools were set on disciplining the body and the will into military obedience. The legacy of the Trust and the Strathcona system lingers still, both in the tedium of squads and the exaggerated emphasis on discipline in many physical education classes, and in the designation of school sports as extracurricular activities that are less important than intellectual pursuits. There were some vocal opponents to the system—even well-respected educators such as Ethel Mary Cartwright at McGill (and later the University of Saskatchewan)—but they were easily overcome by the large machinery of the Strathcona system in the 1920s and 1930s.[87] It was not until the 1940s—when the first degree programs for training in physical education were established at the University of Toronto, McGill, and the Universities of Western Ontario and British Columbia—that sports and games received legitimate curricular attention.[88] Although interscholastic and intercollegiate competition in every conceivable sport was fully established for both boys and girls during the twenties and thirties,[89] it was reserved strictly for skilled athletes.

Between 1850 and 1930, physical education and sports and games developed quite separately within Ontario's (and Canada's) schools and universities. Physical education was regimented—it had a distinctly disciplinary component—and was only loosely accepted as part of the curriculum. Sports and games were extracurricular activities, open to interested and elite students or gifted athletes. By 1933, the third, revised *Strathcona Syllabus* included a wide variety of provisions for games and sports; however, it was still a matter of the training and/or inclination of individual teachers or boards of education as to whether games and sports became curricular. The Strathcona Trust was *the* major provision for curricular physical education from 1910 until about the period coinciding with the end of the Second World War and the first university physical education degree graduates. By and large, funds from the Trust were funnelled towards the cadet movement in Canada,[90] although the Ontario committee of the Strathcona Trust published a significant teaching manual, *Physical Education in Rural Schools*,[91] for distribution to rural schools beginning in 1954. As indirect as the federal government's role was in the administration of the Trust—in essence, local provincial committees managed the Trust in co-operation with the various departments of education—it was a significant and important precedent for federal government involvement in fitness/physical education and, to a limited extent, sport.

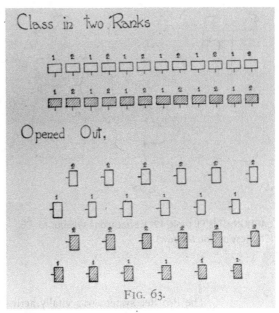

PE Class 'squad' formation, 1911. Strathcona syllabus for PE. (Courtesy of Don Morrow)

Pro-Rec in BC and Federal Involvement in Physical Fitness

The same provincially-based leadership was brought to recreation and sport on the west coast of Canada with the inauguration of British Columbia's Pro-Rec (Provincial Recreation) program in 1934.[92] Typically, Pro-Rec involved calisthenics, team sports, track and field events, dancing, and physical fitness activities. Pro-Rec also sponsored swimming galas and organized mass gymnastic displays. The Recreation and Physical Education Branch of the Department of Education—Dr G.M. Weir, Minister of Education, is credited with founding Pro-Rec—provided instructors for the various Pro-Rec activities, along with basic gymnastics apparatus and athletic equipment. In turn, local communities were expected to provide a facility that could serve as a recreation centre. The first Branch director was Ian Eisenhardt (1906–2004), formerly Supervisor of Playgrounds for the Vancouver Parks Board; Eisenhardt successfully administered the program until 1941. The first public recreation system of its kind in the British Empire, the program had as its original intent to provide healthy recreational activities and to combat the 'demoralizing influence of enforced idleness'

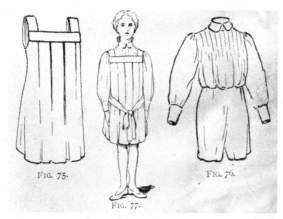

FIG. 75.   FIG. 76.

FIG. 77.

CAPTION: Girls' PE tunic, 1911. Strathcona syllabus for PE. (Courtesy of Don Morrow)

among unemployed youths. Very quickly, the program became available to anyone over the age of 15, whether in school or not. By 1939, the Pro-Rec program boasted 174 recreational activity centres throughout the province and an annual budget of $43,000. In addition to conducting community-based athletic programs, the Recreation and Physical Education Branch published a monthly magazine (*The Gymnast*) and produced a series of radio broadcasts entitled *Gym of the Air*. Pro-Rec officials were active in promoting the youth hostel movement and, during the Second World War, in organizing patriotic activities and displays. As well, Pro-Rec was associated with several programs designed to combat juvenile delinquency.

The Pro-Rec system was vitally active until the early 1950s. Its programs were very popular—some displays drew 10,000 spectators—and it seemed to attract federal attention. For example, some of the costs associated with the Pro-Rec movement in British Columbia were met by the federal government. The federal Unemployment and Agricultural Assistance Act (1937) established a Dominion-Provincial Youth Training Program to fund projects for physical training and health education for unemployed young people. Ottawa subsequently contributed to BC's Pro-Rec program through the Youth Training Act (1939), the Vocational Training Co-ordination Act (1941), and the National Physical Fitness Act (1943).[93] The implementation of the latter Act more significantly represented direct federal government involvement in and promotion of physical activities and fitness for Canadians.

As early as 1937, the League of Nations recommended that member countries establish national fitness programs. The Canadian House of Commons recognized this suggestion but with a clear perspective that sport was the prerogative of 'amateur' sports groups or associations and that sport might properly be the domain of provincial governments. What seemed to spur the Canadian government was the news, real or contrived, that a plurality of Canadian men who tried to enlist for the war were rejected based on low fitness levels.[94] On 24 July 1943 the National Physical Fitness Act (NFPA) was assented in Parliament and its first director, not surprisingly, was Major Ian Eisenhardt. The Act provided for a National Council on Physical Fitness consisting of representatives from each participating province; their charge was to promote the physical fitness of the people of Canada. Its aims were broad, such as to 'assist in the extension of physical education' in the schools and to 'encourage and correlate all activities relating to the physical development of the people through sports, athletics and other similar pursuits.'[95] A total amount of $225,000 was made available to carry out these objectives and it was to be distributed on a matching dollar basis to the provinces in proportion to provincial populations.[96]

The broad scope of the NFPA led to the program being put under the Welfare branch of the Department of National Health and Welfare—an interesting decision considering fitness is treated as more of a health than welfare domain today. What quickly became apparent

Upward Jump in Threes

Note the grasp; the jumper must stiffen her arms so that the supporters may assist her spring. A useful way of taking the exercise is for the jumper to take two or three small skip jumps followed by a deep knee bending before springing into the air. Two or three consecutive high springs can then be taken.

FIG. 58.

Sideways Jump

The Jumper springs over the ropes from side to side with rebound, on the spot or moving forward.

FIG. 60.

Upward Jump with leg parting

This may be taken on the spot following two or three preliminary skip jumps or following a short run and a double take-off.

FIG. 59.

Running High Jump over an obstacle   FIG. 61.

This exercise requires skilful co-operation on the part of the supporters and should not be attempted unless careful preliminary training has been given in jumping and supporting. Care must be taken not to hinder the jumper.

Play-form exercises from 1933 Strathcona manual. (Courtesy of Don Morrow)

to the National Council was that the program's aims were lofty—at one point, one of the stated objectives was to ensure that every Canadian child received one month of canoeing each year—and the funding was woefully inadequate. For example, while Ontario could get as much as $75,000 annually from the government, Prince Edward Island was eligible for only $1,800.[97] Moreover, it was never made explicit whether the National Council was to act in an advisory capacity or if it might have any executive authority. That dilemma continued to affect the administration of the Act until 1951 when the Council won its executive power—too little too late. Three years later, the NFPA was repealed without one dissenting vote in the House of Commons. It may be that the Act was conceived during wartime and that fitness retained its Strathcona-like associations with militarism or military preparedness. Never precise enough in its statement of purpose, the Act did not provide an opportunity to implement sound programs.[98] There were, however, some notable achievements and legacies from the NFPA. In some respects, the NFPA was a kind of testing ground or bridge from former ways of administering fitness and sport on a virtual ad hoc basis to a systematized approach to managing sport and fitness on a more public level. One of the distinct outcomes of the NFPA had been the promotion and implementation of physical education degree programs via the National Council; the long-term effects of training professionals in fitness, exercise, and sport would pay dividends in the future. In addition, the Council had arranged meetings with several sport governing bodies, thereby setting the precedent for what would become a sports advisory council in 1959. The purpose of this advisory council was to give organized sport a forum to discuss issues and problems and to present a unified voice for sport in Canada. This part of the bridgework of the NFPA led directly to the passage of the Fitness and Amateur Sport Act in 1961.

Whereas the Strathcona Trust, the Pro-Rec, and the NFPA had been important precedents for government involvement in sport, in reality, they all dabbled—almost gingerly—in fitness and sport. By the 1950s, the world of sport and sport in the world had assumed greater cultural significance. For example, with respect to the Olympic Games, the Cold War had profound effects on the character, intensity, and political importance of that international festival (see Chapter 11). As one researcher noted, 'the sport of the international arena was becoming a theatre for the achievement of national prestige through success in sport.'[99] Whereas Canada had been so 'successful' in Olympic competition prior to the Second World War, by 1960, in 'unofficial' rankings by country, Canada finished twenty-sixth out of 53 countries competing at the Summer Games and eighth out of 16 at the Winter Games. And more particularly discouraging to Canada's perceived superiority in hockey, the USSR won the gold medal in 1956 and the United States was victorious in 1960.[100] To some members of Parliament, the hockey situation was a 'national embarrassment'.[101] Perhaps the most publicized reaction to the Canadian 'situation' was a speech delivered to the Canadian Medical Association by the **Duke of Edinburgh** in 1959. In it, the Duke took Canadians to task for their apparent complacency regarding physical fitness and said it was essential that some scheme be established to

The Fitness Issue and the Creation of ParticipACTION

With respect to fitness and educating Canadians about fitness (and to some extent, sport), one important spin-off development from the Act occurred near the end of the 1960S. In 1968, the same year that the Task Force was appointed, Prime Minister Pierre Trudeau hired a management consultant firm, P.S. Ross and Partners, to review the system of fitness and recreation being supported by the government and to assess the fitness levels of Canadians. The firm's two-volume report was multi-faceted in its recommendations; the most functionally significant of these was a recommendation to set up a private, not-for-profit communications agency to promote fitness among the Canadian population. In 1971, Sport Participation Canada or 'ParticipACTION' was created in direct response to this suggestion. Its role was to sell the concept of physical fitness as a product to Canadians.

It was a controversial issue, a delicate process to motivate people to improve their personal levels of fitness. Poster campaigns, radio campaigns, television and other media campaigns, a test community in Saskatoon, private company co-operation, and self-funding of its programs were quickly implemented.[104] For 30 years, until its dissolution in 2001, ParticipACTION was a significant and successful force: at one point during the 1990s, its cost–benefit ratio was calculated at 35:1. In catalyzing the whole fitness movement its advertisements seemed to both tease and be poignant—'Don't run for the bus, you might not make it,' mocked one of the early posters—and ubiquitous. The action-oriented symbol of the corporation, a stylized, coloured representation of a human body in motion, became synonymous with the concept of fitness. In 2004, ParticipACTION was revitalized and re-established at a meeting of the Canadian Public Health Association via leaders from the whole fields of active living and health promotion in Canada.[105]

Young recreational squash player, a product of the late-twentieth century fitness boom. (Courtesy of Don Morrow)

encourage all Canadians to participate in sport and recreation.[102] This speech seemed to affect public thinking about Canadian fitness. A high-profile member of the royal family had mildly chastised Canadians. And it echoed fitness radio personality Lloyd Percival's frequent fitness messages on his show, *Sport College of the Air*. In 1956, Percival presented a brief on the 'physical fitness deficiencies in Canada' to the Liberal government but it was more warmly received when the Sports Advisory Council represented it to the Conservative government in 1960.[103] All of these factors were significant in the Diefenbaker government's decision to move directly into the arena of amateur sport and fitness administration in 1961; presumably, the government recognized that professional sport was a complex business in its own right and therefore elected to stay with amateur sport and the concept of fitness. The derivation and implementation of the 1961 Fitness and Amateur Sport Act are discussed in Chapter 10.

Conclusions

Clearly, institutionally organized sport, physical education, and physical fitness have had a checkered history of intersections and societal sanction. Canadian educators supported sport, for the most part, as an extracurricular activity. Drill, fitness, and health were generally regarded as more curricular even though only minimal attention was paid to promoting and teaching those concepts until about the middle of the twentieth century. The very fact that ParticipACTION was created attests to the lack of impact that physical education seems to have had in educating Canadians about fitness and/or instilling fitness behaviours within the educational system.

Related Websites

Egerton Ryerson
http://www.ryerson.ca/archives/naylor.html

The Pro-Rec movement
http://records.viu.ca/homeroom/content/Topics/Programs/pro-rec.htm

ParticipACTION
http://www.participaction.com/en-us/Splash.aspx

ParticipACTION History
http://journal.cpha.ca/index.php/cjph/article/view/1459/1648

Strathcona Trust
http://records.viu.ca/homeroom/Content/Topics/Programs/PHYSED.HTM

Canadian Interuniversity Sport Information
http://www.universitysport.ca/

Online History Resources for Students
http://canada.gc.ca/acanada/acPubList.jsp?font=0&lang=eng&categoryId=151&parentCategoryId=85&level=3

Study Questions

1. At various periods of time, how has Ontario's educational system reflected gender biases in sport?
2. Why would public educational systems be reluctant to include sport in the curriculum? How does this compare to music or art in the curriculum?
3. How might pupils have responded to physical education classes prior to the Second World War?
4. What has been and what is the perception of the role of sports in Canada's educational institutions?
5. Examine the advertisement examples and communication strategies of ParticipACTION (from the websites listed above). How would you assess the motivational goals and impact of this company?

CHAPTER 10

Sport and the National

———◆◆◆———

It is impossible to account for the whereabouts of every Canadian yesterday afternoon, but it is safe to assume one thing: If there wasn't a television in the room, chances are nobody was there. . . . cities in the rest of the country were downright spooky. Busy streets and typically bustling shopping malls looked like ghost towns as people spent the afternoon inside and in front of the TV. But when the final seconds ticked away and Canada won the gold medal, joyous fans streamed down bustling Yonge Street in downtown Toronto, many draped in flags and clad in red and white. Some leaned precariously out of car windows as they leaned on their car horns. One fan was seen sprinting down the street, clad in nothing but a Canadian flag. 'It's the greatest thing I've ever seen in my life,' said Sue Murray from Flin Flon, Man. 'I'm a happy, happy person today. I cried. We all cried. Fifty years without a gold medal. We deserve it.' 'That was better than losing my virginity!' screamed one fan in the frenzied moments after Canada won gold.[1]

The Canadian men's hockey team won the gold medal at the Salt Lake City Winter Olympics in 2002, and the press responded typically. It is evident from the media announcements and the quotations selected by reporters that this event was considered a significant moment by many Canadians. Some said it was their most noteworthy memory since the Canadian NHL representatives defeated the Soviet national team in the Summit Series of 1972. Others pointed to Donovan Bailey's victory in the 100-metre race in Atlanta in 1996, Nancy Greene's gold medals in skiing in 1968, Catriona Le May Doan's Olympic and world championship speed-skating victories, Marilyn Bell's Lake Ontario swim in 1954, Barbara Ann Scott's Olympic medal in 1948, perhaps even Ben Johnson's short-lived world record run in Seoul in 1988. Table 10.1 lists some of the landmark achievements in Canadian sport and important events related to sport over the past century and a half that have had a nation-building effect for Canadians.

All of these athletic triumphs elicited significant attention in the Canadian press, evidence of their newsworthiness as well as their considerable national importance. Such attention demonstrates the privileged place of sport in the construction of images and myths of national identity, or what one might refer to as the national imagination. Although it is a concept that would merit considerable analysis, 'national imagination' might, for the present purpose, be defined simply as what animates and motivates the nation, that is, what counts as being important to Canadians as Canadians. The national media, where most Canadians receive information and news, provides a reliable bellwether of such feelings of Canadianness.

Table 10.1 Building the Nation: Events and Cultural Icons

1851	World Exposition—the Crystal Palace
1860	Prince of Wales visit to British North America
1867	World rowing championship—the Paris Crew
1868	Dominion of Canada Rifle Association—federally funded sport organization
1872	Rifle team to Britain
1876	Lacrosse tour
1880	Ned Hanlan—world rowing champion
1883	Lacrosse tour—sponsored by the Department of Agriculture
1890	Louis Rubenstein—world figure-skating champion
1895	T.H. Hayhurst—Queen's Prize in rifle shooting
1900	George Orton—Paris Olympic steeplechase champion
1904	Olympic champions in St Louis: Étienne Desmarteau; George S. Lyon; lacrosse
1908	Government funds Olympic team
1915–40	Edmonton Commercial Graduates Basketball Club
1920	Winnipeg Falcons win hockey tournament at Antwerp Olympics
1924	Toronto Granites win hockey gold at first Winter Olympics in Chamonix
1928	Matchless Six—Canada's athletic champions in Amsterdam: Ethel Smith, Myrtle Cook, Fanny, Rosenfeld, Jane Bell, Ethel Catherwood, and Jean Thompson
1928	Percy Williams—100-metre and 200-metre dash champion in Amsterdam
1943	National Physical Fitness Act
1948	Barbara Ann Scott—Olympic figure-skating gold in St Moritz
1952	Edmonton Mercuries—last men's Olympic hockey gold in the twentieth century
1961	Act to Encourage Fitness and Amateur Sport
1967	Expo '67 and Canada Games
1969	Federal government Task Force on Sport for Canadians
1970	Proposed sports policy for Canadians
1971	Sport Canada and Recreation Canada
1972	Canada–Soviet hockey series
1973	Fitness and Amateur Sport Directorate
1973	Game Plan '76
1976	Montreal Olympic Games
1979	Iona Campagnolo's White Paper on Sport
1982	Best Ever '88
1986	Expo '86
1988	Calgary Winter Olympic Games
1988	Federal Sport Task Force—Toward 2000
1988	Ben Johnson disqualified at Seoul Olympics
1990	Dubin Report on the use of performance-enhancing drugs in sport
1996	Donovan Bailey wins 100-metre dash at Atlanta Olympics, setting world and Olympic records

1998	Mills Report examines economic impact of sport and the issue of federal involvement in sport funding
2002	Men's and women's hockey gold medals—Salt Lake City Olympics
2003	Mike Weir wins the Masters golf tournament at Augusta, Georgia
2003	Vancouver wins bid to host Winter Olympics 2010
2004	National Hockey League locks out players
2005	'Own the Podium', to enable Canada to win the most medals in 2010, is launched
2010	Vancouver Winter Olympic Games

We have discussed how sport played a role in the development of ideas about masculinity, femininity, and Aboriginal cultural identity, and what is true of masculinity or Aboriginality is also true of a national identity and its connection to sporting events. For a significant relationship to be drawn between sporting prowess and Canadian identity, social actors (such as parents with children) and institutions (such as the media) must recognize the relationship and consider it meaningful. At the same time, meanings about national identity are almost always partial and do not connect to the practical experiences of *all* of the population. The significance of sport and the national may include some yet exclude others, as we shall see in regard to hockey.

Throughout Canadian history, mythologies and images of national identity have been created to support specific political and economic agendas from the time of Confederation to the present day. Implicit in the idea of nationhood is the understanding that Canada and Canadians have often sought to establish a national identity in distinction from other nations, especially the United States. To remain meaningful, fresh, and modern, these myths and images have been reworked significantly time and again. Thus, national identity is not only something that must be actively produced, but it must be continually reproduced and updated if it is to sustain its capacity to motivate.[2]

Victories of individual athletes and teams are, and have always been, represented in the popular press (more recently on television and over the Internet) as national or Canadian victories. Individuals seeking to recognize these achievements typically have used the public venues of their time—newspapers, commemorative books, then television programs, and lists of 'most significant victories of the century' (particularly as the twentieth century ended), and, later, halls of fame. While ice hockey may not presently be important to all or even the majority of Canadians, one cannot overstate its historical significance in creating a Canadian national identity. The inescapable reach of hockey into the lives of Canadians has been described as almost an organic connection, a 'natural extension of seasonal rhythms'.[3] Indeed, the passionate fascination historians hold for determining when and where Canadians played the first hockey game speaks volumes to the sheer cultural significance of the sport in sustaining the Canadian national narrative.[4] Yet, other sports and individuals remain on the margins of national consciousness. The achievements of women and Aboriginals, for example, are conspicuously absent from the rolls of cultural honour, particularly with respect to sport.[5] The women's gold medal victory in hockey at Salt Lake City in 2002 drew considerable media attention but, predictably, less than the men's identical feat. Other victories by the women's hockey team and other sporting events involving the achievements of Canadian women not related to the Winter Games received little or no press. Whose identities, then, do sport victories represent, when a dominant collective identity can be imagined or invented or can be based on common or dominant social practices, sometimes at the expense of individual or marginalized identities and customs?[6]

If these forums represent the national imagination, one might expect them to stand for 'Canadianness' in all of its diversities—language, religion, region, and ethnicities. In Canadian history, sport has not transcended these cultural differences; rather, it has tended to reinforce or reproduce them. The meanings produced through sport in the construction of national identities seem fragile and temporary. Yet, mythologies have always been important to people. Moreover, hockey remains central for individuals who seek to elaborate an ostensibly unified Canadian national identity. In this respect, hockey invented Canadians as much as Canadians invented hockey. How does a form of culture become so ubiquitous? For the promoters of Canadianness, it was not always hockey, and hockey alone, that defined 'the national identity'. Government officials, community and business leaders, and patriotic citizens used public ceremonies, holiday festivals, and cultural events to invoke images of nationhood and the national, from the early agricultural competitions of the 1820s to hockey victories in the twentieth century, to the Vancouver Olympics of 2010.

Creating Early Impressions

Following the period of European conquest of the New World, citizens in the geographical territory of present-day Canada had competing views about nationhood and identity. In the first instance, culturally diverse Aboriginal groups inhabited the territories, followed in the second instance by Europeans, Americans, and Loyalists, diverse in language, religion, and cultural practices. One could argue that there have always been competing versions of Canadian identities, some strategically positioned in historically specific moments and eras to achieve certain economic, political, and social ends, others marginalized, repressed, even forgotten. It is difficult to determine, historically, whether concerns relative to a shared national identity were on the average person's mind at any given time—until such times when individuals attempted to produce sentiments of national identity to mobilize others to achieve specific goals. For example, in the early nineteenth century it was evident in the laws and customs established in British North America that some citizens embraced the cultural connections to Britain, many seeking to create similar living conditions and social activities.[7] It is also evident that competing values and customs existed in Lower Canada and later in Quebec. Even groups that leaned towards British imperialism had diverse opinions about the connection to Britain, as people have in regard to the US, and during the Confederation era opinions varied as to what the new nation, the Dominion of Canada, should be.[8] However, in all circumstances, during all eras, sports and games remained fundamental to individual and group identities and to the kinds of cultural messages popularized at home and offered for consumption abroad.

The British North American tour of the Prince of Wales, son of Queen Victoria, in 1860 is a case in point. At that time, government officials, community leaders, and colonists in various regions attempted to display their achievements, public decorum, and cultural strengths, in addition to their deference to the Crown and allegiance to the Empire. The Legislature of the Province of Canada had invited Queen Victoria to commemorate officially the opening of the Victoria Bridge in Montreal, to enable Her Majesty to 'witness the progress and prosperity', and to 'judge the importance of [the] Province of Canada'. Government officials also suggested that the tour would give Canadians an opportunity to unite 'in their expressions of loyalty and attachment to the Throne and Empire'.[9] Government officials financed grandiose celebrations in Newfoundland, Nova Scotia, New Brunswick, Prince Edward Island, Quebec, and Ontario, greeting the Prince with welcoming ceremonies, dances, dinners, parades, fireworks, music, displays of military arms, and sporting events. In addition to presenting displays of the local militias, demonstrating that Canadians were prepared to defend the territories of the Empire, sports and cultural pageants entertained the royal contingent, illustrating selected colonial pastimes for their approval. A demonstration of lacrosse in Montreal, a game between Montreal Lacrosse Club members and a combined Iroquois-Algonkian team, inaugurated a royal fascination with Aboriginal groups and the sport of lacrosse that persisted for the remainder of the century.[10]

The newspapers and official recorders of the Prince's contingent interpreted Aboriginal participation in the civic events both positively and negatively. Some accounts noted with approval the distances that Aboriginal groups travelled to greet the Prince, while others mocked their appearances, songs, and dances, and explicitly sought to denigrate all Natives as uncivilized, savage people, in sharp contrast to Her Majesty's civilized Caucasian subjects.[11]

Organizers strategically arranged parades of men in uniform, including militiamen, firemen, and fraternal organizations loyal to the Crown, and presented a group of the biggest, strongest lumbermen and voyageurs in the Ottawa–Hull region, an impressive visible representation of Canadian manhood. Evidently, they wished to illustrate unique aspects of the developing colonies through representations of both work and play, showing initiative and pledging loyalty at a time when the neighbouring United States, on the brink of civil war, was growing in economic influence and military power.[12] These formal celebrations helped to create public images through linking the themes of pageantry with the ideas of progress, prosperity, relative independence, and economic development of British North America. At local levels, civic celebrations—including Queen Victoria's birthday on May 24th—presented similar but more regular opportunities to demonstrate loyalty to the Crown, while promoting local boosterism and competitiveness between towns.[13] State visits brought these impressions to those outsiders in attendance as well as to those who read about the events in the newspapers overseas.

The intent, partly, was to demonstrate that the colonies were competitive and economically productive. A successful Empire required productive colonies. Yet, it was also important to create similar impressions abroad to attract immigrant settlers, farmers, and businessmen, as well as the sport hunters and fishermen who paid to visit the Canadas. Colonists were no strangers to the idea of competition or productivity; agricultural societies formed in the 1820s to improve farming techniques and encourage people to compete with one another in measuring their success in producing farm and domestic goods. By mid-century, the governments of most regions of British North America funded agricultural associations, local fairs and exhibitions, and plowing matches. Membership in agricultural associations in Canada East (Quebec) surpassed 10,000 in 1866.[14] Farm families socialized at fairs and competitive events, while showing off their crops, preserves, or plowing techniques; authors of agriculture reports, by contrast, impressed their superiors by describing such affairs in the language of progress, productivity, and competitiveness, highlighting their value in terms of contribution to the nation's welfare. One author argued that the agricultural shows: 'subserve[d] the chief objects of their institution—excitement of interest, emulation, and circulation of agricultural intelligence . . . . The whole range of exhibition gave satisfactory indication that the farming economy of the country was advancing.'[15]

Making the Local International

Comparable to agricultural fairs in political intent, but organized on a much larger scale, world's fairs and expositions of the nineteenth century provided the most significant venues for the display of scientific, technological, and cultural progress.[16] England hosted the first world's fair at the Crystal Palace in London in 1851. Architectural achievements such as the Crystal Palace itself and the Eiffel Tower in Paris were centrepieces speaking to the modern themes of the fairs. The British expositions celebrated the Empire and the 'benevolent' power of British colonial policies, while at the same time they promoted a new social interest in industrial and engineering progress and economic achievement. World's fair displays introduced scientific, technological, and product innovations and novelties that organizers hoped would impress and amaze the throngs of spectators. Products such as Coleman's Mustard (Paris 1878) and Goodyear's 'India rubber' (Philadelphia 1876) made their debuts at world's fairs.[17] Canadian officials described the Chicago Fair of 1893 in the language of social promise held by the future: 'The World's Columbian Exposition . . . was full of wonders—the triumphs of science, of art, and of industry in all its forms; it was a bewildering forecast of the legacy which the energy and skill and civilization of the expiring century will bequeath to its successor.'[18]

Countries that sent exhibits and products jealously competed with one another for national prestige. Members of the American press, for example, alleged that machines exhibited by Canada at the Universal Exhibition at Paris in 1855 were 'surreptitious imitations of American inventions'.[19] The international competitiveness fostered by these cultural spectacles created opportunities to celebrate nationhood and country beyond immediate and local experiences.[20] Hence Canadian contingents, similar to the other colonies of Empire, participated in world's fairs throughout the second half of the nineteenth century. Between the Confederation of provinces in 1867 and 1908, the Dominion government spent over $2 million sending goods, exhibits, and officials to world's fairs and expositions.[21]

The early exhibits focused on Canada as a sportsmen's paradise. Displays of big-game animals and fish were juxtaposed with information and maps expressing the general theme of Canada: a resource-rich land awaiting exploration and colonization. Sir Charles Tupper, executive commissioner of the Canadian section at the Colonial and Indian exhibition at South Kensington in 1886, remarked:

> It is to J.H. Hubbard, of Winnipeg, that the Dominion is indebted for the most comprehensive exposition of her riches of the chase. . . . I have described the attractions of the agricultural trophy at the west end of the Central Gallery. Mr. Hubbard's trophy of wild animals and birds at the west end formed a fitting complement to it. The former attracted the farmer and intending settler, the latter the wealthy nobleman and gentleman intent on sport. . . . Mr. Hubbard's game trophy was the chief attraction in the whole Exhibition to the classes of wealth and leisure, and was the means of sending to the Dominion many parties of distinguished sportsmen. . . . The collection was constantly visited by persons of royal or aristocratic rank, and

it would have been impossible to contrive any more effectual means of guiding the powerful sporting element of England in the direction of Canada.[22]

At the same time, the Canadian government attempted to balance the resource-based images of Canada with the interests of its growing manufacturing sector. To promote its tourist industry, the Canadian Pacific Railroad actively promoted the Canadian Rockies and hotels at Banff and Lake Louise.[23] Other companies displayed fishing rods, oars, pleasure boats and yachts, croquet balls, cricket and baseball bats, lacrosse sticks, bicycles, pianos, organs, and Canadian whisky.[24] The intrigue of uninhabited regions of the country, of the natural beauty of its mountains, lakes, and prairies, joined with a northern character theme presenting Canadians as robust, hearty individuals,[25] had to be qualified by increasing emphasis on manufacturing accomplishments. To be competitive with other countries, and to encourage immigration, Canada had to appear to be modern, its growing towns safe and inhabitable.

These investments by the Canadian government were part of broader domestic and international plans to develop the West and to improve trade. Prime Minister John A. Macdonald's National Policy envisioned that prairie and hinterland settlers would produce raw goods and resources to be shipped to central Canada for the production of manufactured goods.[26] The plan required settlers to populate the West. Displays at world's fairs advertised to prospective immigrants, and immigration agents stationed overseas provided information, lectures, and encouragement to fair visitors and implored them to consider moving to Canada. The social values attributed to prizes and awards at world's fairs represented Canadian industrial and agricultural competitiveness to the outside, but these meanings could be turned inward, as well, to promote national identity, particularly in a country as diverse as Canada, where people often clashed over language, religious, educational, and regional issues. The press announced the potential of 'Canadian' victories as ostensibly unifying social events, even though such constructed national identities remained mythological in more regional and local contexts.

Making Sport 'National'

Politicians and the central Canadian business elite engineered Confederation, in part, to control trade and tariffs in support of manufacturing industries and not necessarily because it made sense to the daily affairs of the average person. Indeed, citizens often had more in common with their southern neighbours than with other Canadians in more distant regions. Fishermen in Halifax, for example, had more in common with fishermen from Cape Cod than with farmers in Quebec or Ontario. In many respects, in the immediate post-Confederation period, Canada, as a nation, existed only abstractly in the minds of its people. One approach to nation-building, or making sense out of the new administrative structures and economic developments, federal and provincial, was to mobilize regional and cultural loyalties under the guise of national interests, through new national symbols or contributions to the Dominion. Accurate or not, events, titles, policies, and competitions could be arbitrarily positioned as 'national', in name alone, thereby attributing more significance to what in essence were regional affairs.

In this process of nation-building, sport, by virtue of its popularity, factored strategically.[27] Indeed, the victory of Canadian rowers, the Paris Crew, over Europe's best in 1867 at the Paris Exposition received more world press attention than Confederation itself.[28] The Dominion of Canada Rifle Association (DRA), formed in 1868, was Canada's first federally-funded national sport organization. Rifle shooting was a competitive sport given national significance by federal administrators, particularly parliamentarians and the Department of the Militia. Rifle shooting had been popular in British North America, particularly since the withdrawal of the garrison troops in the early 1860s. The American Civil War alerted Canadian and British authorities to the vulnerability of Canadian territories and to the nation's complete dependence on Britain for military support.[29] Mobilizing a volunteer force made the most sense to both governments in terms of expense and geographical convenience. In the new Dominion of Canada, mobilizing men to service was relatively easy; any militia movement or military training could be suffused with ideas of patriotism, loyalty, and the natural duty of protecting one's homeland. The social meanings about shooting were salient at the level of the nation much as they made sense at the level of the personal—an activity that was fun and competitive but in defence of both nation and family was also manly and patriotic.[30]

The federal government, through its regional militia representatives, encouraged the organization of regional and local associations and funded associations by purchasing or renting rifle ranges and by providing targets, rifles, and ammunition. By the late 1860s, provincial or regional associations existed in Nova Scotia, New Brunswick, Prince Edward Island, and Ontario, and the DRA received annual grants of $10,000.[31] Federal government expenditures to promote competitive rifle shooting between 1868 and 1908 exceeded $1.5 million. The DRA held its first 'national' championship at La Prairie, Quebec, in 1868. Politicians, Crown representatives, and businessmen lent their names to trophies and cups and provided prizes for national, provincial, and local competitions. The official organ of the Canadian Military, the *Military Gazette*, described the new competitions as patriotic ties that bound the diverse regions together:

> Such meetings cannot do otherwise than engender a kindly feeling between the various sections of the Dominion as well as between individuals, and in this may keep up and strengthen the territorial and political links by which we are united together by means of that far stronger and more lasting bond of union—common hopes and aspirations, good fellowship, a firm and honest belief in the bright prospects of our young country, and a determination to uphold its honor and dignity when opportunity offers, a practical training which is presented each year at the D.R.A.[32]

The National Rifle Association of England had first invited British North American teams in 1861 to compete at its annual championships held at Wimbledon. After several invitations, the first team, men from Ontario, competed in England in 1871, funded by the Ontario government. The first Canadian 'national' team competed the following year. From that year through the turn of the century, the federal government funded a national team to represent Canada. The funding strategy received its greatest return when Private T.H. Hayhurst won the coveted Queen's Prize for Canada in 1895; public officials greeted him with parties and celebrations in Montreal, Toronto, and Hamilton when he returned home.[33] In the press and in Parliament, supporters cast the victory in the spirit of nationalism, a victory for Canadians that supposedly transcended all political differences in the nation:

Rifle shooting at the range in Ottawa, c. 1900. (Library and Archives Canada, PA-134824)

this is a victory that I think cannot conflict with the feelings of any religious sect, or of any class of people in Canada. It has been won in a manly sport, a sport that is kept up for the defence of Canada, and for the defence of British possessions.[34]

Another commentator lauded Hayhurst's achievement not in terms of its transcendence of class and religious barriers; rather, the potential of Hayhurst's win to overcome developing regional differences merited attention:

With all of this silly talk about Provincial rights and local interests in connection with the Manitoba school fuss, it is pleasant to see the spirit of camaraderie and oneness that pervades the militia. The Montreal militiamen were just as proud of Hayhurst's victory, and gave the champion marksman just as warm a reception as the members of his own battalion up in Hamilton. The militia has had not a little to do with the welding of the peoples of these once scattered provinces into one solid nationality.[35]

Others chose to identify Hayhurst's win as further evidence of Canadian loyalty to British institutions, the masculinity embedded in competitive sport, and the glory of Empire:

It is gratifying, too, to hear of the popularity of the Canadian victors, not only on Bisley Common, but throughout the length and breadth of England. But after all, it is only what we might have expected of our wholesouled fellow-subjects in the dear old island, which is the shrine of manly sport and fair play, as well as the mother of nations. It is one of the remarkable and satisfactory characteristics of the good fellowship and affection existing between the different branches of the British nation that they reach undiminished in strength across oceans.[36]

Parliamentarians and supporters of the militia and rifle-shooting exercises took full advantage of leveraging sport as an indicator of national identity. They successfully mobilized Canadian men through competitive rifle shooting to become competent shooters, a ready source of trained volunteers who would be prepared for military service should the need arise. Most men, including sportsmen, were not called to service during the late nineteenth century, except to win prizes and competitions for nation, hometown, and family.

These sport competitions also served government policies abroad. Well-schooled national teams displayed becoming decorum while attending the Wimbledon, later Bisley, rifle matches. Supervisors reminded them that the appearance of their camp and uniforms and their behaviour reflected on Canada, and that such decorum was important in attracting potential immigrants. One member of Parliament remarked on the significance of rifle shooting to Canada's competitive reputation internationally: 'The presence of a Canadian team at Wimbledon each year was one of the best means of interesting the people of Great Britain in Canada and of promoting emigration.'[37] Another remarked on the symbolic value of Hayhurst's victory to foreign policy: 'I think this victory has done more to advertise us and to bring Canada to the front, than thousands of dollars could have done, if spent in the ordinary way by the government of Canada.'[38]

International Sport

In addition to the continued success of world's fairs, the emergence of Baron Pierre de Coubertin's Olympic Games, discussed in Chapter 11, provided new venues to define nationhood through the celebration of cultural competitiveness. Indeed, the organizational structure of the Olympics, pitting nation against nation, with team rituals such as the parade of athletes in the opening ceremonies, uniforms, and flags, fused and mutually reinforced notions of nationhood and competition. Coubertin's Games provided opportunities for countries to demonstrate the superior physical strength of their citizens, which could be presented to the public at home as a symbolic expression of supremacy over other nations. The American press, for example, tended to emphasize the significance of the athletics or track and field events because the United States athletes dominated these competitions from the first games in 1896 well into the twentieth century. The American athletes became 'athletic missionaries', symbolizing the cultural supremacy of the United States at home and abroad during the early twentieth century.[39] The Canadian press had its own celebrity athletes too, such as Hamilton's Billy Sherring, who won the marathon race at the Interim or Intercalated Games of 1906, held in Athens.[40] However, the creation of national sporting icons ultimately related directly to their socio-economic and ethnic status and to the contexts of their performances. For example, it was only when he won that the Canadian press celebrated Aboriginal runner Tom Longboat, winner of the prestigious Boston Marathon of 1907 and many other races. It was more usual that the press denigrated Longboat's Aboriginal status with cultural stereotypes, blaming him for losses, questioning his training techniques, and accusing him of being that catch-all—a drunken, lazy Indian. But when he won he was 'Canadian', and grudgingly given some credit. Even then, however, his handlers and managers, who attempted to profit from his abilities, were given unusually extensive acknowledgements.[41]

The North American Indigenous Games

In the colonizing process, for many centuries both the French and the English implemented policies and practices to establish familiar and traditional forms of culture in the new land, while seeking to eradicate the cultural practices of Aboriginals. As a matter of administrative procedure, it was assumed that Aboriginals could be 'civilized' or assimilated if they adopted European traditions. The banning of Aboriginal traditional cultural practices and celebrations and the forced transition to the residential school and reserve system shattered Native cultural life. Government officials were of the opinion that traditional practices such as hunting and trapping, communal sharing of land, and learning from experience on the land did not suit Natives for the newly emerging Canadian society. Older, traditional values were to be replaced by Euro-Canadian social values and a Western, Christian education. In the late nineteenth century traditional dances and ceremonies, including the potlatch, were outlawed; government officials did not understand their spiritual significance. In addition, the giving away of personal possessions during the potlatch ran counter to the principles of accumulation underscored in the Canadian economy.

As discussed earlier in the book, early legislation targeted drinking establishments in all of the colonies and made provisions to control public behaviours considered to be nuisances. Such laws targeted Aboriginals, specifically, on issues of alcohol consumption, frequenting pool halls, and participating in pageants or exhibitions, while additionally outlining clear restrictions on subsistence activities such as hunting and fishing. In the same era that traditional customs were outlawed, however, Europeans remained fascinated by some aspects of Aboriginal culture and appropriated many physical activities and games, re-fashioning them into middle-class sports and competitions. Lacrosse and snowshoe clubs and competitions, for example, had their roots in widespread Native traditions of centuries past. Members of Montreal's sporting clubs instituted rules and competitive regulations, for the most part restricting Aboriginal participation unless a talented 'ringer' was needed for lacrosse or a 'sideshow' of Native men or women could add entertainment value to snowshoe races.[42]

Over time, the Canadian government Indian officials recognized that the reserve system was not working.[43] From the late nineteenth century to the late 1960s, as many as 80 residential schools operated across Canada. Aboriginal children were forced from their families. School teachers and administrators attempted to re-socialize Native children, forcing them to speak English-only, erasing traditional customs and beliefs, cutting their hair, and altering their appearances. In mainstream Canadian schools, where boys performed military drill and both boys and girls participated in calisthenics, private school boys learned the principles of muscular Christianity and the value of sport in building social skills and character. Following the turn of the century, Native children, too, participated in a variety of sports which were part of the broader assimilation strategies employed in the schools. Principles of authority and obedience were embedded in school-organized sporting practices, considered to be fundamental elements required in modern society. Indian agents and school officials engaged in the process of assimilation did not realize that sports presented opportunities for Native children to address these physical experiences on their own terms.[44] Aboriginal youth celebrated their athletic achievements, feeling pride in their heritage and providing outlets for the frustrations superimposed by all other aspects of their incarceration. Sport became an important part of physical expression and a form of cultural resistance.

The Canadian government continued its assimilationist policies toward Natives through the twentieth century until it was forced to make significant changes, both because of the complete destruction of Aboriginal communities and in response to a strong lobby group, the National Indian Brotherhood (NIB), which sought major change. The NIB submitted a proposal to the federal government in 1972 outlining a change in approach to Aboriginal education which would help communities gain control over their own affairs—a new political organization emphasizing engagement instead of coercion. Of all cultural practices enforced in the residential schools, Aboriginal leaders saw value in sport for rekindling community identities and pride in communities, provided that these activities could at least, in part, be self-determined. The goals were twofold: first, to assist Aboriginal athletes to be competitive in the mainstream sport system and, secondly, to establish an all-Native sport system to celebrate distinctiveness and self determination. A failure to adequately fund the Native Sport and Recreation Program in the 1970s gave rise to broader initiatives envisioned by Aboriginal activist and sport leader J. Wilton Littlechild, namely the World Indigenous Nations Games (WIN) and the North American Indigenous Games (NAIG).[45] Littlechild, and fellow Aboriginal leaders Charles Wood and John Fletcher, began to plan the first NAI Games in 1988 to involve Native athletes from the United States and Canada in 17 proposed sports. If the NAI Games could be successful, then Littlechild hoped to gain international support from organizations like the IOC for the WIN Games. When the inaugural NAI Games of 1990 in Edmonton opened, some 2,500 Aboriginal athletes arrived for competition. Promised federal support of this festival dissolved, however, and the Games depended on the City of Edmonton and several Native groups for funding. The NAI Games were held again in 1993 in Prince Albert, Saskatchewan, and again 1995 in Blaine, Minnesota; this time the number of athletes exceeded 8,000. Victoria, BC hosted the Games in 1997, followed by Winnipeg, Manitoba in 2002; Denver, Colorado in 2006 (with 10,000 participants); and the Cowichan Valley, BC, in 2008 (4,500 participants).[46] Historically, sports and physical activity have been used as assimilative tools, wielded to civilize Canada's Aboriginal peoples. The North American Indigenous Games demonstrate how sport has been used by Native people to empower their communities through self-determination and for cultural survival.[47]

The New National Pastime

Just like Aboriginal athletes, women had to be better than average merely to be equal. The Canadian press celebrated the women of the Edmonton Grads for their astonishing series of regional, national, and international basketball victories over the period 1915–40. However, because they were women playing in an era when national sporting accolades were reserved for men, they were relegated to the social page of the newspaper and their athletic achievements were marginalized.[48] Neither did they play what would soon develop into Canada's dominant sport. For men—the dominant group of participants and spectators—the growing significance of the Olympic Games, as *the* international sport competition of the late 1920s and 1930s, coupled with Canadian Olympic ice hockey victories and the solidification of a monopoly over professional hockey by the National Hockey League (NHL) during the early 1930s, vaulted hockey and male hockey players to national iconographic status. A marginal sport such as basketball, played by women moreover, remained a side issue.

The McGill University Hockey Club, 1883. (Courtesy of McGill University Archives, PL007612)

Hockey emerged in the late nineteenth century as a variation of the older sports of **bandy**, **shinty**, **Irish hurley**, and field hockey. The earliest claims to the origin of hockey in Canada include Dartmouth, Nova Scotia (eighteenth century); Fort Franklin (1825);[49] Halifax (early nineteenth century);[50] Montreal (1837); shinty in Kingston (1839); shinty in Toronto (1863); with the first formalized and rule-based match recorded in Montreal in 1875.[51] By 1900, Canadians played hockey in most towns and cities, as did some Americans in the northern United States. As had been the case with baseball, hockey victories and championship teams became significant markers of local identity, most clearly expressed in community boosterism.[52] The Governor-General of Canada, Sir Frederick Arthur Stanley—Lord Stanley—eagerly donated a trophy for a national championship, first contested in 1893.

Initially a trophy representing amateur supremacy, the Stanley Cup was contested by teams from as far away as Dawson City, Yukon.[53] The first professional league, the International Hockey League, originated in the United States in 1904. Rival professional leagues competed for talent, with players moving from team to team, based on lucrative contracts. By 1909, the National Hockey Association emerged as the dominant league; hockey became a business venture, capitalizing on the decades of urban and rural interest in the sport as well as on town boosterism, with professional teams contesting for the Stanley Cup. The league survived challenges from the rival Pacific Coast League to be renamed the National Hockey League in 1917. The NHL ensured its North American prominence by expanding to American cities during the mid to late 1920s.[54]

By this time, Canadian amateur teams had easily defeated the representatives of other countries at the Olympic Games in Antwerp (1920) and at the Winter Games in Chamonix (1924), and St Moritz (1928). Canadian athletes had many successes during this era both in

A hockey match, possibly the first Stanley Cup game, played in the Victoria Rink, Montreal, 1893. (Courtesy of Don Morrow)

the Summer and Winter Olympics. Canadian periodicals celebrated the fame of Canadian players and the impact of their hockey victories overseas. Fred Edwards wrote passionately in *Maclean's* about players who 'roam up and down a dozen lands of Continental Europe spreading the fame of Canada and the Canadian people, causing nice things to be printed about Canada and Canadians in numerous, queer looking foreign publications'.[55]

As the Canadian men's teams gained fame in Europe, reinforcing the idea that hockey was Canada's game, hockey remained very popular in both urban and rural Canada. Women's hockey, too, had a long history but a peak period in popularity and organization was the 1930s. Teams competed for national championships five times during this period, at a time when ice time and finances for travel were major challenges. The Preston Rivulettes were a dominant team in Ontario, winning 10 provincial championships and four national championships during the 1930s. Also of note, at the national level were the Edmonton Rustlers, Winnipeg Eatons, Winnipeg Olympics, and the Charlottetown Islanders.[56]

The Canadian men had been victorious at the Lake Placid Olympics in 1932, but lost the Olympic gold medal in 1936 to an English team staffed in part with Canadian players; they recaptured victory again, after the war years, at the St Moritz Games in 1948. However, the Edmonton Mercuries—winners of the gold medal in Oslo, Norway in 1952—were the last Canadian team to win the Olympic hockey championship in the twentieth century, much to the consternation of hockey leaders, Canadian politicians, and hockey fans.

The broadcast of National Hockey League games, first on radio and later on television, in addition to the long history of local, regional, and national competition and extensive media coverage in the country, had made heroes and cultural icons out of hockey players and rendered hockey *the* Canadian sport. Indeed, the Canadian Broadcasting Corporation (CBC) played a significant role in the creation of this monopoly of national cultural production, but by mid-century the successful and powerful owners of teams based in the United States held the economic and administrative reins of Canada's national sport.[57]

The National Hockey League

CBC Radio's broadcast of NHL games attracted two million Canadian listeners in the early 1930s. By the early 1960s, the so-called original six teams drew television audiences of more than five million to CBC's *Hockey Night in Canada*.[58] Although six teams comprised the NHL from the 1933–34 season until expansion in 1967, other teams existed for periods of time in the previous era: Montreal Canadiens (1917–18); Toronto Arenas (1917–18); St Pats (1919–20); Maple Leafs (1927–28); Boston Bruins (1924–25); Chicago Black Hawks (1926–27); New York Rangers (1926–27); and the Detroit Cougers (1926–27), Falcons (1929–30), and Red Wings (1933–34).[59] Seven more US-based expansion teams joined the NHL by 1974 with the league weathering a challenge from the World Hockey Association from 1972 to 1979. The WHA attracted big-name players such as Bobby Hull, Gordie Howe, Dave Keon, and Frank Mahovolich. When the league folded in 1979, three Canadian franchises joined

Clarence Campbell, president of the National Hockey League, 1946–77. (Chris Lund, Library and Archives Canada, PA-111399)

the NHL, including Quebec, Edmonton, and Winnipeg. The move from Atlanta to Calgary provided seven Canadian teams to the NHL.[60]

During this period, significant changes had taken place in North American hockey—European players entered the WHA and NHL, and expansion brought more fighting into the game. Hockey in the 1970s featured many bench-clearing brawls, as teams like Philadelphia—labelled the 'Broad Street Bullies'—built reputations on toughness and intimidation. Star players such as Wayne Gretzky and Mario Lemieux placed more emphasis on skill, speed, and scoring; they also ushered in an era of escalating salaries and new revenues from television contracts, the sales of team paraphernalia, and corporate boxes. This environment placed considerable pressures on the 'small market' franchises such as Quebec and Winnipeg that could not compete at this economic scale. In response to the Canadian government announcement in 2000 that it would follow the advice of the Mills Report and subsidize professional teams, Canadians vehemently objected. Hockey was important to Canadians but subsidizing the massive salaries of hockey players and owner profits was out of the question. The NHL eventually responded by invoking team salary caps and revenue sharing. Disagreements about profit, caps, and revenue-sharing between team owners and the NHL Players' Association led to a lockout in 2004–5. The league had enjoyed a romantic dedication to the game by its players for decades until they learned that their labour had long been undervalued. Representatives for the players argued that owners underreported profits and that they, the players, did not receive a fair share of revenues. The resolutions to the lockout protected small market teams but limited salaries for players. Team payrolls were capped at $39 million for the 2005–6 season and salaries could not exceed 54 per cent of total league revenues. There are still disagreements about what constitutes gross revenues, and accounting practices are not consistent across the league.[61]

Canadian Football

Played in various forms with animal bladders by Aboriginal Canadians, its modern types arriving with garrison officers and soldiers, football has been played in Canada for a long time. The first rugby football club formed in Montreal in 1868. With the superstar status of the National Football League (NFL) and the NCAA in the United States and the Canadian Football League and CIS in Canada, it is hard to imagine that the current game has its roots in a challenge match between McGill University and Harvard in May of 1874. McGill brought the rugby game and Harvard expected soccer, so the result was a compromise of a game of each type. Later that year, Harvard travelled to McGill, played rugby rules, and returned to the United States to share it with other universities. According to Cosentino, the Americans later adapted the rules and invented the centre snap technique to eliminate the uncertainty of ball possession in the rugby scrum.[62] By the early twentieth century, the game was a combination of rules and scoring of the old rugby game and a new football experiment. In 1931, the forward pass was formally and permanently adopted into the game.

Table 10.2 Moments in Canadian Football

1868	Montreal Football Club
1874	McGill versus Harvard
1874	Toronto Argonauts
1880	Winnipeg Rugby Football Club
1882	Snap back for ball control in the United States
1883	Hamilton Tiger Cats and Ottawa Rough Riders
1897	Introduction of 3 downs to turn over possession of the ball
1898	Yates Cup—formation of the Canadian Intercollegiate Rugby Union, a league of Ontario and Quebec Universities
1909	Grey Cup for the Dominion Championship, until a 1921 an amateur championship between University and city teams
1909	Vanier Cup for Universities Championship
1911	Western Canadian Rugby Football Union
1921	First Grey Cup championship between East and West Teams—Toronto Argonauts defeated the Edmonton Eskimos
1929	American forward pass introduced in the Grey Cup game and adopted in 1931
1930s	American players recruited for pay by Canadian teams
1952	First televised Grey Cup
1956	Canadian Football Council—precursor to the CFL
1956	Touchdown value changed from five to six points, based on the NFL model
1958	Canadian Football League
1968	Prime Minister Trudeau ceremonial kickoff—first colour-televised Grey Cup
1969	Canadian quarterback Russ Jackson in his final season wins the Grey Cup, Most Outstanding Player, and Most Outstanding Canadian Player of the Year
2008	NFL Buffalo Bills host games in Toronto

The Tigers of Hamilton, 1906. (Library and Archives Canada, PA-029178)

Building the Nation

A growing impatience with Canada's successive hockey defeats at the Olympics after 1952 and at world championships fuelled debates over the funding of sport in Canada and the amateur problems in international hockey. Canadians complained that countries like the Soviet Union used their best players—salaried athletes—as members of the Soviet army, while Canada's best hockey players—the NHL professionals—were prevented from playing in the Olympics. Prior to the 1960s, the federal government had deftly avoided the issue of government support for amateur sport. However, the increasing influence of television in the promotion of Cold War nationalism, particularly through the Olympics and world championships, had a significant impact on public attitudes towards funding for sport.[63]

In the Cold War context, physical fitness deficiencies in Canadians became a matter of national security. The Canadian Sports Advisory Council's 1958 brief to the government of Canada stressed health, fitness, and national prestige as some of the benefits of sport.[64] The widely publicized speech of the Duke of Edinburgh on 30 June 1959 also spoke to the physical fitness levels of Canadians.[65] Similar calls for developing physical fitness as a matter of national defence were raised by the President of the United States, John F. Kennedy. If sport and fitness were to be considered issues of national importance, then they could no longer be operated by volunteers and a handful of local organizations.

Prime Minister John Diefenbaker selected the Hockey Hall of Fame to announce that the Canadian government would soon pass legislation to fund amateur sport. The Fitness and Amateur Sport Act, passed in 1961, and the sport programs that followed its passage, signalled that the federal government recognized the cultural significance of sport, its place in international relations, and its potential for the promotion of national unity.[66] The Department of National Health and Welfare administered a budget of $5 million by 1966–67. The Canada Games, inaugurated in 1967, became a highly visible means of demonstrating the unity of provinces at a time of increasing political tension between French-speaking Quebec, the federal government, and English-speaking Canada.[67]

However, in spite of increased funding for amateur sport in the early 1970s, the federal government and hockey leaders had not solved the problem of Canada's poor showing in international hockey. Protesting against the International Ice Hockey Federation and the half-hearted IOC principles of amateurism, Canada boycotted the hockey events of the 1972 and 1976 Winter Olympics.[68] Meanwhile, a hockey series that pitted Canada's best professional hockey players against the best players of the Soviet Union was staged in 1972. The media interpreted the Summit Series as the most significant measure of Canada's international reputation since the Second World War. For hockey enthusiasts, it presented an opportunity to reaffirm that Canadian hockey was the best in the world. For Canadians, generally, it mobilized greater patriotic interest in a cultural event than ever before.[69] In 1972, the Canadian national imagination focused on hockey. Yet, as the century drew to a close and the IOC declared Olympic hockey open to all professionals, the Canadian media could still no more than lament the fact that a gold medal had not been won by the 'first nation of hockey'[70] since 1952. Entrepreneurs selling commemorative video collections had rekindled memories of the 1972 series, but the national sentiments of the day resonated only with those who had experienced that now distant victory.

Hockey Hall of Fame Still a Boys' Club in the Twenty-first Century?

'The Hockey Hall of Fame was founded in 1943 to establish a memorial to those who have developed Canada's great winter sport—ice hockey. Incorporated in 1983, Hockey Hall of Fame and Museum ('HHFM') exists in order to honour and preserve the history of the game of ice hockey, and in particular, those who have made outstanding contributions and achievements in the development of the game' (http://www.hhof.com/html/gi200.shtml).

Curiously, the greatest Canadian female hockey player, Hilda Ranscombe, has not been inducted into the Hockey Hall of Fame. Ranscombe dominated Canadian women's hockey through the 1930s. She was captain of the Preston Rivulettes from 1931–40 and was part of the team that won an estimated 350 games and only lost 3. The Rivulettes won six national championships and 10 Ontario championships during this period. Shirley Cameron was captain of the Edmonton Chimos from 1973–92, leading her team to 19 provincial titles, two national titles, and leading Team Canada to a gold medal at the first women's international tournament in 1987 and the first women's World Championships in 1990. The application nominating her to the Hall was denied in 1995.[71] As of 2010, up to two women per year may be inducted into the Hall in a separate category.

The World Stage

Success in Olympic hockey after 1952 may have been long in coming, but the 'Canadian game' provided ample opportunity for the production of notions of national identity. This has also been true of other events on the world stage. Promoters and event organizers and politicians have given Canadians opportunities to identify with particular national accomplishments through the hosting of international festivals. During the 1960s, 1970s, and 1980s, Canadians were encouraged to show their excitement about hosting world-class events that would announce the 'arrival of Canada on the world stage'. Expo '67 in Montreal, the Summer Olympics of 1976 in Montreal, Expo '86 in Vancouver, and the 1988

Winter Olympics in Calgary were important events in the production of national identity. Although differing in focus, these festivals had common ideological objectives. Canadians were encouraged to think in a global context about international competitiveness and the importance of displaying industrial accomplishments, while organizers presented Canada to foreign visitors and international television audiences as an attractive and modern place in which to live, visit, or invest.

Always, there was to be a legacy of the most modern technological facilities left for the enjoyment of Canadians, a tourist industry that would blossom after the festivals and foreign investment that would be encouraged by the projection of Canada as a competitive nation. Canada was extolled in all of the promotional discourse as a nation of human as well as natural resources, a society whose technological and cultural accomplishments now signalled its emergence as one of the world's leading industrial nations. Canada had 'arrived', and one of the rallying themes of political leaders was that a nation of 20 million people, known until the 1960s for its forests and minerals, now had an opportunity to demonstrate the accomplishments of its people to the whole world. Thus, Georges Valade, member of Parliament for Sainte-Marie, described Expo '67 as a 'tremendous undertaking, unequalled in the whole world, [that] has given Canada an international and world stature'.[72] Even T.C. Douglas celebrated Canadian sophistication in his speech in support of Expo: 'If there are any Canadians who have an inferiority complex about living close to the most technologically advanced nation in the world I am sure such a feeling has been dissipated by the success of Expo 67'.[73]

Encouraging Canadians to think in the global context of competition among nations remained an integral part of the image construction and promotion that ensued at subsequent events. Of Expo '86, British Columbia politician Grace McCarthy suggested: 'It will be the kind of exercise . . . that will make our city of Vancouver and our province of British Columbia truly outstanding players on the world stage in that year.'[74] Upon the close of festivities, Mary Collins, the member for Capilano, claimed that 'we have showcased Canada and the world loves it . . . this country is the best in the world. . . . Our people, our resources, our spirit, and our achievements are second to none.'[75] More than 100 years of nation-building had passed, but the content of promotional rhetoric, intended to mobilize and excite Canadians, remained remarkably similar. As Expo '86 approached, BC Premier W.C. Bennett predicted in the Speech from the Throne:

The world will see British Columbia in a way which has never been the case before. Investors in the key areas of transportation and communication will see our province as a good place to live and a good place to locate and create jobs. The spirit of Expo 86 will live on through a legacy of permanent facilities and community benefits to be enjoyed by future generations throughout the province. But my government believes our greatest heritage will assuredly be the lasting spirit and reputation of having shown the world that we can achieve great things together.[76]

In sport, the language of national and international competitiveness was just as pervasive. The Olympics of 1976 replayed the familiar ambitions, in this case of Mayor Jean Drapeau, to remind the world of Montreal's world-class stature by building facilities more spectacular than those of previous host sites. In Alberta, the Winter Olympics of 1988 were framed as the accomplishment of a new, wealthy, and technologically sophisticated region signifying Calgary's emergence from regional to national and, indeed, international status.

In a very concrete way, moreover, the province wanted to promote the Alberta Rockies as an international, upscale ski destination, and the Winter Games provided an unparalleled opportunity to display the region in this highly competitive market. In a motion of congratulations in the Alberta legislature, one member remarked on the newly constructed image of Calgary after the Olympics: 'I thought, you know, that Calgary is now an international word. I think that's what the Olympics really did for Calgary and the province of Alberta: put us into the international field of commerce and recreation and notoriety.'[77]

Canada's hosting of the 1976 and 1988 Games was the stimulus for the Canadian government to spend more systematically in the area of amateur sport and to restructure Canadian amateur sports to achieve better international results.[78] Game Plan '76 attempted to bring together all administrative stakeholders in elite sport to propel the Canadian Olympic team's performance to tenth at the Montreal Olympics.[79] For 1988, through its Best Ever program, Sport Canada's official targets were that Canada place 'among the three leading Western sporting nations' and the top six nations overall in the 1992 Summer and Winter Olympics and that Canada finish 'first as a nation in the 1990 Commonwealth Games'.[80] For more than a century, sport had been used to demonstrate Canada's competitiveness internationally.

Governments still position athletes as international ambassadors: 'Our athletes help the modern Canada become better known in other countries.'[81] Governments still use sport and event hosting to facilitate international relations abroad and to encourage investment and trade. Indeed, the federal Mills Report, completed in 1998, explored some of the themes for sport that Canadian governments had been pursuing since the immediate post-Confederation period. Its mandate included an examination of: 'the economic impact of sport on a national and regional basis . . . evidence of sport's impact on national unity and how this might be enhanced . . . . The potential scope of, and rationale for, federal involvement—or increased federal involvement—in the promotion of (and participation in) amateur sport in Canada.'[82] With respect to Canada's international policy, the report concluded: 'Each time Canadian athletes win a medal, the country as a whole gains in reputation, as do Canadian industries.'[83] Sport is still a fundamental aspect of nation-building.

At home, the meaning of the national is still turned inward to promote unity, as national identity and national pride are reconstituted around the economic and political projects of the day:

> This is a celebration of excellence. It is a celebration of participation . . . . The Olympics is a dream. It is a fulfillment of a dream for Canada . . . . Today all Canadians celebrate the dream of the Olympics. Today we are proud to be Canadians.[84]

In July 2003, the Vancouver Olympic Bid Corporation president, John Furlong, described the city's victory in national terms: 'We are thankful because the bid pushed us to visualize a better future for our city and for our country. It is such a privilege to stand up here before you and the world representing Vancouver and Canada.'[85] Bid organizers announced the Winter Games of 2010 as another opportunity to display Canada before the world, encapsulating nation as a unified modern project: 'Canada is a meeting place of the world's peoples, and embodies Olympic values. Vancouver's culture is founded on tradition yet is young, on the edge, an international leader in contemporary creativity.'[86] Shallow public relations statements, such as this, once again encouraged Canadians to be motivated by hosting the latest world-class event.

National symbols are an important part of athletic ceremonies at all levels of competition in Canada. (Courtesy of Kevin Wamsley)

In January 2005 a group of partners including Sport Canada, the Canadian Olympic Committee, Winter National Sport Federations, CODA, VANOC, the governments of Canada and British Columbia, and others including corporate partners launched the Own the Podium program, a $110 million support package for elite sport. Sport leaders determined that with more funding and infrastructural support Canada's athletes could win the most medals at the Vancouver Olympics in 2010. The program provides additional money for personalized training, travel, equipment, and a secret research program designed to develop new technologies to improve performances.[87]

Conclusions

Sport has always provided convenient metaphors for nation-builders, and for nationalism, a ready source of cultural content available to mobilize Canadians at both ideological and practical levels. The Canadian public has always been encouraged to admire and respect particular athletes and teams—those possessing the characteristics deemed appropriate in the given era—as ephemeral cultural icons representing the nation. In the media, these depictions of the 'national' athlete have ranged from the simple to the extreme, on occasion imbued with an almost religious significance, as evident from the imagery used in the following excerpt from a story written about the 2002 hockey victory at the Olympics and one of the most potent national figures in recent Canadian history:

Of all of Gretzky's exceptional hours, this might almost have been the finest. It was he who, as executive director, had put this team together, borne the brunt of a nation's soulful expectations, also borne the brunt of a nation's jitters after a poor beginning to this tournament, and now had seen it through to its ultimate triumph. He did all this under the quantum handicap of not having himself on his side on the ice. Gretzky could already walk on water; now he was skating on air.[88]

The victory, it was said, had captured the national imagination, a new set of images and myths to create a Canadian identity, at least for the time being.

* * *

Related Websites

Canadian Football League
http://www.cfl.ca/

National Hockey League
http://www.nhl.com/

Sport Canada
http://www.pch.gc.ca/progs/sc/index_e.cfm

Recreation Canada
http://culturecanada.gc.ca/chdt/interface/interface2.nsf/engdocBasic/18.html

Calgary Olympic Development Association
http://www.coda.ca/

Paul Henderson's Goal to Win the Summit Series
http://archives.cbc.ca/IDC-1-41-163-1005-20/sports/henderson_goal/

Summit Series
http://www.1972summitseries.com/

Own the Podium
http://www.ownthepodium2010.com/

Study Questions

1. What is the most significant moment in Canadian sport that occurred during your lifetime? What are the factors that influence your decision?
2. How has sport been important in the process of nation-building?
3. How did the role of government in sport change between the late nineteenth and late twentieth centuries?
4. How does the notion of gender influence national identity?
5. If we consider sport in national terms, who benefits?
6. Examine Table 10.1. Are there any patterns that you can find? Are there any other events and/or cultural icons you would add?

CHAPTER 11

The Olympic Games

———◆◆◆———

Beginnings

On 2 July 2003, Vancouver, British Columbia won the rights to host the Winter Olympic Games of 2010. Canada was not involved in the first modern Olympics held more than a century ago, in 1896; indeed, only a handful of nations participated and for decades few people were even aware of the Olympic Games. Today, the Olympics are a cultural event of global dimensions; nations invest millions of dollars to improve the performances of their athletes, and cities are clamouring for opportunities to host the games. Having hosted the Summer Games of 1976 in Montreal and the Winter Games of 1988 in Calgary, Canada has sent athletes to the Olympics for more than a century—a long history of participation, significant financial expenditures, and, as is the case for citizens of many other countries of the world, a cultural fascination in the Olympics.

For historians generally, and for the self-proclaimed keepers of the Olympic trust—the **International Olympic Committee** (IOC)—particularly, the most venerated figure in this long history is Baron Pierre de Coubertin. Commonly, he alone is credited with the idea of reviving the ancient games in a modern form; this solo credit is due, in part, to his own efforts. More recently, scholars have demonstrated that his ideas were, in fact, borrowed from other events and his actions were influenced by many social factors. The ancient Greek bond to the god-like Olympians and the religious festival of the Olympic Games, dedicated to the god Zeus and inaugurated around 776 BC, became a focal point of cultural interest for nineteenth-century aristocrats, scholars, and popular enthusiasts who wished to recast the ancient traditions in their own lifetimes.[1] This was true for early Canada as well. Middle- and upper-class elite men of Montreal, including members of Parliament, lawyers, garrison officers, doctors, and businessmen, organized an Olympic Games in 1844, a two-day festival with 29 events under the auspices of the Olympic Athletic Club, to celebrate the sports and games of imperialist Britain—cricket, rowing, and athletics.[2]

The use of the word 'olympic' was not unusual at that time; indeed, with increasing European bourgeois fascination in ancient Greek culture, stirred in part by archaeological excavations of ancient sites, the term was applied to phenomena as diverse as sporting events and beer.[3] In spite of the self-serving recollections of Pierre de Coubertin, the man who took and received full credit for the idea of establishing the modern Olympic Games,[4] there were many Olympic-like festivals, cultural celebrations, competitive precursors, and social influences bearing on the launch of the modern games in 1896. Robert Dover organized the 'Olimpick' or Cotswold Games in rural England, a country festival dating back to the sixteenth century. The educator Guts Muths refers to organizing Olympic contests for children in his book *Gymnastics for Youth* (1794). Professor Gustav Johann Schartau organized the first Scandinavian Games in 1834 in Sweden; Yugoslavian Olympic festivals were held in the 1870s; and the Scots organized Highland Games in Scotland and wherever they emigrated (see Chapter 4). Germans organized Turnfests or gymnastics festivals in the 1800s, and every four years since 1851 the German-American Turners in the United States have held the National Turnfest, the longest running sports festival in the world.[5] The most significant influences on the establishment of an international Olympic festival were the nineteenth-century Greek Olympics, sponsored by the estate of wealthy Greek patriot Evangelos Zappas; the Olympick Games at Much Wenlock, England, organized by Dr William Penny Brookes beginning in 1850; and the theme of cultural competitiveness embedded in the world's fairs and expositions of the late nineteenth century.

The Baron

Pierre de Coubertin was born into a French aristocratic family. As an eight-year-old boy, he was aware of the defeat of the French in 1863 at the hands of Otto von Bismarck and the Germans. The second important intellectual influence on the young Coubertin was French theorist Frederic LePlay, whose writings were dedicated to restoring harmony to a French society rife with class divisions.[6] Coubertin's eventual response to France's lack of military strength was a first-hand examination of the role of physical training in various countries, including Germany, England, the United States, and Canada.[7] Many countries—Sweden, Denmark, and Germany in particular—had incorporated mass movements of gymnastics training as part of their nation-state development, a militaristic response connecting language, history, and physical exercise in the construction and mobilization of national identities. Coubertin was particularly inspired, during his visits to Britain, by the English model of sports and games that had gained favour in the public schools and by the novels of Charles Kingsley (e.g., *Westward Ho*) and Thomas Hughes (*Tom Brown's School Days*) that linked the morals of Christianity with those social prerogatives of manliness or masculinity imparted through competitive sport. Muscular Christianity was the celebration of manhood through vigorous physical sports, tempered by moral values, and transferred to other aspects of life. Like the British imperialists who idealized the character development of boys through 'manly' sports and games that were sometimes quite violent, Coubertin sought to rejuvenate the youth of France through a program of physical education.

Constantly rebuffed in his attempts to insert sport into the curricula of French schools, he turned his creative energies elsewhere. While fully aware of the **Highland Games** and **Turnfests**, but especially aware—through Brookes—of the Greek Olympics of the nineteenth century, Coubertin borrowed primarily from Brookes's ideas. Coubertin witnessed the Much Wenlock games in 1889. Brookes joined John Hulley, one of the organizers of the 1864 Liverpool Olympics, and E.G. Ravenstein, president of the Turner organization in London, to form the National Olympic Organization in 1865, a precursor to the International Olympic Committee.[8] After years of corresponding with the Greeks and supporting their games, Brookes first conceived of an international Olympic games in the fall of 1880. Brookes repeatedly lobbied John Gennadius, representative of the Greek government in London, for the Greeks to stage an international event in Athens, but to no avail.[9] Thus, Coubertin did not conceive an international Olympic games; however, he was responsible for engineering their inauguration and eventual success.

Alongside the public school educators in England, Brookes and Hulley recognized and endorsed the importance of physical fitness for military competence and, by extension, national strength. Brookes spoke in 1862:

[W]hy not direct our attention to the physical improvement of those who are to constitute the living defenders of our freedom? I feel sure that the introduction of a system of gymnastic training into our national schools . . . would be a national good, would be a means of raising up . . . a race of healthy, active, vigorous youths, a noble, manly race, whose reputation for pluck, bodily power, and endurance, would inspire far more terror on the battlefield than the arms they bore.[10]

It was this kind of rhetoric that drew Coubertin and his designs for France into the movement towards Olympic revival. The militarism embodied in men's sport and physical training was evident in Coubertin's plans for French rejuvenation in the early 1890s when he suggested that boys and men who did not shrink from a football scrimmage would surely not cower from the mouth of a Prussian cannon.[11] Coubertin had written nothing about the Olympics before 1889. Yet, it was Coubertin who received the credit for the idea of introducing an international Olympic games at the International Congress held at the Sorbonne in Paris in 1894.

Coubertin announced his intentions to revive the Olympics in 1892 but received no support in France and only mild interest during his trip to the United States in 1893. The Congress of 1894 attracted international delegates—aristocrats, officials, and elites—because the agenda proposed to deal explicitly with the difficult issue of amateurism in sport, the concern of sporting leaders in several nations. Brookes had grown tired of the amateurism debates raised by aristocrats in England but Coubertin recognized that preserving exclusivity in sport was of paramount importance for leaders of influence—politicians and sportsmen of nobility from around the world, the men who would help him see his grandiose plans to fruition. Caspar Whitney, appointed to the IOC in 1900 and president of the American Olympic Committee in 1906, was appalled at the failure of amateurism in the United States and found similar conditions in Britain. Whitney's disdain for the mixing of classes through sport was evident in his conclusion that it was wrong:

to bring together in sport the two divergent elements of society that never by any chance meet elsewhere on even terms. . . . The laboring class are all right in their way; let them go their way in peace, and have their athletics in whatsoever manner suits their inclinations. . . . Let us have our own sport among the more refined elements.[12]

Nineteenth-century elite sportsmen invented the idea of amateurism (see Chapter 5), and organized their sports, memberships, rules, and regulations in Britain and other countries around this concept in order to maintain the exclusivity of sporting gentlemen, under the auspices of what they considered to be preserving the integrity of men and sport. These men popularized and rationalized amateurism and its lofty social ideals, in part by linking it anachronistically to the ancient Greeks and the **ancient Olympic games**. In reality, amateurism was an ideal wielded oppressively by middle- and upper-class sportsmen that had nothing to do with ancient Greece.[13] Under this fabricated rubric of amateurism members of the Montreal Amateur Athletic Association (MAAA) wielded control and influence over sport in central Canada. Thus, in some countries, any discussions about organized sport were coloured by the aristocratic tenets of gentlemanly amateurism and the associations to the classical period of ancient Greece that such men commonly summoned.

Indeed, nostalgic connections to a fictionalized ancient Greek culture were invoked to thrill the aristocratic delegates at Coubertin's Sorbonne Congress in 1894, named the International Congress of Amateurs. Coubertin craftily played on this obsession of aristocrats, placing the establishment of the Olympic Games as an aside on an agenda devoted to the amateur question.[14]

The Early Games

Coubertin's unbridled energies, grounded by a certain political shrewdness and coupled with his skillful management of nostalgia and sentiment, culminated in the selection of Athens, Greece as host of the first international Olympic Games in 1896. Demetrius Vikelas was appointed as the first IOC president.[15] Coubertin himself appointed 14 members to the International Committee of the Olympic Games (later known as the International Olympic Committee), each of them independently wealthy and bound to serve as representatives to their respective nations to ward off any undue influence of governments on the Olympics. None were Canadian. During this early period, the Baron was also careful not to appoint sport leaders with too much power in the international sport federations or in their own nations, as that might also exert an uncontrollable influence upon the IOC.[16] In spite of Coubertin's work to establish the games in 1896 he contributed little to their organization. Crown Prince Constantine of Greece organized committees, solicited financial support to build facilities and to pay for the event, including money from Georges Averoff for the construction of a magnificent stadium. Constantine was directly responsible for the organizational success of the first modern Olympics. By all accounts, the Games of 1896 were very successful, with 13 countries participating and 311 male athletes competing. There were no women; Coubertin and his peers were not interested in women's participation in the Olympics.

Canada did not send a contingent to Athens because such an international competition was beyond the organizational abilities of the Amateur Athletic Union of Canada, not because of a lack of interest or of talented athletes.[17] Athletes competing at the MAAA track and field meet in 1895, it has been suggested, scored better times and distances than the athletes in Athens the following year.[18] The idea of competitiveness in the emerging international sporting arena was not lost upon Canadian boosters.

On the excitement and anticipation generated by the event, the Coubertin-Philemon report of 1896 was unequivocal:

The sacred moment is now to hand. The Games are about to begin. The athletes of the various nationalities who have registered to take part have drawn up in double row in the arena for the arrival of the Royal Family, exciting general interest by the harmonious build of their bodies. A trumpeting is heard. The first event is about to take place. The bands depart from the arena and are placed in various tiers, where at various intervals they play marches.

The contestants who are to take part in the first event emerge from the dressing room at the end of the tunnel. They are all lightly dressed. They are wearing a flannel shirt, short socks, and light shoes. Each has on his breast the number of the order of his registration.[19]

Following the contests in athletics (track and field), cycling, tennis, shooting, fencing, swimming, weightlifting, and gymnastics, the most widely celebrated event was the marathon race. Twenty-five runners spent the night in the town of Marathon on the eve of the modern world's first marathon race. Cyclists, soldiers on horseback, and doctors in carriages trailed the marathoners as they raced towards Athens the next day. Along the route, Spiridon Loues of Greece supposedly stopped at the inn near Pikermi and drank a full glass of wine, asked how many runners were ahead of him, and confidently told onlookers that he would pass them all.[20] A dusty starter arrived at the stadium in Athens on horseback to announce that a Greek runner was leading the race. Coubertin's account reports:

After a few minutes, which seemed centuries, a movement is noticed at the entrance of the stadium. The officers and the members of the committee hasten thither. Finally a man wearing white, sun-burnt, and covered in perspiration, is seen to enter. It is Louis, the victor of the Marathon race. He arrives running, on the right side of the arena, most fatigued, but not to exhaustion, followed by the members of the committee and the ephors who cheer him. The Crown Prince and Prince George run with him, one on either side. The King, when the runner reached his place in the sphendone and bows to him in greeting, gets up and waves his nautical cap, for a long time in deep emotion. Some of the aide-de-camps rush forward, embrace the runner and kiss him. The two princes, who were joined by Prince Nicholas, lift the victor in triumph. The foreign officials applaud with emotion.[21]

The stories and mythologies surrounding the first marathon race, indeed the long distance travelled by the runners, added to the excitement generated by the event. In the early era of the Olympic Games, particularly following the victory of a Greek athlete at the first games, the marathon race was the most anticipated event. Thus began the modern Olympic narrative, juxtaposing image, heroism, and even political ascendancy with athletic contest, positioning the triumphant male athlete at the pinnacle of exemplary, patriotic manhood. Nonetheless, the games of 1896 were set within the social, political, and economic relations of the day, as were all the Olympic Games to follow. The wonderful Olympic stories belied the tensions of class, gender, ethnicity, the social contradictions embedded in modern sport, and the political and military strains between nations, as the Olympic Games provided a new venue for cultural competitiveness among nations striving to assert and represent themselves.[22] Yet, as early as 1896, organizers, participants, and observers confidently

Athens Stadium: site of the 1896 Olympic Games and some events for the Summer Games of 2004. (Courtesy of the International Centre for Olympic Studies, University of Western Ontario)

summoned Olympic sport as a guardian for morality and peace, even though the festival had distinct military and nationalistic foundations. Of course, such rhetoric implicitly endorsed their visions of morality and politics:

> And from the following day the foreigners left in groups for their homelands, dispatched up to the last moment, with signs of affection, and taking with them impressions of affection and admiration for Greece, and with firm conviction, that, according to the Royal sentence that Greece was destined to be the peaceful meeting ground of the Nations, the permanent and continual field of the Olympic Games.[23]

The 'peaceful meeting ground of the Nations' soon found itself defeated and bankrupted as a result of a brief war with Turkey. Coubertin disappointed the Greeks, who wished to secure the Games in perpetuity, by insisting that the IOC award them every four years to the 'great' cities of the world. Coubertin's own Paris was selected for the games of 1900, organized in conjunction with a world exposition, an event with much greater newsworthy prominence at the time.

Since their inauguration in 1851 at the Crystal Palace in London, the Canadian government had spent more than $1 million sending displays of goods and manufactured items to **world's fairs**.[24] News from Paris boldly headlined: 'CANADA BEATS WHOLE WORLD' followed by the subheading, 'In Its Fruit Display at Paris'. These headlines overshadowed news about George Orton, from Strathroy, Ontario, the first Canadian Olympic champion, who won the 2,500-metre steeplechase event, representing the New York Athletic Club and the University of Pennsylvania; Canadian newspapers identified the win as a victory for America.[25] Alex and Dick Grant of St Mary's, Ontario, also competed for the United States team in Paris.

Clearly, the second Olympic Games occurred at the periphery of the world's fair and, tortuously, over a six-month period, in conjunction with the usual length of world's fairs. Consequently, the press and the spectators had difficulty following events, athletes did not know in the broader sense what sort of event they were participating in, and the world learned little about Coubertin's festival. Coubertin viewed the proceedings as humiliating.[26] Conflicts between athletes, team officials, and even cultures over the issue of participating in sport on Sunday marred some of the events, as did the lack of adequate facilities. Charlotte Cooper of Britain became the first female Olympic champion, in tennis, although she was not officially recognized. Women participated in a handful of events since the local organizing committee was responsible for the program, and not Coubertin's IOC.

In spite of Coubertin's eagerness to gain accolades for his new festival and to forget the tribulations of association with the Paris Exposition, the Games of 1904 once again drew organizational support from the culturally more significant world's fair, the **Louisiana Purchase Exposition** in St Louis. The IOC successfully fought off the efforts of James E. Sullivan, secretary of the Amateur Athletic Union of the United States, to gain control over the site selection process, even proposing Buffalo as a hosting site for an Olympic Games in 1901. Coubertin announced that New York was a possibility.[27] Initially the IOC awarded the games to Chicago, whose officials ultimately deferred to St Louis, as opposed to Sullivan's preference for Philadelphia.[28] Such political manoeuvring and struggling over control demonstrated an emerging significance for international sport, one that increasingly concerned nations, including Canada. The individuals who shaped the social and political attitudes were excited by the prospect of a world stage on which to wield the symbolic value of trained men's bodies for domestic and international purposes. Political proponents and sportsmen alike positioned the athletic victor, crowned in international sport competitions, as a signifier of the relative economic and social position of the nation. Athletes of the early twentieth century, then, took their place alongside fruits, agricultural products, manufactured goods, and scientific inventions of the era as indicators of national progress.[29]

In the years leading up to 1904, Coubertin's Olympics received considerable press in the United States.[30] But, once again, the Games were lost among exhibits at the fair. All IOC members but two (neither of whom was Coubertin) refrained from making the voyage to America. However, the St Louis location was much more convenient for Canadian athletes, competing in a contingent of 52 men.[31] Six women from the United States participated in archery. The Americans dominated all athletics events with the exception of the 56-pound weight throw, won by Montreal policeman Étienne Desmarteau. George S. Lyon won the golf competition for Canada; other winners included the Galt association football team and the Winnipeg lacrosse team. The Mohawk lacrosse team from Canada finished third.[32]

However, in another of the great travesties of Olympic celebrations, other Aboriginals and 'non-Caucasians' did not participate in the St Louis Olympics in the same context

Étienne Desmarteau, winner of the 56-pound weight throw at the St Louis Olympics in 1904. (Courtesy of Don Morrow)

as the Mohawks. Rather, organizers selected them from the anthropological exhibits of the fair by virtue of 'race', offering them up for scientists and spectators to interpret racial differences that the events were organized to demonstrate. The *Official Report of the Olympic Games of 1904* boasted that **Anthropology Days**, a two-day sporting event, featured the first sporting competition exclusively organized for 'savages'. For the Physical Culture exhibits, fair organizers showcased individuals who ostensibly repre-sented the uncivilized and savage races from various parts of the world, and situated them in displays to demonstrate how they lived.

Following dialogue between James E. Sullivan, the chief of the Department of Physical Culture, and Dr W.J. McGee, chief of the Department of Anthropology, it was determined that the Aboriginals in the various displays should participate in certain competitions to discern whether they had 'natural' physical abilities. The staged events, judged by American physical educator Dr Luther Halsey Gulick, included some of the running and throwing events of athletics, in addition to pole-climbing and tug-of-war, as well as an exhibition of mud wrestling. The author of the report, Charles Lucas, noted: 'The Pygmies and the Cocopa Indians at the conclusion of the day's sport gave an exhibition of their shinny game, which required team work and the uninteresting exhibition showed conclusively the lack of the necessary brain to make the team and its work a success.'[33]

Officials mobilized many different political and social agendas through sport. In the course of international sport competitions, the Olympics in particular, sporting aficionados and politicians fervently positioned the officially sanctioned male Olympic champion as an exemplar of modern man; the organizers of Anthropology Days used sport to construct distorted social meanings. The embarrassment of the racist debacle and the encumbrance of the world's fair did little for the reputation of Coubertin's Olympic Games.

Two years later and still lobbying to provide a permanent home for the Olympics, the Greeks rejuvenated Coubertin's Olympic concept, in considerable distress following St Louis, by organizing an Olympic festival in 1906 on the 10th anniversary of the first games in Athens. Coubertin, who continued to exert careful and concerted jurisdiction over *his* games, refused to acknowledge the successful event held in Athens in 1906 as official Olympics, arguing that it fell outside of the established four-year cycle. The Athens event became known as the **Interim** or **Intercalated Games**. However, a Canadian contingent participated and Billy Sherring, from Hamilton, won the marathon and enjoyed the pleasure of Prince George running at his side to the finish line in the stadium. Sherring's victory received tremendous press coverage in Canada and stimulated significant interest for participants and spectators in running. Further, international victories at sport championships and the Olympics, including Sherring's marathon win, helped to stimulate a new nationwide interest in sport in Canada during the first two decades of the twentieth century.[34]

England hosted the 1908 Olympic Games. Scheduled for Rome, the eruption of Mount Vesuvius forced the IOC to relocate the festival to London. Canada's marathon hopes rested on the shoulders of Tom Longboat, winner of the prestigious 1907 Boston Marathon. Longboat's celebrated victory in Boston and many long-distance race wins in Canada created significant interest in the Games in London. Longboat and his peers started the marathon at **Windsor Castle**, inaugurating the modern standard length (42.2 km) for the race. Although expected to win, Longboat did not finish the race, leading to speculation on the part of team officials and critics about his character, alcohol and drug consumption, and general laziness. Profiteering managers and a Canadian public eager to rationalize the successes and failures of an Aboriginal athlete blemished Longboat's record-breaking running career. In addition, prior to the London Games the Americans had challenged Longboat's amateur status, attempting to have him banned from the Olympics (see Chapter 4).[35] Canadian team manager John Howard Crocker reported: 'Longboat should have won his race. His sudden collapse and the symptoms shown seem to me to indicate that some form of stimulant was used contrary to the rules of the Games.'[36] Controversies had plagued the marathon event since its inception: in 1896, Greek officials prevented two women, Melpomene and Stamata Revithi, each of whom ran the entire course, from receiving official recognition;[37] Americans accused the winner of the 1900 event, Michel Theato, of taking shortcuts; Fred Lorz jogged into the stadium as the apparent victor in St Louis having received a ride in an automobile; Thomas Hicks, the eventual winner in 1904, was accused of taking strychnine and brandy to complete the race; and Dorando Pietri, who defeated Longboat, was accused of taking strychnine and was disqualified for being assisted by British officials over the finish line.[38]

Bobby Kerr of Hamilton, winner of the 200-metre sprint, was a member of Canada's first Olympic team to be funded by the federal government. Parliament allocated the sum of $15,000 to help defray the team's expenses. Some boosters viewed Kerr and his victory as a national asset or cultural achievement; others debated the notion of providing public money for athletes. Parliamentary member for Grey County, Mr Sproule, argued:

> I regard such a vote as the height of absurdity. I think our country is running too far in the line of games and sports and too little in the direction of useful labour, and to sanction all this by a vote in the federal parliament seems to be going too far.[39]

Nevertheless, politicians were in favour of the Olympic enterprise. The newly established British Olympic Committee had encouraged Governor-General Earl Grey to organize a Canadian team. Grey appointed John Hanbury-Williams to the task. He became Canada's first IOC member and the head of an early Canadian National Olympic Committee that did not receive official status until 1913.[40] This Committee received $2,000 from the Ontario government to defray its expenses for the 1908 Olympic Games; politicians saw value in international sport competition.[41]

A Political Arena

In spite of the emerging rhetoric of peace and goodwill invoked to justify and promote the Games, the competitive structure always pitted athlete versus athlete and nation against nation. The American athletes served as 'athletic missionaries', promoting notions of cultural dominance abroad as 'muscular ministers of the gospel of Americanism, a spectacle which sold better in domestic than foreign markets'.[42] Such national rivalries inevitably rendered all Olympic Games politically charged in a highly visible manner. In 1908, for example, Britain and the United States fought vehemently over procedures, rituals, and officiating, contradicting the so-called amateur ideals and the integrity of sport supposedly upheld through participation in the Olympics. With the increasing cultural significance attributed to these international competitions, such conflicts were broadly replayed in the press, belying any notions that sport was somehow beyond the economic, military, and political purview of relations between countries.[43] Beset with challenges to the authority of the IOC coming from the Americans and displeased with the controversies of 1908, Coubertin wrote about his difficulties with Sullivan:

> I just could not understand Sullivan's attitude here. He shared his team's frenzy and did nothing to try and calm them down. This was followed on his return by a new betrayal; he persuaded the Amateur Athletic Union to appoint a commission for the purpose of forming a new International Olympic Committee and drawing up the statutes of future games. But this time, nobody listened to him.[44]

Politicking within nations created numerous ripples in the early Olympic Games, as the American Olympic decathlon and pentathlon champion of 1912, Jim Thorpe, discovered. The IOC, after intense lobbying by officials from the Amateur Athletic Union (AAU), removed Thorpe's record-breaking performances at the Games in Stockholm, Sweden from the official Olympic records and forfeited his medals after determining that he had breached the amateur code by playing semi-professional baseball in the United States. In principle, Coubertin did not concern himself with the issue of amateurism; however, to secure the prosperity of the Olympic Games for the future, the powerful amateur idealists, he realized, required due consideration. The Stockholm Olympics stood alone, successful, and free from the association with world's fairs, an important achievement that helped to right the Baron's games from their inauspicious beginnings.[45] Canadian George Hodgson, a swimmer from Montreal, won the 1500-metre and 400-metre events, Canada's first two-gold-medal performance at the Olympics. George Goulding of Toronto won the 10,000-metre race walk.[46] Goulding set 12 world records in walking races of various distances that year, including the four-mile indoor world record in New York.[47] Unlike Longboat, who was frequently chastised in the press and by the Canadian sport authorities who sought to trade on his victories (see Chapter 4), Goulding was held up as the paragon of amateur ideals. The Canadian press celebrated these victories widely, as newspapers increasingly tended to equate international sport victories with national strength.

Not completely satisfied with the organization of the Games, despite of the relative success of the festival in Stockholm, Coubertin and the IOC removed control over the athletic program of events from host committees. Moreover, Coubertin voiced his disdain for the participation of women in the Olympics. Ten nations sent a total of 53 women to participate in Stockholm.[48] How could nations and individuals celebrate exemplary masculinity through athletic performance if female athletes were performing similar feats? The inclusion of women in the Olympic Games blurred the lines of distinction, the binary opposites of gender construction, between masculinity and femininity. Thus, in *Review Olympique*, Coubertin implored the world that the Olympic Games were the domain of men, on a base of internationalism, with 'loyalty as a means, arts as a background, and the applause of women as a recompense'.[49] Coubertin later wrote about the significance of Olympic records as indicators of human progress; women, too, had a specific role in the production of records: 'woman's glory rightfully came through the number and quality of children she produced, and that where sports were concerned, her greatest accomplishment was to encourage her sons to excel rather than to seek records for herself.'[50] At this time Coubertin's views were not out of the ordinary for a sportsman and man of his class position; but his opinions carried extraordinary influence in the domain of sport. As it turned out, the First World War led to the cancellation of the Berlin Olympics of 1916, and the issue of women's participation did not emerge again until the Antwerp Games in 1920.

In the meantime, Sigfrid Edstrom, vice-president of the Swedish Olympic Committee, lobbied Coubertin directly to obtain his support for the establishment of an international body to govern athletics. Edstrom was aware of Coubertin's distrust of challenges to the IOC's authority and carefully worded his correspondence so as not to offend the Baron. Edstrom proposed the formation of the **International Amateur Athletics Federation** (IAAF) to solve the various problems of non-standardized competitions at the Olympics. He assured Coubertin that the Olympics would remain the world championships of athletics and that a rival competition would not emerge. In 1913, Edstrom was appointed president of the new IAAF, a governing body for men's athletics and the eventual focal point for lobbyists intent on the inclusion of women's events in the Olympic Games.[51] Edstrom replaced Victor Balck on the IOC; Balck accurately predicted how Edstrom's leadership would influence international sport, calling him the 'strong man of the iaaf who could 'help in cementing the contacts between the IOC and the IFs' (International Federations).[52]

War-damaged Antwerp, Belgium, hosted the Games in 1920, creating 'the rebirth of the Olympic movement from the ashes of the First World War'.[53] In spite of a housing shortage and many economic difficulties, participants and officials considered the Antwerp Games to be successful, although athletes and visitors could not escape the residuals of war, evident in the surroundings and in the political fallout surrounding the event. The absence of invitations for Germany, Hungary, Bulgaria, Turkey, and post-revolution Russia underscored the increasing politicization of the Olympics.

Besides the victory of Earl Thomson in the 110-metre hurdles, Bert Schneider's gold medal in boxing, and Canada's four other medals in boxing, Canada contested for the first ice hockey championship at these Olympics. The amateur champion Winnipeg Falcons easily won, by a goal differential of 28 for and 1 against, ushering in one of the first significant markers of Canadian ice hockey supremacy and of Canada's own athletic missionaries.[54] In 1925, the IOC declared official the first Winter Olympics after athletes had completed the 1924 winter festival competitions in Chamonix, France.

Alice Milliat, president of the Fédération de Société Féminine Sportive de France, proposed in 1919 that the IOC include events in women's athletics on the Olympic programs for 1920 and 1924. The IOC's reluctance to include women's track and field led to the formation of the Fédération Sportive Féminine Internationale (FSFI) in 1921, an organization dedicated to promoting women's sport internationally, and to the establishment of the **Women's Olympic Games**, first held in Paris in 1922. The IOC did not show immediate concern for these successful games, even though Coubertin identified what he called the 'abuse' of the word 'Olympic' as early as 1910.[55] The IOC's growing concern over the application of the word 'Olympic' in other sports festivals, such as the **Workers' Olympics** and the Student Olympics, demonstrated not only concerted efforts towards securing and sustaining exclusivity for its own Olympic Games but also a will to test control over international affairs.

Respecting Coubertin's wishes on the matter, Edstrom waited until the Baron retired as IOC president in 1925 to address women's participation directly. Edstrom was no more in favour of women participating than Coubertin in what were considered to be traditionally men's events, but he realized that the IOC could not stem the tide of women's participation and recognized that women must be included if the IOC and IAAF were to manage international sport competitions for men and women.[56] The newly formed IOC Executive directed the lobbying efforts of Alice Milliat to the IAAF and, eventually, the IAAF recommended the inclusion of five women's events for 1928. In exchange for this 'privilege' the FSFI agreed to: cease using the word 'Olympic' in favour of the suggested International Ladies Games; hand over control of women's athletics to the world body, the IAAF; and accept a five-event athletics program in 1928. The British women's team, in protest of this limited program, boycotted the Amsterdam Olympics.[57]

Full beneficiary of the extensive work of the FSFL, Canada had its best medal-producing performance to date in the Olympic Games of 1928. According to the press, at the Amsterdam Games the 'Matchless Six'—Ethel Catherwood, Fannie 'Bobbie' Rosenfeld, Myrtle Cook, Jane Bell, Jean Thompson, and Ethel Smith—won more 'points' than any other athletics team,[58] including gold medals for Catherwood in the high jump, and for Cook, Rosenfeld, Smith, and Bell in a world record-breaking 4 x 100-metre relay. Canada's Percy Williams won gold in the men's 100- and 200-metre sprints.

The remarkable performances of the Canadian women on the track announced the international arrival of women's athletics, the fruits of resistance against prohibitive Victorian ideologies about the physical limitations of women's bodies. However, these accomplishments were somewhat overshadowed by the exaggerated reactions of officials and spectators to the exhaustion of runners in the women's 800-metre event. In spite of similar symptoms often exhibited by men running the same distance, officials and dignitaries, including the IOC and IAAF members and world press, were disconcerted observing some of the female competitors at various stages of exhaustion and apparently suffering on the track. Partial normalization of participation to women evidently did not entitle them to equally normalized assumptions regarding physiological responses to exercise. But few critics allayed their disquiet at least by acknowledging that many women in the race had

Percy Williams wins the men's 100-metre race in Amsterdam in 1928. (Courtesy of Canada's Sports Hall of Fame)

broken the world record for the 800-metre distance. A reporter from *The Times* of London wrote: 'the half dozen prostrate and obviously distressed forms lying on the grass at the side of the track after the race may not warrant a complete condemnation of the girl athletic championships, but it certainly suggests unpleasant possibilities.'[59]

Members of the IOC and IAAF responded swiftly, calling for the expulsion of women from the Olympic Games. In lively debates between 1928 and 1931, the IOC presidential successor to Coubertin, Count Henri Baillet-Latour of Belgium, proposed that women's participation should be limited to the more 'feminine appropriate, aesthetic' events, such as gymnastics, swimming, fencing, and tennis.[60] These pronouncements, of course, made little sense to the athletically-gifted Matchless Six, Canada's champion athletes. And women's athletics drew support from influential supporters. At the 1930 IAAF Congress, American AAU president Gustavus Kirby threatened to withdraw the United States men's team from the 1932 Games if the IOC prevented women from participating in athletics.[61] Led somewhat by the urging of Edstrom, the IAAF voted 16–6 in favour of continuing women's participation in track and field events. Canada's representative, Dr Arthur Stanley Lamb, voted against women's participation.

After almost a decade of lobbying, Alice Milliat and the FSFI had won the right for women to participate in track and field events in Coubertin's Olympics. But this victory had come at a price. Milliat's successful women's Olympics folded and the FSFI relinquished control over women's athletics to the IAAF. Further, the IAAF prevented women from running races in excess of 200 metres until the 1960s. Milliat's acquiescence demonstrates in part the established cultural significance of Coubertin's Olympics by the late 1920s and the influence of national organizations in governing and controlling athletic participation in select countries. Given the emerging dominance of the Coubertin Olympics, the press attention and identification of the Games as the pre-eminent sport festival, and the relative power of amateur sport organizations, other rival competitions such as the Workers'

Canada's Jean Thompson successfully completes the 800-metre run in Amsterdam in 1928. (Library and Archives Canada, PA-151008)

Olympics eventually suffered the same fate.[62] By the early 1930s, supported by national amateur sport organizations, national Olympic organizations, and for the most part by the international federations,[63] Coubertin's Olympic Games had become solidly entrenched as the most important sporting festival in the world.

The Winter Olympics of 1932 in Lake Placid, New York, marked the fourth Olympic championship for Canada in men's hockey. In Lake Placid another Winnipeg team duplicated the gold medal feat of the original Falcons of 1920. In between, the Toronto Granites of 1924 and the Toronto Grads of 1928 won gold medals. Canadian speed skaters in both men's and women's events won nine medals, although the women's events were labelled 'demonstration' sports, as were curling and sled dog racing, both won by Canadian athletes.[64] The Summer Games of Los Angeles proceeded in 1932 in spite of the economic and social crises of the Great Depression. Against a backdrop of unemployment, homelessness, and soup kitchens, athletes and Hollywood stars mingled at social events and the typical celebrations of the Olympic Games. The overt strategy of Olympic leadership for the next several decades, to sustain the festival within a context of complicated international relations, was to insist repeatedly that sport and politics should not mix. In spite of such rhetoric, national and world politics, as always, suffused the Games with political meanings and actions, rendering Olympic sport the most important venue for cultural conflict and nationalistic competition in the twentieth century.[65]

The Berlin Olympics of 1936 in Hitler's Nazi Germany were explicitly propagandistic, extolling the virtues of National Socialism, the new Germany, and a militaristic racism symbolically made explicit in the decoration of venues, the presence of uniformed soldiers, and the overt discrimination against German-Jewish athletes. Following the severe repression of German Jews across the nation,[66] boycott movements against the 1936 Olympics emerged in countries such as France, the United States, and Canada. The Toronto-based Communist Party newspaper, *The Worker*, led the editorial charge against the Olympics, publishing reports of Nazi atrocities and discrimination through sport in Germany. In general, the popular press supported participation, as did the Canadian Olympic Association and the

Young Men's Christian Association of Canada. The Workers' Sports Associations identified Coubertin's Olympics hosted in Berlin as a fascist event preparing youth for war, argued vehemently against participation, and encouraged athletes to participate in the Workers' Olympics, called the People's Olympics, scheduled for Barcelona that year. The Amateur Athletic Union of Canada did not support alternative sports events such as the Soviet-sponsored competitions in 1935 or the People's Olympics of 1936, and on the issue of the Olympics in Berlin the AAU of C preferred to follow the lead of the British Olympic Association.[67] Pat Forkin, writer for *The Worker*, responded to mainstream press authors who criticized workers' sports:

We workers may be 'mediocre athletes' at times . . . our bodies broken by poor food, poverty engendered disease, rotten factory and living conditions—what else can be expected.

We have no apologies to make whatever about accepting the hospitalities of fellow trade unionists and sports lovers in the Soviet Union.

But when it comes to accepting the Judas offer of the Nazi party which has destroyed all semblance of workers' organizations, has driven our best leaders into hellish concentration camps, has exiled the best thinkers of our class and has sentenced our womenhood into a slave-like existence, we say 'nothing-doing!'[68]

In addition to the smaller contingents sent to the People's Olympics in Barcelona by Canada, the United States, Britain, Belgium, Czechoslovakia, Denmark, Switzerland, Holland, and Norway, the French sent a team of 1,300 athletes and officials.[69] Due to the outbreak of the Spanish Civil War, however, officials cancelled the games. The Canadian athletes heading to Barcelona attempted to join the Olympic team en route to Berlin in Paris but were refused and then suspended by the AAU when they returned to Canada.

A threatened boycott by the Americans posed a more serious threat to the IOC and to Hitler's Olympics. Without the Americans, the sporting world would not view the Olympics as a premiere athletic event and Hitler's campaign of propaganda would have suffered tremendously. The pro-participation faction was led by Avery Brundage, president of the American Olympic Committee, and American IOC member Charles Sherill. Both were concerned with ensuring that Americans would participate in spite of the discrimination against German-Jewish citizens. In an effort to avert a boycott, Sherill met with Hitler to have a Jewish athlete placed on the German team. Always the sport politician, Brundage struck an agreement with IOC president Baillet-Latour to give signing authority over US athletes to the American Olympic Committee, negating the influence of the AAU on the decision to participate in the Games. The boycott movement was led by Jeremiah Mahoney, president of the AAU, and was supported by the extensive correspondence of the American Consul General in Berlin, George Messersmith, who recognized the atrocities perpetrated by the Nazis and the legitimizing opportunities sought by Hitler that would be made available by American participation. In a pamphlet distributed to gain support for the boycott movement, Mahoney wrote: 'The present German government has injected race, religion and politics into sports in general and into the Olympics in particular, and has destroyed their free and independent character.'[70] Brundage retorted that the

Canada and the Olympic Games: Issues and Controversies

1900	Canadians participate for the United States.
1908	Favoured marathoner, Tom Longboat, is unable to finish the race.
1920	Winnipeg Falcons win the demonstration sport of ice hockey.
1928	First women's participation in Track and Field; Canada's Matchless Six reign supreme.
1936	Canada does not win the hockey gold medal.
1936	Famous Edmonton Graduates basketball team tours Europe and wins unofficial Olympic tournament. Basketball for women does not enter the Olympics officially until 1976.
1948	Figure skater Barbara Ann Scott forced to give back her canary yellow convertible in order to participate in the Olympics without violating amateur regulations.
1976	Canada dresses up 'Indians' for the closing ceremonies.
1984	Gold medal canoeist Alwyn Morris holds an eagle feather on the podium.
1988	Ben Johnson tests positive for performance-enhancing drugs.
1988	Protestors line the course of the torch relay to support the cause of the Lubicon Cree in Alberta.
1998	Ross Rebagliati tested positive for marijuana and was disqualified. He later had his gold medal for snowboarding returned.
2002	Medal drought from 1956–98 ends for Canadian men's hockey, with their win at the Salt Lake City Olympic Games.
2005	Canada announces that the Own the Podium program will place Canada first in overall medals at Vancouver in 2010.
2008	Wheelchair racer Chantal Petitclerc wins the Lou Marsh Trophy as Canada's top athlete.

boycott supporters had no right to bring politics to the sphere of athletics. The backroom politicking of Brundage and Sherill eventually secured American participation.[71] Hitler's Olympics eventually attracted wide attention from the world press, a result for which his Minister of Propaganda, Joseph Goebbels, had meticulously planned. Ironically, Avery Brundage earned his appointment to the IOC at the expense of American member Ernst Jahncke, who had urged the IOC to remove the Olympics from Berlin and was subsequently dismissed for his efforts.[72]

With the largest German team ever entered, the Olympics symbolically demonstrated Hitler's initiatives; indeed, the Games overtly displayed the physical power of the nation. A severe setback to Nazi strategies of demonstrating white, Aryan superiority to the world were the four gold medals won by the American black track and field athlete, Jesse Owens. The growing size and popularity of the Olympics created conditions for the invocation of powerful social messages. The triumphs of Jesse Owens were significant in that they ran counter to Hitler's notions of white superiority; however, Owens, like many Olympic athletes in history, was treated as a hero and national exemplar during the Games but upon return to his own country was subject to the typical racist discrimination of the era, resorting to match races against horses and motor vehicles to earn money (not unlike Canada's Ben Johnson a half-century, later after he was stripped of his 100-metre-dash gold medal for having taken performance-enhancing drugs). In many respects, the Olympic Games provided a *tabula rasa* for the press, sport leaders, and politicians to transform athletes into cultural icons. In most instances they could become only temporary heroes, unable to transcend the boundaries of class, gender, and race extant in specific nations. Athletes carried their social and political burdens of home and nation with them, but sport decontextualized such baggage, focusing exclusively on performance. None of these life experiences were represented for observers. Indeed, without sport leaders such as Avery Brundage, president of the IOC from 1952–72, to smooth over the rough edges of human relations, including protest and resistance, the Olympic Games may not have endured beyond the mid-twentieth century.

The Cold War

The Olympics of 1940 and 1944 were cancelled because of the Second World War. In the post-war era, following the defeat of Germany and its allies, two 'superpowers' emerged: the Soviet Union and the United States. The ideological division between the two powers, as well as the military threat they posed to each other and to the rest of the world, solidified and focused international policies in economics, politics, and culture, creating unprecedented tensions, in part because of the nuclear capability of each superpower. Hyper-competition existed between the two superpowers in all areas of industry, science, technology, and perhaps, most visibly, through Olympic sport. In 1952, following the entry of the Soviet Union into the Olympics, athletes noted a change in atmosphere at the Games, a new emphasis not just on winning but that reflected an 'us versus them', capitalism versus communism, West versus East valorization of performance expectations that extended beyond the sports arena to the political and social levels. American decathlete Bob Mathias commented on the issue: 'There were many more pressures on American athletes because of the Russians. They were in a sense the real enemy. You just loved to beat 'em. You just had to beat 'em. This feeling was strong down through the entire team.'[73] Such political bifurcations plagued the IOC during the Cold War: the defeated nations of war did not receive invitations to attend the London Games of 1948; China, Korea, and Germany—all divided as a consequence of military and political events—sought recognition and status in international sport; the Suez Canal crisis divided the Middle East, resulting in limited boycotts of the 1956 Melbourne Games; the Soviet military repression in Hungary created a near-riot in the water polo match between the Hungarian and Soviet teams in Melbourne; and the increased symbolic value attributed to gold medals accelerated individual and state-sponsored performance-enhancing drug programs.[74] World records throughout the twentieth century became indicators of national progress for all of the quantitative or measured sports, with the Olympics as their most prominent arena for display.

The Cold War formula equating medals with national and cultural supremacy ushered in new levels of women's participation, energized by the Soviet Union and matched by the United States. However, this occurred at some cost with respect to gendered representations of performance capability. A case in point was the iconographic positioning of Barbara Ann Scott, Canada's champion figure skater, as the ideal feminine athlete (see Chapter 7). The IOC and international sport leadership—as well as the popular press—actively channelled women into feminine-appropriate, artistic sports such as figure skating, gymnastics, and diving. The Olympic Games helped to sustain a newly wrought post-Victorian gender order that included female athletes within its own hierarchy of relations where representations of female athletes called 'darlings', 'pixies', 'dolls', and 'mermaids'[75] produced a subordinate positioning by shifting the focus from physical performance to beauty; an aesthetic femininity was ensured through popular discourse, feminine sportswear, and Olympic pageant costuming.[76] The feminization of the qualitative or judged sports, between 1930 and 1972, created social crises in two important areas. By the early 1970s, the most popular women's events in the Olympics were gymnastics in the Summer Games and figure skating in the Winter Games. Record-breaking of all sorts even outside of sport, from space travel to parachuting from hot-air balloons, was linked to rampant Cold War nationalism. It also fuelled the popularity of the quantitative sports and operationalized the twentieth-century mechanical notion of human progress, recognized and endorsed by Coubertin himself in 1930.[77] The qualitative sports of the Olympics answered the call to progress and captivated audiences by increasing the complexity of routines and the difficulty of moves in sports such as diving, gymnastics, and figure skating. A consequence of executing more complex jumps on ice and more complicated routines in gymnastics was the requirement for smaller and, therefore, younger women.[78] This eventually led to the introduction of child athletes at the Olympics, and the judging and coaching communities began to obsess over size and weight controls for young athletes, putting pressure on the self-concept of girls in particular, one of the bases of eating and body image disorders.[79]

The feminization process, more focused in the 1930s, served in part to alleviate concerns that sport masculinized women. However, a consequence of this shift was the feminization of those men who participated in the so-called artistic sports, particularly figure skating. Men's gymnastics, which exuded a long-standing national masculine tradition in Europe that embellished the overt publicly displayed musculature of the male gymnast, complicated the issue of the male aesthetic.

Canada has had a long history of participation in Olympic figure skating, with numerous champions both male and female. Indeed, the performances of winter sports athletes most often raised Canadian hopes for Olympic medals. Arguably, the performance of men's Olympic hockey teams provided Canada with its international competitive sport identity. Indeed, after dominating ice hockey in all Olympic Games to 1952—with the exception of a silver medal in 1936[80] due in part to the performance of Canadian players enlisted by the champion British team—expectations for Canadian successes in hockey were high. In part, poor international sport performances, particularly at the Olympic Games, led to federal legislation in 1961 to promote and develop amateur sport in Canada.[81] Faced with the state-sponsored sport systems of European nations and the university athletic scholarships of the United States, Canada responded by establishing federal subsidies for elite 'amateur' athletes. By the early 1970s, athletes from many countries, East and West, had worn thin the residual notion of amateurism, jealously defended by Avery Brundage during his entire presidency.[82] In one of his final conflicts over amateurism, Brundage expelled Austrian skier Karl Schranz from the 1972 Winter Games for receiving corporate money. His response to Brundage signified a changing era for Olympic athletes: 'The Russians are subsidized by their own government and all international athletes get help from one source or another. It's an emphasis on the wrong principle. I think the Olympics should be a contest of all sportsmen, with no regard for color, race, or wealth.'[83]

Massacres and Protests

In spite of pressing Cold War issues, the battles of Avery Brundage over po.. amateurism, **apartheid** in South Africa, and debates over increasing commercializau. of the Games, the Olympics continued to grow in popularity and in national Olympic committee membership. Satellite television in the 1960s vastly increased the TV audience for the Olympics, and countries such as Japan in 1964 used the Olympics to broadcast their economic and cultural 'arrival' to international audiences.[84] Subsequent to the 1964 Tokyo Games, controversy, crises, and corruption in the form of boycotts, security disasters, scandal, and exploding financial costs plagued the IOC.

Given the magnitude of the Olympic Games in terms of size, number of athletes, and media demands, the costs of hosting were enormous. Japan spent more than a billion dollars in 1964 in preparation for the Games; Sydney spent more than six times that amount in 2000. Even though financing the Games had always been an issue, nations were still willing to invest energy and capital into hosting this global event. In 1968, citizens of Mexico City protested lavish expenditures and the idea of hosting the Games in a city rife with unemployment and poverty and in a country run by an oppressive regime. After the Mexican government thwarted a planned peaceful march by 10,000 citizens, the protestors gathered in the Plaza of Tlatelolco to listen to speeches. In the 'worst crime in Olympic history',[85] the army moved in on the unarmed demonstrators and opened fire, killing an estimated 325 people and wounding more than 1,000. The IOC distanced itself from the massacre, its human consequences downplayed by the Mexican government as well as the foreign press.[86] It remains one of the most horrific yet least discussed tragedies in Olympic history.[87]

Relieved that the Games would proceed as planned, the IOC then faced a significant protest on the part of black American athletes, who chose to use the moment of crowning glory on the podium to protest the endemic discrimination against black people in the United States and other parts of the world. The American sociologist Harry Edwards, who had attempted to convince black athletes to boycott the Games, encouraged those who decided to participate to protest in their own way. An enduring image of protest in Olympic Games history is that of John Carlos and Tommy Smith, with gloved fists raised and standing in black socks, on the victory podium in Mexico City. A furious United States Olympic Committee ordered the athletes home within 48 hours. President Brundage indignantly retorted: 'The nasty demonstration against the United States flag by Negroes ... had nothing to do with sport.'[88]

Millions of spectators from around the world received the message; the Olympic Games, through widespread television coverage, offered a stage from which political expressions might be enunciated. Four years later, members of a Palestinian organization called Black September chose to use the 1972 Munich Games to draw attention to the plight of Palestinians, who effectively had lost their homeland with creation of the Jewish state of Israel in 1948. With lax security provisions in Munich, the group easily made its way into the Olympic Village during the pre-dawn hours and took members of the Israeli team hostage, demanding release of Arab political prisoners held in Israeli jails. Israeli wrestlers Moshe Weinberg and Shmuel Rodensky were killed almost immediately in the attack. After failed negotiations, the Palestinians and hostages moved to an abandoned airfield where German authorities agreed to provide them safe passage to Egypt. Instead, an ambush was planned. Inept planning and execution of the rescue attempt resulted in the death of all of the remaining hostages and five of the eight terrorists. Brundage, acting alone, cancelled Olympic events that day and arranged a memorial service in the stadium.[89] The IOC determined that the Munich Games would continue, a decision praised by some and condemned as inhuman by others.[90]

Speaking at the memorial service, Brundage once again drew the ire of critics when he conflated the Munich tragedy with the pressures on the IOC to expel the Rhodesian team to avoid a boycott by African nations. The IOC rendered its decision on the issue in reaction to protests against widespread racial discrimination in Rhodesia. Previously, Eastern bloc support of black African nations and constant lobbying against Avery Brundage had ultimately resulted in the expulsion of South Africa from the Olympics in 1970.[91] In 1972 an aging Brundage handed over the presidency of the IOC to Ireland's Lord Killanin. This change marked the end of an era within the Olympic Games.

Money, Boycotts, Drugs, and Scandal

A new urgency for security, an increasing concern for the financial stability of the IOC, alarm over drug-enhanced performances, and Cold War politics that produced major boycotts marked Killanen's term as IOC president. In 1976 Canada hosted its first Olympic Games in Montreal. Flamboyant mayor Jean Drapeau won the bid for Montreal after flying IOC members to Expo '67 the previous decade to impress them with the city. All of their expenses were paid.[92] The mayor promised modest, self-financed games. In one of the memorable statements on Olympic financing, he claimed: 'The Montreal Olympics can no more have a deficit than a man can have a baby.'[93] Prodded by an enthusiastic Drapeau, architect Roger Taillibert designed brilliant and complex facilities, unrivalled by those at previous Olympic Games. However, spiralling inflation, cost overruns, labour disputes, and private decisions by Drapeau all hampered the organizing committee. Construction remained incomplete at the time of the opening ceremonies. Yet, the games were excellent for spectators and well organized for the athletes.[94]

Against a backdrop of national tensions between French and English Canada and federal and provincial governments, political controversies clouded the festivities. The two-China issue was not yet resolved and the Canadian government, based on its 1970 one-China policy, refused to issue visas to the athletes from the Republic of China unless they participated as 'Taiwan'. The Taiwanese athletes were called home. The IOC refused to accede to the lobbying efforts of African nations that wanted New Zealand removed from the Games for its earlier rugby team tour of South Africa. As a result, 22 teams from Africa left Montreal.

In their attempts to display aspects of Canadian multiculturalism, organizers drafted a program to portray Aboriginal culture in the closing ceremonies, which included costumes and teepees, colour-coded to match the colours of the five Olympic rings. Organizers invited some 200 First Nations people to participate in a program featuring elaborate dancing. Added to the First Nations contingent were 250 non-Aboriginals painted to look like Natives, all dancing to the music of *La Danse Sauvage*.[95] Aboriginal leaders vowed that such a travesty would never happen again.[96]

A new federal funding initiative for high-performance sport (Game Plan) was implemented in the early 1970s. In spite of Game Plan's fivefold increase in funding for athletes and the creation of three categories of payments for elite athletes,[97] Canada became the first host nation in Olympic history not to win a gold medal.

Television revenues, a corporate sponsorship program, an Olympic lottery, and ticket sales were supposed to finance the Games without a deficit. When the Montreal Olympics ended, the province of Quebec and the city of Montreal absorbed a billion-dollar deficit, shared 80–20 between the province and the city. This debt will not be retired until 2012.[98] The IOC, long dependent on television revenues exclusively for its finances and marred by criticism of the financial debacle of Montreal, established a worldwide marketing program, The Olympic Program, or TOP, implemented in 1985.[99] Before the inauguration of TOP, major boycotts further compromised the integrity of the games. Following the invasion of Afghanistan by the Soviets in December 1979, the United States and its political allies boycotted the Moscow Games of 1980 and the Soviets retaliated with a boycott of the Los Angeles Games of 1984. Initially committed to going to Moscow, Canada decided to boycott following a telephone call from United States President Jimmy Carter to Prime Minister Joe Clark, although Great Britain did send a team to the 1980 Games. Over the course of the twentieth century, Canada's cultural and political allegiance had shifted from Britain to the United States.

The Los Angeles Games of 1984 became a watershed Olympic event, highlighted by a distinct shift from the era of Cold War politics to the outright commercialization of the festival. Lord Killanin's failing health led to his replacement by Juan Antonio Samaranch in 1980. For Samaranch, who promoted the participation of the best athletes in the world, professional or otherwise, the issue of amateurism was dead. Following preliminary meetings with athletic shoe magnate Horst Dassler, the TOP (known now as The Olympic Partners) program was conceived, and, coupled with significant increases in the costs of television rights, the IOC's financial stability was ensured well beyond the end of the twentieth century.[100]

Following the massacres in Mexico City and Munich and the massive debts of Montreal, Los Angeles remained the only host city expressing an interest in hosting the Summer Games of 1984. Peter Ueberroth, head of the organizing committee and later commissioner of Major League Baseball, adopted a corporate-style leadership approach and successfully solicited corporate sponsorship to offset greatly the costs of the Games. The sponsorship program, television revenues, and the use of existing athletic facilities that, for the most part, required only upgrading rather than new construction resulted in a profit of approximately $225 million. After this financial success, the IOC encouraged all hosting National Olympic Committees and organizing committees to establish national sponsorship programs. Samaranch's presidential legacy, following the appointment of Canada's Richard Pound as chair of the Television Rights Negotiation Commission, quickened the pace of 'the IOC's transition to a corporate entity'.[101]

During this era, cities began to view hosting the Olympic Games as an opportunity to acquire facilities and infrastructure and to make money. Thus, the votes of IOC members to award the Games to bidding cities began to have a significant financial impact.

Calgary became the first host city to benefit from the TOP sponsorship program and, further, received an unprecedented sum of money from television rights revenues. The American Broadcasting Corporation (ABC) paid US $309 million for the rights; ABC had paid only $10 million for the rights in Montreal and the larger summer festival.[102] Like other host cities in Olympic history, Calgary had to build elaborate venues for the winter sports,

The United States responds to the Soviet boycott. (Courtesy of the International Centre for Olympic Studies, University of Western Ontario)

accommodations for athletes, and facilities to provide for the burgeoning media industry. In spite of such phenomenal revenues, the Canadian government, the province of Alberta, and the city of Calgary spent between $400–$500 million for the construction of the Olympic speed-skating oval, Canada Olympic Park, where the ski jumping, bobsleigh, and luge facilities were located, and infrastructural developments such as road construction and a light-rail transit system.[103] Following the Games, the organizing committee transferred $60 million to the Calgary Olympic Development Association (CODA), a private organization that provides funds to maintain facilities and subsidizes elite national and local sports.[104] From its hosting experience, Calgary came to define itself as an Olympic city through further tourism development strategies and by hosting international events using some of the Olympic facilities. Although access to many of the facilities remain the prerogative of elite and junior elite athletes, the University of Calgary venues, particularly the Oval, have been widely used by the community.

Considered in Olympic circles to have been a success, the Calgary Games were made possible only through the work of thousands of volunteers, organized by paid staff and a well-compensated executive. As in any massive construction project and significant cultural enterprise carried out in the context of local, national, and international politics, Calgary experienced its share of controversy. Significant issues included a controversial display of Aboriginal artifacts on loan from museums from around the world; a Torch Relay boycotted by the Lubicon Cree of Alberta, who protested a lack of recognition by the federal government and the destruction of traditional hunting grounds by oil companies; the dismissal of volunteers and employees; environmental concerns over site selection; the intense campaign by the Canadian Olympic Association to prevent the use of Olympic symbols and insignia for commercial purposes; and the presence of athletes such as British ski jumper Eddie 'the Eagle' Edwards and the Jamaican bobsled team, who gained celebrity status mainly for ineptness or inexperience in their chosen sports.[105]

Prior to the Summer Olympics in Seoul in 1988, the rivalry between 100-metre sprinters Ben Johnson of Canada and Carl Lewis of the United States intensified, receiving considerable attention in the world sporting press. Throughout the twentieth century to the present day, from the flying finish of Charlie Paddock in Antwerp in 1920 to the world record-breaking performances of Lewis and Johnson and, in 1996, of Donovan Bailey, the men's Olympic sprint victory came to signify the pinnacle of sport performance in the world. Lucrative sponsorship opportunities awaited the holder of the title 'World's Fastest Man'. Johnson's victory over Lewis and his world record performance in Seoul set off celebrations across Canada, including a nationally broadcast congratulatory telephone call from Prime Minister Brian Mulroney. An IOC press conference announcing that Johnson had tested positive for anabolic steroids abruptly halted the victory celebrations. The high-profile case sent shock waves throughout the sporting world, particularly in the sport of track and field, and the IOC implemented more stringent, regular drug tests for all athletes. The fact remained that athletes in the Olympic Games had always looked for methods, products, alcohol, and drugs to enhance their performances. Cold War nationalism accelerated and systematized the process for teams and the commercialization of sport rendered drug-taking endemic at the individual level.

Corporate sponsorship became the new foundation of the Olympics during the 1980s. (Courtesy of the International Centre for Olympic Studies, University of Western Ontario)

The East Germans, in particular, have been condemned for their systematic use of drug laboratories and for administering steroids to unsuspecting athletes. The Johnson case raised the world's level of awareness; in shame, Canada responded with an investigative inquiry, the Dubin Commission. Despite this, in the late twentieth and early twenty-first centuries, athletes continue to dope their bodies with substances and techniques designed to enhance performance.[106] As a consequence of a major public relations campaign, in 1999 the IOC sponsored an international conference on doping, an outcome of which was the establishment of the **World Anti Doping Agency** (WADA).

Endemic drug issues persisted throughout the 1990s and the cost of hosting the Games increased markedly. The IOC altered the cycle of Winter and Summer Games to a two-year format (until 1992 both were held in the same year) and, at the same time, worldwide sponsors signed on for TOP III and IV. Television rights' fees continued to escalate. For spectators, the Olympic Games remained popular and the IOC itself enjoyed continued financial success.[107] In 1998, another crisis loomed. Evidence demonstrated that the Salt Lake City bid committee had bribed IOC members in exchange for their votes to deliver the Games to the United States in 2002.[108] Previously, British journalist Andrew Jennings had argued that the IOC was corrupt and had engaged in a number of questionable practices, including bribery, sex scandals, and concealed drug test results.[109] Investigations initiated by the United States government disclosed that bid cities, including Toronto, had been providing IOC members with free trips, cash, and lavish gifts in exchange for votes for

The University of Calgary's Olympic Oval is a multi-use facility, widely used by elite athletes and members of the public. Shown here are the two ice surfaces surrounded by the speed-skating oval.

over a decade.[110] Yet, in spite of—or perhaps in many respects a result of—the world press attention to the IOC scandal, Olympic news became more popular than ever. Indeed, the awarding of the 2008 Summer Games in July 2001 and the selection of an IOC president to replace Samaranch were frenzied media events. Samaranch's declaration, early in his presidency, of bringing the Games to all corners of the world, culminated in the selection of Beijing to host the 2008 Games.

Long touted as successor to Samaranch, Canada's Richard Pound was mainly responsible for the economic stability of the IOC. After decades of loyal service, Pound was selected by Samaranch to lead an investigation into allegations of IOC bribery, which resulted in the expulsion of a handful of members and castigation of several others. Pound's standing among his IOC colleagues waned. By the time of the vote for the IOC presidency, Samaranch's support had shifted to Belgium's Jacques Rogge. The IOC elected Rogge by a wide margin. His presidency enjoys the fruits of TOP sponsorship through 2008, capitalizes on a US $4.3 billion television agreement with the American network NBC for the period 2000–8[111] and US $2.2 billion for the years 2010 and 2012.[112] The next media event for the IOC was the selection of the host city for the Winter Olympics of 2010.

The cities of Vancouver, Canada, Salzburg, Austria, and Pyeong Chang, South Korea, were the final candidates selected by the IOC in the fall of 2002. Vancouver and Salzburg led on technical merit.[113] Buoyed by the victories of Salt Lake City in 2002, and the first gold medal in men's hockey since 1952, the IOC *Report* stated that Canadians generally

The Athens white water kayak venue cost $35 million US and is operated as a family theme park after the Olympics. (Courtesy of the International Centre for Olympic Studies, University of Western Ontario)

supported the Vancouver bid.[114] In Vancouver, however, Mayor Larry Campbell conceded to a campaign promise to poll the citizens of Vancouver on their opinion of hosting an Olympics.[115] The plebiscite, held on 22 February 2003, returned 64 per cent in favour of hosting and 36 per cent opposed.[116] The IOC selected Vancouver over Pyeong Chang in July 2003 on the second ballot by a margin of 56–53. The costs of hosting the Olympic Games are a serious issue for the Vancouver Organizing Committee.

The Athens Olympics of 2004 provided what Greek citizens had been coveting for decades—a return to the birthplace of the modern Olympics. Massive infrastructural projects, post-9/11 security, and substantial last-minute preparations escalated costs. Although the facilities were on par with Olympic standards, the Games failed to live up to hopes for the city's revitalization.[117] The Athens Olympics incurred in excess of US $11 billion of public debt.[118] These Games raised the question, once again, what to do with the Olympic facilities when the Games have left town? After touring the facilities just one year after the Games, BBC correspondent Richard Galpin described them as 'empty and silent'.[119]

The Bird's Nest stadium, Beijing, 2008. (Courtesy of Mike Heine)

The always more modest Winter Games, held in Turin, Italy in 2006, still raised the issue of unused facilities but the scale of debt was at a markedly different level, even though the Italian government provided significant funding beyond the Games' original budget.[120] For Canadian sport leaders, medal performances in the Summer and Winter Games remained a stark contrast. Canoeist Adam Van Koeverden, cyclist Lori-Ann Muenzer, and gymnast Kyle Shewfelt won gold medals for Canada at Athens in 2004. In Turin, Canada placed third in the medal count with 24 and speed skater Cindy Klassen won five medals. This result strengthened the opinion that it could be possible for Canada to 'win' the Vancouver Olympics. In Beijing, in the summer of 2008, Canadian athletes matched the gold medal performance in Athens with three, and 18 medals overall.

The 2008 Beijing Games remain unrivalled historically with respect to the amount of money spent on facilities, infrastructure, and ceremonies. The costs of the opening ceremonies, for example, have been estimated at $300 million,[121] with the total costs of hosting and preparing the city estimated between $40 and $50 billion. Since the IOC awarded the Games to Beijing in 2001, the most contentious issue over the following seven years was China's poor human rights record. At issue was China's treatment of prisoners, the persecution of practitioners of Falun Gong, systematic organ harvesting from prisoners, and its relationship with Tibet.[122] These political circumstances received little press between 2001 and 2008, until the torch relay attracted significant, aggressive protests. Beginning with the torch-lighting ceremony in Greece, various forms of protest also marked the route in London, Paris, and San Francisco, including attempts to steal the torch, to snuff out the flame, and the unfurling of protest banners. With the exception of the posting of one banner in Beijing, the Games, surprisingly, did not experience significant political protests.[123] Extensive pre-Games police inspections, deportations, very high levels of security, and a volunteer citizen force of 100,000[124] were likely factors in preventing the disruption of these Games. Swimmer Michael Phelps surpassed the 1972 medal total of seven by Mark Spitz and Usain Bolt of Jamaica obliterated the sprinting field in the 100- and 200-metre races. With the lowering of the Olympic flag and the extinguished Olympic flame, spectators marvelled at the sheer spectacle of the Beijing Games, wondering if London in 2012 would go to such lengths.

The Olympic flame will now travel from Beijing to Vancouver, winding its way through the provinces. For the 2010 Games, in addition to new Winter Olympic facilities, the supporting infrastructure includes a major upgrade to the convention centre, a new urban transit system from the airport to downtown Vancouver, and significant upgrades to the Sea to Sky Highway between Whistler and Vancouver.

Conclusions

Canada's more than century-long participation in Coubertin's Olympic Games enters a new chapter with the upcoming Vancouver Winter Olympics. The federal government has increased funding to help Canadian athletes achieve better results. The international prestige derived from Olympic gold medals is still important to national governments. The Olympic victories of Canadian athletes such as Percy Williams and Barbara Ann Scott and the early Canadian hockey teams cemented the symbiotic relationship of international sport performance, national competitiveness, and national pride; the Cold War emphasis on human performance, and the general perception that Canada's lack of medals in the Games after the Second World War was shameful, and led to significant federal government involvement in and funding of elite sport. The Canadian media ensured that the victories of athletes such as sprinter Donovan Bailey and speed skater Cindy Klassen would not be forgotten. Canadian athletes would not play second fiddle to a fruit display again.

Related Websites

International Centre for Olympic Studies
http://www.uwo.ca/olympic/

International Olympic Committee
http://www.olympic.org/uk/index_uk.asp

Canadian Olympic Athletes: Images
http://www.nlc-bnc.ca/olympians/

Beijing 2008
http://en.beijing2008.cn/

Vancouver 2010
http://www.winter2010.com

Study Questions

1. Why has the Canadian government provided financial support for Olympic athletes to attend the Olympic Games?
2. How has the notion of amateurism influenced our perceptions about the Olympic Games and the athletes involved?

3. What are some of the challenges that have faced Canadian athletes, historically, since the inception of the Olympic Games?
4. How have the Olympics influenced the Canadian sport system and the funding of athletes over the past 50 years?
5. Why do Canadians expect their athletes to win international hockey championships, particularly Olympic gold medals?
6. Some researchers critically label the Olympic Games as an 'aristocracy of muscle'. What do they mean? Do you agree?
7. Are the Olympic Games an appropriate venue for political protest?

CHAPTER 12

Sport in Canada: Current Issues

For thousands of years, people have cooperated, competed, and played on the landscape that is now Canada. Physical contests are exciting, full of cultural meanings for both the participants and the spectators. They are also portals to events of historical and contemporary significance that offer social insights into who we are and what is important to us. Physical activity has been important across the ages. Although context, venue, and meanings are vastly different now, one can easily imagine, for example, that the Jesuit missionary Jean de Brébeuf must have been as amazed and excited watching the Hurons play lacrosse during his early travels in New France in 1636 as today's first-time spectator at a professional lacrosse game at Toronto's Air Canada Centre or Calgary's Saddledome. Vast as the changes in the social landscape over those intervening 400 years may have been, as historians we endeavour to make sense out of some of the changes that have taken place, and identify what remnants of older traditions and practices endure, what has been lost, and what new sports and games have emerged as popular forms of culture in the present. To understand sport and physical activity today, it helps to draw upon historical and sociological sources to help us to frame our questions and to seek answers to various issues extant in sport. Why are some sports more popular? Why do some sports attract more attention and resources? Who participates? How do sports relate to broader social institutions and relations of power and influence? What does sport tell us about ourselves? This final chapter briefly examines issues in contemporary sport and offers some commentary in respect to the various historical contexts discussed in the previous chapters.

One of the most remarkable aspects of sport in contemporary Canada is the breadth of activities which interest people as spectators and participants. One could argue that there is a physical activity for everyone—vigorous, light, high-level, risk-filled, violent, passive—from massive stadia venues, high intensity and full-time training elite levels, expensive sports at the Olympic Games or world championship level, to pick-up hockey or slo-pitch games or private, living-room based activities such as the Nintendo Wii Fit movement game. Participation can range from a full-time occupation as professional athlete, to being a spectator, to the citizen who, though not really interested, cannot escape sports headlines, taxes directed towards local rinks, or a federal budget with a line item that will pay for hosting major festivals such as the Olympic Games. Sport is ubiquitous in the Canadian cultural landscape.

Telepro Sports

In the Canadian social landscape, particularly with respect to sport in the media, professional sport has won the day, as Bruce Kidd argued in 1996.[1] It would be difficult for the sporting elites of the late nineteenth century, the middle- and upper middle-class amateurs, to imagine that corporate structures and capitalist enterprise would one day control sport in Canada, and that the notion of amateurism would be non-existent. History points us, however, to the growing appeal of professional sports and star players evident in the last decades of the nineteenth century. Promoters leveraged the excitement of the game and the abilities of the players so that sports performances became consumable, and somewhat affordable, goods. Further, the old amateur club models made no sense to working-class people, preventing any sort of organic connection to the broader community under those terms. It was a general appeal to national sentiment, competition, and identity that drew people to the elite-level amateur sports and to events such as the Olympics. Following on the heels of professional baseball's popularity, the monopoly secured by the National Hockey League by the 1930s was powerful, and the only opposition to complete control were the machinations of amateurism coming from the International Olympic Committee (IOC) and amateur athletic associations. At local levels, spectators followed home-town teams and athletes in sports such as hockey and baseball. The box scores and stories of professional athletes could be followed in the newspaper (see Chapter 7), and radio brought professional baseball and hockey to consumers at little cost. Shortly thereafter, television brought the games to living rooms[2] for a form of mass consumption that had not been experienced. Fans on the west coast or in the prairies could follow and identify with far-away teams such as the Montreal Canadiens or the Toronto Maple Leafs, or even teams from the United States.

The IOC invoked the amateur ideal to distinguish the Olympics from professional sports but, by the 1970s, the concept was dying a slow death. Canadian athletes received minimal government financial support, whereas some Americans had lucrative university scholarships and East Bloc athletes received compensation in the form of preferred housing[3] and training resources or small amounts of money for their mandatory enlistment in the military. IOC president Juan Antonio Samaranch put the nail in the coffin of amateurism in the early 1990s with his claims to provide the 'best of the best' for his corporate clients, The Olympic Partner (TOP) sponsors, and the world's television networks (see Chapter 11). The older form of systemic control and exclusion exerted by middle and upper class men—amateurism—was gone.

For most people, these events—the Olympic Games and professional sports such as NHL hockey, Major League baseball, National Football League (NFL) football, and National Basketball Association (NBA) basketball—are *televised* entertainment. Leagues only grant franchises to large-market cities and even in those centres, ticket prices are too high for working-class families. Upper deck tickets at 2008 prices for the Pittsburgh Steelers of the NFL are listed at approximately $200 each;[4] courtside tickets for the NBA Toronto Raptors ranged from $706 to $1145.[5] Available NHL tickets for a Vancouver Canucks versus Chicago Blackhawks game ranged from $86 to several thousand dollars for a seat in a luxury suite.[6]

These prices generally do not include parking or service charges and, unless your seat is located in a corporate box or suite, refreshments will incur additional costs. One year before the Vancouver 2010 Olympics, short-track speed skating tickets range from $188 to $423, while opening ceremonies tickets for the Games are posted at $423 to $7196 per ticket.[7] Olympic tourists may book travel packages through private companies, some in the range of $3,000 per person for a six-night trip that includes tours, a hotel room, lounge access, and a banquet.[8]

Professional sport franchise management, of course, is quite different from that of the Olympic Games, which create more temporary effects on resources and consumption. Sport franchise owners once operated their teams strictly on the basis of gate receipts and some advertising revenues. In the current market, owners depend on television contracts, advertising, merchandise, and ticket sales for their revenues. Professional sport has become more of a product, targeting, in Whitson's terms, 'free floating consumers' who exercise a range of choices, as opposed to the identification with home teams and home players of previous eras. Commercial branding has replaced the invocation of local, regional, or national affinities.[9]

While Canadians became more exposed to American television in the 1970s, the more recent reach of satellite television, the emergence of the sports networks, and pay-per-view sport events changed the sport entertainment landscape and the packaging of sports for consumers. In Canada, The Sports Network (TSN) was established in 1984 as the first national provider of sports programming exclusively. Currently, Canadians may choose between alternatives Sportsnet, the SCORE, and several specialty channels such as the Fight Network, the Fishing Channel, the Golf Channel, and comprehensive channel packages for all of the major North American professional sports. Unlike the 1970s, when the major television networks offered sports coverage to viewers for free, the sports channels are billed through packages that incur fees in addition to basic cable or satellite programming. Specialty channels, such as the NHL network or NASCAR, cost a subscriber hundreds of dollars for the season, in addition to other purchased programming.[10]

The landscape for viewing has certainly changed in the past 30 years and the marketing of sports television and the acquisition of lucrative television contracts have become more significant for franchise owners.[11] For example, Marc Lavoie reports the following distribution of television revenues to each major North American sports franchise per year in current contracts: baseball, $18.6 million; basketball, $31.7 million; NFL football, $68.7 million; and hockey, $4.9 million.[12] It is true, though, that as viewership costs continue to increase, sports consumers have access to other, free sources for viewing game scores, stories, and highlight film. News/sports corporations maintain specific-content websites, all major professional sports teams have websites, and the popular Youtube website provides a searchable database of replay videos which includes sports of all kinds.[13]

Players' salaries have increased substantially in the past 30 years, in all sports. Increasing revenues from television contracts and merchandise sales, players' union demands, salary disclosure, and rival leagues have played roles specific to each sport. Salary disclosure and union demands to share profits with NHL owners, for example, boosted hockey salaries markedly.[14] The average salary for NHL players in 1970 was $26,000; in 2006–07 the NHL average salary was $1.98 million.[15] In 2008–09 the highest-paid NHL player was Dany Heatley of the Ottawa Senators, who earned $10 million for the season.[16] Ben Roethlisberger, quarterback of the NFL's Pittsburgh Steelers earned $27.9 million in 2008,[17] And the highest-paid NBA player of 2008 was Kevin Garnett of the Boston Celtics, who earned $24 million.[18] Professional athletes also have opportunities to secure private contracts with corporate sponsors. *Sports Illustrated* reports that with tour winnings and endorsements combined, golfer Tiger Woods earned $127.9 million in 2007.[19] The average employee salary in Canada that year was just over $38,000.[20]

Despite the popularity of football in Canada, and the existence of leagues for all ages for boys and young men across the country, the Canadian Football League (CFL), unlike the NFL, has not secured major television contracts and ticket revenues remain the primary source of income for its franchises. Once earning 50 per cent of NFL salaries (in 1975), CFL players earned just over 5 per cent of the average NFL salary, or $75,000, in 2006.[21] The Grey Cup championship of 2008 between the Calgary Stampeders and the Montreal Allouettes drew just over 2.4 million viewers in Canada. In comparison, the 2008 NFL Super Bowl game between the New York Giants and New England Patriots drew more than 4.2 million Canadian spectators.[22] From time to time, the Canadian media raises the issue of the quality of play in both leagues, pitting NFL fans against CFL fans.[23] Without question, both leagues profile big, fast, talented players emerging mainly from the NCAA football system, with some Canadian players, who all play in similar working conditions and environments. Differences in equipment, preparation, training camps, stadia, atmosphere, staff, coaching are not easily discernable; players such as Warren Moon and Jeff Garcia starred in both leagues. Yet profile, salaries, and spectatorship differ significantly.

Body Break: Sport as Work

As discussed earlier in the book, fur traders competed with one another, testing skills used in their trade for fun and to reaffirm physical hierarchies. Middle- and upper-class men competed with other men of similar status for fun and for competition within social hierarchies but not in 'work' environments. Tavern-goers wrestled, arm wrestled, and fought with fists to settle scores and to enjoy and assert their physical abilities but only the gamblers made some form of living within these social settings. Professional athletes found a market for their skills in limited capacities in the late nineteenth century and, to a greater extent, by the early 1920s. Since then, and more recently in the past four to five decades, the sport workplace has emerged as a more complex, unique environment with a network of relationships reaching between owners, coaches, players, and fans.

For generations, environments such as in the NFL, CFL, and all of the major leagues, have been glamorized to the extent that many consider professional sport to be 'play' for grown men who earn large salaries, lead luxurious lifestyles, and are significantly removed from the day-to-day lives of average people. While salaries are disproportionately high in our common sense understanding, professional athletes work in specific conditions that would elsewhere not be tolerated by law or within common standards of health and safety.[24]

Through this process, the professional sport environment has become normative, indeed reinforced, by admiring spectators and ticket buyers, who helped to create star images for players and what they represented in a world that seemed so far removed from daily life. Imagine, for example, meanings and values inherent in the sports world superimposed in other settings: an autoworker signing autographs after his or her shift; a bank executive from Halifax trading a clerk to Victoria for 'future considerations'; a Petro Canada gas station attendant sent out by his supervisor to fight an Esso rival across the street; an elementary teacher who conducts classes with a broken wrist, not telling anyone, for fear of being replaced by another teacher; a lawyer screaming obscenities or throwing a water bottle at a judge because she didn't agree with the judge's decision. This is not to suggest that competitive physical environments do not exist in the traditional workplace; rather, unique sub-cultural values have emerged in sport, which position certain ideas—which would not be accepted outside of sport—about strength, toughness, masculinity, risk, and violence in social hierarchies that are understood, accepted, and celebrated.

Pain, Injury, and Risk

Chapter 8 discusses the historical factors which led to the establishment and acceptance of gender hierarchies in sport. These factors help us understand codes of masculine honour and practice in sport and why athletes consent to these conditions, and even protect what appear to be rather negative or harmful practices, in their environments of competition and training. As Young suggests, athletes consent to participating in harmful or dangerous environments because, historically, they have had little power in the definition of the working conditions in the sport workplace.[25] In order to benefit from the systems of reward extant in the sport, players must adhere to codes of conduct or they risk demotion, ostracization, or ridicule. Careers for athletes are structured, for the most part, on a prescriptive basis, with years of service in minor leagues, attending training camps, responding to coaches and personal trainers, and meeting the expectations of parents, peers, and media. Children learn not only from television broadcasts and sports reporting; they become part of lived environments, where personal traits and values are taught as much as skill, technique, and strategy. Hundreds of hours each year are invested in these competitive experiences, so the exposure to particular codes of conduct is far-reaching. Children learn how to 'own' one another through skilled moves or speed, or physical domination. Children learn to cheer when opponents or even teammates during practice, are levelled by hard tackles or body checks. Spectacular hits are valued, perhaps even more valued than skilled, technical moves. Children learn early what constitutes 'cowardly' behaviour in the sport setting or, conversely, how to respond when physically dominating another player.[26] Individuals who exhibit valued physical and technical skills are revered within the sport hierarchy, and identified as those who show promise to move on to the next level. These skills and techniques serve young players well, for achieving success in sport.

Along the way, however, in most North American sports children learn to or are pressured into ignoring or suppressing 'unwanted' signals indicating pain and injury. Enduring, or playing through pain, has been a fundamental part of sport for decades that is both inculcated from early ages and demanded at the professional level.[27] The concept has become so normalized that athletes are taught that there are different types of pain—those which require medical attention and those for which 'nagging' must be tolerated. At all levels of competitive sport, athletes attempt to reach the highest levels and cling to the opportunities available to them; as a matter of course, they desperately compete for a position on the team. Inability to play due to bodily pain or injury becomes an obstacle to success. For some, this implies the threat of being replaced by a rival player; in other words, the 'natural' progression through the competitive ranks is halted. In addition to issues of advancement, coaches and peers may ostracize players whose acceptance of injury is perceived to jeopardize the team's success. Consequently, coaches expect players to continue playing

In sports such as football boys pursuing CFL or NFL dreams begin training early. (Courtesy of Kevin Wamsley)

through discomfort and injuries, and so do their peers. Even those not familiar with competitive sport environments understand that the language of weakness invokes labels of 'femininity' to categorize a victim of a schoolyard injury or a childhood fall: 'wimp', 'pussy', 'chicken-shit', 'baby'. A normalizing strategy for addressing pain and injury is to honour it, to represent it as a sort of 'war wound'.[28] In 1964, NHL player Bobby Baun returned to the ice after breaking a bone in his leg; he went on to score the overtime, winning goal in game six of the Stanley Cup play-offs.[29] Baun's return in spite of his injury has become iconic in hockey lore and his actions represent an enduring message to athletes who experience pain. And, these strategies are not just invoked by male athletes. Young and White found that competitive female athletes displayed similar attitudes toward pain and injury.[30]

Honouring Injury Recovery and Rehabilitation

Each season, the NHL hosts an awards ceremony to honour its best players. These awards include, for example, the most valuable player, the top goaltender, the best defenseman, the best coach, the best rookie, and the most sportsmanlike player. In the company of these prestigious awards is the Bill Masterton trophy, which is awarded by the Professional Hockey Writers' Association to the player who best 'exemplifies the qualities of perseverance, sportsmanship and dedication to hockey'.[31] Bill Masterton was a rookie player for the Minnesota North Stars in the NHL. He was killed during the 1968 season when he struck his head on the ice after being checked by two players. Since the trophy was first awarded after the 1967–68 season, the writers have voted for athletes who were considered to be hard-working, team players, defensive players, players working extensively for charities, and players who fought back from disease and injury. Since 1985, however, with the exception of only a few players, the Masterton trophy has been awarded to players who have battled health and injury problems. These have included multiple knee injuries, spine injuries, various forms of cancer, surgeries, meningitis, and concussions. In a way, the recovery process has become ritualized in professional hockey and the Masterson trophy now signifies this process by normalizing risk[32] and rewarding athletes who have worked hard to recover and who were able to return to the ice under trying circumstances. Young et al. refer to a concomitant recovery of identity in rehabilitation, whereby some athletes are willing to risk long-term disability to regain their pre-injury sense of self.[33] It follows then, in many respects, that the argument raised by Gruneau and Whitson about preserving masculine pride in the context of losing in hockey is also applicable in the context of injury and rehabilitation. They maintain that fighting hard and not quitting or admitting defeat 'have been minimum conditions for symbolically maintaining the integrity of masculine identity in a losing cause'.[34] Young, White, and McTeer have suggested that following serious injury, athletes feel a certain betrayal by their bodies and a sense of disempowerment (or loss of masculine integrity) through the whole process. Fighting hard, or refusing to quit, during rehabilitation or the 'comeback' provides a focal point for the re-assertion of that lost sense of self, functioning as a marker of masculine identity.[35]

While at one level the reproduction of appropriate and valued masculinities and both short- and long-term health issues are important points of analysis, at another level the economic concerns of players and owners and labour relationships cannot be disconnected from gender ordering. As much as the players have been commodified as financial and community 'investments' by owners, it is in fact hockey culture, providing, for the average player, only short-term employment, that has engineered a certain dependency on 'that last big contract' before retirement, the contract that will supposedly solidify the player's financial standing after hockey. And yet, within that culture, the immediacy of economic concerns is transposed into the language of masculinity and perseverance. The language that describes the recovery process and the comeback speaks generally about the benefit to hockey and the immediate impact on the injured player's team; and the successful comeback player is praised for showing character, determination, perseverance, and even toughness following a difficult rehabilitation program—all valued qualities that can be used to replace the masculine traits habitually attributed to the healthy professional hockey player. Players return, then, with reconstructed bodies. For example, the 1996 Masterton trophy winner, Gary Roberts of the Calgary Flames, was told after two operations on his neck that because of the injuries that he had sustained a return to hockey would mean permanent disability. He then spent six months 'reconstructing' his body, adding 'layers' of muscle in appropriate areas so that he might play again. The physical component of the comeback, however, is only a part of the injury process, and can't be disconnected from emotional, ideological, or even economic considerations. The 1990 Masterton winner, Gord Kluzak of the Boston Bruins, was known by his teammates as 'Gordzilla' because of his seeming immunity to physical impairment; he finally retired after having 11 knee operations in six years. In between operations, Kluzak rode an exercise bike for hours while the team practised. On their way back from the ice, players ritually checked his knee for swelling to gauge the prospects for his comeback. Indeed the procedures of rehabilitation and the comeback are as ritualized and normalized as off-season training or mid-season practice.

Until recent decades, the responsibility to let injured players return to the ice often remained with the player. However, all major league professional teams now have physicians who consult the team on player health, along with a group of athletic therapists, trainers, and physiotherapists. The short-term health of players is more carefully monitored; yet long-term health does not receive the same public consideration or press. From the perspective of owners, marquee players have a direct and immediate short-term impact on gate receipts and team paraphernalia sales. Bobby Orr, for example, was one of the first marquee players to receive considerable North American press for a series of knee injuries. At a time when gate receipts were the dominant source of revenues for owners, the presence of Orr in the line-up significantly affected gate takes in Boston, Minnesota, and Pittsburgh. Yet, even though Orr was the most popular and skilled player of his time, has had a lasting impact on the style of play in the NHL, and won the best defensemen award eight times and the league's most valuable player award three times, when it appeared as though he might not recover from his fifth knee operation (in seven years), the Bruins showed little interest in him. The line between franchise hero and financial liability became distinctly thin for Bobby Orr.

Focusing on athletes who successfully return to the ice, however, the comeback remains a significant part of the mid-season subtexts generated by the sport media. As part of public relations and event hype, special ceremonies are often provided for star players, such as the frenzy around Mario Lemieux and the press build-ups for former role players like Cam Neely and Wendel Clark. So much excitement was built around Lemieux's first comeback from a herniated disc that coach Bob Johnson had to warn his players to stay focused. During Lemieux's third comeback, after yet another back operation and treatment for Hodgkin's disease, the Pittsburgh Penguins built pre-game celebrations around the event, announcing his arrival to the ice after all of the other players and then following up with a blast of fireworks. Lemieux won the Masterton trophy in 1993. The rewards for returning to the ice after months of painful rehabilitation, however, can be short-lived. In the celebrated cases of Gord Kluzak, Cam Neely, Tim Kerr, and Pat Lafontaine, expectations for playing were only on a game-to-game basis. They were Masterton trophy winners, one and all.

The emergent infrastructural support provided by professional sport teams in the form of extensive medical and rehabilitation programs corresponds to the ideological support provided by positive media representations of personal character and toughness. This reinforces a culture of risk that is, in part, also reproduced by the players and coaches themselves. The Masterton trophy provides implicit legitimacy to violent play, painful injury, rehabilitation, and the acceptance of the risks of long-term disability directly related to comebacks after serious injuries. The list of operations and catastrophic injuries sustained by Masterton winners is lengthy, but tends to become overshadowed by the public representation of their resolve to return to play and, perhaps more distinctly, by the lack of concern shown for their health after hockey.

Following Masterton's death on the ice, players such as Chicago's Stan Mikita and Pit Martin broke longstanding hockey tradition and chose to wear helmets. Martin, the 1970 Masterton winner, claimed that team management actively encouraged players not to wear helmets. Even as recently as the early 1990s, players such as Craig Mctavish received extra contract bonuses to play without a helmet. The New York Rangers' Jean Ratelle was the first player awarded the Masterton trophy for an injury-related comeback; in 1971, he was awarded the trophy for returning successfully after a spinal fusion operation. The Flyers' famously toothless captain Bobby Clarke won the next year; despite requiring 70 units of insulin a day for his diabetes condition, Clarke played in the NHL for 15 seasons. Lowell Macdonald won the Masterton trophy in 1973, explicitly in recognition for his comeback from six knee operations. Rod Gilbert, of the New York Rangers and winner of the trophy in 1975, had two spinal fusion operations in junior hockey after catching a skate on some garbage lying on the ice. He was forced to wear a steel corset in order to play and refused an operation which would have alleviated his pain. Tim Kerr, the winner of the 1989 Masterton trophy, endured five shoulder operations before he retired. As mentioned above, Gord Kluzak was awarded the trophy in 1990 after his eleventh knee operation. Goaltender Mark

Fitzpatrick won it in 1992 after enduring muscle and joint pain and swollen feet, hands, and forearms from a rare white blood cell disorder caused by vitamin supplements. The now-retired 1994 winner, Cam Neely, carries a brick-sized mass of calcified muscle in his left thigh because of hockey injuries. Pat Lafontaine, the 1995 Masterton winner, suffered extended bouts of memory loss and dizziness caused by a series of concussions over the course of his career.[36]

Another statistic commonly recorded in professional sport which reveals the sub-cultural attitude towards injury is the number of consecutive games played. In hockey, the record holder is called the 'Ironman', a prestigious title that is valued by coaches, managers, owners, players, and fans. Doug Jarvis won the Masterton in 1987 after playing 962 consecutive NHL games. There was tremendous media and public attention when Cal Ripken Jr broke the major league baseball record for consecutive games. The 'Ironman' records in professional sport speak volumes about the widespread understanding that injury is considered to be an everyday part of sport and players who practice and play without injury time-off are very unique. The Jarvis record and his position as hockey's Ironman distinguish the labour

Former NHL star Pat Lafontaine, who won the Masterton trophy in 1995, was named to the Hall of Fame on 11 June 2003. Lafontaine scored 468 goals and 545 assists in his 15 seasons with the New York Islanders, Buffalo, and the New York Rangers. (© Reuters/CORBIS)

relationship in hockey as being symbolic for both management and players—ownership has a direct economic interest in the durability of players, and the social meanings attached to the Ironman distinction are constructed as significant markers of self definition for the players. The sports page of the *Calgary Herald* newspaper, for example, reported in 1997 that Edmonton Oiler Doug Weight's consecutive game streak had ended at 314. Weight played for several weeks with cracked vertebrae, which to him felt as if 'someone was sticking a needle in my back all night'.[37]

The meanings associated with consecutive games played are not dissimilar from those linked to players who launch successful comebacks from injury and disease. In a sense, the Masterton trophy is a tribute to 'Ironmen' of a different sort. Yet, the common denominator for hockey culture is a performance-based notion of the able body and the capacity to play, regardless of long-term health. The values of perseverance, sportsmanship, and dedication have recently been directed for the most part towards the celebration of multiple rehabilitations and the '**comeback**', two key stages in the normalized injury process within hockey culture.[38] The injury process is legitimized throughout hockey in its labour relationships; media representations; subcultural attitudes towards violence, pain, and rehabilitation; and in the common popular cultural understanding of hockey. Perhaps one of the best indicators of the levels of social acceptance and complicity is that the injury process in hockey should generate widespread empathy but not anger or concern. Although from time to time, former players with chronic pain such as Rich Sutter[39] and with lifelong disability such as Jim Harrison[40] speak out against the appalling treatment of hockey players and their post-career suffering, the voices from within the game remain silenced by ideological loyalties to a socially constructed sense of traditional masculine 'propriety' in hockey. The tremendous cultural weight of hockey, moreover, which is sustained in part by pervasive and powerful notions of appropriate and **exemplary masculinities**, makes a reflexive examination of the injury process and the comeback, by direct participants such as players and coaches and complicit representatives such as the sportswriters, a difficult project. Even though Bill Masterton might perhaps be pleased that hockey players are now wearing helmets, it now seems that the trophy awarded in his name tends to legitimize and reinforce an often dehumanizing sense of physicality in professional hockey culture.

The CBC program, *The Fifth Estate*, aired a documentary entitled 'Head Games' in November 2008. CBC reported startling information on the life expectancy of athletes in professional football. In the NFL, if a playing career is longer than five years, the life expectancy is 55 (52 for linemen)—20 years less than the rest of the male population. The documentary focused on the careers of Edmonton Eskimos linemen Bill Stevenson, York Hentschel, and David Boone. All were members of the five-time Grey Cup champion Eskimos teams from 1978–82. All suffered multiple concussions over the course of their careers, and all suffered from symptoms of depression, substance abuse, severe difficulties in their private lives, and all died prematurely.[41] A Scripps Howard News Service study of 3,850 football players over the past 100 years stated that these athletes were at a 52 per cent greater risk for dying of heart disease, relating primarily to weight and obesity. The study also noted that 'the average weight in the NFL has grown by 10 per cent since 1985 to a current [2006] average of 248 pounds. The heaviest position, offensive tackle, went from 281 pounds two decades ago to 318 pounds.'[42]

Sport Violence

As discussed in Chapter 8, no other institutionalized cultural activity in Canadian history has contributed more to naturalizing violence in society than sport. Historically, sport leagues have been permitted by the judiciary to police themselves, that is, to solve their own problems when it came to assault and violence on the field or ice. The issue received considerable press in the last quarter of the twentieth century but significant change in sport has not been forthcoming. Fans watched in horror, in September 2007, when NFL Buffalo Bills player Kevin Everett suffered a catastrophic spine injury following helmet-to-helmet contact when he tackled the Denver Bronco, Domenik Hickson. Unlike Mike Utley, a guard for the Detroit Lions who suffered an injury which paralyzed him below the chest, Everett walked again.[43] In professional hockey, it has been typical that violence and fighting receive significant press, immediately following a serious incident where harm has been inflicted. On Friday 5 January 2009 Whitby Dunlops hockey player Don Sanderson died in hospital, three weeks after his head hit the ice during a hockey fight.[44]

Less than two weeks later, the Ontario Hockey League (OHL) Commissioner David Branch announced a new rule prohibiting players from removing helmets to engage in fighting.[45] While the rule change dealt specifically with the common practice of OHL players purposefully removing their helmets to fight, it did not address the fact the fighting is not only permitted in the highest levels of Canadian hockey, it is encouraged and celebrated. As a result of Steve Moore's career-ending injuries caused by Todd Bertuzzi's blindside punch to Moore's head, these issues received some public debate in 2004 and beyond. Police charged Bertuzzi with assault, he pled guilty, and, in addition to one year's probation, he performed 80 hours of community service. Had he assaulted Moore in a similar fashion, off the ice, it is likely that the punishment would have been more severe. Marty McSorley was found guilty of assault in 2000 after slashing Donald Brashear in the head, causing him to lose consciousness and hit his head on the ice. He was sentenced to 18 months probation.[46] The NHL suspended both players but did nothing to address the issue of on-ice violence and fighting.

In spite of 66 charges of assault in hockey between 1905 and 1982, the NHL has done little to curb violence or fighting in the game.[47] In fact, the expansion of the NHL in the late 1960s led to the development of new tactics of intimidation and violence as competitive strategies, to offset imbalances of talent between teams. Players took on roles as fighters to protect star players or to change the momentum of a game. Fighting is a normalized part of hockey—players still argue that fighting is part of the game. One of the corollary arguments has it that fighting serves as a 'safety valve' in a game where tensions build to levels of imminent volatility.[48] Violent stick work, it is argued, would replace fighting and injuries would be much more severe. Apply the same logic to a hypothetical model of 'road rage' or conflict between motorists on the street: we would have to permit fist fights between motorists in traffic to settle their differences to release the tension created by driving and competing for space in dense and congested traffic; otherwise, recourse to any available weapon to create more serious injuries might occur—keys, tire irons, brief cases. How is it that in Canada's official national sports of summer and winter, lacrosse and hockey, fighting has been endorsed by owners, coaches, players, the media, and spectators, while in other high contact sports, such as football, fighting is rare? In sports where space is contested hotly, with less contact, such as in basketball and soccer, fighting is also rare.

The incidence and severity of risks, injuries, fighting, and the widespread support to sustain violence in sport, do not occur in a social vacuum. From the earliest days of duels and tavern fights, there has always been public violence in sport and recreational activities, tolerated to a great extent by law. For example, as a socially constructed activity, boxing has endured various acts of legislation against it, the deaths of boxers, and the long-term disabilities caused by repeated head trauma. Sport entrepreneur Vince McMahon has earned millions of dollars in professional wrestling, trading upon the public interest[49] in violent masculinity—the juxtaposition of body building and **hypermuscularity**, Hollywood-styled plotlines and acting, physical skill and risky manoeuvres, and technical stunts.[50] As athletic performance, professional wrestling, which is now a combination of sports entertainment, extensive weight training, stunt training, and character acting, is a unique and arduous occupation requiring the right combination of bodily attributes, unique skills, and character traits.[51] Pro-wrestlers meet a demanding schedule with cards of events which take them across North America and sometimes overseas. Size and appearance play a significant role in determining a wrestler's marketability. Hypermuscularity has become a staple attribute, in

Death Too Young: Professional Wrestlers Who Died Before 50[53]

Ring Name	Name	Age
Andre the Giant	Andre Rousimoff	46
Adrian Adonis	Keith Franke	34
Flyin' Brian Pillman		35
Ravishing Rick Rude	Richard Rood	40
Mr Perfect	Curt Henning	44
British Bulldog	David Smith	39
Yokozuna	Rodney Anoia	34
Miss Elizabeth	Elizabeth Hulette	42
The Blue Blazer	Owen Hart	34
Hawk	Michael Hegstrand	45
Hercules Hernandez	Raymond Hernandez	46
Eddie Guerrero		38
Bam Bam Bigelow	Scott Bigelow	45
Chris Benoit		40
Crush	Brian Adams	44
Sensational Queen	Sherri Martel	49
Big Boss Man	Ray Traylor	41
Punisher / Test	Andrew Martin	33

addition to height and weight, residual aspects of human circus shows of earlier eras. Andre the Giant, for example, at 7 feet 2 inches tall and 500 pounds, was one of the most popular wrestlers of the twentieth century. Several factors in the wrestling profession, including size, drug consumption, dangerous stunts, and a heavy reliance on automobile transportation to meet demanding schedules have been cited as contributing to an unusually long list of wrestlers who have died relatively young.[52]

More recently, however, wrestling extravaganzas have been challenged by the popularity of **mixed martial arts** contests of various sorts, particularly Ultimate Fighting Championship (UFC) events which pit opponents against each other who use boxing, kicking, and wrestling in combination to achieve a knock-out, submission, stopped fight, or win by points. A tremendous amount of blood is spilled during these events, knock-outs are brutal, and bones are broken. The popularity of UFC speaks volumes about society's current lust for violent entertainment. *Sports Illustrated* claimed in 2006 that ultimate fighting had surpassed boxing in popularity.[54] This was clearly evident in Canada when the UFC champion, Canadian fighter George St Pierre, was named Sportsnet athlete of the year in 2008. (On the other hand, St Pierre was not even nominated for the prestigious Lou Marsh trophy won by multiple Olympic medal winner Chantal Peticlerc that year.) Like boxing and professional wrestling, UFC derives significant revenues from pay-per-view events, and now draws accolades from the celebrity crowd that used to grace the major boxing events. One of the most viewed pay-per-view events,[55] UFC made its debut in Canada with UFC 83 in Montreal in April 2008, but the activity remains illegal in Ontario, under Section 83 of the Criminal Code. United States Senator, and later Presidential candidate, John McCain called the activity 'human cockfighting.'[56]

Gender Discrimination

Women, too, in recent decades have entered the ranks of violent sports such as boxing and mixed martial arts. Just as the Preston Rivulettes hockey team fought opponents on a regular basis and body checked their way to four national championships during the 1930s, female athletes have not been averse to rough play and violence.[57] Debi Purcell started her website, FighterGirls.com, to promote women's mixed martial arts. The site lists hundreds of wrestlers, submission wrestlers, kickboxers, boxers, mixed martial arts competitors, and boasts more than 26,000 members in its chat forum.[58] The increase in the number of females participating in violent sports is an indication of the fact that there are more opportunities for women to participate in sport than ever. At the Beijing Olympics, 4,746 female athletes participated, representing 42 per cent of all athletes competing.[59]

However, the Canadian Association for the Advancement of Women and Sport and Physical Activity (CAAWS) reports that 11–14-year-old girls were less likely to participate in sport in 2005 than 1992.[60] Reflecting on the issue of women's participation, generally, Lenskyj disputes the notion that as long as girls and women are better supported, have more resources, and have better role models, there will be full participation in sport. These **liberal** approaches, she argues, do not address the systemic barriers that women encounter in sport.[61] As mentioned above, professional sport and its values dominate the Canadian landscape. These values privilege men and tend to subordinate women. A gender order in sport has been reproduced and sustained since the nineteenth century; one need only follow the structure of professional sport, opportunities presented for professional female athletes, salaries and prize money, team ownership and senior management, and coaching and staff opportunities. There is significant resistance to permitting the best female athletes to participate on men's teams or in individual competitions such as golf and tennis. Lenskyj contends that, as long as women participate in a model of sport that favours men, women will not experience full participation. In this model, there will always be a **sexualization** of female athletes in the media, expectations of compulsory heterosexuality, and harassment. Concomitantly, in its promotion of hierarchies of masculinity, of the physical and psychological domination of others, and of **homophobia**, many men do not directly benefit from this model either.

The elite sport training model, too, has always played a significant role in sustaining a gender order in and through sport. When the Olympic athletes marched into the stadium in Beijing in 2008, men and women wore different uniforms, spectators and home viewers had different expectations for males and females, television broadcasts created different stories about them, and the Internet presented selective pictures and edited clips of the Olympic experience. These men and women pursued the same goals, they trained equally hard, yet their social experiences and the ways they are remembered are remarkably different. Such is the case, historically, as men and women have experienced sport differently and, indeed, it has been the conscious effort of sport leaders, media personnel, fans, and spectators to create oppositional classifications in the social meanings which contextualize men's and women's sport. We have discussed this in earlier chapters. Yet, in spite of considerable retrenchment of this vast cultural crevice, there are still, in the twenty-first century, significant differences with respect to sport in people's perceptions of what is appropriately masculine and feminine. In other words, at all levels, from the International Olympic Committee (IOC) to the armchair spectator, people have expectations about how men and women should look and behave.

Even though girls and young women now bring their own physical styles to sport, sport leaders fear the dropping levels of participation. (Courtesy of Kevin Wamsley)

Since the first meeting at the Sorbonne in 1894, this sort of categorizing and delimiting has always been a fundamental aspect of the Olympic Games, on issues of class and gender, and more implicitly, race.[62] The Olympic Games are one of the dominant institutions which reproduce the present gender order in sports, a system of unequal and sometimes oppressive relations between men and women or different masculinities and femininities. Such orders may be constructed by force or by collusion, and they are not static; people may be coerced into oppressive relationships or they may consent to participating. Western society's professional sports and sporting institutions, such as the Olympic Games, endorse heterosexuality and reinforce the privilege and power of heterosexual men over all other men and over all women.[63]

As argued earlier in this book, no other global institution in the twentieth century did more to increase women's sport participation than the Olympic Games.[64] The Cold War was the most influential force in popularizing the Olympic Games in the twentieth century, and the widespread inclusion of Soviet women into the Olympic sports program set off a chain reaction among western nations to match their achievements in the race for medals. In this respect, the Olympics have contributed to narrowing the gap which defined the cultural boundaries delimiting the importance of women in relation to men in sport. But these gains in participation have come at some cost.

The Cold War and Beyond: Gender, Performance, and Performance Enhancement

The widespread adoption of Henri Didon's dictum 'Citius, Altius, Fortius' ('Swifter, Higher, Stronger') as the Olympic motto has literally been the death knell for some athletes. Cultural fascination with the idea of human progress, conceived broadly in the nineteenth century and institutionalized in the twentieth century, has led to remarkable scientific, medical, and cultural achievements but, unfortunately, the obsession with progress and the perceived symbolic and economic value of sport has led to extensive drug use and the ritual abuse of men's and women's bodies.[65] Breaking records—to surmount the constraints of height, weight, distance—is the compulsion of our time, shared by athletes, coaches, administrators, sports leaders, and fans alike.

The unrestrained celebration of human performance has always been fundamental to the Olympic Games. The organized production of performance, for the most part a twentieth-century fetish, has inspired the disciplines of physical education, exercise physiology, biomechanics, and coaching. International politics and the pursuit of the symbolic capital of sport now position the Olympic Games as a significant aspect of international policy and expenditure for most nations. For the United States, the Soviet Union, and their respective allies, elite male athletes provided the **symbolic capital** to advance their respective political ideologies as the most visible alternative to an unthinkable nuclear war.[66] However, the unfortunate corollary to the emergence of **hyper-competition** has been the physical toll on human bodies, male and female. With the exception of the space program, there has never been a cultural field so hotly contested, with so many physical, human, and monetary resources leveraged, as in and through sport during the Cold War period. However, the problematic consequences to men's and women's bodies have been manifold, including catastrophic injuries, drug-related illnesses and side effects, risk-related and coincidental accidents, and generally unhealthy and extreme bodily practices.

For some men, particularly in strength and speed-related events, a directive toward full-time training, weight lifting, dieting, extensive drug-taking programs, physiotherapy, and physical rehabilitation inherent in mid- to late-twentieth-century sporting culture entailed an implicit directive forward. In Western nations, in this context, it was the strength of the *male* athlete that came to be positioned as a more salient aspect of Cold War sport politics; media, athlete, and coach alike refused to view female athletes in Western nations in the same light as female athletes from communist countries. Thus, the focus in the West shifted once again to the feminized sports, as opposed to the heavy events dominated by Eastern female athletes. For male athletes, however, accusations concerning performance-enhancing substances from East or West did not seem to warrant as much public attention until the Ben Johnson scandal of 1988 (see Chapter 6). By that time, the Olympic movement had long been complicit in the creation of a culture of high performance rife with the abuse of human bodies through drug-taking, over-training, and chronic, sometimes life-threatening injuries. Indeed, pushing the human body past its physiological limits remains a fundamental part of the rhetoric employed in the systematic selling of the Olympics to all corners of the world.[67]

With the International Association of Athletics Federations (IAAF) and IOC usurpation of control over the organization and regulation of sport for women, coupled with the gendered interpretations of female performance manifested in the increasing reach of the sport media, and combined with the hyper-competition of the Cold War era, the foundations were established for significant crises in women's sport competition. The Olympic Games historically have been, in part, the cause of serious problems in women's sport. Certainly, as a result of long histories of male domination in sport, most consumers of competitive sport were receptive to the imagery of the 'strong' man and 'graceful' woman created during the celebration of the Olympic Games. But the channelling of women and girls into feminized sports gave rise to the challenge to sustain these sports over the long term, in the face of the dominance of measurable and quantifiable performance sports. Unlike those sports, the qualitative, judged events required more sustained imagination over time to maintain public interest. Such sports found it necessary to reinvent themselves on a continual basis by recalibrating the scales and standards by which cumulative enhancements of performance could be measured, thereby retaining the ideal of progress in these sports that allowed them to remain as marketable as the quantifiable events. Consequently, over a period of 30 years, the sports of gymnastics, diving, and figure skating continuously adopted increasingly difficult codes of adjudication to sustain the illusion of progress.[68] It became evident in the late 1960s and early 1970s that once women's bodies reached a certain age or stage of physical maturity, physical growth and bodily shape impeded movement in space, particularly for somersaulting actions and other complex patterns of movement. The average strength to body weight ratio diminishes for women as they grow older. For male gymnasts, this was not a problem within the context of ever-increasing levels of difficulty in the sport. For female gymnasts and figure skaters, however, a distinct process of '**kindertraining**' within these sports occurred in response. As single somersaults turned to doubles and gymnastics manoeuvres became ever more difficult, elite athletes competed at younger and younger ages, and with smaller physical frames. In collusion with international and national federations, judges were responsible for qualitative changes in these sports inasmuch as their scoring represented implicit statements about the desirable female body. The occasional private yet explicit comment to particular athletes about losing weight added to the impact.[69] It became clear in the 1970s, to coaches and administrators that 'girl' athletes would win medals; consequently they had to be recruited and trained at much younger ages. Coaches, who were untrained in the physiology of exercise and ignorant of nutritional requirements, developed unrealistic, unhealthy expectations for their female athletes.[70] Indeed, at the greatest extremes of abuse, it has been reported that female gymnasts were impregnated to delay the normal physical changes of puberty, to increase flexibility, or to increase levels of endurance.[71]

Over several decades, IOC leadership played a significant role in feminizing women's sports and the Games themselves did more to popularize the so-called 'aesthetic' sports than any other international competition. Consequently, women's gymnastics and figure skating from the mid-1970s to the present have been plagued by eating disorders, over-training, and decreasing ages of children in elite sport training centres.[72] The treatment of these athletes by the sporting community has been no less than pathologically disturbing. And coaches, administrators, broadcasters, and spectators must all share the blame. These intolerable circumstances raise some serious questions about modern sport; indeed, is it reasonable to ask young children to train several hours a day? Is it reasonable for a sport body to impose codes of difficulty and judging expectations which require increasingly smaller bodies, with potentially damaging, low levels of body fat? The IOC responded to sustained criticism by turning to the international body, Federation Internationale de Gymnastique (FIG). In 2009, the minimum age for all gymnasts participating in FIG events, including the world championships in the year preceding the Olympic Games, will be 16 years of age.[73]

As discussed earlier, another major issue for high performance sport was doping. Ingesting performance-enhancing substances has plagued the professional sports as well, particularly baseball, as the home-run hitters such as Barry Bonds, Mark McGuire, Sammy Sosa, Jose Canseco, and Jason Giambi ran afoul with authorities. Canada's response to the widely publicized Ben Johnson steroid scandal of 1988 was the Dubin Inquiry, commissioned by Prime Minister Brian Mulroney. The Inquiry disclosed that elite athletes at the highest levels were routinely using performance enhancers. The doping problem was endemic. While the Inquiry served to counteract the embarrassment of the Canadian sport system and its leaders, more stringent doping control mechanisms were put in place. The World Anti-Doping Agency (WADA) was formed in 1999, with headquarters in Montreal, as an arms-length organization of the IOC.

Since the 1970s, the results of drug testing have received significant press, and particularly since 1988, even though doping has existed within the Olympics and the Tour de France for many decades.[74] The elite sport community is concerned, in the first instance, that doping is a form of cheating and, in the second instance, that taking drugs may be dangerous or unhealthy. Long-term studies of the affects of steroids on human health have not been conducted, so the evidence is limited. Some studies suggest that small doses taken under medical supervision do not cause significant harm.[75] Kirkwood argues that we need to look beyond the traditional models of drug ingestion as cheating and examine why athletes take drugs to improve their performances or to increase size or why people take drugs to alter their appearances or their weight.[76] Further, it is difficult to raise the issue of what substances are healthy, within the context of high performance or professional sport, given the extreme training programs, competitive pressures, catastrophic and chronic injuries, violence to self and others, and hours of daily training for decades which constitute significant stresses upon an athlete's body over a lifespan. High level sport is not a healthy enterprise and, for the athletes specifically, this can be very difficult to discern. Beamish and Ritchie rightfully argue: '[f]or athletes, whose lives are spent right in the middle of the demands of high-performance sport, the distinction between health and pathology is even more difficult to make because tolerance for what is acceptable is increased imperceptibly each day and over the span of a career until it is changed dramatically.'[77]

There are many issues in contemporary sport, too many to discuss adequately here. Issues of race, gender, and social class are prevalent in society as they are prevalent in sport. Sport has different meanings for different people; it is significant for some and not so for others. Sport has created opportunities but it has also reinforced or created barriers in society. Sport today is not the sport of the nineteenth century, but neither is it better or worse. Sport and physical activity have always been an important part of Canadian history. Canadians take great pleasure in the various aspects of participating and watching. If we understand sport, we understand ourselves to a degree and that, in part, has been our mission in this text.

Related Websites

The World Anti –Doping Agency
http://www.wada-ama.org/en

Canadian Centre for Ethics in Sport
http://www.cces.ca

National Hockey League
http://www.nhl.com

Canadian Football League
http://www.cfl.ca

National Football League
http://www.nfl.com

National Basketball Association
http://www.nba.com

Major League Baseball
http://mlb.mlb.com/index.jsp

National Lacrosse League
http://www.nll.com

Ultimate Fighting Championship
http://www.ufc.com

World Wrestling Entertainment
http://www.wwe.com

Study Questions

1. Why is fighting tolerated in hockey but not in football and basketball?
2. What are the indicators that men and women are treated differently in sport?
3. Why would high-level athletes compete in environments which compromise their health and safety?
4. How did the idea of progress influence competition in sports both during and since the era of the Cold War?
5. Why do different standards and levels of tolerance for violence exist for sport in relation to broader society?
6. What roles do spectators assume within the economic model that sanctions exorbitant salaries for star athletes?

Notes

Chapter 2 Games and Contests in Early Canada

1. Cited from Michael Heine, *Arctic Sports: A Training and Resource Manual*, 2nd edn. Traditional Aboriginal Sport Coaching Resources, vol. 2 (Yellowknife: Sport North Federation, 2002), ch. 1, 3–4, from Knud Rasmussen, *Intellectual Culture of the Igloolik Eskimo* (Report of the Fifth Thule Expedition 1921–4), 1.

2. J.V. Wright, *A History of the Native People of Canada* (Hull: Canadian Museum of Civilization, 1995), 1–21.

3. We have limited our brief analysis to recent in-depth research on Aboriginal games, which incorporates Aboriginal voices, and to games that have had far-reaching influences in the post-Victorian period. For an excellent overview of the variety of games and traditions, see Morris Mott, 'Games and Contests of the First "Manitobans"', in Mott, ed., *Sports in Canada: Historical Readings* (Toronto: Copp Clark Pitman, 1989), 18–27.

4. See, for example, Victoria Paraschak, 'Native Sport History: Pitfalls and Promises', *CJHS* 20, 1 (May 1989): 57–68; Paraschak, 'Racialized Spaces: Cultural Regulation, Aboriginal Agency and Powwows', *Avante* 2 (1996): 7–18; Paraschak, 'Sport Festivals and Race Relations in the Northwest Territories of Canada', in Grant Jarvie, ed., *Sport, Racism and Ethnicity* (London, England: Falmer Press, 1991), 74–93; Paraschak, 'Variations in Race Relations: Native Peoples in Sport in Canada', *Sociology of Sport Journal* 14, 1 (1997): 1–27; Paraschak, Michael Heine, and James McAra, 'Native and Academic Knowledge Interests: A Dilemma', in Kevin B. Wamsley, ed., *Method and Methodology in Sport and Cultural History* (Dubuque, Iowa: Brown & Benchmark, 1995), 62–8; Michael Heine, 'Gwich'in Tsii'in: A History of Gwich'in Athapaskan Games', PhD dissertation (University of Alberta, 1995); John Bloom, *To Show What an Indian Can Do: Sports at Native American Boarding Schools* (Minneapolis: University of Minnesota Press, 2000).

5. Secondary source analyses include but are not limited to: George Eisen, 'Games and Sporting Diversions of the North American Indians as Reflected in American Historical Writings of the Sixteenth and Seventeenth Centuries', *CJHSPE* 9, 1 (May 1978): 58–85; Edward Norbeck and Claire R. Farrer, eds., *Forms of Play of Native North Americans* (St Paul, Minn.: West Publishing, 1979); Stewart Culin, 'Games of the North American Indians', *Twenty-Fourth Annual Report of the Bureau of American Ethnology to the Smithsonian Institution, 1902–03* (Washington: US Government, 1907).

6. R. Douglas Francis, Richard Jones, and Donald B. Smith, *Origins: Canadian History to Confederation* (Toronto: Holt, Rinehart and Winston, 1988), 7–9. See also the map in Roger L. Nichols, *Indians in the United States and Canada: A Comparative History* (Lincoln: University of Nebraska Press, 1998), xxviii–xxix.

7. Michael Heine, Dene Games: *A Culture and Resource Manual*, Traditional Aboriginal Sport Coaching Resources, vol. 1 (Yellowknife: Sport North Federation, 1999), ch. 1, 4.

8. Ibid., ch. 1, 11.

9. Ibid., ch. 1, 15–19.

10. Heine, *Arctic Sports*, ch. 1, 40–1. The arm pull is a tug-of-war type contest, determined solely by strength. The two players sit opposite one another at close range and lock arms. On the referee or judge's signal, the opponents pull slowly backward until one of them is pulled out of position. The opponent loses if an arm is pulled to a straight position, if the opponent is pulled over forward, or if the opponent's arm is pulled to and touches one's chest. Ibid., ch. 4, 104–5. During the finger pull, opponents lock middle fingers as they face one another on the floor. They attempt to extend the opponent's arm or force the opponent to concede. Ibid., ch. 2, 33. There are other variations of these competitions. There are many variations of the high kick, including two-foot, one-foot, Alaskan, swing kick, toe kicks, and back extension kicks. The object of the high kick contests is to kick a suspended object with the appropriate footwork, landings, and contact required in each specific event. Ibid., ch. 4, 24–49.

11. Ibid., ch. 1, 7–9.

12. Heine, *Dene Games*, ch. 1, 19, from Tupou Pulu, *Beliefs from Nikolai* (Fairbanks: National Bilingual Materials Development Centre, Rural Education University of Alaska-Fairbanks, 1981).

13. William N. Fenton, *The Great Law and the Longhouse: A Political History of the Iroquois Confederacy* (Norman: University of Oklahoma Press, 1988), 24.

14. Heine, *Dene Games*, ch. 2, 15.

15. Ibid.

16. See Heine's extensive descriptions of these and many other games in *Arctic Sports* and *Dene Games*.

17. Mike Heine, with Ruth Caroll and Harvey Scott, *Traditional Dene Games: A Resourcebook, Games the Dene Elders Remember from the Old Days* (Yellowknife: Municipal and Community Affairs, n.d.), 105.

18. Mott, 'Games and Contests', 21; Heine, *Dene Games*, ch. 2, 185–6.

19. Donald M. Fisher, *Lacrosse: A History of the Game* (Baltimore: Johns Hopkins University Press, 2002), 12.

20. Ibid., 13–14.

21. In addition to Fisher, see also James A. Teit, *Tewaarathon (Lacrosse): Akwesasne's Story of Our National Game* (North American Indian Traveling College, 1978); Thomas Vennum Jr, *American Indian Lacrosse: Little Brother of War* (Washington: Smithsonian Institution Press, 1994); Michael A. Salter, 'The Effect of Acculturation on the Game of Lacrosse and Its Role as an Agent of Indian Survival', *CJHSPE* 3 (May 1972): 28–43.

22. Fisher, *Lacrosse*, 11–17.

23. Mott, 'Games and Contests', 20–1.

24. Ibid.

25. See for example, Bruce G. Trigger, 'The Road to Affluence: A Reassessment of Early Huron Responses to European Contact', in Ken S. Coates and Robin Fisher, eds, *Out of the Background: Readings on Canadian Native History* (Toronto: Irwin, 1998), 4–16.

26. Fisher, *Lacrosse*, 22.

27. Nichols, *Indians*, xiii.

28. Peter Cook argues that the general description of exchange relations between Aboriginals and Europeans as the 'fur trade' is misleading given the tremendous variety of goods exchanged. See 'Symbolic and Material Exchange in Intercultural Diplomacy: The French and the Hodenosaunee in the Early Eighteenth Century', in Jo-Anne Fiske, Susan Sleeper-Smith, and William Wicken, eds, *New Faces of the Fur Trade: Selected Papers of the Seventh North American Fur Trade Conference, Halifax, Nova Scotia, 1995* (East Lansing: Michigan State University, 1998), 75–100.

29. 'Les Voyages du Sieur de Champlain 1613', in H.P. Biggar and W.F. Ganong, eds, *The Works of Samuel de Champlain*, 6 vols, vol. 1, part III, book 1 (1604–7) (Toronto: Champlain Society, 1922), 447–8.

30. [Marc Lescarbot], *Nova Francia London 1609* (Amsterdam: Theatrum Orbis Terrarum, 1977), 111.

31. Frances et al., *Origins*, 67. See Alan Metcalfe's extensive descriptions of the physical capacities of these men in 'The Form and Function of Physical Activity in New France, 1534–1759', *CJHSPE* 1, 1 (May 1970): 45–64.

32. Francis Parkman, *The Old Regime in Canada* (Boston: Little, Brown, 1899), 151.

33. Metcalfe's 'Form and Function of Physical Activity' clearly demonstrates the ambivalence of the French governors to the fur traders.

34. Ibid., 57, from Raymond Douville and J. Casanova, *Daily Life in Early Canada* (London: Allen and Unwin, 1968), 150.

35. Parkman, *The Old Regime in Canada*, 178.

36. Sylvia Van Kirk, '"Women in Between": Indian Women in Fur Trade Society in Western Canada', in Coates and Fisher, eds, *Out of the Background*, 102–17.

37. Susan Sleeper-Smith, 'Furs and Female Kin Networks: The World of Marie Reaume L'archevêque Chevalier', in Fiske et al., eds, *New Faces of the Fur Trade*, 62.

38. Helen Hornbeck Ranner, 'The Career of Joseph La France, Coureur de Bois in the Upper Great Lakes', in Jennifer S.H. Brown, W.J. Eccles, and Donald P. Heldman, eds, *The Fur Trade Revisited: Selected Papers of the Sixth North American Fur Trade Conference, Mackinac Island, Michigan, 1991* (East Lansing: Michigan State University Press, 1994), 171–87.

39. See Frances et al., *Origins*, 76–9.

40. Jan Noel, 'New France: Les femmes favorisées', in Veronica Strong-Boag and Anita Clair Fellman, eds, *Rethinking Canada: The Promise of Women's History*, 3rd edn (Toronto: Oxford University Press, 2002), 34–56.

41. Frances et al., *Origins*, 79–80.

42. Noel, 'New France'.

43. Frances et al., *Origins*, 96–7.

44. A.R.M. Lower, *Canadians in the Making* (Toronto: Longman's Green and Co., 1958), 77.

45. Parkman, *The Old Regime in Canada*, 147.

46. Frances et al., *Origins*, 162–5.

47. Carolyn Podruchny, 'Unfair Masters and Rascally Servants? Labour Relations Among Bourgeois, Clerks and Voyageurs in the Montreal Fur Trade, 1780–1821', *Labour/Le Travail* 43 (Spring 1999), 43–70.

48. Carolyn Podruchny, 'Baptizing Novices: Ritual Moments among French Canadian Voyageurs in the Montreal Fur Trade, 1780–1821', *CHR* 83 (June 2002): 167.

49. Ronald S. Lappage, 'The Physical Feats of the Voyageur', *CJHS* 15, 1 (May 1984): 31.

50. Podruchny, 'Unfair Masters', 48.

51. Podruchny, 'Baptizing Novices', 165–95.

52. Konrad Gross, 'Coureurs-De-Bois, Voyageurs, and Trappers: The Fur Trade and the Emergence of an Ignored Canadian Literary Tradition', *Canadian Literature* 127 (Winter 1990): 69–93.

53. Lappage, 'Physical Feats', 33–4.

54. C.E.S. Franks, *The Canoe and White Water* (Toronto: University of Toronto Press, 1977), 136.

55. Podruchny, 'Unfair Masters', 56–7.

56. Ibid., 56.

57. W.J. Eccles, *The Canadian Frontier 1534–1760* (Toronto: Holt, Rinehart and Winston, 1969), 191.

58. Carolyn Podruchny, 'Festivities, Fortitude, and Fraternalism: Fur Trade Masculinity and the Beaver Club, 1785–1827', in Fiske et al., eds, *New Faces of the Fur Trade*, 31–52.

59. Gross, 'Coureurs-De-Bois, Voyageurs, and Trappers', 84, from *The Young Fur Traders* (London: P.R. Gawthorn, n.d.), 196.

60. Ibid., 85, from 'The Voyageurs of Canada', *British American Magazine* 1 (1863): 473.

Chapter 3 Games, Pastimes, and Sporting Life in British North America

1. Kevin B. Wamsley and Robert S. Kossuth, 'Fighting It Out in Nineteenth-Century Upper Canada/Canada West: Masculinities and Physical Challenges in the Tavern', *JSH* 27, 3 (Fall 2000): 413.

2. W.L. Morton, *The Kingdom of Canada: A General History from Earliest Times* (Toronto: McClelland & Stewart, 1972.)

3. See J.K. Johnson, *Becoming Prominent—Regional Leadership in Upper Canada 1791–1841* (Montreal and Kingston: McGill-Queen's University Press, 1989); E.M. Richards, 'The Joneses of Brockville and The Family Compact', *Ontario History* 60 (1969): 169–84; M.S. Cross, 'The Age of Gentility: The Formation of the Aristocracy in the Ottawa Valley', *Canadian Historical Association Annual Report* (1967): 105–17. On the concept of 'like-mindedness' and loyalty, see S.F. Wise, 'God's Peculiar Peoples', in W.L. Morton, ed., *The Shield of Achilles* (Toronto: McClelland & Stewart, 1968), 36–61.

4. Nancy B. Bouchier, *For the Love of the Game: Amateur Sport in Small-Town Ontario 1838–1895* (Montreal and Kingston: McGill-Queen's University Press, 2003), 14–15.

5. The Constitutional Act of 1791 set aside one-seventh of all lands for the support of the Protestant clergy. Later, payments for the lands went directly to the Governor and Executive Council, bypassing the elected Assembly and preventing non-Anglicans from access to the fund.

6. *Montreal Gazette*, 2 Apr. 1810.

7. Bruce Curtis, 'Representation and State Formation in the Canadas, 1790–1850', *Studies in Political Economy* 28 (1989): 61.

8. Ibid., 65. See also Alan Greer, 'The Birth of the Police in Canada', in Greer and Ian Radforth, eds, *Colonial Leviathan—State Formation in Mid-Nineteenth-Century Canada* (Toronto: University of Toronto Press, 1992), 17–49.

9. E. Guillet, *Pioneer Days in Upper Canada* (Toronto: University of Toronto Press, 1970); *Pioneer Inns and Taverns*, 4 vols (Toronto: Toronto Ontario Publishing Co., 1954–8); Wamsley and Kossuth, 'Fighting It Out', 405–30; H. Christie, 'The Function of the Tavern in Toronto, 1834–1875, with Special Reference to Sport', Master's thesis (University of Windsor, 1973).

10. *Statutes of Upper Canada*, 33 Geo. III, cap. XII.

11. Ibid., 58 Geo. III, cap. II.

12. See Suzanne Morton's discussion about gambling and moral reform in *At Odds: Gambling and Canadians 1919–1969* (Toronto: University of Toronto Press, 2003); Kevin B. Wamsley, 'State Formation and Institutionalized Racism: Gambling Laws in Nineteenth and Early Twentieth Century Canada', *SHR* 29, 1 (May 1998): 77–85.

13. On the notoriety of billiards as a social vice, see Peter L. Lindsay, 'A History of Sport in Canada, 1807–1867', PhD dissertation (University of Alberta, 1969), 264–6.

14. *Statutes of Lower Canada*, 41 Geo., cap. XII.

15. Kevin B. Wamsley, 'Legislation and Leisure in 19th Century Canada', PhD dissertation (University of Alberta, 1992), 62.

16. Wayne Simpson, 'The Elite and Sport Membership in Toronto, 1827–1881', PhD dissertation (University of Alberta, 1987), 330.

17. *Statutes of Lower Canada*, 4 Will. IV, cap. VII.

18. Ibid., 3 Geo. IV, cap. XXI.

19. Governments funded local agricultural societies and mechanics' institutes as the educational alternatives to the tavern for the 'improvement' of working citizens and the betterment of the provinces, generally. See, for example, Darren Ferry, 'On Common Ground: Voluntary Associations and the

Construction of Community in Victorian Canada', PhD dissertation (McMaster University, 2003).

20. Wamsley, 'Legislation and Leisure', 52–8, for a brief discussion of early legislation in the Canadas, Nova Scotia, New Brunswick, and Prince Edward Island.

21. M.A. Garland and J.J. Talman, 'Pioneer Drinking Habits and the Rise of Temperance Agitation in Upper Canada Prior to 1840', in F.H. Armstrong, H.A. Stevenson, D.J. Wilson, and Talman, eds, *Aspects of Nineteenth Century Ontario* (Toronto: University of Toronto Press, 1974), 171–93.

22. J.K. Chapman, 'The Mid-Nineteenth Century Temperance Movement in New Brunswick and Maine', *CHR* 35 (1954): 44–5.

23. See Guillet, *Pioneer Days*.

24. Kevin B. Wamsley and M. Heine, 'Sabbath Legislation and State Formation in 19th Century Canada', *Avante* 1, 2 (1995): 44–57.

25. Ibid.

26. Lindsay, 'History of Sport', 260, 274.

27. *Montreal Gazette*, 5 Mar. 1810.

28. Donald Guay, 'Problèmes de l'Intégration du Sport dans la Société Canadienne 1830–1865: Le Cas des Courses de Chevaux', *CJHSPE* 4, 2 (Dec. 1973): 70–92; Alan Metcalfe, 'The Form and Function of Physical Activity in New France, 1534–1759', *CJHSPE* 1, 1, (May 1970): 45–64. In *Canada's Sporting Heroes* (Don Mills: General Publishing, 1974), S.F. Wise and Douglas Fisher cite the Quebec *Gazette*, 5 July 1764, as evidence of an early horse-racing event on a race ground. Howell argues that racing grounds such as the track established by Nova Scotia Governor William Campbell by 1768 served to curtail the more dangerous and impromptu street racing. See also Colin Howell, *Blood, Sweat, and Cheers: Sport and the Making of Modern Canada* (Toronto: University of Toronto Press, 2001), 18.

29. *Statutes of Lower Canada*, 7 Geo IV, cap. III.

30. *Montreal Gazette*, 5 Mar. 1810.

31. *Statutes of Prince Edward Island*, 6 William IV, cap. VII.

32. Kevin B. Wamsley, 'Good Clean Sport and a Deer Apiece: Game Legislation and State Formation in Nineteenth Century Canada', *CJHS* 25, 2 (Dec. 1994): 1–20.

33. Patricia Jasen, *Wild Things: Nature, Culture, and Tourism in Ontario 1790–1914* (Toronto: University of Toronto Press, 1995); John MacKenzie, *Empire of Nature: Hunting, Conservation, and British Imperialism* (Manchester: Manchester University Press, 1988).

34. See Nancy B. Bouchier and Ken Cruikshank, 'Sportsmen and Pothunters: Class, Conservation and the Fishing of Hamilton Harbour, 1850–1914', *SHR* 28 (1997): 1–18; Wamsley, 'Good Clean Sport'.

35. On this sort of tension in the construction of masculine identity, see Elizabeth Vibert, 'Real Men Hunt Buffalo: Masculinity, Race and Class in British Fur Traders' Narratives', in Catherine Hall, ed., *Cultures of Empire: A Reader* (London: Routledge, 2000); Greg Gillespie, 'Sport and "Masculinities" in Early Nineteenth-Century Ontario: The British Travellers' Image', *Ontario History* 92, 2 (Autumn 2000): 113–26; Greg Gillespie and Kevin B. Wamsley, '"My Chief Object—Fine Heads": Big Game Hunting, Imperialism, and Masculinities in the British North American West', *Proceedings of the North American Society of Sport History Conference*, 2002.

36. Greg Gillespie, 'The Imperial Embrace: British Sportsmen and the Appropriation of Landscape in Nineteenth Century Canada', PhD dissertation (University of Western Ontario, 2001).

37. Ibid., 191.

38. See Raymond Williams, *Problems in Materialism and Culture* (London: Verso and NLB, 1980), referring to the 'scientization' of nature.

39. Wamsley, 'Legislation and Leisure', 76.

40. Michael Payne, 'The Sports, Games, Recreations, and Pastimes of the Fur

Traders: Leisure at York Factory', in Morris Mott, ed., *Sports in Canada: Historical Readings* (Mississauga, Ont.: Copp Clark Pitman, 1989), 54. Note the class distinction drawn between the gentlemen and the average trader.

41. Ibid., 50–77.

42. Peter L. Lindsay, 'The Impact of Military Garrisons on the Development of Sport in British North America', *CJHSPE* 1, 1 (Dec. 1970), 34.

43. See Wamsley and Kossuth, 'Fighting it Out'; Judith Fingard, *The Dark Side of Life in Victorian Halifax* (Nova Scotia: Pottersfield, 1989); Alan Greer, 'The Birth of the Police in Canada,' in Greer and Ian Radforth, eds, *Colonial Leviathan: State Formation in Mid-Nineteenth-Century Canada* (Toronto: University of Toronto Press, 1992), 17–49.

44. Carolyn Podruchny credits Margaret Creighton for this argument in 'American Mariners and the Rites of Manhood, 1830–1870', in Colin Howell and Richard J. Twomey, eds, *Jack Tar in History: Essays in the History of Maritime Life and Labour* (Fredericton: Acadiensis Press, 1991), 132–63.

45. See Kevin B. Wamsley, 'The Public Importance of Men and the Importance of Public Men: Sport and Masculinity in 19th Century Canada', in Philip White and Kevin Young, eds, *Sport and Gender in Canada* (Toronto: Oxford University Press, 1999), 24–39.

46. John A. Stevenson, *Curling in Ontario, 1846–1946* (Toronto: Ontario Curling Association, 1950), 23–4. See also Gerald Redmond, *The Sporting Scots of Nineteenth Century Canada* (Toronto: Associated Press, 1982).

47. Redmond, *The Sporting Scots*, 107, note 7.

48. Ibid., 104; Guillet, *Pioneer Days*, 208–9, from John McNair, *The Channel Stane, or Sweeping Frae the Rinks*, 4 vols (1883–5), I, 73–4.

49. Redmond, *The Sporting Scots*, 109–11.

50. R. Douglas Francis, Richard Jones, and Donald B. Smith, *Origins: Canadian History to Confederation* (Toronto: Holt, Rinehart and Winston, 1988), 236.

51. Wise and Fisher, *Sporting Heroes*, 21.

52. Alan Metcalfe, *Canada Learns To Play: The Emergence of Organized Sport, 1807–1914*

53. (Toronto: McClelland & Stewart, 1987), 22.

54. Lindsay, 'The Impact of Military Garrisons', 33–44.

55. Robert Nye, *Masculinity and Male Codes of Honour in Modern France* (Oxford: Oxford University Press, 1993).

56. Cecilia Morgan, 'In Search of the Phantom Misnamed Honour: Dueling in Upper Canada', *CHR* 76 (1995): 529–62.

57. R. Connell, *Masculinities* (Berkeley: University of California Press, 1995); see also Wamsley and Kossuth, 'Fighting It Out'. Punishments meted out during this era, such as public hangings, whippings, and incarceration in open stockades, also lend support to Connell's arguments about violence and intimidation in unstable regimes.

58. Morgan, 'In Search of the Phantom Misnamed Honour', 530.

59. Ibid., 542–3.

60. *Kingston Gazette*, 28 Apr. 1812.

61. M. Ann Hall, *The Girl and the Game: A History of Women's Sport in Canada* (Peterborough, Ont.: Broadview Press, 2002), 6.

62. Edwin C. Guillet, 'Amusements and Social Life in the Rural Districts', in Morris Mott, ed., *Sports in Canada: Historical Readings* (Mississauga, Ont.: Copp Clark Pitman, 1989), 40–1, citing Joseph Pickering, *Inquiries of an Emigrant* (1831), 2 Nov. 1826.

63. Wamsley and Kossuth, 'Fighting It Out'.

64. Guillet, 'Amusements and Social Life', 154–5. The chivaree or charivari was conducted after a wedding, when the bride and groom differed markedly in age or if local citizens

considered the marriage to be too soon after the death of the previous spouse, or later, just for fun. Participants attacked the newlyweds during the night, making loud noises with pots and pans or horse bells until the husband brought alcohol from the house. Sometimes fights occurred or more serious threats, such as plugging the chimney, resulted in death. But, for the most part, they were considered fun and relatively harmless. See also Bryan D. Palmer, 'Discordant Music: Chivaries and Whitecapping in Nineteenth Century North America', *Labour/Le Travailleur* 1 (1978): 5–62.

65. Guillet, *Pioneer Days*, 119–40.

66. Wise and Fisher, *Sporting Heroes*, 6–7.

67. Both men, remembered for astonishing feats of strength, are recorded in accounts as being over seven feet tall and weighing over 400 pounds. See *Iron Game History* 1, 1 (Feb. 1990): 5; Don Morrow et al., *A Concise History of Sport in Canada* (Toronto: Oxford University Press, 1989), 41; Ben Weider, *The Strongest Man in History: Louis Cyr* (Toronto: Mitchell Press, 1976).

68. Bouchier, *For the Love of the Game*, 13.

69. Ibid., 15; also Nancy B. Bouchier, 'Aristocrats and Their Noble Sport: Woodstock Officers and Cricket During the Rebellion Era', *CJHS* 20, 1 (May 1989): 16–31.

70. S.F. Wise, 'Sport and Class Values in Old Ontario and Quebec', in Morris Mott, ed., *Sports in Canada: Historical Readings* (Toronto: Copp Clark Pitman, 1989), 115–16.

71. J.G. Hodgins, *Schools and Colleges of Ontario, 1792–1910*, vol. 1 (Toronto: K.K. Cameron, 1910), 198. See also David W. Brown, 'Sport, Darwinism and Canadian Private Schooling to 1918', *CJHSPE* 26, 1 (May 1985): 27–37; Richard Gruneau, *Class, Sports and Social Development* (Amherst: University of Massachusetts Press, 1983).

72. See G.M. Craig, ed., *Lord Durham's Report* (Toronto: McClelland & Stewart, 1971); S.J.R. Noel, *Patrons, Clients, Brokers—*

Ontario Society and Politics, 1791–1896 (Toronto: University of Toronto Press, 1990); Ian Radforth, 'Sydenham and Utilitarian Reform', in Alan Greer and Radforth, eds, *Colonial Leviathan: State Formation in Mid-Nineteenth-Century Canada* (Toronto: University of Toronto Press, 1992), 64–102.

73. David Mills, *The Idea of Loyalty in Upper Canada, 1784–1850* (Montreal and Kingston: McGill-Queen's University Press, 1988).

74. Cornelius Cunningham, Joshua Gillean Doane, Amos Pearly, and Albert Clark, charged with treason, were hanged in London. Samuel Lount and Peter Mathews were tried and hanged in Toronto. *History of the County of Middlesex, Canada* (Toronto and London: Goodspeed Publishers, 1889), 120–2. See also J.M. Beattie, 'Attitudes towards Crime and Punishment in Upper Canada, 1830–1850: A Documentary Study', (Toronto: Working Paper of the Centre of Criminology, University of Toronto, 1977), 1–8.

75. G.P. de Glazebrook, *A History of Transportation in Canada* (Toronto: Ryerson Press, 1938); P. Baskerville, 'Transportation, Social Change, and State Formation, Upper Canada, 1841–1864,' in Alan Greer and Ian Radforth, eds, *Colonial Leviathan: State Formation in Mid-Nineteenth-Century Canada* (Toronto: University of Toronto Press, 1992), 230–56; P.A. Baskerville, 'The Boardroom and Beyond: Aspects of the Upper Canadian Railroad Community', PhD dissertation (Queen's University, 1974); G. Davison, 'Francis Hincks and the Politics of Interest', PhD dissertation (University of Alberta, 1989).

76. See Wamsley, 'Legislation and Leisure', 105–22.

77. *Journals of the Legislative Assembly, Province of Canada*, 1849, Appendix ZZZ.

78. S.D. Clarke, *Church and Sect in Canada* (Toronto: University of Toronto Press, 1971). See also E.J. Dick, 'From Temperance to Prohibition in 19th Century Nova Scotia', *Dalhousie Review* 61 (1981): 530–53.

79. J.K. Chapman, 'The Mid-Nineteenth Century Temperance Movement in New Brunswick and Maine', *CHR* 35 (1954): 44–5.

80. *Statutes of the Province of Canada*, 9 Vic., cap. XI; *Journals of the Legislative Assembly, Province of Canada*, 1847, Appendix A, No. 30.

81. Garland and Talman, 'Pioneer Drinking Habits', 171–93.

82. Letter to the editor of the *Kingston Chronicle and Gazette*, 12 Dec. 1840.

83. Bouchier, *For the Love of the Game*, 12. *Journals of the Legislative Assembly, Province of Canada*, 1849, Appendix ZZZ.

84. Judith Fingard, *The Dark Side of Life in Victorian Halifax* (Porter's Lake, NS: Pottersfield, 1989), citing the *Annual Reports* of the City of Halifax.

85. Treating was the reciprocal social practice of buying rounds of alcohol. Those on the receiving end were obliged to drink and return the favour at a later date.

86. See Wamsley and Kossuth, 'Fighting It Out'; C.A. Joyce, 'From Left Field: Sport and Class in Toronto, 1845–1886', PhD dissertation (Queen's University, 1997), 118, citing *The Daily Leader*, 14 Apr. 1854; Christie, 'The Function of the Tavern in Toronto'; Peter DeLottinville, 'Joe Beef of Montreal: Working-Class Culture and the Tavern, 1869–1889', *Labour/Le Travailleur* 8/9 (1981–2): 9–40.

87. Howell, *Blood, Sweat and Cheers*, 12.

88. DeLottinville, 'Joe Beef'.

89. C. Warsh, '"John Barleycorn Must Die": An Introduction to the Social History of Alcohol', in C. Warsh, ed., *Drink in Canada: Historical Essays* (Montreal and Kingston: McGill-Queen's University Press, 1993), 3–26.

90. Celia Morgan, *Public Men and Virtuous Women: The Gendered Languages of Religion and Politics in Upper Canada, 1791–1850* (Toronto: University of Toronto Press,

1996), 163–9; C. Warsh, '"Oh, Lord, pour a cordial in her wounded heart": The Drinking Woman in Victorian and Edwardian Canada', in Warsh, *Drink in Canada*, 70–91.

91. Wamsley and Kossuth, 'Fighting It Out,' particularly the examples from London, Hamilton, and Kingston.

92. *Statutes of the Province of Canada*, 10, 11 Vic., cap. VI.

93. Morgan, 'In Search of the Phantom Misnamed Honour'.

94. See Michael Kimmel, *Manhood in America: A Cultural History* (New York: Free Press, 1996); Mark C. Carnes and Clyde Griffen, eds, *Meanings for Manhood: Constructions of Masculinity in Victorian America* (Chicago: University of Chicago Press, 1990); J. Tosh, *A Man's Place: Masculinity and the Middle-Class Home in Victorian England* (New Haven: Yale University Press, 1999), 53–78; N. Vance, *Sinews of the Spirit: The Ideal of Christian Manliness in Victorian Literature and Religious Thought* (Cambridge: Cambridge University Press, 1985); J.A. Mangan, *Manliness and Morality: Middle Class Masculinity in Britain and America, 1800–1940* (New York: St Martin's Press, 1987).

95. J.W. Grant, *A Profusion of Spires: Religion in Nineteenth-Century Ontario* (Toronto: University of Toronto Press, 1988).

96. *Montreal Gazette*, 27 Feb. 1845; *British Colonist*, 4 Mar. 1845; *Toronto Globe*, 11 Mar. 1845; *Montreal Gazette*, 25 Feb. 1845.

97. *Statutes of the Province of Canada*, 8 Vic., cap. XLV.

98. See M. Beckman, S. Langmead, and J. Black, *The Best Gift: A Record of the Carnegie Libraries in Ontario* (Toronto: Dundurn Press, 1984).

99. Bouchier, *For the Love of the Game*, 31–59; Nancy B. Bouchier, 'The 24th of May is the Queen's Birthday: Civic Holidays and the Rise of Amateurism in Nineteenth-Century Canadian Towns', *IJHS* 10, 2 (Aug. 1993): 159–92.

100. Wamsley, 'Legislation and Leisure', 131–47; Wamsley, 'Good Clean Sport'.

101. Lindsay, 'The Impact of Military Garrisons', 38–9.

102. Bouchier, *For the Love of the Game*, 91, reports a match between the Woodstock Cricket Club and the London garrison in 1845.

103. Robert D. Day, 'The British Garrison at Halifax: Its Contribution to the Development of Sport in the Community', in Mott, ed., *Sports in Canada*, 32. See also Lindsay, 'The Impact of Military Garrisons'.

104. Kevin B. Wamsley, 'Rough and Ready, Sometimes Fancy, but Always Manly: Exploring the Social World of the Garrison Soldier in Nineteenth Century London'. Paper presented to the North American Society for Sport History, annual conference, London, Ont., 2001.

105. Day, 'The British Garrison', 34–5.

106. Alan Metcalfe, 'The Evolution of Organized Physical Recreation in Montreal, 1840–1895', *Histoire Sociale/Social History* 11, 21 (1978): 144–66; Metcalfe, *Canada Learns To Play*.

Chapter 4 Transitions to and Control of Organized Sport in the Nineteenth Century

1. Ian F. Jobling, 'Sport in Nineteenth Century Canada: The Effects of Technological Changes in its Development', PhD dissertation (University of Alberta, 1970). Most of the information on technological change is taken from this source.

2. Ibid., 9–12.

3. See, for example, Trent Frayne and Peter Gzowski, *Great Canadian Sports Stories: A Century of Competition* (Toronto: Canadian Centennial Publishing Company, 1965), 64.

4. See, for example, an editorial that chastised steamer captains at a Toronto regatta in *Toronto Globe*, 10 Sept. 1881.

5. Pierre Berton, *The Last Spike: The Great Railway 1881–1885* (Toronto: McClelland & Stewart, 1971).

6. See William Humber, *Cheering for the Home Team: The Story of Baseball in Canada* (Erin, Ont.: Boston Mills Press, 1983).

7. Frank Cosentino, 'Ned Hanlan—Canada's Premier Oarsman: A Case Study in Nineteenth Century Professionalism', *CJHS* 5, 2 (Dec. 1974): 8.

8. Jobling, 'Sport in Nineteenth Century Canada', 47–70.

9. *Novascotian*, 18 Sept. 1833, cited ibid., 77–8.

10. See Don Morrow, 'The Little Men of Iron: The 1902 Montreal Hockey Club', *CJHS* 7, 1 (May 1981): 51–65. Also see Richard Gruneau and David Whitson, *Hockey Night in Canada* (Toronto: Garamond Press, 1993).

11. Lindsay, 'History of Sport'.

12. Ibid.

13. Donald M. Fisher, *Lacrosse: A History of the Game* (Baltimore: Johns Hopkins University Press, 2002), 256–8.

14. Eaton's catalogues in Canada carried lacrosse sticks and baseball equipment advertisements by 1900.

15. Jobling, 'Sport in Nineteenth Century Canada', 181.

16. Ibid., 185–94.

17. Margaret Ann Hall, 'A History of Women's Sport in Canada Prior to World War I', Master's thesis (University of Alberta, 1968), 86–92. See also M. Ann Hall, *The Girl and the Game* (Peterborough, Ont.: Broadview Press, 2002), 15–21; Helen Lenskyj, *Out of Bounds: Women, Sport and Sexuality* (Toronto: Women's Press, 1986), 59–64.

18. S.F. Wise and D. Fisher, *Canada's Sporting Heroes* (Don Mills, Ont.: General Publishing, 1974), 13–14.

19. Information on the Montreal Curling Club is synthesized from R. Wayne Simpson, 'The Influence of the Montreal Curling Club on the Development of Curling 1807–1857', Master's thesis (University of Western Ontario, 1980).

20. Ibid.

21. Jobling, 'Sport in Nineteenth Century Canada', 229–35.

22. Simpson, 'The Influence of the Montreal Curling Club'.

23. Alan Metcalfe, 'The Evolution of Organized Physical Recreation in Montreal, 1840–1895', *Histoire Sociale/Social History* 11, 21 (May 1978): 144. Heavy reliance was placed on this seminal article for background information on the chronological development of Montreal sport.

24. As quoted in P.C. McIntosh, *Physical Education in England Since 1800* (London: G. Bell and Sons, 1968), 70.

25. See Mark Moss, *Manliness and Militarism: Educating Young Boys in Ontario for War* (Toronto: Oxford University Press, 2001), especially chapters 2 and 7.

26. See P.L. Lindsay, 'The Impact of the Military Garrisons on the Development of Sport in British North America', *CJHSPE* 1, 1 (May 1970): 33. Material on the Montreal garrison was gleaned from this article.

27. Alan Metcalfe, 'Organized Sport and Social Stratification in Montreal, 1840–1901', in R.S. Gruneau and J.G. Albinson, eds, *Canadian Sport: Sociological Perspectives* (Don Mills, Ont.: Addison-Wesley [Canada], 1976), 78–9.

28. Material on snowshoeing is from Don Morrow, 'The Knights of the Snowshoe: A Study of the Evolution of Sport in Nineteenth Century Montreal', *JSH* 15, 1 (Spring 1988): 5–40.

29. *Montreal Gazette*, 16 Jan. 1873.

30. H.W. Becket, *The Montreal Snow Shoe Club: Its History and Record* (Montreal: Becket Brothers, 1882), 44–5. This 521-page book is an excellent period piece on Montreal snowshoeing.

31. Morrow, 'The Knights of the Snowshoe', 22.

32. Information on the Victoria Skating Rink was taken from D. Rosenberg, D. Morrow, and A.J. Young, 'A Quiet Contribution: Louis Rubenstein', *CJHS* 12, 1 (May 1981): 51–65.

33. See Don Morrow, 'Frozen Festivals: Ceremony and the *Carnaval* in the Montreal Winter Carnivals, 1883–1889', *SHR* 27, 2 (Nov. 1996): 173–90.

34. *Montreal Daily Star*, 8 Feb. 1889.

35. The photograph is in the Notman Archives at the McCord Museum of Canadian History in Montreal. It is reprinted on the cover of *Fact and Fiction: Canadian Painting and Photography, 1860–1900* (Montreal: Plow and Watters, 1979).

36. Colin Howell, *Northern Sandlots—A Social History of Maritime Baseball* (Toronto: University of Toronto Press, 1995), 14.

37. B. Schrodt, R. Baka, and G. Redmond, *Sport Canadiana* (Edmonton: Executive Sport Publications, 1980), 23. See Howell, *Northern Sandlots*, 13–30, for the sport's organization in the Maritimes.

38. Don Morrow, A Sporting Evolution: The Montreal Amateur Athletic Association, 1881–1981 (Montreal: Graphics Group, 1981), 37–41.

39. Don Morrow, 'The Powerhouse of Canadian Sport: The Montreal Amateur Athletic Association, Inception to 1909', *JSH* 8, 3 (Winter 1981): 21–2.

40. Material on the MAAA is synthesized from ibid. and from Morrow, *A Sporting Evolution*.

41. Morrow, 'Frozen Festivals', 173–90.

42. *Montreal Daily Star*, 15 Dec. 1883.

43. See Morrow, 'The Little Men of Iron', 63–5.

44. Metcalfe, 'Evolution of Physical Recreation in Montreal', 161–4.

45. Barbara Pinto, 'Ain't Misbehavin': The Montreal Shamrock Lacrosse Club Fans, 1868–1884', Master's thesis (University of Western Ontario, 1990), 56. This study is particularly instructive in the way it counterpoints middle-class sporting

values with those of the working classes, such as the Irish. The Scots did dominate the organization and dispersion of many sports in Canada. And yet, the Irish greatly outnumbered the Scots during the nineteenth century. To date, very little has been written about the Irish influence on Canadian sport. Two notable exceptions are Pinto, 'Ain't Misbehavin': The Montreal Shamrock Lacrosse Club Fans', and Dennis P. Ryan, 'Irish Catholic Sport, Identity and Integration in Toronto, 1858–1920', Master's thesis (University of Western Ontario, 2000). However, both studies are specific to local clubs and, therefore, extrapolation to the Irish in Canada as a complete group is, as yet, difficult to do.

46. Bruce Kidd, *The Struggle for Canadian Sport* (Toronto: University of Toronto Press, 1996), 27.

47. See Howard J. Savage, *American College Athletics* (New York: Carnegie Foundation, 1929), 46; Savage, *Games and Sports in British Public Schools and Universities* (New York: Carnegie Foundation, 1928).

48. Savage, *Games and Sports in British Public Schools and Universities*, 194–6.

49. Ibid., 196.

50. See, for example, Allen Guttmann, *From Ritual to Record: The Nature of Modern Sports* (New York: Columbia University Press, 1978), 31.

51. Savage, *American College Athletics*, 37.

52. Cited in Keith L. Lansley, 'The Amateur Athletic Union of Canada and Changing Concepts of Amateurism', PhD dissertation (University of Alberta, 1971), 17. This dissertation is a major source for the information on amateur rules and regulations in this chapter.

53. Peter L. Lindsay, 'The Impact of the Military Garrisons on the Development of Sport in British North America', *CJHSPE* 1, 1 (May 1970): 34.

54. Frank Cosentino, 'A History of the Concept of Professionalism in Canadian Sport', PhD

dissertation (University of Alberta, 1973), 28–9.

55. Ibid., 29–31.

56. See Gerald Redmond, 'The Scots and Sport in Nineteenth Century Canada', PhD dissertation (University of Alberta, 1972), 197–264.

57. Don Morrow, 'The Powerhouse of Canadian Sport: The Montreal Amateur Athletic Association, Inception to 1909', *JSH* 8, 1 (1981): 35.

58. Lansley, 'The Amateur Athletic Union of Canada', 30–1.

59. See Kidd, *The Struggle for Canadian Sport*, 28. Also see John Holt, 'Amateurism and its Interpretation: The Social Origins of British Sport', *Innovation in Social Science Research* 5, 4 (1992): 29; Nancy Bouchier, '"For the Love of the Game and the Honour of the Town": Organized Sport, Local Culture and Middle Class Hegemony in Two Ontario Towns, 1838–1895', PhD dissertation (University of Western Ontario, 1990), 198.

60. Bouchier, '"For the Love of the Game"', 197–9.

61. Frank Cosentino, 'A History of the Concept of Professionalism in Canadian Sport', 134–5.

62. Ibid., 146–75.

63. Ibid., 176.

64. Lansley, 'The Amateur Athletic Union of Canada'.

65. Ibid.

66. Ibid., 57.

67. Ibid. There is no evidence of any such promotion of physical exercise/education by the CAAU.

68. Respective trophies for these three sports were the Stanley Cup, donated in 1893, the Minto Cup, donated in 1901, and the Grey Cup, donated in 1909.

69. *Minutes of the Meetings of the Board of Governors of the CAAU*, 1901–5.

70. Ibid., 6 May 1904, 124–5.

71. See Don Morrow, 'A Case Study in Amateur Conflict: The Athletic War in Canada, 1906–1908', *British Journal of Sports History* 3, 2 (1986): 176–8.

72. *Minutes of the Meetings of the Board of Governors of the CAAU*, 26 June 1905, 149–52.

73. *Minutes of the Meetings of the Directors of the MAAA*, Minute Book No. 7, 21 Nov. 1904, 17–18.

74. *Montreal Daily Star*, 30 Apr. 1906. 30

75. Ibid., 27 Apr. 1906.

76. Ibid., 8, 11, 12, 14 Sept. 1906. The 14 September issue is filled with arguments concerning the perceived benefits of the concept and practice of amateurs playing with and against professionals.

77. Morrow, 'A Case Study in Amateur Conflict', 179.

78. *Montreal Daily Star*, 1 Feb. 1907.

79. *Minutes of the 25th Annual Meeting of the CAAU*, 9 Nov. 1908, 4. By November 1909, as the athletic war drew to an end, the CAAU listed 1,200 member clubs with 75,000 affiliated athletes. *Minutes of the 26th Annual Meeting of the CAAU*, 27 Nov. 1909.

80. *Montreal Daily Star*, 2 Dec. 1907.

81. Ibid., 21 Dec. 1907. The same message appeared in 1908: ibid., 19 Dec. 1908.

82. Morrow, 'A Case Study in Amateur Conflict', 183.

83. *Ottawa Journal*, 24 July 1908.

84. For more information on Longboat's career and the many controversies that plagued his career, see, Bruce Kidd, *Tom Longboat* (Don Mills: Fitzhenry and Whiteside, 1980), 65 pages, and Bruce Kidd, 'In Defense of Tom Longboat' in *Canadian Journal of History of Sport* Vol. 14, No. 1 (May, 1983), 34–63.

85. *Toronto Telegram*, 22 Apr. 1909.

86. *Montreal Daily Star*, 7 Sept. 1909.

87. *Minutes of the Meetings of the CAAU Board of Directors*, 1 Oct. 1909.

88. Kidd, *The Struggle for Canadian Sport*, 35–7.

89. *Minutes of the 2nd Annual Meeting of the AAU of Canada*, 27 Nov. 1911, n.p.

90. Cosentino, 'History of the Concept of Professionalism', 197. This source forms the basis for much of the discussion on the development of professionalism in Canadian sport.

91. *Toronto Daily Star*, 7 Aug. 1906.

92. Cosentino, 'History of the Concept of Professionalism', 223.

93. See Stacy L. Lorenz, 'In the Field of Sport at Home and Abroad: Sports Coverage in Canadian Daily Newspapers, 1850–1914', *SHR* 34, 2 (Nov. 2003): 151–3.

94. See Don Reddick, *The Dawson City Seven* (Fredericton: Goose Lane, 1993).

95. H.H. Roxborough, *The Stanley Cup Story* (Toronto: McGraw-Hill Ryerson, 1971), 29.

96. Contract Adopted by the National Hockey Association of Canada, 1910, reprinted in full in Cosentino, 'History of the Concept of Professionalism', 531–2. Cosentino also notes that the Canadian Lacrosse Association in 1887 published its player agreement in the *Toronto Mail*, 25 June 1887. It is reprinted ibid., 530. The CLA agreement was more a letter of agreement than a contract.

97. See, for example, Eric Whitehead, *Cyclone Taylor: A Hockey Legend* (Toronto: Doubleday Canada, 1977), for an excellent biographical analysis of one of Canada's earliest professional hockey heroes.

98. Cosentino, 'History of the Concept of Professionalism', 242.

99. Some historians look at the professionalization of hockey and the NHL monopoly as the key ingredients in bringing about such drastic changes in the game as to ruin its identity, cultural significance, and community roots. See Bruce Kidd and

John Macfarlane, *The Death of Hockey* (Toronto: New Press, 1972). The jacket cover of the book carries a poignant image of a detached hand, presumably the NHL personified, squeezing the lifeblood out of a puck.

100. For a historical account of the team, see Frank Cosentino, *The Renfrew Millionaires: The Valley Boys of Winter 1910* (Burnstown, Ont.: General Store Publishing House, 1990).

101. The source for material on the PCHL is Cosentino, 'History of the Concept of Professionalism', 243–7.

102. Ibid., pp. 247–50.

103. Lansley, 'The Amateur Athletic Union of Canada', 83.

104. Frank Cosentino and Glynn Leyshon, *Olympic Gold: Canada's Winners in the Summer Games* (Toronto: Holt, Rinehart and Winston of Canada, 1975).

105. See Kidd and Macfarlane, *The Death of Hockey*.

106. Foster Hewitt, *Foster Hewitt, His Own Story* (Toronto: Ryerson Press, 1967).

Chapter 5 Case Studies in the Growth and Institutionalization of Sport: Lacrosse and Baseball

1. The most comprehensive history of the game of lacrosse is Donald M. Fisher, *Lacrosse: A History of the Game* (Baltimore: Johns Hopkins University Press, 2002). Most of the book focuses more broadly on North America, but Chapter 1, 'The Birth of Modern Lacrosse in Canada, 1860–1914', provides a clear analysis of the game's origins and developments to 1914.

2. M.A. Salter, 'The Relationship of Lacrosse to Physical Survival Among Early North American Indian Tribes', in *Proceedings of the Second World Symposium on the History of Sport and Physical Education* (Banff, Alta, June 1971), 95–106. See also Fisher, *Lacrosse*, 1–24.

3. M. Jette, 'Primitive Indian Lacrosse—Skill or Slaughter', in *Proceedings of the Second World Symposium on the History of Sport and Physical Education* (Banff, Alta, June 1971), 107–26.

4. Both Salter's and Jette's works cited above attest to the skills required and the values that were believed to be a component of lacrosse. By far the most definitive source on early Indian lacrosse, underscoring its nuances and skills, is Stewart Culin, *Games of the North American Indians* (New York: Dover, 1975), 562–616.

5. Ibid., 562–3.

6. Ibid., 563.

7. P.L. Lindsay, 'A History of Sport in Canada, 1807–1867', PhD dissertation (University of Alberta, 1969), 114.

8. Ibid., 115.

9. Don Morrow, *A Sporting Evolution: The Montreal Amateur Athletic Association 1881–1981* (Montreal: Graphics Group, 1981), 14–25.

10. The photograph is by Notman and depicts 10 players in high-button shirts, bow ties, white trousers, and peaked caps.

11. Lindsay, 'History of Sport', 117.

12. See Alan Metcalfe, 'Sport and Athletics: A Case Study of Lacrosse in Canada, 1840–1889', *JSH* 3, 1 (Spring 1976), 1–5.

13. *Montreal Gazette*, 23 Aug, 1860.

14. Ibid., 28 Aug. 1860.

15. Goal-Keeper, *The Game of Lacrosse* (Montreal: M. Longmore Co., 1860).

16. *Montreal Gazette*, 15 Sept. 1860.

17. As cited in Christina A. Burr, 'The Process of Evolution of Competitive Sport: A Study of Senior Lacrosse in Canada, 1844 to 1914', Master's thesis (University of Western Ontario, 1986), Appendix A, 255. See also Don Morrow, 'The Institutionalization of Sport: A Case Study of Canadian Lacrosse, 1844–1914', *IJHS* 9, 2 (Aug. 1992): 236–51.

18. Text of a speech delivered by George N. Beers, grandson of Dr George W. Beers, to the Merit Awards Banquet at the Canadian Lacrosse Association annual convention in Vancouver, 24 Nov. 1973. Mr Beers cites his grandfather's birth year as 1841 but most historical sources list it as 1843.

19. P.L. Lindsay, 'George Beers and the National Game Concept: A Behavioural Approach', in *Proceedings of the Second Canadian Symposium on the History of Sport and Physical Education*, Windsor, Ont. (May 1972), 27–8. Lindsay's article on Beers is the basis of the information used here to determine Beers's influence in promoting lacrosse.

20. See George W. Beers, 'A Rival to Cricket', *Chambers Journal* 18 (6 Dec. 1862): 366–8; 'The Voyageurs of Canada', *British American Magazine* 1 (1863): 472–9; 'Canada in Winter', *British American Magazine* 2 (1864): 166–71.

21. Henry Roxborough, One Hundred-Not Out: The Story of Nineteenth Century Canadian Sport (Toronto: Ryerson Press, 1966), 173.

22. *Montreal Gazette*, 8 Aug. 1867.

23. The convention concept was discussed in the *Montreal Gazette* as early as 29 July and 12 August 1867. See Burr, 'The Process of Evolution', 60, 102.

24. *Montreal Gazette*, 30 Sept. 1867.

25. Lindsay, 'History of Sport', 123.

26. Roxborough, *One Hundred-Not Out*, 16.

27. Culin, *Games of the North American Indians*, 563.

28. G.W. Beers, *Lacrosse: The National Game of Canada* (Montreal: Dawson Brothers, 1869).

29. Ibid., 57–8. In 'Canadian Sports', *Century Magazine* 14 (May–Oct. 1877): 507, Beers also states: 'The game of lacrosse, which was adopted as the national game of Canada on the 1st of July, 1859 . . . .' This 21-page article romanticizes and promotes lacrosse, snow-shoeing, and tobogganing as the quintessential Canadian sports.

30. See, for example, K.G. Jones and T.G. Vellathottam, 'The Myth of Canada's National Sport', *Journal of the Canadian Association for Health, Physical Education and Recreation* 41, 1 (Sept.–Oct. 1974): 33–6. Douglas Fisher examined every major Canadian newspaper and all relevant parliamentary documents between 1860 and 1870 and found no mention of lacrosse's enactment as a national game. See Fisher, *Lacrosse: A History of the Game*, 35. Both lacrosse and ice hockey were officially recognized as the national sports of Canada by the National Sports of Canada Act of federal Parliament on 12 May 1994. The declaration was: 'The game commonly known as ice hockey is hereby recognized and declared to be the national winter sport of Canada and the game commonly known as lacrosse is hereby recognized and declared to be the national summer sport of Canada.' See the full text of the Act at (as of April 2004).

31. Lindsay, 'History of Sport', 130 (emphasis added).

32. Ibid., 125.

33. *Montreal Gazette*, 23 Oct. 1867, cited ibid., 126.

34. Lindsay, 'History of Sport', 130.

35. Beers, 'Canadian Sports', 512.

36. A.E. Cox. 'A History of Sports in Canada, 1868–1900', PhD dissertation (University of Alberta, 1969), 138.

37. Alan Metcalfe, *Canada Learns To Play: The Emergence of Organized Sport, 1807–1914* (Toronto: McClelland & Stewart, 1987), 196. The discussion on the Shamrocks is based on Metcalfe's discussion, 196–203.

38. Ibid., 197.

39. Burr, 'The Process of Evolution', 76.

40. *Montreal Gazette*, 13 Sept. 1875.

41. Burr, 'The Process of Evolution', 84.

42. Metcalfe, *Canada Learns To Play*, 201.

43. See *Montreal Gazette*, 4 Oct. 1869, 16 Oct. 1876, cited in Burr, 'The Process of Evolution', 110.

44. *Laws of Lacrosse and Constitution of the National Lacrosse Association of Canada.* Revised and adopted 7 June 1878 (Toronto: Robert Marshall, 1878), 23.

45. Burr, 'The Process of Evolution', 78–9.

46. Metcalfe, 'Sport and Athletics', 6–15.

47. 'Hints to Players by a Native', *Canadian Magazine* 1 (July–Dec. 1871): 120–4, 248–54.

48. W.K. McNaught, *Lacrosse and How to Play It* (Toronto: Robert Marshall, 1873). A prominent Toronto player, McNaught copied Beers's text and issued it under a different title. In 1883 McNaught was elected president of the NALA.

49. G.W. Beers, 'The Ocean Travels of Lacrosse', *Athletic Leaves* (Sept. 1888): 42.

50. Don Morrow, 'The Canadian Image Abroad: The Great Lacrosse Tours of 1876 and 1883', in *Proceedings of the Fifth Canadian Symposium on the History of Sport*, Toronto (Aug. 1982), 10–21.

51. *Montreal Herald* press clipping, 1875, in the Montreal Amateur Athletic Association Scrapbook, vol. 15, 124; ibid., 165, 176.

52. MAAA Scrapbook, press clipping, 165.

53. *Toronto Globe*, 13 July 1876.

54. *Montreal Gazette*, 1 May 1876.

55. MAAA Scrapbook, vol. 15, 192.

56. *Toronto Globe*, 28 Apr. 1883.

57. *Montreal Gazette*, 14 Aug. 1883; Beers, 'The Ocean Travels of Lacrosse', 42–3.

58. *Toronto Globe*, 29 June 1883.

59. Ibid.

60. See *Sessional Papers*, vol. 8, under the report of the Canadian Minister of Agriculture.

61. *Toronto Globe*, 18 Aug. 1883.

62. *Laws of Lacrosse*, amended 10 Apr. 1883, by the NALA, cited in Morrow, *A Sporting Evolution*, 209–10.

63. H.H. Allingharn, 'Lacrosse in the Maritime Provinces', *Dominion Illustrated Monthly* (1892): 225–33.

64. Metcalfe, *Canada Learns To Play*, 204–5.

65. Burr, 'The Process of Evolution', 121–2.

66. Metcalfe, *Canada Learns To Play*, 207.

67. Ibid.

68. *Toronto Globe*, 29 Mar. 1902.

69. Cox, 'History of Sports in Canada', 144.

70. *Mainland Guardian* (New Westminster), 28 Sept. 1890. cited in ibid., 145.

71. Burr, 'The Process of Evolution', 157.

72. *Toronto Globe*, 8 July 1911.

73. J.A.P. Day, 'The 1908 New Westminster Salmonbellies', *Proceedings of the First Canadian Symposium on the History of Sport and Physical Education*, Edmonton (May 1970), 225. For greater ease of handling the ball, the Salmonbellies also used a shorter lacrosse stick than most teams.

74. Burr, 'The Process of Evolution', 135–41.

75. Ibid., 141.

76. Don Morrow, 'A Case Study in Amateur Conflict: The Athletic War in Canada', *British Journal of Sports History* 3, 2 (Sept. 1986): 177–86.

77. Burr, 'The Process of Evolution', 198–209.

78. Metcalfe, *Canada Learns To Play*, 207–9. Joe Lally, Canadian lacrosse stick manufacturer and entrepreneur, was a significant exception in his efforts to promote lacrosse at grassroots levels. See Chapter 10 on organized sport and technological changes.

79. T.G. Vellathottam and K.G. Jones, 'Highlights in the Development of Canadian Lacrosse to 1931', *CJHSPE* 5, 2 (Dec. 1974): 46–7.

80. David Q. Voigt, *American Baseball: From the Gentleman's Sport to the Commissioner*

System (University Park: Penn State University Press, 1983), I, 5–8.

81. Ibid., 8. These rules were actually written for the club by Alexander Cartwright in 1846. Earlier versions or forerunners of the game in the United States also have been documented.

82. The letter, and a discussion of its significance, is published by N.B. Bouchier and R.K. Barney in 'A Critical Examination of a Source on Early Ontario Baseball: The Reminiscence of Adam E. Ford', *JSH* (Spring 1988): 75–90. Most of this section is based on this publication.

83. William Humber, *Cheering for the Home Team: The Story of Baseball in Canada* (Erin, Ont.: Boston Mills Press, 1983), 28. Lindsay, 'History of Sport', 80, cites 1859 as the date of the first recorded game in Hamilton. Given the known existence of at least four teams in 1859—the Burlington Club, the Barton Club, the Hamilton Maple Leafs, the Canadian Pioneer Club of Toronto—an earlier date seems more logical. Lindsay goes so far as to call Hamilton 'the baseball centre of North America' during this period.

84. Bryan D. Palmer, *A Culture in Conflict: Skilled Workers and Industrial Capitalism in Hamilton, Ontario 1860–1914* (Montreal and Kingston: McGill-Queen's University Press, 1979), 53.

85. Ibid., 52. Palmer remarks that baseball was almost a 'matter of course' at union picnics and that whole teams would turn out at funerals of a fellow team member as a kind of 'bond of solidarity cementing the working-class community'. Ibid., 54, 36. His deduction that scores of 73–4 and 58–35, common during the 1860s and 1870s, were strong evidence of 'raucous' affairs and much 'merriment' shows a lack of understanding of the nature of baseball at the time. Batters could wait for the pitch of their choice, fielders were inept and without gloves, and the emphasis was on base-running and scoring.

86. Nancy Bouchier, '"For the Love of the Game and the Honour of the Town": Organized Sport, Local Culture, and Middle Class Hegemony in Two Ontario Towns, 1838–1895', PhD dissertation (University of Western Ontario, 1990), 255.

87. Lindsay, 'History of Sport', 80.

88. William Humber, 'Cheering for the Home Team: Baseball and Town Life in 19th Century Ontario', *Proceedings of the Fifth Canadian Symposium on the History of Sport and Physical Education* (University of Toronto, Aug. 1982), 192.

89. See *Ingersoll Chronicle*, 20 July 1882, 12 July 1884, 16 July 1885, 17 June 1886, and 26 July 1889, for accounts of middle-class games.

90. *Woodstock Sentinel*, 3 Sept. 1875. Examples abound in the *Sentinel* of this level of competition through to the mid-1880s in Woodstock.

91. *Hamilton Spectator*, 29 Sept. 1864.

92. Lindsay, 'History of Sport', points out that baseball, among other games, was prohibited in Montreal's public parks by an 1865 municipal ordinance that carried a five-dollar penalty for infractions. It is likely that baseball was perceived as a children's game that was a nuisance activity within the serenity of a public park. See also Alexander J. Young, *Beyond Heroes: A Sport History of Nova Scotia* (Hantsport, NS: Lancelot Press, 1988), I, 95.

93. *Toronto Globe*, 17 Aug. 1867.

94. The same *Brampton Times* excerpt is quoted in W. Perkins Bull, *From Rattlesnake Hunt to Hockey: The History of Sports in Canada and of the Sportsmen of Peel 1798–1934* (Toronto: George J. McLeod, 1934), 324, 327. Brampton never did develop as a nineteenth-century baseball town. Lacrosse was its dominant sport in the last third of the century.

95. See Bouchier, 'For the Love of the Game and the Honour of the Town', 261–6.

96. Humber, *Cheering for the Home Team*, 28. For the most current history of the Guelph Maple Leafs and the London Tecumsehs,

see Spencer Lang, 'Experimenting with Professional Baseball: An Examination of the Guelph Maple Leafs and the London Tecumsehs in Canadian Baseball's First Professional Era', Master's thesis (University of Western Ontario, 2003).

97. *New York Clipper*, 19 June 1869.

98. Humber, 'Cheering for the Home Team', 194–5.

99. *Hamilton Spectator*, 11 Aug. 1864. The citizens of Woodstock donated American silver dollars that were melted down and crafted in 1864 into an elegant ball of regulation size. The Silver Ball is pictured in the *Star Weekly*, 19 July 1924.

100. Sleeman Papers, University of Guelph. One newspaper article in the 1880s actually suggested renaming the town Sleemanville.

101. *Guelph Evening Mercury*, 5 Aug. 1869.

102. Metcalfe, *Canada Learns To Play*, 86.

103. 'Club Rules', 1874, in Sleeman Papers.

104. *Toronto Globe*, 9 Apr. 1876.

105. Canadian Base Ball Association Constitution, By-Laws, Playing Rules, Championship Code, 1876, in William Bryce, *Canadian Base Ball Guide for 1876* (London, Ont.: Bryce, 1876), 37–42. This *Guide* was a promotional device of the CBBA.

106. Tecumseh Baseball Club of London Minute Book, June 1868 to May 1872. This Minute Book was written in a formal style by the secretary of the club, whose object was to 'impart, foster and perpetuate the game of Base Ball and to advance the interests of its members' (p. 2). The team was scheduled to practise three days per week at 5:00 p.m. and the club paid all necessary expenses during match games (players' expenses, equipment, umpire, and scorer). Most of the Minute Book entries are businesslike committee meeting items—an indication of increasing organization creeping into baseball.

107. Sleeman Papers and selected issues of the *London Advertiser*, 1876–80.

108. Humber, *Cheering for the Home Team*, 40.

109. The general trend in baseball, not Englehart's specific part in it, has been paraphrased from R. Gruneau, *Class, Sports, and Social Development* (Amherst: University of Massachusetts Press, 1983), 116–17. Gruneau's remarks were pointed specifically at Canadian professional baseball. He noted that the entrepreneurial orientation 'crystallized' after 1910. We would argue it happened much earlier, even with Sleeman's role; it may have proliferated after 1910.

110. *London Daily Advertiser*, 2 Sept. 1876.

111. *Toronto Globe*, 12 Sept. 1876, cited in Cox, 'History of Sports in Canada', 46.

112. *London Daily Advertiser*, 11 July 1878.

113. Ibid.

114. Metcalfe, *Canada Learns To Play*, 88–9.

115. See ibid., 86.

116. See Cox, 'History of Sports in Canada', 54–5, for a description of the leagues in Ontario and Quebec that came in and out of existence as late as 1895 to 1900.

117. Brian Flood, *Saint John: A Sporting Tradition* (Saint John: Neptune Publishing, 1985), 71. This source is heavily relied upon for Maritime baseball history in this chapter, along with Colin D. Howell, *Northern Sandlots: A Social History of Maritime Baseball* (Toronto: University of Toronto Press 1995).

118. Flood, *Saint John*, 74.

119. Ibid., 75–80, 125.

120. Cox, 'History of Sports in Canada', 53.

121. Flood, *Saint John*, 78.

122. Ibid., 121–9.

123. H. Charles Ballem, *Abegweit Dynasty 1899–1954: The Story of the Abegweit Amateur Athletic Association* (Summerside, PEI: Williams and Crue, 1986), 53.

124. M. Mott, 'The First Pro Sports League on the Prairies: The Manitoba Baseball League

of 1886', *CJHS* (Dec. 1984): 62–3. References to Winnipeg baseball history are based on this article.

125. Ibid., 62–9.

126. Humber, *Cheering for the Home Team*, 69.

127. Metcalfe, *Canada Learns To Play*, 94–5.

128. Barry Broadfoot, *The Pioneer Years 1895–1914: Memories of Settlers Who Opened the West* (Toronto: Doubleday Canada, 1976), 337.

129. Humber, *Cheering for the Home Team*, 53. Humber cites the formation of the Crescents team in 1868 at St John's, Quebec, but there is no documentation of baseball games in Quebec (outside of Montreal) at that early period.

130. *Annual Report of the MAAA*, 1886 to 1889.

131. Bull, *From Rattlesnake Hunt to Hockey*, 327.

132. Ibid., 337.

133. Metcalfe, *Canada Learns to Play*, 166

134. W.A. Hewitt, *Down the Stretch: Recollections of a Pioneer Sportsman and Journalist* (Toronto: Ryerson, 1958), 122.

135. Louis Cauz, *Baseball's Back in Town: A History of Baseball in Toronto* (Toronto: Controlled Media Corporation, 1977), 17.

136. Cox, 'History of Sports in Canada', 53.

137. *Saturday Night*, 22 June 1895, 6.

138. Kevin G. Jones, 'Sport in Canada, 1900–1920', PhD dissertation (University of Alberta, 1970), 36.

139. Paul O'Neill, *The Oldest City: The Story of St. John's Newfoundland* (Don Mills, Ont.: Musson Book Co., 1975), I, 331.

140. Ballem, *Abegweit Dynasty*, 90–1.

141. Flood, *Saint John*, 130, 164–5.

142. Young, *Beyond Heroes*, I, 104.

143. Ibid., 107.

144. Humber, *Cheering for the Home Team*, 69–73.

145. Ibid., 79–80.

146. Jones, 'Sport in Canada', 43–7.

147. Ibid., 53–5.

148. *Toronto Globe*, 24 May 1917.

149. Metcalfe, *Canada Learns To Play*, 85, 88. Metcalfe used the cities of Halifax, Montreal, Toronto, Winnipeg, Edmonton, Vancouver, and Victoria in his sample.

150. E. Janice Waters, 'A Content Analysis of the Sport Section in Selected Canadian Newspapers 1927 to 1935', Master's thesis (University of Western Ontario, 1981), 24–52.

151. M. Ann Hall, *The Girl and the Game: A History of Women's Sport in Canada* (Peterborough, Ont.: Broadview Press, 2002), 42–5.

152. Ibid. Hall's book is an excellent resource and history for learning about the development and organization of a wide variety of sports for women in Canada. See also Bruce Kidd, *The Struggle for Canadian Sport* (Toronto: University of Toronto Press, 1996), esp. 94–145.

153. Hewitt, *Down the Stretch*, 123; Cauz, *Baseball's Back in Town*, 35.

154. Cauz, *Baseball's Back in Town*, 36.

155. *Saturday Night*, 16 May 1908, 11.

156. Ibid.

157. Ibid., 15 May 1909, 10.

158. Hewitt, *Down the Stretch*, 135–6.

159. *Saturday Night*, 1 June 1912, 6.

160. Harvey Frommer, 'Jackie Robinson as a Montreal Royal', *Proceedings of the Fifth Canadian Symposium on the History of Sport and Physical Education* (University of Toronto, Aug. 1982), 122–8. For a complete discussion of Robinson's time with the Royals, see Jules Tygiel, *Baseball's Great Experiment: Jackie Robinson and His Legacy* (New York: Oxford University Press, 1983), 99–143.

161. For a fine reminiscence of the Royals in the 1940s and later, see Mordecai Richler, 'Expansion: Up from the Minors in Montreal', in Daniel Okrent and Harris Lewine, eds, *The Ultimate Baseball Book* (Boston: Houghton Mifflin, 1988).

162. Humber, *Cheering for the Home Team*, ch. 7.

163. Ibid., 106.

164. Tygiel, *Baseball's Great Experiment*, 143; Sam Martin in the *Pittsburgh Courier*, 12 Oct. 1946.

165. We are grateful to William Dendy for providing information on the stadium.

166. Cauz, *Baseball's Back in Town*, was the source for much of the information in the following passage on the Leafs during the 1930s and after, and on the Blue Jays.

Chapter 6 Stars and Heroes: Hanlan, Rubenstein, Cyr, Scott, and Johnson

1. See R. Holt, J.A. Mangan, and P. Lanfranchi, eds, *European Heroes: Myth, Identity, Sport* (London: Frank Cass, 1996), for a discussion of this perspective on examining heroes in social context. See also, Don Morrow, 'The Myth of the Hero in Canadian Sport History', *CJHS* 23, 2 (Dec. 1992): 72–83.

2. A.E. Cox, 'A History of Sport in Canada, 1868 to 1900', PhD dissertation (University of Alberta, 1969), 286. Information on early rowing leading up to Hanlan's exploits was taken from this source, unless otherwise indicated.

3. B. Flood, *Saint John: A Sporting Tradition* (Saint John: Neptune Publishing, 1985), 15–17.

4. Robert S. Hunter, *Rowing in Canada* (Hamilton: Davis-Lisson, 1933), 13–17.

5. Flood, *Saint John*, 33.

6. Hunter, *Rowing in Canada*, 27.

7. The *Toronto Globe* and *Telegram* carried daily messages about American centennial festivities and Canadian contributions to displays or ceremonial occasions.

8. Frank Cosentino, 'Ned Hanlan—Canada's Premier Oarsman: A Case Study in Nineteenth Century Professionalism', *CJHSPE* 5, 2 (Dec. 1974): 8. Background information on Hanlan was derived from this source and from Hunter, *Rowing in Canada*.

9. Cosentino, 'Ned Hanlan', 8.

10. Hunter, *Rowing in Canada*, 29–30. Cosentino relies on Hunter for the allegation.

11. *Sketches of the Champion Oarsmen: Hanlan and Courtney* (Montreal: Callehan and Co., Printers, 1878).

12. Hunter, *Rowing in Canada*, 29.

13. Cosentino, 'Ned Hanlan', 10.

14. *Toronto Mail*, 2 Oct. 1878.

15. Cosentino, 'Ned Hanlan', 10.

16. Hunter, *Rowing in Canada*, 30.

17. Cosentino, 'Ned Hanlan', 11.

18. *Toronto Globe*, 15 July 1879.

19. Pierre Berton, 'Ned Hanlan and the Golden Age of Sculling', in Berton, *My Country: The Remarkable Past* (Toronto: McClelland & Stewart, 1976), 204–5.

20. J. Batten, *Champions* (Toronto: New Press, 1971), 53, as cited in Cosentino, 'Ned Hanlan', 12.

21. *Toronto Globe*, 19 Aug. 1879, brackets ours.

22. Ibid., 14 July 1879.

23. H. Roxborough, 'The Boy in Blue', in Roxborough, *Great Days in Canadian Sport* (Toronto: Ryerson Press, 1957), 15.

24. *Toronto Mail*, 4 Oct. 1880.

25. Race events were culled from a variety of sources, including Hunter, Cosentino, and Berton.

26. Hunter, *Rowing in Canada*, 33.

27. Ibid.

28. Cosentino, 'Ned Hanlan', 15.

29. Brown, 'Edward Hanlan, The World Sculling

Champion Visits Australia', *CJHSPE* 11, 2 (Dec. 1980): 1–44.

30. Ibid.

31. *Toronto Globe*, 28 Apr. 1883.

32. Berton, 'Ned Hanlan and the Golden Age', 211.

33. Cosentino, 'Ned Hanlan', 16–17.

34. This section on Rubenstein is based on D. Rosenberg, D. Morrow, and A.J. Young, 'A Quiet Contribution: Louis Rubenstein', *CJHS* 13, 1 (May 1982): 1–18.

35. *Illustrated Police News*, 28 Feb. 1885.

36. *Montreal Gazette*, 19 Feb. 1885.

37. Rubenstein Scrapbook, property of the YMHA Montreal.

38. *Montreal Gazette*, 23 Feb. 1889.

39. See *Montreal Gazette*, 8 Feb. 1883, 23 Jan. 1885.

40. Ibid., 8 Feb. 1883.

41. Ibid., 26 Jan. 1886, for example.

42. A copy of the circular was printed in the *Montreal Gazette* on 1 Nov. 1887.

43. The list was published in the *Gazette* on 18 Jan. 1888.

44. *Montreal Gazette*, 22 Feb. 1884.

45. *Spirit of the Times*, 27 Feb. 1886; *Montreal Daily Star*, 5 Feb. 1886.

46. *Montreal Gazette*, 23 Jan. 1888, 31 Jan. 1889.

47. Ibid., 23 Feb. 1889.

48. Ibid., 15 Jan. 1889.

49. Ibid., 7 Mar. 1888.

50. Ibid., 30 Dec. 1889.

51. Ibid., 15 Mar. 1890.

52. Ibid., 14 Mar. 1890.

53. *Montreal Daily Star*, 10 Feb. 1891.

54. *Montreal Gazette*, 30 Jan. 1895.

55. Ibid., 14 Feb. 1890.

56. Ibid.

57. Ibid., 14–18 Feb. 1890.

58. B. Postal et al., *Encyclopedia of Jews in Sport* (New York: Block Publishing, 1965), 341.

59. No copies of this book have been found. The only reference to it was in one newspaper article written near the end of Rubenstein's athletic career.

60. *Annual Report of the Montreal Amateur Athletic Association*, 1884–87.

61. *Montreal Gazette*, 1 Apr. 1899.

62. Don Morrow, *A Sporting Evolution: The Montreal Amateur Athletic Association, 1881 to 1981* (Montreal: Graphics Group, 1981), 47.

63. *Montreal Daily Star*, 6 Feb., 12 Dec. 1895.

64. Ibid., 20 Feb. 1897.

65. Ibid., 2 Feb. 1907, 6 Feb. 1909.

66. Ibid., 24 June 1911.

67. *Annual Report* of the *MAAA*, 1912–13.

68. *Montreal Daily Star*, 5 Jan. 1916.

69. S.F. Wise and D. Fisher, *Canada's Sporting Heroes: Their Lives and Times* (Don Mills, Ont.: General Publishing, 1974), 214.

70. Personal interview with Rabbi Charles Bender, 19 Dec. 1980.

71. See, for example, *Montreal Gazette*, 1 Aug. 1888, 17 Mar. 1898.

72. Frank Andrews, *Rejoice We Conquer* (Toronto: New Line Fraternity, 1960), 13–14.

73. *Montreal Gazette*, 6 Jan. 1931.

74. B. Weider, *The Strongest Man in History: Louis Cyr* (Toronto: Mitchell Press, 1976). Weider is also the author of *Les Hommes Forts du Quebec* (Montreal: Editions du jour, 1973). The latter work focuses primarily on Cyr. These, plus newspaper articles written at the time of Cyr's death in 1912, are the principal sources for information on Cyr.

75. Weider, *The Strongest Man*, 3–13.

76. S.F. Wise, 'Sport and Class Values in Old Ontario and Quebec', in W.H. Heick and R. Graham, eds, *His Own Man: Essays in Honour of A.R.M. Lower* (Montreal and Kingston: McGill-Queen's University Press, 1974), 96.

77. Weider, *The Strongest Man*, 31; and Wise and Fisher, *Canada's Sporting Heroes*, 141.

78. Wise and Fisher, *Canada's Sporting Heroes*, 63–7.

79. Ibid., 141.

80. David R. Norwood, 'The Sport Hero Concept and Louis Cyr', Master's thesis (University of Windsor, 1971), 40.

81. *Le Devoir*, 11 Nov. 1912.

82. *Montreal Daily Star*, 7 May 1896, as cited in Norwood, 'The Sport Hero Concept', 39.

83. Weider, *The Strongest Man*, 766.

84. Norwood, 'The Sport Hero Concept', 39.

85. *Calgary Herald*, 24 Dec. 1891.

86. Weider, *The Strongest Man*, 89–93.

87. *Le Devoir*, 11 Nov. 1912.

88. Norwood, 'The Sport Hero Concept'.

89. Don Morrow, 'Sweetheart Sport: Barbara Ann Scott and the Post World War Two Image of the Female Athlete in Canada', *CJHS* 28, 1 (May 1987): 36–54. Most of the background information on Scott is taken from this source.

90. David Young, *The Golden Age of Canadian Figure Skating* (Toronto: Summerhill Press, 1984), 7.

91. Nigel Brown, *Ice Skating: A History* (New York: A.S. Barnes & Co., 1979), 177.

92. Young, *The Golden Age*, 63.

93. Her tutor, Sylvia Seeley, remained with her for 10 years. *Ottawa Citizen*, 7 Mar. 1947.

94. *Maclean's*, 15 Feb. 1949.

95. Sidney Hook, *The Hero in History: A Study in Limitation and Possibility* (Boston: Beacon Press, 1955), 151–83. Rubenstein was very likely more eventful than event-making, though a case could be made for both in his case.

96. *Time*, 26 Jan. 1948.

97. Ibid., brackets ours.

98. *Ottawa Citizen*, 13 Mar. 1947.

99. Ibid.

100. *Newsweek*, 5 Feb. 1968.

101. These dolls are treasured heirlooms to this day, available on E-bay for about $600.

102. *Maclean's*, 15 Feb. 1949.

103. For a full discussion of image-making, especially the making of the female image in sport, see A. Bowman and D. Daniels, 'A Shifting Gaze: The Changing Photographic Representation of Women Athletes', *Canadian Women's Studies* 15 (1995): 84–8; D. Hilliard, 'Media Images of Male and Female Professional Athletes: An Interpretive Analysis of Magazine Articles', *Sociology of Sport Journal* 1 (1984): 251–62; D. McDonald, 'The Golden Age of Sport in Canada', *Canadian Women Studies* 15 (1995): 12–15.

104. *Time*, 2 Feb. 1948.

105. Young, *The Golden Age*, 77.

106. These descriptors were taken randomly from newspapers across Canada—the *Vancouver Sun*, *Halifax Herald*, *Toronto Daily Star*, *Ottawa Citizen*, and *Montreal Gazette*. Thus, the press was consistent in describing her perceived femininity.

107. See, for example, *Toronto Daily Star*, 11 Mar. 1947; *Ottawa Citizen*, 17 Feb., 7 Mar. 1947, 9 Mar. 1948.

108. *Ottawa Citizen*, 17 Feb. 1947. Her 1947 world championship 'costume' was put 'on display' in a Toronto department store window—a perfect reflection of the manner in which she was displayed herself. *Toronto Daily Star*, 8 Mar. 1947.

109. *Montreal Gazette*, 7 Feb. 1948.

110. *Ottawa Citizen*, 17 Feb. 1947.

111. *Halifax Herald*, 8 Mar. 1948.

112. See, for example, *Toronto Daily Star*, 11 Mar. 1947; *Ottawa Citizen*, 20 Mar. 1947. At Toronto's 1947 reception, Mayor Saunders actually thanked the mayor of Ottawa for 'lending Toronto its wonderful daughter'. The inference, of course, is that Scott was property for display.

113. *Toronto Daily Star*, 12 Mar. 1947.

114. *Ottawa Citizen*, 7 Feb. 1948.

115. *Halifax Herald*, 8 Mar. 1948, 1.

116. *Ottawa Citizen*, 9 Mar. 1948. The poem is reprinted, in full, in this newspaper edition.

117. After her world championship victory in 1947, the city of Ottawa presented her with a canary yellow convertible complete with the licence plate engraved with 47U1. Prior to her participation in the 1948 Olympic Games, the gift became an issue regarding her amateur status and she returned the gift. See *Ottawa Citizen*, 7, 8, 10 Mar. 1947. Also see Stephen R. Wenn, 'Give Me the Keys Please: Avery Brundage, Canadian Journalists and the Barbara Ann Scott Phaeton Affair', *JSH* 18, 2 (1991): 241–54.

118. *Saturday Night*, 14 Feb. 1948.

119. *Maclean's*, 15 Jan. 1951.

120. Toronto Daily Star, 4 Mar. 1947.

121. *Ottawa Citizen*, 9 Mar. 1948.

122. Ibid., 17 Feb. 1947.

123. B.A. Scott, *Skate With Me* (New York: Doubleday, 1950); B.A. Scott and M. Kirby, *Skating for Beginners* (New York: Alfred A. Knopf, 1953). The latter book went through four printings in 10 years and was copyrighted by Scott's professional corporation, the St Lawrence Foundation. C. Moore, *She Skated Into Our Hearts* (Toronto: McClelland & Stewart, 1948).

124. S. Swan, 'Barbara Ann, Are You Still Happy?', *Chatelaine* (Nov. 1975): 51, brackets ours.

125. Duperreault, Jean R. 'L'Affaire Richard: A Situational Analysis of the Montreal Hockey Riot of 1955' *CJHS* 12, 1 (1981): 107–22. Background information on the Riots and Richard's career statistics are extracted from this source.

126. *Globe and Mail*, 18 March 1955. Richard's prowess has been remembered not only through his hockey records and accelerated induction into the Hockey Hall of Fame (in 1961), but also through Roch Carrier's classic children's story and National Film Board production of *The Hockey Sweater* (Montreal: Tundra Books, 1985), 24 pages. In 2005, Director Charles Binané released a well-reviewed movie entitled *The Rocket*; it starred Roy Dupuis as Richard. See the Internet Movie Database at http://www.imdb.com/title/tt0460505/, accessed 25 October 2008.

127. Batten, *Champions*, 53; see the description of the events under the Ned Hanlan section at the start of this chapter.

128. M. Kram, 'Ben Still Needs to Run', *Outside Magazine* (December 1998), 12.

129. Unless otherwise stated, all background information on Johnson is taken from James R. Christie, *Ben Johnson: The Fastest Man on Earth* (Toronto: McClelland-Bantam Inc., 1988).

130. Listen to the 22 April 1980 CBC broadcast of the boycott decision at http://archives.cbc.ca/sports/olympics/clips/3662/, accessed 14 October 2008.

131. Christie, *Ben Johnson: The Fastest Man on Earth*, 66.

132. *Globe and Mail*, 11 December 2006; and *Wikipedia*, http://en.wikipedia.org/wiki/Lou_Marsh_Trophy, accessed 1 December 2008.

133. See www.gg.ca/honours/. He was actually appointed to the Order on 29 December 1986, just prior to his flurry of indoor world record performances; however, he was not invested until the following April. His citation is: 'World record holder for the indoor 60-metre run, this Ontarian has proved himself to be the world's fastest

human being and has broken Canadian, Commonwealth and World Cup 100-metre records. Recipient of the Norton Crowe Award for Male Athlete of the Year for 1985, "Big Ben" was the winner of the 1986 Lou Marsh Trophy as Canada's top athlete.'

134. *Canadian Encyclopedia*, accessed online at www.thecanadianencyclopedia.com, accessed 8 February 2005; also, see Christie's dramatization of the events of the World Championships, those involving Ben and his arch-rival Carl Lewis, in *Ben Johnson: The Fastest Man on Earth*, 87–92.

135. See http://en.wikipedia.org/wiki/Ben_Johnson _(athlete), accessed 18 November 2008.

136. The 'Big Ben' epithet was very common in the national media. It seemed to be the manner in which the media endeared Johnson to Canadians. Even Johnson's Order of Canada citation used the term. See endnote 131 above.

137. See the CBC archives at http://archives.cbc. ca/sports/drugs_sports/clips/8700/ for a media report of interviews with several disappointed Canadians and doubting broadcasters that was aired about two weeks before the Seoul Games.

138. See http://www.oilersheritage.com/history/ dynasty_highlights_gretzkytrade.html, accessed 1 November 2008, for an account of the Great One's trade.

139. John B. Lee, *The Hockey Player Sonnets* (Waterloo, Penumbra Press, 1991), 28.

140. Don Morrow, 'Olympic Masculinity: An Analysis of Canadian Newspapers During the 1976, 1988, and the 2000 Summer Olympic Games' in *The Global Nexus Engaged: Past, Present, and Future Interdisciplinary Olympic Studies* (London, Ont.: The University of Western Ontario, 2002), 123–34. Most of the background information on the 1988 Games and descriptions of Johnson are taken from this source.

141. YouTube currently carries the full race at http://www.youtube.com/watch?v=cCh5 QswxQ6k, accessed 1 December 2008.

142. Toronto Sun, 26 September 1988.

143. Morrow, 'Olympic Masculinity'.

144. Ibid.

145. William Oscar Johnson and Kenny Moore, 'The Loser', *Sports Illustrated*, 3 October 1988, at http://vault.sportsillustrated.cnn. com/, accessed online 15 November 2008.

146. When the hearings ended in October of 1989, the television program, *As It Happens* presented an audio collage of the inquiry's 'most gripping moments'. The collage can be heard at http://archives.cbc.ca/sports/ drugs_sports/clips/8964/, accessed 15 October 2008. The hearings cost Canadian taxpayers some $3.6 million.

147. Charlie Francis, *Speed Trap: Inside the Biggest Scandal in Olympic History* (Toronto: Lester and Orpen Denny's, 1990).

148. See https://www.trackandfieldnews.com/ archive/aoy.html, accessed 1 December 2008.

149. Steven J. Jackson, 'Exorcizing the Ghost: Donovan Bailey, Ben Johnson and the Politics of Canadian Identity' *Media, Culture and Society* 26, 1 (2004): 126.

150. Ibid., 126–8. Jackson's article contains a litany of documented media racial stereotypes.

151. Ibid., 129.

152. See, *The Boston Globe*, 28 April 2005, for a story by Stan Grosfield that documents other banned substance users in the years following the 1988 Olympic Games.

153. The Cheetah ad can be seen at http:// www.youtube.com/watch?v=KlL1vl601rk, accessed 1 December 2008.

154. *Toronto Star*, 15 August 2008.

155. Ibid., 28 December 2008.

Chapter 7 Sports Journalism and the Media

1. See Marshal McLuhan, *Understanding Media: The Extensions of Man* (New York: McGraw-Hill, 1964), for a full explanation of McLuhan's theories about the media.

2. See http://www.thecanadianpress.com/home. aspx?ID=58, accessed 8 November 2008.

3. For a more contemporary analysis of the media's impact on Canadian sport, see Steve Jackson, Jay Scherer, and Scott G. Martyn, 'Sport and the Media' in *Canadian Sport Sociology*, Jane Crossman, ed. (Toronto: Nelson, 2008), 177–195.

4. Ian F. Jobling, 'Sport in Nineteenth Century Canada: The Effects of Technological Changes in its Development', PhD dissertation (University of Alberta, 1970), 71–138 on 'Communication Changes'. See also Chapter 4 in this text for the discussion of the telegraph's impact on sport.

5. William A. Hewitt, *Down the Stretch: Recollections of a Pioneer Sportsman and Journalist* (Toronto: Ryerson Press, 1958), 18.

6. *Toronto Daily Star*, 9 March 1936. Marsh died two days earlier; this issue of the Star was filled with tributes to him as well as facts and stories about his career.

7. *The Evening Citizen*, Ottawa, 5 March 1936.

8. *Toronto Daily Star*, 9 March 1936, brackets ours.

9. Ibid. Phil Edwards was a winner of five bronze medals in middle distance running events in three successive Olympic Games, 1928 to 1936 inclusive. A graduate of New York and McGill universities, Edwards was self-trained and self-coached.

10. To date, hockey star Wayne Gretzky has won the award on four occasions, more times than any other athlete; figure skater Barbara Ann Scott (see Chapter 7) has won it 3 times, the most frequent winner among Canadian female athletes.

11. Don Morrow, 'Lou Marsh: The Pick and Shovel of Canadian Sporting Journalism', *CJHS* 14, 1 (May 1983): 21–33. A great deal of the material on Marsh's involvement in sport is taken from this source.

12. Bruce Kidd has suggested that Marsh's involvement with Longboat was suspi- cious, at best. Kidd provides a number of examples of outright racist comments in his columns. Though not unusual in the press of the era, the comments did have strong tones of racism. Moreover, Kidd sug- gests that Marsh had the best opportunity to provide the overdose of strychnine to Longboat during the 1908 Olympic mara- thon because trainers and coaches were allowed to accompany their athletes along the marathon routes. See Bruce Kidd, 'In Defense of Tom Longboat', *CJHS* 14, 1 (May 1983): 43–4, and 49–52.

13. *Montreal Star*, 5 March 1936.

14. *Toronto Daily Star*, 5 March 1936.

15. Ibid., 5–9 March 1936. The Star was filled with tributes and stories about Marsh. Many of his colleagues attempted to describe the nature of his writing style in those issues.

16. Ibid., 2 January 1931, brackets ours.

17. This claim is based upon the many, many comments from Canadian and American sportswriters who were quoted directly in the *Toronto Daily Star* from 5–9 March 1936. Journalists, writers, and readers alike were unanimous in their testaments to Marsh's sports writing allure.

18. Ibid., 8 February 1927. Until the mid 1920s, even-man hockey was common, even in the NHL. The seventh position was a rover.

19. Ibid., 15 February 1926.

20. Ibid., 10 July 1928.

21. Ibid., 27 August 1928. The three-star marks were separators Marsh used throughout his column, likely intended to maintain the terse, punchy format.

22. Ibid., 2 May 1933.

23. Ibid., 23 June 1930.

24. Ibid., 5 January 1931.

25. Ibid., 27 May 1925.

26. Ibid., 29 September 1927.

27. Ibid., 8 June 1931.

28. Ibid., 5 January 1929.

29. Ibid., 16 September 1931.

30. Ibid. 11 February 1928.

31. See, for example, his columns in ibid., 10 November 1935, 13 November 1934, 23 May 1927, 1 December 1925, and 19 February 1936.

32. Ibid., 29 August 1928.

33. Ibid., 16 December 1925.

34. Ibid., 12 March 1931. 'Gutta percha' is the hardened rubber material used as an insulator in electrical wires, in dental fillings, and, in Marsh's realm, the core of golf balls.

35. Ibid., 6 February 1928 (Jim Douglas); 5 January 1931 (Louis Rubenstein, see Chapter 7); and 1 June 1931 (Joseph Herdsman).

36. Ibid., 8 September 1933. Note that Hanlan died 25 years earlier; forgotten or never known by contemporary Torontonians, Hanlan was still revered at that time.

37. Marsh may have been instrumental in launching the Santa Claus fund-raiser which is still in existence at the time of this book's publication.

38. Ibid., 7 September 1927.

39. Ibid., 23 October 1926. The *Bluenose* is the ship etched into one side of the Canadian dime.

40. *Winnipeg Tribune*, 5 March 1936, and *Vancouver Sun*, 5 March 1936.

41. S.F. Wise and Douglas Fisher, *Canada's Sporting Heroes: Their Lives and Times* (Don Mills: General Publishing Company, 1974), 311.

42. Bruce Kidd, 'Forgotten Foremother: Alexandrine Gibb', *Canadian Association for the Advancement of Women in Sport (CAAWS) Action Bulletin* (Winter, 1994), reprinted at http://www.caaws.ca/e/milestones/women_history/alexandrine_gibb.cfm, accessed 18 November 2008. Gibb was the driving force in organizing the women's branch, the Women's Amateur Athletic Federation, of the Amateur Athletic Union of Canada governing body of amateur sport. In addition, it was Gibb's initiative more than anyone else that enabled a group of Canadian track athletes to attend the 1928 Amsterdam Olympics; the six women who participated in the first Olympic Games to include women in track and field competitions, amassed more medals than any other women's team at the Games.

43. Honouring Canada's Sporting Heroes, the Canadian Sports Hall of Fame biographies, Ted Reeve biography, at http://www.cshof.ca/hm_profile.php?i=366, accessed 11 November 2008.

44. Ibid.

45. *The Globe*, 13 November 1931.

46. J.T. Scanlon, 'Sports in the Daily Press in Canada'. Mimeographed, unpublished paper prepared for Sport Canada, Ottawa, 1970.

47. See Ronald S. Lappage, 'Selected Sports in Canadian Society, 1921–1939'. Unpublished doctoral dissertation, University of Alberta, 1974.

48. J.E. Waters, 'A Content Analysis of the Sport Section of in Selected Canadian Newspapers, 1927–1935'. Unpublished Master's thesis, The University of Western Ontario, 1981.

49. Ibid., 12–65.

50. *Toronto Telegram*, 7 October 1929.

51. Ibid., 8 October 1928.

52. Ibid., 13 October 1930.

53. Ibid., 27 July 1931.

54. Ibid., 27 October 1930.

55. Ibid., 3 July 1928.

56. Ibid., 21 January 1929.

57. Ibid.

58. Ibid., 29 July 1929. Thompson was from Penetanguishene, hence the sobriquet 'Penetang.'

59. Ibid., 3 July 1928.

60. Ibid., 9 July 1928.

61. Ibid., 11 July 1932, brackets ours.

62. Ibid., 11 January 1932.

63. Ibid., 6 October 1930.

64. The Edmonton Graduates basketball team is perhaps the best known example of women's elite level competitive sport during the 1920s and 1930s.

65. The *Toronto Daily Star* carried basic, factual coverage for these games and teams. See, for example, 10 June 1925.

66. *Globe and Mail*, 20 March 1985.

67. *The Toronto Daily Star*, 3 July 1928.

68. Ibid., 13 August 1928. Lou Marsh, also in attendance at the event, corroborated Gibb's interpretation and called the starter's methods at least inconsistent. Ibid.

69. Henry Roxborough, *Canada at the Olympics* (Toronto: The Ryerson Press), 71–3, gives a recollected account of the race.

70. Ibid., 4 August 1928.

71. 'Celebrating Women's Achievements', National Library of Canada, available at http://www.nlc-bnc.ca2/12h12-225-e.html, accessed 15 February 2008.

72. The records held by Cook through to 1931 for the 100-metre event was 12.0 seconds, also a world record; in the 60-yard sprint, her record time was 7.0 seconds. *Montreal Daily Star*, 9 May 1931.

73. Currently writing for the *Globe and Mail*, Blatchford is one of the country's most respected and widely read journalists. Most recently, she wrote an acclaimed *Fifteen Days: Stories of Bravery, Friendship, Life and Death from Inside the New Canadian Army* (Toronto: Doubleday Canada, 2007) concerning frontline stories of Canadians serving in Afghanistan.

74. *Toronto Daily Star*, 8 July 1976.

75. She began to write her column in the second week of that month andcontinued to write for the *Star* for 40 years. Background infor-

mation on Cook's career and some of her column examples are taken from Pamela Lewis 'Myrtle Cook: Her Role in Promoting Women's Sport in Canada'. Unpublished paper, The University of Western Ontario, 1978. See also, Ann Hall, *The Girl and the Game: A History of Women's Sport in Canada* (Peterborough: Broadview Press, 2002) for interspersed and various discussions of Cook's impact on Canadian sport as athlete, coach, administrator, and journalist.

76. *Montreal Daily Star*, 22 April 1929.

77. Ibid., 15 May 1929.

78. Ibid., 12 June 1929. The Caledonian Society incorporated 100-yard dash and high jump events for women for the first time at their annual meet in 1929. Ibid., 14 June 1929.

79. *Toronto Daily Star*, 15 August 1928.

80. *Montreal Daily Star*, 10 June 1929.

81. Ibid., 17 August 1929.

82. Ibid., 9 January 1930.

83. Ibid. The column on 28 October 1929 is an example of her exploration and description of Hitomi's career; Johnson's solo flight is detailed on 29 October 1930.

84. Ibid., 30 July 1931.

85. Ibid., 16 January 1931.

86. *Globe and Mail*, 10 December 1957.

87. Ibid., 20 March 1985. See also, Athletics Canada, Rules and By-laws, Rule 261, page 4, available at http://www.athletics.ca/files// Governance/AC%20RULES%20SECTION %20V%20(241-270)%20-2008%20(EN). PDF, accessed 9 November 2008. The Myrtle Cook Trophy was first awarded in 1963 and is awarded annually to 'the Most Outstanding Youth (17 and under) athlete in any discipline of Athletics. Male and Female athletes are to be considered'.

88. Joseph Levy, Danny Rosenberg, and Avi Hyman, 'Fanny "Bobbie" Rosenfeld: Canada's Woman Athlete of the Half Century', *Journal of Sport History* 26, 2 (199): 392–6. Rosenfeld was also honoured

with her picture on a 1996 Canadian 45-cent stamp.

89. Ibid., 5 November 1938.

90. http://jwa.org/exhibits/wov/rosenfeld/, accessed 18 October 2007. She actually wrote the column over a 21-year span.

91. The columns are reprinted from ibid.

Chapter 8 Gender, Body, and Sport

1. Many historians and sociologists have used this term. See, for example, R.W. Connell, *The Men and the Boys* (Cambridge: Polity Press, 2000), 12; Brian Pronger, *The Arena of Masculinity: Sports, Homosexuality, and the Meaning of Sex* (Toronto: Summerhill Press, 1990).

2. Michael Heine, *Arctic Sports: A Training and Resource Manual* (Calgary: Triad Press, 1998).

3. See Carol Devens, 'Separate Confrontations: Gender as a Factor in Indian Adaption to European Colonization in New France', in Veronica Strong-Boag and Anita Clair Fellman, eds, *Rethinking Canada: The Promise of Women's History*, 3rd edn (Toronto: Oxford University Press, 1986), 11–32; Sylvia Van Kirk, '"Women in Between": Indian Women in Fur Trade Society in Western Canada', in Ken S. Coates and Robin Fisher, eds, *Out of the Background: Readings on Canadian Native History* (Toronto: Irwin Publishing, 1998), 102–17; Susan Sleeper-Smith, 'Furs and Female Kin Networks: The World of Marie Reaume l'archevêque Chavalier', in Jo-Anne Fiske, Susan Sleeper-Smith, and William Wicken, eds, *New Faces of the Fur Trade: Selected Papers of the Seventh North American Fur Trade Conference, Halifax, Nova Scotia, 1995* (East Lansing: Michigan State University Press, 1998).

4. Bruce G. Trigger, 'The Road to Affluence: A Reassessment of Early Huron Responses to European Contact', in Coates and Fisher, eds, *Out of the Background*.

5. Kevin B. Wamsley, 'The Public Importance of Men and the Importance of Public Men: Sport and Masculinity in 19th Century Canada', in Philip White and Kevin Young, eds, *Sport and Gender in Canada* (Toronto: Oxford University Press, 1999), 24–39.

6. Michael Payne, 'The Sports, Games, Recreations, and Pastimes of the Fur Traders: Leisure at York Factory', in Morris Mott, ed., *Sports in Canada: Historical Readings* (Mississauga, Ont.: Copp Clark Pitman, 1989), 50–77; Ronald S. Lappage, 'The Physical Feats of the Voyageur', *CJHS* 15, 1 (May 1984): 30–7.

7. Jan Noel, 'New France: Les femmes favourisées,' in Strong-Boag and Fellman, *Rethinking Canada*, 34–56; Janice Potter, 'Patriarchy and Paternalism: The Case of the Eastern Ontario Loyalist Women', ibid., 57–69.

8. Nancy M. Theriot, *The Biosocial Construction of Femininity: Mothers and Daughters in Nineteenth-Century America* (New York: Greenwood Press, 1988), 25.

9. Cecilia Morgan, *Public Men and Virtuous Women: The Gendered Languages of Religion and Politics in Upper Canada, 1791–1850* (Toronto: University of Toronto Press, 1996), 54.

10. Ibid.

11. Ibid., 37.

12. Nancy B. Bouchier, *For the Love of the Game: Amateur Sport in Small-Town Ontario 1838–1895* (Montreal and Kingston: McGill-Queen's University Press, 2003), 88–94.

13. Ibid., 91.

14. Alan Greer, 'The Birth of the Police in Canada', in Alan Greer and Ian Radforth, eds, *Colonial Leviathan: State Formation in Mid-Nineteenth-Century Canada* (Toronto: University of Toronto Press, 1992), 17–49.

15. See *History of the County of Middlesex, Canada* (Toronto and London: Goodspeed, Publishers), 1889, 120–2; J.M. Beattie, 'Attitudes Towards Crime and Punishment in Upper Canada, 1830–1850: A Documentary Study' (Toronto: Working Paper of the

Centre of Criminology, University of Toronto, 1977), 1–8.

16. Wamsley, 'The Public Importance of Men'.

17. Ibid.; Kevin B. Wamsley, 'Legislation and Leisure in 19th Century Canada', PhD dissertation (University of Alberta, 1992); Bouchier, *For the Love of the Game*, 31–59.

18. Noel, 'New France', 46.

19. Rusty Bitterman, 'Women and the Escheat Movement: The Politics of Everyday Life on Prince Edward Island', in Strong-Boag and Fellman, *Rethinking Canada*, 79–92.

20. Kevin B. Wamsley and Robert S. Kossuth, 'Fighting It Out in Nineteenth-Century Upper Canada/Canada West: Masculinities and Physical Challenges in the Tavern', *JSH* 27, 3 (Fall 2000): 405–30.

21. Wamsley, 'Legislation and Leisure'.

22. Wamsley and Kossuth, 'Fighting It Out'.

23. Norman Feltes, *This Side of Heaven: Determining the Donnelly Murders, 1880* (Toronto: University of Toronto Press, 1999).

24. Wamsley and Kossuth, 'Fighting It Out'.

25. Ibid.

26. Ibid.

27. See Eric Dunning's discussion of violence as fun in *Sport Matters: Sociological Studies of Sport, Violence, and Civilization* (London: Routledge, 1999).

28. Theriot, *The Biosocial Construction of Femininity*, 39–40.

29. Ibid., 44.

30. Don Morrow, 'The Knights of the Snowshoe: A Study of the Evolution of Sport in Nineteenth Century Montreal', *JSH* 15, 1 (1988): 5–40.

31. Judith Fingard, 'Masculinity, Fraternity, and Respectability in Halifax at the Turn of the Century', in Joy Parr and Mark Rosenfeld, eds, *Gender and History in Canada* (Toronto: Copp Clark, 1996), 211–24.

32. Morrow, 'The Knights of the Snowshoe', 22–4.

33. Greg Gillespie and Kevin B. Wamsley, '"My Chief Object—Fine Heads": Big Game Hunting, Imperialism, and Masculinities in the British North American West', *Proceedings* of the North American Society of Sport History Conference, 2002; Elizabeth Vibert, 'Real Men Hunt Buffalo: Masculinity, Race and Class in British Fur Traders' Narratives', in Parr and Rosenfeld, eds, *Gender and History*, 50–67.

34. M. Ann Hall, *The Girl and the Game. A History of Women's Sport in Canada* (Peterborough, Ont.: Broadview Press, 2002), 7–9.

35. Morrow, 'Knights of the Snowshoe'.

36. Jihang Park, 'Sport, Dress Reform and the Emancipation of Women in Victorian England: A Reappraisal', *IJHS* 6, 1 (May 1989): 10.

37. Theriot, *The Biosocial Construction of Femininity*, 45.

38. Francis Hoffman and Ryan Taylor, *Much To Be Done: Private Life in Ontario from Victorian Diaries* (Toronto: Natural Heritage/Natural History Inc., 1996), 219, from the Diary of Forbes Geddes, 22 Oct. 1862, Hamilton Public Library, Special Collections, Archives File.

39. Ibid., 217, Geddes Diary, 22 Feb. 1862.

40. See Hall's description of the pedestrian contests in *The Girl and the Game*, 8–9; Kevin B. Wamsley, 'Cultural Signification and National Ideologies: Rifle Shooting in Late Nineteenth-Century Canada', *Social History* 20, 1 (1995): 63–72.

41. Clifford Putney, Muscular Christianity: Manhood and Sports in Protestant America, 1880–1920 (Cambridge, Mass.: Harvard University Press, 2001), 3.

42. Lynne Marks, *Revivals and Roller Rinks: Religion, Leisure, and Identity in Late Nineteenth Century Small-Town Ontario* (Toronto: University of Toronto Press, 1996), 33.

43. Ibid.

44. Norman Vance, Sinews of the Spirit—The Ideal of Christian Manliness in Victorian Literature *and Religious Thought* (Cambridge: Cambridge University Press, 1985), 2. See also J.A. Mangan, *The Games Ethic and Imperialism: Aspects of the Diffusion of an Ideal* (London: Frank Cass, 1998), esp. 142–67.

45. Jeffrey Richards, 'Introduction' to J.A. Mangan, *Athleticism in the Victorian and Edwardian Public School* (London: Frank Cass, 2000), xxiii.

46. Morrow, 'Knights of the Snowshoe', see the 'Song of the Montreal Snow Shoe Club'.

47. Mangan, *Athleticism*, 189, citing Norman Gale, 'The Female Boy', in *More Cricket Songs* (London, 1905), 15.

48. David W. Brown, 'Sport, Darwinism and Canadian Private Schooling to 1918', *CJHS* 26, 1 (May 1985): 31, citing T. Aldwell, *Conquering the Last Fortier* (Seattle: Artcraft Engraving and Electic Company, 1950), 5–6.

49. S. Houston and A. Prentice, *Schooling and Schools in 19th Century Ontario* (Toronto: University of Toronto Press, 1988).

50. Wamsley, 'Cultural Signification and National Ideologies'.

51. Don Morrow et al., *A Concise History of Sport in Canada* (Toronto: Oxford University Press, 1989), 78–9.

52. Hall, *The Girl and the Game*, 27.

53. Ibid., 30–3.

54. Leigh Summers, *Bound to Please: A History of the Victorian Corset* (New York: Berg, 2001).

55. Geoffry Bilson, *A Darkened House: Cholera in Nineteenth Century Canada* (Toronto: University of Toronto Press, 1980); Michael Bliss, *Plague: A Story of Smallpox in Montreal* (Toronto: HarperCollins, 1991).

56. Patricia A. Vertinsky, *The Eternally Wounded Woman: Women, Doctors, and Exercise in the Late Nineteenth Century* (Urbana: University of Illinois Press, 1994).

57. Ibid., 39, citing 'The Obstetrical Society meeting to consider the proposition of the council for the removal of Mr. I.B. Brown', *British Medical Journal* 1 (1867): 396.

58. Vertinsky, *The Eternally Wounded Woman*.

59. Helen Lenskyj, *Out of Bounds: Women, Sport and Sexuality* (Toronto: Women's Press, 1986), 17.

60. Vertinsky, *The Eternally Wounded Woman*, 52–3.

61. Ibid., 39–40.

62. James C. Whorton, 'Athlete's Heart: The Medical Debate over Athleticism, 1870–1920', *JSH* 9, 1 (Spring 1982): 30–52.

63. Lenskyj, *Out of Bounds*, 19–20.

64. Wamsley, 'Legislation and Leisure'.

65. Lenskyj, *Out of Bounds*, 20–2.

66. Park, 'Sport, Dress Reform and the Emancipation of Women', 14.

67. Amanda Schweinbenz, 'All Dressed Up and Nowhere to Run: Women's Uniforms and Clothing in the Olympic Games from 1900 to 1932', Master's thesis (University of Western Ontario, 2001).

68. Ibid., 28–41.

69. Tobias Smollett, *The Expedition of Humphrey Clinker* (London: Penguin Books, 1967), 213.

70. Vertinsky, *The Eternally Wounded Woman*, 12–15; M. Danyet Cunningham, 'Limitations Reconsidered: The Interplay between Women's Capabilities and Menstrual Mythology Evident in the *American Physical Education Review*, 1896–1929', Master's thesis (University of Western Ontario, 1990), 27–8.

71. S.F. Wise and Douglas Fisher, *Canada's Sporting Heroes* (Don Mills, Ont.: General Publishing, 1974), 21.

72. Canon R.W. Norman, 'Shorter Consecutive

School Hours', *The Educational Record* 1, 1 (1881): 5, cited in Graham Ivan Neil, 'A History of Physical Education in the Protestant Schools of Quebec', Master's thesis (McGill University, 1963), 24 (London, Ont.: ICOS archives).

73. Glen Norcliffe, *The Ride to Modernity: The Bicycle in Canada, 1869–1900* (Toronto: University of Toronto Press, 2001), 182.

74. Robert S. Kossuth and Kevin B. Wamsley, 'Cycles of Manhood: Pedaling Respectability in Early Ontario Bicycle Clubs', *SHR* 34, 2 (Nov. 2003), citing John Woodforde, *The Story of the Bicycle* (New York: Universe Books, 1970), 41.

75. Ibid.

76. Lenskyj, *Out of Bounds*, 20; Hall, *The Girl and the Game*, 18–19.

77. Hall, *The Girl and the Game*, 18; Schweinbenz, 'All Dressed Up', 36–47.

78. Lenskyj, *Out of Bounds*, 60.

79. Schweinbenz, 'All Dressed Up', 36.

80. Chris Armstrong and H.V. Nelles, *The Revenge of the Methodist Bicycle Company* (Toronto: Peter Martin Associates, 1977).

81. Hall, *The Girl and the Game*, 27–33.

82. Lenskyj, *Out of Bounds*, 62.

83. Ibid., 39.

84. Colin Howell, *Northern Sandlots—A Social History of Maritime Baseball* (Toronto: University of Toronto Press, 1995).

85. Alan Metcalfe, 'Sport and Athletics: A Case Study of Lacrosse in Canada', *Journal of Sport History* 3, 1 (Spring 1976): 1–19; Bouchier, *For the Love of the Game*, 129.

86. Varda Burstyn, *The Rites of Men: Manhood, Politics, and the Culture of Sport* (Toronto: University of Toronto Press, 1999).

87. Wamsley, 'Legislation and Leisure', 219–20.

88. Peter L. Lindsay and David Howell, 'Social Gospel and the Young Boy Problem, 1895–1925', *CJHS* 17, 1 (May 1986): 75–87.

89. Howell, *Northern Sandlots*; Spencer Lang, 'Importing Professional Baseball: An Examination of the Guelph Maple Leafs and London Tecumsehs 1872–1878, Master's thesis (University of Western Ontario, 2003); Richard Gruneau and David Whitson, *Hockey Night in Canada: Sport, Identities, and Cultural Politics* (Toronto: Garamond Press, 1993).

90. Gruneau and Whitson, *Hockey Night in Canada*, 74–6.

91. Kevin Young and Kevin B. Wamsley, 'State Complicity in Sports Assault and the Gender Order in Twentieth Century Canada: Preliminary Observations', *Avante* 2, 2 (1996): 51–69.

92. Ibid.

93. Kevin B. Wamsley and David Whitson, 'Celebrating Violent Masculinities: The Boxing Death of Luther McCarty', *JSH* 25, 3 (Fall 1998): 419–31.

94. Ibid.

95. Ibid.; Alan Metcalfe, 'The Evolution of Organized Physical Recreation in Montreal, 1840–1895', in Morris Mott, ed., *Sports in Canada: Historical Readings* (Toronto: Copp Clark Pitman, 1989), 130–55; Robert S. Kossuth, 'Constructing a Stage for Play: Sport, Recreation, and Leisure in London, Ontario, 1867–1914', PhD dissertation (University of Western Ontario, 2002); Bouchier, *For the Love of the Game*, Ch. 3, n. 108.

96. Wamsley and Whitson, 'Celebrating Violent Masculinities'. See John Terrence Jackson, 'Tommy Burns: World Heavyweight Boxing Champion', Master's thesis (University of Western Ontario, 1985).

97. A.J. 'Sandy' Young, *Beyond Heroes: A History of Sport in Nova Scotia* (Hantsport, NS: Lancelot Press, 1988), 34–40.

98. Wamsley and Whitson, 'Celebrating Violent Masculinities'.

99. Hall, *The Girl and the Game*, 37.

100. Kevin B. Wamsley and Greg Gillespie, 'The Prince of Wales Tour and the Construction

of British Sporting Masculinity in Nineteenth-Century Canada', Proceedings of the North American Society for Sport History, Columbus, Ohio, 2003; Bouchier, *For the Love of the Game*, 38; Marks, *Revivals and Roller Rinks*, 118.

101. Marks, Revivals and Roller Rinks, 116–20.

102. Howell, Northern Sandlots, 99–100.

103. Kenneth R. Dutton, *The Perfectible Body: The Western Ideal of Male Physical Development* (New York: Continuum, 1995), 119–25.

104. Lenskyj, *Out of Bounds*, 63.

105. Ibid., 92–129.

106. Susan L. Forbes, 'The Influence of the Social Reform Movement and T. Eaton Company's Business Practices on the Leisure of Eaton's Female Employees During the Early Twentieth Century', PhD dissertation (University of Western Ontario, 1998). See also John Byl, 'The Margaret Eaton School, 1901–1942: Women's Education in Elocution, Drama, and Physical Education', PhD dissertation (State University of New York at Buffalo, 1992).

107. Hall, *The Girl and the Game*, 34–6.

108. This story was captured by the National Film Board's celebratory film, *Shooting Stars*.

109. Cathy Macdonald, 'The Edmonton Grads: Canada's Most Successful Team, A History and Analysis of Their Success', Master's thesis (University of Windsor, 1976); Elaine Chalus, 'The Edmonton Commercial Graduates: Women's History, An Integrationist Approach', in E.A. Corbet and A.W. Rasporich, eds, *Winter Sports in the West* (Calgary: Historical Society of Alberta, 1990), 69–86.

110. Kevin B. Wamsley, 'Power and Privilege in Historiography: Constructing Percy Page', *SHR* 28, 2 (Nov. 1997): 146–55.

111. Amanda Schweinbenz and Kevin B. Wamsley, 'Lilies, Pixies, Mermaids, and Sweethearts: The Feminization of Olympic Female Athletes in the Popular Media',

paper presented at conference of ISCPES, Windsor, Ont., 2001.

112. Lenskyj, *Out of Bounds*, 78.

113. Kevin B. Wamsley, 'Symbolic Body Practices: Gender Configurations in the Early Olympic Games', *Proceedings*, North American Society for Sport History, Banff, Alta, May 2000.

114. Schweinbenz, 'All Dressed Up'.

115. Henry Roxborough, *One Hundred-Not Out: The Story of Nineteenth Century Canadian Sport* (Toronto: Ryerson Press, 1966), 83.

116. Hall, *The Girl and the Game*, 46–51.

117. Bruce Kidd, *The Struggle for Canadian Sport* (Toronto: University of Toronto Press, 1996), 116–19.

118. Hall, *The Girl and the Game*, 50.

119. Kidd, *Struggle for Canadian Sport*, 123–4; Lenskyj, *Out of Bounds*, 69.

120. *Chatham Daily News*, 'Movie Sparks Fond Memories for Stanton', date unknown, Stanton family scrapbook, Chatham.

121. Personal interview with Nancy Meredith, daughter of Marion Watson, by Shannon Stanojevic, 4 Nov. 1998.

122. Hall, *The Girl and the Game*, 104–13.

123. Gruneau and Whitson, *Hockey Night in Canada*, 131–73.

124. Ibid., 175–96.

125. Mariah Burton Nelson, *The Stronger Women Get, the More Men Love Football: Sexism and the American Culture of Sports* (New York: Harcourt Brace, 1994).

126. John D. Fair, *Muscletown USA: Bob Hoffman and the Manly Culture of York Barbell* (University Park: Pennsylvania State University Press, 1999).

127. Dutton, *The Perfectible Body*, 139–41.

128. Alan Klein, *Little Big Men: Bodybuilding Subculture and Gender Construction* (Albany: State University of New York Press, 1993).

129. Dutton, *The Perfectible Body*, 144–7.

130. Janice Rodney, 'Fitness Magazines and Body Ideal', unpublished paper, ICOS archives, London, Ont., 2003.

131. Susan Bordo, 'Reading the Slender Body', in E. Jacobus, E. Fox Keller, and S. Shuttleworth, eds, *Body Politics: Women and the Discourse of Science* (New York: Routledge, 1990), 83–112; C. Spitzack, *Confessing Excess: Women and the Politics of Body Reduction* (Albany: State University of New York Press, 1990).

132. Hall, *The Girl and the Game*, 127.

133. Ibid., 181.

134. Ibid.

135. Kevin Young and Philip White, 'Sport, Physical Danger and Injury: The Experiences of Elite Women Athletes', *Journal of Sport and Social Issues* 19 (1995): 45–61.

136. Kevin B. Wamsley, 'Organizing Gender in the Modern Olympic Games'. Keynote address to the Singapore Olympic Academy, 2000; K.D. Brownell, J. Rodin, and J.H. Wilmore, eds, *Eating, Body Weight and Performance in Athletics* (Philadelphia: Lea & Febiger, 1992).

Chapter 9 Physical Education, School Sport, and Physical Fitness

1. E.B. Houghton, *Physical Culture* (Toronto: Warwick and Sons, 1886), 38.

2. Michael Dinning, 'The Role of the Government of Canada and the Province of Ontario in the Implementation of the Fitness and Amateur Sport Act, 1961–1974', Master's thesis (University of Western Ontario, 1974), 37.

3. The full title of the Trust was, The Strathcona Trust: For the Encouragement of Physical and Military Training in Public Schools. See Don Morrow, 'The Strathcona Trust in Ontario, 1911–1939', *CJHS* 8, 1 (May 1977): 72–90.

4. See J.H. Passmore, 'Teacher Education', in M.L. Van Vliet, *Physical Education in Canada* (Scarborough, Ont.: Prentice-Hall of Canada, 1965), 55–6; F. Cosentino and M.L. Howell, *A History of Physical Education in Canada* (Toronto: General Publishing, 1971), 26–30.

5. Morrow, 'The Strathcona Trust'; J.A. McDiarmid, 'The Strathcona Trust: Its Influence on Physical Education', in *Proceedings of the First Canadian Symposium on the History of Sport and Physical Education*, Edmonton, 13–16 May 1970, 395–413.

6. A.S. Lamb, 'Physical Education in Canada', *Canadian Physical Education Association* (1933–4): 4, as cited in R.S. Lappage, 'Selected Sports and Canadian Society, 1921–1939', PhD dissertation (University of Alberta, 1974), 224–5.

7. See, J.D. Eaton, 'The Life and Professional Contributions of Arthur Stanley Lamb, M.D., to Physical Education in Canada', PhD dissertation (Ohio State University, 1964), 181–5.

8. Norman O. Brown, *Life against Death the Psychoanalytic Meaning of History* (Middletown, Conn.: Wesleyan University Press, 1959), 31, brackets ours.

9. W.T. Newham and A.S. Nease, *The Professional Teacher in Ontario: The Heritage, Responsibilities and Practices* (Toronto: Ryerson Press, 1965), 1, 19.

10. J.G. Althouse, 'The Ontario Teacher: An Historical Account of Progress, 1800–1900', Doctor of Pedagogy dissertation (University of Toronto, 1929), 1–18.

11. J.G. Hodgins, *Documentary History of Education in Upper Canada* (Toronto: Warwick Brothers and Rutter Printers, 1897), vol. 5, 272. A 'closet' was the term used to refer, at times, to an outdoor toilet facility.

12. E.C. Bockus, 'The Common Schools of Upper Canada, 1786–1840', Master's thesis (McGill University, 1967), 122.

13. J.G. Hodgins, *The Establishment of Schools and Colleges in Ontario, 1792–1910* (Toronto: L.K. Cameron, 1910), vol. 2, 143.

14. Ibid., vol. 1, 9. The 'Old Blue School' merged with Upper Canada College in the late 1820s and 1830s. They were two schools at one location during that period, eventually becoming just UCC. The original six-acre plot of land owned by the Home District School was given to Upper Canada College as its permanent site.

15. Hodgins, *Documentary History of Education in Upper Canada*, vol. 1, 293.

16. Cited ibid., 354.

17. Susan E. Houston, 'Politics, Schools and Social Change in Upper Canada between 1836 and 1846', Master's thesis (University of Toronto, 1967), 16–50. The quotation from the Duncombe report is taken from Houston, p. 16.

18. Egerton Ryerson, *The Story of My Life*, ed. J.G. Hodgins (Toronto: William Briggs, 1883), 342–3.

19. Peter L. Lindsay, 'A History of Sport in Canada, 1807–1867', PhD dissertation (University of Alberta, 1969), 197–218.

20. Ryerson, *The Story of My Life*, 40. 'The primary and dominant motive of his life was religious', wrote Ryerson's principal biographer, C.B. Sissons, in *Egerton Ryerson: His Life and Letters* (Toronto: Clarke Irwin and Company, 1937), vol. 10, 3.

21. C.B. Sissons, ed., *My Dearest Sophie: Letters from Egerton Ryerson to His Daughter* (Toronto: Ryerson Press, 1969), 3, 75, 87.

22. Ibid., 83.

23. Ryerson considered Arnold 'one of England's most distinguished and enlightened educationists'. Egerton Ryerson, ed., *Journal of Education for Upper Canada* 6, 1 (Jan. 1853): 16.

24. See J.A. Mangan, *Athleticism in the Victorian Edwardian Public School* (London: Falmer Press, 1981); Mangan, *The Games Ethic and Imperialism: Aspects of the Diffusion of an Idea* (New York: Viking Penguin, 1985), esp. 142–67.

25. Hodgins, *The Establishment of Schools and Colleges in Ontario*, vol. 6, 161–2.

26. Hodgins, *Documentary History of Education*, vol. 10, 6.

27. Ibid., 245.

28. N.F. Davin, *The Irishman in Canada* (Toronto: Maclear and Co., 1877), 620–2.

29. *Annual Report of the Superintendent of Education for Upper Canada*, 1853, 113; *Annual Report of the Superintendent of Education for Ontario*, 1869, 67.

30. E.H. Johnson, *A Brief History of Canadian Education* (Toronto: McGraw-Hill of Canada, 1968), 78

31. A Marling, *A Brief History of Public and High School Textbooks Authorized for the Province of Ontario 1846–1889* (Toronto: Warwick and Sons, 1890), 36.

32. A selection of these and other articles are reprinted in F. Consentino and M. Howell, *A History of Physical Education in Canada* (Don Mills, Ont.: General Publishing, 1971), 73–98.

33. Egerton Ryerson, ed., *Journal of Education for Upper Canada* 10, 8 (Aug. 1857): 115–16.

34. See ibid., 15, 8 (Aug. 1862): 113–14, for three articles pertaining to military drill and military training.

35. Ibid., 19, 10 (Oct. 1866): 145–54.

36. Ibid., 30, 7 (June 1877): 89–90.

37. Hodgins, *The Establishment of Schools and Colleges in Ontario*, vol. 1, 26.

38. *Journal of Education for Upper Canada* 8, 2 (Feb. 1855): 29.

39. Hodgins, *The Establishment of Schools and Colleges in Ontario*, vol. 1, 86, 94.

40. Lindsay, 'History of Sport in Canada', 335.

41. A.E. Cox, 'A History of Sports in Canada, 1868–1900', PhD dissertation (University of Alberta, 1969), 391.

42. See G. Redmond, *The Sporting Scots of Nineteenth Century Canada* (Toronto:

Associated University Presses, 1982), 159–213.

43. Althouse, 'The Ontario Teacher', 179.

44. W.N. Bell, *The Development of the Ontario High School* (Toronto: University of Toronto Press, 1918), 159, 146.

45. Ontario Archives, Department of Education, Record Group 2, Series p, p-2, Coole No. LV, Box 50, Physical Culture.

46. *Annual Report of the Minister of Ontario for the Province of Ontario,* 1889, 195.

47. See, for example, G.M. Shutt, *The High Schools of Guelph* (Toronto: University of Toronto Press, 1961), 36, 66.

48. James L. Hughes, *Manual of Drill and Calisthenics* (Toronto: W.J. Gage and Company, 1957), 274.

49. E.C. Phillips, *The Development of Education in Canada* (Toronto: W.J. Gage and Company, 1957), 274.

50. They were Lieutenant-General Sir Sam Hughes (later, federal Minister of Militia), Major-General John Hughes, and Brigadier-General William St Peter Hughes. L. Pierce, *Fifty Years of Public Services: A Life of James L. Hughes* (Toronto: Oxford University Press, 1924), 122. In fact, Sam Hughes was instrumental in supporting the implementation of the Strathcona Trust.

51. E.B. Houghton, *Physical Culture* (Toronto: Warwick and Sons, 1886).

52. *Annual Report of the Minister of Education for Ontario,* 1887, 1889, and 1899.

53. Houghton, *Physical Culture,* 13.

54. Ibid., 220.

55. E.T. White, *Public School Text-Books in Ontario* (London: The Chas. Chapman Co., 1922), 71.

56. *Proceedings of the Ontario Education Association,* 1890–1908.

57. J.D. Wilson, R.M. Stamp, and L-P. Audet, eds, *Canadian Education: A History*

(Scarborough, Ont.: Prentice-Hall of Canada, 1970), 318.

58. *Minutes and Proceedings of the Dominion Educational Association,* 1892, 224.

59. *The Educational Journal* 6 (1892): 173.

60. W.B. McMurrich and H.N. Roberts, *The School Law of Ontario* (Toronto: Goodwin Law Book and Publishing Office, 1894), 300.

61. *Annual Report of the Minister of Education for the Province of Ontario,* 1891 to 1897.

62. Ontario Archives, Department of Education, Record Group 2, Series P, p-2, Select Files, 1885–1913, Box 38.

63. *Regulations of the Education Department, Province of Ontario* (Toronto: L.K. Cameron, 1907), 10–11.

64. F. Consentino, *Canadian Football: The Grey Cup Years* (Toronto: Musson, 1969), 13.

65. T.A. Reed, *The Blue and White: A Record of Fifty Years of Athletic Endeavour at the University of Toronto* (Toronto: University of Toronto Press, 1944), 90–2.

66. Ibid., 188; H. Roxborough, *One Hundred-Not Out: The Story of Nineteenth Century Canadian Sport* (Toronto: Ryerson Press, 1966), 140–1.

67. Cox, 'History of Sports in Canada', 400–2.

68. R.J. Moriarty, 'The Organizational History of the Canadian Intercollegiate Athletic Union Central (C.I.A.U.C.) 1906–1955', PhD dissertation (Ohio State University, 1971).

69. Ibid., 107–8. For a specific analysis of the development of athletics and the underlying philosophy of athleticism at the University of Toronto prior to the Second World War, see, Catherine Gidney, 'The Athletics-Physical Education Dichotomy Revisited: The Case of the University of Toronto, 1900–1940' *SHR* 37, 2 (November, 2006), 130–149.

70. H.J. Savage, 'American College Athletics', *Bulletin of the Carnegie Foundation for the*

Advancement of Teaching, no. 23 (Boston: Merrymount Press, 1929), 25.

71. Cosentino, *Canadian Football,* 26–59.

72. See, for example, *Toronto Globe,* 17 Oct. 1922.

73. *Toronto Telegram,* 27 Oct. 1930, brackets ours.

74. Queen's won three consecutive Grey Cup championships between 1922 and 1924. See Cosentino, *Canadian Football,* 55–9.

75. K. Jones, 'Sport in Canada 1900–1920', PhD dissertation (University of Alberta 1970), 423.

76. See G.J. Burke, 'An Historical Study of Intercollegiate Athletics at the University of Western Ontario 1908–1945', Master's thesis (University of Western Ontario, 1979), 103–8.

77. The full text of Title IX is available at http://www.usdoj.gov/crt/cor/coord/titleixstat.php, accessed 8 November 2008.

78. Information on the modern era of the CIAU and CIS was extracted from the CIS history at http://www.universitysport.ca/e/about/history.cfm, accessed 8 November 2008.

79. Jones, 'Sport in Canada', 420–33.

80. J.A. Morris, *Prescott 1810–1967* (Prescott, Ont.: St Lawrence Printing Company, 1967), 77.

81. K. Beattie, *Ridley: The Story of a School* (St Catharines, Ont.: Ridley College, 1962), vol. 1, 318.

82. *Debates of the House of Commons,* vol. 90, 1909, 3200–1.

83. Hardy and H.M. Cochrane, eds, *Centennial Story: The Board of Education for the City of Toronto 1850–1950* (Toronto: Thomas Nelson and Sons, 1950), 281.

84. Ibid.

85. *Annual Report to the Minister of Education for Ontario,* 1911, 254.

86. Morrow, 'The Strathcona Trust'.

87. See Yvette Walton, 'The Life and Professional Contribution of Ethel Mary Cartwright, 1880–1955', Master's thesis (University of Western Ontario, 1976).

88. Don Morrow, 'Physical Education', in James H.Marsh, ed., *The Canadian Encyclopedia,* vol. 3 (Edmonton: Hurtig, 1985), 1666.

89. R.S. Lappage, 'Selected Sports and Canadian Society 1921–1939', PhD dissertation (University of Alberta, 1974), 228–40.

90. G.J. Burke, 'Good for the Boy and the Nation: Military Drill and the Cadet Movement in Ontario Public Schools 1865–1911', PhD dissertation (University of Toronto, 1996).

91. *Physical Education in Rural Schools: A Guide to Teachers in the Development of a Programme Suited to the Needs of Rural Schools,* published by the Strathcona Trust Committee (Ontario) (Toronto: Hunter Rose Company, 1954). See also Lorne Sawula, 'Notes on the Strathcona Trust', *CJHS* 5, 1 (May 1974): 56–61.

92. The major source of information on the Pro-Rec movement is Barbara Schrodt, 'Federal Programmes of Physical Recreation and Fitness: The Contributions of Ian Eisenhardt and BC's Pro-Rec', *CJHS* 15, 2 (Dec. 1984): 45–61. See also Schrodt, 'A History of Pro-Rec: The British Columbia Provincial Recreation Program, 1934–1953', PhD dissertation (University of Alberta, 1979).

93. In 2001, at the age of 94, Ian Eisenhardt exuded a highly active lifestyle. In that year he participated in two long-distance runs in his native Denmark. He is a tireless campaigner for physical education in schools and a strong advocate for the development of the Trans-Canada Trail. Eisenhardt was recently honoured with an induction into the Order of Canada and a Lifetime Achievement Award from Sports Canada, mainly for his pioneering achievements in physical fitness promotion both nationally and internationally.

94. Lorne Sawula, 'Why 1970 Not Before?', *CJHS* 4, 2 (Dec. 1973): 45–7; J. Thomas West,

'Physical Fitness, Sport and the Federal Government', *CJHS* 4, 2 (Dec. 1973): 34–5.

95. Sawula, 'Why 1970 Not Before?', 47.

96. Schrodt, 'Federal Programmes', 54.

97. West, 'Physical Fitness', 38.

98. Eric Broom and Richard Baka, *Canadian Governments and Sport* (Ottawa: CAHPER, 1979), 8.

99. Michael Dinning, 'The Role of the Government of Canada and the Province of Ontario in the Implementation of the Fitness and Amateur Sport Act, 1961–1974', Master's thesis (University of Western Ontario, 1974), 48. This research was used in analyzing the impact of this Act during its first 13 years of existence.

100. Johan Louw, 'Canada's Participation at the Olympic Games', PhD dissertation (University of Alberta, 1971), 433.

101. Dinning, 'The Role of the Government', 48.

102. Van Vliet, *Physical Education in Canada*, 245; Darwin S. Semotiuk, 'The Development of a Theoretical Framework for the Role of the National Government in Sport and Physical Education and its Application to Canada', PhD dissertation (Ohio State University, 1971).

103. Dinning, 'The Role of the Government', 52–4. Percival wrote *The Hockey Handbook* in 1951. Trivialized in its day, it received a huge boost coincident with the 1972 Canada–USSR hockey series when the USSR coach said the book was his hockey manual. Percival's legacy is reflected in the establishment of the Toronto-based Fitness Institute in 1963, a forerunner in the concept of large, fitness-promoting facilities in Canada. After going through several transformations over the years, inclusive of reassigned ownership to American-based Heinz Company of Pittsburgh in 1988, it is now owned by the Cambridge Group, the same company that currently owns the Montreal Athletic Association (formerly the Montreal Amateur Athletic Association). See the Fitness Club's his-tory at http://www.thefitnessinstitute.ca/about_history.html.

104. Richard S.P. Baka, 'ParticipACTION: An Examination of its Role in Promoting Physical Fitness in Canada', Master's thesis (University of Western Ontario, 1975).

105. See, 'ParticipACTION—The Mouse That Roared: A Marketing and Communications Success Story', *Canadian Journal of Public Health* 95, Supplement 2 (May/June 2004): S1–S44. Available online at http://journal.cpha.ca/index.php/cjph/article/view/1459/1648, accessed 15 November 2008.

Chapter 10 Sport and the National

1. James McCarton, 'A coast-to-coast cel-ebration: Canada comes together to share in Olympic hockey triumph'. Available at http://www.canada.com/sports/Olympics/news/story.html.

2. K.B. Wamsley and David Whitson, 'Representations of Competitiveness: International Sport Festivals and Expositions in the Production of National Identity', *Proceedings* of the North American Society for Sport History, Albuquerque, New Mexico, 1993.

3. Richard Gruneau and David Whitson, *Hockey Night in Canada: Sport, Identities, and Cultural Politics* (Toronto: Garamond Press, 1993), 3.

4. Michel Vigneault, 'Tentative de Responses sur les Origines du Hockey Moderne', *CJHS* 20, 2 (Dec. 1989): 15–26; Donald Guay, 'Les Origines du Hockey', *CJHS* 20, 1 (May 1989): 32–46.

5. M. Ann Hall, *The Girl and the Game: A History of Women's Sport in Canada* (Peterborough, Ont.: Broadview Press, 2002), 212–15.

6. Benedict Anderson's often-cited notion of nations as imagined communities is appro-priate here, particularly for a country as cul-turally diverse as Canada. See his *Imagined Communities: Reflections on the Origin and*

Spread of Nationalism, rev. edn (London: Verso, 1991).

7. Nancy B. Bouchier, *For the Love of the Game: Amateur Sport in Small Town Ontario 1838– 1895* (Montreal and Kingston: McGill-Queen's University Press, 2003).

8. Carl Berger, *The Sense of Power: Studies in the Ideas of Canadian Imperialism 1867– 1914* (Toronto: University of Toronto Press, 1970).

9. Kevin B. Wamsley and Greg Gillespie, 'The Prince of Wales Tour and the Construction of British Sporting Masculinity in Nineteenth-Century Canada', *Proceedings of the North American Society for Sport History*, Columbus, Ohio, 2003, citing Henry J. Morgan, *The Tour of H.R.H. the Prince of Wales through British America and the United States by a British Canadian* (Montreal: J. Lovell, 1860), 13, from the address presented by Sir Henry Smith, Speaker of the House of Assembly, Wed., 4 May 1859, brackets ours.

10. Ian Radforth, 'Performance, Politics, and Representation: Aboriginal People and the 1860 Royal Tour of Canada', *CHR* 84, 1 (2003): 1–32.

11. Ibid.; Wamsley and Gillespie, 'Prince of Wales Tour'.

12. Wamsley and Gillespie, 'Prince of Wales Tour'.

13. Bouchier, *For the Love of the Game*, 31–59.

14. Kevin Wamsley, 'Legislation and Leisure in 19th Century Canada', PhD dissertation (University of Alberta, 1992), 141.

15. Ibid., citing *Journals of the Legislative Assembly*, Province of Canada, 1847, Appendix E, brackets ours.

16. Douglas A. Brown, 'Aggressive, Progressive and Up-to-Date: The Sport Program at Toronto's Industrial Exhibition, 1879–1910', *SHR* 32, 2 (Nov. 2001): 70–109.

17. C. Breckenridge, 'The Aesthetics and Politics of Colonial Collecting', *Comparative Studies in Society and History* 31, 3 (1989): 211.

18. *Sessional Papers*, Dominion of Canada, 1894, No. 8g.

19. *Journals of the Legislative Assembly*, Province of Canada, 1856, App. 56.

20. Wamsley and Whitson, 'Representations of Competitiveness'.

21. Wamsley, 'Legislation and Leisure', 274.

22. Ibid., 275–6, citing *Sessional Papers*, Dominion of Canada, 1887, No. 12.

23. E.J. Hart, *The Selling of Canada: The CPR and the Beginnings of Canadian Tourism* (Banff, Alta: Altitude Publishing, 1983).

24. Wamsley, 'Legislation and Leisure', 276.

25. David W. Brown, 'The Northern Character Theme and Sport in Nineteenth Century Canada', *CJHS* 20, 1 (May 1989): 51.

26. C. Brown, 'The Nationalism of the National Policy', in R.D. Douglas and D.B. Smith, eds, *Readings in Canadian History: Post-Confederation* (Toronto: Holt, Rinehart and Winston, 1986), 45–51.

27. Wamsley, 'Legislation and Leisure', 251–80.

28. See S.F. Wise and D. Fisher, *Canada's Sporting Heroes* (Don Mills, Ont.: General Publishing, 1974), 112–13; Barbara Schrodt, Gerald Redmond, and Richard Baka, eds, *Sport Canadiana* (Edmonton: Executive Sport Publications, n.d.).

29. J.H. Siddons, *The Canadian Volunteers Hand-Book: Military Facts and Suggestions Adapted to Field Service* (Toronto: Bollo & Adam, 1863).

30. Kevin B. Wamsley, 'Cultural Signification and National Ideologies: Rifle Shooting in Late Nineteenth-Century Canada', *Social History* 20, 1 (1995): 63–72.

31. Ibid.

32. Ibid., citing the *Canadian Military Gazette*, 29 July 1886.

33. Ibid., 70.

34. Ibid., 71, citing *Debates of the House of Commons*, 22 July 1895.

35. Ibid. 70, citing *Canadian Military Gazette*, 15 Aug. 1895.

36. Ibid., citing *Canadian Military Gazette*, 1 Aug. 1895.

37. Ibid., citing *Debates of the House of Commons*, 26 Feb. 1875.

38. Ibid., citing *Debates of the House of Commons*, 22 July 1895.

39. Mark Dyreson, *Making the American Team: Sport, Culture, and the Olympic Experience* (Urbana: University of Illinois Press, 1998).

40. As discussed in Chapter 11, the IOC did not officially recognize these games because they were outside of the traditional four-year cycle. They were the games 'in between'.

41. Bruce Kidd, 'In Defense of Tom Longboat', *CJHS* 14, 1 (May 1983): 34–63; J. Wilton Littlechild, 'Tom Longboat: Canada's Outstanding Indian Athlete', Master's thesis (University of Alberta, 1975).

42. Don Morrow, 'The Knights of the Snowshoe: A Study of the Evolution of Sport in Nineteenth Century Montreal', *Journal of Sport History*, 15, 1 (1988): 5–40.

43. Sally Weaver, *Making Canadian Indian Policy: The Hidden Agenda, 1968–1970* (Toronto: University of Toronto Press, 1981).

44. John Bloom, *To Show What an Indian Can Do: Sports at Native American Boarding Schools* (Minneapolis, MN: University of Minnesota Press, 2000).

45. Janice M. Forsyth, 'From Assimilation to Self-Determination: The Emergence of J. Wilton Littlechild's North American Indigenous Games, 1763–1997', Master's thesis (University of Western Ontario, 2000).

46. *Vancouver Sun*, 5 August 2008, Available at http://www.canada.com/vancouversun/news/westcoastnews/story.html?id=d5b9c27b-0de9-4802-87f5-76c8e27edf25, accessed 20 November 2008.

47. Janice Forsyth and Kevin B. Wamsley,

'"Native to Native…We'll Recapture Our Spirits": The World Indigenous Nations Games and North American Indigenous Games as Cultural Resistance', *The International Journal of the History of Sport*, 23, 2 (2006): 294–314.

48. Kevin B. Wamsley, 'Power and Privilege in Historiography: Constructing Percy Page', *SHR* 28, 2 (Nov. 1997): 146–55.

49. See http://www.nlc-bnc.ca/hockey/h36-2003-3.html.

50. Colin Howell, *Blood, Sweat and Cheers: Sport and the Making of Modern Canada* (Toronto: University of Toronto Press, 2001), 44.

51. Don Morrow, et al., *A Concise History of Sport in Canada* (Toronto: Oxford University Press, 1989), 169–72.

52. Paul Voisey, *Vulcan: The Making of a Prairie Community* (Toronto: University of Toronto Press, 1988).

53. Michael K. Heine, and Kevin B. Wamsley, 'Kickfest at Dawson City: Native Peoples and the Sports of the Klondike Gold Rush', *SHR* 27, 1 (1996): 72–86.

54. Morrow et al., *A Concise History*, 183–93.

55. Ron S. Lappage, 'The Role of Sport in Canada's Interaction with Europe and Britain 1919–1939', *Proceedings of the Third Canadian Symposium on the History of Sport and Physical Education*, Dalhousie University, Halifax, 1974, 5, citing Frederick Edwards, 'Envoys on Ice', *Maclean's*, 15 Oct. 1934, 8.

56. Carly Adams, '"Queens of the Ice Lanes": The Preston Rivulettes and Women's Hockey in Canada, 1931–1940', *Sport History Review*, 39 (2008): 1–29.

57. Bruce Kidd, *The Struggle for Canadian Sport* (Toronto: University of Toronto Press, 1996), 259.

58. David Whitson and Richard Gruneau, eds, *Artificial Ice: Hockey, Culture, and Commerce* (Peterborough, Ont.: Broadview Press, 2006), 3.

59. Bruce Kidd, *The Struggle for Canadian Sport* (Toronto: University of Toronto Press, 1996), 200–1.

60. Morrow et al., *A Concise History*, 218–19.

61. See Mark Rosenstraub, 'Playing With the Big Boys: Smaller Markets, Competitive Balance, and the Hope for a Championship Team', in Whitson and Gruneau, *Hockey Night*, 143–62.

62. Frank Cosentino, 'Football', in Morrow et al., *A Concise History*, 144.

63. Donald Macintosh, with Tom Bedecki and C.E.S. Franks, *Sport and Politics in Canada* (Kingston and Montreal: McGill-Queen's University Press, 1987), 10–29.

64. C. Westland, *Fitness and Amateur Sport in Canada, The Federal Government's Programme: An Historical Perspective* (Ottawa: Canadian Parks and Recreation Association, 1979).

65. Duke of Edinburgh, Speech delivered to the Canadian Medical Association, Toronto, 30 June 1959.

66. Ibid.

67. Westland, *Fitness and Amateur Sport*, 37–41.

68. John MacDougall, 'A Professional Fight in an Amateur Arena: Canada's Struggle for an Open Ice Hockey World Championship', unpublished paper, 2002, ICOS Archives.

69. Gruneau and Whitson, *Hockey Night*, 249.

70. The Molson Brewing Company, in recent ad campaigns, played a significant role in promoting hockey as the national pastime, and its 'Joe Canadian' rant referred to Canada as the first nation of hockey.

71. Carly Adams and Kevin B. Wamsley, 'Moments of Silence in Shallow Halls of Greatness: The Hockey Hall of Fame and the Politics of Representation', in Colin D. Howell, ed., *Putting it on Ice, Volume III, Women's Hockey: Gender Issues On and Off the Ice* (Halifax: Gorsebrook Research Institute, 2005), 13–18.

72. *Debates of the House of Commons*, 24 Oct. 1967.

73. Ibid., 24 Oct. 1960.

74. *Debates of the Legislative Assembly*, British Columbia, 12 Dec. 1980.

75. Ibid., 2 Oct. 1986.

76. Ibid., 4 Mar. 1985.

77. *Alberta Hansard*, 18 Mar. 1988.

78. Macintosh et al., *Sport and Politics*.

79. Ibid., 85–8.

80. Government of Canada, *Toward 2000: Building Canada's Sport System*, 36. See the analysis of these programs in Donald Macintosh and David Whitson, *The Game Planners: Transforming Canada's Sport System* (Montreal and Kingston: McGill-Queen's University Press, 1990), 17–25.

81. Government of Canada, *Toward 2000*, 7.

82. See http://www.parl.gc.ca/InfoComDoc/36/1/SINS/Studies/Reports/sinsrp05/04-rep-e.htm.

83. Ibid., 27.

84. *Debates of the House of Commons*, 22 Feb. 1988.

85. Jeff Lee, 'Today We Have Moved a Mountain', *Vancouver Sun*, 3 July 2003.

86. *Vancouver 2010 Candidate City Bid Book*, vol. 3, 121.

87. http://www.ownthepodium2010.com/; Gary Kingston, 'Own the Podium Strategy Still "Top Secret" material'. Available at http://www.financialpost.com/story.html?id=1007877, accessed 28 Nov. 2008.

88. Greg Baum, 'Canada Finally Breaks the Ice', available at http://www.theage.com/au/articles/2002/02/25/1014471629082.html.

Chapter 11 The Olympic Games

1. This point is borrowed from Bruce Kidd, 'The Myth of the Ancient Games', in Alan Tomlinson and Garry Whannel, eds, *Five*

Ring Circus: Money, Power and Politics at the Olympic Games (London and Sydney: Pluto Press, 1984), 71–83.

2. Alan Metcalfe, 'Organized Sport and Social Stratification in Montreal, 1840–1901', in Richard Gruneau and John Albinson, eds, *Canadian Sport: Sociological Perspectives* (Don Mills, Ont.: Addison-Wesley, 1976), 77–101.

3. See Kidd, 'The Myth of the Ancient Games'; Alfred E. Senn, *Power, Politics, and the Olympic Games: A History of the Power Brokers, Events, and Controversies That Shaped the Games* (Champaign, Ill.: Human Kinetics, 1999), 20–1. During the 1860s in London, Ontario, Bishop Hellmuth organized an informal Hellmuth College Olympics accompanied by parading of the garrison men and music by the Royal Rifles. In the following years, the organizers awarded gold medals to event winners, and spectators numbered over 500; at the same time, tavern owners sold Olympic beer in downtown London. Jim Fogarty, 'Hellmuth College: A Pre-Olympic Festival Held in London, Ontario's Backyard', unpublished paper, 1998, ICOS Archives.

4. See David C. Young, 'The Origins of the Modern Olympics: A New Version', *IJHS* 4 (1987): 271–300; Pierre de Coubertin, 'Why I Revived the Olympic Games', in Jeffrey O. Seagrave and Donald Chu, eds, *The Olympic Games in Transition* (Champaign, Ill.: Human Kinetics, 1988), 101–6, originally published in *Fortnightly Review* 90 (July 1908): 110–15.

5. See, for example, David C. Young, *The Olympic Myth of Greek Amateur Athletics* (Chicago: Ares Publishers, 1984); David C. Young, *The Modern Olympics: A Struggle for Revival* (Baltimore: Johns Hopkins University Press, 1996); John J. MacAloon, *This Great Symbol: Pierre de Coubertin and the Origins of the Modern Olympic Games* (Chicago: University of Chicago Press, 1981); Allen Guttmann, *The Olympics: A History of the Modern Games* (Urbana: University of Illinois Press, 1992); Senn, *Power, Politics,*

and the Olympic Games; Gerald Redmond, 'Toward Modern Revival of the Olympic Games: The Various "Pseudo-Olympics" of the 19th Century', in Seagrave and Chu, eds, *Olympic Games in Transition*, 71–87; Robert K. Barney, 'For Such Olympic Games: German-American Turnfests as Preludes to the Modern Olympic Games', in Fernand Landry, Marc Landry, and Magdeleine Yerles, eds, *Sport . . . The Third Millennium* (Sainte Foy: Les Presses de l'Université Laval), 697–706.

6. Guttmann, *The Olympics*, 7.

7. See Michel Vigneault, 'The Visit of Pierre de Coubertin to Montreal in 1889: Muscles or Brain for the French Canadian?', *Proceedings of the North American Society for Sport History*, Pennsylvania State University, 1999.

8. Young, *The Modern Olympics*, 30–5.

9. Ibid.

10. Ibid., 31, brackets ours.

11. Robert A. Nye, *Masculinity and Male Codes of Honor in Modern France* (New York: Oxford University Press, 1993), 220.

12. Young, *The Olympic Myth*, 26.

13. Ibid., 28–56.

14. Ibid., 60–1.

15. On the complexities of these selections and their political significance, see David Young's extensive elaboration in *The Modern Olympics*, 81–105.

16. Robert K. Barney, Malcolm Scott, and Rachel Moore, 'Old Boys at Work and Play: The International Olympic Committee and Canadian Co-option, 1928–1946', *OLYMPIKA: The International Journal of Olympic Studies* 8 (1999): 81–2.

17. Bruce Kidd, 'The First COA Presidents', *OLYMPIKA: The International Journal of Olympic Studies* 3 (1994): 107–10.

18. Henry Roxborough, *Canada at the Olympics* (Toronto: Ryerson Press, 1965), 18.

19. The Baron de Coubertin, Timoleon Philemon, Politis, and Charalambos Anninos, *The Olympic Games of 1896*, trans. 1966 (Lausanne : International Olympic Committee, 1983), 133. Originally printed by Charles Beck, Athens and Le Soudier, Paris, 1896.

20. Ibid., 143.

21. Ibid., 143–4.

22. Narratives about sport, then, must be viewed critically to provide the historical context in which to understand them. Taken at face value, a narrative always privileges the voice of the speaker and the specific interests embedded in the story. Critically appraising narratives permits us to view some of the social forces that remain unseen, yet to appreciate the significance of the material and the experiences of those who participated in the event that is being remembered.

23. Ibid., 155.

24. Kevin Wamsley, 'Legislation and Leisure in 19th Century Canada', PhD dissertation (University of Alberta, 1992), 520–53.

25. Kevin B. Wamsley, 'American Boys in Paris: Canadian Participation in the Games of 1900', in Robert K. Barney, Kevin B. Wamsley, Scott G. Martyn, and Gordon H. MacDonald, eds, *Global and Cultural Critique: Problematizing the Olympic Games* (London, Ont.: ICOS, 1998), 135–40.

26. Senn, *Power, Politics, and the Olympic Games*, 25; Guttmann, *The Olympics*, 22.

27. Bill Mallon, *The 1904 Olympic Games: Results for All Competitors in All Events, with Commentary* (Jefferson, NC: McFarland, 1999), 4–5.

28. Guttmann, *The Olympics*, 24–5.

29. See Mark Dyreson, *Making the American Team: Sport, Culture, and the Olympic Experience* (Urbana: University of Illinois Press, 1998); Dyreson, 'America's Athletic Missionaries: Political Performance, Olympic Spectacle and the Quest for an American National Culture', *OLYMPIKA: The International Journal of Olympic Studies* 1 (1992): 70–91.

30. Robert Knight Barney, 'Born from Dilemma: America Awakens to the Modern Olympic Games, 1901–1903', *OLYMPIKA: The International Journal of Olympic Studies* 1 (1992): 92–135.

31. Mallon, *The 1904 Olympic Games*, 233.

32. Ibid., 233–4.

33. Ibid., 207–9.

34. See Kevin G. Jones, 'Sport in Canada—1900 to 1920', PhD dissertation (University of Alberta, 1970).

35. See Bruce Kidd, 'In Defense of Tom Longboat', *CJHS* 14, 1 (May 1983): 34–63; Wilton Littlechild, 'Tom Longboat: Canada's Outstanding Indian Athlete', Master's thesis (University of Alberta, 1975).

36. Don Morrow, Mary Keyes, Wayne Simpson, Frank Cosentino, and Ron Lappage, *A Concise History of Sport in Canada* (Toronto: Oxford University Press, 1989), 290, citing John Howard Crocker, *Report of the First Canadian Olympic Athletic Team (1908)*, 4.

37. Bill Mallon and Ture Widland, *The 1896 Games: Results for All Competitors in All Events, with Commentary* (Jefferson, NC: McFarland, 1998), 14.

38. Senn, *Power, Politics, and the Olympic Games*, 24.

39. *Debates of the House of Commons*, 15 July 1908.

40. See Kidd, 'The First COA Presidents'; Barney et al., 'Old Boys at Work and Play'.

41. *Sessional Papers*, Province of Ontario, 1909, No. 1.

42. Dyreson, 'America's Athletic Missionaries', 84.

43. See George R. Matthews, 'The Controversial Olympic Games of 1908 as Viewed by the *New York Times* and the *Times of London*', *JSH* 7, 2 (Summer 1980): 40–53.

44. John Lucas, 'Early Olympic Antagonists:

Pierre de Coubertin versus James E. Sullivan', *Stadion* 3, 2 (1977): 271, citing Pierre de Coubertin, *Memoires Olympiques* (Lausanne: Bureau International de pedagogie sportive, 1931), 92.

45. See Guttmann, *The Olympics*, 32–5.

46. Roxborough, *Canada at the Olympics*, 49–51.

47. Jones, 'Sport in Canada', 203.

48. Bill Mallon and Ture Widland, *The 1912 Olympic Games: Results for All Competitors in All Events, with Commentary* (Jefferson, NC: McFarland, 2002), 57.

49. Sheila Mitchell, 'Women's Participation in the Olympic Games, 1900–1926', *JSH* 4, 2 (Summer 1977): 214, citing Pierre de Coubertin, 'Sports and the Feminine Aux Jeux Olympique', *Revue Olympique* (Jan. 1912): 109.

50. Betty Spears, 'Women in the Olympics: An Unresolved Problem', in P. Graham and H. Ueberhorst, eds, *The Modern Olympics* (New York: Leisure Press, 1972), 63.

51. Guy Schultz, 'The IAAF and the IOC: Their Relationship and its Impact on Women's Participation in Track and Field at the Olympic Games, 1912–1932' Master's thesis (University of Western Ontario, 2000).

52. '19th IOC Session: Antwerp 1920', in *The IOC Sessions: 1894–1955* (Lausanne: IOC, 1989), 97.

53. Roland Renson, *The Games Reborn: The VIIth Olympiad Antwerp 1920* (Antwerp: Pandora, 1996), 7.

54. Roxborough, *Canada at the Olympics*, 53–5. The American press and sporting leaders had always placed the most significance on the athletics competitions where the United States dominated. The Canadian press came to place emphasis on the significance of hockey and the dominance of Canadian men. Roxborough (56) reports that one spectator, so thrilled by the skating abilities of Mike Gooderman, offered $100 for his skates.

55. Robert K. Barney, Stephen R. Wenn, and Scott G. Martyn, *Selling the Five Rings: The International Olympic Committee and the Rise of Olympic Commercialism* (Salt Lake City: University of Utah Press, 2002), 29.

56. Kevin B. Wamsley and Guy Schulz, 'Rogues and Bedfellows: The IOC and the Incorporation of the FSFI', in Kevin B. Wamsley, Scott G. Martyn, Gordon H. MacDonald, and Robert K. Barney, eds, *Bridging Three Centuries: Intellectual Crossroads and the Modern Olympic Movement* (London, Ont.: ICOS, 2000), 113–18.

57. IOC and IAAF members disagreed on the issue of women's participation. Dr Arthur Stanley Lamb, Canadian member of the IAAE, for example, was opposed. See Amanda Schweinbenz, 'All Dressed Up and No Where to Run: Women's Uniforms and Clothing in the Olympics Games from 1900 to 1932', Master's thesis (University of Western Ontario, 2001), 124–8; M. Ann Hall, *The Girl and the Game: A History of Women's Sport in Canada* (Peterborough, Ont.: Broadview Press, 2002), 51, citing George Pallett, *Women's Athletics* (London: Normal Press, 1955).

58. Hall, *The Girl and the Game*, 53.

59. *The Times* (London), 3 Aug. 1928.

60. 'IOC Executive Session, 23–25 July 1929', The Executive Committee: Part I, Meetings 1–84, 1921–69, (Lausanne: IOC, 1992), 50.

61. IOC *Minutes, Tenth Congress, Berlin 20–21 May 1930* (Stockholm: Swedish National Archives, 1930), 18–19.

62. See Bruce Kidd, '"We Must Maintain a Balance between Propaganda and Serious Athletics": The Workers' Sport Movement in Canada, 1924–36', in Morris Mott, ed, *Sports in Canada: Historical Readings* (Toronto: Copp Clark Pitman, 1989), 247–64.

63. See Gordon H. MacDonald, 'Regime Creation, Maintenance, and Change: A History of Relations between the International Olympic Committee and

International Sports Federations, 1894–1968', PhD dissertation (University of Western Ontario, 1998).

64. Roxborough, *Canada at the Olympics*, 171–2.

65. See Richard Espy, *The Politics of the Olympic Games* (Berkeley: University of California Press, 1979); John Hoberman, *The Olympic Crisis: Sports, Politics and the Moral Order* (New Rochelle, NY: Caratzas, 1986); Kevin B. Wamsley, 'The Global Sport Monopoly: A Synopsis of 20th Century Olympic Politics', *International Journal* 57, 3 (Summer 2002): 395–410.

66. See Richard D. Mandell, *The Nazi Olympics* (New York: Macmillan, 1971); Allen Guttmann, *The Games Must Go On: Avery Brundage and the Olympic Movement* (New York: Columbia University Press, 1984).

67. Bruce Kidd, 'Canadian Opposition to the 1936 Olympics in Germany', *CJHSPE* 9, 2 (Dec. 1978): 20–40. See also James Riordan, 'The Worker's Olympics', in Alan Tomlinson and Garry Whannel, eds, *Five Ring Circus: Money, Power and Politics at the Olympic Games* (London: Pluto Press, 1984), 98–112; Bruce Kidd, *The Struggle for Canadian Sport* (Toronto: University of Toronto Press 1996), 146–83.

68. Kidd, 'Canadian Opposition', 29, citing *The Worker*, 19 Nov. 1935.

69. Bruce Kidd, 'The Popular Front and the 1936 Olympics', *CJHSPE* 11, 1 (May 1980): 17.

70. Senn, *Power, Politics, and the Olympic Games*, 55, citing Jeremiah T. Mahoney, 'Germany Has Violated the Olympic Code!' (New York: Committee on Fair Play in Sports, 1935).

71. See Stephen R. Wenn, 'A Suitable Policy of Neutrality? FDR and the Question of American Participation in the 1936 Olympics', *IJHS* 8, 3 (Dec. 1991): 319–35; Stephen R. Wenn, 'A Tale of Two Diplomats: George S. Messersmith and Charles H. Sherrill on Proposed American Participation

in the Berlin Olympics', *JSH* 16, 1 (Spring 1989): 27–43; Carolyn Marvin, 'Avery Brundage and American Participation in the 1936 Olympics', *Journal of American Studies* 16 (Apr. 1982): 81–106.

72. Senn, *Power, Politics, and the Olympic Games*, 55.

73. Guttmann, *The Olympics*, 97, citing Jim Scott, *Bob Mathias* (Englewood Cliffs, NJ: Prentice-Hall, 1952).

74. See Espy, *The Politics of the Olympic Games*, 31–122; Senn, *Power, Politics, and the Olympic Games*, 84–109; Guttmann, *The Olympics*, 85–102. On performance enhancement, see John Hoberman, *Mortal Engines: The Science of Performance and the Dehumanization of Sport* (New York: Free Press, 1992).

75. Amanda Schweinbenz and Kevin B. Wamsley, 'Lilies, Pixies, Mermaids, and Sweethearts: The Feminization of Olympic Female Athletes in the Popular Media', paper presented at the annual conference of the International Society for Comparative Sport and Physical Education, Windsor, 2001; Kevin B. Wamsley, 'The Organization of Gender in the Modern Olympic Games', keynote address to the Singapore Olympic Academy, Singapore, Sept. 2000.

76. Schweinbenz, 'All Dressed Up and Nowhere To Run', 131–57.

77. Norbert Müller, *Pierre de Coubertin 1863–1937: Olympism, Selected Writings* (Lausanne: International Olympic Committee, 2000), 749.

78. Kevin B. Wamsley, 'Laying Olympism to Rest', paper presented at the conference, 'Post-Olympism?', Aarhus, Denmark, Sept. 2002.

79. Joan Ryan, Little Girls in Pretty Boxes: The Making and Breaking of Elite Gymnasts and Figure Skaters (New York: Doubleday, 1995); see also Wamsley, 'Organization of Gender'.

80. See John Wong, 'Sport Networks on Ice: The Canadian Experience at the 1936 Olympic

Hockey Tournament', *SHR* 34, 2 (Nov. 2003): 190–212.

81. Donald Macintosh, with Tom Bedecki and C.E.S. Franks, *Sport and Politics in Canada: Federal Government Involvement since 1961* (Montreal and Kingston: McGill-Queen's University Press), 10–41.

82. Andrew Strenk, 'Amateurism: The Myth and the Reality', in Seagrave and Chu, eds, *Olympic Games in Transition*, 303–28.

83. Espy, *The Politics of the Olympic Games*, 138, citing *New York Times*, 31 Jan. 1972.

84. Barney et al., 'Old Boys at Work and Play', 81.

85. Hoberman, *Olympic Crisis*, 1.

86. See Octavio Paz, *The Other Mexico: Critique of the Pyramid* (New York: Grove Press, 1972).

87. Hoberman, *Olympic Crisis*, 14.

88. Guttmann, *The Olympics*, 132.

89. Ibid., 139.

90. Ibid., 140.

91. Ibid., 134. See also Shayne P. Quick, 'Black Knight Checks White King: The Conflict between African Bloc Nations and Avery Brundage during the 1960s', Master's thesis (University of Western Ontario, 1987).

92. See Nick Auf der Maur, *The Billion Dollar Game: Jean Drapeau and the 1976 Olympics* (Toronto: James Lorimer, 1976).

93. Morrow et al., *A Concise History*, 301, citing *New York Times*, 15 Oct. 1974. See also Don Morrow, 'Olympic Masculinity: An Analysis of Canadian Newspapers During the 1976, 1988, and 2000 Olympic Games', in Kevin B. Wamsley, Robert K. Barney, and Scott G. Martyn, eds, *The Global Nexus Engaged: Past, Present, Future Interdisciplinary Olympic Studies* (London, Ont.: ICOS, 2002), 123–34.

94. Bruce Kidd, 'Montreal 1976: The Games of the XXth Olympiad', in John E. Findling and Kimberley D. Pelle, eds, *Historical Dictionary of the Modern Olympic Movement* (Westport, Conn.: Greenwood Press, 1996), 153–60.

95. Janice Forsyth, 'Teepees and Tomahawks: Aboriginal Cultural Representation at the 1976 Olympic Games', in Wamsley et al., eds, *The Global Nexus Engaged*, 71–6.

96. Janice Forsyth, 'From Assimilation to Self-Determination: The Emergence of J. Wilton Littlechild's North American Indigenous Games, 1763–1997', Master's thesis (University of Western Ontario, 2000), 95–6.

97. Macintosh et al., *Sport and Politics in Canada*, 85–8.

98. Barney et al., *Selling the Five Rings*, 164.

99. Ibid., 159.

100. Ibid.

101. Ibid., 202.

102. Scott G. Martyn, 'The Struggle for Financial Autonomy: The IOC and the Historical Emergence of Corporate Sponsorship, 1896–2000', PhD dissertation (University of Western Ontario, 2000), 229–30.

103. Anthony G. Church, 'The Sacred Cow: Calgary and the XV Olympic Winter Games', Master's thesis (University of Western Ontario, 2003), 24–53.

104. Ibid, 143, summarized from the Statement of Revenue, Expenditures, and Fund Balance, 16 Apr. 1982 to 31 Mar. 1993, Coopers and Lybrand Chartered Accountants, Calgary, 30 Apr. 1993.

105. See Kevin B. Wamsley and Michael K. Heine, 'Tradition, modernity, and the construction of civic identity: the Calgary Olympics', *OLYMPIKA: The International Journal of Olympic Studies* 5 (1996): 81–90; Wamsley and Heine, 'Don't Mess with the Relay, It's Bad Medicine: Aboriginal Culture and the 1988 Winter Olympic Games', in Robert K. Barney, Scott G. Martyn, Douglas A. Brown, and Gordon H. MacDonald, eds, *Olympic Perspectives* (London, Ont.: ICOS, 1996), 173–8.

106. See Wayne Wilson and Edward Derse, eds, *Doping in Elite Sport: The Politics of Drugs in the Olympic Movement* (Champaign, Ill.: Human Kinetics, 2001).

107. Martyn, 'The Struggle for Financial Autonomy'.

108. Douglas Booth, 'Gifts of Corruption? Ambiguities of Obligation in the Olympic Movement,' *OLYMPIKA: The International Journal of Olympic Studies* 8 (1999): 43–68.

109. See Vyv Simson and Andrew Jennings, *The Lords of the Rings: Power, Money and Drugs in the Modern Olympics* (Toronto: Stoddart, 1992); Andrew Jennings, *The New Lords of the Rings: Olympic Corruption and How to Buy Gold Medals* (London: Pocket Books, 1996); Andrew Jennings and Clare Sambrook, *The Great Olympic Swindle: When the World Wanted Its Games Back* (London: Simon and Schuster, 2000).

110. Booth, 'Gifts of Corruption?'

111. Martyn, 'The Struggle for Financial Autonomy', 239–40.

112. 'NBC Lands Olympics with $2 Billion Bid', available at http://www.tsn.ca.

113. *Report of the IOC Evaluation Commission for the Olympic Winter Games in 2010*, ICOS Archives, University of Western Ontario, London.

114. Ibid., 58.

115. Karenn Krangle, 'Council Approves $538,000 Olympic Vote', available at http://www.vnc.bc.ca/ioc/pdfs/Council%20Approves%20Olympic%20Vote%20%2012.11.2002%20-%20Vancouver%20Sun.pdf.

116. See http://www.winter2010.com/NewsAndEvents/News/NewsItems/CoVNewsRelease.htm.

117. 'As Olympic glow fades, Athens questions $15 billion cost', available at http://www.csmonitor.com/2008/0721/p04s0-wogn.html.

118. See http://newsvote.bbc.co.ok/mpaps/page-tools/print/news.bbc.co.uk/1/hi/business/3649268.s.

119. 'Olympic stadiums' uncertain future', available at http://news.bbc.co.uk/1/hi/world/europe/4168658.stm.

120. 'Turin Olympic Games still facing budget shortfall', available at http://www.dailycommercialnews.com/article/20050209850.

121. These figures are not 'official' and remain speculative. Olympic-fact historian Bill Mallon compared Olympic Games costs per athlete in his Beijing blog (http://www.sports-reference.com/olympics/blog/?p=9), and NBC Action News reported the same figure (http://www.nbcactionnews.com/content/olympics/story.aspx?content_id=b4d0b56b-a85a-4c80-a647-6de2119146ac).

122. People's Republic of China: The Olympics countdown—Broken promises, available at http://www.amnesty.org/en/library/asset/ASA17/089/2008/en/824a9d66-5724-11dd-90eb-ff4596860802/asa170892008eng.html; David Matas and Hon. David Kilgour, *Bloody Harvest, Revised Report into Allegations of Organ Harvesting of Falun Gong Practitioners in China*, 31 January 2007, available at http://organharvestinvestigation.net.

123. This is not to downplay the stabbing/suicide incident in Beijing or the suicide bombing that killed 11 people in Western China. Rather, it is surprising that, given the anti-China protests, major on-site protests did not occur.

Chapter 12: Sport in Canada: Current Issues

1. Bruce Kidd, *The Struggle for Canadian Sport* (Toronto: University of Toronto Press, 1996), 262–70.

2. Richard Gruneau and David Whitson, *Hockey Night in Canada* (Aurora, Ont.: Garamond Press, 1993).

3. Hart Cantelon, 'Amateurism, High-Performance Sport, and the Olympics', in Kevin Young and Kevin B. Wamsley, eds,

Global Olympics: Historical and Sociological Studies of the Modern Olympic Games (Amsterdam: Elsevier Press, 2005), 97.

4. Search completed through the Ticketsnow website, where the corporation Ticketmaster has been accused of inflating prices. See http://www.nowtoronto.com/news/story.cfm?content=162999.

5. Search completed through the Ticketmaster website. Tickets at the highest levels of the Air Canada Centre are available at $12.50.

6. Search completed through Ticketsnow.

7. Search completed through Ticketsnow. Service charges for the most expensive tickets are over $1,000 per ticket.

8. Ludis Tours, available at http://www.ludus-tours.com/van_pkg.shtml.

9. David Whitson, 'Globalization', in Jane Crossman, ed., *Canadian Sport Sociology*, 2nd ed., (Toronto: Thompson/Nelson, 2008), 239–56.

10. NHL Centre Ice, offered by Bell Expressvu, for example, costs $149 for programming between December and February alone and is subject to local viewing blackouts, according to existing contract arrangements with the sports channels, see http://www.bell.ca/shopping/PrsShpTv_PPV_Landing.page?selectedtab=2&MovieId=Top&first=0&Title=NHL%C2%AE%20Centre%20Ice; the NASCAR Hot Pass for 2008–09 sells for $159, see http://www.bell.ca/shopping/PrsShpTv_PPV_Landing.page?selectedtab=2&MovieId=Top&first=0&Title=NASCAR%20HotPass.

11. The NFL's current contract extending from 2006–11 with Fox, CBS, and NBC is $8 billion. See 'NFL signs new television contract', available at http://www.outsidethebeltway.com/archives/nfl_signs_new_television_contract.

12. Marc Lavoie, 'The Economics of Sport and the NHL Lockout', in Jane Crossman, ed., *Canadian Sport Sociology*, 2nd ed. (Toronto: Thomson Nelson, 2008), 203.

13. See http://ca.youtube.com for searchable video postings.

14. For a discussion of labour relations between owners and players, see David Cruise and Alison Griffiths, *Net Worth: Exploding the Myths of Pro Hockey* (Toronto: Penguin Books, 1992). See also Russ Conway, *Game Misconduct: Alan Eagleson and the Corruption of Hockey* (Toronto: Macfarlane Walter & Ross, 1995).

15. Lavoie, 'The Economics of Sport and the NHL Lockout', 203.

16. According to the *Globe and Mail*; see http://static.fantasysports.ca/NHLSalaryData/globe/top100avg-Overall-salary.html.

17. http://content.usatoday.com/sports/football/nfl/salaries/top25.aspx?year=2008.

18. http://www.sportscity.com/NBA-Salaries/.

19. Jonah Freedman, 'Ranking the 50 highest-earning athletes in the U.S.', available at http://sportsillustrated.cnn.com/more/specials/fortunate50.

20. Lavoie, 'The Economics of Sport and the NHL Lockout', 203.

21. Lavoie, 'The Economics of Sport and the NHL Lockout', 199.

22. Robert Ballantyne, 'Super Bowl lives up to its title in Canada...but the big game still isn't as popular up north', available at http://www.popjournalism.ca/magazine/2008/02/10/super-bowl-lives-up-to-its-title-in-canada/.

23. See http://www.montrealgazette.com/opinion/letters/debate/1013513/story.html; http://newsgroups.derkeiler.com/Archive/Rec/rec.sport.football.canadian/2008-06/msg00031.html.

24. Kevin Young discusses the institutional pressures applied within professional sport which encourage athletes to participate in work environments that are often dangerous and violent, and to embrace such behaviour as masculine or manly in 'Violence in the Workplace of Professional Sport from Victimological and Cultural Studies Perspectives',

International Review for the Sociology of Sport 26, 3 (1991).

25. Young, 'Violence in the Workplace of Professional Sport', 3.

26. See David Whitson, 'Sport in the social construction of masculinity', in M.A. Messner and D. Sabo, eds, *Sport, Men, and the Gender Order: Critical Feminist Perspectives* (Champaign, Ill.: Human Kinetics, 1990), 19–30.

27. Kevin Young, Philip White, and William McTeer, 'Body Talk: Male athletes reflect on sport injury and pain', *Sociology of Sport Journal* 11 (1994): 175–94.

28. Michael A. Messner, 'When bodies are weapons: Masculinity and violence in sport', *International Review for the Sociology of Sport* 25, 3 (1990): 203–16.

29. See the video clip of Baun's injury and goal at http://archives.cbc.ca/clip.asp?IDClip=15101.

30. Kevin Young and Philip White, 'Sport, physical danger, and injury: The experience of elite women athletes', *Journal of Sport and Social Issues* 19 (1995): 45–61.

31. See http://www.nhl.com/trophies/masterton.html.

32. Howard L. Nixon, 'Social pressure, social support, and help seeking for pain and injury in college sports networks', *Journal of Sport and Social Issues* 13 (1994): 340–55.

33. Young, et al., 'Body Talk'.

34. Gruneau and Whitson, *Hockey Night in Canada*, 67–8.

35. Young et al., 'Body Talk'.

36. Profiles of Masterton trophy winners can be viewed online at http://www.legendsofhockey.net:8080/LegendsOfHockey/jsp/SilverwareTrophyWinners.jsp?tro=BMT.

37. *Calgary Daily Herald*, 22 February 1997.

38. This argument points to a sub cultural focus on the injury process, while recognizing that recovery from disease unrelated to hockey is a quite different matter, even though body recovery remains the theme.

39. *Calgary Daily Herald*, 18 January 1996.

40. *Calgary Daily Herald*, 26 January 1996.

41. See http://www.cbc.ca/sports/football/story/2008/11/19/fifthestate-headgames.html?ref=rss.

42. Thomas Hargrove, 'Heavy NFL players twice as likely to die before 50', 31 January 2006. Available at http://sports.espn.go.com/nfl/news/story?id=2313476.

43. 'Report: Doctor says Everett has voluntary movement of arms, legs', 12 September, 2007. Available at http://sports.espn.go.com/nfl/news/story?id=3014742.

44. Mike Edgell, 'Sanderson remembered as a hero, friend by family: Hockey player died last week after he cracked head on ice', 5 January 2009. Available at http://www.calgaryherald.com/Sanderson+remembered+hero+friend+family/1146722/story.html.

45. 'New helmet rules for Ont. hockey league in light of player death: Players planning to fight one another must keep them on, or face misconduct', 14 January 2009. Available at http://www.calgaryherald.com/Sports/helmet+rules+hockey+league+light+player+death/1176604/story.html.

46. Kevin B. Wamsley, 'Sport and Social Problems', in Jane Crossman, ed., *Canadian Sport Sociology*, 2nd ed. (Toronto: Thomson Nelson, 2008), 147.

47. Kevin Young and Kevin B. Wamsley, 'State Complicity in Sports Assault and the Gender Order in Twentieth Century Canada: Preliminary Observations', *Avante* 2, 2 (1996): 51–69.

48. On the theory of catharsis and safety valve, see K. Lorenz, *On Aggression* (New York: Harcourt, Brace, & Jovanovich, 1966).

49. See M. Atkinson, 'Fifty million viewers can't be wrong: Professional wrestling, sports-entertainment, and mimesis', *Sociology of Sport Journal* 19, 1 (2002): 63–5.

50. On the origins of wrestling and the shift to entertainment spectacle, see Keith Greenberg, *Pro wrestling: From carnivals to cable TV* (Minneapolis, Minn.: LernerSports, 2000); see also Michael R. Ball, *Professional wrestling as ritual drama in American popular culture* (Lewiston, NY: Edwin Mellen Press, 1990).

51. By character gimmick, I mean the ability to sell a persona to the audience, given the plot lines established by the wrestling organization, such as ECW or the WWF, or what character persona the wrestler brings to the promoter; see Patrice Oppliger, *Wrestling and hypermasculinity* (Jefferson, NC: McFarland, 2004).

52. The point here is that the list is particularly lengthy and unusual within one profession and that this material warrants further research.

53. These are but a few examples. Internet sites claim causes of death for each wrestler but these are not verified. Common examples include heart attack, drug overdose, suicide, car accident, with the exception of Owen Hart who died in 1999 during a failed ring stunt whereby he plunged to his death from over 70 feet. See, for example, http://www.foxnews.com/story/0,2933,286844,00.html; http://prowrestling.about.com/od/whatsrealwhatsfake/a/wrestlersdeaths.htm; http://www.wwecritic.com/dead-wwfwwe-wrestlers-that-died-in-the-last-10-years/; http://www.pwwew.net/people/dead.htm.

54. 'Sports' monster in the closet: Ultimate Fighting's popularity continues to rise', available at http://sports.espn.go.com/nfl/news/story?id=3014742.

55. Steve Buffery, 'Ontario's Ultimate Stalemate: Against a tide of popularity and precedent, province stands firm in its reluctance to join the mixed martial arts boom', available at http://slam.canoe.ca/Slam/Fighting/MixedMartialArts/2008/02/22/4868565-sun.html.

56. Dennis Cauchon, 'Amateur fighting rounds up crowds and controversy', available at http://www.usatoday.com/news/nation/2006-03-27-toughman-popularity_x.htm.

57. Carly Adams and Kevin B. Wamsley, 'Table Scraps: Violence in Women's Sport in Early Canada', Paper presented to the *North American Society for the Sociology of Sport*, Montreal, 2003.

58. See http://www.fightergirls.com.

59. See http://www.olympic.org.

60. See http://www.caaws.ca/e/index.cfm.

61. Helen J. Lenskyj, 'Women's Issues and Gender Relations', in Jane Crossman, ed., *Canadian Sport Sociology*, 2nd ed. (Toronto: Thomson Nelson, 2008), 99–117.

62. Kevin B. Wamsley and Gertrud Pfister, 'Olympic Men and Women: The Politics of Gender in the Modern Games', in Kevin Young and Kevin Wamsley, eds, *Global Olympics: Historical and Sociological Studies of the Modern Games* (Oxford: Elsevier Press, 2005), 103–26.

63. The issue of gender is also elaborated clearly in J. Coakley's *Sport in Society: Issues and Controversies* (St. Louis: Moseby, 1994); more elaborately in R.W. Connell, *Masculinities* (Los Angeles: University of California Press, 1995); M. Ann. Hall, *Feminism and Sporting Bodies: Essays on Theory and Practice* (Champaign, Ill.: Human Kinetics, 1996); and M. Messner and D. Sabo, *Sport, Men, and the Gender Order* (Champaign, Ill.: Human Kinetics, 1990).

64. For an extensive examination of these issues of women's participation in sport, see for example J. Hargreaves, *Sporting Females: Critical Issues in the History and Sociology of Women's Sports* (London: Routledge, 1994).

65. See John Hoberman, *Mortal Engines: The Science of Performance and the Dehumanization of Sport* (New York: Free Press, 1992).

66. See Alfred E. Senn, *Power, Politics, and the Olympic Games* (Champaign, Ill.: Human Kinetics, 1999).

67. Hoberman, *Mortal Engines*.

68. Kevin B. Wamsley and Gordon MacDonald, 'Child's Play: Decreasing Size and Increasing Risk in Women's Olympic Gymnastics', in Nigel B. Crowther, Robert K. Barney, Michael K. Heine, eds, *Eighth International Symposium for Olympic Research*, London, Ont., 2006.

69. Joan Ryan, *Little Girls in Pretty Boxes: The Making and Breaking of Elite Gymnasts and Figure Skaters* (New York: Doubleday, 1995).

70. Caroline Davis, 'Eating Disorders, Physical Activity, and Sport: Biological, Psychological, and Sociological Factors', in Philip White and Kevin Young, eds, *Sport and Gender in Canada* (Don Mills, Ont.: Oxford University Press, 1999), 85–106; John H. Salmela, with Bernard Petiot, Madeleine Hallé, and Guy Régnier, *Competitive Behaviors of Olympic Gymnasts* (Springfield, Ill.: Charles C. Thomas Publisher, 1980); Patrick J. O'Connor, Richard D. Lewis, and Andrea Boyd, 'Health Concerns of Artistic Women Gymnasts', *Sports Medicine* 21, 5 (May 1996): 321; Jorunn Sundgot-Borgen, 'Eating Disorders in Female Athletes', *Sports Medicine* 17, 3 (1994): 176–88.

71. Jacquelin Magnay, 'Supermums are on drugs, naturally', 9 December 2006. See http://www.smh.com.au/news/sport/super-mums-are-on-drugs-naturally/2006/12/08/1165081155039.html.

72. See 'The costs that children pay: Young Athletes Need Child Law Protection', in P. Donnelly, ed., *Taking Sport Seriously* (Toronto: Thompson, 1997), 189–95.

73. Wamsley and MacDonald, 342.

74. Jan Todd and Terry Todd, 'Significant events in the history of drug testing and the Olympic movement: 1960–1999', in Wayne Wilson and E. Derse, eds, *Doping in Elite Sport: The Politics of Drugs in the Olympic Movement* (Champaign, Ill.: Human Kinetics, 2000), 65–128.

75. A. Schneider and R. Butcher, 'An ethical analysis of drug testing', in Wayne Wilson and E. Derse, eds, *Doping in Elite Sport: The Politics of Drugs in the Olympic Movement* (Champaign, Ill.: Human Kinetics, 2000), 129–52.

76. Ken Kirkwood, 'Out of the Olympic closet: Abandoning prohibitions on doping in favour of a harm reduction approach.' Unpublished dissertation, London, Ont.: The University of Western Ontario, 2004.

77. Rob Beamish and Ian Ritchie, *Fastest, Highest, Strongest: A Critique of High-performance Sport* (New York and London: Routledge, 2006), 142.

Glossary of Key Terms

Agricultural societies: encouraged by government to improve farming skills

Alexander Henry: fur trader and entrepreneur of the late eighteenth century

Ancient Olympic games: religious/athletic festival to honour the Greek gods, 776 BCE–393 AD

Anthropology Days: organized within the Louisiana Purchase Exposition in St. Louis; organizers brought in Aboriginal peoples from North America and beyond to display them in artificial villages

Anti-Semitism: overt or indirect hostility or prejudice toward Jews

Apartheid: policies of racial separation enforced in South Africa from 1948–90

Articles of agreement: written, formalized rules for particular nineteenth century sporting competitions such as track and field, rowing, and figure skating; participants were asked to sign the 'articles' in agreement

Associated Press: the world's oldest and largest news-gathering organization

Axel spins: a figure skating jump using a forward take-off from a forward outside edge of one foot to land on the back outside edge of the opposite foot

Bandy: played on ice with stick and ball, invented after shinty and hurling

Barge: a large, flat bottomed boat built for river and canal conveyance of heavy cargoes

Bees: work groups, with some compensation, organized for jobs which required more people

Bier: stand on which a coffin is placed to lie in state

Blacksmith's bellows: fan-shaped mechanical apparatus used to fan a blacksmith's forge or fire in order to increase the heat

Bluenose: famous Nova Scotian racing schooner of the 1920s and 1930s; Bluenose image still appears on most Canadian-minted dimes

Blutcher's Army: leader of the Prussian army during the Napoleonic Wars

Bobby soxers: zealous teenage fans of singers Bonaventure Station

Boosterism: the act of promoting one's town, city, or organization

British North America Act: the first (1867) of a series of acts that are at the core of the constitution of Canada

Brobdignagian: anything of colossal size

Bush masculinity: sense of manliness determined by survival and work physical skills, influencing relationships to women and other men

Canadian Press: bilingual national news agency created in 1917

Challenge matches: prior to leagues and sport schedules, teams or players issued challenges to other teams or players

Charlie McCarthy: ventriloquist Edgar Bergen's puppet

Château Clique: ruling elites in Lower Canada

Chivaree: an evening event targeting a newly-wed couple with harmless and harmful pranks; sometimes severe if the community did not approve of the marriage

CIS: Canadian Interuniversity Sport

Civil War (US): a war between a state and some political faction arising within the state; in this text, refers to the American Civil War, which occurred from 1861–65

Closets (washrooms): the proper name for outdoor toilets contained in small sheds

Colonial or colonialism: refers to the process by which a nation extends its sovereignty over a new territory often displacing indigenous peoples

Comeback: the process of returning to the line-up for an injured player or a retired player

Confederation: the union of the British North American colonies of New Brunswick, Nova Scotia and Canada (Canada being an earlier 1841 union of Lower Canada and Upper Canada), achieved 1 July 1867 under the new name, Dominion of Canada

Confrontational competitions: physical competitions such as wrestling or fighting

Continental Sunday: permitted certain pleasurable activities on Sundays, as opposed to the strict Protestant Sunday

Cooper, James Fennimore: prolific and popular American writer of the nineteenth century

CPR Telegraph Company: the Canadian Pacific Railway's establishment of an adjunct communication company with telegraph lines paralleling railway lines and telegraph operators providing the communications usually via Morse code

Crimean War (1854–56): was fought over the desire by various European powers to dominate the Ottoman Empire

Dominion Day: a commemoration of the achievement of national status; celebrated on the first of July in Canada

Double Salchows: a figure skating jump with a take-off from a back inside edge and landing on the back outside edge of the opposite foot after two rotations in the air

Duke of Edinburgh: the titular designation of Prince Phillip, current husband of English Queen Elizabeth

Eurocentric: placing European cultural values first

Exemplary masculinities: celebrated traits of manhood, held up for admiration

Fairs: local social festivals organized to celebrate the harvest and display farm goods

Family Compact: Upper Canada elites of political influence, usually Anglican, former officers, and Tories

First Nations: first peoples of Canada

Fowling: bird hunting

Funeral Cortege: the procession to accompany the funeral casket in tribute to the deceased; originally on foot, then horseback, currently by car

Garrison: military post

Garrison officers: officers of a garrison

Gender polarities: traditional distinctions in 'maleness' and 'femaleness' in behaviour and appearance; such binary pairs, in part, define each other by their opposition

Gendered: organization of social relations according to traditional notions of masculinity and femininity

Griffintown: the popular name given to the former south-western downtown part of Montreal, Quebec; it existed from the 1820s until the 1960s and was mainly populated by Irish immigrants and their descendants

Guernsey: a knitted wool sweater or jersey

Habitants: early French settlers

Hawkers: an individual or private vendor of goods or products

Highland Games: the Scottish Highland Games have a long history; the Scots established versions of the Games when they emigrated to other countries

Homophobia: a fear and distrust of homosexuality that considers the behaviour to be somehow unnatural or immoral

House of Assembly: the legislature or lower house in parliaments

Hyper-competition: outcomes are so important that competitors will use whatever methods and resources necessary to win

Hypermuscularity: an exaggerated and extremely developed musculature

Iliad, The: together with *The Odyssey*, one of two epic Greek poems said to be written by Homer around the eighth or ninth centuries BCE (Before the Christian Era)

Indian clubs: wooden exercise and juggling equipment common in nineteenth-century gymnasia

Industrial Revolution: a period in which fundamental changes occurred in agriculture, textile and metal manufacture, transportation, and so forth

Interim or Intercalated Games: the 1906 Games in Athens to commemorate the 10th anniversary of the inaugural modern Olympics; the IOC has never recognized these Games as part of the official cycle of Olympics

International Amateur Athletics Federation: formed in 1914, the IAAF is the world governing body for athletics or track and field

International Olympic Committee (IOC): the appointed governing body for the modern Olympic Games

Irish hurling: game played with a stick and leather ball; dates back centuries

Ironman: the distinction given in professional sports to the player with the most consecutive games without absence

Keel: the large or central beam around which the hull of ship is built

Kindertraining: placing young children in adult environments of sport competition, training, and preparation

Last spike: final spike driven into the Canadian Pacific Railway at Craigellachie, British Columbia on 9:22 AM, 7 November 1885 by railroad financier Sir Donald Smith (Lord Strathcona)

Liberal: a theoretical approach in the social sciences that views problems of inequality in terms of opportunity and resources, as opposed to more systemic issues

Lord Strathcona: Canadian adventurer Donald Smith, who made his fortune building and financing railroads

Louisiana Purchase Exposition: held to celebrate the anniversary of the purchase of the state of Louisiana, its transfer from Spain to France and then to the United States for the sum of $15 million

Lower Canada College: prestigious coeducational, independent day school in Montreal

Loyalists: Americans who remained faithful to the British crown

Masons: worldwide fraternal organization; also known as freemasons

Methodist: a person of United Methodist religious faith

Militia Department: name accorded to what is currently labelled the Department of National Defense

Militia Muster Day: the enrolment of members of the militia

Mixed martial arts: a contest between two athletes who use a variety of blows—hand, foot, elbow—in combination with wrestling to defeat one another

Muscular Christianity: an athletic Christian; a strong body tempered by Christian values

NCAA: National Collegiate Athletic Association (in the United States)

New France: French colonies extending from present-day Newfoundland to North Western Ontario, ceded to Britain in 1763

Notman photographic firm: the Montreal

photographic company established by William Notman in 1856

Oral traditions: sharing community traditions and values through stories

Orangemen: a Protestant fraternal organization

Order of Canada: Canada's highest civilian honour, recognizing a lifetime of outstanding achievement, dedication to the community, and service to the nation

Pogroms: a form of riot or violent attacks directed against a particular group or ethnicity

Pontiac Rebellion: a war launched in 1763 by North American Indians who were dissatisfied with British policies in the Great Lakes region

Prince of Wales: title traditionally granted to the Heir Apparent to the reigning monarch of the United Kingdom

Queen's Own Rifles: infantry regiment of the Canadian forces

Quiet Revolution: 1960s period of intense changes in the province of Quebec; changes were characterized by the secularization of society, the creation of a welfare state, and the realignment of politics into federalist and separatist factions

Racism: the unfounded belief that race is the primary determinant of human traits; often represented by discriminatory behaviours of one group over another

Report on Education: the common schools' report (late 1930s) written by physician, politician, and educator Charles Duncombe

Residential schools: institutions established by American and Canadian governments to 'Christianize' and 'educate' Aboriginals

Rowdyism: real or perceived disorderly conduct or behaviour

Sampson (or Samson): Old Testament figure possessed of tremendous physical strength

Sculling: a form of rowing where a rower (or each rower, if more than one is in the craft) is possessed of two oars

Seigneuries: tracts of land sold to land barons and rented to habitants

Sexism: the belief or attitude that one gender or sex is inferior to or less valuable than the other

Sexualization: a process of treating people as objects of desire, without establishing a personal relationship with them

Shinny: derived from shinty; a pick-up or informal hockey game

Shinty: stick and ball game with Scottish origins

Social Darwinism: an extension of Darwin's often quoted biological reference 'survival of the fittest', extended to apply social values and distinctions between people

Stag leaps: a figure skating jump so-named because the skater's air position resembles a deer in full flight

Stanozolol: a synthetic anabolic steroid derived from testosterone; developed in 1961

Steamboat: a ship in which the primary means of propulsion is steam power

Subsistence techniques: related to survival skills such as hunting or running

Symbolic capital: from the French social theorist, Pierre Bourdieu, referring to the honour and prestige held by an individual in particular social settings

TOP: The Olympic Programme, now termed The Olympic Partners; the exclusive sponsorship arrangement between global corporations and the IOC

Traditional games: activities passed down through generations of families and communities

Turnfests: gymnastics competitions; originated in Germany but also established in the United States and Canada

Vitai Lampada: Sir Henry Newbolt's famous nineteenth-century poem that celebrates the character traits and bravado developed in cricket carried over to war

Windsor Castle: the traditional home of Britain's monarch; the Royal Family asked that the start of the marathon race for the London Olympics in 1908 be at the castle and the end be at Shepherd's Bush stadium; this now constitutes the standardized marathon race distance

Winter Carnivals: dances, winter sporting events, and civic and cultural festivities celebrated in a carnival-like atmosphere during winter

Women's Olympic Games: held in 1922, 1926, 1930, and 1934

Workers' Olympics: an outgrowth of the worker's sports club organized by trade unions and socialist parties; first held in 1921, the Worker's Olympics attracted 250,000 spectators and 80,000 worker athletes to Vienna for the 1931 Games

World Anti Doping Agency (WADA): established in 1999 by the IOC to organize testing and combat drug use in sport

World's fairs: international events of large scale, generally held over a two- or three-month period, with displays of technology, architecture, manufacturing, and culture

Bibliography of Canadian Sport History

CHR   *Canadian Historical Review*

CJHS   *Canadian Journal of History of Sport*

CJHSPE   *Canadian Journal for the History of Sport and Physical Education*

ICOS   International Centre for Olympic Studies, University of Western Ontario

IJHS   *International Journal of the History of Sport*

IRSS   *International Review for the Sociology of Sport*

JCPES   *Journal of Comparative Physical Education and Sport*

JSH   *Journal of Sports History*

LAC   *Library and Archives Canada*

SHR   *Sport History Review*

Articles

Abbott, Frank. 'Cold Cash and Ice Palaces: The Quebec Winter Carnival of 1894', *CHR* 69, 2 (June 1988): 167–202.

Adams, C. 'Softball and the Female Community: Pauline Perron, Pro Ball Player, Outsider, 1926-1951', *JSH* 33, 3 (Fall 2006): 323–43.

———. 'Queens of the Ice Lanes: The Preston Rivulettes and Women's Hockey in Canada, 1931–1940', *SHR* 39, 1 (2008): 1–29.

———, & Stevens, J. 'Change and Grassroots Movement: Re-conceptualizing Women's Governance in Canada', *International Journal of Sport Management and Marketing [Special Ed. Managing Policy and Politics in Sport]* 2, 4 (2007): 344–61.

Anderson, Robin John. 'On the Edge of the Baseball Map with the 1908 Vancouver Beavers', *CHR* 77, 4 (Dec. 1996): 538–74.

Andrew, Caroline, Jean Harvey, and Don Dawson. 'Evolution of Local State Activity: Recreation Policy in Toronto', *Leisure Studies* 13, 1 (June 1994): 1–16.

Armstrong, Jerry. 'How the Calgary Stampede Began', *Old West* 6, 3 (Spring 1970): 30–3, 86–7.

Atkinson, M. 'Fifty million viewers can't be wrong: Professional wrestling, sports-entertainment, and mimesis', *Sociology of Sport Journal* 19, 1 (March 2002): 63–5.

Ayre, John. 'Berlin 1936: Canadian Dancers at Hitler's Olympics', *The Beaver* 76, 1 (Feb.–Mar. 1996): 35–42.

Baka, Richard. 'Canadian Federal Government Policy and the 1976 Summer Olympics', *CAHPER Journal* (Mar.–Apr. 1976): 52–60.

——— and David Hoy. 'Political Aspects of Canadian Participation in the Commonwealth Games: 1930–1978', *CAHPER Journal* 44, 4 (Mar.–Apr. 1978): 6–14, 24.

Ballem, Charles H. 'Missing from the Canadian Sport Scene: Native Athletes', *CJHS* 14, 2 (Dec. 1983): 33–43.

———. 'Bill Halpenny, First Island Olympian', *The Island* 15 (Spring/Summer 1984): 23–7.

———. 'Reflections on a Sport Dynasty: The Abegweit Amateur Athletic Association (1884–1954)', *CJHS* 18, 1 (May 1987): 1–18.

Barman, Jean. 'Sports and the Development of Character', in Mott (1989: 234–46).

Barney, Robert Knight. 'Diamond Rituals: Baseball in Canadian Culture', in Peter Levine, ed., *Baseball History*, vol. 2. Westport, Conn.: Meckler Books, 1989, 1–21.

———. 'Born From Dilemma: America Awakens to the Modern Olympic Games, 1901–1903', *OLYMPIKA: The International Journal of Olympic Studies* 1 (1992): 92–135.

———, Malcolm Scott, and Rachel Moore. 'Old Boys at Work and Play: The International Olympic Committee and Canadian Co-option, 1928–1946', *OLYMPIKA: The International Journal of Olympic Studies* 8 (1999): 81–104.

Baskin, Cyndy. 'Tom Longboat: The Caledonian Cyclone', *Ontario Indian* 6 (June 1982): 30–7, 52.

Beck, Jason. 'The Forgotten Games: Fifth British Empire and Commonwealth Games, Vancouver, 1954', *SHR* **35**, 1 (May 2004): 32–63.

Benidickson, Jamie. 'Recreational Canoeing in Ontario before the First World War', *CJHSPE* 9, 2 (Dec. 1978): 41–57.

Bernard, David L. 'The Guelph Maple Leafs: A Cultural Indicator of Southern Ontario', *Ontario History* 84, 3 (Sept. 1992): 211–23.

———. 'Sports Promotion in the Western Canadian City: The Example of Early Edmonton', *Urban History Review* 12, 2 (Oct. 1983): 47–56.

———. 'Winter Sports in the Early Urban Environment of Prairie Canada', in Corbet and Rasporich (1990: 52–68).

Blackstock, C.R. 'De Coubertin and Tait McKenzie', *CAHPER Journal* 42, 4 (Mar.–Apr. 1976): 8–9.

Booth, Douglas. 'Gifts of Corruption?: Ambiguities of Obligation in the Olympic Movement', *OLYMPIKA: The International Journal of Olympic Studies* 8 (1999): 43–68.

Bouchier, Nancy B. 'Aristocrats and Their Noble Sport: Woodstock Officers and Cricket during the Rebellion Era', *CJHS* 20, 1 (May 1989): 16–31.

———. 'Strictly Honorable Races: Woodstock's Driving Park Association and Nineteenth Century Small Town Civic Holidays', *CJHS* 24, 1 (May 1993): 29–51.

———. 'The 24th of May is the Queen's Birthday: Civic Holidays and the Rise of Amateurism in 19th Century Canadian Towns', *IJHS* 10, 2 (Aug. 1993): 159–92.

———. 'Idealized Middle-Class Sport for a Young Nation: Lacrosse in Nineteenth Century Ontario Towns, 1871–1891', *Journal of Canadian Studies* 29, 2 (Summer 1994): 89–110. Reprinted in Norman Knowles, ed., *Age of Transition: Readings in Canadian Social History, 1800–1900*. Toronto: Harcourt Brace Canada, 1998, 334–53.

———. 'Canadian Sport History', *Acadiensis* 28, 1 (Autumn 1998): 98–102.

——— and Robert Knight Barney. 'A Critical Examination of a Source on Early Ontario Baseball: The Reminiscences of Adam E. Ford', *IJHS* 15, 1 (1988): 75–90.

——— and Ken Cruikshank. 'Sportsmen and Pothunters: Class, Conservation and the Fishing of Hamilton Harbour, 1850–1914', *SHR* 28 (1997): 1–18.

——— and ———. 'Reflections on Creating Critical Sport History for a Popular Audience: The People and the Bay', *JSH* 25, 2 (Summer 1998): 309–16.

Brown, Andrea. 'Edward Hanlan: The World Sculling Champion visits Australia', *CJHSPE* 11, 2 (Dec. 1980): 1–44.

Brown, David W. 'The Rise and Fall of Rugby Football League in Nova Scotia, 1946–1956', *CJHSPE* 10, 2 (Dec. 1979): 52–75.

———. 'Sport, Darwinism and Canadian Private Schooling to1918', *CJHS* 16, 1 (May1985): 27–37.

———. 'Militarism and Canadian Private Education: Ideal and Practice, 1861–1918', *CJHS* 1, 7 (May 1986): 46–59.

———. 'Prevailing Attitudes Towards Sport, Physical Exercise and Society in the 1870s: Impressions from Canadian Periodicals', *CJHS* 17, 2 (Dec. 1986): 58–70.

———. 'Canadian Imperialism and Sporting Exchanges: The Nineteenth Century Cultural Experience of Cricket and Lacrosse', *CJHS* 18, 1 (May 1987): 55–66.

———. 'The Northern Character Theme and Sport in Nineteenth Century Canada', *CJHS* 20, 1 (May 1989): 47–56.

Brown, Douglas A. 'Thoroughbred Horse-Racing Receives an Imperialist Nod: The Parliamentary Debate on Legalizing Gambling in Canada, 1910', *IJHS* 2, 2 (Aug. 1994): 252–69.

———. 'Aggressive, Progressive and Up-to-Date: The Sport Program at Toronto's Industrial Exhibition, 1879–1910', *SHR* 32, 2 (Nov. 2001): 70–109.

Byl, John. 'Why Physical Educators should know about the Margaret Eaton School', *CAHPER Journal* (Spring 1993): 10–13.

———. 'Directing Physical Education in the Canadian YWCAs: Margaret Eaton School's Influence, 1901–1947.' *SHR* 27, 2 (1996): 139–54.

Cameron, Silver Donald. 'The Bluenose', *Canadian Geographic* 3 (April–May 1984): 20–5.

Cavanaugh, Richard P. 'The Development of Canadian Sports Broadcasting, 1920–78', *Canadian Journal of Communications* 17, 3 (Summer 1992): 301–18.

Cavett, Mary E., H. John Selwood, and John C. Lehr. 'Social Philosophy and the Early Development of Winnipeg Public Parks', *Urban History Review* 11 (June 1982): 27–39.

Charters, David A. 'It's a Guy Thing: The Experience of Women in Canadian Sports Car Competition', *SHR* 37, 2 (Nov. 2006): 83–99.

Christie, Todd. 'The Eddie Shore–Ace Bailey Incident of 1933: One of the Greatest Tragedies in Canadian Sports History', *CJHS* 19, 1 (May 1988): 63–76.

Cheska, Alyce. 'Ball Game Participation of North American Indian Women', in Howell (1982: 29–34).

———. 'The Antigonish Highland Games: A Community's Involvement in the Scottish Festival of Eastern Canada', *Nova Scotia Historical Review* 3, 1 (1983): 51–63.

Colpitts, George W. 'Fish and Game Association in Southern Alberta, 1907–1928', *Alberta History* 42, 4 (Autumn 1994): 16–26.

Conlin, Paul. 'The Cold War and Canadian Nationalism on Ice: Federal Government Involvement in International Ice Hockey During the 1960s', *CJHS* 25, 2 (Dec. 1994): 50–68.

Cooper, David Bernard. 'Canadians Declare "It Isn't Cricket": A Century of Rejection of the Imperial Game', *JSH* 26, 1 (Spring 1999): 51–81.

Cosentino, Frank. 'Ned Hanlan—Canada's Premier Oarsman: A Case Study in Nineteenth Century Professionalism', *CJHSPE* 5, 2 (Dec. 1974): 5–17.

Cosentino, Frank. 'Ned Hanlan—Canada's Premier Oarsman: A Case Study of Nineteenth Century Professionalism', *Ontario History* 66, 4 (1974): 241–50.

———. 'A History of the Concept of Professionalism in Canadian Sport', *CJHSPE* 6, 2 (Dec. 1975): 75–81.

——— and Glynn Leyshon. 'Gold Medal for Canada—Triumph of an Underdog',

CAHPER Journal (Mar.–Apr. 1976): 19–26.

———. 'Sport in the Land of the Beaver, Eagle, and Bear', *CAHPER Journal* 44, 5 (May–June 1978): 15–17, 40–1; 44, 6 (July–Aug. 1978): 26–9.

Cruikshank, Ken, and Nancy B. Bouchier. 'Dirty Spaces: Environment, the State and Recreational Swimming in Hamilton Harbour, 1870–1946', *SHR* 29 (1998): 59–76.

——— and ———. '"The Heritage of the People Closed Against Them": Class, Environment, and the Shaping of the Burlington Beach, 1870s–1980s', *Urban History Review* 30, 1 (Oct. 2001): 40–55.

——— and ———. '"The Pictures Are Great but the Text Is a Bit of a Downer": Creating Ways of Seeing and the Challenge of Exhibiting Critical History', *CHR* (Mar. 1999): 96–113.

Cumbo, Enrico. 'Sports and Inter-Ethnic Relations at Camp Petawawa', *Polyphony* 7, 1 (Spring–Summer 1985): 31.

Dauphinias, Paul. 'A Class Act: French-Canadians in Organized Sport, 1840–1910', *IJHS* 7, 3 (Dec. 1990): 432–9.

Day, Robert D. 'Sport in Poetry: A Nineteenth Century Newspaper Study of Chatham, Ontario Journals', *CJHSPE* 10, 1 (May 1980): 62–82.

———. 'Ethnic Soccer Clubs in London, Canada: A Study in Assimilation', *International Review of Sport Sociology* 16, 1 (1981): 37–52.

DeLottinville, Peter. 'Joe Beef of Montreal: Working Class Culture and the Tavern, 1869–1889', *Labour/Le Travailleur* 8/9 (1981–2): 9–40.

Dewar, John. 'Saskatchewan Basketball Beginnings (1891–1922)', *Saskatchewan History* 41, 3 (Autumn 1989): 89–112.

Dufresne, Sylvie. 'The Winter Carnival of Montreal, 1803–1889', *Urban History Review* 11, 3 (Feb. 1983): 25–45.

Dunning, T.P. 'Convict Leisure and Recreation: The North American Experience in Van Dieman's Land, 1840–1847', *Sporting Traditions* 9, 2 (May 1993): 3–15.

Duperreault, Jean R. 'L'Affaire Richard: A Situational Analysis of the Montreal Hockey Riot of 1955', *CJHS* 12, 1 (May 1981): 66–83.

Earle, Neil. 'Hockey as Canadian Popular Culture: Team Canada 1972, Television, and the Canadian Identity', *Journal of Canadian Studies* 30, 2 (Summer 1995): 107–22.

Eastman, Wayne. 'Religion and Sport: The Denominational Colleges. The Genesis of Physical Education in Newfoundland', *CJHS* 19, 2 (Dec. 1988): 30–49.

———. 'School Athletic Organizations and Professional Associations for Physical Educators: A Retrospect of Interfacing (1900–1986)', *CJHS* 20, 2 (Dec. 1989): 49–63.

Eisen, George. 'Games and Sporting Diversions of the North American Indian as Reflected in American Historical Writings of the Sixteenth and Seventeenth Centuries', *CJHSPE* 9, 1 (May 1978): 58–95.

Eyford, Ryan. 'From Prairie Goolies to Canadian Cyclones: The Transformation of the 1920 Winnipeg Falcons', *SHR* 37, 1 (May 2006): 5–18.

Farnham, Katharine. 'Skiing in the Alberta Coal Branch', *Alberta History* 45, 3 (Summer 1997): 12–14.

Field, Russell. 'Passive Participation: The Selling of Spectacle and the Construction of Maple Leaf Gardens, 1931', *SHR* 33, 1 (May 2002): 35–50.

Files, James. 'Smocks and Jocks: The Establishment of the Ontario Ministry of Culture and Recreation, 1974', *Ontario History* 83, 3 (Sept. 1991): 209–23.

Fisher, Donald M. '"Splendid But Undesirable Isolation": Recasting Canada's National Game as Box Lacrosse, 1931–1932', *SHR* 36, 2 (Nov. 2005): 115–29.

Fogarty, Jim. 'Hellmuth College: A Pre-Olympic Festival Held in London, Ontario's Backyard', unpublished paper, 1998, ICOS Archives.

Forsyth, J. 'After the Fur Trade: First Nations Women in Canadian History, 1850-1950', *Atlantis* 29, 2 (2005): 69–78.

——. 'The Indian Act and the (Re)shaping of Canadian Aboriginal Sport Practices', *International Journal of Canadian Studies* 35 (2007): 95–111.

——. 'To My Sisters in the Field', *Pimatisiwin: A Journal of Aboriginal and Indigenous Community Health* 5, 1: 155–68.

——, & Heine, M. 'A Higher Degree of Social Organization: Jan Eisenhardt and Canadian Aboriginal Sport Policy in the 1950s', *JSH* 35, 2 (2008): 401–17.

——, & Wamsley, K. 'Native to Native We'll Recapture Our Spirits: The World Indigenous Nations Games and North American Indigenous Games as Cultural Resistance', *IJHS* 23, 2 (2006): 294–314.

Franks, C.E.S. 'White Water Canoeing: An Aspect of Canadian Socio-Economic History', *Queen's Quarterly* 82, 2 (Summer 1975): 175–88.

Fudge, Paul H. 'The North West Mounted Police and Their Influence on Sport in Western Canada, 1873–1905', *Journal of the West* 22, 1 (Jan. 1983): 30–6.

Galasso, P.J. 'The Involvement of the Canadian Federal Government in Sport and Fitness', *CJHSPE* 3, 2 (Dec. 1972): 42–61.

Gear, James L. 'Factors Influencing the Development of Government Sponsored Physical Fitness Programmes in Canada from 1850 to 1972', *CJHSPE* 4, 2 (Dec. 1973): 1–25.

George, Judith Jenkins. 'The Fad of North American Women's Endurance Swimming during the Post World War I Era', *CJHS* 25, 1 (1995): 52–72.

Gidney, Catherine. 'The Athletics–Physical Education Dichotomy Revisited: The Case

of the University of Toronto, 1900–1940', *SHR* 37, 2 (Nov. 2006): 130–49.

Gillespie, Greg. 'Roderick McLennan, Professionalism, and the Emergence of the Athlete in Caledonian Games', *SHR* 31, 1 (2000): 43–63.

——. 'Sport and "Masculinities" in Early Nineteenth-Century Ontario: The British Travellers' Image', *Ontario History* 92, 2 (Autumn 2000): 113–26.

——. 'The United States Military Academy–Royal Military College of Canada Hockey Rivalry', *IJHS* 17, 1 (Mar. 2000): 94–112.

——. 'Wickets in the West: Cricket, Culture, and Constructed Images of Nineteenth Century Canada', *JSH* 27, 1 (Spring 2000): 51–66.

——, and K. Wamsley. 'Clandestine Means: The Aristocratic British Hunting code and Early Game Legislation in Nineteenth-Century Canada', *Sporting Traditions: The Australian Journal of Sport History* 22, 1 (2005): 99–120.

Greene, David L. 'Early Pioneer Sports in Saskatchewan', *Saskatchewan History* 14, 3 (1961): 110–13.

Gregorovich, Andrew. 'Sports Achievements of Ukrainian Canadians', *Forum* no. 52 (Fall 1982): 23–8

Guay, Donald. 'Problèmes de l'Intégration du Sport dans la Société Canadienne 1830–1865: Le Cas des Courses de Chevaux', *CJHSPE* 4, 2 (Dec. 1973): 70–92.

——. 'Les Origines du Hockey', *CJHS* 20, 1 (May 1989): 32–46.

——. *L'histoire du Hockey au Québec*. Montreal: Les Editions JCL, 1990.

Hall, M. Ann. 'Rarely Have We Asked Why: Reflections on Canadian Women's Experience in Sport', *Atlantis* 6, 1 (Fall 1980): 51–60.

——. 'Alexandrine Gibb: In No Man's Land of Sport', *IJHS* 18, 1 (Mar. 2001): 149–72.

Harding-Milburn, Wanda. 'The Chatham All-Stars: An Interview with Kingsley Terrell', *Polyphony* 7, 1 (Spring/Summer 1985): 111.

Harrigan, Patrick J. 'Asserting Authority: The Canadian Intercollegiate Athletic Union, 1961–1975', *SHR* 37, 2 (Nov. 2006): 150–75.

———. 'The Controversy about Athletic Scholarships in Canadian Universities: A Historical Perspective', *SHR* 32, 2 (Nov. 2001): 140–68.

Harvey, Jean, and Christine Dallaire. 'La Division des Loisirs du Conseil Canadien du Bien-être (1934–1958), Les Travailleurs Sociaux et la Constitution du Champ Sportif Canadian', *CJHS* 25, 1 (May 1994): 29–49.

Heard, Clark P. 'Sport and Image during World War II: The Issue of Intercollegiate Football Continuation at the University of Western Ontario', *SHR* 27, 2 (1996): 155–72.

Heine, Michael K., and Kevin B. Wamsley. 'Kickfest at Dawson City: Native Peoples and the Sports of the Klondike Gold Rush', *SHR* 27, 1 (1996): 72–86.

Henderson, Robert. 'Every Trail Has a Story: The Heritage Context as Adventure', in J. Miles and S. Priest, eds, *Adventure Education*. State College, Penn.: Venture Publishing, 1990.

Hickey, Colm. 'For All That Was Good, Noble and True': A Middle Class Martial Icon of Canadian Patriotism and British Imperialism. John Lovell Dashwood, Canada and the Great War', *IJHS* 22, 4 (July 2005): 722–44.

Homel, Gene Howard. 'Sliders and Backsliders: Toronto's Sunday Tobogganing Controversy of 1912', *Urban History Review* 10, 2 (Oct. 1981): 25–34.

Hotchkiss, Ron. 'The Matchless Six: Canadian Women at the Olympics, 1928', *Beaver* (Oct.–Nov. 1993): 23–42.

Howell, Colin. 'Baseball, Class and Community in the Maritime Provinces, 1870–1910', *Social History* 22, 44 (Nov. 1989): 270–1.

———. 'On Metcalfe, Marx, and Materialism: Reflections on the Writing of Sport History in the Post-modern Age', *SHR* 29 1 (May 1998): 96–102.

———. 'Two Outs; or Yogi Berra, Sport and Maritime Historiography', *Acadiensis* 29, 1 (Autumn, 1999): 106–21.

———. 'Of Remembering and Forgetting: From Ritual to Record and Beyond', *SHR* 32, 1 (May 2001): 12–18.

——— and Christopher Fletcher. 'Modernization Theory and the Traditional Sporting Practices of Native People in Eastern Canada', *JCPES* 19, 2 (1997): 79–84.

Huel, Raymond. 'The Creation of the Alpine Club of Canada: An Early Manifestation of Canadian Nationalism', *Prairie Forum* 15, 1 (Spring 1990): 25–43.

Humber, William. 'Spirit of the Black Bear: Lacrosse our Native Sport Flourishes in Obscurity', *Idler* 24 (1989): 32–6.

——— and Raja Eves. 'The Baseball Tradition in Western Canada', *Baseball Research Journal* (1982): 137–41.

Jackson, Steven J. 'Exorcizing the Ghost: Donovan Bailey, Ben Johnson and the Politics of Canadian Identity', *Media, Culture and Society* 26, 1 (Jan. 2004): 121–41.

Janson, Gilles. 'Sport et modernité: *Le Devoir*, 1910–1920', in Robert Comeau and Luc Derochers, eds, *Le Devoir: Un journal indépendant (1910–1995)*. Quebec: Presses de l'Université du Québec, 1996, 80–92.

Jette, Shannon. 'Little/Big Ball: The Vancouver Asahi Baseball Story', *SHR* 38, 1 (May 2007): 1–16.

Jokisipilä, Markku. 'Maple Leaf, Hammer, and Sickle: International Ice Hockey During the Cold War', *SHR* 37, 1 (May 2006): 36–53.

Jones, Kevin G. 'Developments in Amateurism and Professionalism in Early 20th

Century Canada', *JSH* 2, 1 (Spring 1975): 29–40

——— and T. George Vellathottam. 'Highlights in the Development of Canadian Lacrosse to 1931', *CJHSPE* 5, 2 (Dec. 1974): 31–47.

——— and ———. 'The Myth of Canada's National Sport', *CAHPER Journal* (Sept.–Oct. 1974): 33–6.

Joyce, C.A. Tony. 'Alan Metcalfe, Maverick, Marx and Methodology', *CJHS* 18, 2 (Dec. 1987): 58–69.

———. 'Sport and the Cash Nexus in Nineteenth Century Toronto', *SHR* 30, 2 (Nov. 1999): 140–67.

———. 'Canadian Sport and State Control: Toronto 1845–86', *IJHS* 16 (Mar. 1999): 22–37.

Kearney, Mark. '"Abner Who?" Baseball's Canadian Roots', *The Beaver* 74, 5 (Oct.–Nov. 1994): 12–17.

Keesing-Tobias, Lenore. 'Baggataway: History of Lacrosse', *Ontario Indian* 5, 6 (June 1982): 21–3.

Kendall, Brian. 'Sportsmen at War: Conn Smythe and Co. Man the Bofors—And Play a Little Baseball', *The Beaver* 72, 2 (April–May 1992): 31–6.

Kidd, Bruce. 'Canadian Opposition to the 1936 Olympics in Germany', *CJHSPE* 9, 2 (Dec. 1978): 20–40.

———. 'Reflections on the 8th Commonwealth Games', *CJHSPE* 9, 2 (1978): 105–28.

———. 'Sport, Dependency and the Canadian State', in H. Cantelon and R. Gruneau, eds, *Sport, Culture, and the Modern State*. Toronto: University of Toronto Press, 1982, 281–303.

———. 'In Defense of Tom Longboat', *CJHS* 14, 1 (May 1983): 34–63.

———. 'The myth of the ancient Games', in Alan Tomlinson and Garry Whannel, eds, *Five Ring Circus: Money, Power and Politics at the Olympic Games*. London and Sydney: Pluto Press, 1984, 71–83.

———. 'Sports and Masculinity', *Queen's Quarterly* 94, 1 (Spring 1987): 116–31.

———. 'The Toronto Olympic Commitment: Towards a Social Contract for the Olympic Games', *OLYMPIKA: The International Journal of Olympic Studies* 1 (1992): 154–67.

———. 'Culture Wars of the Montreal Olympics', *IRSS* 27, 2 (1992): 151–64.

———. 'The First COA Presidents', *OLYMPIKA: The International Journal of Olympic Studies* 3 (1994):107–10.

———. 'Making the Pros Pay for Amateur Sports: The Ontario Athletic Commission, 1920–1947', *Ontario History* 87, 2 (June 1995): 105–28.

———. 'Montreal 1976: The Games of the XXth Olympiad', in John E. Findling and Kimberly D. Pelle, eds, *Historical Dictionary of the Modern Olympic Movement*. Westport, Conn., Greenwood Press, 1996, 153–60.

———. 'The Making of a Hockey Artifact: A Review of the Hockey Hall of Fame', *CJHS* 23, 3 (Fall 1996): 328–40.

———. 'Muscular Christianity and value-centred sport: The Legacy of Tom Brown in Canada', *IJHS* 23, 5 (August 2006): 701–13.

———. 'Ontario and the Ambition of Sports', *Ontario History* 90, 2 (Autumn 1998): 157–72.

Killan, Gerald. 'Mowat and a Park Policy for Niagara Falls, 1873–1887', *Ontario History* 70, 2 (Mar.1978): 115–35.

Klassen, Henry C. 'Bicycles and Automobiles in Early Calgary', *Alberta History* 24, 2 (1976): 1–8.

Kossuth, Robert. 'Transition and Assimilation: English Rugby and Canadian Football in Halifax, Nova Scotia, 1930–1955', *Football Studies: Journal of the Football Studies Group* 2, 2 (1999): 18–36.

———. 'Dangerous Waters: Victorian Decorum, Swimmer Safety, and the Establishment of Public Bathing Facilities in London (Canada)', *IJHS* 22, 5 (Sept. 2005): 796–815.

———. 'Men on the Closing Range: Early Rodeo Competition in the Southern Northwest Territories/Alberta', *Sporting Traditions* 24, 1–2 (Nov. 2007): 23–42.

———. 'Spaces and Places to Play: The Formation of a Municipal Parks System in London, Ontario, 1867–1914', *Ontario History* XCVII, 2 (Autumn 2005): 160–90.

——— and Kevin B. Wamsley. 'Cycles of Manhood: Pedaling Respectability in Ontario's Forest City', *SHR* 34, 2 (2003): 168–89.

Kupfer, Charles. 'Crabs in the Grey Cup: Baltimore's Canadian Football Sojourn, 1994–95', *IJHS*, 24, 1 (Mar. 2006): 49–66.

Laforce, Gina L. 'The Alpine Club of Canada, 1906 to 1929: Modernization, Canadian Nationalism, and Anglo-Saxon Mountaineering', *Canadian Alpine Journal* 12 (1979): 39–47.

Lamb, Patrick. 'Deacon White, Sportsman', *Alberta History* 37, 1 (Winter 1989): 23–27.

Lappage, Ronald S. 'Sport as an Expression of Western and Maritime Discontent in Canada between the Wars', *CJHSPE* 8, 1 (May 1977): 50–71.

———. 'British Columbia's Contribution to the Dominion-Provincial Youth Training Program through the Provincial-Recreation Program', *CJHSPE* 9, 1 (May 1978): 86–93.

———. 'A Sporting Life', *Alberta History* 26, 2 (1978): 13–20.

———. 'The Physical Feats of the Voyageur', *CJHS* 15, 1 (May 1984): 30–7.

———. 'The Kenora Thistles Stanley Cup Trail', *CJHS* 19, 2 (Dec. 1988): 79–100.

Lathrop, Anna H. 'Elegance and Expression, Sweat and Strength: A Portrait of the Margaret Eaton Schools (1901–1941) through the Life History of Emma Scott

Nasmith, Mary G. Hamilton, and Florence A. Somers', *Vitae Scholasticae* 16, 1 (1997): 69–92.

———. 'Strap an Axe to Your Belt: Camp Counselor Training and the Socialization of Women at the Margaret Eaton School', *SHR* 32, 2 (Nov. 2001): 110–25.

Leiper, Jean M. 'Stampeding Toward the Olympic Games: Calgary '88', *Journal of the West* 26, 1 (Jan. 1987): 26–33.

Lennox, Brian. 'Nova Scotia's Forgotten Boxing Heroes: Roy Mitchell and Terrence 'Tiger' Warrington', *Nova Scotia Historical Review* 12, 2 (1992): 3–46.

Lenskyj, Helen. 'Femininity First: Sport and Physical Education for Ontario Girls, 1890–1930', *CJHS* 13, 2 (Dec. 1982): 4–17. Reprinted in Mott (1989: 187–200).

———. 'We Want to Play . . . We'll Play', *Canadian Woman Studies* 4, 3 (1983): 15–18.

———. 'Putting the Physical into Education: The Politics of Teaching Women's Sport History in High School', *History and Social Sciences Teacher* 25, 3 (Spring 1990): 138–45.

———. 'Common Sense and Physiology: North American Medical Views on Women and Sport, 1890–1930', *CJHS* 21, 1 (May 1990): 49–60.

———. 'Training for "True Womanhood": Physical Education for Girls in Ontario Schools, 1890–1920', *Historical Studies in Education* 2, 2 (Fall 1990): 205–24.

———. 'Good Sports: Feminists Organizing on Sport Issues in the 1970s and 1980s', *Resources for Feminist Research/Documentation sur la recherche féministe* 20, 3/4 (1991): 130–5.

———. 'Whose Sport? Whose Tradition? Canadian Women and Sport in the Twentieth Century', *IJHS* 9, 1 (Apr. 1992): 141–50.

———. 'When Winners Are Losers: Toronto and Sydney Bids for the Summer Olympics',

Journal of Sport and Social Issues 20, 4 (Nov. 1996): 392–410.

Lewis, Guy. 'Canadian Influence on American Collegiate Sport', *CJHSPE* 1, 2 (Dec. 1970): 7–17.

Levitt, Cyril, and William Shaffir. 'Baseball and Ethnic Violence in Toronto: The Case of the Christie Pits Riot, August 16, 1933', *Polyphony* 7, 1 (1985): 67.

Levy, Joseph, Danny Rosenberg, and Avi Hyman. 'Fanny "Bobbie" Rosenfeld: Canada's Woman Athlete of the Half Century', *JSH* 26, 2 (Summer 1999): 392–6.

Leyshon, Glynn A. 'Wobble to Glory: George Goulding, Pedestrian', *The Beaver* 71, 4 (Aug.–Sept. 1991): 19–25.

———. 'The Friendly Games: Hamilton Hosts the First British Empire Games', *The Beaver* 74, 4 (Aug.–Sept. 1994): 15–21.

———. 'Forgotten Heroes: Canada's Athletes at the Olympics', *The Beaver* 76, 3 (June–July 1996): 21–4.

Lindsay, Peter L. 'The Impact of Military Garrisons on the Development of Sport in British North America', *CJHSPE* 1, 1 (Dec. 1970): 33–44.

———. 'Woman's Place in Nineteenth Century Canadian Sport', *Canadian Women's Studies* 1, 4 (1979): 22–4.

——— and David Howell. 'Social Gospel and the Young Boy Problem, 1895–1925', *CJHS* 17, 1 (May 1986): 75–87.

Lorenz, Stacy L. 'Bowing Down to Babe Ruth: Major League Baseball and Canadian Popular Culture, 1920–1929', *CJHS* 26, 1 (May 1995): 22–39.

———. 'A Lively Interest on the Prairies: Western Canada, the Mass Media, and a World of Sport, 1870–1939', *JSH* 27, 2 (Summer 2000): 195–228.

———. '"In the Field of Sport at Home and Abroad": Sports Coverage in Canadian Daily Newspapers, 1850–1914', *SHR* 34, 2 (2003): 133–67.

Lund, Rolf T. 'The Development of Skiing in Banff', *Alberta History* 25, 4 (1977): 26–30.

———. 'Skiing in Canada: The Early Years', *The Beaver* 308, 3 (1977): 48–53.

———. 'Recreational Skiing in the Canadian Rockies', *Alberta History* 25, 4 (1977): 30–4.

———. 'Skiing on the Prairies', *Saskatchewan History* 32, 1 (1979): 29–34.

Macdonald, Cathy. 'Hamilton's Hurdler: Betty Taylor', *Canadian Woman Studies/Les Cahiers de la Femme* no. 3 (Spring 1983): 19–26.

Macintosh, Donald, Donna Greenhorn, and David Black. 'Canadian Diplomacy and the 1978 Edmonton Commonwealth Games', *JSH* 19, 1 (1992): 26–55.

MacKinnon, Dan. 'Myth, Memory, and the Kitchener-Waterloo Dutchmen in Canadian International Hockey', *SHR* 31, 1 (Nov. 2000): 1–27.

MacLeod, David. 'A Live Vaccine: The YMCA and Male Adolescence in the United States and Canada, 1870–1920', *Social History* 11, 21 (May 1978): 1–25.

MacLellan R, and R.C. Watson. 'Smitting to Spitting: Eighty Years of Ice Hockey in Canadian Courts', *CJHS* 17, 2 (Dec. 1986): 10–27.

McNutt, Steve. 'Shifting Objectives: The Development of Male Physical Education in Nova Scotia from 1867 to 1913', *CJHS* 22, 1 (May 1991): 32–51.

Markham, Susan E. 'The Impact of Prairie and Maritime Reformers and Boosters on the Development of Parks and Playgrounds, 1880 to 1930', *Loisir et société/Society and Leisure* 14, 1 (Spring 1991): 219–33.

Marvine, Dee. 'Fanny Sperry Wowed 'Em at First Calgary Stampede', *American West* (Aug. 1987): 30–7.

Marsh, John. 'The Changing Skiing Scene in Canada', *Canadian Geographical Journal* 90, 2 (1975): 4–13.

———. 'The History and Character of Recreational Use of the Mt. Sir Sanford Area, Selkirk Mountains, BC', *Canadian Alpine Journal* 60 (1977): 38–40.

Mason, Courtney W. 'Rethinking the Revival of the Glengarry Highland Games: Modernity, Identity, and Tourism in Rural Canada', *SHR* 36, 2 (Nov. 2005): 130–53.

Mason, Daniel S. 'Professional Sports Facilities and Developing Urban Communities: Vancouver's Recreation Park, 1905–1912', *Urban History Review* 26, 1 (Oct. 1997): 43–51.

———. 'The International Hockey League and the Professionalization of Ice Hockey, 1904–1907', *JSH* 25, 1 (1998): 1–17.

——— and Barbara Schrodt. 'Hockey's First Professional Team: The Portage Lakes Hockey Club of Houghton, Michigan', *SHR* 27, 1 (1996): 49–71.

Massicotte, Jean-Paul. 'L'Eglise et Le Loisir au Québec au XXe Siècle', *CJHS* 8, 2 (Dec. 1982): 45–55.

———. 'Role Ethno-Historique de la Racquette', *CJHS* 17, 1 (May 1986): 1–10.

———. 'Traine et Glissoire à Travers l'Histoire du Québec', *CJHS* 19, 2 (Dec. 1988): 62–78.

———. 'Les Anglophones et le Sport en Maurice', *CJHS* 22, 1 (May 1991): 9–19.

——— and Claude Lessard. 'Le Chasse en Nouvelle-France au XVIIe Siècle', *CJHSPE* 5, 2 (Dec. 1974): 18–30.

McDonald, Robert A.J. '"Holy Retreat" or "Practical Breathing Spot"?: Class Perceptions of Vancouver's Stanley Park, 1910–1913', *CHR* 65, 2 (1984): 127–53.

McIntyre, Bruce R. 'Which Uniform to Serve the War: Hockey in Canada versus Military Service during World War Two', *CJHS* 24, 2 (Dec. 1993): 68–90.

McKee, William C. 'The Vancouver Park System, 1886–1929: A Product of Local Businessmen', *Urban History Review* 7, 3 (1978): 33–49.

McKelvey, J.A. 'A Story of Recent Football at Queen's', *Queen's Quarterly* 35, 3 (Feb. 1982): 288–96.

Metcalfe, Alan. 'The Form and Function of Physical Activity in New France, 1534–1759', *CJHSPE* 1, 1 (May 1970): 45–64.

———. 'Some Background Influences on Nineteenth Century Canadian Sport and Physical Education', *CJHSPE* 5, 1 (May 1974): 62–73.

———. 'Physical Education in Ontario during the Nineteenth Century', *CAHPER Journal* 37, 1 (Sept.–Oct. 1974): 29–33.

———. 'Sport and Athletics: A Case Study of Lacrosse in Canada', *JSH* 3, 1 (1976): 1–19.

———. 'The Evolution of Organized Physical Recreation in Montreal, 1840–1895', *Histoire Sociale/Social History* 9, 1 (May 1978): 144–66.

———. 'Working Class Physical Recreation in Montreal', *Working Papers in the Sociological Study of Sport and Income* 1, 2 (1978): 27–34.

———. 'The Urban Response to the Demand for Sporting Facilities: A Case Study of Ten Ontario Towns/Cities, 1919–1939', *Urban History Review* 12, 2 (Oct. 1983): 31–46.

———. 'The Anatomy of Power in Amateur Sport in Ontario, 1918–1936', *CJHS* 22, 2 (Dec. 1991): 47–66.

———. 'Power: A Case Study of the Ontario Hockey Association, 1890–1936', *JSH* 19, 1 (1992): 5–25.

———. 'The Meaning of Amateurism: A Case Study of Canadian Sport, 1884–1970', *CJHS* 26, 2 (Dec. 1995): 33–48.

Meyer-Dries, Laurie. 'Indians Bygone Past: The Banff Indian Days, 1902–1945', *Past Imperfect* 2 (1993): 7–28.

Mickelson, Glen. 'Indians and Rodeo', *Alberta History* 35 (Summer 1987): 13–19.

————. 'Games Indians Played', *Alberta History* 41, 3 (Summer 1993): 2–8.

————. 'Rumble on the Range: Chuckwagon Racing's 75th Anniversary', *Alberta History* 46, 2 (Spring 1998): 20–6.

————. 'The Sport of Kings in Victorian Canada', *The Beaver* 76, 4 (Aug.–Sept. 1996): 18–21.

Mitchinson, Wendy. 'The YWCA and Reform in the Nineteenth Century', *Social History* 12, 24 (Nov. 1979): 368–84.

Mizener, David. 'Competitive Plowing and Organized Sport in the Ontario Countryside, 1911–1940', *JSH* 33, 3 (Fall 2006): 299–321.

Moore, Bruce. 'For the Love of Sport', *The Beaver* 76, 4 (Aug.–Sept. 1996): 53–5.

Moore, Katharine. '"The Warmth of Comradeship": The First British Empire Games and Imperial Solidarity', *IJHS* 6, 2 (1989): 242–51.

————. 'A Divergence of Interests: Canada's Role in the Politics and Sport of the British Empire during the 1920s', *CJHS* 21, 1 (May 1990): 21–9.

Morgan, E.C. 'Pioneer Recreation and Social Life', *Saskatchewan History* 38, 2 (Spring 1965): 41–54.

Morrow, Don. 'The Strathcona Trust in Ontario, 1911–1939', *CJHSPE* 8, 1 (May 1977): 72–90.

————. 'Lionel Pretoria Conacher', *JSH* 6, 1 (1979): 5–37.

————. 'The Powerhouse of Canadian Sport: The Montreal Amateur Athletic Association, Inception to 1909', *JSH* 8, 3 (1981): 20–39.

————. 'Lou Marsh: The Pick and Shovel of Canadian Sporting Journalism', *CJHS* 14, 1 (May 1983): 21–33.

————. 'Canadian Sport History: A Critical Essay', *JSH* 10, 1 (Spring 1983): 67–79.

————. 'A Case Study in Amateur Conflict: The Athletic War in Canada, 1906–08', *British Journal of Sports History* 3, 2 (1986): 183–90.

————. 'Sweetheart Sport, Barbara Ann Scott and the Post-World War II Image of the Female Athlete in Canada', *CJHS* 18, 1 (May 1987): 36–54.

————. 'The Knights of the Snowshoe: A Study of the Evolution of Sport in Nineteenth Century Montreal', *JSH* 15, 1 (1988): 5–40.

————. 'The Institutionalization of Sport: A Case Study of Canadian Lacrosse, 1844–1914', *IJHS* 9, 2 (Aug. 1992): 236–51.

————. 'The Myth of the Hero in Canadian Sport History', *CJHS* 23, 2 (Dec. 1992): 72–83.

————. 'With Craft and Guile: Canada's Jimmy McLarnin and the Business of Welterweight Boxing during the Great Depression', *CJHS* 26, 1 (May 1995): 40–51.

————. 'Frozen Festivals: Ceremony and the Carnival in Montreal Winter Carnivals, 1883–1889', *SHR* 27, 2 (1996): 173–90.

———— and Terry Jackson. 'Boxing's Interregnum: How Good was Tommy Burns, World Heavyweight Boxing Champion, 1906–1908', *CJHS* 24, 2 (Dec. 1993): 30–46.

———— and Glynn Leyshon. 'George Goulding: A Case Study in Sporting Excellence', *CJHS* 18, 2 (Dec. 1987): 26–51.

————, Alexander J. Young, and Danny Rosenberg. 'A Quiet Contribution: Louis Rubinstein', *CJHS* 8, 1 (May 1982): 1–17.

————. 'A Riotous Reflection: The Heroic, Richard, and Canadian Sport History', *Journal of Canadian Sport Studies* 1, 1 (2004): 48–53.

————. 'Timelessness and Historicity of the Game in Ken Dryden's *The Game*', *SHR* 37, 1 (2006): 54–68.

Moss, Robert. 'Cricket in Nova Scotia during the Nineteenth Century', *CJHSPE* 9, 2 (Dec. 1978): 58–75.

Mott, Morris. 'One Town's Team: Souris and Its Lacrosse Club, 1887–1906', *Manitoba History* 1 (1980): 10–16.

——. 'The British Protestant Pioneers and the Establishment of Manly Sports in Manitoba, 1870–1886', *JSH* 7, 3 (1980): 25–36.

——. 'Canadian Sports History: Some Comments to Urban Historians', *Urban History Review* 12, 2 (Oct. 1983): 25–9.

——. 'One Solution to the Urban Crisis: Manly Sports and Winnipeggers, 1900–1914', *Urban History Review* 12, 2 (Oct. 1983): 57–70.

——. 'The First Pro Sports League on the Prairies: The Manitoba Baseball League of 1886', *CJHS* 15, 2 (Dec. 1984): 62–9.

——. 'Ball Games in the Canadian West: An Historical Outline', *Journal of the West* 23, 4 (1984): 19–25.

——. 'Flawed Games, Splendid Ceremonies: The Hockey of the Winnipeg Vics, 1890–1903', *Prairie Forum* 10, 1 (Spring 1985): 169–87.

——. 'Here's to the Roarin' Game: An Affectionate Look at Early Canada's Favourite Sport', *Material History Review* 35 (Spring 1992): 53–6.

—— and John Allardyce. 'Curling Capital: How Winnipeg Became the Roaring Game's Leading City, 1876–1903', *CJHS* 19, 1 (May 1988): 1–14.

Murray, Heather. 'Making the Modern: Twenty-five Years of the Margaret Eaton School of Literature and Expression', *Essays in Theatre* 10, 1 (1991): 39–57.

Mutimer, Brian. 'Great Men, Vagaries and Canadian Football', *CJHS* 21, 1 (May 1990): 77–83.

Newman, P. 'Voyageurs: Those Magnificent River Rats', *Canadian Geographic* 197, 6 (1987): 40–9.

O'Connor, Patrick J., Richard D. Lewis, and Andrea Boyd. 'Health Concerns of Artistic Women Gymnasts', *Sports Medicine* 21, 5 (May 1996): 321.

Olafson, Gordon A. 'The History of Bill C-131', *CJHSPE* 1, 1 (May 1970): 65–86.

Paraschak, Victoria. 'Native Sport History: Pitfalls and Promises', *CJHS* 20, 1 (May 1989): 57–68.

——. 'Organized Sport for Native Females on the Six Nations Reserve, Ontario, from 1968 to 1980: A Comparison of Dominant and Emergent Sport Systems', *CJHS* 21, 2 (Dec. 1990): 70–80.

——. 'The Native Sport and Recreation Program, 1972–1981: Patterns of Resistance, Patterns of Reproduction', *CJHS* 26, 2 (Dec. 1995): 1–18.

——. 'Invisible But Not Absent: Aboriginal Women in Sport and Recreation', *Canadian Women's Studies* 15 (1995): 71–2.

——. 'Racialized Spaces: Cultural Regulation, Aboriginal Agency and Powwows', *Avante* 2 (1996): 7–18.

——. 'Variations in Race Relations: Native Peoples in Sport in Canada', *Sociology of Sport Journal* 14, 1 (1997): 1–27.

——. 'Reasonable Amusements: Connecting the Strands of Physical Culture in Native Lives', *SHR* 29, 1 (May 1998): 121–31.

Peacock, Shane. 'The Toronto Huskies: Pro Basketball's False Start', *The Beaver* 76, 5 (Oct.–Nov. 1996): 33–8.

Pearce, W. 'Establishment of National Parks in the Rockies', *Alberta Historical Review* 10 (1962): 8–17.

Popovic, M., and D. Morrow. 'Stomping the Shadow: The Elevation of Snowboarding to the Olympic Pedestal from a Jungian Perspective', *SHR* 39, 2 (2008): 170–91.

Pound, Richard W., and G.A. Paton. '"Whistler's Father": The Life and Times of Andrew Sidney Dawes in Canadian Post-World War II Olympic Affairs', *OLYMPIKA* 17 (2008): 41–100.

Rae, Lorne W. 'It Was Real Baseball', *Saskatchewan History* 43, 1 (1991): 50–2.

Ranson, Diane. 'The Saskatoon Lily: A Biography of Ethel Catherwood', *Saskatchewan History* 41, 3 (Autumn 1989): 81–98.

Redmond, Gerald. 'Apart from the Trust Fund: Some Other Contributions of Lord Strathcona to Canadian Recreation and Sport', *CJHSPE* 4, 2 (1973): 59–69.

————. 'The Olympic City of 1844 and 1976: Reflections upon Montreal in the History of Canadian Sport', *CAHPER Journal* (Mar.–Apr. 1976): 43–50.

————. 'The First Tom Brown's Schooldays: Origins and Evolution of Muscular Christianity in Children's Literature, 1762–1857', *Quest* (1978): 4–18.

————. 'Some Aspects of Organized Sport and Leisure in Nineteenth Century Canada', *Society and Leisure* 2, 1 (1979): 73–100.

————. 'Imperial Viceregal Patronage: The Governors-General of Canada and Sport in the Dominion, 1867–1909', *IJHS* 6, 2 (Sept. 1989): 193–217.

Renson, Roland, Danielle De Kegel, and Herman Smulders. 'The Folk Roots of Games: Games and Ethnic Identity among Flemish Canadian Immigrants', *CJHS* 14, 2 (Dec. 1983): 69–79.

Reynolds, Mark. 'The Great Canadian Foot Race', *The Beaver* (Aug.–Sept. 2000): 30–1.

Roberts, Terry. 'The Influence of the British Upper Class on the Development of the Value Claim for Sport in the Public Education System of Upper Canada from 1830 to 1875', *CJHSPE* 4, 1 (May 1973): 27–47.

Robidoux, Michael. 'Historical Interpretations of First Nations Masculinity and its influence on Canada's Sport Heritage', *IJHS* 23, 2 (Mar. 2006): 267–84.

Robinson, Zac. 'The Golden Years of Canadian Mountaineering: Asserted Ethics, Form, and Style, 1886–1925', *SHR* 35, 1 (May 2004): 1–19.

————, and P. Reichwein. 'Canada's Everest? Rethinking the First Ascent of Mount Logan and the Politics of Nationhood, 1925', *SHR* 35, 2 (Nov. 2004): 95–121.

Ross, Andrew J. 'The Paradox of Conn Smythe: Hockey, Memory, and the Second World War', *SHR* 37, 1 (May 2006): 19–35.

Rush, Anita. 'The Bicycle Boom of the Gay Nineties: A Reassessment', *Material History Bulletin* (Fall 1983): 1–12.

Ryan, D., and K. Wamsley. 'The Fighting Irish of Toronto: Sport and Irish Catholic Identity at St. Michael's College, 1906–1916', *Sport in Society* 10, 3 (2007): 495–513.

————, and K. Wamsley. 'A Grand Game of Hurling and Football: Sport and Irish Nationalism in Old Toronto', *Canadian Journal of Irish Studies* 30, 1 (2004): 21–31.

Salter, Michael A. 'The Effect of Acculturation on the Game of Lacrosse and on its Role as an Agent of Indian Survival', *CJHSPE* 3, 1 (May 1972): 28–43.

————. 'L'Ordre de Bon Temps: A Functional Analysis', *JSH* 3, 2 (1976): 111–19.

————. 'Play in Ritual: An Ethnohistorical Overview of Native North America', *Stadion* 3, 2 (1977): 230–43.

————. 'Games, Goods and Gods: An Analysis of Iroquoian Gambling', *Canadian Journal of Applied Sports Science* 4, 2 (June 1979): 160–4.

————. 'Baggataway to Lacrosse: A Case Study in Acculturation', *CJHS* 26, 2 (Dec. 1995): 49–64.

Sangster, Joan. 'The Softball Solution: Female Workers, Male Managers, and the Operation of Paternalism at Westclox, 1923–1960', *Labour/Le Travail* 32 (1993): 139–66.

Savoie, Mark. 'Broken Time and Broken Hearts: The Maritimes and the Selection of Canada's 1936 Olympic Hockey Team', *SHR* 31, 2 (Nov. 2000): 120–38.

Sawula, Lorne W. 'Why 1970, Why Not Before?', *CJHSPE* 4, 2 (Dec. 1973): 43–58.

———. 'Notes on the Strathcona Trust', *CJHSPE* 5, 1 (May 1974): 56–61.

Schrodt, Barbara. 'Canadian Women at the Olympics: 1924 to 1972', *CAHPER Journal* 44, 4 (Mar.–Apr. 1976): 34–42.

———. 'Sabbatarianism and Sport in Canadian Society', *JSH* 4, 1 (1977): 22–33.

———. 'Canadian Women at the Commonwealth Games: 1930–1974', *CAHPER Journal* 44, 4 (1978): 30–7.

———. 'Changes in the Governance of Amateur Sport in Canada', *CJHS* 14, 1 (May 1983): 1–20.

———. 'Federal Programmes of Physical Recreation and Fitness: The Contributions of Ian Eisenhardt and BC's Pro-Rec', *CJHS* 15, 2 (Dec. 1984): 45–61.

———. 'Sport at the Fair: The Promotion of Urban Sport by the Vancouver Exhibition, 1910–1985', *Journal of the West* 26, 1 (Jan. 1987): 71–9.

———. 'Taking the Tram: Travelling to Sport and Recreation Activities on Greater Vancouver's Interurban Railway—1890s to 1920s', *CJHS* 19, 1 (May 1988): 52–62.

———. 'Problems of Periodization in Canadian Sport History', *CJHS* 21, 1 (May 1990): 65–76.

———. 'Control of Sports Facilities in Early Vancouver: The Brockton Point Athletic Association at Stanley Park, 1880–1913', *CJHS* 23, 2 (Dec. 1992): 26–53.

———. 'Vancouver's Dynastic Domination of Canadian Senior Women's Basketball: 1942 to 1967', *CJHS* 26, 2 (Dec. 1995): 19–32.

Schweinbenz, Amanda N. 'Racing for Equality in Women's Competitive International Rowing: An Examination of the Change of Women's Racing Distance from 1000 metres to 2000 metres', *SHR* 39 (2008): 30–44.

———. 'Paddling Against the Current: An Analysis of Oarswomen's Entrance into the 1954 European Rowing Champions', *JSH* 33, 1 (Fall 2006): 401–20.

Smith, Geoffrey S. 'The Roar of Greasepaint, The Smell of the Crown', *Queen's Quarterly* 103, 3 (Fall 1996): 502–19.

Smith, Michael J. 'Graceful Athleticism or Robust Womanhood: The Sporting Culture of Women in Victorian Nova Scotia, 1870–1914', *Journal of Canadian Studies* 23, 1 and 2 (Spring–Summer 1988): 120–37.

———. 'Sport and Society: Towards a Synthetic History?', *Acadiensis* 18, 2 (Spring 1989): 150–8.

———. 'There's No Penalty When You Hit the Fence: Sporting Activities in Central and Eastern Nova Scotia, 1880s to 1920s', *SHR* 27, 2 (1996): 191–203.

Sokolyk, K.W. 'The Role of Ukrainian Sports, Teams, Clubs and Leagues, 1924–52', *Journal of Ukrainian Studies* 16, 1/2 (1991): 133.

Summers, John. 'Coldest Sport in the World: Ice-Boating on Toronto Harbour, 1824–1941', *Material History Review* 35 (1992): 35–46.

———. 'Probably the Most Beautiful Rowboat Afloat: The Form and Meaning of the St. Lawrence Skiff', *Material History Review* 48 (Fall 1998): 13–25.

Swain, S. 'History of Ontario Women's Intercollegiate Athletic Association OWIAA', *CAHPER Journal* 49, 2 (1982): 26–8.

Swain, Stephen. 'I Stole This from a Tragically Hip Song: Stories of Bill Barilko', *SHR* 39, 2 (Nov. 2008): 152–69.

Teetzel, Sarah. 'Sports, Medicine, and the Emergence of Sports Medicine in the Olympic Games: The Canadian Example', *JSH* 34, 1 (2007): 75–86.

Tolton, Gord. 'Dreams of a Western Showman: Guy Weadick and the First Calgary Stampede', *Canadian West Magazine* 9, 1 (Jan.–Mar. 1993): 36–45.

Trovato, Frank. 'The Stanley Cup of Hockey and Suicides in Quebec, 1951–1992', *Social Forces* 77, 1 (Sept. 1998): 105–26.

Varpalotai, Aniko. 'A "Safe Place" for Leisure and Learning—The Girl Guides of Canada', *Loisir et société/Society and Leisure* 15, 1 (Spring 1992): 115–33.

Vertinsky, Patricia. 'The Effect of Changing Attitudes toward Sexual Morality upon the Promotion of Physical Education for Women in 19th Century America', *CJHSPE* 7, 2 (1976): 26–38.

———. 'God, Science and the Marketplace: The Bases for Exercise Prescriptions for Females in Nineteenth Century North America', *CJHS* 17, 1 (May 1986): 38–45.

———. 'Feminist Charlotte Perkins Gilman's Pursuit of Health and Fitness as a Strategy for Emancipation', *JSH* 16, 1 (Spring 1989): 5–26.

———. 'Sport and Exercise for Old Women: Images of the Elderly in the Medical and Popular Literature at the Turn of the Century', *IJHS* 9, 1 (Apr. 1992): 83–104.

Vigneault, Michel. 'La Diffusion du Hockey à Montréal, 1895–1910', *CJHS* 17, 1 (May 1986): 60–74.

———. 'Tentative de Responses sur les Origines du Hockey Moderne', *CJHS* 20, 2 (Dec. 1989): 15–26.

Wamsley, Kevin B. 'Strangers in the 18th Hole: The Evolution of Golf in Edmonton and the Establishment of Canada's First Municipal Golf Course, 1896–1914', *CJHS* 20, 2 (Dec. 1989): 1–14.

———. 'Good Clean Sport and a Deer Apiece: Game Legislation and State Formation in Nineteenth Century Canada', *CJHS* 25, 2 (Dec. 1994): 1–20.

———. 'Cultural Signification and National Ideologies: Rifle Shooting in Late Nineteenth-Century Canada', *Social History* 20, 1 (1995): 63–72.

———. 'Nineteenth Century Sport Tours, State Formation, and Canadian Foreign Policy', *Sporting Traditions* 13, 2 (1997): 73–89.

———. 'Power and Privilege in Historiography: Constructing Percy Page', *SHR* 28, 2 (Nov. 1997): 146–55.

———. 'State Formation and Institutionalized Racism: Gambling Laws in Nineteenth and Early Twentieth Century Canada', *SHR* 29, 1 (May 1998): 77–85.

———. 'The Global Sport Monopoly: A Synopsis of 20th Century Olympic Politics', *International Journal* 57, 3 (Summer 2002): 395–410.

——— and Michael K. Heine. 'Sabbath Legislation and State Formation in 19th Century Canada', *Avante* 1, 2 (1995): 44–57.

——— and ———. 'Tradition Modernity, and the Construction of Civic Identity: The Calgary Olympics', *OLYMPIKA: The International Journal of Olympic Studies* 5 (1996): 81–90.

——— and Robert S. Kossuth. 'Fighting it Out in Nineteenth Century Upper Canada/Canada West: Masculinities and Physical Challenges in the Tavern', *JSH* 27, 3 (Fall 2000): 405–30.

——— and David Whitson. 'Celebrating Violent Masculinities: The Boxing Death of Luther McCarty', *JSH* 25, 3 (Fall 1998): 419–31.

——— and Kevin Young. 'State Complicity in Sports Assault and the Gender Order in Twentieth Century Canada: Preliminary Observations', *Avante* 2, 2 (1996): 51–69.

Watson, Ronald C., and Gregory D. Rickwood. 'Stewards of Ice Hockey: A Historical Review of Safety Rules in Canadian Amateur Ice Hockey', *SHR* 30, 1 (1999): 27–38.

Watts, Heather M. 'Nat Butler and Burns Pierce: Nova Scotian Heroes of the Cycle Tracks', *Nova Scotia Historical Review* 2, 2 (1982): 4–8.

Weadick, Guy. 'Origins of the Calgary Stampede', *Alberta Historical Review* 14, 4 (Autumn 1966): 20–4.

Wenn, Stephen R. 'A Tale of Two Diplomats: George S. Messersmith and Charles H. Sherrill on Proposed American Participation in the Berlin Olympics', *JSH* 16, 1 (Spring 1989): 27–43.

———. 'A Call to Arms: A Sidney Dawes Campaign for C.C.A. Independence', *CJHS* 21, 3 (Dec. 1990): 33–46.

———. 'Give Me the Keys Please: Avery Brundage, Canadian Journalists, and the Barbara Scott Phaeton Affair', *JSH* 18, 2 (1991): 241–54.

———. 'A Suitable Policy of Neutrality? FDR and the Question of American Participation in the 1936 Olympics', *IJHS* 8, 3 (Dec. 1991): 319–35.

———. 'Television Rights Negotiations and the 1976 Montreal Olympics', *SHR* 27, 2 (1996): 111–38.

West, J. Thomas. 'Physical Fitness, Sport and the Federal Government, 1909 to 1954', *CJHSPE* 4, 2 (Dec. 1973): 26–42.

Whalen, James M. 'Kings of the Ice: Hockey's First Golden Age', *The Beaver* 74, 1 (Feb.– Mar. 1994): 28–36.

White, Philip, Peter Donnelly, and John Nauright. 'Citizens, Cities and Sports Teams', *Policy Options/Options politiques* 18, 3 (May 1997): 9–12.

Whitson, D. 'Sport and Hegemony: On the Construction of the Dominant Culture', *Sociology of Sport Journal* 1 (1984): 64–75.

——— and D. Macintosh. 'Becoming a World-Class City: Hallmark Events and Sport Franchises in the Growth Strategies of Western Canadian Cities', *Sociology of Sport Journal* 10 (1993): 221–40.

Williams, Trevor. 'Cheap Rates, Special Trains and Canadian Sport in the 1850s', *CJHSPE* 12, 2 (Dec. 1981): 84–93.

Wilson, J.J. 'Skating to Armageddon: Canada, Hockey and the First World War', *IJHS* 22, 3 (May 2005): 315-343.

Wilson, L.J. Roy. 'Medicine Hat—The Sporting Town, 1883–1905', *CJHS* 16, 2 (Dec. 1985): 15–32.

Wong, John. 'Sport Networks on Ice: The Canadian Experience at the 1936 Olympic Hockey Tournament', *SHR* 34, 2 (Nov. 2003): 190–212.

Wong, John. 'From Rat Portage to Kenora: The Death of a (Big-Time) Hockey Dream', *JSH* 33, 2 (Summer 2006): 175–91.

Xing, Xiaoyan, A. Church, N. O'Reilly, A. Pegoraro, J. Nadeau, A. Schweinbenz, L. Heslop, and S. Benoit. 'Essays in Olympic Games Host and Bid City Marketing: Conflicting Views and Suggestions for Future Study', *International Journal of Sports Marketing & Sponsorship* (2008): 169–83.

Young, A.J. 'Sandy'. 'A Nova Scotian Perspective of Canadian Sport History after the Metcalfe Attack', *SHR* 29, 1 (May 1998): 86–95.

Young, Alexander, Jr. 'The Boston Tarbaby', *Nova Scotia Historical Quarterly* 4, 3 (1974): 277–98.

———. 'Sport for Women in the 1920s and 1930s', *Nova Scotia Sports Heritage Centre* (Sept. 1982): 14–15.

Young, Kevin. 'Violence in the Workplace of Professional Sport from Victimological and Cultural Studies Perspectives', *IRSS* 26, 3 (1991).

———, P. White, and W. McTeer. 'Body Talk: Male Athletes Reflect on Sport Injury and Pain', *Sociology of Sport Journal* 11 (1994): 175–94.

———, and P. White. 'Sport, Physical Danger, and Injury: The Experience of Elite Women Athletes', *Journal of Sport and Social Issues* 19, (1995): 45–61.

Zakus, Dwight H. 'A Genesis of the Canadian Sport System in Pierre Trudeau's Political

Philosophy and Agenda', *SHR* 27, 1 (1996): 30–48.

Zweig, Eric. 'Playing Football the Canadian Way', *The Beaver* 75, 5 (Oct.–Nov. 1995): 24–9.

———. 'Meet Me in St. Louis: Our First "Official" Olympiad', *The Beaver* 76, 3 (June–July 1996): 25–8.

Books and Chapters in Books

Adams, C. 'Body Check: Women's Olympic Ice Hockey and the Process of Incorporation', in *Cultural Relations Old and New: The Transitory Olympic Ethos*. London, Ontario: International Centre for Olympic Studies, The University of Western Ontario, 2004, 141–50.

———, and Wamsley, K.B. 'Moments of Silence in Shallow Halls of Greatness: The Hockey Hall of Fame and the Politics of Representation', in *Women's Hockey: On and Off the Ice*. Halifax, Nova Scotia: Centre for the Study of Sport and Community Health, 2005.

Armstrong, Chris, and H. V. Nelles. *The Revenge of the Methodist Bicycle Company*. Toronto: P. Martin, 1977.

Auf der Maur, Nick. *The Billion Dollar Game: Jean Drapeau and the 1976 Olympics*. Toronto: James Lorimer, 1976.

Ballem, Charles H. *Abegweit Dynasty: The Story of the Abegweit Amateur Athletic Association, 1899–1954*. Charlottetown: Prince Edward Island Museum and Heritage Foundation, 1986.

Barman, Jean. 'Sports and the Development of Character', in Mott (1989: 234–46).

Barman, Jean. *Growing Up British in British Columbia: Boys in Private Schools*. Vancouver: University of British Columbia Press, 1984.

Barney, Robert K., Stephen R. Wenn, and Scott G. Martyn. *Selling the Five Rings: The International Olympic Committee and the Rise of Olympic Commercialism*. Salt Lake City: University of Utah Press, 2002.

Beamish, Rob, and Ian Ritchie. *Fastest, Highest, Strongest: A Critique of High-performance Sport*. New York and London: Routledge, 2006.

Bella, L. *Parks for Profit*. Montreal: Harvest House, 1987.

Betke, Carl. 'The Social Significance of Sport in the City: Edmonton in the 1920s', in A.R. McCormack and Ian MacPherson, eds, *Cities in the West: Papers of the Western Canadian Urban History Conference*. Winnipeg: University of Winnipeg, 1974, 211–35.

Benidickson, Jamie. *Idleness, Water, and a Canoe: Reflections on Paddling for Pleasure*. Toronto: University of Toronto Press, 1997.

Bouchier, Nancy B. *For the Love of the Game: Amateur Sport in Small-Town Ontario, 1838–1895*. Montreal and Kingston: McGill-Queens University Press, 2003.

——— and Ken Cruikshank. *The People and the Bay: A Popular History of Hamilton Harbour*. Hamilton: OWAHC, 1997.

Bratton, Robert D. *Canadian Volleyball: A History to 1967*. Ottawa: Canadian Volleyball Association, 1972.

Bray, Cathy. 'Gender and the Political Economy of Canadian Sport', in Nancy Theberge and Peter Donnelly, eds, *Sport and the Sociological Imagination*. Fort Worth: Texas Christian University Press, 1984, 104–24.

Bull, W. Perkins. *From Rattlesnake Hunt to Hockey: The History of Sports in Canada and the Sportsmen of Peel 1798–1934*. Toronto: George J. McLeod, 1934.

Cantelon, Hart. 'Amateurism, High-Performance Sport, and the Olympics', in Kevin Young and Kevin B. Wamsley, eds, *Global Olympics: Historical and Sociological Studies of the Modern Olympic Games*. Amsterdam: Elsevier Press.

———, and Robert Hollands, eds. *Leisure, Sport and Working Class Cultures:*

Theory and History. Toronto: Garamond Press, 1988.

Cauz, Louis. *Baseball's Back in Town: A History of Baseball in Toronto*. Toronto: Controlled Media Corporation, 1977.

Chalus, Elaine. 'The Edmonton Commercial Graduates: Women's History: An Integrationist Approach', in Corbet and Rasporich (1990: 69–86).

Christie, James R. *Ben Johnson: The Fastest Man on Earth*. Toronto: McClelland-Bantam Inc., 1988.

Cochrane, Jean, Abby Hoffman, and Pat Kincaid. *Women in Canadian Life: Sports*. Toronto: Fitzhenry & Whiteside, 1977.

Conrad, Peter C. *In the Winning Lane: A History of Competitive Swimming in Saskatchewan*. Regina: Swim Saskatchewan, 1990.

Conway, Russ. *Game Misconduct: Alan Eagleson and the Corruption of Hockey*. Toronto: Macfarlane Walter & Ross, 1995.

Corbet, E.A., and A.W. Rasporich, eds. *Winter Sports in the West*. Calgary: Historical Society of Alberta, 1990.

Cosentino, Frank. *Canadian Football—the Grey Cup Years*. Toronto: Musson, 1969.

———. *Ned Hanlan*. Toronto: Fitzhenry & Whiteside, 1978.

———. *Not Bad Eh? Great Moments in Canadian Sports History*. Burnstown, Ont.: General Store Publishing, 1990.

———. *The Renfrew Millionaires: Valley Boys of Winter, 1910*. Burnstown, Ont.: General Store Publishing, 1990.

———. *A Passing Game: A History of the CFL*. Winnipeg: Bain & Cox, 1995.

———. *Almonte's Brothers of the Wind: R. Tait McKenzie and James Naismith*. Burnstown, Ont.: General Store Publishing, 1996.

———. *Afros, Aboriginals and Amateur Sport in Pre-World War One Canada*. Ottawa: Canadian Historical Association, Canada's Ethnic Group Series, 1998.

——— and Max Howell. *History of Physical Education in Canada*. Toronto: General Publishing, 1971.

——— and Glynn Leyshon. *Olympic Gold: Canadian Winners of the Summer Games*. Toronto: Holt, Rinehart & Winston, 1975.

——— and Don Morrow. *Lionel Conacher*. Toronto: Fitzhenry & Whiteside, 1981.

Cruise David, and Griffiths, Alison. *Net Worth: Exploding the Myths of Pro Hockey*. Toronto: Penguin Books, 1992.

Culin, Stewart. 'Games of the North American Indians', in *Twenty-Fourth Annual Report of the Bureau of American Ethnology to the Smithsonian Institution, 1902–03*. Washington: US Government, 1907.

Daub, Merv. *Gael Force: A Century of Football at Queen's University*. Montreal and Kingston: McGill-Queen's University Press, 1996.

Davis, Caroline. 'Eating Disorders, Physical Activity, and Sport: Biological, Psychological, and Sociological Factors', in Philip White and Kevin Young, *Sport and Gender in Canada*. Don Mills, Ont.: Oxford University Press, 1999, 85–106.

Dheensaw, Cleve. *Island of Champions: A Sporting History of Vancouver Island*. Victoria: Orca Book Publishers, 1988.

———. *The Commonwealth Games: The First 60 Years, 1930–1990*. Victoria: Orca Book Publishers, 1994.

Dodds, E. *Canadian Turf Recollections and Other Sketches*. Toronto, 1909.

Dryden, Ken. *The Game: A Thoughtful and Provocative Look at a Life in Hockey*. Toronto: Macmillan Canada, 1983.

Dubin, Charles L. *Commission of Inquiry into the Use of Drugs and Banned Practices Intended to Increase Athletic Performance*. Ottawa: Canadian Government Publication Centre, Supply and Services, 1990.

Ferguson, Bob. *Who's Who in Canadian Sport*.

Scarborough, Ont.: Prentice-Hall of Canada, 1977.

Fisher, Donald M. *Lacrosse: A History of the Game.* Baltimore: Johns Hopkins University Press, 2002.

Flood, Brian. *Saint John: A Sporting Tradition, 1785–1985.* Saint John: Neptune Publishing Co., 1985.

Forsyth, J. 'Aboriginal Leisure in Canada', in Ron McCarville and Kelly MacKay, eds, *Leisure for Canadians.* State College, Penn.: Venture Publishing Inc., 2007.

———, and K. Wamsley. 'Symbols without Substance: Aboriginal Peoples and the Illusions of Olympic Ceremonies', in Kevin Young and Kevin Wamsley, eds, *Global Olympics: Historical and Sociological Studies of the Modern Games.* Oxford, UK: Elsevier Press, 2005.

Forsyth, Janice. 'Teepees and Tomahawks: Aboriginal Cultural Representation at the 1976 Olympic Games', in Kevin B. Wamsley, Robert K. Barney, and Scott G. Martyn, eds, *The Global Nexus Engaged: Past, Present, Future Interdisciplinary Olympic Studies.* London, Ont.: ICOS, 2002, 71–6.

Francis, Charlie. *Speed Trap: Inside the Biggest Scandal in Olympic History.* Toronto: Lester and Orpen Denny's, 1990.

Franks, C.E.S. *The Canoe and White Water.* Toronto: University of Toronto Press, 1977.

Giles, A., and J. Forsyth. 'The Empire's Eden: British Hunters, Travel Writing, and Imperialism in Nineteenth-Century Canada', in Jean Manroe and Dale Miner, eds, *The Culture of Hunting in Canada.* Vancouver: University of British Columbia Press, 2006.

Gillespie, Greg. *Hunting for Empire: Narratives of Sport in Rupert's Land, 1840–1870.* Vancouver: University of British Columbia Press, 2007.

Gregson, Ian. *Irresistible Force: Disability Sport in Canada.* Victoria: Polestar Books, 1999.

Gruneau, Richard. *Class, Sports and Social Development.* Amherst: University of Massachusetts Press, 1983.

Gruneau, Richard. 'Modernization or Hegemony: Two Views on Sport and Social Development', in Jean Harvey and Hart Cantelon, eds, *Not Just a Game.* Ottawa: University of Ottawa Press, 1988, 9–32.

——— and David Whitson. *Hockey Night in Canada: Sport, Identities, and Cultural Politics.* Toronto: Garamond Press, 1993.

Guay, Donald. *Le Sport et La Société Canadienne au XIXème Siècle.* Quebec City: Université Laval, 1977.

———. *L'Histoire de l'Éducation Physique au Québec; Conceptions et Événements (1830–1980).* Chicoutimi: Gaetan Morin & Associés, 1981.

———. *Histoires Vraies de la Chasse au Québec.* Montreal: VLB, 1983.

———. *Histoires des Courses de Chevaux au Québec.* Montreal: VLB, 1985.

———. *Introduction à l'Histoire des Sports au Québec.* Montreal: VLB, 1987.

———. *La conquête du sport: Le sport et la société québécoise au XIXème siècle.* Outrement: Lanctot, 1997.

Gurney, Helen. *Girls' Sports: A Century of Progress.* Don Mills, Ont.: OFSAA, 1979.

———. *A Century to Remember, 1892–1993: Women's Sport at the University of Toronto.* Toronto: University of Toronto Women's T-Holders' Association, 1993.

Hall, Ann, and Dorothy Richardson. *Fair Ball: Towards Sex Equality in Canadian Sport.* Ottawa: Canadian Advisory Council on the Status of Women, 1982.

Hall, M. Ann. *The Girl and the Game. A History of Women's Sport in Canada.* Peterborough, Ont.: Broadview Press, 2002.

———. 'Women and Sport: From Liberal Activism to Radical Cultural Struggle', in S. Burt and Lorraine Code, eds, *Changing*

Methods: Feminists Transforming Practice. Peterborough, Ont.: Broadview Press, 1995, 265–300.

Heine, Michael. *Arctic Sports: A Training and Resource Manual.* Calgary: Triad Press, 1998.

———. *Dene Games: A Culture and Resource Manual.* Calgary: Triad Press, 1999.

———, with Ruth Carroll and Harvey Scott. *Traditional Dene Games: A Resource book, Games the Dene Elders Remember from the Old Days.* Yellowknife: Northwest Territories Municipal and Community Affairs, 1995.

Hewitt, W.A. *Down the Stretch: Recollections of a Pioneer Sportsman and Journalist.* Toronto: Ryerson Press, 1958.

Hodgins, Bruce, and Margaret Hobbs. *Nastawgan: The Canadian North by Canoe and Snowshoe.* Toronto: Betelgeuse Books, 1985.

Howell, Colin. *Northern Sandlots—A Social History of Maritime Baseball.* Toronto: University of Toronto Press, 1995.

———. *Blood, Sweat and Cheers: Sport and the Making of Modern Canada.* Toronto: University of Toronto Press, 2001.

Howell, M.L., and Nancy Howell. *Sports and Games in Canadian Life: 1700 to the Present.* Toronto: Macmillan, 1969.

Howell, M.L., and R.A. Howell, eds. *History of Sport in Canada.* Champaign, Ill.: Stipes Publishing Company, 1981.

Howell, Reet, ed. *Her Story in Sport: A Historical Anthology of Women in Sports.* West Point NY: Leisure Press, 1982.

Hubbard, R.H. 'Viceregal Influences on Canadian Society', in W.L. Morton, ed., *The Shield of Achilles.* Toronto: McClelland & Stewart, 1968, 256–74.

Humber, William. *Cheering on the Home Team.* Erin Mills, Ont.: Boston Mills Press, 1983.

———. *Freewheeling: The Story of Bicycling in Canada.* Erin Mills, Ont.: Boston Mills Press, 1986.

———. *Lets Play Ball: Inside the Perfect Game.* Toronto: Lester & Orpen Dennys/Royal Ontario Museum, 1989.

———. *Diamonds of the North: A Concise History of Baseball in Canada.* Toronto: Oxford University Press, 1995.

——— and John St. James, eds. *All I Thought About Was Baseball: Writings on a Canadian Pastime.* Toronto: University of Toronto Press, 1996.

Hunter, Robert S. *Rowing in Canada.* Hamilton, Ont.: Davis-Lisson, 1933.

Innis, Mary Quayle. *Unfold the Years: A History of the Young Women's Christian Association in Canada.* Toronto: McClelland & Stewart, 1949.

Janson, Gilles. *Enparons-nous du sport: Les Canadiens française et le sport au XIXème siècle.* Montreal: Guerin, 1995.

Jasen, Patricia. *Wild Things: Nature, Culture, and Tourism in Ontario, 1790–1914.* Toronto: University of Toronto Press, 1995.

Jobling, Ian. 'Urbanization and Sport in Canada, 1867–1900', in Richard Gruneau and John Albinson, eds, *Canadian Sport: Sociological Perspectives.* Don Mills, Ont.: Addison-Wesley (Canada), 1976, 64–76.

Kearney, Mark. *Champions: A British Columbia Sports Album.* Vancouver: Douglas & McIntyre, 1985.

Kendrick, Martyn. *Advantage Canada: A Tennis Centenary.* Toronto: McGraw-Hill Ryerson, 1990.

Kerr, Rev. J. *Curling in Canada and the United States: A Record of the Tour of the Scottish Team, 1902–1903, and of the Game in the Dominion and the Republic.* Toronto: Toronto News Co., 1904.

Kidd, Bruce. *Tom Longboat.* Toronto: Fitzhenry & Whiteside, 1981.

———. *The Struggle for Canadian Sport.* Toronto: University of Toronto Press, 1996.

———. *Political Economy of Sport*. Ottawa: CAHPER, 1979.

———. 'The Men's Cultural Centre: Sports and the Dynamic of Women's Oppression/ Men's Repression', in Michael A. Messner and Donald F. Sabo, eds, *Sport, Men and the Gender Order: Critical Feminist Perspectives*. Champaign Ill.: HK Press, 1990.

——— and John Macfarlane. *The Death of Hockey*. Toronto: New Press, 1972.

Killan, Gerald. *Protected Places: A History of Ontario's Provincial Parks System*. Toronto: Dundurn Press, 1993.

Lenskyj, Helen. *Out of Bounds: Women, Sport and Sexuality*. Toronto: Women's Press, 1986.

———. *Women, Sport and Physical Activity: Selected Research Themes*. Ottawa: Ministry of Supply and Services, 1994.

Lavoie, Marc. 'The Economics of Sport and the NHL Lockout', in Jane Crossman, eds, *Canadian Sport Sociology*, 2nd ed. Toronto: Nelson, 2008.

Lee, John B. *The Hockey Player Sonnets*. Waterloo: Penumbra Press, 1991.

Lenskyj, Helen J. *Out of Bounds: Women, Sport, and Sexuality*. California: Women's Press, 1987.

———. 'Women's Issues and Gender Relations', in Jane Crossman, eds, *Canadian Sport Sociology*, 2nd ed. Toronto: Nelson, 2008, 99–117.

———. 'Canadian Women and Physical Activity, 1890–1930: Media Views', in J.A. Mangan and R.J. Park, eds, *From Fair Sex to Feminism: Sport and the Socialization of Women in the Industrial and Post-Industrial Eras*. London: Frank Cass, 1987, 208–34.

Leslie, Susan, ed. *In the Western Mountains: Early Mountaineering in British Columbia*. Victoria: Archives of British Columbia Oral History Program, 1980.

Leyshon, Glynn. *Of Mats and Men: The Story of Canadian Amateur and Olympic Wrestling from 1600 to 1984*. London, Ont.: Sports Dynamics, 1984.

Leveridge, Bill. *Fair Sport: A History of Sports at the Canadian National Exhibition 1879– 1977 Inclusive*. Toronto: CNE, 1978.

Levitt, Cyril B., and William Shaffir *The Riot at Christie Pitts*. Toronto: Lester and Orpen Dennys, 1987.

Lindsay, P. 'George Beers and the National Game Concept: A Behavioural Approach', *Proceedings of the Second Canadian Symposium on the History of Sport and Physical Education* (1972): 27–44.

———. 'Woman's Place in Nineteenth Century Canadian Sport', in Howell (1982).

——— and R. Hess. 'The Sporting Elites in Late Nineteenth Century Edmonton: The Case of Cycling', *North American Society for Sport History Proceedings* (1990): 42–3.

Lothian, W.F. *A History of Canada's National Parks*. Ottawa: Parks Canada, 1976.

McFarlane, Brian. *One Hundred Years of Hockey*. Toronto: Deneau, 1989.

———. *Proud Past, Bright Future: One Hundred Years of Canadian Women's Hockey*. Toronto: Stoddart, 1994.

McFarland, Elsie Marie. *The Development of Public Recreation in Canada*. Vanier, Que.: Canadian Parks-Recreation Association, 1970.

Macintosh, Donald, Tom Bedecki, and C.E.S. Franks. *Sport and Politics in Canada: Federal Government Involvement since 1961*. Montreal and Kingston: McGill-Queen's University Press, 1987.

——— 'Intercollegiate Athletics in Canadian Universities: A Historical Perspective', in A.W. Taylor, ed., *The Role of Interuniversity Athletics: A Canadian Perspective*. London, Ont.: Sports Dynamics, 1986, 3–7.

——— and Michael Hawes. *Sport and Canadian Diplomacy*. Montreal and Kingston: McGill-Queens University Press, 1994.

—— and David Whitson. *The Game Planners: Transforming Canada's Sport System.* Montreal and Kingston: McGill-Queen's University Press, 1990.

McKay, Jim. *Managing Gender: Affirmative Action and Organizational Power in Australian, Canadian and New Zealand Sport.* Albany, NY: State University of New York Press, 1997.

MacKenzie, John. *Empire of Nature: Hunting, Conservation, and British Imperialism.* Manchester: Manchester University Press, 1988.

Marks, Lynne. *Revivals and Roller Rinks: Religion, Leisure, and Identity in Late Nineteenth Century Small-Town Ontario.* Toronto: University of Toronto Press, 1996.

Metcalfe, Alan. *Canada Learns To Play: The Emergence of Organized Sport, 1807–1914.* Toronto: McClelland & Stewart, 1987.

——. 'Organized Sport and Social Stratification in Montreal, 1840–1901', in Richard Gruneau and John Albinson, eds, *Canadian Sport: Sociological Perspectives.* Don Mills, Ont.: Addison-Wesley (Canada), 1976, 77–101.

——. 'The Growth of Organized Sport and the Development of Amateurism in Canada, 1807–1914', in Jean Harvey and Hart Cantelon, eds, *Not Just a Game.* Ottawa: University of Ottawa Press, 1988, 33–50.

——. 'Leisure, Sport and Working Class Culture: Some Insights from Montreal and the North-East Coalfield of England', in Hart Cantelon and Robert Hollands, eds, *Leisure, Sport and Working Class Cultures: Theory and History.* Toronto: Garamond Press, 1988, 65–76.

Mitchell, Shelia. 'The Development of Women's Organized Sport in the 1920s: A Study of the Canadian Ladies Golf Union', in Reet Howell, ed., *Her Story in Sport: A Historical Anthology of Women in Sports.* West Point, NY: Leisure Press, 1982, 564–71.

Mitchinson, Wendy. 'Early Women's Organizations and Social Reform: Prelude to the Welfare State', in A. Moscovitch and J. Albert, eds, *The Benevolent State: The Growth of Social Welfare in Canada.* Toronto: Garamond, 1987, 77–92.

Morrow, Don. *A Sporting Evolution: Montreal Amateur Athletic Association, 1881–1981.* Montreal: Montreal Amateur Athletic Association and Don Morrow, 1981.

——. 'The Canadian Image Abroad: The Great Lacrosse Tours of 1876 and 1883', *Proceedings of the Fifth Canadian Symposium on the History of Sport* (1982): 11–23.

——, Mary Keyes, Wayne Simpson, Frank Cosentino, and Ron Lappage. *A Concise History of Sport in Canada.* Toronto: Oxford University Press, 1989.

——'Quarrington's Hockey Schtick: A Literary Analysis' in Collin D. Howell, eds., *Putting it on Ice.* Halifax, Canada: Gorsebrook Research Institute, 2001.

——. 'Olympic Masculinity: An Analysis of Canadian Newspapers During the 1976, 1988, and 2000 Olympic Games', in *The Global Nexus Engaged: Proceedings of the Sixth International Symposium for Olympic Research* (2002): 123–35.

——, and Kevin B. Wamsley. *Sport in Canada: A History.* Don Mills, Ont.: Oxford University Press, 2005.

——, 'Canadian Sport in Historical Perspective' in Jane Crossman, eds, *Canadian Sport Sociology*, 2nd ed. Toronto: Nelson, 2008, 41–60.

Moss, Mark. *Manliness and Militarism: Educating Young Boys in Ontario for War.* Toronto: Oxford University Press, 2001.

Mott, Morris, ed. *Sports in Canada: Historical Readings.* Toronto: Copp Clark Pitman, 1989.

——. 'The Problems of Professionalism: The Manitoba Amateur Athletic Association and the Fight against Pro Hockey, 1904–

1911', in Corbet and Rasporich (1990: 132–42).

———. 'Academic and Popular History, or Humour and the Sports Historian', in Wamsley (1995: 162–71).

——— and John Allardyce. *Curling Capital: Winnipeg and the Roarin' Game, 1876 to 1988*. Winnipeg: University of Manitoba Press, 1989.

Mutimer, Brian T.P. *History of Squash Racquets in Canada*. Calgary: Triad Press, 1988.

Norbeck, Edward, and Claire R. Farrer, eds. *Forms of Play of Native North Americans*. St Paul, Minn.: West Publishing, 1979.

Norton, Wayne. 'Fair Manipulators of the Twisted Hickory: Women's Hockey in Fernie, 1919–1926', in Wayne Norton and Naomi Miller, eds, *The Forgotten Side of the Border: British Columbia's Elk Valley and Crowsnest Pass*. Kamloops, BC: Plateau Press, 1998, 206–16.

Oppliger, Patrice. *Wrestling and Hypermasculinity*. Jefferson, NC: McFarland, 2004.

Palmer, Bryan. *A Culture in Conflict: Skilled Workers and Industrial Conflict in Hamilton, Ontario, 1860–1914*. Montreal and Kingston: McGill-Queen's University Press, 1979.

Pakes, Fraser. '"Skill To Do Comes of Doing": Purpose in Traditional Indian Winter Games and Pastimes', in Corbet and Rasporich (1990: 26–37).

Parkes, A.E. Marie. *The Development of Women's Athletics at the University of Toronto*. Toronto:

Paraschak, Vicky. 'Sport Festivals and Race Relations in the Northwest Territories of Canada', in Grant Jarvie, ed., *Sport, Racism and Ethnicity*. London: Falmer Press, 1991, 74–93.

———. 'A Sporting Chance? The Governing of Aboriginal Sport', in Dave Headon, Joy Hooton, and Donald Horne, eds, *The Abundant Culture: Meaning and Significance in Everyday Australia*. Sydney: Allen and Unwin, 1995, 187–97.

———. 'An Examination of Sport for Aboriginal Females of the Six Nations Reserve, Ontario from 1968 to 1980', in Christine Miller and Patricia Chuchryk, eds, *Women of the First Nations: Power, Wisdom, and Strength*. Winnipeg: University of Manitoba Press, 1996, 83–96.

———. 'Native American Sporting Competitions', in David Levinson and Karen Christensen, eds, *Encyclopedia of World Sport: From Ancient Times to the Present*, vol. 2. Denver: ABC-CLIO, 1996, 679–83.

———. 'Native Canadians and Sport: A Clash of Cultural Values', in Luke Uche, ed., *North-South Information Culture: Trends in Global Communications and Research Paradigms*. Lagos: Longman Nigeria PLC, 1996, 99–113.

———. 'Billy Mills'; 'National Indian Activities Association'; 'Native American Sports'; 'Jim Thorpe', in George Kirsch, Othello Harris, and Claire Nolte, eds, *Encyclopedia of Ethnicity and Sports in the United States*. Westport, Conn.: Greenwood Press, 2000, 316–17, 328–9, 329–35, 461–2.

———. 'Knowing Ourselves Through the "Other": Indigenous Peoples in Sport in Canada', in Robyn Jones and Kathleen Armour, eds, *Sociology of Sport: Theory and Practice*. Essex: Longman, 2000, 153–66.

———. 'Native American Games and Sports'; 'Ryneldi Becenti: A Role Model for Her People', in Karen Christensen, Allen Guttmann, and Gertrude Pfister, eds, *International Encyclopedia of Women and Sports*. New York: Macmillan Reference, 2001, 788–91.

———. Michael Heine, and James McAra. 'Native and Academic Knowledge Interests: A Dilemma', in Wamsley (1995: 62–8).

Paton, Garth A. 'The Historical Background and Present Status of Canadian Physical

Education', in E.F. Zeigler, ed., *History of Physical Education and Sport in the United States and Canada*. Champaign, Ill.: Stipes, 1975, 432–49.

Pitters-Caswell, Marian. 'Women's Participation in Sporting Activities as an Indicator of a Feminist Movement in Canada between 1867 and 1914', in Howell (1982).

Raffan, J., and B. Horwood, eds. *Canexus: The Canoe in Canadian Culture*. Toronto: Betelgeuse Books, 1988.

Ransom, Diane. *Pioneers and Performers: University of Saskatchewan Sport, 1909–1984*. Saskatoon: Modern Press, 1984.

Redick, Don. *The Dawson City Seven*. Fredericton, NB: Goose Land, 1993.

Redmond, Gerald. *The Caledonian Games in Nineteenth Century America*. Cranbury, NJ: Associated Universities Press, 1971.

———. *Sport and Ethnic Groups in Canada*. Ottawa: CAHPER, 1978.

———. *The Sporting Scots of Nineteenth-Century Canada*. Toronto: Associated Press, 1982.

———. *Wayne Gretzky: The Great One*. Toronto: ECW Press, 1986.

———. 'Cricket', in James H. Marsh, ed., *The Canadian Encyclopedia*. Edmonton: Hurtig, 1988, 534–5.

———. 'The Development of Curling in Western Canada', in Corbet and Rasporich (1990: 112–23).

Reed, T.A. *The Blue and White: A Record of Athletic Endeavour at the University of Toronto*. Toronto: University of Toronto Press, 1944.

Riordan, James. 'The Worker's Olympics', in Alan Tomlinson and Garry Whannel, eds, *Five Ring Circus: Money, Power and Politics at the Olympic Games*. London: Pluto Press, 1984, 98–112.

Robinson, Laura. *She Shoots, She Scores: Canadian Perspectives on Women and Sport*. Toronto: Thompson, 1997.

Rosenstraub, Mark. 'Playing with the Big Boys: Smaller Markets, Competitive Balance, and the Hope for a Championship Team', in Whitson and Gruneau (2006: 143–62).

Roxborough, Henry. *Great Days in Canadian Sport*. Toronto: Ryerson Press, 1957.

———. *One Hundred—Not Out: The Story of Nineteenth Century Canadian Sport*. Toronto: Ryerson Press, 1966.

———. *Canada at the Olympics*. Toronto: Ryerson Press, 1969.

———. *The Stanley Cup Story*. Toronto: McGraw-Hill Ryerson, 1971.

Rutherford, Paul. *When Television was Young: Prime Time Canada, 1952–67*. Toronto: University of Toronto Press, 1990.

Ryan, Doreen. 'The Development of Speed Skating in Western Canada from a Personal Perspective', in Corbet and Rasporich (1990: 124–31).

Salmela, Jonh H., and B. Petiot, M. Hallé, and G. Régnier. *Competitive Behaviors of Olympic Gymnasts*. Springfield, Ill.: Charles C. Thomas Publisher, 1980.

Sandford, R.W. *The Canadian Alps: The History of Mountaineering in Canada*. Banff, AB: Altitude Publishing, 1990.

Sandland, Tom. *Something about Bicycling in Newfoundland*. St John's: Tom Sandland, 1983.

Schweinbenz, Amanda N. 'Beyond the Hockey Arena: Canadian Sport Historiography', in J.R. Nauright and S. Pope, eds, *Routledge Companion to Sports History*. New York and London: Routledge Press, 2009.

Smith, Cyndi. *Off the Beaten Track: Women Adventurers and Mountaineers in Western Canada*. Jasper, AB: Coyote Books, 1989.

Sparks, Robert, T. Dwehirst, S. Jette, and A. Schweinbenz. 'Historical Hangovers or Burning Possibilities: Regulation, Adaptation and Brand Equity in Tobacco and Alcohol Sponsorship', in John Amis and T. Bettina Cornwall, eds,

Global Sport Sponsorship. Oxford, UK: Berg, 2005.

Stebbins, Robert A. *Canadian Football: The View from the Helmet*. London, Ont.: Centre for Social and Humanistic Studies, University of Western Ontario, 1987.

Stevenson, John A. *Curling in Ontario, 1846–1946*. Toronto: OCA, 1950.

Stubbs, Lewis St George. *Shoestring Glory: A Prairie History of Semi-Pro Ball*. Winnipeg: Turnstone Press, 1996.

Teit, James A. *Tewaarathon (Lacrosse): Akwesasne's Story of Our National Game*. Cornwall Island, Ont.: North American Indian Travelling College, 1978.

Tillotson, Shirley M. *The Public at Play. Gender and the Politics of Recreation in Post-War Ontario*. Toronto: University of Toronto Press, 2000.

Valverde, Mariana. *The Age of Light, Soap and Water: Moral Reform in English Canada, 1885–1925*. Toronto: McClelland & Stewart, 1991.

Vaughan, Garth. *The Puck Starts Here: The Origin of Canada's Great Winter Game, Ice Hockey*. Fredericton, NB: Goose Lane, 1996.

Vennum, Thomas, Jr. *American Indian Lacrosse: Little Brother of War*. Washington: Smithsonian Institute Press, 1994.

Wamsley, Kevin B. *Method and Methodology in Sport and Cultural History*. Dubuque, Iowa: Brown and Benchmark, 1995.

———. 'Calgary 1988: XVth Olympic Winter Games', in John E. Findling and Kimberly D. Pelle, eds, *Historical Dictionary of the Modern Olympic Movement*. Westport, Conn.: Greenwood Press, 1996, 310–17.

——— and M. Heine. 'Don't Mess with the Relay, It's Bad Medicine: Aboriginal Culture and the 1988 Winter Olympic Games', in Robert K. Barney, Scott G. Martyn, Douglas A. Brown, and Gordon H. MacDonald, eds, *Olympic Perspectives*. London, Ont.: ICOS, 1996, 173–8.

———. 'American Boys in Paris: Canadian Participation in the Games of 1900', in Robert K. Barney, Kevin B. Wamsley, Scott G. Martyn, and Gordon H. MacDonald, eds, *Global and Cultural Critique: Problematizing the Olympic Games*. London, Ont.: ICOS, 1998, 135–40.

———. 'Laying Olympism to Rest', in John Bale and Mette Krogh Christensen, eds, *Post-Olympism? Questioning Sport in the Twenty-First Century*. Oxford: Berg, 2004, 231–42.

———. 'Introduction: Coubertin's Olympic Games: The Greatest Show on Earth' in Kevin Young and Kevin B. Wamsley, eds, *Global Olympics: Historical and Sociological Studies of the Modern Games*. Oxford: Elsevier Press, 2005.

———. 'Sport and Social Problems', in Jane Crossman, ed., *Canadian Sport Sociology*, 2nd ed. Toronto, Ont.: Thomson, 2007.

———. 'The Public Importance of Men and the Importance of Public Men: Sport and Masculinity in 19th Century Canada', in K. Young and P. White eds, *Sport and Gender in Cananda*, 2nd ed. Don Mills, Ont.: Oxford University Press, 2007.

———. 'Womanizing Olympic Athletes: Policy and Practice during the Avery Brundage Era', in G.P. Schaus and Stephen R. Wenn, eds, *Onward to the Olympics: Historical Perspectives on the Olympic Games*. Waterloo, Ont.: Wilfred Laurier Press, 2007.

———, and M. Heine. 'Fair Game: Indigenous Peoples and the Physical Culture Exhibits of World Expositions', in M. Lammer, E. Mertin, and T. Terret, eds, *New Aspects of Sport History*. Cologne, Germany: Academia, 2007.

———, and G. Pfister. 'Olympic Men and Women: The Politics of Gender in the Modern Games', in Kevin Young and Kevin B. Wamsley, eds, *Global Olympics: Historical and Sociological Studies of the Modern Games*. Oxford: Elsevier Press, 2005.

_____, and D. Whitson. 'Celebrating Violent Masculinities: The Boxing Death of Luther McCarty', in James Opp and John C. Walsh, eds, *Home, Work, and Play: Situating Canadian Social History, 1840–1980*. Don Mills, Ont.: Oxford University Press, 2006.

Watts, Heather. *Silent Steeds: Cycling in Nova Scotia to 1900*. Halifax: Nova Scotia Museum, 1985.

Weider, Ben. *The Strongest Man in History—Louis Cyr*. Toronto: Mitchell Press, 1976.

Wetherell, Donald G. 'A Season of Mixed Blessings: Winter and Leisure in Alberta before World War II', in Corbet and Rasporich (1990: 38–51).

Weyand, Alexander M., and Milton R. Roberts. *The Lacrosse Story*. Baltimore: H & A Herman, 1965.

White, Philip, and Kevin Young, eds. *Sport and Gender in Canada*. Toronto: Oxford University Press, 1999.

Whitehead, Eric. *Cyclone Taylor: A Hockey Legend*. Toronto: Doubleday, 1977.

Whitson, David. 'Globalization', in Jane Crossman, ed., *Canadian Sport Sociology*, 2nd ed. Toronto: Nelson, 2008, 239–56.

_____, and R. Gruneau, eds., *Artificial Ice: Hockey, Culture, and Commerce*. Peterborough, ON: Broadview Press, 2006.

Wetherell, Donald G., and Irene Kmet. *Useful Pleasures: The Shaping of Leisure in Alberta, 1896–1945*. Regina: Great Plains Research Centre, 1990.

Wieting, Stephen G., and Danny Lamoureux. 'Curling in Canada', in Wieting, ed., *Sport and Memory in North America*. London: Frank Cass, 2001, 140–53.

Wise, S.F. 'Sport and Class Values in Old Ontario and Quebec', in W.H. Heick and Roger Graham, eds, *His Own Man: Essays in Honour of Arthur Reginald Marsden Lower*. Montreal and Kingston: McGill-Queen's University Press, 1974, 93–117.

——— and Douglas Fisher. *Canada's Sporting Heroes*. Don Mills, Ont.: General Publishing, 1974.

Yeo, William B. 'Making Banff a Year-Round Park', in Corbet and Rasporich (1990: 87–98).

Young, A.J. 'Sandy'. *Beyond Heroes: A History of Sport in Nova Scotia*, 2 vols. Hantsport, NS: Lancelot Press, 1988.

Young, David. *The Golden Age of Canadian Figure Skating*. Toronto: Summerhill Press, 1984.

Young, Scott. *War on Ice: Canada in International Hockey*. Toronto: McClelland & Stewart 1976.

———. *100 Years of Dropping the Puck: A History of the OHA*. Toronto: McClelland & Stewart, 1989.

Zeman, Brenda. *Hockey Heritage: Eighty-eight Years of Puck Chasing in Saskatchewan*. Regina: Saskatchewan Sports Hall of Fame, 1983.

———. *To Run with Longboat: Twelve Stories of Indian Athletes in Canada*. Edmonton: GMS2 Ventures, 1988.

Zeman, Gary W. *Alberta on Ice: The History of Hockey in Alberta since 1893*. Edmonton: Westweb Press, 1985.

Dissertations, Theses, and Unpublished Manuscripts

Adams, Carly. 'Communities of Their Own: Women's Sport and Recreation in London, Ontario, 1920-1951', PhD dissertation, University of Western Ontario, 2007.

Adams, William. 'Competitive Paddling on the Dartmouth Lakes, 1846–1950', Master's thesis, Dalhousie University, 1974.

Amis, John Matthew. 'A Critical Analysis of the Development of Soccer in Nova Scotia', Master's thesis, Dalhousie University, 1992.

Anderson, David F. 'A Synthesis of the Canadian Federal Government Policies in Amateur Sports, Fitness and Recreation Since 1961',

PhD dissertation, University of Northern Colorado, 1974.

Andrew, Dale. 'Crowded Memories: The Origins, Growth, and Decay of Selected Memorial Arenas in Ontario', Master's thesis, University of Western Ontario, 2003.

Baka, Richard S.P. 'ParticipACTION: An Examination of its Role in Promoting Physical Fitness in Canada', Master's thesis, University of Western Ontario, 1975.

————. 'A History of Provincial Government Involvement in Sport in Western Canada', PhD dissertation, University of Alberta, 1978.

Bedecki, T.G. 'Modern Sport as an Instrument of National Policy with Reference to Canada and Selected Countries', PhD dissertation, Ohio State University, 1971.

Beedling, William Paul. 'Henry Robert "Bob" Pearce: A Biography', Master's thesis, University of Western Ontario, 1981.

Beesley, Diane. 'Walter Dean and Sunnyside: A Study of Waterfront Recreation in Toronto, 1880–1930', Master's thesis, University of Toronto, 1996.

Bell, Robert John. 'A History of Tennis at the University of Alberta', Education thesis, University of Alberta, 1994.

Berridge, Mavis. 'The Development of the Red Cross Water Safety Service and the Royal Life-Saving Society in Canada', Master's thesis, University of Wisconsin, 1966.

Blackburn, Cecil. 'The Development of Sports in Alberta, 1900–1918', Master's thesis, University of Alberta, 1974.

Bonney-James, Timothy Damian. 'More Than a Game: The Interaction of Sport and Community in Guelph', Master's thesis, University of Guelph, 1997.

Bouchier, Nancy B. 'Social Class and Organized Sport in Nineteenth Century Ontario: A Case Study of Sport in a Small Town—Ingersoll, Ontario, 1860–1894', Master's thesis, University of Western Ontario, 1982.

————. 'For the Love of the Game and the Honour of the Town: Organized Sport, Local Culture and Middle Class Hegemony in Two Ontario Towns, 1838–1895', PhD dissertation, University of Western Ontario, 1990.

Bowie, G.W. 'The History and Trends of Curling', Master's thesis, Washington State University, 1962.

Brock, Laura Helen. 'Beyond Domesticity: The Use and Value of Women's Leisure Time in Halifax, 1880–1930', Master's thesis, St Mary's University, 1998.

Brooks, Anne Stephanie. 'An Athletic Biography of a Champion Canadian Sculler: Jacob Gill Gaudaur 1858–1937', Master's thesis, University of Western Ontario, 1981.

Brown, David. 'The History and Development of Organized Canadian Football in Nova Scotia', Master's thesis, Dalhousie University, 1979.

————. 'Athleticism in Selected Canadian Private Schools for Boys to 1918', PhD dissertation, University of Alberta, 1984.

Brown, Douglas A. 'Theories of Beauty and Modern Sport: Pierre De Coubertin's Aesthetic Imperative for the Modern Olympic Movement, 1894–1914', PhD dissertation, University of Western Ontario, 1997.

Buma, P. Michael, 'Refereeing Identity: The Cultural Work of Canadian Hockey Novels', PhD dissertation, University of Western Ontario, 2008.

Burke, G.J. 'An Historical Study of Intercollegiate Athletics at the University of Western Ontario, 1908–1945', Master's thesis, University of Western Ontario, 1979.

Burr, Christina A. 'The Process of Evolution of Competitive Sport: A Study of Senior Lacrosse in Canada, 1844 to 1914', Master's thesis, University of Western Ontario, 1986.

Byl, John. 'Objectives and Involvement in Dance and Physically Active Games in the Christian Reformed Denomination and in its Congregations in Chatham, Ontario, 1926–1981', Master's thesis, University of Windsor, 1983.

———. 'The Margaret Eaton School, 1901–1942: Women's Education in Elocution, Drama, and Physical Education', PhD dissertation, SUNY Buffalo, 1992.

Cavanaugh, Richard Patrick. 'Cultural Production and Reproduction of Power: Political Economy, Public Television and High Performance Sport in Canada', PhD dissertation, Carleton University, 1989.

Christie, Howard A. 'The Function of the Tavern in Toronto, 1834 to 1875 with Special Reference to Sport', Master's thesis, University of Windsor, 1973.

Church, Anthony G. 'The Sacred Cow: Calgary and the XV Olympic Winter Games', Master's thesis, University of Western Ontario, 2003.

———, 'Pressure Groups and Canadian Sport Policy: A Neo-Pluralist Examination of Policy Development', PhD dissertation, University of Western Ontario, 2008.

Churchill, Kristopher Lloyd. 'Character Building and Gender Socialization in Early Private Youth Camp in Ontario', Master's thesis, University of Guelph, 1991.

Colpitts, George W. 'Science, Streams and Sport: Trout Conservation in Southern Alberta, 1900–1930', Master's thesis, University of Calgary, 1994.

Cooper, David Bernard. 'Canadians Declare "It Isn't Cricket": A Colonial Reflection of the Imperial Game', Master's thesis, University of Toronto, 1996.

Cosentino, Frank. 'A History of Canadian Football, 1909–1968', Master's thesis, University of Alberta, 1969.

———. 'A History of the Concept of Professionalism in Canadian Sport', PhD dissertation, University of Alberta, 1973.

Cossarin, Mark A. 'Joyride: Manifestation of the 1890s Bicycle Craze in Toronto', Master's thesis, University of Western Ontario, 1993.

Cox, A.E. 'A History of Sport in Canada, 1868–1900', PhD dissertation, University of Alberta, 1969.

Davidson, S.A. 'A History of Sports and Games in Eastern Canada Prior to World War I', PhD dissertation, Columbia University, 1951.

Davies, R.M. 'A History of Rugby in Nova Scotia', Master's thesis, Dalhousie University, 1979.

Day, Robert Douglas. 'Impulse to Addiction: A Narrative History of Sport in Chatham, Ontario, 1790–1895', Master's thesis, University of Western Ontario, 1977.

———. 'The British Army and Sport in Canada: Case Studies of the Garrisons at Halifax, Montreal and Kingston to 1871', PhD dissertation, University of Alberta, 1981.

Duppereault, Jean. 'Forty-Five Years of Roadracing in Nova Scotia, 1900–45', Master's thesis, Dalhousie University, 1979.

East, Jocelyn. 'Sport, Éthique et Culture au Québec de 1960 à 1995', Master's thesis, Université Laval, 1995.

Eaton, J.D. 'The Life and Professional Contributions of Arthur Stanley Lamb, M.D. to Physical Education in Canada', PhD dissertation, Ohio State University, 1964.

Echenberg, Havi. 'Sport as a Social Response to Urbanization: A Case Study: London, Ontario, 1850–1900', Master's thesis, University of Western Ontario, 1979.

Ecker, Glen. 'An Outline History of the Development of Football in Hamilton, 1860–1960', unpublished ms, Hamilton Public Library Special Collections, n.d.

———. 'Historical Development of Public Recreation in Great Britain and Hamilton, 1830–1880', unpublished ms, Hamilton Public Library Special Collections, n.d.

Eckert, H. 'The Development of Physical Education and Recreation in Alberta', Master's thesis, University of Alberta, 1953.

Files, James. 'The Ministry of Culture and Recreation and Cultural Changes in Ontario', PhD dissertation, University of Waterloo, 1991.

Forbes, Susan L. 'The Influence of the Social Reform Movement and T. Eaton Company's Business Practices on the Leisure of Eaton's Female Employees During the Early Twentieth Century', PhD dissertation, University of Western Ontario, 1998.

Forsyth, Janice. 'From Assimilation to Self-Determination: The Emergence of J. Wilton Littlechild's North American Indigenous Games, 1763–1997', Master's thesis, University of Western Ontario, 2000.

———, 'The Power to Define: A History of the Tom Longboat Awards, 1951–2001', PhD dissertation, University of Western Ontario, 2005.

Gillespie, Greg. 'The Imperial Embrace: British Sportsmen and the Appropriation of Landscape in Nineteenth Century Canada', PhD dissertation, University of Western Ontario, 2001.

Gillis, Sheldon. 'Putting it on Ice: A Social History of Hockey in the Maritimes, 1880–1914', Master's thesis, St Mary's University, 1996.

Gray, Wendy. 'The Origin and Evolution of the German-Canadian Turnverein Movement, Waterloo County, Canada West, 1850–1875', Master's thesis, University of Western Ontario, 1990.

Hall, Margaret Ann. 'A History of Women's Sport in Canada Prior to World War I', Master's thesis, University of Alberta, 1968.

Hallett, W.D. 'A History of Federal Government Involvement in the Development of Sport in Canada, 1943–1979', PhD dissertation, University of Alberta, 1981.

Heard, Clark Patrick. 'Sideshows and the Main Tent: A Social History of the Symbiotic Relationship between the University of Western Ontario and Its Senior Intercollegiate League Football Program, 1929–1970', Master's thesis, University of Western Ontario, 1996.

Heine, Michael K. 'The Enculturative Function of Play Behaviour and Games among the Tlingit Indians of Southeast Alaska', Master's thesis, University of Western Ontario, 1984.

———. 'Gwich'in Tsii'in: A History of Gwich'in Athapaskan Games', PhD dissertation, University of Alberta, 1995.

Hess, Robert M. 'A Social History of Cycling in Edmonton, 1890–1897', Master's thesis, University of Alberta, 1991.

Howell, David F. 'History of Horseracing in Halifax, Nova Scotia, 1747–1867', Master's thesis, Dalhousie University, 1972.

———. 'The Social Gospel in Canadian Protestantism, 1895–1925', PhD dissertation, University of Alberta, 1980.

Hudson, Michael James. 'An Examination into the Development of Golf Courses in Nova Scotia', Master's thesis, Dalhousie University, 1998.

Huskins, Bonnie L. 'Public Celebrations in Victorian St. John and Halifax', PhD dissertation, Dalhousie University, 1991.

Jackson, John Terrance. 'Tommy Burns: World Heavyweight Boxing Champion', Master's thesis, University of Western Ontario, 1985.

Jackson, Steven J. 'Sport, Crisis, and Canadian Identity in 1988: A Cultural Analysis', PhD dissertation, University of Illinois, 1992.

Jobling, Ian. 'Sport in Nineteenth Century Canada: Their Effects of Technological Changes in its Development', PhD dissertation, University of Alberta, 1970.

Jones, K.G. 'Sport in Canada, 1900–1920', PhD dissertation, University of Alberta, 1970.

Joyce, Charles Anthony. 'At Close of Play: The Evolution of Cricket in London, Ontario, 1836–1902', Master's thesis, University of Western Ontario, 1988.

———. 'From Left Field: Sport and Class in Toronto, 1845–1886', PhD dissertation, Queen's University, 1997.

———. 'No Change in the Batting Order. A Study of Social Class and Nineteenth Century London Cricketers, 1860–1900', unpublished ms, University of Western Ontario, n.d.

———. 'The London Asylum: A Not So Crazy Place for Cricket. A Study of Two Selected Components of Institutionalization in the Asylum Cricket Club, 1877–1902', Master's thesis, University of Western Ontario, 1986.

Kennedy, John Robinson. 'A History of the Development of the Coaching Certification Programme in Canada', PhD dissertation, Ohio State University, 1981.

Key, John W. 'Socio-Cultural Characteristics and the Image of the Urban Anglo-Canadian Athletic Hero, 1920–1939', Master's thesis, University of Windsor, 1982.

Keyes, Mary Elanor. 'John Howard Crocker LL.D., 1870–1959', Master's thesis, University of Western Ontario, 1965.

———. 'The History of the Women's Athletic Committee of the Canadian Association for Health, Physical Education, and Recreation, 1940–1973', PhD dissertation, Ohio State University, 1980.

Kidd, Bruce. 'Improvers, Feminists, Capitalists and Socialists: Shaping Canadian Sport in the 1920s and 1930s', PhD dissertation, York University, 1990.

Kimber, Nancy. 'The Wanderers Amateur Athletic Club of Halifax, 1882–1925: Its Contribution to Amateur Sport', Master's thesis, Dalhousie University, 1974.

Kirkwood, Ken. 'Out of the Olympic Closet: Abandoning prohibitions on doping in favour of a harm reduction approach',

PhD dissertation, University of Western Ontario, 2004.

Kossuth, Robert. 'The Decline of English Rugby and the Rise of Canadian Football in Halifax, 1930 to 1954', Master's thesis, University of Windsor, 1996.

———. 'Constructing a Stage for Play: Sport, Recreation, and Leisure in London, Ontario, 1867–1914', PhD dissertation, University of Western Ontario, 2002.

Kolesnyk, Kristina, 'Globalization and Sport: Athletic Talent Migration to Canada', Master's thesis, University of Western Ontario, 2004.

Kurtz, Morris. 'A History of the 1972 Canada–USSR Ice Hockey Series', PhD dissertation, Pennsylvania State University, 1981.

Lamb, Patrick. 'A History of Rugby Football in Edmonton', Master's thesis, University of Alberta, 1990.

Landry, Blaise James. 'Nova Scotia's Success in Paddling at the Canada Summer Games, 1969–1993', Master's thesis, Dalhousie University, 1995.

Lang, Spencer. 'Importing Professional Baseball: An Examination of the Guelph Maple Leafs and London Tecumsehs 1872–1878', Master's thesis, University of Western Ontario, 2003.

Lansley, Keith L. 'The Amateur Athletic Union of Canada and Changing Concepts of Amateurism', PhD dissertation, University of Alberta, 1971.

Laporte, R.E. 'The Development of Parks in Regina, 1882–1930: Private Initiatives and Public Policy', Master's thesis, University of Regina, 1986.

Lappage, Ronald. 'Selected Sports and Canadian Society, 1921–1939', PhD dissertation, University of Alberta, 1974.

Lathrop, Anna H. 'Elegance and Expression, Sweat and Strength: Body Training, Physical Culture and Female Embodiment in Women's Education at the Margaret

Eaton Schools (1901–1941)', PhD dissertation, University of Toronto, 1997.

Laubman, Katherine M. 'A Historical-Ethnographic Account of a Canadian Woman in Sport 1920–1938: The Story of Margaret (Bell) Gibson', Master's thesis, University of British Columbia, 1991.

Laurendeau, W. Edward. 'Sport and Canadian Culture in the Border Cities, 1867 to 1929', Master's thesis, University of Windsor, 1971.

Lawrence-Harper, Janis. 'Change in a Feminist Organization: The Canadian Association for the Advancement of Women and Sport and Physical Activity, 1981–1991', Master's thesis, University of Alberta, 1993.

Lennox, Brian D. 'Nova Scotia's Black Boxers. A History of Champions', Master's thesis, Dalhousie University, 1990.

Lenskyj, Helen. 'The Role of Physical Education in the Socialization of Girls in Ontario, 1890–1930', PhD dissertation, Ontario Institute for Studies in Education, 1983.

Lewis, Pam. 'Fitness and Amateur Sport Branch Policies as They Pertain to Women in Canada, 1974–1979. Master's thesis, University of Western Ontario, 1980.

Lindsay, Andrew J. 'The Decline of Professional Boxing in Toronto, 1920–1993', Master's thesis, University of Windsor, 1994.

Lindsay, Peter. 'A History of Sport in Canada, 1807–1867', PhD dissertation, University of Alberta, 1969.

Littlechild, Wilton. 'Tom Longboat: Canada's Outstanding Indian Athlete', Master's thesis, University of Alberta, 1975.

Loiselle, Richard. 'Wheelchair Sports: Development in Canada and its Impact on the Rehabilitation of the Physically Disabled', Master's thesis, Dalhousie University, 1973.

Louie, Siri Winoma. 'Gender in the Alpine Club of Canada, 1906–1940', Master's thesis, University of Calgary, 1996.

Lund, Rolf. 'A History of Skiing in Canada Prior to 1940', Master's thesis, University of Alberta, 1971.

McBryde, John. 'The Bipartite Development of Men's and Women's Field Hockey in Canada in the Context of Separate International Hockey Federations', Master's thesis, University of British Columbia, 1986.

Macdonald, Cathy. 'The Edmonton Grads, Canada's Most Successful Team: A History and Analysis of Their Success', Master's thesis, University of Windsor, 1976.

MacFarland, John M. 'A History of the Role Played by the Military in the Development of Competitive Sport in Nova Scotia, 1930–1969', PhD dissertation, Springfield College, 1978.

McLaughlin, M.K. 'Vice Regal Patronage of Canadian Sport: 1867–1916', Master's thesis, University of Alberta, 1981.

MacNeill, Margaret E. 'Olympic Power Plays: A Social Analysis of CTV's Production of the 1988 Winter Olympic Ice Hockey Tournament', PhD dissertation, Simon Fraser University, 1994.

Manning, Richard P. 'Recreating Man: Hunting and Angling in Victorian Canada', Master's thesis, Carleton University, 1994.

Markham, Susan E. 'The Development of Parks and Playgrounds in Selected Canadian Prairie Cities: 1880–1930', PhD dissertation, University of Alberta, 1988.

Marks, Lynne. 'Religion and Leisure in Three Ontario Towns, 1883–1929', PhD dissertation, York University, 1993.

Marsh, John S. 'Man, Landscape and Recreation in Glacier National Park, British Columbia, 1880 to Present', PhD dissertation, University of Calgary, 1971.

Mitchell, Shelia L. 'The Organizational Development of Women's Competitive Sport in Canada in the 1920s', Master's thesis, University of Windsor, 1976.

Mitchell McKie, Leila Gay. 'Voluntary Youth Organizations in Toronto, 1880–1930', PhD dissertation, York University, 1983.

Mitchelson, E.B. 'The Evolution of Men's Basketball in Canada, 1892–1936', Master's thesis, University of Alberta, 1968.

Mitchener, E.A. 'William Pearce and Federal Government Activity in Western Canada 1882–1904', PhD dissertation, University of Alberta, 1971.

Moriarty, Richard. 'The Organizational History of the Canadian Intercollegiate Athletic Union Central, 1906–1955', PhD dissertation, Ohio State University, 1971.

Morrow, Don L. 'An Historical Study of the Development of the Intramural Program at the University of Western Ontario, 1878–1972', Master's thesis, University of Western Ontario, 1972.

———. 'Selected Topics in the History of Physical Education in Ontario: From Dr. Egerton Ryerson to the Strathcona Trust, 1844–1939', PhD dissertation, University of Alberta, 1975.

Mott, Morris Kenneth. 'Manly Sports and Manitobans, Settlement Days to World War One', PhD dissertation, Queen's University, 1980.

Myers, James D. 'Hard Times-Hard Ball: The Cape Breton Colliery League, 1936–1939', Master's thesis, St Mary's University, 1997.

Myrer, Joseph William. 'The Canadianization of Intercollegiate Football in Ontario and Quebec from 1897–192', Master's thesis, University of Windsor, 1977.

Nattrass, Susan Marie. 'Sport and Television in Canada: 1952 to 1982', PhD dissertation, University of Alberta, 1988.

Norwood, David R. 'The Sport Hero Concept and Louis Cyr', Master's thesis, University of Windsor, 1982.

Nurmberg, R. 'A History of Competitive Gymnastics in Canada', Master's thesis, University of Alberta, 1970.

O'Bonsawin, Christine. 'Failed TEST: Aboriginal Sport Policy and the Olympian Firth Sisters', Master's thesis, University of Western Ontario, 2002.

———. 'Spectacles, Policy, and Social Memory: Images of Canadian Indians at World's Fairs and Olympic Games', PhD dissertation, University of Western Ontario, 2006.

O'Hanley, J.A. 'Women in Non-Traditional Sport: The Rise and Popularity of Women's Rugby in Canada', Master's thesis, Queen's University, 1999.

Olafson, Pauline. 'Sport, Physical Education and the Ideal Girl in Selected Ontario Denominational Schools, 1970–1930', Master's thesis, University of Windsor, 1990.

Paraschak, Victoria A. 'Selected Factors Associated with the Enactment of the 1961 Fitness and Amateur Sport Act', Master's thesis, University of Windsor, 1978.

Parratt, Catriona B. 'Sport and Hegemony: Windsor c.1895 to c.1929', Master's thesis, University of Windsor, 1985.

Pearson, Robert Harry. 'Montreal's Delorimer Downs Baseball Stadium as Business and Centre of Mass Culture, 1928–1960', Master's thesis, Queen's University, 1999.

Pederson, Diana L. 'The YMCA in Canada, 1870–1920: A Movement to Meet a Spiritual, Civic, and National Need', PhD dissertation, Carleton University, 1987.

Pinto, Barbara S. 'Ain't Misbehavin': The Montreal Shamrock Lacrosse Club Fans, 1868 to 1884', Master's thesis, University of Western Ontario, 1990.

Pitters-Caswell, Marian. 'Women's Participation in Sporting Activities as an Indicator of Femininity and Cultural Evolution in Toronto, 1910 to 1920', Master's thesis, University of Windsor, 1975.

Ponic, Pamela L. 'Herstory: The Structuring of the Fitness and Amateur Sport Branch's Women's Program: 1970–1988', Master's thesis, University of Windsor, 1994.

Popovic, Megan. 'Shredding and Jibbing: The Subculture and Evolution of Snowboarding in Canada', Master's thesis, University of Western Ontario, 2005.

Purcell, John W. 'English Sport and Canadian Culture in Toronto, 1867 to 1911', Master's thesis, University of Windsor, 1974.

Ransom, Diane. 'The Saskatoon Lily: A Biography of Ethel Catherwood', Master's thesis, University of Saskatchewan, 1986.

Redmond, Gerald. 'The Scots and Sport in Nineteenth Century Canada', PhD dissertation, University of Alberta, 1972.

Reid, John E. 'Sports and Games in Alberta before 1900', Master's thesis, University of Alberta, 1969.

Reichwein, PearlAnn. 'Beyond the Visionary Mountain: The Alpine Club of Canada and the Canadian National Park Idea, 1906 to 1969', PhD dissertation, Carleton University, 1998.

Reid, Daniel B. 'The Amateur Athletic Union of the United States and the Canadian Amateur Athletic Union, 1897–1914: A Study of International Sporting Relations', Master's thesis, University of Western Ontario, 1990.

Reilly, C. 'Attitudes to Women in Sport with Emphasis on the Peterborough Area, 1870 to 1914', Master's thesis, Trent University, 1986.

Robertson, Cathy E.M. 'Recreational Facilities and Community: Stouffville, Ontario, 1888–1971', Master's thesis, University of Windsor, 1987.

Rose, Ainsley B. 'An Historical Account of Canada's Participation in International Ice Hockey: 1948–1970', Master's thesis, University of Western Ontario, 1976.

Ross, Andrew, 'Hockey Capital: Commerce, Culture and the National Hockey League, 1917–1967', PhD dissertation, University of Western Ontario, 2008.

Routledge, P. 'The North-West Mounted Police and Their Influence on the Sporting and Social Life of the North West Territories, 1870–1904', Master's thesis, University of Alberta, 1978.

Ryan, Dennis. 'Irish Catholic Sport, Identity, and Integration in Toronto, 1858–1920', Master's thesis, University of Western Ontario, 2000.

Salter, Michael A. 'Games in Ritual: A Study of Selected North American Tribes', PhD dissertation, University of Alberta, 1972.

Savoie, Mark. 'Baseball and Cricket in Fredericton and Saint John: The Origin and Evolution of the Two Sports and the Socio-Economic Status of Those Who Played', Master's thesis, University of Western Ontario, 1994.

Sawula, Lorne W. 'The National Physical Fitness Act of Canada, 1943–1954', PhD dissertation, University of Alberta, 1977.

Schrodt, P. Barbara. 'A History of Pro-Rec: The British Columbia Provincial Recreation Programme, 1934 to 1953', PhD dissertation, University of Alberta, 1979.

Schweinbenz, Amanda. 'All Dressed Up and No Where to Run: Women's Uniforms and Clothing in the Olympics Games from 1900 to 1932', Master's thesis, University of Western Ontario, 2001.

Seglins, David. 'Just Part of the Game: Violence, Hockey and Masculinity in Central Canada, 1890–1910', Master's thesis, Queen's University, 1995.

Short, George D. 'Sport and Economic Growth in the Windsor Area, 1919 to 1939', Master's thesis, University of Windsor, 1972.

Sills, M.C. 'The History of Physical Education in Nova Scotia with Particular Attention to the Elementary Schools', Master's thesis, Dalhousie University, 1976.

Simpson, Robert Wayne. 'The Influence of the Montreal Curling Club on the Development of Curling in the Canadas, 1807–1857', Master's thesis, University of Western Ontario, 1980.

————. 'The Elite and Sport Club Membership in Toronto, 1827–1881', PhD dissertation, University of Alberta, 1987.

Sojczynski, Jan. 'Sport Club Executives and Occupational Structure: A Case Study of Chatham, Ontario, 1855–1895', unpublished ms, University of Windsor, 1983.

Stephens, G.P. 'A History of Basketball in Halifax, 1894–1930', Master's thesis, Dalhousie University, 1977.

Stevens, Julie A. 'The Development of Women's Hockey: An Explanation of Structure and Change within the Canadian Hockey System', Master's thesis, Queen's University, 1992.

Stidwell, Howard. 'The History of the Canadian Olympic Association', Master's thesis, University of Ottawa, 1982.

Sturrock, D.N. 'A History of Rugby Football in Canada', Master's thesis, University of Alberta, 1971.

Sultzback, Michael C. 'Canadian Schooner Bluenose, 1921–1946', Master's thesis, Dalhousie University, 1978.

Swain, Derek Anthony. 'A History of Sport in British Columbia to 1895: A Chronicle of Significant Developments and Events', Master's thesis, University of British Columbia, 1977.

Swift, Jessica, 'Under the Floodlights: Coxwell Stadium and the East Toronto Ladies Softball League 1947–1965', Master's thesis, University of Western Ontario, 2006.

Tillotson, Shirley M. 'Gender, Recreation and the Welfare State in Ontario, 1945–61', PhD dissertation, Queen's University, 1994.

Timothy Damian, Bonney-James. 'More Than a Game: The Interaction of Sport and Community in Guelph', Master's thesis, University of Guelph, 1997.

Vankirk, S. 'The Development of National Park Policy in Canada's Mountain National Parks 1885–1930', Master's thesis, University of Alberta, 1969.

Vellathottam, George T. 'A History of Lacrosse in Canada', Master's thesis, University of Alberta, 1967.

Vigneault, Michel. 'The Cultural Diffusion of Hockey in Montreal, 1890–1910', Master's thesis, University of Windsor, 1986.

————. 'La naissance d'un sport organizé au Canada: le hockey à Montreal, 1875–1917', PhD dissertation, Université Laval, 2001.

Walton, Yvette M. 'The Life and Professional Contributions of Ethel Mary Cartwright (1880–1955)', Master's thesis, University of Western Ontario, 1976.

Wamsley, Kevin. 'Legislation and Leisure in 19th Century Canada', PhD dissertation, University of Alberta, 1992.

Waters, Janice Evelyn. 'A Content Analysis of the Sport Section in Selected Canadian Newspapers, 1927 to 1935', Master's thesis, University of Western Ontario, 1981.

Waters, Gregory J. 'Operating on the Border: A History of the Commercial Promotion, Moral Suppression and State Regulation of the Thoroughbred Racing Industry in Windsor, Ontario, 1884 to 1936', Master's thesis, University of Windsor, 1992.

Watkins, Glenn G. 'Professional Team Sports and Competition Policy: A Case Study of the Canadian Football League', PhD dissertation, University of Alberta, 1972.

Watson, G.G. 'Sport and Games in Ontario Private Schools, 1830–1930', Master's thesis, University of Alberta, 1970.

Watson, James Douglas. 'G.O.L.F. Gentlemen On, Ladies Follow: Class, Gender and Golf, 1873–1914', Master's thesis, Laurentian University, 1995.

White, Gregory. 'Icing the Puck: The Origins, Rise and Decline of Newfoundland's Senior Hockey, 1896–1996', Master's thesis, Memorial University, 1997.

Wilkie, D.R. 'Fitness and Amateur Sport Act in Alberta', Master's thesis, University of Alberta, 1968.

Williams, Beverly. 'Leisure as Contested Terrain in Nineteenth Century Halifax', Master's thesis, St Mary's University, 1991.

Proceedings of Canadian Symposia on the History of Sport

1st Canadian Symposium, Edmonton, 1970.

2nd Canadian Symposium, Windsor, Ont., 1972.

3rd Canadian Symposium, Halifax, 1974.

4th Canadian Symposium, Vancouver, 1979.

5th Canadian Symposium, Toronto, 1982.

6th Canadian Symposium, London, Ont., 1988.

7th Canadian Symposium, Calgary, 1994.

8th Canadian Symposium, St Catharines, Ont., 2001.

Index

Guides to Writing from Oxford University Press

Oxford University Press Canada publishes a wide range of writing guides for students in all disciplines. Some of our bestselling titles are described below.

Making Sense: A Student's Guide to Research and Writing, Sixth Edition
(revised with up-to-date MLA and APA documentation guidelines)

MARGOT NORTHEY • JOAN McKIBBIN

Making Sense is one of a series of concise, readable guides on research and writing for all levels of undergraduate study. Designed specifically for students in the humanities, *Making Sense* outlines general principles of style, grammar, and usage, while covering issues such as how to prepare illustrations, write business reports, give oral presentations, write tests and exams, and prepare resumés and application letters. The four major documentation styles used in the humanities—MLA, APA, CMS, and CSE—are all covered in detail. The updated sixth edition has added material on evaluating Internet sources, avoiding plagiarism, and how to prepare an annotated bibliography, as well as new and updated examples throughout. A concise reference guide detailing common errors and symbols is located on the inside front cover.

CONTENTS: 1. Writing and Thinking. 2. Writing an Essay. 3. Writing a Book Report. 4. Writing a Lab Report. 5. Writing a Business Report. 6. Using Illustrations. 7. Documenting Sources. 8. Giving an Oral Presentation. 9. Writing Examinations. 10. Writing a Resumé and Letter of Application. 11. Writing with Style. 12. Common Errors in Grammar and Usage. 13. Punctuation. 14. Misused Words and Phrases. Glossary.

Paper, 2010, 208 pp., ISBN 9780195440034

Communicating in Geography and the Environmental Sciences, Canadian Edition

IAIN HAY • PHILIP GILES

Intended for students studying geography and the environmental sciences, this first Canadian edition is a concise yet comprehensive guide to effective communication. Focussing on why strong written and verbal communication skills are so important in this field, the authors demonstrate how to develop these skills to produce high quality work. Drawing on Canadian sources and examples, the text examines the communication forms that students will encounter throughout their academic careers, including essays, lab reports, reviews, posters, graphs, tables, maps, oral presentations, and exams.

CONTENTS: 1. Writing an Essay. 2. Writing a Report. 3. Writing an Annotated Bibliography, Summary, or Review. 4. Finding, Evaluating, and Using Sources. 5. Referencing and Language Matters. 6. Making a Poster. 7. Communicating with Graphs and Tables. 8. Communicating with Maps. 9. Preparing and Delivering an Oral Presentation. 10. Writing for the Media. 11. Succeeding in Examinations. Glossary.

Paper, 2011, 312 pp., ISBN 9780195436419

Guides to Writing from Oxford University Press

Oxford University Press Canada publishes a wide range of writing guides for students in all disciplines. Some of our bestselling titles are described below.

Writing in the Social Sciences: A Guide for Term Papers and Book Reviews

JAKE MULLER

Designed for students new to academic writing, *Writing in the Social Sciences* is a clear, step-by-step guide to the entire writing process. Students will learn how to select and research a topic, develop and refine their ideas into a comprehensive outline, and convert the outline into a research paper or book report. An inductive approach leads students through the process of selecting a topic, conducting research, and writing arguments using a pre-designed outline in order to come up with a well-developed thesis. Appendices include an answer key, a summary of common grammatical terms, and two sample outlines for social science term papers.

CONTENTS: Introduction–Preparing for Your Social Science Term Paper and Book Review. 1. Learning the Basic Social Science Argumentative Format and Process. 2. Researching to Create an Aim and Arguments. 3. Referencing Your Sources: Some Basic APA Styles. 4. Researching to Define Concepts in the Aim, Organizing Arguments, and Drafting a Conclusion. 5. Writing the First Social Science Term Paper. 6. Writing the First Social Science Book Review. Appendices.

Paper, 2010, 168 pp., ISBN 9780195430264

Writing with Style: Grammar in Context

HEATHER PYRCZ

This concise guidebook helps students understand the intricacies of grammar in order to improve their writing skills. A variety of well-known literary quotes and excerpts contextualize grammar principles and are accompanied by a range of simple to complex writing exercises. The author uses the method of first breaking down the quotation into its grammatical elements and then rebuilding it to examine how the elements and devices create or enhance meaning, demonstrating how the featured writer has used a sophisticated knowledge of language to communicate effectively. Innovative and engaging, *Writing with Style: Grammar in Context* features classic and contemporary literary and non-literary quotations, as well as Canadian, international, and minority voices. Headnotes accompanied by a photo introduce each author, and self-testing quotation analyses, discussion questions, an extensive guide to style and grammar terms, and suggestions for further reading facilitate student understanding of key concepts. The result is an indispensable grammar guide for any course with a writing component.

CONTENTS: Part I. Lessons. 1. Jane Austen—Parts of a Sentence: Subject, Predicate. 2. Franz Kafka—Parts of Speech. 3. Margaret Atwood—Nouns, Simple Sentences, Figures of Speech. 4. James Joyce—Verbs: Principal Parts, Tense. 5. Dylan Thomas—Verbs: Finite/Verbal, Intransitive/Transitive. 6. Pearl S. Buck—Verbs: Mood. 7. French Feminists—Parts of a Sentence: Subject, Object. 8. Gabriel Garcia Marquez—Adjectives, Adverbs. 9. André Gide—Simple Sentences, Phrases. 10. Heraclitus—Compound Sentences, Independent Clauses, Parallel Constructions. 11. Oscar Wilde—Compound Sentences, Parataxis, Conjunctions. 12. Virginia Woolf—Compound Sentences, Freight Trains, Triads. 13. Graham Greene—Complex Sentences, Dependent Clauses. 14. Hannah Arendt—Complex Sentences, Dependent Clauses, Subordinating Conjunctions. 15. Martin Luther King, Jr.—Clauses. 16. Johann Wolfgang von Goethe—Punctuating Clauses, Restrictive and Non-restrictive Clauses. 17. David Suzuki—Compound-Complex Sentences, Analogies. 18. Barbara Gowdy—Fragments, Pronouns, Tone. 19. Angela Carter—Interruption, Allusion. 20. A Cornucopia of Voices—Figures of Speech: Metaphor, Simile. 21. A Plethora of Voices—Emphatic Devices: Repetition. 22. George Elliott Clarke—Emphatic Devices: Accumulation. 23. Simone Weil—Emphatic Devices: Rhythm. 24. *The Oxford English Dictionary*—Diction. Review. Part II. Excerpts. 25. Don McKay—Clarity. 26. Charles Dickens—Emphatic Devices. 27. Peter Sanger—Diction. 28. Harry Thurston—Description. 29. Doris Lessing—Flow. 30. Barack Obama—Parallel Constructions, Anaphora. 31. Annie Dillard—Poetic Devices in Prose. 32. Phil Fontaine—Eloquence, Tense. 33. Thomas Carlyle—Last Word. Guide to Style and Grammar Terms. Five Readings for Enlightenment, Pleasure, and Whimsy. Quotation Analysis.

Paper, 2010, 136 pp., ISBN 9780195431735

Guides to Writing from Oxford University Press

Oxford University Press Canada publishes a wide range of writing guides for students in all disciplines. Some of our bestselling titles are described below.

Practical Grammar: A Canadian Writer's Resource, Second Edition

MAXINE RUVINSKY

Practical Grammar offers students of all levels and disciplines a succinct and comprehensive overview of the basics of English grammar. It includes clear and concise explanations of important grammatical concepts, information on citation, expert advice on avoiding common errors, review exercises and drills, and tips on research and writing techniques. *Practical Grammar* is a valuable addition to any class with a focus on writing or a written component and can serve as a reference throughout students' academic careers. The new edition includes additional exercises and updated pedagogical features, as well as a concise explanation of common proofreaders' marks printed on the inside covers.

CONTENTS: A Note to the Reader. A Note to the Instructor. Part I. Grammar Basics. 1. Parts of Speech. 2. Sentence Structure. 3. Verbs Revisited. Part II. Elementary Errors. 4. Subject–Verb Agreement. 5. Pronoun–Antecedent Agreement and Pronoun Case. 6. Diction and Danglers. Part III. Points of Style. 7. Parallelism and Faulty Constructions. 8. Punctuation. Part IV. Writing Essentials. 9. Writing Well: A Compendium of Tips. 10. Style and Documentation. Answers to Review Exercises. Glossary of Grammatical Terms. Online Student Resources at www.oupcanada.com/Ruvinsky2e: Grammar and Spelling Diagnostic Websites. CMS Documentation Guidelines.

Paper, 2009, 248 pp., ISBN 9780195430141

Making Sense in the Social Sciences: A Student's Guide to Research and Writing, Fourth Edition (revised with up-to-date MLA and APA documentation guidelines)

MARGOT NORTHEY • LORNE TEPPERMAN • PATRIZIA ALBANESE

Making Sense in the Social Sciences is one of a popular series of concise guides to research and writing designed for students at all levels of undergraduate study in the social sciences. It outlines general principles of style, grammar, and usage, while covering issues such as how to conduct sociological research, how to write reports, and how to document sources. This fourth edition includes valuable new material on evaluating Internet sources and avoiding plagiarism, as well as new and updated examples.

CONTENTS: 1. Writing and Thinking. 2. Designing a Project. 3. Theorizing about a Project. 4. Using Quantitative Data. 5. Using Qualitative Data. 6. Exercising Judgment and Good Ethics. 7. Arguing and Writing with Style. 8. Planning and Organizing an Essay or Report. 9. Writing an Essay or Exam. 10. Documentation. 11. Common Errors in Grammar and Usage. 12. Punctuation. 13. Misused Words and Phrases. Glossary I: Social Science. Glossary II: Grammar.

Paper, 2009, 296 pp., ISBN 9780195439939

Guides to Writing from Oxford University Press

Oxford University Press Canada publishes a wide range of writing guides for students in all disciplines.

The Concise Canadian Writer's Handbook

WILLIAM E. MESSENGER • JAN DE BRUYN • JUDY BROWN • RAMONA MONTAGNES

The Concise Canadian Writer's Handbook is a streamlined, coil-bound, full-colour version of the well-established *Canadian Writer's Handbook* that instructors have come to know and trust. The concise edition uses the accessible, well-organized, classroom-tested structure of the full volume, featuring descriptions and examples of the entire writing process, from basic grammar to constructing sentences and paragraphs to proofreading and editing. Also included are English as an Additional Language tools, up-to-date examples, and advice on avoiding plagiarism and achieving academic integrity. The latest documentation guidelines have also been added to ensure students have access to the most current resources available. A comprehensive list of marking symbols and abbreviations located on the inside back cover directs students to sections in the handbook that discuss specific writing problems, such as faulty parallelism (fp, //) or dangling modifiers (dm). Students will also value the new design, tabs for easy navigation, and the easy-to-use format, all of which make this a valuable reference throughout academic life and beyond.

CONTENTS: Part I. Principles of Composition. 1. Kinds of Paragraphs. 2. Paragraph Unity. 3. Paragraph Coherence. 4. Coherence through Organization: Beginning, Middle, and Ending. 5. Structural Coherence. 6. Emphasis in Paragraphs. 7. Length of Paragraphs. 8. Essays: Unity, Coherence, and Emphasis. 9. The Process of Planning, Writing, and Revising an Essay. 10. Argument: Writing to Convince or Persuade. 11. Writing In-class Essays and Essay Examinations. Part II. Understanding Sentences. 12. Sentence Patterns and Conventions. Part III. Parts of Speech. 13. Nouns. 14. Pronouns. 15. Agreement of Pronouns with Their Antecedents. 16. Reference of Pronouns. 17. Verbs. 18. Agreement between Subject and Verb. 19. Adjectives. 20. Adverbs. 21. Verbals: Infinitives, Participles, and Gerunds. 22. Prepositions. 23. Conjunctions. 24. Interjections. Part IV. Writing Effective Sentences. 25. Subject, Verb, Object, Complement. 26. Modifiers. 27. Sentence Length. 28. Sentence Variety. 29. Emphasis in Sentences. 30. Analyzing Sentences. 31. Sentence Coherence. 32. Fragments. 33. Comma Splices. 34. Run-on (Fused) Sentences. 35. Misplaced Modifiers. 36. Dangling Modifiers. 37. Mixed Constructions. 38. Faulty Alignment. 39. Shifts in Perspective: Inconsistent Point of View. 40. Faulty Parallelism. 41. Faulty Coordination: Logic, Emphasis, and Unity. 42. Faulty Logic. Part V. Punctuation. 43. Internal Punctuation: Comma, Semicolon, Colon, Dash. *How to Use Commas, Semicolons, Colons, and Dashes*: 44. Between Independent Clauses. 45. To Set Off Adverbial Clauses. 46. To Set Off Introductory and Concluding Words and Phrases. 47. To Set Off Concluding Summaries and Appositives. 48. To Set Off Nonrestrictive Elements. 49. Between Items in a Series. 50. Punctuating Sentence Interrupters. 51. Parentheses. 52. Brackets. 53. End Punctuation: Period, Question Mark, and Exclamation Point. 54. Punctuation with Quotations: Using Quotation Marks. 55. Avoiding Common Errors in Punctuation. Part VI. Mechanics and Spelling. 56. Formatting an Essay. 57. Abbreviations. 58. Capitalization. 59. Titles. 60. Italics. 61. Numerals. 62. Spelling Rules and Common Causes of Error. Part VII. Diction. 63. About Dictionaries. 64. Level. 65. Figurative Language. 66. Concrete and Abstract Diction; Weak Generalizations. 67. Connotation and Denotation. 68. Euphemism. 69. Wrong Word. 70. Idiom. 71. Wordiness, Jargon, and Associated Problems. 72. Usage: A Checklist of Troublesome Words and Phrases. Part VIII. Research, Writing, and Documentation. 73. The Library and the Internet. 74. The Research Plan: Data and Sources. 75. Taking Notes. 76. Writing the Essay. 77. Acknowledging Sources. 78. Quotation, Paraphrase, Summary, and Plagiarism. 79. Documentation. 80. A Sample MLA Research Paper with Comments. 81. Other Methods of Documentation. Appendix: Checklists for Use in Revising, Editing, and Proofreading.

SUPPLEMENTS: *Printed Student Workbook (ISBN 9780195433999)*. Includes over 150 exercises that range in difficulty from basic to more complex so that students can practise their skills as they advance through a course. A complete answer key at the back of the workbook gives students the opportunity to check their progress and comprehension. *FREE Online Student Workbook at www.oupcanada.com/CCWH.* Includes 95 practice exercises and a complete answer key.

Paper, 2009, 512 pp., ISBN 9780195430387

The Making Sense Series

Celebrating 25 years

Margot Northey with Joan McKibbin
MAKING SENSE
A Student's Guide to Research and Writing
Sixth Edition

Margot Northey, David B. Knight, and Dianne Draper
MAKING SENSE IN GEOGRAPHY AND ENVIRONMENTAL SCIENCES
A Student's Guide to Research and Writing
Fourth Edition

Margot Northey and Judi Jewinski
MAKING SENSE IN ENGINEERING AND THE TECHNICAL SCIENCES
A Student's Guide to Research and Writing
Third Edition

Margot Northey, Lorne Tepperman, and Patrizia Albanese
MAKING SENSE IN THE SOCIAL SCIENCES
A Student's Guide to Research and Writing
Fourth Edition

Margot Northey and Patrick von Aderkas
MAKING SENSE IN THE LIFE SCIENCES
A Student's Guide to Research and Writing

About Oxford University Press

Oxford University Press (often referred to as 'OUP') is one of the oldest publishing companies in the world, as well as one of the largest. Its imprint carries authority, its editorial and production standards are high, and its range of interests is wide. It is a department of the University of Oxford, and like the University as a whole, it is devoted to the spread of knowledge: any surplus generated by the Press through its activities is directed toward the publication of works which further scholarship and education, or to encouraging and sustaining research on which these books may be based.

The Press dates its origins back to the fifteenth century. The first book to be printed in Oxford—the *Commentary on the Apostles' Creed*, attributed to St Jerome, by Theodoric Rood—was issued in 1478, only two years after Caxton set up the first printing press in England, and barely a quarter-century following the invention of the printing press by Johann Gutenberg in 1450.

Matters developed in a somewhat haphazard fashion over the following century, with a number of short-lived private businesses, some patronized by Oxford University, taking the field. But in 1586, the University itself obtained a decree from the Star Chamber confirming its privilege to print books. In the same year, Oxford University lent £100—a small fortune at that time—to a local bookseller, Joseph Barnes, to set up a press. Barnes produced many books now prized by collectors, including the first books printed at Oxford in Greek (1586) and Hebrew (1596), and Captain John Smith's *Map of Virginia* (1612). The Great Charter, secured by Archbishop Laud from King Charles I in 1632, increased the independence and latitude of the press, entitling the University to print 'all manner of books', and approximately 300 books were printed before Barnes retired in 1617.

In 1633, the University first appointed delegates to oversee printing and publishing activities. Minute books recording their deliberations date back to 1668, and the Press as it exists today began to develop in a recognizable form from that time. To this day, the worldwide Press' activities are overseen by delegates, who are appointed from the academic staff of Oxford University to 'have charge of the affairs of the Press' and to govern it under the University statutes. The delegates are actively involved in the publishing program and maintain an active dialogue with editors in their specialist subject areas. The operations of the Press as a whole are overseen by a board that includes the vice chancellor of the University and other University administrators, as well as a number of delegates and officers of the Press.

The University established its right to print the King James Authorized Version of the Bible in the seventeenth century. This 'Bible Privilege' formed the basis of a successful publishing business throughout the next two centuries and was the spur for OUP's expansion. In London, the Press established a Bible warehouse, which later grew into a major publisher of books with educational and cultural content aimed at the general reader. Then, OUP began to expand internationally, starting with the opening of an American office in New York in 1896 and the Canadian branch in 1904.

Today, the OUP group of publishing companies constitutes the world's largest university press—larger than all of North America's university presses and Cambridge University Press combined. Worldwide, OUP publishes more than 6,000 new titles a year and employs approximately 5,000 people in 50 countries. As a result of its diverse, international publishing program, the 'Oxford University Press' imprimatur has become familiar world-wide, standing for scholarly, educational, and research excellence and authority.

Few if any organizations publish a more diverse range of titles than Oxford, including scholarly works in all academic disciplines; bibles; music reference works as well as sheet music; textbooks; children's books; materials for teaching English as a foreign language; dictionaries and reference books; professional books in fields such as law, brain science, and medicine; academic journals; and a burgeoning online publishing program of electronic resources and publications. Oxford and New York are the two largest publishing centres within the Press, but other publishing programs of significant size and scope exist the world over, in such countries as Canada, Australia, China, India, Kenya, Malaysia, Mexico, Pakistan, South Africa, and Spain.

Additional information about Oxford University Press is available at our global website: www.oup.com.

About Oxford University Press Canada

OUP Canada: A Brief History

The Canadian branch of Oxford University Press was established in 1904. It was the first overseas branch to be set up after an office was established in New York in 1896. Although the branch did not open until 1904, the first book published for the Canadian market actually appeared eight years earlier—a hymnal for the Presbyterian Church of Canada.

Before the twentieth century, the main suppliers of books to the trade in Canada were the Copp Clark Company, the W.J. Gage Company, and the Methodist Bookroom (in 1919 renamed The Ryerson Press after its founder, Egerton Ryerson). These three firms acted as 'jobbers' for other lines that were later to be represented either directly by branches of their parent houses or by exclusive Canadian agents. Prior to 1904, Oxford books had been sold in Canada by S.G. Wilkinson, who, based in London, England, travelled across Canada as far west as Winnipeg. Wilkinson did a large trade with S.B. (Sam) Gundy, the wholesale and trade manager of the Methodist Bookroom. When Oxford University Press opened its own branch in Canada, Gundy, already familiar with Oxford books, was invited to become its first manager. The premises were at 25 Richmond Street West and, lacking an elevator of any kind, were hardly ideal for a publishing house.

In 1929, the branch moved to Amen House, located at 480 University Avenue, and in 1936, after Gundy's death, the branch became closely allied with Clarke, Irwin and Company under W.C. Clarke. This association continued until 1949 when Clarke, Irwin moved to a separate location on St Clair Avenue West. In 1963, the Press moved to a new building at 70 Wynford Drive

OUP Canada's first home, at 25 Richmond Street West in Toronto.

The original reception area and library at 70 Wynford Drive. The library was later removed to make room for offices.

An etching of Amen House on University Avenue, created by Stanley Turner.

in Don Mills, which served it well for the next 46 years. By 2009, however, the branch had outgrown the 70 Wynford site. An extensive search process culminated in the move that November to a split-site configuration. The offices relocated to new premises at the Shops at Don Mills, an innovative retail/office/residential development, while the warehouse moved to a site in Brampton that not only offered more affordable rent and carrying charges but also provided a modern high-bay space much closer to major customers and Pearson International Airport.

Today OUP Canada is a major publisher of higher education, school, and English-as-a-second-language textbooks, as well as a significant trade and reference publisher. The Higher Education Division publishes both introductory and upper-level texts in such disciplines as sociology, anthropology, social work, English literature and composition, geography, history, political science, religious studies, and engineering. The division publishes more than 60 new Canadian texts and 150 student and instructor supplements each year, and derives about 60 per cent of its total sales from books and other learning materials written, edited, and published in Canada.

Some of the many books recently published by Oxford University Press Canada.